T0189062

Communications
in Computer and Information Science   **1268**

Commenced Publication in 2007
Founding and Former Series Editors:
Simone Diniz Junqueira Barbosa, Phoebe Chen, Alfredo Cuzzocrea,
Xiaoyong Du, Orhun Kara, Ting Liu, Krishna M. Sivalingam,
Dominik Ślęzak, Takashi Washio, Xiaokang Yang, and Junsong Yuan

Editorial Board Members

More information about this series at http://www.springer.com/series/7899

Shui Yu · Peter Mueller ·
Jiangbo Qian (Eds.)

Security and Privacy
in Digital Economy

First International Conference, SPDE 2020
Quzhou, China, October 30 – November 1, 2020
Proceedings

 Springer

Editors
Shui Yu 🆔
University of Technology Sydney
Sydney, NSW, Australia

Jiangbo Qian
Ningbo University
Ningbo, China

Peter Mueller
IBM Zurich Research Laboratory
Zurich, Switzerland

ISSN 1865-0929   ISSN 1865-0937   (electronic)
Communications in Computer and Information Science
ISBN 978-981-15-9128-0   ISBN 978-981-15-9129-7   (eBook)
https://doi.org/10.1007/978-981-15-9129-7

This Springer imprint is published by the registered company Springer Nature Singapore Pte Ltd.
The registered company address is: 152 Beach Road, #21-01/04 Gateway East, Singapore 189721, Singapore

Preface

This volume contains the selected papers from the First International Conference on Security and Privacy in Digital Economy (SPDE 2020), which was held in Quzhou, China, during October 30 – November 1, 2020. The event was organized by the Southeast Digital Economy Development Institute and Ningbo University, both located in China, and it was co-organized by University of Technology Sydney and Deakin University, both located in Australia

The purpose of SPDE 2020 is to offer a timely venue for researchers and industry partners in the framework of the digital economy to present and discuss their latest results in security and privacy-related work. The security and privacy concerns are critical issues in this booming digital economy. The vulnerability and potential threats of the new techniques are yet to be examined, solutions are yet to be tested and confirmed in practice. For example, we need detection method against generative adversarial network-based attacks, fraud, and cheating in digital economy ecosystems need to be detected and solved. We fully believe the solutions depend on the extensive collaboration between academia and industry, and depend on cross-disciplinary efforts from the law and social science. SPDE 2020 focused on the security and privacy issues in the digital economy from the following perspectives: network security, privacy protection, anomaly and intrusion detection, trust computation and forensics, attacks and countermeasures, covert communication, security protocol, anonymous communication, and security and privacy from social science. SPDE 2020's Organizing Committee presented 5 cutting-edge keynotes from the international leading researchers, and 10 invited talks from the distinguished experts on the front line of the security domain. To enhance communication between young researchers and renowned scholars, we held a special panel session entitled "How to Publish Papers in Top Conferences/Journals? Questions and Answers." All accepted and presented papers at SPDE 2020 were contested for the paper awards in a variety of tracks.

SPDE 2020 received 132 papers, which were contributed from several countries such as China, Australia, Greece, and India. All the submitted manuscripts were peer reviewed in a single-blind fashion by at least three qualified reviewers chosen from our Technical Committee members based on their qualifications. Eventually, 49 papers were finally accepted for publication, yielding an acceptance ratio of about 37.12%. Note that, due to the negative impact of COVID-19, we had to run SPDE 2020 as a virtual event. Nevertheless, SPDE 2020 attracted numerous attendees, with heated discussion in the virtual meeting rooms.

The editors would like to express their sincere appreciation and thanks to all the members of the SPDE 2020 Organizing Committee and the Technical Program Committee for their tremendous efforts. Without their dedication, it would have been impossible to host a successful SPDE 2020. The editors would also like to thank all the authors for their contributions. Finally, we express special thanks to Springer for publishing the proceedings of SPDE 2020.

November 2020

Shui Yu
Peter Mueller
Jiangbo Qian

Organization

General Chairs

George Karagiannidis   Aristotle University of Thessaloniki, Greece
Zhensheng Zhang   Boeing (retired), USA

Program Committee Chairs

Shui Yu   University of Technology Sydney, Australia
Peter Mueller   IBM Zurich Research Laboratory, Switzerland
Jiangbo Qian   Ningbo University, China

Special Issue Chairs

Ruidong Li   NICT, Japan
Lianyong Qi   Qufu Normal University, China

Publication Chairs

Keshav Sood   Deakin University, Australia
Li Dong   Ningbo University, China

Publicity Chairs

Danda Rawat   Howard University, USA
Youyang Qu   Deakin University, Australia

Local Chairs

Zhijun Xie   Ningbo University, China
Lang Lin   Southeast Digital Economic Development Institute,
         China

Webmaster

Gui Rao   Southeast Digital Economic Development Institute,
         China

Program Committee

Claudio Ardagna   Università degli Studi di Milano, Italy
Ilija Basicevic   University of Novi Sad, Serbia

Zhibo Wang	Wuhan University, China
Haizhou Wang	Sichuan University, China
Boyang Wang	University of Cincinnati, USA
Weichao Wang	University of North Carolina at Charlotte, USA
Zhang Wei	Nanjing University Posts and Telecommunications, China
Lifei Wei	Shanghai Ocean University, China
Haiqin Wu	University of Copenhagen, Denmark
Xiaotong Wu	Nanjing Normal University, China
Xin-Wen Wu	Indiana University of Pennsylvania, USA
Tao Wu	Chongqing University of Posts and Telecommunications, China
Tao Xiang	Chongqing University, China
Ke Xiao	North China University of Technology, China
Liang Xiao	Xiamen University, China
Mengjun Xie	The University of Tennessee at Chattanooga, USA
Yi Xie	Sun Yat-sen University, China
Xiaofei Xing	Guangzhou University, China
Hu Xiong	University of Science and Technology of China, China
Jin Xu	Tsinghua University, China
Lei Xu	Texas A&M University, USA
Kuai Xu	Arizona State University, USA
Guangquan Xu	Tianjin University, China
Zheng Yan	Xidian University, China
Dayong Ye	University of Wollongong, Australia
Yong Yu	Shaanxi Normal University, China
Jiawei Yuan	University of Massachusetts Dartmouth, USA
Yuan Zhang	University of Electronic Science and Technology of China, China
Rui Zhang	University of Delaware, USA
Yuan Zhang	Nanjing University, China
Mingyue Zhang	Nanjing University of Science and Technology, China
Weizhe Zhang	Harbin Institute of Technology, China
Qingyi Zhu	Chongqing University of Posts and Telecommunications, China
Xiaoyan Zhu	Xidian University, China

Additional Reviewers

Nicola Bena
Matthias Börsig
Bruno Dalmazo
Jia Duan
Bogdan Groza
Camil Jichici
Hicham Lakhlef
Yuzhen Lin
Xuying Meng
Hyun Min Song

Munkenyi Mukhandi
Pal-Ştefan Murva
Francesco Renna
Alessandra Rizzardi
Weiwei Sun
Donghua Wang
Jie Wang
Marek Wehmer
Liyao Xiang
Xueyuan Zhang

Contents

Anomaly and Intrusion Detection

Trust Computation and Forensics

Attacks and Countermeasures

Security and Privacy from Social Science

Cyberspace Security

Detection and Defense Against DDoS Attack on SDN Controller Based on Spatiotemporal Feature

Yan Xu[1,2]([⊠]) [iD], Jinxing Ma[1] [iD], and Sheng Zhong[2]

[1] School of Computer Science and Technology, Anhui University, Hefei 230601, China
xuyan@ahu.edu.cn
[2] State Key Laboratory for Novel Software Technology, Nanjing University, Nanjing 210023, China

Abstract. Software defined network (SDN) is an important part of the next generation computer network. The controller enables SDN to provide flexible data processing and programmable functions, which is the core of SDN. Once the controller is paralyzed, the whole network will be disrupted. DDoS attack targeting the controller will pose a great threat to SDN. However, most of the existing DDoS attack detection schemes only focus on the temporal or content feature of network data, it is easy to fail to detect attack or produce misjudgment. In this paper, we use the temporal and spatial feature of network data to detect DDoS attack on SDN Controller. Furthermore, flow table is used to defend against DDoS attack. We used the DARPA data set to perform experiments, and compared the performance with other scheme. The results show that our scheme can accurately detect DDoS attack and defend against it efficiently.

Keywords: SDN · DDoS attack · CNN-LSTM · Spatiotemporal feature · Network defense mechanisms

1 Introduction

Software-Defined Networking(SDN) is a new network architecture that can manage network traffic more effectively than traditional networks. By virtue of the separation of the control plane and forwarding plane, SDN can not only realize flexible network traffic regulation, but also easily accomplish advanced functions such as route management through programming. These functions can only achieve through complex device configurations in traditional network [1]. However, the introduction of phase separation technology between the control plane and forwarding plane also leads to some security issues. The centralization of logic function makes the SDN control plane vulnerable to malicious attacks, which in turn leads to a single point of failure [2]. Therefore, network security issues are seen as one of the most urgent problems in the SDN architecture [3].

© Springer Nature Singapore Pte Ltd. 2020
S. Yu et al. (Eds.): SPDE 2020, CCIS 1268, pp. 3–18, 2020.
https://doi.org/10.1007/978-981-15-9129-7_1

DDoS attack on SDN Controller have received widespread attention since the controller is the core of SDN. In DDoS attack on SDN Controller, attackers constantly consume controller's resources in order to make the controller unable to provide normal services [4–6]. Eventually, if the controller cannot provide normal services, the entire network will be greatly affected or even paralyzed [7]. In recent years, many researchers have proposed some detection schemes to detect DDoS attack on SDN Controller. However, since the OF(OpenFlow) switch will send the packet to the controller after receiving the unknown packet, an attacker can use the OF switch to send the attack packet to the controller indirectly. This mechanism makes DDoS attack on SDN Controller difficult to detect.

This paper designed and implemented a scheme to detect and defense DDoS attack on SDN Controller. In this scheme, packets are first processed into samples that can reflect the change of traffic over a period of time [8,9]. For detection, the deep neural network built by Convolution Neural Network(CNN) and Long Short Term Memory(LSTM) will conduct attack detection on the generated samples. For defense, the scheme uses lightweight calculation to identify the attacker to block the attack traffic without affecting the normal service provided by the victim. It can be seen from the experimental results that the proposed scheme can accurately detect a variety of attacks type and block the attack traffic while making the victim continue to provide normal services. The contributions of this paper are summarized as follows:

- We design a novel preprocessing stage. At this stage, the scheme constructs samples that can reflect the spatial-temporal characteristics of the data flow by extracting features such as joint entropy and number of hosts that reflect the state changes of the data flow.
- We built a module containing a deep neural network model to detect DDoS attacks on the controller. As the samples can reflect the spatial and temporal characteristic of the data flow, the deep network model is constructed by CNN and LSTM. This is because CNN can effectively extract the spatial structure of data, and LSTM is the best choice when processing sequential data. As a result, the model can perform high-precision DDoS attack detection.
- A module to defend DDoS attack on SDN Controller is deployed in the scheme. The module uses lightweight computation to exactly determine the attacker's attributes based on the flow table information and install defensive flow entry to handle the attack packet so that the victim can still provide normal services.

The rest of this paper is organized as follows. Section 2 introduces the background knowledge of the scheme, and Sect. 3 mainly describes the related work. As for Sect. 4, it illustrates the details of the scheme. The evaluation result is provided in Sect. 5. Finally, in Sect. 6, this paper will be concluded.

2 Background

In this section, we will introduce the SDN architecture and OpenFlow protocol.

2.1 Software Defined Network

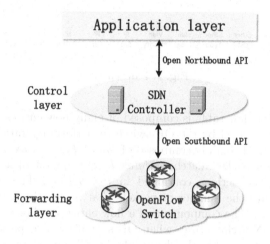

Fig. 1. SDN architecture

SDN has a layered structure as shown in Fig. 1. It consists of application, control and forwarding layer.

- Application layer: The application layer contains many applications that provide different functions. These applications communicate with controllers using northbound interface according to their network requirements [10].
- Control layer: The control layer is the brain of SDN, integrating all logic processing capabilities, which is the biggest difference between SDN and traditional network. This layer can program the network resources, update the forwarding rules dynamically and manage the network more flexibly than the traditional network. The main object of the control layer is the controller, which can generate network traffic operation instructions according to the requirements of various applications in the application layer, and sends the generated operation instructions to the forwarding layer through the southbound interface, indicating how the forwarding devices work.
- Forwarding layer: The forwarding layer consists of several OF switches. Different from the forwarding devices in the traditional network, OF switches can only forward the corresponding data packets according to the instructions sent by the controller, and has no logical processing function.

2.2 OpenFlow

OpenFlow is the protocol followed by the interaction between control layer and forwarding layer [11]. There is a flow table in each OF switch according to

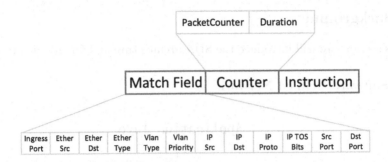

Fig. 2. Flow entry

OpenFlow 1.0. The flow table is composed of many flow entries, which instruct the data packets received by the OF switch to perform operations such as forwarding. Flow entry is mainly composed of *Match Fields*, *Counter* and *Instructions*. Each time a packet matches *Match Fields* content of a flow entry, the packet performs the actions contained in *instructions*. The function of the *Counter* is to count the number of packets that match the current flow entry and other statistics. The components of a flow entry are shown in Fig. 2.

Under the SDN architecture, when OF switch receives packet that do not match any flow entry within the flow table, it will send the packet to the controller. The controller first generate the processing action and then installs the action as a flow entry into OF switch to handle the mismatched packet. Due to this special mechanism, OF switch can perform fine-grained data flow processing compared to switch in traditional networks. However, attackers also can use the mechanism to launch DDoS attacks.

Since the controller integrates all the logical processing capabilities and can generate instructions to adjust the work of the forwarding device. Therefore, it is feasible to use the controller to obtain data flow and bring it into the established attack detection module for attack detection. On the other hand, the information contained in the flow table can be obtained using the controller to analyze the attributes of the attacker when a DDoS attack is detected. As a result, the scheme is applicable to SDN.

3   Related Work

In this section, we briefly introduce and analyze the existing DDoS attack detection and defense schemes in SDN.

The scheme based on statistics carries out statistical inference test on data flow, and treating data flow that do not conform to the statistical models as attack data to achieve DDoS attack detection [12,13]. AvantGuard [14] is a scheme to improve the security of DDoS attack detection. It introduces two modules on OF switch. These modules implement attack detection by classifying TCP SYN requests and triggering corresponding actions according to the classification results. However, this scheme can only detect a single type of DDoS attack

(TCP SYN Flood). In 2015, Wang and Jia [15] proposed a scheme to detect DDoS attacks by calculating the IP address entropy of data flow in the network. It can accurately detect DDoS attacks, while it does not provide a defense method for DDoS attacks. In 2017, a scheme to detect unknown attacks via OF switch was proposed by Kalkan et al. [16]. The scheme incorporates intelligence features into the OF switch that enable OF switch to perform independent operations on packets. The act of providing intelligence for OF switch allows the scheme to not only accurately detect known DDoS attacks, but also detect unknown types of DDoS attacks. However, the concept of "capable switch" violates the concept of separate the control plane from the forwarding plane in SDN.

The detection scheme based on machine learning detects DDoS attacks by using a variety of machine learning algorithms to train the detection model [17–19]. In [20], the authors use naive bayes, support vector machine(SVM) algorithms to detect DDoS attacks. The scheme can quickly distinguish the abnormal flow yet the detection accuracy is low. Similarly, SD-Anti-DDoS [21] is proposed to detect DDoS attacks in a fast and efficient manner by Cui et al. The scheme can reduce the load of the controller and OF switch by setting the attack detection trigger to respond to the abnormal attack more quickly. The scheme can detect DDoS attacks that trigger a large number of *packet_in* messages in a short period of time.

In 2018, Cui [22] et al. proposed a time-based detection scheme. The article proposes that the principle of DDoS Attack on SDN Controller is to trigger a large number of packet-in packets, so the attack must result in a sharp drop in the hit rate. As a result, The scheme uses the hit rate of the flow entry as a feature to detect DDoS attack on SDN Controller. This scheme can detect DDoS attack on SDN Controller, but it ignores the spatial feature of the data.

In the above schemes, the feature used is content features basically. Attackers can easily trick detection scheme by adjusting the content of the data packet. In [23], the authors find that the joint entropy can more accurately and flexibly reflect the change of the current data flow state. Since the DDoS attack is inevitably accompanied by the change of feature entropy, it is necessary to use joint entropy to more accurately detect DDoS attack on SDN Controller. In addition, as attack packets often come from different hosts manipulated by attackers, DDoS attacks are often accompanied by an explosion in the number of hosts. Therefore, the number of hosts can also be used as a spatial feature to effectively reflect the current flow changes.

4   The Designed Scheme

In this section, we will describes the details of the proposed scheme. The scheme consists of three modules: Flow process module, Attack detection module and Active defense module. Figure 3 depicts the process of the proposed scheme.

– *Flow Process Module*: This module consists of two-part: Flow collection and Feature process. Flow collection mainly collects packets from the unknown data flow sent by the OF switch to the controller and flow table information for the OF switch. The function of Feature process is to calculate the corresponding feature value according to the extracted packet header information, and forms the sample X.

- *Attack Detection Module*: This module mainly contains a deep neural network model composed of CNN and LSTM, which is responsible for detecting DDoS attack on SDN Controller. The model detects the received the sample X and sends the detection results to Active defense module.
- *Active Defense Module*: According to the detection results sent by Attack detection module and the flow table information, this module will generate the defensive flow entry to defend against DDoS attack on SDN controller.

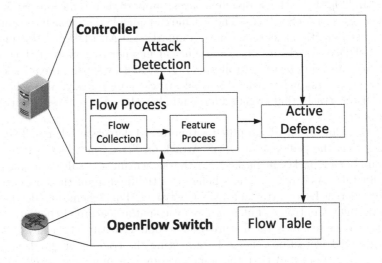

Fig. 3. System architecture of our scheme

4.1 Flow Process Module

Flow process module is embedded in the controller. In SDN, the OF switch send packets that do not match any of the flow entry to the controller. With this mechanism, unknown packets received by the OF switch can be easily collected.

Flow Collection : To detect DDoS attack on SDN Controller, Flow collection collect the different attributes of the unknown packet. The most important attributes of TCP/IP packets headers are: source IP address (IP_{src}), destination IP address (IP_{dst}), source port (P_{src}), destination port (P_{dst}), packet size (PKT_{size}), protocol type (PKT_{type}). These attributes can be represented as a collection:

$$flow = \{IP_{src}, IP_{dst}, P_{src}, P_{dst}, PKT_{size}, PKT_{type}\}$$

When an unknown TCP/IP packet arrives at the controller, Flow collection will collect the property values in the collection *flow* from the packet header. After a period of time, Flow collection consolidates the value received during this period into *Flow*.

In [24], the author compares the time-based and packet-based period determination, and concludes that the packet-based period determination is more effective. So we choose packet-based period determination. Because of this, *Flow* will send to Feature process after Flow collection receives α packets. At the same time, Flow collection will query the OF switch flow table information and sends it to Active defense module. The contents of *Flow* are shown below:

$$Flow = \{flow_1, flow_2, ..., flow_\alpha\}$$

Feature Process : In 1948, the concept of information entropy was presented by Shannon [25]. It can be used to describe the randomness of a random variable. If we consider two independent random variables at the same time. The joint-entropy of random event X and Y is defined as:

$$H(XY) = -\sum_{i=1}^{N}\sum_{j=1}^{M} p(x_i y_j) log_2(p(x_i y_j)) \tag{1}$$

where $p(x_i y_j)$ is the probability of event$(X = x_i, Y = y_j)$, i = 1,2,...,N and j = 1,2,...,M.

Algorithm 1. Framework of ensemble learning for our scheme.

Require: The set of receive *Flow*; The set of attribute pairs $\mathbb{A}$; The number of packets received in a period α;

Ensure: Sample X

1: Initialize the set of joint-entropy $\mathbb{JC}_{\mathbb{A}}$;
2: **for** (a_1, a_2) in $\mathbb{A}$ **do**
3:     Initialize dictionary of counting *count_table*
4:     **for** Each *flow* in *Flow* **do**
5:         **if** $(flow.a_1, flow.a_2) \in count\_table$ **then**
6:             count_table.add$((flow.a_1, flow.a_2),1)$
7:         **else**
8:             count_table$[(flow.a_1, flow.a_2)]$ += 1
9:         **end if**
10:     **end for**
11:     **for** Each c in *count_table* **do**
12:         $P = c.key/\alpha$
13:         $\mathbb{JC}_{\mathbb{A}}.(a_1, a_2)$+ = $P * \log(P)$
14:     **end for**
15:     $\mathbb{JC}_{\mathbb{A}}.(a_1, a_2)/ = \log_2(\alpha)$
16: **end for**
17: X = $(\mathbb{JC}_{\mathbb{A}}, Duration, NUM)$
18: **return** X

In normal traffic, the packet received by the OF switch is random, so the entropy value of normal flow is usually large. In contrast, in a DDoS attack, the entropy of some attributes of attack packet drops dramatically. In the same way, the joint-entropy of the attribute pairs composed of these attributes has the same trend [23]. In addition, when a DDoS attack on SDN Controller occurs, attack packets received by the OF switch increase significantly and the number of hosts corresponding to the flow will increase. At the same time, the duration of the flow containing attack packets will also be shortened. These features can be extracted to reflect changes in the spatial characteristics of the flow.

The attributes in the collection *flow* constitute the attribute pair. There attribute pairs form a collection $\mathbb{A}$. The contents of collection $\mathbb{A}$ are shown below:

$$\mathbb{A} = \{(IP_{src}, IP_{dst}), (IP_{src}, IP_{dst}), ..., (PKT_{size}, PKT_{type})\}$$

We use A_i represents the ith element of the collection $\mathbb{A}$, JC_{A_i} represents the corresponding joint-entropy value of A_i, respectively. For example, $A_1 = (IP_{src}, IP_{dst})$. JC_{A_1} represents the joint-entropy of attribute pair consisting of source IP address and destination IP address. The process of Feature process is shown in algorithm 1.

Finally, Feature process generates the sample X, which represents the characteristics of the flow. *Duration* and *NUM* represents the duration of *Flow* and the number of hosts in the *Flow*, respectively.

4.2 Attack Detection Module

In this module, we construct a deep neural network model to detect DDoS attack on SDN Controller. The view of the model is shown in Fig. 4. We choose the CNN-LSTM as the core of the model. Since CNN has been proved to be able to extract the spatial feature of data efficiently. LSTM is not only good at processing sequential data, but also avoids the gradient disappearance during training [26,27].

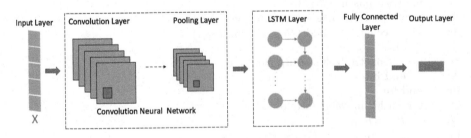

Fig. 4. Overall CNN-LSTM module

The model consists of input layer, convolution layer, pooling layer, LSTM layer, full connection layer and output layer, which are combined according to linear structure. The data of the input layer is the sample X. The sample first is processed by the convolutional neural network composed of the convolution layer and pooling layer. The convolution layer extracts features of high dimensional by performing convolution operation on the sample X, while the pooling layer compresses and reduces dimensions of features of high dimensional extracted by the convolution layer to simplify the complexity of network computation. In this model, we set the convolutional kernel of the convolutional layer as 3 and the step size as 1. In order to speed up the training progress of the model, we use the ReLU function as the activation function of the convolutional layer.

$$ReLU(x) = max(0, x) \qquad (2)$$

After the convolution network processing, the output of the high-dimensional spatial feature with the sample X will be input into the LSTM layer for further processing. The LSTM layer consists of several layers of LSTM units. With the introduction of the concept of cell, LSTM can effectively recognize the implied temporal relationship between large sequential data. Therefore, the output processed by LSTM layer has the spatial-temporal characteristics of sample X.

Finally, the output of the LSTM layer, after being processed by the fully connected layer, will generate the final output through an output layer to determine whether the current network is under DDoS attack. For the output layer classifier, we use the value of the Softmax function as the output.

$$Softmax(x_i) = \frac{e^{x_i}}{\sum_j e^{x_j}} \qquad (3)$$

All in all, the sample X obtained will be brought into the trained model, and the model will classify the sample X according to the feature it has. The detection results will send to Active Defense Module.

4.3   Active Defense Module

After receiving the results from Attack detection module. Active defense module will select suspicious flow entries to determine the attacker's attribute value, and generate defensive flow entry to defend against DDoS attacks.

As mentioned above, most DDoS attacks on SDN Controller leverage the OpenFlow processing mechanism. There DDoS attacks consume controller resources quickly by generating as many attack packets as possible. Suspicious flow entries are those generated by attack packets. Since they are generated by attack packets, this means that suspicious flow entries typically match to fewer packets and have a longer lifetime than normal flow entries. At the same time, the traffic matching of these flow entries often has a high asymmetry characteristic.

When the number of matched packets of any flow entry is lower than the mean A_p, this module will calculate the duration and asymmetric flow rate of the flow entry, and compare with the mean values of A_s and A_f respectively. If all of these values are above the mean values, this flow entry is considered as

Table 1. Defensive flow entry

Priority	Match field	Counter	Instructions
Minimal	$IP_{Src} = A_{ack}$	...	Actions = Drop

a suspicious flow entry. Through the suspicious flow entry, defensive flow entry will generated. An example of a defensive flow entry is shown in Table 1.

The function of this flow entry is to drop all packets sent from the A_{ack} address. A_{ack} is believed to be the IP address of the attacker. These attributes can be obtained from suspicious flow entry that are generated by the attacker.

Although the defensive flow entry can effectively block the attack packets from the attacker, sometimes it may also block legitimate packets sent by normal users. So this module will remove the defensive flow entry immediately after the DDoS attack is over to mitigate its impact. We believe that the attack still occurs when a large number of unknown packets are sent to the victim. Therefore, the defensive flow entry will match a large number of packets. By calculating the ratio of the number of packets that matched the defensive flow entry to the normal flow entry, we can determine whether the attack is over. The calculation formula is as follows:

$$N_n = \frac{1}{C_n} \sum_{i \in T_n} FlowCount_i \tag{4}$$

$$N_d = \frac{1}{C_d} \sum_{j \in T_d} FlowCount_j \tag{5}$$

The T_n, T_d represents the set of normal flow entry and defensive flow entry in the OF switch, and the C_n, C_d represents the number of flow entries of sets T_n and T_d, respectively. Finally, we will get the ratio of the number of matched packets between the normal flow entries and the defensive flow entries. And if the result satisfies Eq. 6, we judge that the victim is no longer under the DDoS attack, and remove the defensive flow entry.

$$\frac{N_d}{N_n} < \lambda \tag{6}$$

5 Experiments and Evaluation

5.1 Experiment

DARPA1999 data set [28] is selected to verify the effectiveness of the scheme. By making comparative experiments, we found that when set $\alpha = 100$, that is, one hundred packets are collected as a processing period, the effect of the whole scheme is the best. In addition, we set up several groups of control tests, and

Table 2. Threshold test

Value of the λ	Precision	Misjudgment rate
5	1.00	0.43
7	0.98	0.31
10	0.93	0.14
15	0.81	0.06
20	0.43	0.03

select different values of λ for each group of tests to determine the most suitable value. The experimental results are shown in Table 2. Finally, we found that when $\lambda = 10$, defensive flow entry can correctly block the flow of data from attackers and have little effect on normal data. The parameters used in the experiment and their meanings are shown in Table 3.

Table 3. System parameters

Term	Explanation
$flow$	A collection of data packet header properties
$Flow$	A collection of data collected over a period
$\mathbb{A}$	A collection of attribute pairs formed by the combination of collected data packet header attributes
$\mathbb{JC_A}$	The set of joint entropy corresponding to the attribute pairs in set $\mathbb{A}$
$count\_table$	A dictionary that stores and counts the value of a pair of features in a period and the number of times the value
α	The number of data packets collected in a period ($\alpha = 100$ in our experiment)
A_p	The average of the number of packets matched by the flow entries
A_s	The average duration of flow entries
A_f	The average flow rate of flow entries asymmetric flow
λ	Threshold for the ratio of the number of matched packets between the defensive and normal flow entry

We use Mininet [29] as the network simulator, which can help us build a network topology similar to the real environment. We also use OpenDayLight, an open source controller, as SDN controller. As for verifying that the scheme can effectively block the traffic of DDoS attack, we simulated several DDoS attacks. The types and duration of simulated DDoS attacks are shown in Table 4. And for the southbound interface protocol, we chose OpenFlow1.3, since it is the most commonly used protocol in the industry. The simulation runs on an 8GRAM, Intel Core i5-4590 3.30GHz CPU with Ubuntu 14.04OS.

5.2 Performance Metrics

We conduct comparative experiments with the scheme proposed in [22]. Because the scheme [22] takes into account the time feature of a DDoS attack and achieves good results in the detection and defense of DDoS Attack on SDN Controller.

Table 4. Attack description

Attack Type	Principal	Start Time(s)	End Time(s)
Portsweep	Attacker sends some packet to every port of the target network to determine which host is available to attack	100	160
Ipsweep	Attacker sends some packet to every host of the target network to determine which host is available to attack	100	160
smurf	Attacker sends massive ICMP packets with forged source IP address to the target host, then the target host replies to all nonexistent source Hosts, and become too busy to handle other legitimate packets	340	400
neptune	Attacker sends massive SYN packets with different ports to target host, then the target host replies every SYN packet and waits, finally All the ports of target host are occupied	460	490

We use the ACC(Accuracy), P(Precision) and R(Recall) for evaluating the parameters of the detection efficiency. The parameters are defined as follows:

– *Accuracy(ACC)*:the proportion of data samples that are correctly classified to the total data samples.

$$ACC = \frac{TP+TN}{TP+TN+FP+FN}$$

Table 5. Accuracy, precision and recall

	Accuracy	Precision	Recall
LSTM	0.922	0.948	0.936
CNN	0.907	0.939	0.947
BPNN(Proposed by [22])	0.827	0.921	0.91
CNN-LSTM(Our Proposed)	**0.943**	**0.988**	**0.954**

- *Precision(P)*:the proportion of true attack samples in the attack samples determined by the algorithm.

$$P = \frac{TP}{TP + TN}$$

- *Recall(R)*:the proportion of the attack samples that have been correctly determined to the total attack samples.

$$R = \frac{TP}{TP + FN}$$

The experimental results are shown in Table 5. This proposed scheme can detect DDoS attack on SDN Controller more efficiently, because it can extract the spatial and temporal characteristics of the data flow.

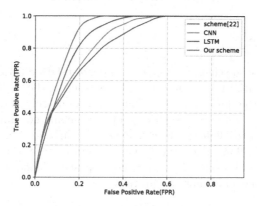

Fig. 5. ROC curve comparison for different algorithms

TP(True Positive) represents the number of samples that the detection algorithm correctly determines to be attacked. TN(True Negative) represents the number of normal samples that are determined correctly. In that vein, FP(False Positive) is the number of normal samples that are incorrectly identified as attack samples. FN(False Negative) represents the number of attack samples that are incorrectly determined as normal samples.

The Receiver Operating Characteristic(ROC)curve, as a standard measure of classifier classification, can reflect the performance of the classifier. As shown in Fig. 5, the scheme proposed is superior in detecting DDoS attack on SDN Controller.

The CPU consumption rate of the victim host is shown in Fig. 6. Since this scheme can quickly detect the attack and send out the defensive flow entry to block the attack data, so that the CPU utilization of the victim service can always maintain the normal state. Compared with the scheme [22], the defensive flow entry issued by our method can regulate network traffic in a more granular way instead of directly cutting off the traffic sent to the victim's IP address, so the CPU consumption rate of this scheme is lower.

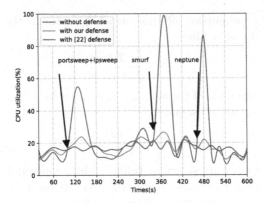

Fig. 6. System CPU utilization

6   Conclusion

This paper proposes a scheme to detect and defense DDoS attack on SDN Controller based on spatial-temporal feature. By extracting the spatial and temporal characteristics of the data flow, the scheme can accurately detect DDoS attack on SDN Controller. The defense module of the scheme generates the defensive flow entry through the lightweight calculation to carry on the fine-grained regulation to the data flow. The experiment is operated on the DARPA1999 data set. The experimental results show that the proposed scheme could detect DDoS attack on SDN Controller more accurately.

References

1. Lopes, F.A., et al.: A software engineering perspective on sdn programmability. IEEE Commun. Surveys Tuts. **18**(2), 1255–1272 (2016). https://doi.org/10.1109/COMST.2015.2501026
2. Scotthayward, S., Sriram, N., Sakir, S.: A survey of security in software defined networks. IEEE Commun. Surveys Tuts. **18**(1), 623–654 (2016). https://doi.org/10.1109/COMST.2015.2453114
3. Swami, R., Mayank, D., Virender, R.: Software-defined networking-based ddos defense mechanisms. ACM Comput. Surveys **52**(2), 1–36 (2019). https://doi.org/10.1145/3301614
4. Yan, Q., et al.: Software-defined networking (sdn) and distributed denial of service (ddos) attacks in cloud computing environments: a survey, some research issues, and challenges. IEEE Commun. Surveys Tuts. **18**(1), 602–622 (2016). https://doi.org/10.1109/COMST.2015.2487361
5. Praseed, A., Santhi, T.P.: DDOS attacks at the application layer: challenges and research perspectives for safeguarding web applications. IEEE Commun. Surveys Tuts. **21**(1), 661–685 (2019). https://doi.org/10.1109/COMST.2018.2870658
6. Han, B., et al.: OverWatch: a cross-plane DDOS attack defense framework with collaborative intelligence in SDN. Secur. Commun. Netw. 1–15 (2018) https://doi.org/10.1155/2018/9649643

7. Wang, Y., et al.: SGS: safe-guard scheme for protecting control plane against ddos attacks in software-defined networking. IEEE Access 34699–34710 (2019) https://doi.org/10.1109/ACCESS.2019.2895092
8. Kalkan, K., Gurkan, G., Fatih, A.: Defense mechanisms against ddos attacks in sdn environment. IEEE Commun. Mag. **55**(9), 175–179 (2017). https://doi.org/10.1109/MCOM.2017.1600970
9. Kumar, K., Joshi, R. C., Singh, K.: A distributed approach using entropy to detect DDoS attacks in ISP domain. In: International Conference on Signal Processing, pp. 331–337. (2007). https://doi.org/10.1109/ICSCN.2007.350758
10. Barki, L., et al.: Detection of distributed denial of service attacks in software defined networks. In: Advances in Computing and Communications, pp. 2576–2581 (2016). https://doi.org/10.1109/ICACCI.2016.7732445
11. Mckeown, Nick, et al. "OpenFlow: enabling innovation in campus networks." acm special interest group on data communication (2008): 69–74. https://doi.org/10.1145/1355734.1355746
12. Xu, Y., Yong, L.: DDoS attack detection under SDN context. In: IEEE International Conference Computer And Communications, pp. 1–9 (2016). https://doi.org/10.1109/INFOCOM.2016.752450
13. Kumar, P., et al.: SAFETY: early detection and mitigation of TCP SYN flood utilizing entropy in SDN. IEEE Trans. Netw. Service Manag. **15**(4), 1545–1559 (2018). https://doi.org/10.1109/TNSM.2018.2861741
14. Shin, S., et al.: AVANT-GUARD: scalable and vigilant switch flow management in software-defined networks. In: Computer and Communications Security, pp. 413–424 (2013) https://doi.org/10.1145/2508859.2516684
15. Wang, R., Zhiping, J., Lei, J.: An entropy-based distributed ddos detection mechanism in software-defined networking. In: Trust, Security and Privacy in Computing and Communications, pp. 310–317 (2015) https://doi.org/10.1109/Trustcom.2015.389
16. Kalkan, K., Gurkan, G., Fatih, A.: SDNScore: A statistical defense mechanism against DDoS attacks in SDN environment. In: International Symposium on Computers and Communications, pp. 669–675 (2017). https://doi.org/10.1109/ISCC.2017.8024605
17. Xie, J., et al.: A survey of machine learning techniques applied to software defined networking (sdn): research issues and challenges. IEEE Commun. Surveys Tuts. **21**(1), 393–430 (2019). https://doi.org/10.1109/COMST.2018.2866942
18. Latah, M., Levent, T.: Artificial intelligence enabled software-defined networking: a comprehensive overview. IET networks **8**(2), 79–99 (2019). https://doi.org/10.1049/iet-net.2018.5082
19. Dayal, N., et al.: Research trends in security and ddos in sdn. Secur. Commun. Netw. **9**(18), 6386–6411 (2016). https://doi.org/10.1002/sec.1759
20. Deepa, S., Deepa, L.: Detection of ddos attack on sdn control plane using hybrid machine learning techniques. In: International Conference on Smart Systems and Inventive Technology, pp. 299–303 (2018) https://doi.org/10.1109/ICSSIT.2018.8748836
21. Cui, Y., et al.: SD-Anti-DDoS: fast and efficient ddos defense in software-defined networks. J. Netw. Comput. Appl. **68**, 65–79 (2016). https://doi.org/10.1016/j.jnca.2016.04.005
22. Cui, J., He, J., Xu, Y., Zhong, H.: TDDAD: time-based detection and defense scheme against ddos attack on sdn controller. In: Susilo, W., Yang, G. (eds.) ACISP 2018. LNCS, vol. 10946, pp. 649–665. Springer, Cham (2018). https://doi.org/10.1007/978-3-319-93638-3_37

23. Mao, J., Weijun, D., Fuke, S.: DDoS flooding attack detection based on joint-entropy with multiple traffic features. In: trust security and privacy in computing and communications, pp. 237–243 (2018). https://doi.org/10.1109/TrustCom/BigDataSE.2018.00045
24. Kim, Y., et al.: Packetscore: statistics-based overload control against distributed denial-of-service attacks. In: International Conference on Computer Communications, pp. 2594–2604 (2004). https://doi.org/10.1109/INFCOM.2004.1354679
25. Shannon, C.E.: Prediction and entropy of printed English. Bell Syst. Tech. J. **30**(1), 50–64 (1951). https://doi.org/10.1002/j.1538-7305.1951.tb01366.x
26. Cui, J., et al.: Comparative study of CNN and RNN for deep learning based intrusion detection system. In: International Conference on Cloud Computing, pp. 159–170 (2018). https://doi.org/10.1007/978-3-030-00018-9_15
27. Zhai, S., et al.: Deep structured energy based models for anomaly detection. In: International Conference on Machine Learning, pp. 1100–1109 (2016)
28. MITLincolnLaboratory:DARPA 1999 Intrusion Detection Data Set. https://www.LL.mit.edu/ideval/docs/attackDB.html
29. Mininet. http://mininet.org/

Trusted Link-Separation Multipath Selection for Software-Defined Wireless Sensor Networks in Adversarial Environments

Pu Zhao, Wentao Zhao, Qiang Liu$^{(\boxtimes)}$ ⓘ, and Anbang Wang

College of Computer, National University of Defense Technology,
Changsha 410000, Hunan, China
qiangliu06@nudt.edu.cn

Abstract. Compared to conventional Wireless Sensor Networks (WSNs), Software-Defined WSNs (SD-WSNs) introduce the software defined networking (SDN) paradigm to offer more adaptivity, flexibility and scalability. Research on reliable and trusted routing for SD-WSNs is a fundamental but very challenging task due to their unstable wireless connectivity, low security assurance and diverse inner adversaries. Hence, we propose a trusted link-separation multipath selection method for SD-WSNs in adversarial environments by jointly considering routing efficiency and security. Specifically, we introduce a Bayesian model to evaluate the nodes' trustworthiness based on their communication behaviors. After that, we formulate the trusted link-separation multipath selection as a multi-objective optimization problem. Then, we generate k trusted link-separation paths by solving the optimization problem using a greedy algorithm. Comparative experiments using six different topologies, including three random networks (Waxman, ER random graphs, and WS small-world topologies) and three real ones (Cernet, Bandcon, and DFN), validate the superior performance of the proposed method compared with the delay-first and the trust-first baseline routing schemes.

Keywords: Software-Defined Wireless Sensor Networks · Trusted routing · Link-separation multipath selection · Multi-objective optimization · Malicious node detection.

1 Introduction

Wireless Sensor Networks (WSNs) consist of a large number of sensor nodes with embedded processors, limited processing and storage capacities, and wireless tranceivers in a self-organization manner. Basically, WSNs are widely used

The corresponding author of this paper is Qiang Liu. The work is supported by National Key Research and Development Program of China (No. 2018YFB0204301), National Natural Science Foundation of China (No. 61702539 and U1811462), Hunan Provincial Natural Science Foundation of China (No. 2018JJ3611), and NUDT Research Project (No. ZK-18-03-47).

© Springer Nature Singapore Pte Ltd. 2020
S. Yu et al. (Eds.): SPDE 2020, CCIS 1268, pp. 19–32, 2020.
https://doi.org/10.1007/978-981-15-9129-7_2

in many mission-critical applications such as surveillance, tracking and monitoring. As the software defined networking (SDN) has been commonly regarded as a key enabling technology of 5G and beyond 5G networks, it is intuitive to integrate WSNs with SDN, resulting in software-defined WSNs (SD-WSNs) [19]. Therefore, SD-WSNs are able to offer global view of network topologies, centralized resource management, fast traffic relaying, intelligent decision using machine learning and programmable capability.

The WSNs usually is deployed in unmanned surveillance or hostile areas. Due to its open characteristic of working environments, limited computing/storage capability of SD-WSN nodes, unstable wireless connectivity, low security assurance and diverse inner adversaries. The WSNs suffer from poor communication performance, sudden node failure and security threats launched by malicious nodes. For example, an adversary can physically capture some WSNs nodes or remotely gain the administrative privilege of these nodes via exploiting software vulnerabilities to launch proxy attacks, which will compromise network security and data privacy. To defend against diverse security threats, a great number of research works have been proposed [1,10,16], including but not limited to intrusion detection/prevention, authentication and authorization, access control, secure routing protocols, and node security reinforcement mechanisms. However, most of these protection techniques are deployed as security patches to overcome different weakness points of wireless networks, which is passive, time consuming and suffering high maintenance cost. Therefore, considering security at the beginning when designing a wireless networking system is highly valuable to provide proactive immune capabilities towards security threats. In this paper, we focus on routing path selection because it is a fundamental problem in any one networking system. Recalling the characteristics of SD-WSNs, we argue that a well-defined path selection scheme for SD-WSNs should jointly consider security, reliability, redundancy, load balance and relaying efficiency. To fill this gap, we adopt the prevailing zero trust design philosophy and study on trusted link-separation multipath selection for SD-WSNs in adversarial environments.

Generally speaking, the research on trusted routing path selection includes two key tasks, i.e., (1) a trust measurement method towards all network nodes [4] and (2) a secure and efficient path selection algorithm for generating communication paths that do not choose those nodes with low trust values as relays. Regarding the former task, many researchers have investigated network monitoring using trust management systems and intrusion detection systems (IDSs) to identify the genuine and malicious users [8,13,18]. These methods calculated trust values by weighting the packet loss rates of network nodes, link reliability and other factors. Hence, they could defeat black hole, Denial-of-Service (DoS) and other attacks. However, they are weak to identify malicious behaviors of untrusted network nodes such as stealing or tampering sensitive information. On the other hand, designing a high-performance IDS is also challening due to lots of false positives and false negatives [15]. In [9,11], a Bayesian model is used to compute reputation scores by statistically updating beta probability density functions. Regarding the latter task, most existing works on secure routing protocols mainly emphasize on security rather than quality-of-service (QoS) guarantee [2,3,6,14]. Moreover, previous research on link-separation multipath selection schemes [5,7,17] did not solve the Head of Line (HOL) blocking problem due to the fact that different routing paths had varied latency, resulting in out-of-order arrival of packets at the same destination node [12]. Consequently, the packets transmitted via low-latency routing paths must wait for those via high-latency paths for data assembling, which induced a significant decrease of network throughput.

To address the above challenges, we propose a trusted link-separation multipath selection method for SD-WSNs using multi-objective optimization. Specifically, we first utilize a Bayesian model to obtain the nodes' reputation from their communication behaviors. Then, their trustworthiness is evaluated by judging their reputation values. After that, we formulate the k trusted link-separation multipath selection problem as a multi-objective optimization one aiming to maximize the trust values but to minimize the relay latency and the delay difference of resulting paths. After solving the optimization problem, we generate k link-separation paths with the maximal trust values but the minimal delay difference among them. The main contributions of this paper are summarized as follows:

(1) We formulate a multi-objective optimization problem to obtain k trusted link-separation paths by jointly considering their trust values, minimal path latency and delay difference among them.

(2) We propose a heuristic algorithm to solve the above optimization problem. Specifically, the algorithm first uses a modified Dijkstra shortest path algorithm to find a set of candidate paths between a source and a destination. Then, the algorithm adopts a greedy method to select k link-separation paths from the candidate path set.

The rest of this paper is organized as follows: Sect. 2 presents the evaluation of node trustworthiness. Section 3 gives a detailed description of the proposed method. Section 4 shows comparative results to demonstrate the superior performance of the proposed method. Finally, Sect. 5 gives conclusion remarks.

2   Evaluation of Node Trustworthiness

2.1   System Model of SD-WSNs

A typical architecture of WSN is usually composed of a base station and a number of sensor nodes. Basically, a SD-WSN consists of a control node representing a centralized SDN controller and a number of nodes that serve as distributed SDN switches. Note that the SDN controller can be implemented in a dedicated hardware deployed in base station, and the SDN switches can be deployed in the sensor nodes. The SDN controller communicates with distributed switches using southbound interfaces such as OpenFlow and Netconf to construct a global view of SD-WSNs. After that, the controller is able to make path selection decisions and to instruct switches taking assigned actions with respect to specific types of network traffic.

In this work, the proposed method is implemented in the SDN controller. The SDN controller calculates the reputation values of WSN nodes via a Bayesian model. The controller obtains the flow table information of SDN switches through the standard southbound interface. Then, the controller can detect abnormal data traffic by calculating the information entropy of the corresponding flow table items. Finally, a data set of <node address, the number of abnormal packets> is fed into the Bayesian model.

2.2   The Used Bayesian Model

Basically, the Bayesian Model in statistics is an inference method where Bayesian rules are used to update the expected probability estimated for a hypothesis. In this work, we apply the model to calculate the reputation values of sensor nodes in SD-WSNs.

For the sake of description, we term N as the total number of packets originated from a node v. E_N^M means an event that N packets are sent by the node v, where M packets are identified as normal ones by existing threat identification systems. Moreover, E_{Normal} denotes an event that a normal packet is sent by v. $P(E)$ represents the probability of the occurance of an event E. Furthermore, we assume that the distribution of observing E_N^M is approximately Binomial, which is formally defined as

$$P(E_N^M | P(E_{Normal}) = p) = C_N^M p^M (1-p)^{N-M}. \tag{1}$$

To quantitatively evaluate the reputation of v (denoted by Γ_v), we adopt the Bayesian inference method to calculate the probability of an event (termed as E_{Normal}^{N+1}) that the $(N+1)$th packet originated from v_s is normal. Hence, we have

$$\Gamma_v = P(E_{Normal}^{N+1} | E_N^M) = \frac{P(E_{Normal}^{N+1}, E_N^M)}{P(E_N^M)}, \tag{2}$$

where

$$P(E_N^M) = \int_0^1 \left(P(E_N^M | P(E_{Normal}) = p) f(p) \right) dp, \tag{3}$$

$$P(E_{Normal}^{N+1}, E_N^M) = \int_0^1 \left(P(E_N^M | P(E_{Normal}) = p) p f(p) \right) dp. \tag{4}$$

Since we have no prior knowledge regarding p, we further assume that p is determined by a uniform distribution and $p \in [0, 1]$. Finally, we can simply rewrite the Eq. (2) to

$$\Gamma_v = \frac{M+1}{N+2} \tag{5}$$

Let L be the total number of WSN nodes. In each time window, the SDN controller maintains a matrix $\{[N_{i,j}, M_{i,j}]\}_{i,j}$ $(i \neq j, 1 \leq i, j \leq L)$ to record the values of variables N and M regarding the communication from a node v_i to its neighboring node v_j. Then, the SDN controller can obtain all SD-WSN nodes' reputation values according to the Eq. (5).

2.3 Calculation of Node Trustworthiness

Typically, the SDN controller is responsible for the calculation of node trustworthiness. It first calculates the reputation values of WSN nodes as mentioned before. After that, it converts these reputation values to corresponding trust values (Ψ) according to a pre-defined mapping table, which is shown in Table 1. Based on simulation results in [11], we set the lower threshold of Γ to 0.72. If the reputation value of a node v satisfies $\Gamma_v \leq 0.72$, then v is regarded as a malicious node. Furthermore, we divide the trusted nodes into three groups with different trust levels, i.e., High ($\Psi = 3$), Medium ($\Psi = 2$) and Low ($\Psi = 1$), for the ease of multi-objective optimization when determining multiple link-separation paths. Note that those nodes with similar reputation values have the same contributions towards routing security.

Table 1. Mapping table from reputation to trust values

Reputation (Γ)	Trust level	Trust value (Ψ)
$(0.92, 1]$	High	3
$(0.82, 0.92]$	Medium	2
$(0.72, 0.82]$	Low	1
$[0, 0.72]$	Malicious	0

3 Details of the Proposed Method

The goal of trusted link-separation multipath selection is to generate k link-separation paths with the maximal trust values but the minimal relay latency and delay difference. Hence, we first formulate the task to a multi-objective optimization problem. After solving the optimization problem, we obtain the resulting routing paths.

3.1 Problem Formulation

For the sake of description, we use a unweighted graph $G = (V, E, D)$ to model a SD-WSN, where V is a non-empty set of vertices with a size of $L = |V|$, $E = \{\langle v_i, v_j \rangle | i \neq j, v_i, v_j \in V\}$ is an edge set, where $\langle v_i, v_j \rangle$ refers to a direct communication link from v_i to v_j. D is a set of forwarding delay, where $d_i \in D$ $(i = 1, 2, 3, \cdots, L)$ denotes the forwarding delay of the node v_i.

Definition 1 (Routing Path): A routing path $p_{s,t}$ from a source node v_s to a destination v_t is defined as

$$p_{s,t} = \{\langle v_s, v_1 \rangle, \langle v_1, v_2 \rangle \cdots, \langle v_{m-1}, v_m \rangle, \langle v_m, v_t \rangle\}, \tag{6}$$

where $v_s \neq v_1$, $v_m \neq v_t$, and $\forall v_i, v_j$, if $i \neq j$, then $v_i \neq v_j$ $(i, j \in 1, \cdots, m-1)$. Based on the definition of routing path, we further define $P_{s,t}^k$ as a set of k link-separation paths from v_s to v_t, i.e.,

$$P_{s,t}^k = \{p_{s,t}^i\}_{i=1}^k, \tag{7}$$

where $\forall i \neq j, p_{s,t}^i \cap p_{s,t}^j = \emptyset$ $(1 \leq i, j \leq k)$.

Definition 2 (Path Trust Level): The trust level of a path $p_{s,t}$ from v_s to v_t is defined as

$$PTL(p_{s,t}) = \min(\Psi_1, \Psi_2, \cdots, \Psi_{m-1}, \Psi_m), \tag{8}$$

where Ψ_j is the trust value of the relay v_j $(1 \leq j \leq m)$.

Based on the definition (8), the maximal path trust level ($MPTL$) of the k link-separation paths from v_s to v_t ($P_{s,t}^k$) is

$$MPTL(P_{s,t}^k) = \max(PTL(p_{s,t}^1), PTL(p_{s,t}^2), \cdots, PTL(p_{s,t}^k)). \tag{9}$$

Definition 3 (Path Forwarding Delay): The forwarding delay of a path $p_{s,t}$ from v_s to v_t is defined as

$$PFD(p_{s,t}) = d_s + \sum_{i=1}^m d_i. \tag{10}$$

d_i represents the forwarding delay of node v_i. Thus, the minimal path forwarding delay ($MPFD$) of $P_{s,t}^k$ is calculated by

$$MPFD(P_{s,t}^k) = \min(PFD(p_{s,t}^1), PFD(p_{s,t}^2), \cdots, PFD(p_{s,t}^k)). \tag{11}$$

Finally, the optimization model is described as follows:

$$\begin{aligned}
\textbf{Maximize:} \quad & MPTL(P_{s,t}^k), \\
\textbf{Minimize:} \quad & PFD(p_{s,t}^l) - PFD(p_{s,t}^m), \\
\textbf{Minimize:} \quad & MPFD(P_{s,t}^k) \\
\textbf{Subject to:} \quad &
\end{aligned} \tag{12}$$

$$\begin{aligned}
& \forall p_{s,t}^i, p_{s,t}^j \in P_{s,t}^k, p_{s,t}^i \cap p_{s,t}^j = \emptyset, \\
& p_{s,t}^l = \arg\max(PFD(p_{s,t}^1), PFD(p_{s,t}^2), \cdots, PFD(p_{s,t}^k)), \\
& p_{s,t}^m = \arg\min(PFD(p_{s,t}^1), PFD(p_{s,t}^2), \cdots, PFD(p_{s,t}^k)), \\
& 1 \leq l \leq k, 1 \leq m \leq k.
\end{aligned} \tag{13}$$

3.2   Problem Solving Using Greedy Algorithms

To solve the multi-objective optimization problem defined in (12) and (13), we propose a heuristic algorithm to obtain an approximately optimal solution. The proposed algorithm first uses a modified Dijkstra shortest path algorithm to find a set of candidate paths between a source and a destination. Then, the algorithm adopts a greedy method to select k trusted link-separation paths from the candidate path set.

The algorithm of candidate path set generation is shown in Algorithm 1. We introduce a *relaxation operation* to update the $MPTL$ and $MPFD$ of a routing path set $P_{s,o}$. Formally speaking, given a source node v_s and an edge $\langle v_u, v_o \rangle$, if $MPTL(P_{s,o}) < \min(MPTL(P_{s,u}), \Psi_{v_o})$, then $MPTL(P_{s,o}) = \min(MPTL(P_{s,u}), \Psi_{v_o})$; if $MPFD(P_{s,o}) < MPFD(P_{s,u}) + PFD(\langle v_u, v_o \rangle)$, $MP\text{-}FD(P_{s,o}) = MPFD(P_{s,u}) + PFD(\langle v_u, v_o \rangle)$. Moreover, we introduce a *record operation* to record the path $p_{s,u} \cup \{\langle v_u, v_o \rangle\}$ from v_s to v_o, its trust value, i.e., $PTL(p_{s,u} \cup \{\langle v_u, v_o \rangle\})$, and its forwarding delay, i.e., $PFD(p_{s,u} \cup \{\langle v_u, v_o \rangle\})$ after performing the *relaxation operation* on the edge $\langle v_u, v_o \rangle$. Finally, the algorithm outputs all candidate paths from v_s to v_t.

After generating all candidate paths from the source node v_s to the destination v_t, we further select k link-separation paths $P_{s,t}^k$, considering to maximize the $MPTL$ of k link-separation paths and minimize PFD differences among these paths. Similar to the link-separation path selection algorithm described in our previous work [19], we first sort all candidate paths from v_s to v_t in descending order according to their path forwarding delays. Then, we introduce a two-dimensional matrix LSR with a size of $m \times m$ to record the link-separation relationships of m candidate paths: $\forall i \neq j$, $p_{s,t}^i \in P_{s,t}$, $p_{s,t}^j \in P_{s,t}$, if $p_{s,t}^i \cap p_{s,t}^j = \emptyset$, then $LSR[i][j] = LSR[j][i] = 1$; otherwise, $LSR[i][j] = LSR[j][i] = 0$. Besides, $\forall i$, $LSR[i][i] = 0$ ($1 \leq i \leq m$). After that, we obtain k link-separation paths based on the matrix LSR.

3.3   Time Complexity Analysis of the Proposed Method

As described in the Algorithm 1, all nodes in the topology graph $G(V, E)$ need to be accessed at the stage of candidate path set generation. We use a modified bubble sorting method to select nodes with the *maximal path trust level*. Therefore, the time complexity of accessing $|V|$ nodes is $O(|V|^2)$. Finally, the total time complexity of candidate path generation is $O(|V|^2)$.

At the stage of k link-separation path selection, the time complexity of checking out whether or not two candidate paths are link-separated is $O(|V-1|^2)$. Therefore, the time complexity of generating the matrix LSR is $O(C_m^2 \cdot |V-1|^2)$. Each iteration can find a set of k link-separation paths, if there exists k link-separation paths in the candidate paths. the time complexity of each iteration is $O(k \cdot m)$. There are at most m iterations. Finally, the time complexity of k link-separation path selection is $O(C_m^2 \cdot |V-1|^2 + k \cdot m^2)$.

Based on the above analysis, the total time complexity of the proposed method is $O((|V|^2) + C_m^2 \cdot |V-1|^2 + k \cdot m^2)$.

Algorithm 1. Pseudocode of Candidate Path Set Generation.

Require: A topology graph $G(V, E)$, a source node v_s and a destination node v_t $(s \neq t)$

Ensure: $P_{s,t}$: A candidate path set from v_s to v_t

1: Initialization: $MPTL(P_{s,s}) = \infty$, $MPFD(P_{s,s}) = 0$, $bVisited(v_s) = $ **False**;

2: Initialization: $\forall u \neq s$, $v_u \in V$, $MPTL(P_{s,u}) = 0$, $MPFD(P_{s,u}) = 0$, $bVisited(v_u) = $ **False**;

3: **if** $\exists i$, $v_i \in V$ **and** $bVisited(v_i) = $ **False and** $i = \arg\max_j MPTL(P_{s,j})$ **then**

4:     **if** $\forall j \neq i$, $bVisited(v_j) = $ **False and** $MPTL(P_{s,j}) < MPTL(P_{s,i})$ **then**

5:         $bVisited(v_i) = $ **True**;

6:         Do *relaxation operation* towards all neighbor nodes of v_i and then do *record operation*;

7:     **else if** $\exists j \neq i$, $MPTL(P_{s,j}) = MPTL(P_{s,i})$ **and** $bVisited(v_j) = $ **False then**

8:         **if** $MPFD(P_{s,j}) < MPFD(P_{s,i})$ **then**

9:             $bVisited(v_j) = $ **True**;

10:            Do *relaxation operation* towards all neighbor nodes of v_j and then do *record operation*;

11:        **else if** $MPFD(P_{s,j}) > MPFD(P_{s,i})$ **then**

12:            $bVisited(v_i) = $ **True**;

13:            Do *relaxation operation* towards all neighbor nodes of v_i and then do *record operation*;

14:        **else**

15:            Randomly select a node from v_i and v_j and set its $bVisited$ to **True**;

16:            Do *relaxation operation* and *record operation*;

17:        **end if**

18:     **end if**

19: **end if**

20: **if** $\forall i$, $bVisited(v_i) = $ **True then**

21:     Checking the path record from v_s to v_t to find a candidate routing path set $P_{s,t}$, each path of which has information of PTL and PFD;

22:     **return** The candidate routing path set $P_{s,t}$;

23: **else**

24:     **Goto** line 3;

25: **end if**

---

4 Performance Evaluation

To demonstrate the effectiveness and the superior performance of the proposed method (PA), we compare it with two baseline routing schemes named the delay-first algorithm (DA) and the trust-first algorithm (TA). Basically, the DA and the TA can find out routing paths with the least path forwarding delay and the highest path reputation value, respectively. Moreover, we conducted comparative experiments using three different types of random network topologies, i.e., Waxman, ER random graphs, and WS small-world topologies and three real

networks i.e., Cernet deployed in China[1], Bandcon deployed in the United States
and Europe[2], and DFN deployed in Germany[3].

Figure 1, 2 and 3 demonstrate the superior performance of the proposed
method when generating link-separation paths over the above three random
topologies, where $k = 3$, the nodes 0 and 9 are assigned to be the source and the
destination nodes, respectively. Figure 4, 5 and 6 show the superior performance
of the proposed algorithm in real networks, where $k = 3$, source nodes are set to
node 21, node 1, and node 50, destination nodes are set to node 24, node 21, and
node 46. Note that the mark (δ, γ) along with each routing path represents that
the forwarding delay of the corresponding path is δ (μs), and its reputation value
is γ. Moreover, the blue dotted, the red dotted and the green solid lines show the
resulting paths generated by the proposed method, the DA and the TA schemes,
respectively. The malicious nodes are marked with red circles. We can see from
Fig. 1, 2, 3, 4, and 6 that the proposed method successfully finds out 3 link-
separation paths, which is in line with our expectations ($k = 3$). But in Fig. 5,
the proposed method only finds out 2 link-separation paths. Because in Bandcon,
the degree of source node 1 and destination node 21 all are 2, obviously, there
are no more than 2 link separation paths in Fig. 5. Furthermore, all resulting
paths do not take malicious nodes as their transmission relays, and the PFD
values of these paths do not have significant differences. The results demonstrate
that the proposed method can enhance the security of transmission paths.

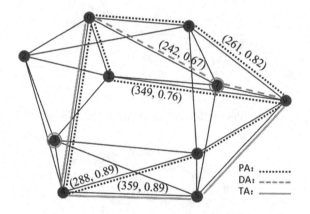

Fig. 1. Comparative results of different methods in the Waxman random graph.

To show the routing efficiency of resulting paths generated by the proposed
method, we further conducted multiple groups of comparative experiments over
six Waxman random graphs with different network sizes ranging from 10 to 60.
Figure 7 illstrates the comparative results of the multipath forwarding delay

---

[1] Access URL: http://www.topology-zoo.org/files/Cernet.gml.
[2] Access URL: http://www.topology-zoo.org/files/Bandcon.gml.
[3] Access URL: http://www.topology-zoo.org/files/Dfn.gml.

28   P. Zhao et al.

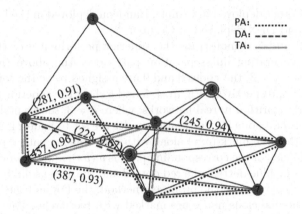

Fig. 2. Comparative results of different methods in ER random graph.

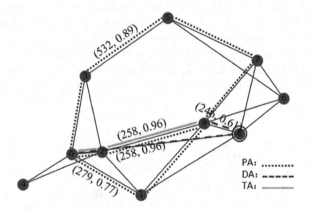

Fig. 3. Comparative results of different methods in the WS small-world networks.

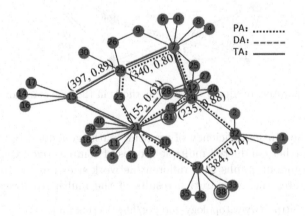

Fig. 4. Comparative results of different methods in Cernet.

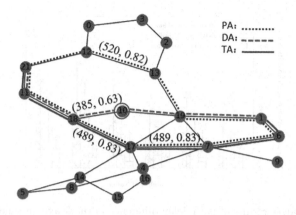

Fig. 5. Comparative results of different methods in Bandcon.

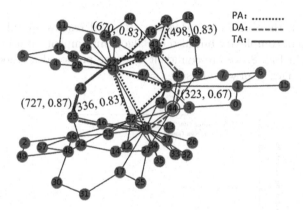

Fig. 6. Comparative results of different methods in DFN.

difference (μs), where each bar is obtained by calculating the mean value of results from 10 independent runs of experiments. From Fig. 7, we find that the multipath delay difference of the PA is smaller (larger) than that of the TA (DA) algorithm. Note that the results of DA objectively represent the minimum delay differences of multiple paths under a specific network topology, which are regarded as the baseline results in this case. Hence, the comparative results validate that the proposed method can make a good tradeoff between the efficiency and the security of resulting transmission paths in adversarial environments.

Lastly, we examine the time cost of the proposed method with different network sizes. Figure 8 shows the average running time of the proposed method versus the number of nodes, where those data points on the red line are obtained by measuring the time cost of running the proposed method in a computer with Intel Core i7-8550U CPU at 1.8GHz and 4G of RAM. We find that the difference between the theoretical and the real results becomes much larger with an increase of the node number. It is rational because the theoretical results reflect

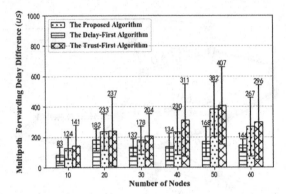

Fig. 7. Comparative results of path delay difference in the Waxman random graphs of different sizes.

the time cost in the worse case. However, the real results are affected by not only the problem complexity but also the algorithm implementation. According to the results in Fig. 8, we are confident that the proposed method is scalable and has advantages of practical usage.

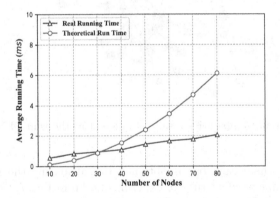

Fig. 8. The running time of the proposed method versus the number of nodes.

5   Conclusions

To solve the secure routing problem in SD-WSNs, we have proposed a trusted link-separation multipath selection method using multi-objective optimization. The proposed method adopts the Bayesian model to calculate the nodes' reputation values, which are then used to evaluate the node trustworthiness. After that, it proposes a multi-objective optimization model to formulate the multipath selection problem with the goals of maximizing the trust values but minimizing the relay latency and the delay difference of resulting paths. Comparative results demonstrate that the proposed method can enhance the routing security and the routing efficiency of transmission paths.

References

1. Alrawi, O., Lever, C., Antonakakis, M., Monrose, F.: Sok: Security evaluation of home-based iot deployments. In: 2019 IEEE Symposium on Security and Privacy (SP). pp. 1362–1380, IEEE (2019)
2. Baranov, N., Bashkin, V., Bashkin, M.: A lightweight cryptographic scheme of route hiding for the on-demand route discovery algorithms. In: 2018 7th Mediterranean Conference on Embedded Computing (MECO). pp. 1–4, IEEE (2018)
3. Boychev, I.Z.: Research algorithms to optimize the drone route used for security. In: 2018 IEEE XXVII International Scientific Conference Electronics-ET. pp. 1–4, IEEE (2018)
4. Cho, J.H., Swami, A., Chen, R.: A survey on trust management for mobile ad hoc networks. IEEE Commun. Surveys Tuts. 13(4), 562–583 (2010)
5. Duan, J., Wang, Z., Wu, C.: Responsive multipath tcp in sdn-based datacenters. In: IEEE International Conference on Communications (2015)
6. Javed, M., Zeadally, S.: Repguide: Reputation-based route guidance using internet of vehicles. IEEE Commun. Mag. 2(4), 81–87 (2018)
7. Koerner, M., Kao, O.: Evaluating sdn based rack-to-rack multi-path switching for data-center networks. Procedia Comput. Sci. 34, 118–125 (2014)
8. Vinoth Kumar, V., Ramamoorthy, S.: Secure adhoc on-demand multipath distance vector routing in MANET. In: Mandal, J.K., Saha, G., Kandar, D., Maji, A.K. (eds.) Proceedings of the International Conference on Computing and Communication Systems. LNNS, vol. 24, pp. 49–63. Springer, Singapore (2018). https://doi.org/10.1007/978-981-10-6890-4_5
9. Liu, K.: Information theoretic framework of trust modeling and evaluation for ad hoc networks. IEEE J. Sel. Areas Commun. 24(2), 305–317 (2006)
10. Luckie, M., Beverly, R., Koga, R., Keys, K., Kroll, J.A., claffy, k.: Network hygiene, incentives, and regulation: Deployment of source address validation in the internet. In: Proceedings of the 2019 ACM SIGSAC Conference on Computer and Communications Security. pp. 465–480 (2019)
11. Meng, Y., Li, W., Kwok, L.: Evaluation of detecting malicious nodes using bayesian model in wireless intrusion detection. In: Lopez, J., Huang, X., Sandhu, R. (eds.) NSS 2013. LNCS, vol. 7873, pp. 40–53. Springer, Heidelberg (2013). https://doi.org/10.1007/978-3-642-38631-2_4
12. Paasch, C., Ferlin, S., Alay, O., Bonaventure, O.: Experimental evaluation of multipath tcp schedulers. In: Proceedings of the 2014 ACM SIGCOMM workshop on Capacity sharing workshop. pp. 27–32, ACM (2014)
13. Rajeswari, A.R., Kulothungan, K., Ganapathy, S., Kannan, A.: A trusted fuzzy based stable and secure routing algorithm for effective communication in mobile adhoc networks. Peer Peer Netw. Appl. 12(5), 1076–1096 (2019). https://doi.org/10.1007/s12083-019-00766-8
14. Shin, D., Yun, K., Kim, J., Astillo, P.V., Kim, J.N., You, I.: A security protocol for route optimization in dmm-based smart home iot networks. IEEE Access 7, 142531–142550 (2019)

15. Sommer, R., Paxson, V.: Outside the closed world: On using machine learning for network intrusion detection. In: 2010 IEEE Symposium on Security and Privacy (2010)
16. Valente, J., Wynn, M.A., Cardenas, A.A.: Stealing, spying, and abusing: consequences of attacks on internet of things devices. IEEE Secur. Priv. **17**(5), 10–21 (2019)
17. Wang, X.: Study on the Technology and Prototype of Software-Defined Mobile Ad-Hoc Networking. Ph.D. thesis, Nanjing University of Posts and Telecommunications (2015)
18. Zhang, T., Yan, L., Yang, Y.: Trust evaluation method for clustered wireless sensor networks based on cloud model. Wirel. Netw. **24**(3), 777–797 (2016). https://doi.org/10.1007/s11276-016-1368-y
19. Zhao, P., Zhao, W., Liu, Q.: Multi-objective link-separation multipath selection using k max-min for software-defined manets. In: Proceedings of the 15th International Conference on Mobile Ad-hoc and Sensor Networks (MSN 2019). pp. 259–264, IEEE (2019)

Secure Radio Frequency DCS Watermark-Aided Physical Layer Authentication Design for NB-IoT Systems

Hongqing Huang[1,2] and Lin Zhang[1,2(✉)]

[1] School of Electronics and Information Technology, Sun Yat-sen University,
Guangzhou 510006, China
isszl@mail.sysu.edu.cn
[2] Shandong Provincial Key Laboratory of Wireless Communication Technologies,
Jinan, China

Abstract. Narrow band Internet of Things (NB-IoT) systems suffer from malicious attacks due to the broadcasting properties of wireless channels. Active attackers would falsify the transmitted data or the controlling signaling to interfere with the information transmissions for legitimate users. In order to combat the active attacks, in this paper, we propose to apply the differential constellation shifting (DCS) radio frequency (RF) watermark to enhance the security of authentications. In our design, the DCS-aided RF watermarking is utilized to hide the authentication tags, and we construct the differential watermarked symbol pairs which consist of host and watermark symbols with a specific watermarking strength. At the receiver, by calculating the difference and the summation of the watermarked symbol pairs, both host and watermark symbols can be securely and reliably recovered. Simulation results demonstrate that our proposed schemes can effectively improve the bit error rate (BER) performances while the security performances outperform the benchmark watermark systems.

Keywords: Differential constellation shifting (DCS) · Narrow band Internet of Things (NB-IoT) · Radio frequency (RF) watermark · Security and reliability

1 Introduction

Internet of Things (IoT) is the extension of the traditional Internet that aims at connecting every object to the Internet and construct massive machine-to-machine communication network [11]. Since the diversity and fragmentization of

This work is partially supported by Guangdong Basic and Applied Basic Research Foundation (No. 2020A1515010703), the open research fund from Shandong Provincial Key Lab. of Wireless Communication Technologies (No. SDKLWCT-2019-05), Key Research and Development and Transformation Plan of Science and Technology Program for Tibet Autonomous Region (No. XZ201901-GB-16) and National Science Foundation of China (No. 61602531).

S. Yu et al. (Eds.): SPDE 2020, CCIS 1268, pp. 33–49, 2020.
https://doi.org/10.1007/978-981-15-9129-7_3

application scenarios severely limit the popularization of IoT system, the third Generation Partnership Project (3GPP) specified the standard of narrow band Internet of Things (NB-IoT) as a novel low power wide area (LPWA) technology in 2016 [1], which utilizes authorized frequency bands and cellular technology to access user ends so that the NB-IoT terminals could be easily integrated with the 5th Generation (5G) network. Benefit from the narrow band techniques and simplified architecture, NB-IoT system has advantages of low-cost, widespread, large-scale connections and low-power dissipations, while guaranteeing the robust transmission [18].

However, due to the broadcasting properties of wireless channels, the NB-IoT systems are vulnerable to malicious passive and active attacks. Passive attackers are who eavesdrop the information without interfere the system, whereas, active attackers would falsify the information-bearing data or the controlling signalling to impose interference to the legitimate communications, thereby causing more serious damages. In order to combat active attackers and ensure the security of system, the legitimacy of received signal must be authenticated, and user should protect the authentication tags from falsification.

The authentication mechanism in traditional wireless communication standard requires complex signaling exchange operations in high layers, which is not suitable to massive NB-IoT system with limited resource [3]. However, physical layer authentication (PLA) techniques have more advantages in terms of computational complexity, communication overhead and security reliability. In general, PLA techniques utilize the inherent physical characteristics of hardware devices or wireless signals. For instance, the uncontrollable factors in hardware manufacturing process bring randomness to the electrical characteristics of the devices, thus, hardware fingerprint techniques can utilize these unique characteristics to authenticate the validity of devices by constructing physically unclonable functions (PUF) circuits [6]. However, the hardware aging will affect the authentication reliability of hardware fingerprint techniques. When attacker is able to collect plentiful enough "Challenge-Response" pairs, it can build prediction model to simulate the response of PUF circuits to arbitrary challenges.

Likewise, the wireless channels between transmitter and receiver also have randomness and uniqueness, thus the channel frequency response of wireless channel can be exploited as fingerprint for signal authentication [15]. In order to reduce the complexity, Demirabas et al. propose to use received signal strength to authenticate the signal validity [5]. Besides, Liu et al. also propose to utilize the amplitude and delay of channel impulse response to further authenticate the location and time domain characteristics of user devices [9]. However, since the channel characteristics are usually uncontrollable, the reliability of channel-based authentication schemes will degrade severely in time-varying channel.

Without using the inherent characteristics of devices or channel, physical layer watermark techniques embed the artificially generated authentication information into the host signal to enhance the reliability of authentication. In traditional physical layer watermark schemes, the authentication information will be modulated as spread spectrum (SS) signal to be embedded into host signals, which generally are image or video signals thereby reduce visual interference [4,12]. However, SS watermark will increase the bit error rate (BER) of wireless signal and degrade the communication reliability. Malvar et al. propose improved SS watermark scheme to reduce the interference to host signal [10] and the capacity performance and security level are further studied [14,16]. However, the SS-based watermark schemes require extra bandwidth and only provide low watermark transmission rate.

Therefore, constellation-based RF watermark methods are proposed to improve the watermark transmission rate, such as the constellation rotation (CR) scheme [8], the constellation shifting (CS) and the improved constellation shifting (ICS) schemes [13,17], by deviating constellation points. Nevertheless, the traditional CS methods induce interferences to the host signals since the embedded watermark signals are treated as noises at the receiver and the rotated constellations may shorten the Euclidean distances between constellation points. Thus the error rate of host signals will increase, thereby leading to reliability degradations.

In our previous research work [7], we present a differential constellation shifting (DCS) aided RF watermark scheme to improve reliability performance while providing secure transmissions. In this paper, we propose a DCS watermark-aided physical layer authentication (PLA) mechanism for NB-IoT systems.

In our design, we propose to generate the authentication tag by using the cryptographic hash function, then we hide the secret authentication tag behind the shifted constellations as the watermark bits. After that, we embed the watermark bits into both real and imaginary parts of adjacent constellation symbols in a differential way. Since NB-IoT systems allow the host signals to be repetitively transmitted 128 times in the uplink and 2048 times in the downlink [1], the reliability of authentication tag transmissions could be guaranteed for legitimate users.

At the receiver, the receivers could extract the authentication tag reliably and securely to validate the identity of users. Furthermore, we provide theoretical analyses of the bit error rate, the efficiency, the authentication performance and the key security. Then simulation results demonstrate the secure and reliable performances achieved by the proposed design.

Briefly, the main contributions include: (1) we propose to hide the authentication tag behind the information bits as watermark data to combat active attacks; (2) we propose to use the cryptographic hash function to generate the tag of the signal, then present a DCS watermark aided authentication mechanisms to enhance security performances while providing reliable transmissions; (3) we derive theoretical bit error rate expressions, and analyze the efficiency as well as security performances.

The rest of the paper is organized as follows. Section 2 presents the system model and the proposed DCS-aided authentication mechanism for NB-IoT systems. Then the theoretical analysis and simulation results are respectively provided by Sect. 3 and Sect. 4. Finally, Sect. 5 concludes our findings.

2   DCS-Aided NB-IoT PLA System

In this section, we present the active attack model, then we present the DCS-aided NB-IoT PLA design in detail. Then we provide the details of the proposed differential constellation shifting aided physical layer authentication mechanism.

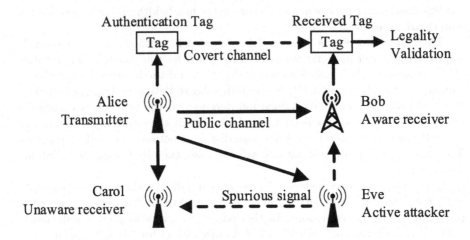

Fig. 1. The active attack model.

2.1   Active Attack Model

Figure 1 shows the active attack model considered in our design. The active attacker Eve keeps eavesdropping the signals sent by Alice, then injects the spurious signals into the legitimate signals to deceive the receivers into accepting the malicious signals or into refusing to receive the legitimate signals, which are defined as the impersonation and the substitution respectively. To combat these active attacks, Alice generates an authentication tag that is sent along with the legitimate signal through a specific covert channel. The aware receiver Bob is able to extract the tag from received signals, then the tag is used to verify the legality and integrity of received signals. By contrast, the unaware receiver Carol cannot extract the authentication tag, and thus is vulnerable to active attacks.

Therefore, the security of authentication plays the vital role to protect the tag from being learned. If the malicious active attackers luckily learn the secret authentication tag, they might also send signals to Bob to interfere with the communications. As a result, the security performance could not be guaranteed. In order to address this issue, we propose to hide the authentication tag behind information bits to prevent eavesdropping as follows.

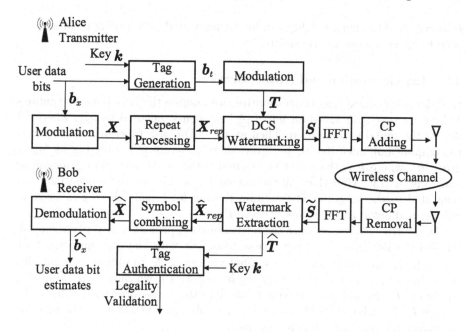

Fig. 2. The DCS-aided NB-IoT PLA system model.

2.2 System Model

Figure 2 shows the proposed DCS-aided NB-IoT PLA system model. This system has two bit streams to be transmitted, i.e. user data bits b_x and watermark bits b_t, where b_t is also regarded as authentication tag that used to verify the validity of transmitter. Without loss of the generality, both b_x and b_t are assumed to be uniformly distributed [13].

In the process of transmitter, the tag bits b_t are firstly generated via an encrypted hash function as $b_t = g(b_x, k)$. The hash function $g(\cdot)$ can map b_x of the arbitrary length to a tag b_t with the fixed length using the key k shared between transceivers [2]. Then both b_x and b_t are conducted with quadrature phase shift keying (QPSK) modulation [1] to form host symbol vectors $X \in \mathbb{C}^{L \times 1}$ and watermark symbol vectors $T \in \mathbb{C}^{L \times 1}$, where $\mathbb{C}$ denotes the complex vector space and L is the vector length. After X and T are repeated for M times, we embed watermark symbols T and its replicas into host symbols X to construct the watermarked symbol matrix $S \in \mathbb{C}^{L \times M}$ via DCS scheme. After the inverse fast Fourier transform (IFFT) and adding the cyclic prefix (CP), the signals will be sent over the wireless channel.

The receiver conducts reverse operations. After the CP removal and the fast Fourier transform (FFT), we can recover the watermark symbol vector $\widehat{T}$ and the host symbol vector $\widehat{X}$ from the received symbol matrix $\widetilde{S}$ by calculating the difference or the summation of the columns of $\widetilde{S}$. Finally, we demodulate $\widehat{T}$ and $\widehat{X}$ via the QPSK demodulation module and recover their estimates $\widehat{b}_t$ and $\widehat{b}_x$, respectively. The signal validity can be authenticated by verifying recovered tag with key k that same as transmitter.

2.3   Tag Generation and Authentication

In order to generate tags in transmitter, we assume the user data b_x contains B bits, we first split the data into $\lceil \frac{B}{128} \rceil$ segments, denoted as b_{xn}, where $\lceil \cdot \rceil$ denote the round up operation. Then we use MD5 hash function, which is easy to compute but infeasible to be inverted, to generate a 128-bit tag as $b_{tn} = g(b_{xn}, k)$, where k is the secret key shared between the legitimate transmitter and receiver [13]. After that, all the output b_{tn} will be spliced sequentially and truncated to the length of B to obtain the tag b_t. Finally the tag message b_t will be modulated as tag symbol vector T.

At the receiver, we conduct the authentication processes to verify the legality and the integrity of received message signals with the corresponding hash tags. Firstly, we demodulate the symbol vectors of $\widehat{X}$ to obtain data bits $\widehat{b}_x$. Secondly, we generate the reference tag $b_t^r = g(\widehat{b}_x, k)$, which is then modulated to obtain T_r. In addition, we could calculate the cross-correlation value c_i by $c_i = \Re(T_r^H \widehat{T})$, where $\widehat{T}$ is the received tag symbol and $\Re(\cdot)$ denotes the function to extract the real part of a specific data.

At last, Bob performs the hypothesis test as

$$\begin{cases} H_0 & : \quad \text{The tag is incorrect.} \\ H_1 & : \quad \text{The tag is correct.} \end{cases} \tag{1}$$

where H_0 implies that the tag does not match the message signal or there is no authentication tag embedded, in this case, the signal is determined to be illegal. By contrast, H_1 implies that the signal contains the correct tag to certify the validity. The confidence of information transmissions and the security performances are analyzed as follows.

2.4   DCS Aided RF Watermark Design

As mentioned above and illustrated by Fig. 3, in our DCS design, after repeating X and T for M times, we obtain the matrix $X_{rep} \in \mathbb{C}^{L \times M}$ and $T_{rep} \in \mathbb{C}^{L \times M}$. Then one half of watermark column vectors in T_{rep} are selected to be subtracted from the corresponding vectors in X_{rep}, while the addition operation will be performed on another half of vectors, thereby we obtain $M/2$ differential watermarked symbol vector pairs.

Specifically, let $X_n = a_n + jb_n$ and $T_n = c_n + jd_n$ respectively denote the n_{th} element of vectors in X_{rep} and T_{rep}, where $a_n, b_n\, c_n, d_n \in \{1, -1\}$. After the differential watermarking, we obtain S for transmissions, wherein the elements $S_n^{k_i^+}$ and $S_n^{k_i^-}$ are derived by

$$S_n^{k_i^+} = \sqrt{1-\alpha} X_n + \sqrt{\alpha} T_n$$
$$S_n^{k_i^-} = \sqrt{1-\alpha} X_n - \sqrt{\alpha} T_n \tag{2}$$

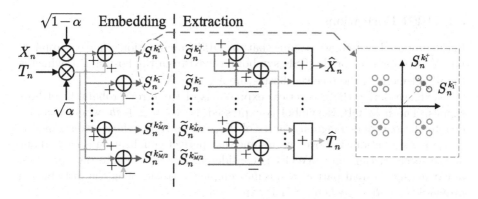

Fig. 3. The embedding and extraction process of DCS scheme.

where $k_i^+ = 2i - 1$ or $k_i^- = 2i$ is the vector index corresponding to "added" columns or "subtracted" column, $i \in [1, M/2]$ denotes the index of the pair of the host symbol and the watermark symbol, $n \in [1, L]$ is the element index, and α denotes the embedding strength. In general, embedding strength is $\alpha < 0.5$ to keep the covertness of the watermark. From Fig. 3, we can see that the original constellation points are shifted as $S_n^{k_i^+}$ and $S_n^{k_i^-}$.

At the receiver, after transmissions over additive white Gaussian noise (AWGN) channel, the received symbol matrix is expressed as $\tilde{S} = S + w$ where $w \in \mathbb{C}^{L \times M}$ is the Gaussian white noise with the power of $P_n = 2\sigma^2$ whose elements follow $w \sim \mathcal{CN}(0, 2\sigma^2)$. Then we extract the watermark symbol from the differential symbol pairs as below

$$\widehat{T}_n = \sum_{i=1}^{M/2} \tilde{S}_n^{k_i^+} - \tilde{S}_n^{k_i^-} = M\sqrt{\alpha}(c_n + jd_n) + \underbrace{\sum_{i=1}^{M/2} w_i^+ - w_i^-}_{W_w} \tag{3}$$

where $W_w \sim \mathcal{CN}(0, 2M\sigma^2)$ is the linear combination of M independent complex Gaussian variables. Similarly, we obtain the estimates of the host symbol as

$$\widehat{X}_n = \sum_{i=1}^{M/2} \tilde{S}_n^{k_i^+} + \tilde{S}_n^{k_i^-} = M\sqrt{1-\alpha}(a_n + jb_n) + \underbrace{\sum_{i=1}^{M/2} w_i^+ + w_i^-}_{W_h} \tag{4}$$

where $W_h \sim \mathcal{CN}(0, 2M\sigma^2)$.

Subsequently, the estimates of the user data bits $\widehat{b}_x$ and watermark bits $\widehat{b}_t$ can be obtained from the QPSK demodulation.

3   Performance Analysis

In this section, we will derive the BER expressions, and analyze the spectrum efficiency and the authentication performance.

3.1   BER Derivations

In the proposed system, we assume that the QPSK modulation scheme is applied. Let $\widehat{X}_n$ denote a restored QPSK symbol received from the host signal, which is the nth element in the received host symbol vector $\widehat{X}$.

Next, we derive the theoretical expressions of the error probability of host signals. The host QPSK symbol is expressed as $X_n = a + jb$, where a and b denote the real and imaginary parts of X_n, respectively, whose value range is $\{-1, 1\}$. As mentioned above, we assume that perfect equalization is carried out at the receiver, thus only AWGN is considered. Let $\Re(\cdot)$ denote the operation of extracting the real part of a specific complex variable, then the distribution probability of $\Re(\widehat{X}_n)$ when $a = 1$ is expressed as

$$p_1(x) = \frac{1}{\sqrt{2\pi}\sqrt{M\sigma^2}} \exp\left(-\frac{(x - M\sqrt{1-\alpha})^2}{2(M\sigma^2)}\right). \tag{5}$$

Set the decision threshold as 0, thus the decision error that the estimate of $a = 1$ is wrongly decided as $\hat{a} = -1$ is expressed by

$$P_{e1} = \int_{-\infty}^{0} \frac{1}{\sqrt{2\pi}\sqrt{M\sigma^2}} \exp\left(-\frac{\left(x - M\sqrt{1-\alpha}\right)^2}{2\left(M\sigma^2\right)}\right) dx$$

$$= Q\left(\sqrt{M(1-\alpha)\gamma}\right) \tag{6}$$

where $Q(x) = \int_x^{\infty} \frac{1}{\sqrt{2\pi}} e^{-\frac{t^2}{2}} dt$ denotes the right tail function of the standard normal distribution.

Likewise, the distribution probability of $\Re(\widehat{X}_n)$ when $a = -1$ is

$$p_0(x) = \frac{1}{\sqrt{2\pi}\sqrt{M\sigma^2}} \exp\left(-\frac{(x + M\sqrt{1-\alpha})^2}{2(M\sigma^2)}\right). \tag{7}$$

Hence we could obtain the error probability of wrongly deciding the estimate of $a = -1$ as $\hat{a} = 1$ as $P_{e0} = Q\left(\sqrt{M(1-\alpha)\gamma}\right)$, which is the same as P_{e1}. Accordingly, the BER expression of real parts of host symbol is $P_{er} = Q\left(\sqrt{M(1-\alpha)\gamma}\right)$.

In the same way, we could also obtain the BER expression of imaginary parts, which has the same expression as P_{er}. Accordingly, we could derive the BER expression of host symbols as

$$P_e^H = Q\left(\sqrt{M(1-\alpha)\gamma}\right). \tag{8}$$

Similarly, we can also derive the BER expression of watermark symbols as

$$P_e^W = Q\left(\sqrt{M\alpha\gamma}\right). \tag{9}$$

3.2   Efficiency Analysis

As presented by Table 1, the spectral efficiency (SE) performances of host signals and watermark signals are compared with the counterpart schemes of improved constellation shifting (ICS) scheme [17] and the spread spectrum (SS) scheme [20]. In our proposed NB-IoT system, we assume that the bandwidth of 200 kHz is divided into 12 subcarriers, while in the time domain, a subframe consists of 14 symbols per second.

Table 1. Spectral efficiency (bit/s/Hz) comparison

Schemes	Host signal	Watermark signal
ICS [17]	1.68	1.68
SS [20]	0.5115	4×10^{-4}
DCS $M = 2, 4, 8$	0.84, 0.42, 0.21	0.84, 0.42, 0.21

The ICS scheme [17] proposes to embed one QPSK watermark symbol into each host symbol, hence the spectral efficiency is $R = 12 \times 2 \times 14 \times 10^3/(200 \times 10^3) = 1.68$ bit/s/Hz. On the other hand, the SS scheme [20], which utilizes the spread spectrum technique, can only achieve 12 bps watermark transmission rate with 30 kHz bandwidth, resulting in lower SE than that of ICS scheme.

Notably, in our proposed DCS system, due to the repetitive transmissions, the SE is not higher than that of the ICS scheme. Naturally, the SE decreases with the increasing repeat times M. Nevertheless, thanks to the differential watermarking, the DCS scheme can achieve higher watermark capacity than that of ICS system especially when the NB-IoT terminals operate at low power mode and the SNR is relatively lower, which will be discussed in detail in Sect. 4.

3.3   Authentication Performance

Suppose the receiver can reliably retrieve the symbol $\widehat{\boldsymbol{X}}_i$, which indicates that $\boldsymbol{T}_r = \boldsymbol{T}$. Thus, for the hypothesis H_1, we have

$$
\begin{aligned}
c_i|H_1 &= \Re\left(\boldsymbol{T}_r^H \widehat{\boldsymbol{T}'}\right) \\
&= \|\boldsymbol{T}\|_2^2 + \frac{1}{M}\sqrt{\frac{1}{\alpha}}\Re\left(\boldsymbol{T}_r^H \boldsymbol{w}_t'\right)
\end{aligned}
\tag{10}
$$

where $\|\cdot\|_2$ denotes 2-norm of the vector. Then we can evaluate the numerical expectation of c_i as $\mathbb{E}(c_i|H_1) = Lp_x^2$, and the variance as $var(c_i|H_1) = \frac{L}{M}\frac{1}{\alpha}p_x^2\sigma^2$, where p_x^2 denotes the power of symbols in $\widehat{\boldsymbol{X}}_i$. When QPSK is employed, we have $p_x^2 = 2$, while for BPSK symbols, $p_x^2 = 1$.

For the hypothesis H_0, the signal sent by attacker does not contain the valid tag, so that we assume $\boldsymbol{T} = 0$ and $\widehat{\boldsymbol{T}} = \boldsymbol{w}_t'$, then we have

$$c_i|H_0 = \frac{1}{M}\sqrt{\frac{1}{\alpha}}\Re\left(\boldsymbol{T}_r^H \boldsymbol{w}_t'\right) \tag{11}$$

where the numerical expectation and variance of c_i are respectively $\mathbb{E}(c_i|H_0) = 0$ and $var(c_i|H_0) = \frac{L}{M}\frac{1}{\alpha}p_x^2\sigma^2$.

Consequently, the hypothesis test problem can be transformed as:

$$\begin{cases} H_0 & : c_i \sim \mathcal{N}\left(0, \frac{L}{M}\frac{1}{\alpha}p_x^2\sigma^2\right) \\ H_1 & : c_i \sim \mathcal{N}\left(Lp_x^2, \frac{L}{M}\frac{1}{\alpha}p_x^2\sigma^2\right). \end{cases} \tag{12}$$

The authentication performance in terms of the probability of false alarm and the detection probability could reflect the confidence of information transmissions. Namely, lower false alarm probability or high detection probability means that the confidence of information transmissions is also higher.

To be more explicit, let η denote the probability of false alarm that H_0 is mistaken as H_1, and ψ denotes the probability of detection that H_1 is correctly judged as H_1. Given a threshold c_0, the probabilities of false alarm and detection are represented as:

$$\begin{aligned} \eta &= P_{FA} = P\left(c_i > c_0|H_0\right) \\ \psi &= P_D = P\left(c_i > c_0|H_1\right). \end{aligned} \tag{13}$$

For a given false alarm rate η constraint, we could derive the corresponding threshold c_{i0} as

$$c_0 = arg\min_{c_i}\Phi\left(\frac{c_i}{\sigma_0}\right) \geqslant 1 - \eta \tag{14}$$

where $\Phi(x)$ is the cumulative distribution function of standard Gaussian distribution and $\sigma_0^2 = Lp_x^2\sigma^2/(M\alpha)$. Furthermore, we can also obtain the probability of detection ψ as

$$\psi = Q\left(\frac{c_0 - Lp_x^2}{\sigma_0}\right) \tag{15}$$

where $Q(x) = 1 - \Phi(x)$ denotes the complementary error function.

3.4   Security of Authentication Tags

The foremost goal of the attackers is to obtain the correct key $\boldsymbol{k}$ to launch active attacks. For the attackers who occasionally have the knowledge of the hash function $g(\cdot)$ of the authentication system, if they can recover the authentication tags reliably, then in sufficiently large enough observation time slots, they might retrieve the authentication key $\boldsymbol{k}$ by using the brute-force exhaustive searching method. By contrast, if the received tag could not be reliably obtained, the key space $\mathcal{K}$ required for searching will expand exponentially, which easily goes beyond the computation capacity of attackers.

Hence, we propose to use the tag equivocation to measure the uncertainty of authentication tag for attackers, which is defined as the entropy of the observed tags expressed as [19]:

$$H\left(\widehat{\boldsymbol{b}}_t | \widetilde{\boldsymbol{S}}\right) = P_e \log_2 \frac{1}{P_e} + (1 - P_e) \log_2 \frac{1}{(1 - P_e)} \tag{16}$$

where $\widehat{\boldsymbol{b}}_t$ denotes estimated tag bits and $\widetilde{\boldsymbol{S}}$ denotes received symbol matrix. Besides, P_e denotes the bit error probability of the tag signal that eavesdropped by attacker Eve.

Suppose the attacker only knows how to extract the tag of the leader device, but is not aware of the embedded signal of member devices. Thus it will regard the embedded message and the tag signal of members as noises. Therefore, when the attacker tries to recover the embedded authentication tag of the leader, it will be greatly interfered with by other embedded signals, which would lead to higher tag equivocation to the active attacker. Thus the confidence of information transmissions could be enhanced.

4   Simulation Results

In this section, we will present the simulation results to verify the effectiveness of the theoretical analysis. Then we will evaluate and compare our proposed DCS-aided NB-IoT PLA system with the counterpart systems in terms of the reliability, the capacity, and security.

In the simulations, in the considered NB-IoT scenario, the QPSK modulation is employed, and 16-point IFFT/FFT operation is performed with 12 effective subcarriers per OFDM frame. In addition, for each SNR, we transmit 10^4 frames. The hardware platform we use includes central processing unit (CPU) of Intel Core i7-4700HQ and random access memory (RAM) of 8.00 GB.

4.1   BER Performance

Firstly, Fig. 4a and Fig. 4b respectively compares BER performances of watermarking symbols and host symbols of the proposed DCS systems with those of the ICS scheme with $\alpha = 0.3$ [17]. It can be seen that the proposed DCS systems achieve much better reliability performances than those of ICS systems. Moreover, for proposed DCS systems, the simulated BER of watermark signals and host signals match the theoretical BER evaluated with Eq. (9) and Eq. (8). Additionally, we can also notice that the BER performances can be further improved with larger M thanks to the repetitive transmissions of the information-bearing signals.

4.2   Watermark Capacity

Next, we demonstrate the watermark capacity performance of proposed DCS systems and ICS systems by evaluating $C = R_b(1 + (1 - P_e)\log_2(1 - P_e) + P_e \log_2 P_e)$ [17], where P_e is the watermark error probability and watermark

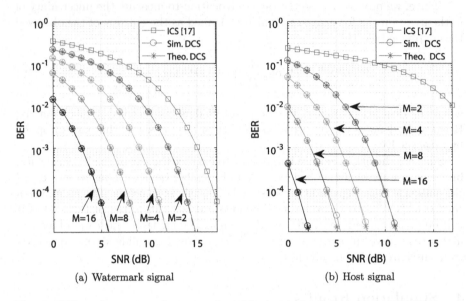

Fig. 4. BER performances of watermark and host signals of the proposed DCS system and the ICS system [17].

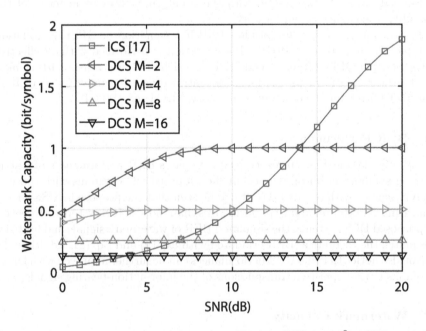

Fig. 5. The watermark capacity performances. The host BER is 10^{-3} at SNR = 12 dB.

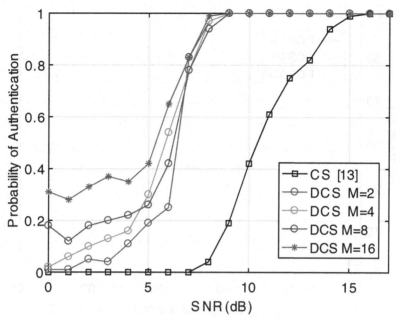

(a) Probability of authentication

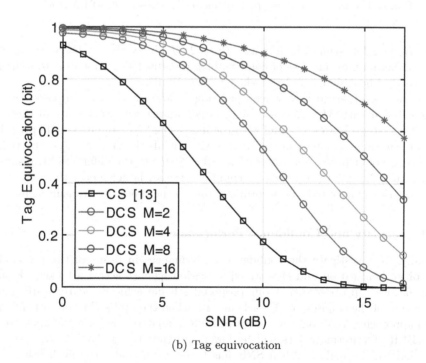

(b) Tag equivocation

Fig. 6. The confidence performance comparison in terms of the probability of authentication and the tag equivocation between the proposed system and the CS system [13]. (a) The host BER is 10^{-3} at SNR = 10 dB. $\eta = 1\%$. (b) The watermark BER is 10^{-3} at SNR = 14 dB.

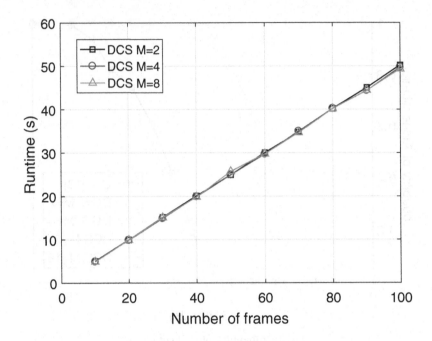

Fig. 7. The time complexity performances of proposed DCS-PLA scheme.

rate $R_b = 2$ bit/symbol in ICS and $R_b = 2/M$ bit/symbol in DCS scheme in Fig. 5. Notably, for fairness of comparisons, we adjust the value of α to remain the BER of host signals is 10^{-3} when SNR is 12 dB.

It can be observed that when operating at lower SNR, the proposed DCS-aided design with $M = 2$ can achieve larger watermark capacity than that of the ICS system. However, along with the increasing SNR, the ICS could provide larger watermark capacity at the BER of 10^{-3}, while the proposed system would approach about half of the watermark capacity due to the differential transmissions when $M = 2$. In addition, we could observe for larger repeat times M, the watermark capacity reduces accordingly due to the repetitive transmissions.

4.3 Security and Confidence Performances

Finally, we investigate the confidence performances in terms of the probability of authentication and the tag equivocation against active attackers. From Fig. 6a, we can observe that our proposed scheme achieves nearly 6 dB gain than that of the counterpart CS scheme [13] when the probability of authentication approaches 1. More over, when the SNR is relatively lower, as M increases, the BER of watermark bits will be lower and thus the probability of authentication will be higher. When SNR has larger value, since the authentication performances are mainly determined by the host signals and the BER of host signals are similar, the probability of authentication will approach 1. Thus the proposed system could achieve secure transmissions.

In addition, Fig. 6b shows that the tag equivocation of the CS scheme drops to zero rapidly when SNR is 15 dB, while the tag equivocation of the proposed scheme still remains higher than that of the CS scheme. More over, when M increases, the embedding strength required to achieve the same BER become smaller, thus error probability of watermark bits recovered by attacker will increase. Accordingly, the tag equivocation will enhance and the security performances will be improved.

4.4   Execution Time Performance

Furthermore, Fig. 7 illustrates the execution time performance of proposed DCS-PLA scheme, where x-axis denotes the number of OFDM frames and y-axis denotes the runtime of process. We can observe that the runtime of the process of transmission and reception is linear with the number of frames, because the computational complexity mainly results from the cryptographic hash function, which is linear process. The repetition time M only has slight effect to the runtime, therefore increasing M can improve the system performance while avoiding excessive computations.

5   Conclusion

In this paper, we propose to hide the authentication tag with the DCS aided RF watermark scheme to enhance the security with improved reliability performances. We first generate the authentication tags with the hash function, then we embed tag bits into one host signal in differential way and design the authentication mechanisms to combat the active attacks. Thus only the legitimate user could get authorized using the secret authentication tag, while active attackers could not authorize the identity, thereby enhancing the security performances. Subsequently, we derive the theoretical BER expressions and analyze the SE as well as the security of the authentication tag transmissions. Simulation results validate the theoretical analysis, and demonstrate that our proposed DCS-aided authentication design can achieve better reliability and security performances, while remaining the satisfactory watermark capacity. Therefore, with the DCS-aided authentication, the NB-IoT systems could enhance the security performances with no loss of reliability performance. Further research work could be done on the application of DCS watermarking to protect the information from the passive attacks.

References

1. 3GPP: Evolved universal terrestrial radio access (E-UTRA) physical channels and modulation (TS 36.211 V 13.2.0 Rel. 13), August 2016
2. Menezes, A.J., van Oorschot, P.C., Vanstone, S.A.: Handbook of Applied Cryptography. CRC Press, Boca Raton (1997)
3. Cao, J., Yu, P., Ma, M., Gao, W.: Fast authentication and data transfer scheme for massive NB-IoT devices in 3GPP 5G network. IEEE Internet Things J. **6**(2), 1561–1575 (2019)
4. Cox, I.J., Miller, M.L., McKellips, A.L.: Watermarking as communications with side information. Proc. IEEE **87**(7), 1127–1141 (1999)
5. Demirbas, M., Song, Y.: An RSSI-based scheme for sybil attack detection in wireless sensor networks. In: Proceedings of 2006 International Symposium on a World of Wireless, Mobile and Multimedia Networks (WoWMoM 2006), Buffalo-Niagara Falls, NY, USA, 26–29 June, pp. 5 pp.-570. IEEE Press, Piscataway (2006)
6. Halak, B., Zwolinski, M., Mispan, M.S.: Overview of PUF-based hardware security solutions for the internet of things. In: Proceedings of 2016 IEEE 59th International Midwest Symposium on Circuits and Systems (MWSCAS), Abu Dhabi, United Arab Emirates, 16–19 October, pp. 1–4. IEEE Press, Piscataway (2016)
7. Huang, H., Zhang, L.: Reliable and secure constellation shifting aided differential radio frequency watermark design for NB-IoT systems. IEEE Commu. Lett. **23**(12), 2262–2265 (2019)
8. Jiang, T., Zeng, H., Yan, Q., Lou, W., Hou, Y.T.: On the limitation of embedding cryptographic signature for primary transmitter authentication. IEEE Wireless Commun. Lett. **1**(4), 324–327 (2012)
9. Liu, F.J., Wang, X., Tang, H.: Robust physical layer authentication using inherent properties of channel impulse response. In: Proceedings of 2011 - MILCOM 2011 Military Communications Conference, Baltimore, MD, USA, 7–10 November, pp. 538–542. IEEE Press, Piscataway (2011)
10. Malvar, H.S., Florencio, D.A.F.: Improved spread spectrum: a new modulation technique for robust watermarking. IEEE Trans. Signal Process. **51**(4), 898–905 (2003)
11. Perera, C., Liu, C.H., Jayawardena, S., Chen, M.: A survey on Internet of Things from industrial market perspective. IEEE Access **2**, 1660–1679 (2014)
12. Tirkel, A.Z., Osborne, C.F., Van Schyndel, R.G.: Image watermarking-a spread spectrum application. In: Proceedings of ISSSTA 1995 International Symposium on Spread Spectrum Techniques and Applications, Mainz, Germany, 25 September, vol. 2, pp. 785–789. IEEE Press, Piscataway (1996)
13. Verma, G., Yu, P., Sadler, B.M.: Physical layer authentication via fingerprint embedding using software-defined radios. IEEE Access **3**, 81–88 (2015)
14. Wang, Y., Zhu, G., Kwong, S., Shi, Y.: A study on the security levels of spread-spectrum embedding schemes in the WOA framework. IEEE Trans. Cybern. **48**(8), 2307–2320 (2018)
15. Xiao, L., Greenstein, L., Mandayam, N., Trappe, W.: Fingerprints in the ether: using the physical layer for wireless authentication. In: Proceedings of 2007 IEEE International Conference on Communications, Glasgow, UK, 24–28 June, pp. 4646–4651. IEEE Press, Piscataway (2007)
16. Xie, X., Xu, Z., Xie, H.: Channel capacity analysis of spread spectrum watermarking in radio frequency signals. IEEE Access **5**, 14749–14756 (2017)

17. Xu, Z., Yuan, W.: Watermark BER and channel capacity analysis for QPSK-based RF watermarking by constellation dithering in AWGN channel. IEEE Signal Process. Lett. **24**(7), 1068–1072 (2017)
18. Yang, B., Zhang, L., Qiao, D., Zhao, G., Imran, M.A.: Narrowband Internet of Things (NB-IoT) and LTE systems co-existence analysis. In: Proceedings of IEEE Global Communications Conference (GLOBECOM), pp. 1–6 (2018)
19. Yu, P.L., Baras, J.S., Sadler, B.M.: Physical-layer authentication. IEEE Trans. Inf. Forensics Security **3**(1), 38–51 (2008)
20. Yu, Z., Jingyong, X., Yongxiang, L., Yong, C., Qiongli, L.: A spectrum watermark embedding and extracting method based on spread spectrum technique. In: Proceedings of 2016 IEEE International Conference on Electronic Information and Communication Technology (ICEICT), pp. 16–22 (2016)

Protecting the Data Plane of SDN From Malicious Flow Entries Based on P4

Yifang Zhi[1,2], Li Yang[2(✉)], Gaolei Yang[2], and Yuehong Zhang[3]

[1] Science and Technology on Communication Information Security Control
Laboratory, Jiaxing, China
[2] Xidian University, Xi'an, China
`yangli@xidian.edu.cn`
[3] PLA Air Force Xi'an Flight Academy, Xi'an, China

Abstract. In Software-defined network (SDN), the switching devices on the data plane rely on the flow entries issued by controllers to forward packets. Therefore, the correctness of flow entries becomes critical. However, the lack of security mechanism in SDN architecture makes the packet forwarding on the data plane easy to be damaged by malicious flow entries. In this paper, we argue that a malicious controller can easily issue malicious flow entries to hinder packets from being forwarded correctly on the data plane. We present a scheme based on P4 to detect and locate malicious flow entries on the data plane. Moreover, we implement the prototype of our scheme and extensive experiments to show that the proposed scheme can prevent malicious flow entries from damaging the packet forwarding of the data plane with trivial overheads.

Keywords: SDN · P4 · Malicious detection · Flow entry

1 Introduction

In Software-defined network (SDN), controllers issue flow entries to the data plane and the switch devices on the data plane forward packets according to the flow entries [8]. Different from the traditional network, the SDN flow entries are only generated by the controller. However, the switching device in the traditional network can generate packet forwarding rules by itself according to some routing protocols, such as RIP and OSPF. Such packet forwarding mechanism in SDN can significantly simplify network management, but also introduces a new threat: a malicious controller can issue malicious flow entries to disrupt packet forwarding on the data plane.

The controller abstracts network programmability as high-level APIs and offers them to SDN applications for the support of various network functions including issuing flow entries [11]. Therefore, malicious applications can easily call the controller's APIs to issue malicious flow entries. Several attempts have been made to prevent malicious applications from sending malicious flow entries. Many proposals adopt permission control to limit the APIs which can be used by

© Springer Nature Singapore Pte Ltd. 2020
S. Yu et al. (Eds.): SPDE 2020, CCIS 1268, pp. 50–64, 2020.
https://doi.org/10.1007/978-981-15-9129-7_4

each application [6, 12, 15]. However, these controls cannot prevent compromised applications after deployment from issuing malicious flow entries. Some studies [7, 13] monitor each inserted flow entry and check whether it has any negative impact on the data plane, but they are unable to identify the threats which are caused by a set of flow entries. Other works [4, 9, 10] implements Byzantine fault tolerance [2] by assigning multiple controllers to the switch, thereby preventing the distribution of malicious flow entries. However, their methods cannot prevent the malicious flow entries directly sent from the controller without any request from switches.

No matter what method is used, they all put the detection of malicious flow entries on the control plane. Therefore, these methods will bring much overhead to the control plane. Different from the prior studies, we implement the detection of malicious flow entries on the data plane based on P4 for the first time. P4 [1] is a language designed to program packet forwarding functions on the data plane. It allows for the definition of new packet formats as necessary to meet some specific demands. P4 also allows for the flexible allocation of device memory [5], which makes it possible to store some necessary information on the switching devices to detect malicious flow entries. In this paper, we try to exploit the abundant features provided by P4 to realize the detection of malicious flow entries on the data plane. The overall method is described in the following.

In our scheme, we first classify malicious flow entries according to their characteristics. For different types of malicious flow entries, we design different detection methods based on P4. We utilize P4's flexible memory allocation and custom packet header mechanism to implement the detection methods we designed. And we design a confirmation method to locate malicious flow entries on the data plane.

The main contributions of this paper are summarized below.

- We summarize the types of malicious flow entries in SDN, and we analyse the characteristics of different types of malicious flow entries and their impact on data plane packet forwarding.
- We design different detection methods for different types of malicious flow entries based on P4 on the data plane for the first time, and we design a method for locating malicious flow entries based on P4.
- We implement the prototype of our scheme and extensive experiments to show that our scheme can detect malicious flow entries on the data plane and locate malicious flow entries with trivial overheads.

The rest of this paper is organized as follows. Section 2 introduces the background information and threat model. Section 3 details our methodology. Section 4 gives the implementation and experiment. Section 5 offers related work. Finally, we conclude this paper in Sect. 6.

2 Preliminary

This section reviews the background knowledge and discusses our threat model.

2.1 Background

OpenFlow and P4. OpenFlow is the original southbound interface of SDN and has become the de facto standard protocol [18]. The OpenFlow interface started simple, with the abstraction of a single table of flow entries that could match packets on a dozen header fields (e.g., MAC addresses, IP addresses, protocol, TCP/UDP port numbers, etc.) [1]. As the network becomes complex, the specification has grown increasingly more complicated, with many more header fields and multiple stages of rule tables. Rather than repeatedly extending the OpenFlow specification, P4 is designed to program packet parsing and matching flow entries functions of switching devices.

Communication in SDN Architecture. Communications between hosts in SDN architecture is realized by flow entries. The flow entries can only be generated by the controller and delivered by the controller to the switch. In general, controller has two ways to issue the flow entry, including active and passive. In passive model, after the switch fails to match the flow entry when forwarding a packet, it will send a request to the controller, and the controller sends the corresponding flow entries to the switch after computing. In active model, the controller can directly issue flow entries to any switch without request. Generally, most controllers open the interface for issuing flow entries. The SDN applications or network administrator can call this interface to issue flow entries.

2.2 Threat Model

In our model, we assume that there is a malicious controller that may be deployed with a malicious application or controlled by an adversary, and this controller has the ability to issue flow entries. We focus on the process of issuing malicious flow entries by the malicious controller and detecting the malicious flow entries on the data plane. After our summary of previous related research [4,6,7,9,11–13,15–17], malicious flow rules can be divided into three categories.

- **Wrong Destination:** One or series of flow entries that can guide packets to the wrong destination.
- **Loop:** One or series of flow entries that can guide packets to loop endlessly between switching devices.
- **Black Hole:** One or series of flow entries that can guide packets to a switching device that does not have the flow entries related to process the packets.

To better illustrate these three kinds of malicious flow entries, we take the communication between *Host1* and *Host2* as an example. As shown in Fig. 1a, a malicious controller issue a flow entry to *Switch1* to change the forwarding path into the red dotted line. In this case, the packets from *Host1* to *Host2* will be routed to *Host3*, which is a wrong destination. As shown in Fig. 1b, a malicious controller issue flow entries to *Switch2* and *Switch3* to guide the packets from *Host1* to *Host2* will be routed endless between *Switch1*, *Switch2* and *Switch3*,

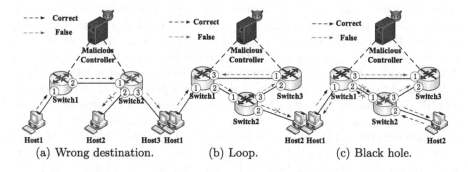

(a) Wrong destination.   (b) Loop.   (c) Black hole.

Fig. 1. Malicious flow entries examples.

causing a loop. As shown in Fig. 1c, a malicious controller issue flow entries to *Switch1* and *Switch2* to forward the packets between H1 and H2 to *Switch3*. *Switch3* does not have flow entries to process the packets and will drop the received packets. In this case, *Switch3* is like a black hole, attracting all the data packets, causing the hosts to fail to communicate.

Our goal is to detect these three kinds of malicious flow entries on the data plane based on P4. We assume that malicious nodes only exist in the control plane, that is, the switching devices on the data plane should strictly obey their specifications. We also assume that a trusted network administrator whose mission is to determine which flow entries on which switches are malicious flow entries after the switches on the data plane detect abnormal.

3 Detection Scheme Based on P4

This section will discuss how to realize the detection of malicious flow entries on the data plane based on P4. We separate our scheme into two phases: detection phase and confirmation phase. The detection phase detects abnormal packets forwarding caused by the three kinds of malicious flow entries in the data plane and send an alert to administrator if an abnormality is detected. In the confirmation phase, after receiving the alert, the administrator will send a probe packet to determine which flow entries on which switches are causing the abnormal.

3.1 Detection Method

We try to exploit the abundant features provided by P4 to realize the detection for the three kinds of malicious flow entries messages in Sect. 2.2. The detailed methods of detecting three kinds of malicious flow entries are proposed below.

Wrong Destination. The main idea to realize the detection of such malicious flow entry is to let switches store the locations of hosts. In the initial phase of a communication, the host initiating the communication will first query the ARP cache table to obtain the MAC address of the gateway. If the MAC address of the gateway is not queried, the host will send an ARP request. The ARP request will contain the IP address and MAC address of the host. Therefore, it is reasonable for the gateway switch to store the hosts it connects to based on ARP requests, which does not introduce much overhead and is effective. The switch should maintain a table to bind the switch's port number, MAC address and IP address information of each host. In order to support the dynamic nature of the network, the connection positions of the hosts can be changed, so the information in this table should also be variable. The switch should update the table's content based on each ARP request it receives. When the gateway switch stores information about the hosts it is connected to, the gateway switch can detect malicious flow entries at the end of the packet forwarding path.

Loop. In the normal process of forwarding data packets, the same data packet cannot be forwarded twice by the same switching device [3]. Otherwise, the forwarding path must not be optimal. Based on this fact, we can confirm that if a packet is forwarded twice by the same switching device, there is a loop forwarding on the data plane. Therefore, the main idea to realize the detection of such malicious flow entry is to let the switch remember the packets that have been processed. Instead of storing forwarded packets on the switch, we exploit the P4's flexible definition of packet format function to design a packet header and switches can leave their own traces on the header. As shown in Fig. 2, *Host1* sends *Packet1* to *Host2*. In the correct forwarding path, When *Switch1* receives *Packet1*, it will add a specific header to the original packet, leave its own trace on the added header and send the packet to *Switch2*. *Switch2* will check if there is any trace of itself on the specific header of the received packet, and if not, add its own trace. When forwarding the packet to *Host2*, *Switch2* will remove the specific headers to recover the specific packet into the normal data packet so that *Host2* can identify this packet. However, in the false forwarding path, *Switch2* will forward *Packet3* to *Switch3*. *Switch3* will add its own trace on the specific header and forward *Packet5* to *Switch1*. In this case, *Switch1* will find that there is already its own trace on the packet. Therefore, *Switch1* can confirm that there is loop forwarding on the data plane.

Black Hole. The key feature of this kind of malicious flow entries is that a switch in the forwarding process does not have related flow entries to process the packets, regardless of whether the switch is on the correct forwarding path. Therefore, the main idea to detect such kind of malicious flow entries is to check whether the switch has the relevant flow entries to process each packet. As described in Sect. 2.1, the switches on the forwarding path that do not have relevant flow entries will request the corresponding flow entries from the controller. In this kind of malicious flow entries, a switch acting as a black hole may also request flow entries from the controller. Therefore, in order to distinguish the black hole from the normal process, we need to add the checking logic after the switch requests flow entries.

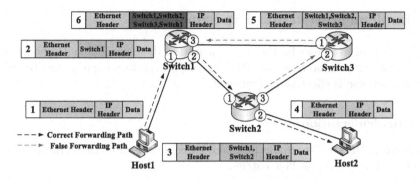

Fig. 2. Loop detection.

3.2 Confirm Malicious Flow Entries

In the confirmation phase, the administrator will send a probe packet to confirm which flow entries caused the anomaly. The formats of the alert packet and the probe packet are shown in Fig. 3.

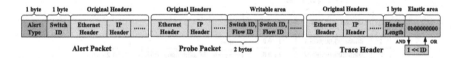

Fig. 3. Packet formats.

When a switch detect the anomaly, it will encapsulate the original packet headers into the alert packet, and add the alert type (wrong destination, loop or black hole) and the ID of the switch to the alert packet. When the administrator receives the alert packet, he can read the original packet header from the alert packet and adds the original packet headers and a write area to the probe packet that is composed of a series of record headers and each record header can record the switch ID and flow entry ID in each forwarding. The administrator will send the probe packet to the switch that at the beginning of the forwarding path through a special management port. When the switch receives the packet from the management port, it will conclude that the packet is the probe packet. The switch will forward the probe packet just like forwarding the original packet because they share the same header. The switches on the forwarding path will write its ID and the ID of matched flow entry into the write area of the probe packet. Similarly, the switch at the end of the forwarding path will also detect the anomaly. The switch will send the probe packet back to the administrator through the management port. The administrator then can learn the malicious flow entries according to the probe packet.

4   Implementation and Experiment

In this section, we describe the implementation details about our scheme. We implement our scheme based on P4$_{16}$. Then, we conduct experiments to prove that our scheme is effective and efficient.

4.1   Implementation

Detection Phase. We totally proposed three detection methods to detect different kinds of malicious flow entries.

In the implementation of the method for detecting wrong destination, the key point is to realize the storage of hosts information. To store hosts information, we need a storage structure that can maintain state. In P4, *Registers* [14] are stateful memories whose values can be read and written by the switch. Unfortunately, we can only define the bit length of the storage type. Therefore, we need to use bit operations to read and write hosts information. As shown in Fig. 4, the instantiation of host information table is made using the *Register* type specialized with 80 bits.

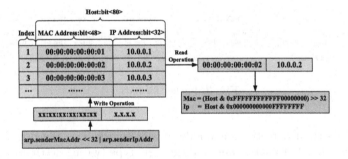

Fig. 4. Host information table.

We use the port number of the switch as the index of the register, the first 48 bits of the elements stored in the register to store the MAC address of the host, and the last 32 bits to store the IP address. We use OR operation and AND operation to realize the write and read of hosts information.

For detecting loop, the key point is to leave a trace of itself in the header of the packet when the switch forwards the packet. We define this trace as the ID of the switch. In P4 networks, The ID of the switch is an integer value that must be set when the switch is turned on, and it is unique in the entire network. To efficiently record the ID of the switch that forwards the packet. We add a custom trace header on the packet. The trace header's format is shown in Fig. 3, after the original headers of the packet we add the trace header that contains the length field and an elastic area. The value of the length field is the byte length of the elastic area.

In the elastic area, the value of each bit represents whether the corresponding switch has forwarded the current packet. The value of the nth bit from the right of the elastic area indicates whether the switch with the ID value n has forwarded the current data packet. If the value is 1, the switch has processed the packet. If the value is 0, the switch has not processed the packet. Therefore, the switch can use AND operation and OR operation to quickly read and set the value of the elastic area.

For detecting black hole, the key point is to realize the detection for flow entry missing. In P4 switch, a *table* describes a match-action unit. Processing a packet using a match-action table executes three steps: key construction, key lookup in a lookup table and action execution. In black hole switches, key lookup step cannot be performed because there is no matched flow entry in the table. Therefore, we should add the flow entry miss detection process on the second step of the match-action table execution process. A *table* can be invoked by calling its *apply* method. The evaluation of the *apply* method sets the *hit* field to *false* and the field *miss* to *true* if a match is not found in the lookup step. Therefore, we can use *miss* field to detect such malicious flow entry.

Confirmation Phase. In the confirmation phase, we need to simulate a network administrator. We use python's scapy library to receive the alert packet and construct probe packet. We first use scapy's sniff function to listen to the NIC of the administrator. If the received packet is an alert packet, then the process of constructing the detection data packet is triggered. When constructing the probe packet, the headers of the original packet in the alert packet is parsed out and encapsulated as the head of the probe packet. We use scapy's API to add a writeable header that is used to record flow entry ID and switch ID. The record header is composed of three fields, including a flag, switch ID and flow entry ID. The purpose of the flag is to facilitate the analysis of the probe packet by the P4 switch. When the flag is 0, it proves that there is another recording header after the current header, and the switch will continue to parse subsequent data according to the format of the recording header. When the flag bit is 1, it proves that the parsing of all the recording headers is finished. In the confirmation phase, when each switch forward the probe packet, it needs to add a new record header to record the switch ID and matched flow entry ID. This process is implemented by using the header stacks structure provided by P4.

Detailed Process. In this section, we will explain the detailed process of our scheme. Our scheme has two parts of the processing flow, including the processing flow of the P4 switch and the processing flow of network administrator.

The Processing Flow of P4 Switch: In our scheme the types of packets processed by the P4 switch include ARP requests, IP packets for normal communication, packets with trace headers, and probe packets. For different types of packets, we defined different packet parsers to parse these packets. The detailed processing flow is shown in Algorithm 1.

Algorithm 1 The processing flow of P4 switch

Require: Parsed packet header: *header*, the port on which the network administrator receives messages: *admin*

Ensure: The packets are sent from the specific port

1: **if** The type of the packet is ARP request **then**
2:    Update the content of the host information table according to the ARP request and reply the ARP response;
3: **else if** The packet is an IP packet **or** the packet has a trace header **or** the packet is a probe packet **then**
4:    **if** Matching flow entries fail **and** unable to get relevant flow entries **then**
5:        Add **Black hole** alert header and set the exit port number to *admin*;
6:    **else**
7:        Confirm the exit port number i according to the matched flow entry;
8:        Obtain the MAC address and IP address from the host information table according to the port number i;
9:        **if** No relevant MAC address and IP address information found **then**
10:            **if** There is a trace header in the *header* **then**
11:                **if** The switch ID's related bit value of trace header is 1 **then**
12:                    Add **Loop** alert header to and set the exit port number to *admin*;
13:                **else**
14:                    Set the corresponding bit value of trace header to 1;
15:                **end if**
16:            **else**
17:                Add trace header to the packet and set the current switch id's corresponding bit value of trace header to 1;
18:            **end if**
19:        **else**
20:            **if** The IP and MAC address information in the *header* is inconsistent with the host informations table **then**
21:                Add **Wrong destination** alert header and set the exit port number to *admin*;
22:            **else**
23:                Remove the trace header and set the packet type to IP packet;
24:            **end if**
25:        **end if**
26:    **end if**
27:    **if** The packet is a probe packet **then**
28:        Record the switch ID and the matched flow entry ID;
29:    **end if**
30:    Forward the packet according to the exit port number;
31: **end if**

As shown in Algorithm 1, the P4 switch will process the packet according to its type. For the ARP request, the switch will update the host information table based on the content of the ARP request. For the probe packet, the switch will record the switch id and flow entry id when forwarding probe packet. For the other packets, the switch will perform the detection methods and generate alert when detecting abnormalities.

The Processing Flow of Administrator: The main processing flow of the administrator includes receiving and parsing the alert packet sent by the switch and generating a probe packet based on the alert packet. The administrator can locate malicious controllers in the cluster according to the probe packets returned by the switches. The detailed processing flow is shown in Algorithm 2.

Algorithm 2 The processing flow of administrator

Require: Alert packet: *alert packet* or the probe packet returned by the switch: *detected packet*
Ensure: Send probe packet to the switch or locate malicious flow entries
 1: Monitor the packets received by the NIC;
 2: **if** The type of the packet is alert packet **then**
 3:     Read the alert type field of the alert packet;
 4:     Read the original packet header from the alert packet;
 5:     Encapsulate the original packet header to the probe packet;
 6:     Add the first record header on the probe packet and set the flag to 1;
 7:     Determine the ingress switch of the original packet according to topology information and send the probe packet to the ingress switch;
 8: **end if**
 9: **if** The type of the packet is *detected packet* **then**
10:     **repeat**
11:         Parse the record header of the *detected packet*;
12:     **until** The flag of the record header is 1;
13:     Determine the malicious flow entries according to the record headers;
14: **end if**

The network administrator will continuously monitor the packets received by the Nic. If the packet is the alert packet, the administrator will generate the probe packet and send it to the ingress switch. If the packet is the probe packet returned by the switch, the administrator can locate malicious flow entries.

4.2   Experiment

We implement our experiments on a Ubuntu 16.04 virtual machine with a 4-core processor and 8 GB memory. We choose Mininet (version 2.3.0d4) to create network topology and load P4 switch to the virtual topology created by Mininet. We first prove the effectiveness of three malicious flow entry detection methods and then evaluate the performance of our solution.

Effectiveness Evaluation. In the effectiveness evaluation experiment, we create the network topology shown in Fig. 5.

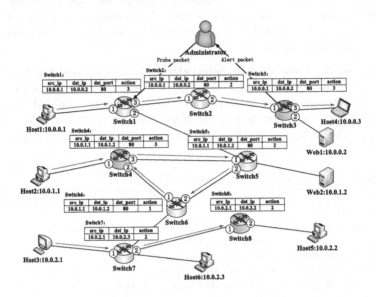

Fig. 5. Effectiveness evaluation.

We first implement experiment to prove the effectiveness of the detection method for the wrong destination. We issue flow entries as shown in Fig. 5 on Switch1, Switch2 and Switch3. This causes the packets sent by Host1 to Web1 to be forwarded to Host4. Due to Switch3 has a host information tale, Switch3 can detect wrong destination. We then test the effectiveness of the detection method for the loop. We implement this experiment on Switch4, Switch5 and Switch6. Switch4 can detect loop forwarding because there is a trace header on the packet. We finally test the effectiveness of the detection method for the black hole on Switch7 and Switch8. The experiment proves that the detection of the flow table matching failure on the Switch8 can successfully detect such malicious flow entries.

Performance Evaluation. After proving the effectiveness of this program, we evaluate the performance of our scheme. We first evaluate the performance of the detection phase, and we separately test the overhead of the three kinds of malicious flow entry detection methods.

For the detection method of the malicious flow entry for the wrong end point, the switch needs to maintain the host information binding table, and the update of the host information table is mainly performed according to the host's ARP request. Therefore, the overhead introduced by this method mainly exists in the processing of the ARP request message by the gateway switch, so we test the time overhead of the switch to process the ARP request of the host and reply the ARP response. During the experiment, we conducted multiple tests with different numbers of hosts connected to the gateway switch, and took the average value as the test result. In order to more accurately reflect the time overhead of the switch to process ARP requests, in each round of testing the overhead for the switch to process the ARP request, we let different numbers of hosts initiate communication requests at the same time, and take the maximum time overhead of processing ARP request as the final result. Then we use the same test method to test the time spent by the switch in processing the ARP request under normal circumstances. We compare the average of the experimental data. The results are shown in Fig. 6a.

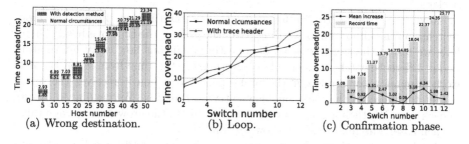

(a) Wrong destination.   (b) Loop.   (c) Confirmation phase.

Fig. 6. Experiment results.

As the number of hosts increases, under normal circumstances the ARP request processing time will gradually increase, and the time overhead with the malicious flow entry detection method will also increase. In the case of the same number of hosts, the time overhead of ARP request processing with the malicious flow entry detection method has increased compared with the time overhead in normal circumstances, but the increase is about 2 ms. Therefore, the detection method of malicious flow entries for wrong destination introduces trivial overhead in processing ARP requests.

For the loop forwarding detection method, the overhead mainly exists in the processing of the trace header by the switch, so when communicating between hosts, the more the number of switches on the communication path, the greater the communication overhead. We test the time cost of forwarding packets on the communication path under a communication path with different numbers of switches and compared with the forwarding time cost under normal circumstances. During the test, the matching fields of the malicious flow entries include source IP address, destination IP address, protocol value, source port number, and destination port number. We use the ICMP Echo Request/Reply message through the ping command on the Mininet simulated host. To test the communication delay, each test generates 10 ICMP Echo Request packets through the ping command and takes the average of the communication delay as the final result. The final experimental results are shown in Fig. 6b.

It can be seen from Fig. 6b that under normal communication conditions, as the number of switches on the communication path increases, the communication time overhead will gradually increase. After adding the trace header and loop forwarding detection, the communication delay has increased compared with the normal situation, but the increase in time overhead is very small, all within 5 ms. Therefore, the detection of loop forwarding will not introduce excessive overhead.

The black hole detection method is only to send an alert packet to the network administrator according to whether the miss field is true after the matching process is completed. The matching flow entry process and the assignment process to the miss field already exist in the original process of processing packet, so this detection method does not affect the performance of the switch in processing packets.

Next, we evaluate the performance of the confirmation phase. The more switches on the abnormal forwarding path, the greater the time overhead. Therefore, we tested the time overhead of collecting malicious flow entry information under different switch numbers. Time overhead is the time from when the network administrator sends out the probe packet to when it receives the probe packet that records the malicious flow entry information. We conducted 5 tests in each case. We then average the data and calculate the growth of average value in each case. The final result is shown in Fig. 6c.

As the number of switches increases, the time overhead for collecting malicious flow entries increases gradually, but even when there are 12 switches on the forwarding path, the time overhead for collecting malicious flow entries is only 25.77 ms. The increase in time overhead is relatively stable. As can be seen from the line chart in the figure, for each additional switch on the forwarding path, the time overhead for collecting malicious flow entries will increase by about 1 ms–4 ms, and the average increase is 2.07 ms. This shows that the increase is also very small. Therefore, the confirmation phase of this solution has good performance both in the time overhead of collecting malicious flow entries or the increase in time overhead. In summary, we can draw the following conclusions:

- The detection method of malicious flow entries based on P4 can successfully detect malicious flow entries of the data plane, which can reduce the workload of the control plane.
- The detection methods of malicious flow entries in the detection phase does not cause excessive impact on the normal communication of the data plane.
- In the confirmation phase, the network administrator can quickly collect malicious flow entries information on the data plane with trivial overhead.

5   Related Work

In this section, we review the efforts being made to protect the data plane of SDN from malicious flow entries. They can be classified into three categories.

Permission Control. Many works adopt permission control to limit the APIs which can be used by each SDN applications [6,12,15]. Permission control can reduce the risks that apps misuse unnecessary APIs or access privileged resources. However, this method cannot prevent compromised applications after deployment from issuing malicious flow entries. What's worse, a legitimate network administrator may issue wrong flow rules due to carelessness. Therefore, this method is not very effective in protecting against malicious flow entries.

Byzantine Fault Tolerance. Some studies [4, 9, 10] utilize Byzantine fault tolerance to prevent malicious data rules from damaging the data plane. Their main idea is to assign multiple controllers to each switch. When a switch requests a flow entry, the request will be sent to multiple controllers and the switch will get replicated flow entries. The switch can then get a correct flow entry by Byzantine fault tolerance, even if there are malicious flow entries in the replicated flow entries. However, this method is only applicable in the case of a controller cluster, and it is not applicable in the case of a single controller. What's worse, this method is not applicable if the controller actively issues flow entries.

Monitoring of Abnormal Behaviors. Other studies [7, 13] monitor each inserted flow entry and check whether it has any negative impact on the data plane. Specifically, FortNOX [13] can detect flow conflicts and VeriFlow [7] verifies network invariants upon forwarding state changes. However, they are unable to identify the threats which are caused by a set of flow entries. Lin et al. [11] propose a method to detect malicious flow entries by building a directed flow graph of the data plane. Their method can detect the threats which are caused by a set of flow entries, but their method is deployed on the controller that can bring extra overhead for the controller.

Different from the prior studies, we implement detection of malicious flow entries on the data plane that can detect multiple types of malicious flow entries. Our method does not bring extra overhead for the controller and the overhead on the data plane is also minimal.

6 Conclusion

In this paper, based on the security problem of malicious flow entries of SDN, we propose a scheme based on P4 that can detect abnormal packet forwarding caused by malicious flow entries and locate malicious flow entries. We divided malicious flow entries into three categories, and designed different detection methods for different types of malicious flow entries. The experiments show that the method can detect and locate malicious flow entries with trivial overheads.

Acknowledgement. The research is partly supported by the National Key Research and Development Project (2017YFB0801805), the Science and Technology on Communication Information Security Control Laboratory under Grant No. 6142106180102 and Nation Natutal Science Foundation of China No. 62072359.

References

1. Bosshart, P., et al.: P4: programming protocol-independent packet processors. Comput. Commun. Rev. **44**(3), 87–95 (2014)

2. de Castro, M.O.T.: Practical Byzantine fault tolerance. Ph.D. thesis, Massachusetts Institute of Technology, Cambridge, MA, USA (2000)
3. Comer, D. (ed.): Internetworking with TCP/IP - Principles, Protocols, and Architectures, 4th edn. Prentice-Hall, Upper Saddle River (2000)
4. Defrawy, K.E., Kaczmarek, T.: Byzantine fault tolerant software-defined networking (SDN) controllers. In: 40th IEEE Annual Computer Software and Applications Conference, COMPSAC Workshops 2016, Atlanta, GA, USA, pp. 208–213 (2016)
5. Hill, J., Aloserij, M., Grosso, P.: Tracking network flows with P4. In: Proceedings of the 5th IEEE/ACM International Workshop on Innovating the Network for Data-Intensive Science, Dallas, TX, USA, 11 November 2018, pp. 23–32 (2018)
6. Jin, X., Gossels, J., Rexford, J., Walker, D.: Covisor: a compositional hypervisor for software-defined networks. In: 12th USENIX Symposium on Networked Systems Design and Implementation, NSDI 2015, Oakland, CA, USA, pp. 87–101 (2015)
7. Khurshid, A., Zhou, W., Caesar, M., Godfrey, B.: Veriflow: verifying network-wide invariants in real time. In: Proceedings of the First Workshop on Hot Topics in Software Defined Networks, HotSDN@SIGCOMM 2012, Helsinki, Finland, pp. 49–54 (2012)
8. Kreutz, D., Ramos, F.M.V., Veríssimo, P.J.E., Rothenberg, C.E., Azodolmolky, S., Uhlig, S.: Software-defined networking: a comprehensive survey. Proc. IEEE **103**(1), 14–76 (2015)
9. Li, H., Li, P., Guo, S., Nayak, A.: Byzantine-resilient secure software-defined networks with multiple controllers in cloud. IEEE Trans. Cloud Comput. **2**(4), 436–447 (2014)
10. Li, H., Li, P., Guo, S., Yu, S.: Byzantine-resilient secure software-defined networks with multiple controllers. In: IEEE International Conference on Communications, ICC 2014, Sydney, Australia, 10–14 June 2014, pp. 695–700 (2014)
11. Lin, C., Li, C., Wang, K.: Setting malicious flow entries against SDN operations: attacks and countermeasures. In: IEEE Conference on Dependable and Secure Computing, DSC 2018, Kaohsiung, Taiwan, pp. 1–8 (2018)
12. Porras, P.A., Cheung, S., Fong, M.W., Skinner, K., Yegneswaran, V.: Securing the software defined network control layer. In: 22nd Annual Network and Distributed System Security Symposium, NDSS 2015, San Diego, California, USA (2015)
13. Porras, P.A., Shin, S., Yegneswaran, V., Fong, M.W., Tyson, M., Gu, G.: A security enforcement kernel for openflow networks. In: Proceedings of the First Workshop on Hot Topics in Software Defined Networks, HotSDN@SIGCOMM 2012, Helsinki, Finland, pp. 121–126 (2012)
14. The P4 Language Consortium: P4$_{16}$ Language Specification. https://p4.org/p4-spec/docs/P4-16-v1.2.0.html
15. Wen, X., Chen, Y., Hu, C., Shi, C., Wang, Y.: Towards a secure controller platform for openflow applications. In: Proceedings of the Second ACM SIGCOMM Workshop on Hot Topics in Software Defined Networking, HotSDN 2013, The Chinese University of Hong Kong, Hong Kong, China, pp. 171–172 (2013)
16. Yu, S., Guo, S., Stojmenovic, I.: Fool me if you can: mimicking attacks and anti-attacks in cyberspace. IEEE Trans. Comput. **64**(1), 139–151 (2015)
17. Yu, S., Wang, G., Zhou, W.: Modeling malicious activities in cyber space. IEEE Netw. **29**(6), 83–87 (2015)
18. Zhi, Y., Yang, L., Yu, S., Ma, J.: BQSV: protecting SDN controller cluster's network topology view based on byzantine quorum system with verification function. In: Vaidya, J., Zhang, X., Li, J. (eds.) CSS 2019. LNCS, vol. 11982, pp. 73–88. Springer, Cham (2019). https://doi.org/10.1007/978-3-030-37337-5_7

High-Speed Network Attack Detection Framework Based on Optimized Feature Selection

Zhicheng Luo[1,2], Weijia Ding[1], Anmin Fu[1], Zhiyi Zhang[2(✉)], and Linjie Zhang[2]

[1] School of Computer Science and Engineering, Nanjing University of Science and Technology, Nanjing, People's Republic of China
[2] Science and Technology on Communication Networks Laboratory, Shijiazhuang, People's Republic of China
ctignzzy@163.com

Abstract. In the era of high-speed information, network technology facilitates our life. When we enjoy the service with high quality, various new intrusion methods have also emerged. Network attacks are more challenging to be detected by security applications under the cover of large-scale flow, threatening the security of cyberspace constantly. In view of the increasingly severe security situation, this paper proposes a high-speed network attack detection framework based on feature selection optimization to overcome the difficulties. It quickly collects data packets through the design of the DPDK mechanism, combines the data sampling method based on the genetic algorithm, and the improved feature selection algorithm to optimize the training model. The integration of incremental learning increases the autonomous detection capability of the framework, which is more suitable for intricate network environments. Finally, we verified the validity of our work by experiments and simulated the actual attacks to test the detection effect in the real network.

Keywords: High-speed network · Attack detection · Feature selection

1 Introduction

Network services have been widely used in various fields. New users, devices, and other things are constantly connected to the network, which has become a part of people's daily life [1]. Higher orders of magnitude bandwidth, faster data links, and more advanced network technologies support new forms of communication services. Although these services provide users with an excellent experience, they also create opportunities for new network attacks [2]. Various abnormal events and attacks may be ignored by the protection mechanism of the firewall, which threatens the operation of the information infrastructure and users' privacy, causing colossal damage to network performance and security.

For the purpose of solving the above issues, network intrusion detection is proposed. Traditional signature-based NIDS usually uses pattern matching technology to detect

© Springer Nature Singapore Pte Ltd. 2020
S. Yu et al. (Eds.): SPDE 2020, CCIS 1268, pp. 65–78, 2020.
https://doi.org/10.1007/978-981-15-9129-7_5

known attacks. The main idea is to build a database of intrusion signatures to compare the current set of activities against the existing signatures and raise the alarm if a match is found [3]. These technologies have high detection accuracy for known intrusions. But there are severe shortcomings in the detection of zero-day attacks, their ability to respond to new types of network attacks cannot meet the protection needs of contemporary network security.

Network flow inspection is an effective alternative method. Cisco first proposed the concept of flow in the context of its NetFlow router feature [4]. A flow can be defined as a sequence of packets with a standard set of features, passing through an observation point in a given period [5]. Typically, flows utilize high-level information about the connection rather than the data itself for transmissions, such as source/destination IP address and source/destination port. It is a good way to monitor communication without checking the contents of the packet. Flow analysis allows for the detection of internal and external behavior (e.g., network configuration errors and policy violations). To a certain extent, it also reduces the amount of data that can be processed, which is more effective than DPI in terms of protecting personal privacy [6, 7] and consuming computing resources.

In recent years, a large number of machine learning and deep learning methods have been introduced into flow-based intrusion detection of abnormal behaviors, which can discover hidden patterns in input data based on the learned knowledge. We could further improve the detection accuracy of attacks and the ability to cope with unknown attacks [8]. However, the accuracy of these systems depends on the integrity of their knowledge of the threats to be detected. Researchers often focus on the optimization of the algorithm to construct the model, so that they ignore the challenges of flow collection and processing in the high-speed network environment [9]. The effect of these methods may be greatly reduced when the system is actually deployed in this way.

Therefore, this paper proposes a flow-based anomaly detection framework in high-speed networks, which can identify the malicious hosts involved by detecting network flows. To summarize, we make the following main contributions:

(1) In the part of data collection, we designed a high-speed packet capture mechanism based on the DPDK [10, 11] to collect the network flow. At the level of packet capture, a reasonable consumption model is used to eliminate the read-write competition and unnecessary memory copying during the packet processing, so as to realize data-parallel processing.
(2) In the part of model training, we optimized the feature selection process of the dataset and classified the flow as malicious and benign, which significantly reduced the time spent on flow analysis and the scale of the network processing traffic.
(3) Our detection framework works in real-time, and we introduced periodic incremental learning on the collected flows, providing more and more autonomy for the system.
(4) We did many experiments to evaluate the detection ability of network attacks.

2 Related Work

In this section, we will review the anomaly detection based on network traffic in recent years. First of all, [8] made a systematic summary of the technology, datasets, and challenges of intrusion detection, from which we draw on the train of thought about the network attack detection. [12] concretely summarized the research status of flow-based intrusion detection technology, which classified and evaluated the architecture of the existing flow-based intrusion detection system.

We can learn from the above survey that most research is based on machine learning to detect abnormal behaviors, which is a mainstream research direction. Specifically, [13] proposed a classification system designed to detect both known as well as previously unseen security threats. The optimization point of the approach is to learn the parameters of the representation automatically from the training data, allowing the classifiers to create robust models of malicious behaviors capable of detecting previously unseen malware variants and behavior changes. In [14], a network intrusion detection system called Flow-hacker was developed, which run the collected traffic on MapReduce to obtain the aggregate traffic and feature vectors. Then the authors combined the unsupervised machine learning classification method to divide the small cluster into malicious or clean traffic. Methods introduced in [15] applied a group of neural networks called auto-encoders to collectively distinguish normal and abnormal flow patterns, which is supported by a feature extraction framework that can effectively track the patterns of each network channel.

For the past few years, the application of attack detection in the high-speed network has been paid much attention. In [16], researchers investigate how malware propagates in networks from a global perspective, and establish a rigorous two layer epidemic model for malware propagation from network to network. Confluo [17] is an end-host stack that can be integrated with existing network management tools to enable monitoring and diagnosis of network-wide events using telemetry data distributed across end-hosts for high-speed networks. [18] proposed a distributed asynchronous NIDS detection model to monitor multi-path routing attacks. In this model, each NIDS scans its own received data packets independently and the adjacent contents between two data packets with consecutive sequence numbers. [19] extended flow-monitoring to application layer HTTP Flows and presented an improved version of the IPFIX-based Signature-based Intrusion Detection System. In [20], a flow-based intrusion detection system (IDS) for high-speed networks using the meta-heuristic scale is proposed. A flow-based approach is applied on request stream to define feature metrics, which are used to define whether the flow is normal or malicious. In [21], the authors proposed BigFlow, an approach capable of processing evolving network traffic while being scalable to large packet rates. BigFlow employs a verification method that checks if the classifier outcome is valid in order to provide reliability.

3   Overview of the Framework

In this section, we will introduce our framework in detail. On the basis of rapid collection and processing of network flow, we optimize the attack detection model to solve the difficulty of responding to unknown patterns when analyzing actual flow. As shown in Fig. 1. The method includes the following steps:

1) Data collection: to collect packets in the network interaction between different hosts or routers belonging to the network infrastructure in real-time.

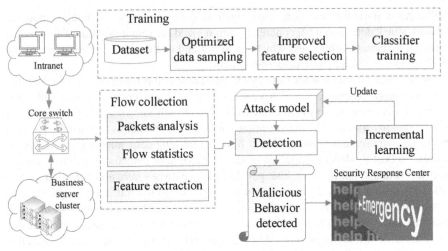

Fig. 1. Overview of the framework architecture

2) Feature extraction: to quickly analyze the collected packets and extract relevant data from them. These data are normalized and then used to create feature vectors that characterize the network flows.
3) Detection: to detect abnormal behavior. For the appropriate dataset, data sampling is optimized based on the genetic algorithm. Besides, we also improve the feature selection algorithm to get better features of flow and then construct the attack model by combining it with the classifier. As for the real-time flow feature vectors in the feature extraction module, they will be matched with the attack model to complete the detection.
4) Incremental learning: to update the knowledge of behavior gradually. Whenever new data is added, the module will reclassify the training results based on the original knowledge base and continuously optimize the detection accuracy.

4   High-Speed Flow Collection Based on DPDK Technology

With the continuous progress of network communication technology, the speed of infor-mation interaction is also increasing, which brings some challenges to the supervision of network data. To meet the data collection task of high-speed networks, we have designed a new flow collection mode based on the open-source DPDK. Compared with the tradi-tional Libpcap capture method based on the Linux protocol stack, this technology can reduce the system packet loss rate and greatly improve the packet capture efficiency. The architecture is shown in Fig. 2.

4.1   Design of High-Speed Data Packet Collection Mechanism

Our method adopts the NIC multi-queue technology, and the traffic load is balanced to different queues of the NIC through RSS called Receive Side Scaling. The DPDK

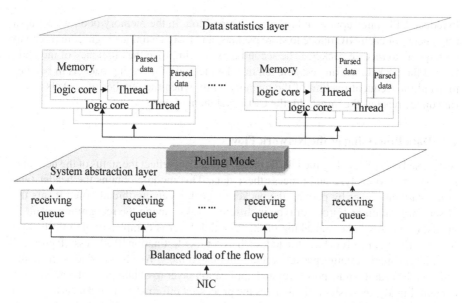

Fig. 2. The architecture of high-speed flow collection based on DPDK technology

user- mode of polling drives the batch receiving of messages. The messages produced by a queue are consumed by a thread bound to a logical core and delivered directly to the user-mode by means of zero-copy. The user-mode memory used to store queue messages for each logical core is independent of each other, so as to reduce the pressure of single-core message reception and processing, which also provides a basis for parallel processing of data leveraging multi-core reception and processing messages.

Since the NIC selects different keywords according to different packet types, it ensures that packets belonging to the same flow can get the same value when calculating the queue index. The next goal is to obtain the RSS keyword of the message and calculate the hash value of the content of the keyword through a hash function. Then the system query the corresponding queue index in the corresponding list in terms of the hash value, determining which NIC queue the packet is specifically allocated to. In the case of NIC with multiple receiving queues, how to allocate resources such as thread, CPU logic core, and memory to consume multi-queue messages is directly related to the processing performance of the whole high-speed packet capture mechanism. Therefore, the system receives packets produced by the queue with a single thread consuming a single NIC, and allocate exclusive memory for each NIC reception queue. Meanwhile, for making full use of the multi-core resources of the server, we introduced the thread binding technology to optimize the three stages of the packets from the NIC to the application.

The packet collection process can be divided into packet capture initialization and packet application processing. The first part is to initialize the system abstraction layer of DPDK so that this module provides the interface of direct interaction with the hardware for subsequent operation. Based on the relevant hardware information obtained by these interfaces, it is necessary for the system to follow certain resource allocation principles to reduce CPU interruption and resource competition. In the memory pool, we set up a ring queue for each NIC queue to store packets, and assign a unique logic core thread to each queue to receive packets. The second part is to improve the efficiency of the CPU to read the packet, and this module applies the method of receiving packets in batches to avoid the frequent reading of the memory. Only when the number of packets in the ring queue reaches the threshold, the CPU read them at once.

4.2   Data Processing of the Network Flow

As the packets collected by the DPDK method could not reflect the status of the network, it is essential to analyze and process these data. This module obtains the header type of the data-link layer by parsing the packet on each receiving thread. Then it sets the offset information and protocol type in different ways, saving the recognition result to the data flow. After the unpacking of the data-link layer is completed, the information from the IP layer needs to be extracted, such as source/destination IP address, IP protocol type, fragmentation status, packet header length, and flags. We also need to perform the same analysis at the transport layer and application layer to obtain port, offset, and flag content. Finally, the system summarizes the processed information into data flows. Each flow includes the following information: quintuple information, VLAN id, timestamp, the direction of the flow, the maximum number of packets detected for each type of the flow, the number of bytes sent from the source to the destination, the number of bytes sent, the number of bytes sent to the destination, etc. After normalizing the data, we create feature vectors according to the corresponding field content to provide the behavioral basis for detection.

5   Detection Model Based on Feature Selection Optimization

UNSW-NB15 [22] dataset is selected to construct the model in this paper, which is more suitable for the research of the intrusion detection system. The dataset was generated by the Australian security lab using the IXIA Perfect Strom tool, which combines the real normal network flows with the artificial attack flows in modern networks. There are 49 features in it, and the attack types include 9 categories: Fuzzers, Analysis, Backdoor, DoS, Exploit, Generic, Reconnaissance, Shellcode, and Worm.

5.1   Data Sampling Based on Genetic Algorithm

Due to the large number and unevenness of category labels in the dataset, the effect of the classifier model will be affected if the data of the training set and the test set are acquired by random sampling. Therefore, we perform sampling optimization on a more significant number of categories based on the overall distribution characteristics of the dataset. After setting the sample proportion on the data of each category, this module obtains different numbers of training data by adjusting the sampling ratio, and generate a set of sampling ratio groups eventually. In this part, we introduce the genetic algorithm to carry out policy search and find the optimal sampling proportion group comprehensively, so that the newly generated training data set can train a more accurate and useful classifier. The algorithm steps are as follows:

Step 1: set the feature of the original dataset as $R = \{r_1, r_2, r_3, r_4 \ldots r_n\}$. Next, feature selection is needed to filter out redundant features.

Step 2: initialize the genetic algorithm. A population is generated here, which is an individual with m chromosomes. With the purpose of avoiding frequent conversion between binary and decimal, the chromosome coding method adopts float coding. The gene of each chromosome is set as $X = \{x_1, x_2, x_3, x_4, x_5, x_6\}$, $x_i \in R$. The genes are different from each other, representing six categories with large numbers, namely Normal, Fuzzers, Reconnaissance, Exploit, DoS and Generic, respectively.

Step 3: evaluate the fitness of chromosome X. From the features of the dataset R, six features contained in the X chromosome gene are selected to form a new data set X'. After setting the random seed value, the X' dataset is divided into a training set and a test set. First, the training set is used to train the classifier model, and then the test set is used for cross-validation. The accuracy rate after cross-validation is used as the fitness evaluation standard for this chromosome.

Step 4: select the chromosome. It adopts roulette to select proportionally and retains the excellent individuals in m chromosomes, screening out the individuals with low adaptability.

Step 5: produce new individuals. Excellent individuals employ crossover operations and mutation operations to produce new individuals to join the population.

Step 6: Re-evaluate the fitness value of each chromosome to check if there are excellent individuals who have reached the set threshold. The algorithm is terminated if there is such an individual; otherwise, skip to the step 4 loop.

5.2 Optimized Mutual Information Feature Selection

After optimizing sampling, some of the most practical features should be selected to reduce the dimension of the dataset and improve the performance of the algorithm. The mutual-information-based feature selection algorithm called MIFS is such a common feature selection algorithm, it exploits mutual information to measure the correlation between candidate features and categories, as well as the redundancy between the selected feature sets. The MIFS standard formula is as follows:

$$J_{MIFS} = I(f_i; C) - \beta \sum_{f_j \in S} I(f_i; f_j) \tag{1}$$

In MIFS algorithm, $I(f_i; C)$ represents the degree of correlation between candidate feature F and target C, and $\sum_{f_j \in S} I(f_i; f_j)$ represents the degree of redundancy between candidate feature F and selected feature set S. We can find that the algorithm does not take the redundancy relationship between the features to be selected and multiple selected features into account through further analysis. It is difficult for the MIFS algorithm to reflect these issues by simply summing the information between the features to be selected and multiple selected features if the redundancy relationship is complicated. Therefore, this paper proposes an improved algorithm based on MIFS. When there are more than two selected features, we add a penalty term $I(f_i; f_j; f_k)$ in the redundancy section to reduce this loss. When the number of selected features is less than two, the MIFS algorithm is still used to select two required feature subsets. After expanding the

MIFS formula, the following formula can be obtained:

$$J_{MIFS} = I(f_i; C) - \beta' \sum_{f_j \in S} \sum_{f_j \in S, k>j} [I(f_i; f_j) + I(f_i; f_k)] \tag{2}$$

The parameter β' regularizes the importance of mutual information between selected features and candidate features. It's required to note that there are multiple relationships between the formula β' and the standard MIFS algorithm parameters β. After adding the redundant terms, the feature selection method of the following formula is obtained:

$$J(f_i) = I(f_i; C) - \beta' \sum_{f_j \in S} \sum_{f_j \in S, k>j} [I(f_i; f_j) + I(f_i; f_k) - I(f_i; f_j; f_k)] \tag{3}$$

The improvement mentioned above optimizes the accuracy of calculating each feature evaluation standard by increasing the amount of redundant information deleted. The algorithm is simply described as follows:

Step 1: initialization. Suppose the set F is an n-dimensional feature set, and the candidate feature set S is empty;
Step 2: calculate the mutual information on the feature target class. Calculate $I(f_i; C)$ for each feature $f_i \in F$ to be selected;
Step 3: calculate the first two features by the MIFS algorithm with two better features.
Step 4: make greedy choices. Calculate mutual information $I(f_i; f_j; f_k), I(f_i; f_k), I(f_i; f_j)$ for all variable pairs $(f_i; f_j; f_k)$. Then we select feature f_i to maximize $J(f_i)$, and f_i will be removed from set F and added to set S. Repeat this step until $|S| = k$.
Step 5: output the result, which is the selected feature set.

Since the amount of information may not fully reflect the association relationship between features, these attributes usually need to be weighted to adjust the degree of feature relevance and redundancy. The adjustment of the weight significantly affects the selection of the feature, so that the correlation and redundancy ratio of the feature can be analyzed and adjusted more flexibly.

5.3 Training and Optimization of the Classifier Model

Finally, we use a variety of classification algorithms in machine learning to predict the results and introduce a voting mechanism to improve detection accuracy. Meanwhile, with the purpose of making the classifier adapt to the changes of various environments and the emergence of new abnormal flow in practical application, we integrate the incremental learning method into the system, so that the classifier model can learn while working in the process of testing, and improve the adaptability of the model. Whenever the data is added, it is not necessary to rebuild all the knowledge bases but to update the changes caused by the new data on the basis of the original knowledge base. In this way, we not only reduce the storage cost but also save the time of subsequent training to get the better training effect of the model.

6   Experimental Evaluation

The framework is deployed on the Ubuntu 18.04 LTS system platform. After the initial filtering of the packets by the firewall, the collector gathers, parses, and extracts flow characteristics from the packets. Finally, the detection engine completes the behavior matching and reports the detected alarm information to the web server so that the network manager can make a timely emergency response. The real network deployment is shown in Fig. 3.

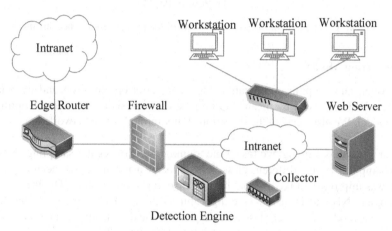

Fig. 3. The network deployment diagram for the framework

6.1   Flow Collection

The advantages and disadvantages of the high-speed packet capture mechanism are mainly measured by the packet loss rate when the message is captured. For the perfor-mance test of the high-speed packet capture mechanism, the system only focuses on the capture performance, so the message will be released immediately after the packet is captured. We increased the network traffic from 0.1 Gbps to 18 Gbps and calculated the packet loss rate of the Libpacp-based capture mechanism and DPDK-based 6-core 6-thread mechanism under different traffic. The result is shown in Fig. 4.

The packet loss rate continues to rise between 0 and 8 Gbps based on Libpcap, and it stabilizes at around 96% after exceeding 8 Gbps. However, the high-speed message capture mechanism designed in this paper, which is based on multi-core and multi-threading, will slowly increase the packet loss rate after the traffic exceeds 4 Gbps, and maintain the rate at about 8% when it reaches 14 Gbps. The improved DPDK-based high-speed message capture mechanism substantially overcomes the shortcomings of traditional technology. On the basis of making full use of the hardware resources, it has obtained better capabilities of data collection.

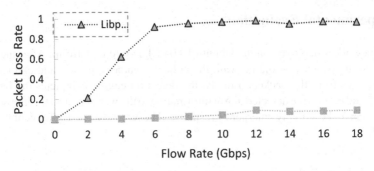

Fig. 4. Comparison of the packet loss rate of the packet capture mechanism

6.2 Detection Model

In this paper, data sampling optimization, feature selection optimization, and incremental learning effect are tested by means of comparative analysis to evaluate the optimized attack model. We also verified the detection ability through some network attacks in the end.

First, for data sampling, we tested the training effect of regular sampling and optimized sampling in five different classifiers. As shown in Fig. 5, the accuracy of the results was improved on the original basis after optimized sampling. The increment of the Gaussian-NB and Decision-Tree algorithm is the most obvious, while the lifting amplitude is modest for other classifiers. In general, the data sampling method based on the genetic algorithm can optimize the training results accordingly.

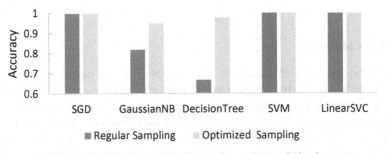

Fig. 5. Comparison of the effects of sampling optimization

Next, in order to better judge whether the feature selection plays a gain effect on the abnormal flow classification model, we introduce more classifiers for comparison based on data sampling optimization. Each classifier's results are taken from the same value of parameter β. The data in Fig. 6 shows that the accuracy of other classifiers is slightly improved, except for a decrease in the results of some classifiers.

As shown in Fig. 7, by calculating the average accuracy of each classifier under the corresponding number of features, we find that the model is enhanced significantly after removing the original redundancy error. In addition, we tested the model after introducing the voting mechanism. The detailed results are shown in Table 1.

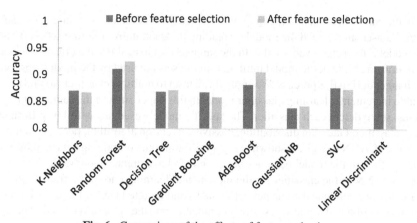

Fig. 6. Comparison of the effects of feature selection

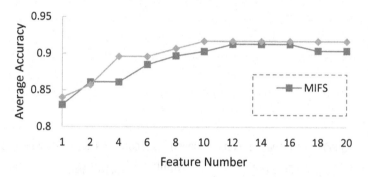

Fig. 7. Comparison of the average accuracy of feature selection algorithms

Table 1. The results of the detection model

Classifier	Accuracy	FAR
K-neighbors	86.73%	13.33%
Random forest	92.51%	5.72%
Decision tree	87.28%	9.81%
Gradient boosting	85.94%	10.18%
Ada-Boost	90.66%	8.13%
Gaussian-NB	84.37%	13.01%
SVM	89.48%	6.13%
Linear discriminant	92.03%	7.02%
Based on voting mechanism	90.75%	7.53%

In the part of incremental learning, we adopted the method of streaming data reading for the dataset, and trained the model by reading the quantitative training set every time. The model is then cross-validated with the same test set to evaluate the effectiveness and prediction error rate of the model until all training sets are used by the model, observing the changes during this process. We apply the dataset to multiple classifiers to find a more suitable incremental learning classifier model in this paper and use the same training set and test set to detect each classifier. The specific models used are as follows: Bernoulli Bayes classifier, Gaussian distribution, passive perception algorithm, perceptron model, SGD model, ANN model. As shown in Fig. 8, as the amount of training data increases, the training effect of the model becomes better and tend to a higher stable value. Therefore, we chose ANN as the classifier for the incremental learning part of the framework.

Finally, we conducted some network attacks and inputted tens of thousands of malicious traffic collected by various security companies into the system. We can find in Fig. 9

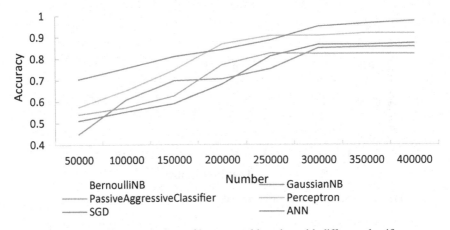

Fig. 8. The effect comparison of incremental learning with different classifiers

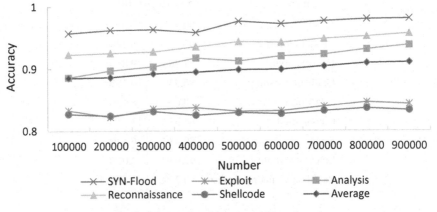

Fig. 9. The results of incremental attack tests

above that the average accuracy of our framework increases steadily as the number of streams increases. The attack mode of exploit/shellcode may have strong invisibility and high complexity, resulting in the lower test effects. But on the whole, the detection model can perform well in practical application deployment.

7 Conclusion and Future Work

This paper presents an attack detection framework for high-speed network flow. It applies the DPDK technology of parallel design to complete the rapid collection of network flow, and the attack detection model through sampling optimization and feature selection optimization to measure the attack events. The integration of incremental learning also increases the autonomous detection capability of the framework, making it more suitable for complex network environments. Experimental evaluation and attack test results show that the framework has an excellent detection effect so that it can be deployed in practical applications. Next, we will carry out the work of tracing the source of network attacks, using the characteristics of the proposed framework to support for the location of network threat sources, so as to restore the whole path of attacks.

Acknowledgment. This work is supported by the Open Project Program of the Science and Technology on Communication Networks Laboratory (BAX19641X006), Postgraduate Research & Practice Innovation Program of Jiangsu Province, China (KYCX19_0344) and CERNET Innovation Project (NGII20190405).

References

1. Kuang, B., Fu, A., Yu, S., Yang, G., Su, M., Zhang, Y.: ESDRA: an efficient and secure distributed remote attestation scheme for IoT swarms. IEEE Internet Things J. **6**(5), 8372–8383 (2019)
2. Kuang, B., Fu, A., Zhou, L., Susilo, W., Zhang, Y.: DO-RA: data-oriented runtime attestation for IoT devices. Comput. Secur. **97**, 101945 (2020)
3. Alazab, A., Abawajy, J., Hobbs, M., Layton, R., Khraisat, A.: Crime toolkits: the productisation of cybercrime. In: 2013 12th IEEE International Conference on Trust, Security and Privacy in Computing and Communications, pp. 1626–1632 (2013)
4. Claise, B.: Cisco systems netflow services export version 9. RFC 3954, RFC Editor, October 2004. http://www.rfc-editor.org/rfc/rfc3954.txt
5. Yu, S., Zhou, W., Jia, W., Guo, S., Xiang, Y., Tang, F.: Discriminating DDoS attacks from flash crowds using flow correlation coefficient. IEEE Trans. Parallel Distrib. Syst. **23**(6), 1073–1080 (2011)
6. Zhou, C., Fu, A., Yu, S., Yang, W., Wang, H., Zhang, Y.: Privacy-preserving federated learning in fog computing. IEEE Internet Things J. (2020). https://doi.org/10.1109/JIOT.2020.2987958
7. Fu, A., Chen, Z., Mu, Y., Susilo, W., Sun, Y., Wu, J.: Cloud-based outsourcing for enabling privacy-preserving large-scale non-negative matrix factorization. IEEE Trans. Serv. Comput. (2019). https://doi.org/10.1109/TSC.2019.2937484
8. Pacheco, F., et al.: Towards the deployment of machine learning solutions in network traffic classification: a systematic survey. IEEE Commun. Surv. Tutor. **21**(2), 1988–2014 (2018)

9. Yu, S., Wang, G., Zhou, W.: Modeling malicious activities in cyber space. IEEE Network **29**(6), 83–87 (2015)
10. Rajesh, R., Ramia, K.B., Kulkarni, M.: Integration of LwIP stack over Intel (R) DPDK for high throughput packet delivery to applications. In: 2014 Fifth International Symposium on Electronic System Design, pp. 130–134. IEEE (2014)
11. Zhu, W., et al.: Research and implementation of high performance traffic processing based on intel DPDK. In: 2018 9th International Symposium on Parallel Architectures, Algorithms and Programming (PAAP), pp. 62–68. IEEE (2018)
12. Umer, M.F., Sher, M., Bi, Y.: Flow-based intrusion detection: techniques and challenges. Comput. Secur. **70**, 238–254 (2017)
13. Bartos, K., Sofka, M., Franc, V.: Optimized invariant representation of network traffic for detecting unseen malware variants. In: 25th {USENIX} Security Symposium ({USENIX} Security 2016), pp. 807–822 (2016)
14. Sacramento, L., et al.: FlowHacker: detecting unknown network attacks in big traffic data using network flows. In: Trust Security and Privacy in Computing and Communications, pp. 567–572 (2018)
15. Mirsky, Y., et al.: Kitsune: an ensemble of autoencoders for online network intrusion detection. In: Network and Distributed System Security Symposium (2018)
16. Yu, S., Gu, G., Barnawi, A., Guo, S., Stojmenovic, I.: Malware propagation in large-scale networks. IEEE Trans. Knowl. Data Eng. **27**(1), 170–179 (2014)
17. Khandelwal, A., Agarwal, R., Stoica, I.: Confluo: distributed monitoring and diagnosis stack for high-speed networks. In: 16th {USENIX} Symposium on Networked Systems Design and Implementation ({NSDI} 2019), pp. 421–436 (2019)
18. Liu, L., et al.: No way to evade: detecting multi-path routing attacks for NIDS. In: 2019 IEEE Global Communications Conference (GLOBECOM), pp. 1–6. IEEE (2019)
19. Erlacher, F., Dressler, F.: On high-speed flow-based intrusion detection using snort-compatible signatures. IEEE Trans. Dependable Secure Comput. (2020)
20. Jyothsna, V., Mukesh, D., Sreedhar, A.N.: A flow-based network intrusion detection system for high-speed networks using meta-heuristic scale. In: Peng, S.-L., Dey, N., Bundele, M. (eds.) Computing and Network Sustainability. LNNS, vol. 75, pp. 337–347. Springer, Singapore (2019). https://doi.org/10.1007/978-981-13-7150-9_36
21. Viegas, E., et al.: Bigflow: real-time and reliable anomaly-based intrusion detection for high-speed networks. Future Gener. Comput. Syst. **93**, 473–485 (2019)
22. https://www.unsw.adfa.edu.au/unsw-canberra-cyber/cybersecurity/ADFA-NB15-Datasets (2015)

CaaS: Enabling Congestion Control as a Service to Optimize WAN Data Transfer

Jiahua Zhu, Xianliang Jiang[✉], Guang Jin, and Penghui Li

Faculty of Electrical Engineering and Computer Science, Ningbo University,
Ningbo 315211, China
1811082205@nbu.edu.cn,jiangxianliang@nbu.edu.cn

Abstract. TCP congestion control is essential for improving performance of data transfer. Traditional TCP congestion control algorithm is designed for the wired network with the assumptive goal of attaing higher throughput as possible for QoE. However, Internet today is constantly evolving and many different network architectures (Cellular network, high BDP network, Wi-Fi network, etc.) coexist for data transfer service. Futhermore, the emerging applications (live video, augmented and virtual reality, Internet-of-Things, etc.) present different requirements (low latency, low packet loss rate, low jitter, etc.) for data transfer service. Unfortunately, operating systems (Windows, MacOS, Android, etc.) today still rigidly stick to the single built-in congestion control algorithm (with Cubic for Linux, MacOS, Android and CTCP for Windows) for all connections, no matter if it is ill-suited for current network condition, or if there are better schemes for use. To tackle above issues, we articulate a vision of providing congestion control as a service to enable: (i) timely deployment of novel congestion control algorithms, (ii) dynamical adaption of congestion control algorithm according to the network condition, (iii) and meeting the diversified QoE preference of applications. We design and implement CaaS in Linux, our preliminary experiment shows the feasibility and benefits of CaaS.

Keywords: Network · Transmission Control Protocol · Congestion control

1 Introduction

Today, almost all Internet applications rely on the Transmission Control Protocol (TCP) to deliver data reliably across the network due to its ability to guarantee reliable data delivery across unreliable network. Although it was not part of TCP's primary design, the most vital element of TCP is congestion control (CC), which significantly determines the performance of data transfer.

Traditional CC is mainly designed for the wired network and with the assumptive goal of achieving high throughput as far as possible to attain ideal QoE. Yet, today, Internet is becoming more and more diverse both in the network technologies and the application requirements for data transfer service.

© Springer Nature Singapore Pte Ltd. 2020
S. Yu et al. (Eds.): SPDE 2020, CCIS 1268, pp. 79–90, 2020.
https://doi.org/10.1007/978-981-15-9129-7_6

For example, the wide area network (WAN) is being enriched with many different communication networks (satellite network, Cellular network, high BDP network, etc.) and is constantly changing and evolving. Available bandwidth, round trip time (RTT) and packet loss rate can vary over many orders of magnitude among these different network links. Traditional TCP underperform in such situations because it is designed with assumptions that not valid any longer in current networks, such as low latency, no channel packet losses, no dynamic link handover, etc.

Furthermore, the emerging applications exhibit different QoE preference for data transfer service. For example, online video applications usually prefer smooth data transfer to reduce jitter. Web browser requires short flow complete time (FCT) [1] to reduce page load time. Applications in the mobile device may prefer low packet loss rate to extend battery life. The file transfer and data storage applications usually persuit high throughput. Yet, many other delay-sensitive applications such as online games and virtual reality require low latency to provide real-time interaction interaction and will suffer from the throughput-oriented TCP design. Such diversity of requirements for data transfer service further makes current throughput-oriented TCP which built in the OS kernel *"A Jack of all trades, master of none"* protocol.

To deliver high quality of data transfer across such diversity, network researchers have proposed numerous new congestion control algorithms for different types of application requirements and different kinds of network environments. For example, Scalable TCP [2], YeAH [3], BIC [4], and CUBIC [5] are proposed for the networks with high BDP. Westwood [15] and Veno [16] are designed to perform well in the wireless networks. Exll [6] and C2TCP [7] are proposed to achieve low latency in cellular networks. While many of them outperform the legacy TCP in their target scenario, few of them are deployed in the real networks. This is because that today's operating systems just stick to the unified built-in CC scheme (with Cubic for Linux, MacOS, Android and CTCP for Windows) all the time. This presents a barrier to the timely deploy of novel CC schemes and makes advance protocol off limits to users. Furthermore, previous study [11] have revealed that the performance of different CC schemes varies significantly across various network conditions (e.g., high BDP links, satellite links, wireless and lossy links), there is no single CC scheme that can outperform all others in all network conditions. In such case, consistent use of a single built-in CC will undoubtedly degrade TCP performance.

Hence, we ask a question: *Can we reconstruct the endpoint congestion control architecture to enable more flexible and efficient CC deployment?* In this paper, We put a vision of providing congestion control as a service (CaaS) to offer three important benefits that are missing in today's endpoint congestion control architecture: (i) deployment flexibility of novel CC schemes, (ii) adaptive congestion control according to specific network conditions, (iii) and satisfy the diversified QoE preference of different applications.

The main contributions of this paper are as follows. Firstly, we present the design of CaaS, including four important components: Offline Learning, Online

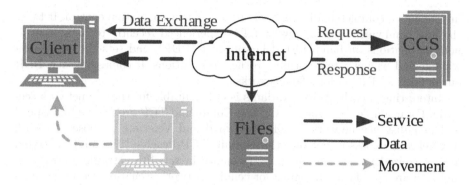

Fig. 1. CaaS architecture.

Matching, Network Change Detection and Algorithm Switching. Secondly, we compare the performance of Caas with legacy congestion control schemes both in the simulation environment and in the real Internet. Preliminary experiment demonstrates the feasibility and superiority of CaaS.

The rest of the paper is organized as follows. Section 2 presents a brief overview of related work. Section 3 details the design of CaaS. In Sect. 4, we evaluate the performance of CaaS. Section 5 provides concluding remarks.

2   Related Work

A. Legacy Congestion Control Schemes. Since the development of Jacobson's TCP Tahoe algorithm in 1988, TCP congestion control over the Internet has been a hot topic for decades because it significantly influences the performance of data transfer. Many researchers have extensively studied and proposed a multitude of enhancements to standard TCP CC. Generally, these CC schemes can be classified into four categories according to their feedbacks: loss-based schemes, delay-based schemes, hybrid schemes and bandwidth-delay-product-based schemes. Loss-based CC protocols, such as HighSpeed [8], BIC, and CUBIC adopt packet loss as the sign of congestion and use an AIMD strategy, which increases the congestion windows (cwnd) if no packet is lost and decreases it on packet losses to avoid copngestion while attaining high network utility. These schemes work well in the wired network with appropriately sized buffers and very little random packet loss. However, they perform poorly in the wireless network which is equipped with large buffers and often experiences high levels of random losses. To tackle with these issues, delay-based schemes, such as Vegas [9] and Hybla [10] use the RTT of packets as an indicator for congestion and keep to reduce queuing delay while achieving high throughput. To take the goodness of both loss-based and delay-based schemes, some hybrid schemes including Compound TCP [12] and TCP Illinois [13] are proposed. They adopt both packet loss and RTT as congestion signal to better predict network congestion. Recently, Google proposed BBR [14], a BDP-based CC protocol which implements a completely different way to implement congestion control. It takes the link bandwidth and the lowest RTT experienced recently to make continuous estimations on bandwidth-delay-product (BDP), and sets the congestion window and pacing rate according to these estimations. It comes out that BBR outperform CUBIC in long fat networks.

Interestingly, each of these variants is only suitable for specific network scenario. For example, Highspeed TCP and Compound TCP are for the high-speed and long-distance networks. TCP Westwood and Veno are proposed to work in wireless networks to enhance throughput. TCP-Peach+ [17] and TCP Hybla are recognized for yielding good performance in satellite networks. Verus [18] and Exll are specifically designed for cellular network scenarios. Despite such a huge set of schemes have been proposed, there is still no "the best TCP" that can always attain best performance across all the possible network conditions. Motivated by this observation, instead of adding just another TCP scheme to such a huge pile of current TCP designs, we focus on providing a platform to dynamically and flexibly deploy these schemes (including the future schemes) in endpoint and enable adaptive congestion control according to specific network scenarios and QoE preference of applications.

B. Learning Based Congestion Control Schemes.   Recently, many researchers have paid attention to machine learning (ML) technologies for Internet congestion control and proposed many interesting learning based CC. These schemes usually construct objective function which involves the throughput, latency, packet loss rate and optimize the function by machine learning technologies. Particularly, Remy [19] uses an offline-trained machine learning model to learn congestion control rules which determine the congestion window sizes based on the latest network conditions. Although Remy provides an effective way to generate CC automatically via machine learning, the rules it learned are mined from the offline data of given network condition, thus is not suitable for other network scenarios. Indigo [11] is another method of learning based CC scheme with the data collected from real network. Indigo learns to "imitate" the oracle rule offline. The oracle is constructed with ideal cwnds given by the emulated bottleneck's bandwidth-delay product. Aurora [16] employs deep reinforcement learning technologies to generate a policy that maps observed network statistics to proper sending rate that maximize data transfer utility. Despite the offline learning based schemes can outperform the heuristic algorithms in some scenarios, they may perform badly in network scenarios they have not been trained for.

To tackle above problem, PCC [21] and Vivace [22] adopt an online learning method. They attempt to find proper sending rate to optimize the utility function via a trial-and-error mechanism. Although online learning can adaptively adjust its strategy according to network dynamics, its performance may diminish in some cases as their greedy exploration could be trapped at a local optimum. It should also be noted that online learning usually has a long convergence time, thus is not suitable for short lived flows and complex scenarios.

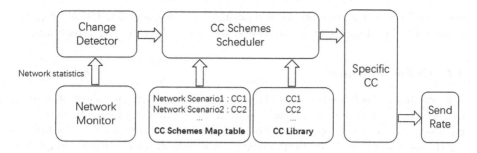

Fig. 2. CaaS Client side framework.

3   System Design

As illustrated above, each CC scheme is only suitable for specific scenario and no single CC scheme is capable of achieving consistent high performance in different network conditions and meet different requirements of applications. Motivated by this, CaaS aims to expedite the deployment of novel CC and distribute the most suitable CC to clients according to network conditions and different QoE requirements of applications in endpoints.

3.1   Overview

At a high-level, CaaS consists of two parts: a server side, termed Congestion Control Server (CCS) and client sides which require congestion control service from CCS, as shown in Fig. 1. The framework of CaaS Client side is shown in Fig. 2. Generally, the server side is responsible for learning the best CC scheme for each network scenario and distributing most suitable CC schemes to clients according to network conditions and application requirements in the client side. The client side can post local network condition information and QoE preference at the suitable time to pull the required CC from CCS, and ship it as a library for congestion control. The downloaded CC modules will be stored in local for future use. We adopt this C/S architecture for timely deployment of new CC schemes.

Congestion control designers can readily publish their new CC scheme by submitting it to the CCS. Each scheme published is required to submit the source code, the design specification for censorship and a statement in the abstract describing scenario where the protocol is recommended or not for use. After that, the CCS will conduct a comprehensive evaluation to check its safety and effectiveness, and decide whether or not to accept it. If adopted, the CC library which holds a set of CC schemes for different application scenarios and the mapping table which maps the network condition to the most suitable CC will be updated to take in new schemes. Some old CC schemes may be replaced if new scheme is more effective in the same or overlapping scenarios. Clients will periodically (about 1–2 weeks) requests the latest mapping table (just 1–3 KB) from the CCS and update the local replica in case that any new CC is adopted in the CCS. We detail main components of CaaS in the following subsections.

3.2 Offline Learning

The optimal CC scheme on a specific network condition can be different across different network conditions, thus it is desirable to find the best CC for every possible network conditions. The offline learning module is responsible for learning the most suitable CC for every given network scenario and output a mapping table which maps a given network condition to the most suitable CC.

To cope with the huge diversity of possible network conditions, we adopt a "divide and conquer" tactic. That is, we divide the possible network conditions in the real world into several sub-scenarios according to the given metric (throughput, rtt, loss rate). In this paper, we assume that the possible network condition varies from 1 Mbit/s to 51 Mbit/s in bandwidth, 10 ms to 200 ms in propagation delay and 0% to 10% in packet loss rate. Then we quantizes each of these three metrics using a quantum (in our experiments, 5 Mbps of bandwidth, 19 ms of delay, 2% of packet loss rate), and obtain 500 sub-scenarios. We simulate each of these sub-scenarios using network simulator Mahimahi [24]. For each sub-scenario, we evaluate the performance of all the CC scheme in the CCS and obtain a performance vector <throughput, delay, loss rate> for each CC scheme. The learning module in the CCS takes the set of performance vectors and determines the best CC for each sub-scenario using a utility function:

$$Utility = w1 * throughput - w2 * delay - w3 * loss, \qquad (1)$$

where $w1$, $w2$, $w3$ are determined by QoE preference of applications. Note that we provide a QoE Control Panel (QCP) in the client side for users to specify customized QoE requirements for different applications. CaaS client will adopt the default parameters if QoE option is not designated by users. Except for the above utility function, we also provide other QoE evaluation indicator, such as flow complete time (FCT) to satisfy QoE requirements for different applications. Finally, we build the mapping table which points out the best CC for every given network condition. Note that every CaaS client will periodically (about 1–2 weeks) access the CCS to get the latest version of this mapping table for online match of best CC.

3.3 Online Matching

When a TCP connection is established, we firstly adopt the default CC scheme (Cubic), because there is no information about network characteristics to decide optimal CC. Note that every CC schemes is responsible for detect network condition while implementing congestion control. So after a while of data transmission, the sender can preliminarily determine the current network condition and find the most suitable CC scheme according to the mapping table. If the desired CC scheme exists locally, client will switch to it directly. Otherwise, client will

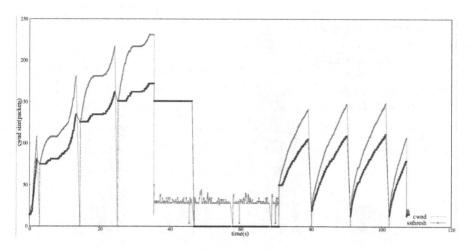

Fig. 3. Hot switch of congestion control schemes.

make a request to the congestion control server (CCS) and switch to the new CC scheme after finishing download. In CaaS, a single CC scheme is approximately 1–3 KB in size, thus it usually takes just a few RTT of time for downloading from server and will not cause too long latency. If the TCP connection is closed when finishing downloade, the new CC will be stored in local for use of next time.

As network condition might change during data transmission, which is common especially for long lived flows, ChangeDetector is continually fed with observations of the network performance metric (throughput, rtt, loss rate) and detect if state has changed. If so, an algorithm switching will be executed to adapt new network condition. We detail Change point detection in next subsection.

3.4 Change Point Detection

Prior work has shown that the network condition along a TCP session is not necessarily a stationary process and might change at different times. For example, mobile phone users in the high-speed rail will undergo frequent handoffs between cellular base stations. Thus, it is desirable to detect such change and adaptively adopt the most suitable CC for new network condition during a TCP connection.

A straightforward way to detect change point of network condition is to continually calculate an exponentially weighted moving average (EWMA) of the related metrics (throughput, RTT, loss rate) samples of TCP flows and check if they reach the threshold values. If so, a new network condition is detected, thus we switch to the new CC for that specific network condition. However, we find this method always leads to frequent and unnecessary switching when these metrics fluctuates, which is very common in practical data transmission.

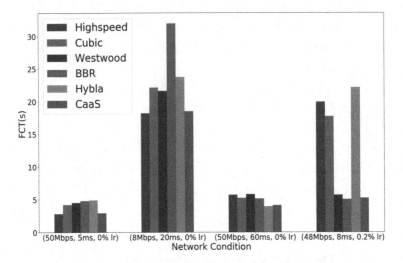

Fig. 4. Flow complete time of different schemes in different network conditions.

Fortunately, according to prior work [25–27], TCP connection metrics can be modeled as a piecewise stationary process which often lasts for tens of seconds or minutes. Motivated by this observation, we use a Bayesian online probabilistic change-point detector [28] which just produce light overhead for computation to detect network condition change. When a TCP connection is created, ChangeDetector is periodically fed with performance metrics, then it calculates mean value and standard deviation of the metrics and detects if new network condition is coming.

3.5 Algorithm Switching

As CaaS dynamically assigns the most suitable congestion control according to connection conditions, algorithm switching should be executed for a single TCP connection when the network condition change is detected. A convenient way to do this is to directly change the congestion control function pointer to another CC module. In this way, however, network throughput will decreases sharply because the sending rate will be initialized to a very small value in the initial phase of a new CC implementation. To ensure smooth transition between algorithms, the new CC is expected to inherit the previous algorithm's sending rate to avoid drastic performance degradation. As for the algorithms employing the pacing mechanism, such as BBR, we set the initial pacing rate to the value of congestion window divided by recent sampled RTT. To test if CaaS client is capable of smooothly switching CC schemes, we switch CC schemes for every 35 s in the order of CUBIC, BBR, Westwood and use tcpprobe tool [23] to observe cwnd. As shown in Fig. 3, each TCP variants perform a different behavior of adjusting cwnd and CaaS is capable of switching different CC at different time.

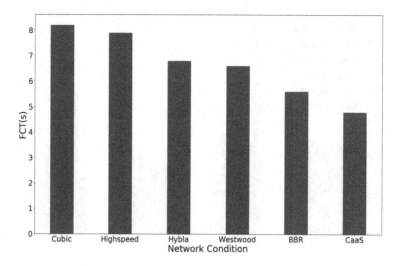

Fig. 5. Flow complete time of different schemes in changing network conditions.

4   Performance Evaluation

To understand and quantify the benefits of CaaS, we evaluated our system both in the network simulator and in the real Internet. Together, these two approaches help us to understand the behavior of CaaS and superiority of it over traditional method. Our test bed consists of 6 clients as data senders and a server as data receiver. In each client, CaaS, Highspeed, Cubic, Westwood, BBR and Hybla are deployed as congestion control scheme respectively. For all clients, we uploaded a file (30 MB) to the server and use transfer completion time (TCT) as the primary performance metric to compare the performance of different CC schemes.

Firstly, we compare the performance of Caas with other schemes in different network scenarios. We randomly generate 4 different network conditions using network simulator Mahimahi. Their link characteristics are (50 Mbps, 60 ms, 0%lr), (50 Mbps, 5 ms, 0%lr), (8 Mbps, 20 ms, 0%lr) and (48 Mbps, 8 ms, 0.2%lr) respectively. In each network condition, clients with different CC schemes send a file to the server. As shown in Fig. 4, every CC scheme has its most suitable network condition and no single CC scheme can outperform all the others in every network condition. Specifically, Hybla achieves best performance in network condition with 50 Mbps bandwidth, 60 ms RTT and 0% loss ratio, but perform worst in other three scenarios. Highspeed outperforms other CC schemes in the first two network conditions but underperforms in the last two scenarios. BBR obtains shortest flow complete time in the network condition with 48 Mbps bandwidth, 8 ms RTT and 0.2% loss ratio, but its performance is significantly worse than other schemes in the network condition with 8 Mbps bandwidth, 20 ms RTT and 0% loss ratio. Fortunately, CaaS always achieves near optimal performance across different network scenarios. This is CaaS can always select the most suitable CC for hosts in different network scenarios.

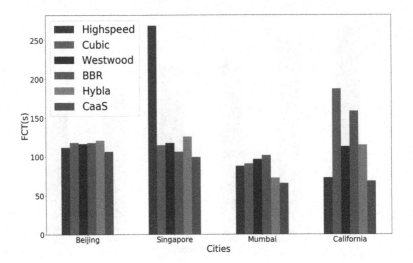

Fig. 6. Flow complete time of different schemes in real Internet.

Secondly, we analyze the performance of CaaS in changing network conditions. The network condition was set to be changed about every 3 s in the order of (48 m, 8 ms, 0.2%lr), (50 m, 60 ms, 0%lr) and (50 m, 5 ms, 0%lr). As shown in Fig. 5, CaaS achieves the shortest flow complete time in data transfer due to its dynamic adjustment CC schemes according to the condition of network. Specifically, we observe that client with CaaS use Cubic as its initial CC, then it switches to BBR at about 0.3 s. After it detects the change of network condition, it switches from BBR to Hybla at about 3.2 s. This proves that CaaS is capable of dynamically switching to the most suitable CC when the network condition is changing.

Thridly, we further evaluate the performance of CaaS in the real Internet. We deploy CaaS in 4 aliyun Web servers from Beijing, Singapore, Mumbai and California respectively. So our local client located in Hangzhou will experience different network characteristics when connecting these Web servers. For each server from different cities, we set client to send a file (300 MB) to server with different CC schemes. As shown in Fig. 6, any specific congestion control algorithm, even the state of the art, cannot excel in diverse network conditions. CaaS can always achieves shorest flow complete time for its adaptive congestion control tactic.

5   Conclusions and Future Work

In this paper, we advocated a vision of providing congestion control as a service to offer flexibility and efficiency benefits for the deploy of novel advanced CC schemes. We implemented a prototype of CaaS to support our argument. Preliminary evaluations confirm that CaaS can transparently deploy suitable CC schemes for clients in different networks, and achieve considerable performance gains as compared to legacy method.

Our prototype system has yielded useful insights for future research of more effective congestion control deploy platform. Our next steps include: 1) further analyze and classify the existing CC schemes to their most suitable network scenario, 2) comprehensively evaluate the overheads of CaaS in terms of CPU usage and extra traffic caused by CC schemes update and 3) improve the performance of the system for short-flow scenarios.

References

1. Dukkipati, N., Mckeown, N.: Why flow-completion time is the right metric for congestion control. ACM SIGCOMM Comput. Commun. Rev. **36**(1), 59–62 (2006)
2. Kelly, T.: Scalable TCP: improving performance in highspeed wide area networks. ACM SIGCOMM Comput. Commun. Rev. **33**(2), 83–91 (2003)
3. Baiocchi, A., Castellani, A.P., Vacirca, F.: YeAH-TCP: yet another highspeed TCP. In: Proceedings of PFLDnet, Roma, Italy, pp. 37–42 (2007)
4. Xu, L., Harfoush, K., Rhee, I.: Binary increase congestion control (BIC) for fast long-distance networks. In: INFOCOM 2004. Twenty-Third Annual Joint Conference of the IEEE Computer and Communications Societies. IEEE (2004)
5. Ha, S., Rhee, I., Xu, L.: CUBIC: a new TCP-friendly high-speed TCP variant. ACM SIGOPS Oper. Syst. Rev. **42**(5), 64–74 (2008)
6. Park, S., et al.: ExLL: an extremely low-latency congestion control for mobile cellular networks. In: The 14th International Conference (2018)
7. Abbasloo, S., Li, T., Xu, Y., et al.: Cellular Controlled Delay TCP (C2TCP). arXiv, Networking and Internet Architecture (2018)
8. Floyd, S.: RFC 3649. https://www.ietf.org/rfc/rfc3649.txt. Accessed 10 June 2019
9. Brakmo, L.S., Peterson, L.L.: TCP Vegas: end to end congestion avoidance on a global Internet. IEEE J. Sel. Areas Commun. **13**(8), 1465–1480 (1995)
10. Caini, C., Firrincieli, R.: TCP Hybla: a TCP enhancement for heterogeneous networks. Int. J. Satell. Commun. Netw. **22**(6), 547–566 (2004)
11. Yan, F.Y., Ma, J., Hill, G.D., et al.: Pantheon: the training ground for internet congestion-control research. In: Usenix Annual Technical Conference, pp. 731–743 (2018)
12. Tan, K., et al.: A compound TCP approach for high-speed and long distance networks. In: Infocom IEEE International Conference on Computer Communications. IEEE (2007)
13. Liu, S., Basar, T., Srikant, R.: TCP-Illinois: a loss-and delay-based congestion control algorithm for high-speed networks. Perform. Eval. **65**(6), 417–440 (2008)
14. Cardwell, N., Cheng, Y., et al.: BBR: congestion-based congestion control. ACM Queue **14**(5), 20–53 (2016)
15. Mascolo, S., Casetti, C., et al.: TCP Westwood: bandwidth estimation for enhanced transport over wireless links. In: 7th ACM Conference on Mobile Computing and Networking (MobiCom), Rome, Italy, pp. 287–297 (2001)
16. Fu, C.P., Liew, S.C.: TCP Veno: TCP enhancement for transmission over wireless access networks. IEEE J. Sel. Area. Commun. **21**(2), 216–228 (2003)
17. Akyildiz, I.F., Zhang, X., et al.: TCP-Peach+: enhancement of TCP-Peach for satellite IP networks. IEEE Commun. Lett. **6**(7), 303–305 (2002)

18. Zaki, Y., Poetsch, T., et al.: Adaptive congestion control for unpredictable cellular networks. ACM SIGCOMM Comput. Commun. Rev. **45**(4), 509–522 (2015)
19. Winstein, K., Balakrishnan, H.: TCP ex Machina: computer-generated congestion control. Comput. Commun. Rev. **43**(4), 123–134 (2013)
20. Jay, N., Rotman, N.H., Godfrey, B., et al.: A deep reinforcement learning perspective on internet congestion control. In: International Conference on Machine Learning, pp. 3050–3059 (2019)
21. Dong, M., Li, Q., et al.: PCC: re-architecting congestion control for consistent high performance. In: Networked Systems Design and Implementation, pp. 395–408 (2015)
22. Dong, M., Meng, T., Zarchy, D., et al.: PCC Vivace: online-learning congestion control. In: Networked Systems Design and Implementation, pp. 343–356 (2018)
23. Linux   TCP   probe.   https://wiki.linuxfoundation.org/networking/tcpprobe. Accessed 12 Oct 2019
24. Netravali, R., Sivaraman, A., Das, S., et al.: Mahimahi: accurate record-and-replay for HTTP. In: Usenix Annual Technical Conference, pp. 417–429 (2015)
25. Balakrishnan, H., Stemm, M., et al.: Analyzing stability in wide-area network performance. Meas. Model. Comput. Syst. **25**(1), 2–12 (1997)
26. Jobin, J., Faloutsos, M., et al.: Understanding the effects of hotspots in wireless cellular networks. In: Proceedings of the Conference of the IEEE Computer and Communications Societies, INFOCOM (2004)
27. Lu, D., Qiao, Y., Dinda, P.A., et al.: Characterizing and predicting TCP throughput on the wide area network. In: IEEE International Conference on Distributed Computing Systems, ICDCS (2005)
28. Ryan Prescott Adams and David JC MacKay: Bayesian Online Changepoint Detection. In arXiv:0710.3742v1 (2007)

Efficient and Evolvable Key Reconciliation Mechanism in Multi-party Networks Based on Automatic Learning Structure

Shuaishuai Zhu[1]([✉]), Yiliang Han[1,2], Xiaoyuan Yang[1,2], and Xuguang Wu[2]

[1] College of Cryptography Engineering,
Engineering University of People's Armed Police, Xi'an 710086, China
zhu_sama@126.com
[2] Key Laboratory of Network and Information Security under the People's Armed
Police, Xi'an 710086, China

Abstract. Key reconciliation protocols are critical components to deploy secure cryptographic primitives in practical applications. In this paper, we demonstrate on these new requirements and try to explore a new design routine in solving the key reconciliation problem in large scale p2p networks with automatic intelligent end user under the notion of evolvable cryptography. We design a new evolvable key reconciliation mechanism (KRM) based on two tricks for the AI user: the observation of shared beacons to evolve based on a deep auto-encoder, and the exchange of observed features as a hint to reconcile a shared key based on a deep paired decoder. For any passive adversary, the KRM is forward provable secure under the linear decoding hardness assumption. Compared with existing schemes, the performance evaluation showed our KRM is practical and quite efficient in communication and time costs, especially in multi-party scenarios.

Keywords: Evolvable cryptography · Key exchange protocol · Automatic learning · Peer-to-peer network · Security model

1 Introduction

While the Internet is entering into the era of artificial intelligence, the development pace of cryptography seems to be delayed. When we focus on designing post-quantum cryptographic primitives, new pattern of requirements and security threats in AI application scenarios boom. Countless of intellectual devices and AI terminals have access to the Internet to share data, features and models,

Supported by the National Natural Science Foundation of China (No. 61572521, U163 6114), National Key Project of Research and Development Plan (2017YFB0802000), Innovative Research Team Project of Engineering University of APF (KYTD201805), Fundamental Research Project of Engineering University of APF (WJY201910).

© Springer Nature Singapore Pte Ltd. 2020
S. Yu et al. (Eds.): SPDE 2020, CCIS 1268, pp. 91–99, 2020.
https://doi.org/10.1007/978-981-15-9129-7_7

which require communication based on large scale of secure sessions. How to efficiently and delicately share a session key in a peer-to-peer AI network is totally
a new topic. The main applying environment of current KEM schemes and key
negotiation protocols are all heavy deployment based on the terminal browsers,
more specially, embedded in the TLS handshake protocols [22]. Why don't deploy
the traditional KEM based on DH or encryption key exchange? Technically, we
sure can do that, but the KEM would become a performance bottleneck and
the advantages of AI users, such as evolvable and cheap in computing power
while costly in communication channels, is neglected in KEM design. In networks involving large scale of AI users like auto-pilots or smart sensor devices,
for the sake of efficiency and global cost of key reconciliation, the current KEM
primitives such as the post-quantum candidates of NIST [2] and current standard schemes of ISO/IEC cannot be directly deployed in p2p scenarios with large
scale of AI users.

The deployment of traditional key exchange protocol in a vast scale p2p
network is awkward and inefficient, because of the high cost of maintaining
independent parameters for each key reconciliation, which brings communication inefficiency, inconvenience and security issue in the long run. In practical
applications like multi-user p2p networks, communication cost is always much
higher than computing cost, so that new KRM construction should occupy lower
message exchange cost. Besides, current KEM and KRM solutions including the
NIST's post-quantum candidates [2] only support fixed system parameters and
configurations in real scenarios, in which the deployment in multi-user p2p networks is clumsy and awkward, and its security cost is expensive to reconcile a
session key in a short slice of connection slot. To solve the above obvious draw-
backs, here we resort to an evolvable design routine to passively or adoptively
generate session keys in p2p networks. Compared with the existing computing
reconciliation based KEMs, we apply a generative methodology based on which
a share secret key is learned and generated from public observation during the
p2p connection. In this section, we try to fundamentally improve these issues by
the constructions of evolvable KRM based on the combination of automatically
learning encoder and decoder (auto-encoder, noted as Ae for short).

2   Related Works

Key Exchange Mechanisms. We assume that key exchange mechanism is
a special instantiation for key encapsulation mechanisms(KEM), which a key
component to encapsulate a cryptographic primitive in the practical communication protocols. For a long time, the discrete logistic based Diffie-Hellman key
exchange is the standard KEM realization [17]. But in the post-quantum KEM,
lattice and LWE based reconciliation [8,9,19] or exchange [3,5–7] take the main
role. The post-quantum KEM usually includes the authenticated protocols like
[13,23], in which signatures or additional verifying structures are applied, and
the direct KEM which is much brief and efficient, such as Ding [8,9], Peikert
[19], and Alkim's NewHope [3,4] that built on Ring-LWE assumption. Also,

there are KEM based on standard LWE assumption, which makes the scheme more brief, such as Frodo protocol [5] and Kyber protocol [6]. Schemes in the first category can easily satisfy strong security like IND-CCA and IND-CCA2 in quantum security model, despite there complex steps and heavy bandwidth costs. KEMs in the second and the third categray may only achieve passively secure, unless safe hash functions or FO transformation [11] are applied, such as Alkim's NewHope.

Generative Secure Communication. The possibility of designing cryptography schemes with the automatic learning techniques such as machine learning and deep learning is discussed firstly in [20]. In the research of KEM, early works focused on how to build secure channels to establish session keys using the method of machine learning [14,18,21]. These automatic approaches cannot generate secure KEM protocols, and their secure keys cannot evolve during further communication. Then for a long period, the research process seems quite hard in handling learning details such as the discrete data training problem [15], the computation overload problem [10] and a less practical outcome. But in recent years, with the widely application of AI technologies and the development of supporting hardware, pure AI based secure communication is becoming an attempting pattern in the future. In 2014, the well-known learning model called generative adversarial network (GAN) [12] appeared, and then it is immediately applied to train a map between an arbitrary input and a target output. The optimized map is then naturally be treated as an encryption or an decryption algorithm. Compared with a mathematical concrete algorithm, the map from a GAN is automatically acquired through statistical adjustment during the training phase. In 2016, Google Brain team [1] published their first secure communication model with automatic negotiated encryption scheme whose security is guaranteed by a passive security model in which the adversary is a third party similar passive learner. As in their demonstration, the receiver can decrypt the message (a 16 bits message sampled in a normal distribution) with overwhelming probability, while the adversary cannot avoid approximately 50% of decoding error with overwhelming probability. But in the continues work of [16], the Google brain's model is found insecure under the attack of stronger adversaries.

3 Construction of Key Reconciliation Mechanism

3.1 System Framework

We first start from constructing KRM in the two party scenario in which our approach can easily be demonstrated. Each user in the network configures a auto-learning system Ae, whose initial state is shared by all users when entering the network. Ae can automatically observe and learn the connection of the recent beacon users which are also leveled users in the network, see Fig. 1. Features f is a transformed representation of the input G_i, and with a complete sample set input, an Ae statistically satisfies $acc(Ae) = P\{G_i = G_{i+1}\} \to 1$.

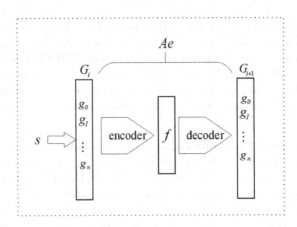

Fig. 1. Auto-encoder structure

3.2 Basic Model: Key Reconciliation Mechanism Within Two Parties

In a peer-to-peer network, there are three types of entities: requesters, responders and beacons. Their computing and storage resources may be vary, but their place in executing p2p protocol is leveled, and their roles may switch in different tasks. KRM within two parties takes the following four steps:

System Init. A set of global parameters are generated, including an secret initial state S_0 of a network auto-encoder ($Ae(n = 2^k, d = 2^{k-\alpha}, G)$ with accuracy threshold η), a secure parameter k, a global identity set $S = \{\cdots, ID_A, \cdots, ID_B \cdots\}$, a collection of beacons $s \in S$, a collision resistant hash function $h(\cdot)$, and a global time tick $i \geq 0$. In each time tick, a beacon scans its connections and sets a vector $g = \{g_0, g_1, \cdots, g_n\}$, $g_i \in \{0, 1\}$, as a current broadcasting beacon sample in S. When $i < 1$, each user observes sample set $s \in S$ and trains Ae_{ID} until $\eta_{ID} \geq \eta$. When $i \geq 1$, the latest state of Ae_{ID} is kept as a secret to evolve new keys in each time tick.

State Evolve. The requestor Alice with ID_A first observes the current beacons s to sample the state of the current network, and obtain a sample set I as the input of Ae. For randomly picked $G_i \in I$, if the accuracy $a \geq \eta$ in decoding G_i, output a feature f and a decoding result G_{i+1} for G_i. Alice runs $\alpha \leftarrow Eval(G'_{i-1}, G'_i)$ to obtains a valid reconciliation threshold. Then he continues to compute $r \leftarrow Rec(G'_{i-1}, G'_i, \alpha)$. Finally, for any user with whom Alice wants to negotiate a key, he sends f to the receiver with ID_B, and computes $k_i \leftarrow h(f||r||ID_A||ID_B)$.

Key Gen. This is a probabilistic procedure. On received the feature f, Bob train his own Ae through the observation of s, and generate a G'_i applying f in Ae. Then Bob runs $\alpha \leftarrow Eval(G'_{i-1}, G'_i)$, and if α exists, he continues to compute $r \leftarrow Rec(G'_{i-1}, G'_i, \alpha)$. Finally, $k_i \leftarrow h(f||r||ID_A||ID_B)$. If α is invalid, then Bob reject f, and jumps to next time tick $i + 1$.

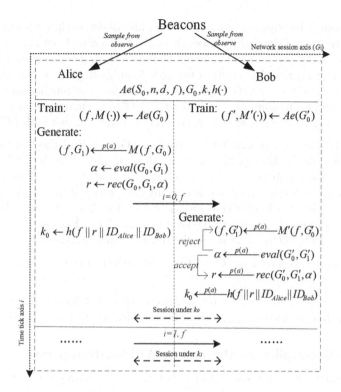

Fig. 2. Basic model with two parties

State Est. Once k_i successfully reconciliated, Alice and Bob establish a connection and update g_{Alice} and g_{Bob} as new beacons from time tick $i + 1$ with probability p (Fig. 2).

3.3 Improved Model: Key Reconciliation Mechanism Within Two Parties

Although the basic model is brief enough with its one-pass message, but its security relies only on the decoder of the responder which may bring expected attack during its instantiation. Besides, a complete passive reconciliation can increase failure probability of the KEM procedure. So we less efficient but more secure variant.

KRM(ID_A, ID_B, S) within two nodes ID_A and ID_B follows five steps:

System Init. A set of global parameters are generated, including an initial state S_0 of two types of network auto-encoders (Ae_{ext} and Ae_{cpr} with accuracy threshold η and feature dimension n, $n > \alpha$ and $d = k/\alpha$ respectively), a secure parameter k, a global identity set $S = \{\cdots, ID_A, \cdots, ID_B \cdots\}$, a collection of beacons $s \in S$, and a collision resistent hash function $h(\cdot)$.

State Evolve. The requestor Alice with ID_A first observes the current beacons s to sample the state of the current network, and obtain a sample set I as the training input of Ae_{ext} and Ae_{cpr}. For randomly picked $G_i \in I$, if the accuracy $a \geq \eta$ in decoding G_i, Ae_{ext} and Ae_{cpr} output features f and f_c and a decoding result G_{i+1} for G_i. Alice runs $\alpha \leftarrow eval(G'_{i-1}, G'_i)$ to obtains a valid reconciliation threshold. Then he continues to compute $r \leftarrow Rec(G'_{i-1}, G'_i, \alpha)$. Finally, for any user with whom Alice wants to negotiate a key, he sends f to the receiver with ID_B.

Key Gen1. This is a probabilistic procedure. On received the feature f, Bob train his own Ae_{ext} through the observation of s, and generate a G'_i applying f in Ae_{ext}. Then Bob runs $\alpha \leftarrow eval(G'_{i-1}, G'_i)$, and if α exists, he continues to compute $r \leftarrow Rec(G'_{i-1}, G'_i, \alpha)$. If α is invalid, then Bob reject f, and jumps to next time tick $i + 1$, else Bob sets $n = k/\alpha$ for Ae_{cpr}. By decoding G'_i in Ae_{cpr}, Bob obtains f_c as the compressed feature of G'_i. Finally, Bob computes $k_i \leftarrow h(f_c||r||ID_A||ID_B)$, and sends the fresh G'_i back to Alice.

Key Gen2. On received an G'_i, Alice generates f_c in Ae_{cpr}, and computes $k_i \leftarrow h(f_c||r||ID_A||ID_B)$.

State Est. Once k_i successfully reconciliated, Alice and Bob establish a connection and update g_{Alice} and g_{Bob} as new beacons from time tick $i + 1$ (Fig. 3).

3.4   Key Reconciliation Mechanism Within Multi-parties

KRM within multi-parties scenario is basically a multi-replica of two parties with one essential problem to handle: extra update of keys for user's dynamic connectivity. With the evolvement of the p2p network, old connections might be disconnected, and new connections might be established according to an average transition probability p. After genesis of the network, it assumed to contain at least $|S| + 2$ nodes including a unique beacon to allocate parameters for dynamic nodes. We extract four types of events: *system init, key evolve, join,* and *drop.* System init is a global event to initialize parameters and prepare local encoders & decoders by observation. The rest operations are used to update keys for connection transition. We apply the improved KRM model to demonstrate the four events of the multi-parties scenario.

System Init. For a p2p network involving at least $|S| + 2$ different nodes where contains an unique initial beacon ID_0 staying online, all global parameters are generated, including an initial state S_0 of two types of network auto-encoders (Ae_{ext} and Ae_{cpr} with accuracy threshold η and feature dimension n, $n > \alpha$ and $d = k/\alpha$ respectively), a secure parameter k, a global identity set $S = \{\cdots, ID_A, \cdots, ID_B \cdots\}$, a collection of beacons $s \in S$, and a collision resistent hash function $h(\cdot)$. Global parameters are allocated by ID_0.

Key Evolve. For every time tick i, any two users $ID_A \in S$ and $ID_B \in S$ who make connection transition in the network make an observation of S and execute $k_i \leftarrow \text{KEM}(ID_A, ID_B, S)$ with each other. On reconciliation success, k_i established, or else the process retry in the next time tick for the same nodes. Finally, after enough time ticks, independent keys are generated between any two users with overwhelming probability.

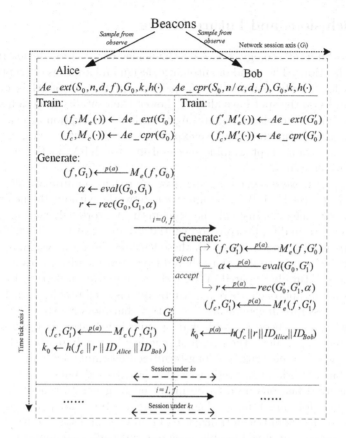

Fig. 3. Improved model with two parties

Join. This is a probabilistic procedure. For new user ID_C joining the network with Ae_{ext} and Ae_{cpr}, ID_0 allocates an S_0, G_0 and the current f for ID_C. Then taking G_0 as the expected state of S, ID_C randomly generates s_i with state transition probability of p. Ae_{ext} and Ae_{cpr} update their state by training on s_i. Taking f as the input of decoder of Ae_ext, ID_C generates G'_{i+1}. Taking G'_{i+1} as the input of encoder of Ae_{cpr} and generates f_c. Finally, ID_C reconciliates with G_0 and G'_{i+1}, computes $k_i \leftarrow h(f_c||r||ID_C||ID_0)$, and sends the fresh G'_i back to ID_0.

Drop. During each time tick i, for any user ID_A's connection state transits, its key stops evolving. The dependency of Ae_{ext} and Ae_{cpr} toward G_i drops after time tick i. Users in a p2p network is free to join and exit, and the transiting probability may vary according to network task, local resources and routine modification. Here we only considered an ideal case of constant state transition probability to comply with the previous correctness base. But if the training results is independent or weak dependent with partial state change of connection graph, the KRM within multi-parties can also be applicable.

4   Conclusions and Future Works

In the late Internet ecology, the AI technologies carry through nearly all the major applications. The trend of automatic design and analysis of cryptographic primitives for specific communication patterns in the era of AI is inevitable. Current works on the spot have already showed their vitality in designing secure communication protocols and analyzing traditional encryption algorithms. Following this interesting direction, we explored the possibility of designing one of the most important cryptographic mechanisms, the KRM in the specific P2P communication scenario.

In this paper, we designed a generative approach to automatically generate the KRM instances for P2P communication networks without the heavy load of frequently key exchange. Instead, the peers in the network only need to randomly observe the surrounding beacons to negotiate shared features. Then each peers generate their own session keys with these features. So far as we know, it is the first generative model to negotiate shared keys, and its advantages in efficiency and briefness naturally required in the P2P communication with vast amount of peers. But in our approach, there are still many unsolved problems, including the unstable success rate in generating shared keys, hardness in extending the width of a satisfying auto-encoder, and lack of standard evaluation in key evolvement. In our current experiment, the length of practical keys only reaches 64~128 bits, which obviously cannot satisfy a long-term secure communication.

In our future work, two directions need to be explored. On security aspect, the state of referred beacons need to be improved to generate random and stable input samples for target peers. Then the architecture and parameters of the generative model should be optimized to obtain wide and stable outputs. On the efficiency aspect, a practical modification of the decoding component is required to polish the randomness of the key evolvement.

References

1. Abadi, M., Andersen, D.G.: Learning to protect communications with adversarial neural cryptography. arXiv preprint arXiv:1610.06918 (2016)
2. Alagic, G., et al.: Status report on the first round of the NIST post-quantum cryptography standardization process. US Department of Commerce, National Institute of Standards and Technology (2019)
3. Alkim, E., et al.: Newhope-algorithm specifications and supporting documentation. Second Round NIST PQC Project Submission Document (2019)
4. Alkim, E., Ducas, L., Pöppelmann, T., Schwabe, P.: Post-quantum key exchange-a new hope. In: 25th {USENIX} Security Symposium ({USENIX} Security 2016), pp. 327–343 (2016)
5. Bos, J., Costello, C., Ducas, L., et al.: Frodo: take off the ring! practical, quantum-secure key exchange from LWE. In: Proceedings of the 2016 ACM SIGSAC Conference on Computer and Communications Security, pp. 1006–1018 (2016)
6. Bos, J., et al.: CRYSTALS-Kyber: a CCA-secure module-lattice-based KEM. In: 2018 IEEE European Symposium on Security and Privacy (EuroS&P), pp. 353–367. IEEE (2018)

7. Bos, J.W., Costello, C., Naehrig, M., Stebila, D.: Post-quantum key exchange for the TLS protocol from the ring learning with errors problem. In: 2015 IEEE Symposium on Security and Privacy, pp. 553–570. IEEE (2015)
8. Ding, J.: New cryptographic constructions using generalized learning with errors problem. IACR Cryptology ePrint Archive, 2012:387 (2012)
9. Ding, J., Takagi, T., Gao, X., Wang, Y.: Ding key exchange. Technical report, National Institute of Standards and Technology (2017)
10. Dudzik, M., Drapik, S., Prusak, J.: Approximation of overloads for a selected tram traction substation using artificial neural networks. Technical Transactions (2016)
11. Fujisaki, E., Okamoto, T.: Secure integration of asymmetric and symmetric encryption schemes. In: Wiener, M. (ed.) CRYPTO 1999. LNCS, vol. 1666, pp. 537–554. Springer, Heidelberg (1999). https://doi.org/10.1007/3-540-48405-1_34
12. Goodfellow, I., et al.: Generative adversarial nets. In: Advances in Neural Information Processing Systems, pp. 2672–2680 (2014)
13. Jiang, H., Zhang, Z., Chen, L., Wang, H., Ma, Z.: IND-CCA-secure key encapsulation mechanism in the quantum random oracle model, revisited. In: Shacham, H., Boldyreva, A. (eds.) CRYPTO 2018. LNCS, vol. 10993, pp. 96–125. Springer, Cham (2018). https://doi.org/10.1007/978-3-319-96878-0_4
14. Klimov, A., Mityagin, A., Shamir, A.: Analysis of neural cryptography. In: Zheng, Y. (ed.) ASIACRYPT 2002. LNCS, vol. 2501, pp. 288–298. Springer, Heidelberg (2002). https://doi.org/10.1007/3-540-36178-2_18
15. Kusner, M.J., Hernández-Lobato, J.M.: GANS for sequences of discrete elements with the Gumbel-Softmax distribution. arXiv preprint arXiv:1611.04051 (2016)
16. Zhou, L., Chen, J., Zhang, Y., Su, C., James, M.A.: Security analysis and new models on the intelligent symmetric key encryption. Comput. Secur. **25**, 14–24 (2019)
17. Maurer, U.M., Wolf, S.: The Diffie-Hellman protocol. Des. Codes Crypt. **19**(2–3), 147–171 (2000)
18. Mislovaty, R., Klein, E., Kanter, I., Kinzel, W.: Security of neural cryptography. In: Proceedings of the 2004 11th IEEE International Conference on Electronics, Circuits and Systems, ICECS 2004, pp. 219–221. IEEE (2004)
19. Peikert, C.: Lattice cryptography for the internet. In: Mosca, M. (ed.) PQCrypto 2014. LNCS, vol. 8772, pp. 197–219. Springer, Cham (2014). https://doi.org/10.1007/978-3-319-11659-4_12
20. Rivest, R.L.: Cryptography and machine learning. In: Imai, H., Rivest, R.L., Matsumoto, T. (eds.) ASIACRYPT 1991. LNCS, vol. 739, pp. 427–439. Springer, Heidelberg (1993). https://doi.org/10.1007/3-540-57332-1_36
21. Ruttor, A.: Neural synchronization and cryptography. arXiv preprint arXiv:0711.2411 (2007)
22. Smith III, T.J., Rai, V.R., Collins, B.M.: Creating and utilizing black keys for the transport layer security (TLS) handshake protocol and method therefor. US Patent App. 15/738,567, 5 July 2018
23. Zhang, J., Zhang, Z., Ding, J., Snook, M., Dagdelen, Ö.: Authenticated key exchange from ideal lattices. In: Oswald, E., Fischlin, M. (eds.) EUROCRYPT 2015. LNCS, vol. 9057, pp. 719–751. Springer, Heidelberg (2015). https://doi.org/10.1007/978-3-662-46803-6_24

CSKB: A Cyber Security Knowledge Base Based on Knowledge Graph

Kun Li, Huachun Zhou$^{(\boxtimes)}$, Zhe Tu, and Bohao Feng

School of Electronic and Information Engineering,
Beijing Jiaotong University, Beijing 100044, China
{kun_li,hchzhou,zhe_tu,bhfeng}@bjtu.edu.cn

Abstract. The access of massive terminal devices has brought new security risks to the existing Internet, so traditional cybersecurity data sets are difficult to reflect the modern and complex network attack environment. Therefore, how to realize the standardization and integration of cybersecurity data, so as to continuously store and update malicious traffic information under massively connected terminals, has become a critical issue to be solved urgently. Therefore, based on the knowledge graph, we built a standardized cybersecurity ontology, and introduced the implementation process of the cybersecurity knowledge base (CSKB) from five stages of knowledge acquisition, knowledge fusion/extraction, know-ledge storage, knowledge inference, and knowledge update, aiming at providing a reliable basis for real-time cybersecurity protection solutions. Experiments prove that the knowledge stored in CSKB can effectively realize the specification and integration of security data.

Keywords: Cyber security data · Knowledge graph · Security ontology · Cyber security knowledge base

1 Introduction

With the rapid development of 5G communication technology, the access of massive terminal devices has brought new security risks to the existing Internet, which in turn threatens user's privacy protection and impacts the security of critical information infrastructure [1, 2]. In the field of cybersecurity, although a series of cybersecurity data sets have been designed, such as KDDCup99 [3], NSL-KDD [4], UNSW-NB15 [5], and CICDDoS2019 [6], etc. They are stored in a CSV file in the form of a two-dimensional table, designed to reflect modern and complex attack environments by designing a comprehensive data set containing normal and abnormal behavior, but they still have some shortcomings: Firstly, cybersecurity data sets capture and analyze traffic in the form of data packets, and put all the characteristics of traffic into data rows, so that they lose the clear relationship between cyber entities and various features. It is difficult to achieve logical preservation of existing data only through data sets; Secondly, each security data set uses its own rules to count traffic and design feature values, resulting

© Springer Nature Singapore Pte Ltd. 2020
S. Yu et al. (Eds.): SPDE 2020, CCIS 1268, pp. 100–113, 2020.
https://doi.org/10.1007/978-981-15-9129-7_8

in a lack of effective correlation with each other, which hinders data mining and knowledge extraction; Finally, the security data set is collected and analyzed under a specific network environment. When faced with traffic information from multiple sources, the data set cannot be updated and expanded regarding the original rules. Therefore, how to effectively use a large amount of existing knowledge and historical accumulation in the field of cybersecurity to achieve the specification and integration of security data, to continuously store and update malicious traffic information under massively connected terminals, has become a critical issue to be solved urgently [7].

On the other hand, in the past decade, research on the construction of knowledge graphs has developed rapidly. As a new knowledge representation method, the knowledge graph represents the relationship between entities in the form of nodes and edges. The efficient query ability, flexible storage mechanism, and update ability of knowledge graph are favored by security researchers [8]. The endless network of threats and the great progress of knowledge graphs have prompted academia to consider how to use knowledge graphs to describe network attack traffic. Among them, related work mainly focuses on attack source traceback [9, 10], which can effectively query and find the evidence and location left by the attack to attribute the source of the attack. However, attack graphs based on specific network environments do not always take into account the dynamic nature of the modern network, especially Distributed Denial of Service (DDoS) attacks [11], so they always lack awareness and classification of malicious attacks on the network. These methods are difficult to meet the needs of the attack and defense parties to quickly and accurately assess the attack success rate and attack revenue [12].

Therefore, we focus on how to build a cybersecurity knowledge base (CSKB) based on the knowledge graph to reflect the modern complex attack environment. The CSKB continuously updates the cybersecurity knowledge through the real-time monitoring system, so as to continuously store and update malicious traffic information under massively connected terminals and achieve network situation awareness and dynamic defense. Specifically, we designed a standardized cybersecurity ontology regarding multi-source security data sets and cybersecurity knowledge, which uniformly describes security element information and implements the function of integrating multi-source and heterogeneous network threat data. Then, we propose a CSKB construction framework based on knowledge graphs and introduce the implementation process of the CSKB from five stages: knowledge acquisition, knowledge fusion/extraction, knowledge storage, knowledge inference, and knowledge update. In particular, we propose a path ranking algorithm *TransFeature* combined with deep learning to achieve knowledge reasoning. Finally, we used the graph database Neo4j to store knowledge in the field of cybersecurity based on the cybersecurity ontology, thereby constructing the CSKB, and showing the comparative analysis between the knowledge in CSKB and various data sets.

The rest of the paper is organized as follows: In Sect. 2, we discuss the related work. In Sect. 3, we explain the construction of cybersecurity ontology. Then, we introduce the construction framework of CSKB based on the knowledge graph and use the graph database Neo4j [13] to store knowledge in the field of cybersecurity in Sect. 4. In Sect. 5, We show a comparative analysis between the knowledge in CSKB and various data sets. At last, Sect. 6 summarizes the paper and future work.

2 Related Work

Recently, many studies have focused on the construction of cybersecurity ontology. Feng et al. [14] focus on Loc/ID split network architectures and provide a related comprehensive survey on their principles, mechanisms, and characteristics. In order to solve the problem of mining and evaluating security information in multi-source heterogeneous networks existing in the Internet of Things (IoT), Xu et al. [15] proposed an IoT cybersecurity situation awareness model based on semantic ontology and user-defined rules. Ontology technology can provide a unified and formal description to solve the problem of semantic heterogeneity in the field of IoT security. Islam et al. [16] analyzed the complexity of integrating safety software systems into safety coordination platforms, and then proposed an ontology-driven method for safety orchestration platforms to automate safety system integration processes. However, the above works only build a general framework for security entities and do not give detailed and standardized cybersecurity ontology construction. This paper refers to various types and characteristics of network attacks to establish a cybersecurity ontology that manages cybersecurity entities at a semantic level.

In addition, several works use knowledge graphs to describe and store modern network attack traffic information. Based on only a limited number of computers and routers involved in the attack session, Yu et al. [9] propose a novel mark-on-demand (MOD) traceability scheme based on the DPM mechanism. Zhu et al. [10] proposed a network attack attribution framework and constructed an air-ground cybersecurity knowledge graph for tracking the source of attacks in the air-ground integrated information network. However, the schemes of these attack graphs do not always consider the dynamic nature of modern networks, so it is difficult to reflect the modern complex attack environment. Our CSKB provides a basis for network situational awareness and dynamic defense by integrating multi-source and heterogeneous security data.

This paper designs a standardized cybersecurity ontology based on multi-source and heterogeneous security data and implements a CSKB by combining knowledge graphs. The CSKB continuously updates the cybersecurity knowledge through the real-time monitoring system, so as to continuously store and update malicious traffic information under massively connected terminals and achieve network situation awareness and dynamic defense.

3 Cyber Security Ontology Construction

Ontology is a set of terms used to describe a field. Its organizational structure is hierarchically structured and can be used as the skeleton and foundation of a knowledge base. Therefore, the goal of building a cybersecurity ontology is to acquire, describe, and represent knowledge in the field of cybersecurity, and to provide a common understanding of cybersecurity knowledge. By determining the commonly recognized terms, we finally give a clear definition of the relationship between concepts or entities from different levels of formal models.

3.1 Process of Cyber Security Ontology Construction

The ontology construction method can be roughly classified as top-down and bottom-up ones. According to the knowledge structure of cyber malicious attacks, we propose a top-down approach to constructing a cybersecurity ontology, as shown in Fig. 1, which aims to describe the types and characteristics of modern network attacks as comprehensively as possible at the semantic level.

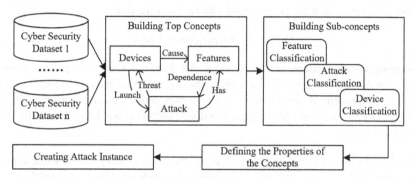

Fig. 1. The process of cybersecurity ontology construction

In order to solve the problem of discrete and independent multi-source heterogeneous cybersecurity data, we collect security data sets that have been widely used in the field of cybersecurity and refer to their experimental environment. First, we constructed the top concepts required by the network attack knowledge conceptual model, including three ontology: device, attack, and feature, and established the relationship between the top concepts. Then, based on the top concepts, we further construct sub-concepts of network attack knowledge. We classify each top concept and provide a detailed description, and describe the internal relationship between each concept by defining object attributes. Finally, by mapping the formatted security data to the ontology model, we add the generated instance to the network attack ontology to describe the relationship between cybersecurity entities.

3.2 Description of Cyber Security Ontology

In this section, we outline the concepts of each layer in the cybersecurity ontology and define the relationship between them.

Top Concepts. As shown in Fig. 1, the top concept contains three ontology: Device, Attack and Feature, and five relationships: Launch, Cause, Threat, Has, and Dependence.

The concept of "Device" represents various physical entities or hardware/software/operating systems from a modern network environment. It may be the source and target of a network attack, as well as the source of attack features.

$$Device \subseteq \forall launch\ Attack\ \cup\ \forall cause\ Feature \tag{1}$$

"Attack" is the core concept in cybersecurity ontology and represents a variety of malicious behaviors in modern networks. It poses a serious threat to devices in the modern network environment. At the same time, different network attacks also have their traffic features.

$$Attack \subseteq \forall threat\ Device \cup \forall has\ Feature \qquad (2)$$

The concept of "Feature" represents the essential features that attack traffic must possess. Different attack types determine different feature values.

$$Feature \subseteq \forall dependence\ Attack \qquad (3)$$

Sub-concepts and Entities. Based on the above three top-level concepts, we expand the category of each concept to further expand the scale of the cybersecurity ontology and achieve a comprehensive and detailed cyber security ontology construction. Since the concepts of upper and lower layers are subordinate relations, we define the relationship attribute as "Has".

We first introduce the classification of device-based sub-concept, as shown in Table 1. Device may be the source and target of modern network attacks, so it should include all hardware, software, and operating systems that may be subjected to or launched attacks. Since the device is a mature ontology, its instantiation has been uniformly described. Therefore, we directly give the cyber security entity corresponding to the device sub-concept based on the experience from the field of cyber security.

Table 1. Device-based sub-concepts

Id	Sub-concepts	Entities
1	Hardware	PC, Mobile device, IXIA etc.
2	Software	Malicious software
3	Operating System	Win7, Win8, Win10, Linux etc.

Next, we analyze the sub-concept classification based on network attacks. The purpose of building the knowledge base is to reflect the modern complex and changing attack environment. Therefore, a comprehensive and meticulous classification of the concept of network attacks, so as to deal with malicious attacks in a targeted manner, is of great significance for achieving network situation awareness and dynamic defense. Unlike device-based sub-concept classification, some network attacks can achieve deeper classification according to their characteristics, especially DDoS attack. As shown in Table 1, referring to multi-source and heterogeneous network attack data, we divide modern network attacks into 8 seed concepts, and also classify each sub-concept in detail, so as to cover the various attack types that appear in modern networks as much as possible.

Table 2. Attack-based sub-concepts

Id	Sub-concepts-1	Sub-concepts-2 (Entities)
1	Fuzzers	FTP Fuzz, Web Fuzz
2	Backdoors	Add root, Sniff user passwords
3	Exploits	SQL injection, Cross-site scripting, Weak password
4	Analysis	Port scan, Spam, Html files penetrations
5	Worms	E-mail, P2P, Vulnerability, Search engine
6	Shellcode	None
7	Reconnaissance	Data collation attack, Sniffing/scanning
8	DDoS	PortMap, NetBIOS, LDAP, MSSQL, UDP, SYN, UDP-Lag, NTP, DNS, SNMP, SSDP, Web, TFTP

By further classifying the sub-concepts of attacks, the types of attacks contained in the underlying concepts directly correspond to the attack entities (Table 2).

Finally, we introduce the classification of feature-based sub-concepts. Different security data sets use different feature extraction tools and lack effective correlation with each other. Therefore, we define and classify feature ontology to realize the specification and integration of multi-source and heterogeneous security data. In order to maintain the scale of the cyber security ontology and ensure a high efficiency of querying the knowledge base, we use the Pearson coefficient to calculate the correlation of each feature value in the data sets, such as NSL-KDD, UNSW-NB15, and CICDDoS2019. Finally, we selected the basic five-tuple features and the five most relevant features as sub-concepts, and explained each feature sub-concept, as shown in Table 3.

Table 3. Feature-based sub-concepts

Id	Sub-concepts	Introduction
1	srcip	Source IP address
2	sport	Source port number
3	dstip	Destination IP address
4	dsport	Destination port number
5	proto	Transaction protocol
6	sbytes	Source to destination bytes
7	sttl	Source to destination time to live
8	sloss	Source packets retransmitted or dropped
9	service	http, ftp, ssh, dns, etc.
10	spkts	Source to destination packet count

3.3 Cyber Security Ontology Implementation

Through the construction of a top-down cyber security ontology, we have established a cyber security ontology that can reflect the types and characteristics of modern network attacks, as shown in Fig. 2. Each node in the ontology represents a concept or entity in cyber security. When the level of the node becomes deeper, the semantics of the entity becomes more specific, but the abstraction of the entity also decreases.

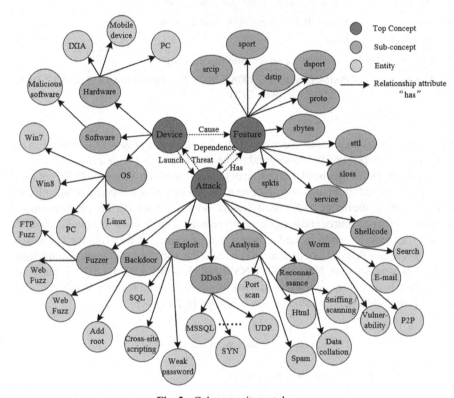

Fig. 2. Cybersecurity ontology

4 Implementation of CSKB

In this section, we will discuss the realization of the CSKB based on the knowledge graph. The implementation process is based on the cyber security ontology in Sect. 3. The implementation process of the CSKB based on knowledge graph we proposed is shown in Fig. 3. It includes five stages: knowledge acquisition, knowledge fusion/extraction, knowledge storage, knowledge inference and knowledge update. Each stage will be explained in the following subsections.

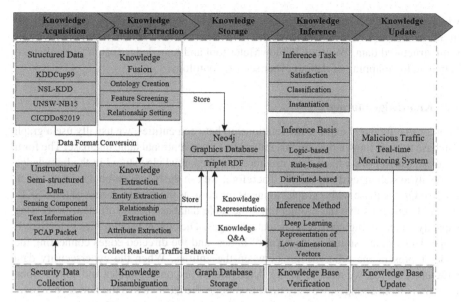

Fig. 3. The solution of constructing CSKB based on knowledge graph

4.1 Knowledge Acquisition and Knowledge Fusion/Extraction

In the previous section, we have constructed a complete cyber security ontology for the CSKB. The process of ontology construction has reflected how to obtain and integrate multi-source security data, and it describes the relationship between cyber security entities and entities. Therefore, we combine the two stages of knowledge acquisition and knowledge fusion/extraction. Based on the cyber security ontology, we can describe how to obtain useful information from multi-source and heterogeneous massive security data and convert it to a triple Resource Description Framework (RDF) format that the graph database can store.

Attack data sources in the field of cyber security are distributed discretely in security databases, PCAP files, security documents, Internet drafts and other media. As shown in Fig. 3, the security data can be divided into structured data, semi-structured data, and unstructured data according to the data type. Above all, structured security data is generally stored in the format of a security data set, and its confidence is usually high. They can be mapped into the cyber security ontology model, and the redundant data can be used for knowledge disambiguation through knowledge fusion technology (such as feature selection). These structured data are an important part of the initial construction of the CSKB. Secondly, part of the attack data is contained in the PCAP format data packets obtained in real-time network attacks. They are called semi-structured data and need to be analyzed using knowledge extraction tools. In turn, they are converted into structured data and stored in a triple RDF format suitable for graph database storage through data fusion. In this paper, we use the CICFlowMeter [17] tool to create reliable features from PCAP files and save them as structured security data sets. Finally, some security documents or Internet drafts usually contain security data without any structure, which can provide a basis for the expansion of cyber security ontology and CSKB. All in all, in the field of cyber security, the main security data comes from structured or semi-structured data. We use CICFlowMeter tool and knowledge fusion technology to complete the mapping of data to cyber security ontology.

4.2 Knowledge Storage

In order to effectively express the relationship between entities, we usually use a graph database to store knowledge graphs, rather than a conventional table database. The form database usually has a fixed data structure, but the knowledge stored in the knowledge graph always changes dynamically. Therefore, we use the Neo4j graph database, which is a NoSQL database with a graph engine as the core, as the storage carrier of the CSKB. It can effectively solve the problem that the table database has insufficient processing capacity when coping with dynamic data changes. The concepts or entities in the Neo4j graph database are stored in the form of nodes, and the directed edges connecting the nodes represent the relationships between the entities. When the cybersecurity data structure changes, we need to add or delete the corresponding nodes and edges; when the data content changes, we only need to modify the attributes of the nodes or edges.

4.3 Knowledge Inference

After the above stages, we have integrated a multi-source and heterogeneous cybersecurity data and used a unified semantic data structure (such as the triple RDF) to store the data in the Neo4j graph database. Finally, a preliminary CSKB was successfully constructed. However, when we collect a large amount of heterogeneous cybersecurity data through knowledge acquisition methods and transform it into the CSKB, the reliability of the data cannot be guaranteed, so we need to complete the classification and recommendation of the data through inference algorithms. Knowledge reasoning can generally be divided into logic-based inference, rule-based inference, and algorithm-based inference. Since cybersecurity data has distinct data features and is more restrictive in logic and rules, we focus on algorithm-based knowledge inference methods to ensure the reliability of security data in the CSKB.

Deep learning can effectively identify the types of network attacks based on input features. Therefore, based on the high-confidence cybersecurity data stored in the CSKB, deep learning can construct a reliable neural network model to identify new types of knowledge. However, the process of deep learning is a black-box model. Therefore, in order to ensure that the knowledge inference process is recognizable, we designed a path sorting algorithm, *TransFeature*, to further verify the reliability of the input safety data content. The process of knowledge inference is shown in Fig. 4.

Deep learning is not the focus of this article, so we choose a Convolutional Neural Network (CNN) consisting of two convolutional layers and two maximum pooling layers as a model for identifying the type of network attack data. We take all the feature entities in the CSKB as the input of CNN and set the corresponding attack entities as labels. After training, we can obtain the trained model to determine the type of attack to which the input security data belongs. According to the judgment of the model, the data that cannot be mapped as the attacking entity in the cybersecurity database is discarded;

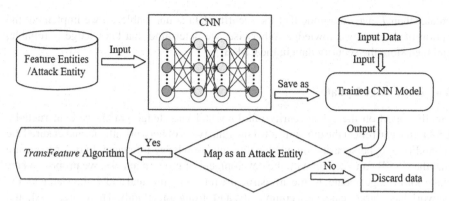

Fig. 4. The process of knowledge inference

The data that can be mapped to a certain attack entity inputs the feature entity into the *TransFeature* algorithm to determine whether the security knowledge is reliable.

TransFeature is the process of learning the low-dimensional vector representation of entities and relationships and comparing entities to achieve the goal of optimization. Due to the particularity of network attack features, it is impossible to describe the type of network attack through a single feature vector, so we define the feature vectors and related calculations as shown in Eqs. (4)–(8).

$$\vec{F_i} = \left(\vec{b_i}, \vec{t_i}, \vec{l_i}, \vec{e_i}, \vec{p_i} \right) \tag{4}$$

$$\vec{F'} = \left(\vec{b'}, \vec{t'}, \vec{l'}, \vec{e'}, \vec{p'} \right) \tag{5}$$

$$\tau_k = \left\| \vec{k} \right\|_{max} - \left\| \vec{k'} \right\| \quad k = b, t, l, e, p \tag{6}$$

$$\vec{T} = \left(\tau_b, \tau_t, \tau_l, \tau_e, \tau_p \right) \tag{7}$$

$$d_i = \left\| \vec{F_i} - \vec{F'} \right\| \tag{8}$$

Among them, the vectors $\vec{b_i}$, $\vec{t_i}$, $\vec{l_i}$, $\vec{e_i}$, $\vec{p_i}$ in Eq. (4) represent the two-dimensional vector representations of feature entities sbytes, sttl, loss, service, and spkts in the i-th data packet. We only select the last five feature entities because they represent the features of the attack packet itself, $\vec{F_i}$ represents the set of feature vectors. The vectors $\vec{b'}$, $\vec{t'}$, $\vec{l'}$, $\vec{e'}$, $\vec{p'}$ in Eq. (5) respectively correspond to the mean vector of each feature vector stored in the CSKB, $\vec{F'}$ represents the mean feature vector set. τ_k in Eq. (6) represents the maximum difference of each feature scalar, and is stored in the threshold vector $\vec{T}$ in Eq. (7). Equation (8) calculates the total distance d_i from the feature vector of the i-th packet to the mean feature vector. Finally, we determine whether the input safety knowledge is reliable by determining the size of d_i and the threshold $\vec{T}$. If d_i is greater than $\vec{T}$, we determine that the security data is unreliable, so we implement the option of discarding knowledge; otherwise, we determine that knowledge is reliable, and then store the security data in the CSKB.

4.4 Knowledge Update

Finally, based on the cybersecurity ontology and knowledge graph, we constructed a CSKB that can reflect the dynamic attributes and types of network attacks and ensured the reliability of cybersecurity knowledge through knowledge inference. In order to ensure that the CSKB can keep up with the development of modern attacks, we propose a new stage, knowledge update. As the infrastructure for generating and undertaking attacks, the network has a large scale, high complexity, and strong uncertainty. Therefore, we should pay attention to the problem of malicious traffic caused by terminal devices in massive connections, and build a large-scale network scenario that can reflect the malicious behavior of modern networks. By establishing a corresponding prototype system, we can monitor malicious traffic in real-time and update knowledge to continuously ensure the real-time and reliability of cybersecurity knowledge.

5 Performance Evaluation

In this section, we show the comparative analysis between the knowledge in CSKB and various data sets. Then, different machine learning techniques have been utilized to compare the classification performance of CSKB with other datasets.

Table 4 shows the comparative analysis between CSKB, NSL-KDD, UNSW-NB15, and CICDDoS2019 datasets. We compared six typical parameters, namely attack families, DDoS attack families, feature extraction tools, number of features, storage format, and data update capability. It can be observed that CSKB has the most attack types compared to the other three datasets. In particular, CSKB also covers 13 DDoS attacks, which can reflect modern attack types to a certain extent. However, by comparison, we found that CSKB has the least number of features. This is because we hope to achieve the specification and integration of multi-source and heterogeneous security data by defining a unified feature ontology classification. What's more, CSKB can continuously filter and update data through the stage of knowledge inference and knowledge update, so it has higher flexibility and scalability.

Since exploring classification methods on the datasets discussed is not the focus of this work, we use Tensorflow [18] to implement five machine learning models for performance analysis. Each model is described as follows:

Logistic Regression (LR): we use the default L2 Regularization to prevent the model from overfitting.
Naive Bayes (NB): the default of Gaussian NB is used.
K-Nearest Neighbor (KNN): we use a cross-validation method to select the optimal K = 6 to balance processing time and classification accuracy.
Decision Tree (DT): Entropy is used as a splitting criterion. In addition, we limit the tree depth to 20 to prevent overfitting.

Table 4. Comparison of datasets

Parameters	NSL-KDD	UNSW-NB15	CICDDoS2019	CSKB
Attack families	4	9	13	30
DDoS attack families	0	0	13	13
Feature extraction tools	Bro-IDS	Bro-IDS, Arugs	CICFlowMeter	CICFlowMeter
Number of features	42	49	80	15
Storage format	CSV	CSV	CSV	Knowledge graph
Data update capability	No	No	No	Yes

Random Forest (RF): the number of base evaluators has a monotonic effect on the accuracy of the RF. The greater the number of evaluators, the better the effect of RF. Therefore, we set the number of evaluators to 100.

When analyzing the performance of the classifier on each data set, the commonly considered indicators are Accuracy, Recall, and F1-Score. Among them, F1-Score is defined as the harmonic mean of Precision and Recall. Finally, we selected the F1-Score as the evaluation indicator. If the F1-Score is larger, the classification performance of the data set is better in the machine learning model.

$$F_1 = 2 \cdot \frac{\text{Precision} \cdot \text{Recall}}{\text{Precision} + \text{Recall}} \in [0, 1] \tag{9}$$

In order to quantitatively analyze the performance of different data sets in each classifier, we set each data set to randomly select 80,000 pieces as the training set and 20,000 pieces as the testing set. The F1-Score obtained for each data set is shown in Fig. 5.

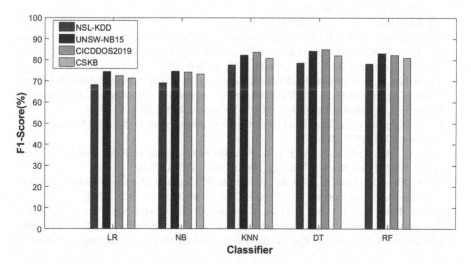

Fig. 5. Comparison of F1-score for NSL-KDD, UNSW-NB15, CICDDoS2019, and CSKB

From Fig. 5, each data set has obtained a high F1-Score in the process of classifying malicious attacks. In addition, it is evident that CSKB equals or betters NSL-KDD on all learning models implemented. Therefore, the experiment proves that the knowledge stored in CSKB effectively realizes the specification and integration of security data.

6 Conclusion

This article is dedicated to solving the problem that traditional security data sets are difficult to reflect the modern and complex network attack environment. We built a standardized cybersecurity ontology based on the knowledge graph and realized CSKB from five stages: knowledge acquisition, knowledge fusion/extraction, knowledge storage, knowledge reasoning, and knowledge update, aiming at fully reflecting the dynamic nature of modern network attacks and providing a reliable basis for real-time cybersecurity protection solutions. Experiments prove that the knowledge stored in CSKB can effectively realize the specification and integration of security data. In future work, we consider expanding CSKB as a communication behavior knowledge base and then establish an intelligent and trusted platform for adaptive memory communication behavior.

Acknowledgement. This paper is supported by National Key R&D Program of China under Grant No. 2018YFA0701604, NSFC under Grant No. 61802014, No. U1530118, and National High Technology of China ("863 program") under Grant No. 2015AA015702.

References

1. Yu, S., Liu, M., Dou, W., Liu, X., Zhou, S.: Networking for big data: a survey. IEEE Commun. Surv. Tutor. **19**(1), 531–549 (2017)
2. Feng, B., Zhou, H., Zhang, H., et al.: HetNet: a flexible architecture for heterogeneous satellite-terrestrial networks. IEEE Network **31**(6), 86–92 (2017)
3. KDD99 (2007). kdd.ics.uci.edu/databases/
4. NSLKDD (2009). nsl.cs.unb.ca/NSLKDD/
5. Moustafa, N., Slay, J.: UNSW-NB15: a comprehensive data set for network intrusion detection systems (UNSW-NB15 network data set). In: 2015 Military Communications and Information Systems Conference (MilCIS), Canberra, ACT, pp. 1–6 (2015)
6. Sharafaldin, I., Lashkari, A.H., Hakak, S., Ghorbani, A.A.: Developing realistic distributed denial of service (DDoS) attack dataset and taxonomy. In: 2019 International Carnahan Conference on Security Technology (ICCST), Chennai, India, pp. 1–8 (2019)
7. Yu, S.: Big privacy: challenges and opportunities of privacy study in the age of big data. IEEE Access **4**, 2751–2763 (2016)
8. Song, Q., Wu, Y., Lin, P., Dong, L.X., Sun, H.: Mining summaries for knowledge graph search. IEEE Trans. Knowl. Data Eng. **30**(10), 1887–1900 (2018)
9. Yu, S., Zhou, W., Guo, S., Guo, M.: A feasible IP traceback framework through dynamic deterministic packet marking. IEEE Trans. Comput. **65**(5), 1418–1427 (2016)
10. Zhu, Z., Jiang, R., Jia, Y., Xu, J., Li, A.: Cyber security knowledge graph based cyber attack attribution framework for space-ground integration information network. In: 2018 IEEE 18th International Conference on Communication Technology (ICCT), Chongqing, pp. 870–874 (2018)

11. Yu, S., Zhou, W., Jia, W., Guo, S., Xiang, Y., Tang, F.: Discriminating DDoS attacks from flash crowds using flow correlation coefficient. IEEE Trans. Parallel Distrib. Syst. **23**(6), 1073–1080 (2012)
12. Yu, S., Wang, G., Zhou, W.: Modeling malicious activities in cyber space. IEEE Network **29**(6), 83–87 (2015)
13. Neo4j (2020). neo4j.com/
14. Feng, B., Zhang, H., Zhou, H., Yu, S.: Locator/identifier split networking: a promising future internet architecture. IEEE Commun. Surv. Tutor. **19**(4), 2927–2948 (2017)
15. Xu, G., Cao, Y., Ren, Y., Li, X., Feng, Z.: Network security situation awareness based on semantic ontology and user-defined rules for internet of things. IEEE Access **5**, 21046–21056 (2017)
16. Islam, C., Babar, M.A., Nepal, S.: An ontology-driven approach to automating the process of integrating security software systems. In: 2019 IEEE/ACM International Conference on Software and System Processes (ICSSP), Montreal, QC, Canada, pp. 54–63 (2019)
17. CICFlowMeter (2017). www.github.com/ISCX/
18. TensorFlow (2020). https://tensorflow.google.cn/

Improvements Based on JWT and RBAC for Spring Security Framework

Gongxuan Zhang[✉], Mingyue Zhang, and Xinyi Fan

School of Computer Science and Engineering, Nanjing University of Science and Technology,
Nanjing 210094, China
gongxuan@njust.edu.cn

Abstract. Authentication and authorization are the two aspects of Spring security system, and they are shortcomings. In this paper, we study the spring security mechanism and some improvements and optimizations based on JSON Web Token and RBAC model. Furthermore, a trust RBAC model is proposed, and we expounded its structure from direct trust and indirect trust. The simulation results show that the method we proposed has a good effect.

Keywords: Authentication · Authorization · JSON Web Token · Role-based access control

1 Introduction

The spring framework was first proposed by Rod Johnson in 2000, and has been a very mature framework since then. Up to now, it has integrated more than 20 modules. The core modules of spring are container based, and different related modules can be customized according to the requirements. Spring is a container framework whose core characteristics are a lightweight inversion of control (IOC) and aspect oriented (AOP) [1]. The former realizes the resource configurable row and promotes loose coupling to a certain extent. The latter simplifies programming, allowing programmers to encapsulate behaviors that affect multiple classes, such as logging and transaction management, into modularity.

An important design goal of spring framework is to integrate more easily with existing J2EE standards and commercial tools [2]. In short, spring's initial goal is not to build another large and comprehensive new framework. It is hoped that spring framework, like a large container, can integrate various existing technologies in various applications quickly and easily, support them, and make developers feel like using simple JavaBeans in the implementation process, and can easily complete the replacement of similar frameworks and tools when necessary. Spring's two key means to achieve this goal are: inversion of control/dependency injection (IOC/DI), and aspect oriented programming (AOP). Among them, IOC/DI is the most basic bottom layer of spring, while AOP is a powerful feature of spring. We can see from the introduction of the three official core modules of spring (as shown in Fig. 1.), the three hottest selling points of spring framework are spring boot, spring cloud, and spring cloud data flow.

The paper is partly supported by NSFC No. 61773206, No. 61272420.

© Springer Nature Singapore Pte Ltd. 2020
S. Yu et al. (Eds.): SPDE 2020, CCIS 1268, pp. 114–128, 2020.
https://doi.org/10.1007/978-981-15-9129-7_9

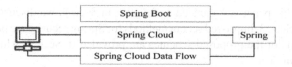

Fig. 1. Core modules of spring framework

Build everything through spring boot, cooperate with everything through spring cloud, and link everything through spring cloud dataflow. These characteristics, in the back of the security issues, spring's many security mechanisms are the cornerstone to ensure its stable position.

Spring security is a security control framework based on spring framework. It abstracts many mechanisms and means of spring on the security level, and implements authentication and authorization in function [3]. Authentication means to verify whether the user is legal through user name, password and other contents. Authorization refers to giving the user some permission to access the page or perform some operations. For example, when a user applies to visit a page, the system will intercept the application and verify whether the user has login and access rights. The system will intercept the user without permission. The security framework will direct the blocked users to the login page.

JSON web token (JWT), as a kind of authentication, is the most popular authentication solution. JWT, which is an open standard based on JSON (RFC7519) [4], is mainly used to deliver statements in the network application environment. In general, JWT is used to transfer user authentication information between the client and authorization server. After authentication, the resource server can send resource information to the client. Because JWT information is usually saved in the HTTP header and needs to be transmitted in the network as authentication information along with HTTP, JWT statements are generally very compact and secure [5]. You can also add some information to the declaration as additional business logic support. JWT can also be used as a signature to implement some encryption or signature verification functions.

RBAC, as a sample of authorization, is role-based access control [6]. The core of RBAC permission control is to introduce the concept of role between user and permission, and use the role to manage permission directly, instead of the user directly associated with permission. By assigning roles to users, the permissions associated with roles can be indirectly assigned to users. When users need to access the limited resources, they need to judge the permissions of the corresponding roles of the users to access the limited resources. RBAC introduces the intermediate concept of role, which makes the authority management level depend on each other. The authority is given to the role and the role is given to the user. This kind of authority design is clear and the management is convenient and efficient. RBAC supports generally accepted security principles: minimum privilege principle, separation of responsibility principle and data abstraction principle [7]. Many extended models have evolved in the development of RBAC. Some of them are not practical in reality, or they are designed based on a specific scenario, and they do not have the universal adaptability value for further research. Among them, the more classic ones with extended value are four conceptual models of $RBAC_0$-$RBAC_3$, which together constitute the RBAC96 model family.

The rest of this paper is organized as follows. In Sect. 2, we discuss some relative works. Then, in Sect. 3, improved secure methods for Spring security are proposed. Some simulation results of the proposed schemes are provided in Sect. 4, which is followed by conclusions in Sect. 5.

2 Related Works

2.1 Spring Security Framework

Spring security framework has good support and implementation in authentication and authorization management, which are the most prominent security issues.

(1) **In terms of identity authentication,** spring security framework supports mainstream authentication methods, such as open id, SSL, HTTP basic authentication, x509, JAAS and LDAP [8].
(2) **In terms of authorization management,** spring security provides support for role access control (RBAC) and access control list (ACL), which enables authorization management based on different models and structures, and fine-grained control of domain objects in applications.

2.2 Identity Authentication

JSON web token (JWT) is widely used as a stateless server authentication method in the distributed web application system. The authentication and permission control process of the traditional server needs a specific server authentication state, the system has a high coupling degree, and the load pressure on specific server is large. The authentication based on JWT is stateless. The token in JWT contains all the information for user identity authentication, so we do not need to store user information in the session, which avoids the session state and realizes the front and back end separation [9]. This makes it easy for us to use the same token to obtain security resources from outside the domain. At the same time, we do not have to defend against Cross Site Request Forgery (CSRF) attacks because we do not use cookies.

At present, there are two kinds of authentication methods available on the market, session based and token based. Session based authentication refers to storing a session ID on the client. Request to carry session during authentication ID, and the server finds the corresponding session from the session data store. In this way, many web sites have token based authentication, which means that all authentication related information is encoded into a token on the server side and signed by the server to ensure that it is not tampered with. Token itself is clear text. The information in the token can include user ID, permission list and user nickname. In this way, as long as the server holds the signature of token and token, it can directly verify the identity of the user is legal. In reality, the main standard of token based authentication is JSON web token (JWT), see [RFC 7519]. The comparison between session based and token based authentication methods is shown in Fig. 2.

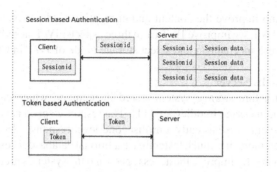

Fig. 2. Comparison between session based and token based authentication

2.3 Authorization Control

Authorization control is based on identity authentication, according to authorization to subdivide access requests, to do further business logic or resource differentiation management. The three core concepts of authorization control are subject, object and attribute.

(1) **Subject** refers to the object that requests resource access. This object can refer to the specific user, or the user's startup process, related services, related devices, etc. the object requests, but the subsequent execution may not be performed by the subject.

(2) **Object** refers to the entity of the accessed resource. The object can refer to all things that can be accessed, operated and managed, information, files, resources, objects and other things, as well as another object.

(3) **The control strategy attribute** is a set of related access rules for subjects to objects. Here, the attribute set of subjects and objects is described [10]. In fact, access control strategy is a kind of authorization behavior in essence. It divides the subject's access to the object into different access rules and authorizes the subject according to the combination of different access rules, which also embodies the object's default to the subject's operation behavior.

3 Improvements of Authentication and Authorization

3.1 Improvement for JWT

In the spring framework, some application scenarios will require a higher level of security. The requirements for user identity authentication and permission control are relatively strict. The user's identity information will be strictly divided. When allocating operable resources, there will also be strict requirements for the division of the minimum required permission. For example, the standard roles in charge of system, audit and security will not be able to access each other's resources to ensure security. This is a high requirement for the mutual exclusion and fine-grained of user identity. When applying JWT to such a security scenario, we need to customize the access rules of resource objects and improve the content and encryption methods of JWT. In view of these problems of JWT, we improve JWT from three aspects: JWT stored in Redis server, JWT dynamic refresh mechanism and select storage mode of JWT in Clients.

JWT Stored in Redis Server

Redis is a data structure storage system stored in memory, which can be used as a database, cache and message middleware [11]. The response speed is very fast. If there is no network problem, it is basically a millisecond level response. As a data structure storage system in memory, it is much faster than traditional database access. Storing token in Redis server can greatly improve the access speed and the system's processing speed of user identity authentication. Secondly, the introduction of middleware to manage token avoids the single point problem. For a distributed system, no matter which service handles the user request, it will be centralized in Redis to obtain token. Token is time-effective, while Redis naturally supports setting expiration time and achieving automatic renewal effect through API provided by some external packages. The identity authentication process stored on Redis with token is designed as follows:

(1) The client requests the user to log in to the server, carrying the account password and other information;
(2) After verifying the information on the server side, a token is generated and sent to the Redis server. Redis sets the expiration time and stores the token information;
(3) At the same time, the server returns token to the client, and the client stores token;
(4) The client carries token to request service from the server;
(5) After receiving the token, the server forwards it to the Redis server to check whether the token exists in the Redis server;
(6) Redis server returns to the server whether the token exists;
(7) If token exists in Redis server, the resource information requested by the user will be sent to the user;
(8) If there is no token in the Redis server, it may be the message that the token in the Redis server is invalid and the server returns the token to the client;
(9) The client user performs the logout and login operation, sends the logout and login message to the server, and the server fails to set the token to the Redis server.

JWT Dynamic Refresh Mechanism

Token is a stateless authentication token stored in the client. In the case of improper use of the user or malicious attack on the network, token will be fraudulently used. At this time, the server can only distinguish whether it is a malicious attacker who fraudulently uses token by comparing IP and other methods. In order to improve its security as much as possible, token will be used in practical applications as much as possible. The failure time is set relatively short. In this case, the time limit of user login is relatively short and frequent login is required. This is obviously not in line with the original intention of JWT. One solution to this problem is to refresh JWT regularly. There are some solutions to this problem. Considering the existing scenarios, this paper proposes a method of the dynamical refreshing token. The dynamic refresh token scheme achieves the dynamic management and use of token by introducing the concept of user active period. During the active period of users, token can always exchange the old token for the new one to continue the system cycle.

Several parameters are defined here:

(1) Refresh timestamp: the meaning of this refresh time stamp is the expiration time of the corresponding token. If the token fails within this refresh time point, the invalid token will be exchanged for a new token

(2) Refresh count: a user-defined period of maximum inactivity, similar to the expiration time of refresh token in traditional models;

(3) Last refresh time: The latest refresh time of the user. If the token does not expire before ZA, the latest refresh time is last refresh time. It is the token expiration time. If the token has expired, then the current time when refreshing is selected.

Save the refresh time method saverefreshtime() in the front-end JS file, which is mainly used to record the active period of the current user's operation. In this active period, the token can be updated dynamically. If it exceeds this period, it will jump to the login page. There are two call points of this method. When the routing switch occurs at the front end and HttpRequest occurs, the call operation is carried out. See Algorithm 1 for the pseudo code of saver fresh time.

Algorithm 1. saveRefreshtime

1: **begin**
2: lastRefreshtime←refreshtime?(new Refreshtime):(new Date());
3: expiretime←TokenExpireTime;
4: refreshCount=1;
5: **if** lastRefreshtime>=nowtime **do**
6: lastRefreshtime←nowtime>expiretime ? nowtime:expiretime;
7: lastRefreshtime←lastRefreshtime+ refreshCount;
8: refreshtime←astRefreshtime;
9: **else**
10:    refreshtime←new Date();
11:    **end if**
12: **end**

Based on the result of the system testing and enabling the token dynamic refresh mechanism, the system will dynamically refresh the token according to the user's active time we set. The refresh process should be transparent to the user, but in order to test the token dynamic refresh mechanism, it is set in token When the user's active time has not expired and the user has any operation on the system, the token will be refreshed, and a prompt box will pop up to indicate that the token is refreshed successfully. The test results are shown in Fig. 3.

Selecting Storage Mode of JWT in Clients

At present, the main way to access token is to use the header and local storage, because this can effectively prevent CSRF (crossing site resource forge) attacks, but it may

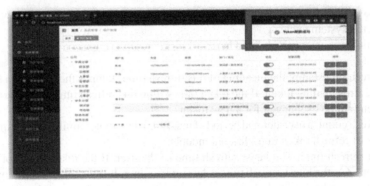

Fig. 3. Test results of dynamic refresh mechanism

increase the possibility of XSS (crossing site script) attacks [12]. The headache of XSS is that it is difficult to ensure that the system can perform the escape operation on all users' input. For example, although 99% of the system is generated by the React framework, there are some special parts. In order to facilitate the use, traditional technologies such as JQuery are adopted. As long as there is a vulnerability, the protection system for XSS is completely invalid.

For this XSS attack, you can also choose to set httponly cookie to store token. Because there is only one resource in the browser that cannot be accessed by scripts. XSS attackers have no way to get authentication information from httponly's cookies. When setting cookies, the following settings are required:

Set-Cookie: access_token = xxxxxxxxxxxxxxxxxx; HttpOnly; Secure; Same-Site = strict; Path =/;

However, even if we use httponly cookies as the storage mode, we are bound to face the threat of CSRF attacks. In traditional page web sites, CSRF token is generally used. This is a very popular practice. Containers such as Tomcat have their own Filter for generating and checking CSRF Token. The workflow of CSRF token is as follows: the client should first request a page with a submission form from the server, and a CSRF token will be embedded in the page returned by the server. When the user submits the form, the CSRF token will be taken together and sent to the server for verification. So, when the server sees the CSRF token, the user can confirm that it is the form interface before submission, so as to avoid the possibility of users submitting forged forms.

3.2 Building Stateless Authentication System Combined with JWT

The identity authentication service is mainly divided into two parts, the authentication from the login request and the authentication from the limited resource access request [13]. Now, we combine spring security and Java JWT to build a stateless authentication system. The methods of request login verification and request limited resource verification are designed as follows.

Request Login Authentication
Spring security login verification is completed by the class of JwtLoginFilter. The verification method is mainly implemented by the authenticationprovider instance of the AuthenticationManager interface through the AuthenticationManager interface attribute within its father class AbstractAuthenticationProcessingFilter. By configurating WebSecurityConfig, the authentication method of AuthenticationProvider is inherited and rewritten in the CustomAuthProvider class. The specific process is shown as follow:

(1) Add login request filter in WebSecurityConfig class. All requests to access/login are processed by this filter.
(2) After the JwtLoginFilter intercepts the login request, it first calls its own attemptAuthentication(), takes out the authentication user information from HTTP request, and then combines it into a certificate object of Authentication user.
(3) After getting the Authentication object, the filter will call authenticate () of the overwrittten CustomAuthProvider class to verify it.
(4) The authenticate () method will take out the user information from the database, add the user permission list to the new credentials and return the success information if the login verification is passed, and return the exception information if the login information is not correct.
(5) JwtLoginFilter will accept the information returned after authentication. If the authentication is successful, a token will be created for the user and returned to the client. If the login request fails to authenticate, a 401 error will be returned.

Request Limited Resource Validation
Add the restricted resource request filter in WebSecurityConfig class to intercept all requests accessing the restricted resource. After receiving the request to intercept, call TokenAuthService. Getauthentication() to authenticate the token in the request.

After the authentication is passed, the returned user credentials are stored in the SecurityContextHolder context information, and then the restricted resource information is sent to the client.

3.3 Improvements of Authorization Control

Based on the discussion in Chapter 2, combined with the application scenarios and the target groups of the security mechanism in this paper, we decided to focus on the improvement of RBAC$_3$.

Improved Design of RBAC Based on Linux Permission
In the Linux file system, the permissions are set as follows: the permission types of files under Linux generally include read, write, and execute, and the corresponding letters are R, W, and X. Linux's permission control subjects are divided into three groups: owner, group and other groups. According to the roles of these three groups, each file can be set with read-write execution permission respectively to realize different granularity permission settings and management.

The permission of the Linux file system uses the mathematical description of bitwise AND. In mathematics, bitwise and operation have the following mathematical expressions. The simple description is the sum of the nth power of 2 and the nth power of 2. After the operation, the n-th power of 2 is obtained.

$$A = 2^a + 2^b + \ldots + 2^n$$

$$A\&2^a = a$$

$$A\&2^b = b$$

$$A\&2^n = n$$

$$A\&2^x = 0 \qquad x \notin \{a, b, \ldots, n\}$$

Through the above mathematical expression, this rule can be applied to the general permission algorithm. Add a number code to each operation item in the permission table, such as operation A-> a, operation B-> b, operation C-> c, operation D -> d, operation E-> e. If a user has permission A and permission C, the user's permission $P = 2^a + 2^c$ can be recorded. When it is necessary to judge whether the user contains the permission x, it can judge the user's permission to the resource quickly and efficiently by bit operation. The biggest advantage of this method is that it can judge the authority quickly, and only do displacement operation in the bottom layer, at the same time, it can also verify multiple authorities together. There are two disadvantages of this method in practical application: the first one is that the same permission code is determined by the mathematical logic of bit and cannot be added twice, and the solution is to check at the business level; the second one is that the number of permissions that a code value can represent is limited, for example, in Java, int takes up 4 bytes, 32 bits, only 32 permission amounts, long can be realized 64 permissions. The solution is to divide permissions into modules, or use byte[] data structure, you can have unlimited storage rights.

Combined with the general model and RBAC3, this paper makes the following improved design, adding long in the role table Type B, the permission data related to the user is stored in the hexadecimal method, and the specific resource permission is stored in the resource data table. When judging whether the user contains certain permission, the user's permission to the resource can be quickly and efficiently judged through the bit by bit operation of the corresponding role of the user. Here, it is assumed that there are three types of permissions in this model, one is system permission, which has information related to system management, such as department, position, permission, role, user, etc., and the type is set to 0 (default); the other is defined as business permission, which is the right required by system related business logic, and the type is set to 1; it is assumed that each type of permission is only 64 If there are more than 64 permissions, the permissions are divided into modules. Each module has 64 permissions. The permission type is used to identify the permission module. The conceptual model is shown in Fig. 4.

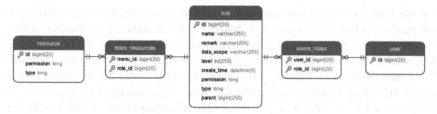

Fig. 4. Conceptual structure

When adding resources, record the permission value from 1 for each time you add resources. The permission amount of each module does not exceed 64. The sum of all permission values in the role corresponding to the storage of the role. When adding and deleting resources, we need to re traverse the roles and recalculate the total permissions.

During permission query, query the total permission recorded by the role corresponding to the user. The sum of permissions and the permission value are operated. If the value is 0, the role does not have the permission. If the value is permission itself, the role has permission.

Dynamic RBAC Model Based on Trust

In view of the problem that the traditional RBAC model lacks the description of the object characteristics and the permissions cannot change dynamically, this paper proposes a dynamic access control model combining trust and RBAC, and the model framework is shown in Fig. 5.

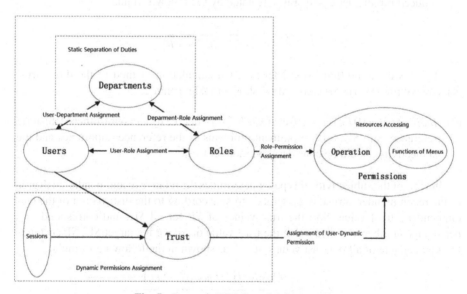

Fig. 5. Dynamic RBAC model framework

In this model, the user's role is judged, and the corresponding authority authorization is obtained according to the user's static role and dynamic trust degree, which can better prevent the unauthorized user's illegal operation and unauthorized access. In the dynamic RBAC model based on trust, the definition of constituent elements and the description of constraint rules are as follows: the subject of trust is called *SP*, the object of trust is called *SU*, when the subject of trust is the owner of resources, the object of trust is the role, and when the subject of trust is the role, the object of trust is the user. How to formally define and accurately measure the trust of entities has always been the research focus of the access control model based on trust. In this paper, trust is divided into two parts: direct trust (hereinafter referred to as *DT*) and indirect trust (hereinafter referred to as *IDT*).

(1) *Direct trust DT.*, which is used to accurately describe *SP*, has two types: direct function trust and direct reference trust. The two trust values are used to stand for direct trust degree as 'DT$_{func}$' of SP-> SU, and direct reference trust as 'DT$_{ref}$' of SP-> SP. DT$_{func}$ is found by Beta distribution function which uses the number of "positive" and "negative" feedbacks as α and β respectively to evaluate direct trust. Positive feedback will be α plus 1, and negative feedback will be β plus 1. In each interaction, *SP* can adjust the direct trust value according to its own experience and historical interaction records. However, this approach cannot quantify the importance and cost of this interaction. In this paper, we define a penalty rate of *PR* to solve the problem of interaction importance. The penalty rate *PR* is used to indicate that when there is negative feedback in important interaction, the negative feedback should be strengthened and the trust value of *SP* to the entity should be reduced rapidly. Direct trust is calculated by the fellow formula.

$$DT = \frac{\alpha^{(t)}}{\alpha^{(t)} + \left(\beta^{(t)} \times PR\right)}$$

Hence, we can preliminarily determine the calculation method of the direct trust value of *SP* for *SU*. The pseudo code is shown in Algorithm 2.

(2) *Indirect trust(IDT).* is used to evaluate SU trust degree by receiving other SP historic reference with SU. Such prominent problems as the reference importance and the subjectivity should be considered in indirect trust.

In view of the subjectivity, this paper determines the relative recommendation degree of the recommender's trust to the target's trust according to the distribution of the recommender's trust value. Sort the trust values of *SP* for all *SU*, and correspond to a percentage number to indicate that the trust value of *SP* for the target *SU*, *SP* accounts for a percentage of all the trust values of *SU*, as shown in the following formula.

$$P_{SU_i}^{SP_h} = \frac{100 \times first\left(DT_{func\,SU_i}^{SP_h}, d_{SP_h}\right)}{C_{SP_h} + 1}$$

After then, we gave some key functions and designed the algorithm for the indirect trust shown as Algorithm 3.

Algorithm 2. Find DT

Input: Parafb, SeqfbSet, Timet, Paraalpha, Parabeta, Penalty PR
Output: Direct Trustdt
1: **function** timef(fb,fbSet,t,alpha,beta)
2: t←t+1
3: k←Max{ fbSet}
4: **if** fb>⌈ $k/2$⌉ **then**
5: alpha←alpha+fb-⌈ $k/2$⌉
6: **else if** fb<⌈ $k/2$⌉
7: alpha←alpha-b+⌈ $k/2$⌉
8: **end if**
9: **end function** 10:
11: **function** dtF(alpah,beta,PR)
12:   dt←alpha/(alpha+(beta*PR))
13:   **return** dt
14: **end function**

---

4 Simulation Results

In this paper, Java language is used to simulate the experiment. The classic advogato data set trust network is used as the initial trust value. The data set has 51127 data, including 6539 nodes. The nodes represent the users of advogato, and the directed side represents the trust relationship. On advogato, the trust link is called "certificate". Three different levels of authentication can be carried out on advogato, corresponding to three different edge trust values, 0.6, 0.8, 1.0, corresponding to basic trust, comparative trust and full trust respectively. Taking these three as the initial trust values, combined with the test process, we will further grade the trust values.

We define a public class 'Trust' to store the advogato dataset and trust related data, among which the key elements are trusteeID, trustedID and trustValue. The common class 'Trans' is defined to store the information of node interaction. The data set of advogato does not include transaction count and time, so we add these parameters to the interaction class. These are the two most critical classes (Table 1).

Algorithm 3. Find Indirect Trust

Input: SP, SU
Output: idt
1: **function** idtf(SP,SU)
2: fenzihe←0,fenmuhe←0
3: **for** all SP2 interacted with SP **do**
4: fenmuhe←fenmuhe+dt(SP,SP2)*wtn(t)
5: **if** dt(SP2,SU) exist **then**
6: fenzihe←fenzihe+dt(SP,SP2)*mdt(h,i,j)*wtn(t)
7: **end if**
8: **end for**
9: **return** fenzihe/fenmuhe 8: **end function**
10: **function** mdt(SP,SP1,SU)
11:    a← ⌊ pf(SP, SU) * (num(SP1) + 1)/100⌋
13:    b←pf(SP,SU)*(num(SP)+1)/100-a
14:    res←0
15:    **if** a>0&&a<num(SP1) **then**
16:        res←first(SP1,a)+b*(first(SP1,a+1)-first(SP1,a))
17:    **else if** a=0 **then**
18:        res←first(SP1,1)
19:    **else if** a=num(SP1) **then**
20:    res←first(SP1,num(SP1))
21:    **end if**
22:    **return** res
23:    **end function**

Table 1. Classification of trust values

Trust rank	Trust class	Permission intensity
[0.9, 1]	Perfect	Absolute
[0.8,0.9]	Better	Strong
[0.6, 0.8]	Basic	Part
[0.4, 0.6]	A little	Weak
[0, 0.4]	No	No

The experimental process is as follows: first, initialize each node and interaction information, randomly pick out the trusted node, conduct interaction operation, and record the interaction information as the initial interaction information; second, filter the initial trust data, pick out the entities with the initial data as the interaction boundary, and then select a random TrustedID, and get all the trust edges from the intersecting boundaries, called SU trust boundary. Through the data of all SP that have interactive records with SU, the trust value of SP to SU is calculated by the above model.

The indirect trust value is calculated in six iterations. In the first iteration, the indirect trust is calculated according to the original data. In the second iteration, the random recommender related to SU is changed to a malicious entity, and the trust value is < 0.4 In the third iteration, two random recommenders are changed to malicious entities. By analogy, the final trust value is calculated. Compared with the relevant models, as shown in Fig. 6, we can see that when there is malicious node recommendation, the indirect trust of this model changes. With the increase of malicious nodes, the indirect trust gradually decreases, which is logical.

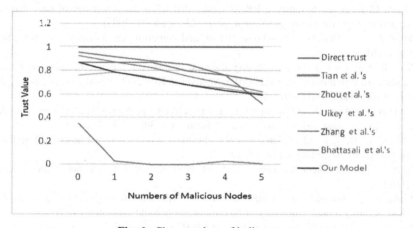

Fig. 6. Changes chart of indirect trust

5 Conclusion

This paper mainly studies the security mechanism under the spring architecture from the two aspects of identity authentication and permission management. In the part of identity authentication, it mainly introduces the shortcomings of JWT and spring security and makes some improvements and optimizations on them. In the authority management part, we mainly analyze the advantages and disadvantages of several authority control models, and improve them. This paper proposes a trust based RBAC model, and expounds the structure of the model from two aspects: direct trust and indirect trust. The process of solving direct trust and indirect trust is studied innovatively, and the pseudo code implementation of the core part is given.

Acknowledgements. This research was partly supported by NSFC No. 61773206, No. 61272420.

References

1. Young, T.: Ministers back web security position Author. Computing, pp. 123–143 (2008)
2. Messmer, E.: Major flaw in Java-based Spring Framework allows remote-code execution by attackers. Network World (Online), pp. 74–91(2013)
3. Wang, S.-Q., et al.: The web security password authentication based the single-block hash functio. IERI Procedia **4**, 13–20 (2013)
4. Jánoky, L.V., et al.: An analysis on the revoking mechanisms for JSON Web Tokens. Int. J. Distrib. Sensor Netw. **14**, 53–66 (2018)
5. Hsu, F.-H., et al.: Web security in a windows system as privacy defender in private browsing mode. Multimedia Tools Appl. **74**(5), 65–78 (2015). https://doi.org/10.1007/s11042-014-2003-5
6. Moon, C.-J., et al.: Symmetric RBAC model that takes the separation of duty and role hierarchies into consideration. Comput. Secur. **23**(2), 85–99 (2003)
7. Yang, Z., et al.: Model of domain based RBAC and supporting technologies. J. Comput. **8**(5), 74–90 (2013)
8. Kim, K., Lee, K.: Real-time processing of spatial attribute information for mobile web based on standard web framework and HTML5. Spatial Inf. Res. **24**(2), 93–101 (2016). https://doi.org/10.1007/s41324-016-0011-4
9. Ghafoorian, M., et al.: A thorough trust and reputation based RBAC model for secure data storage in the cloud. IEEE Trans. Parallel Distrib. Syst. **30**(4), 778–788 (2019)
10. Zheng, H.: Design and implementation of business process driven fine-grained authority control system. Shandong University (2017)
11. Kirda, E., et al.: Client-side cross-site scripting protection. Comput. Secur. **28**(7), 65–71 (2009)
12. Liang, L.: Design and implementation of mobile application management system based on RBAC security model. University of Electronic Science and Technology (2016)
13. Pan, N., et al.: An efficiency approach for RBAC reconfiguration with minimal roles and perturbation. Concurr. Comput.: Pract. Exp. **30**(11), 177–185 (2018)

Privacy Protection

Decentralizing Privacy-Preserving Data Aggregation Scheme Using Blockchain in Smart Grid

Hongbin Fan[1], Yining Liu[2(✉)], and Zhixin Zeng[2]

[1] College of Software and Communication Engineering, Xiangnan University, Chenzhou, Hunan 423000, China
[2] College of Computer Science and Information Security, Guilin University of Electronic Technology, Guilin 541004, China
ynliu@guet.edu.cn

Abstract. As a next-generation power system, the smart grid can implement fine-grained smart metering data collection to optimize energy utilization. In recent years, a large number of privacy-preservation data aggregation schemes have been proposed for smart grid, which relies on trusted third party (TTP) or central authority (CA). If the TTP or CA fails, these schemes become insecure. Therefore, this paper proposes a smart grid data aggregation scheme based on blockchain, which does not rely on TTP or CA and achieves decentralization. In this scheme, the leader election algorithm is used to select a smart meter in the residential area as a mining node to build a block. The node adopts Paillier cryptosystem algorithm to aggregate the user's electricity consumption data. The confidentiality and integrity of user data are guaranteed, which is convenient for billing and power regulation. Security analysis shows that our scheme meets the security and privacy requirements of smart grid data aggregation. The experimental results show that this scheme is more efficient than existing competing schemes in terms of computation and communication overhead.

Keywords: Decentralizing · Privacy-preservation · Data aggregation · Blockchain

1 Introduction

With the rapid development of society and economy, people's demand for electric energy is increasing. However, the aging power system does not keep up with the pace of technological change, and the system architecture remains unchanged, which leads to the decline of power system stability and frequent safety accidents. It brings a lot of inconveniences to people's daily life and causes huge economic losses. For example, in 2012, a large-scale blackout occurred in India, affecting 670 million people. Traditional power system cannot meet the development needs of human society due to inefficiency and fragility. Therefore, smart grid emerges as the times require and becomes a new generation of power network.

© Springer Nature Singapore Pte Ltd. 2020
S. Yu et al. (Eds.): SPDE 2020, CCIS 1268, pp. 131–142, 2020.
https://doi.org/10.1007/978-981-15-9129-7_10

Smart grid is a fully automated power transmission network which based on the physical grid system using sensor measurement technology, communication technology, control technology and computer technology [1]. The information flow between suppliers and users in smart grid is bidirectional, while the traditional power grid adopts the unidirectional centralized system. Users can control the intelligent use of household appliances and equipment at any time according to the floating situation of electricity price in different time periods. Suppliers can automatically monitor the grid, prevent power outages, optimize grid performance, etc. However, the process of smart grid power consumption data collection may lead to the leakage of user privacy information [2, 3].

In recent years, data aggregation, secret sharing [4–6] and differential privacy [7, 8] have attracted attention, which can ensure data collection while effectively protecting user privacy. Data aggregation is one of the most common methods to solve the security and privacy problems of smart grid. Homomorphic encryption is an effective way to protect the privacy of smart meters. Li et al. [9] proposed a privacy-preserving multi-subset data aggregation scheme (PPMA), their scheme based on Paillier cryptosystem, which enables the aggregation of electricity consumption data of different ranges. Liu et al. [10] proposed a privacy-preserving data aggregation without any TTP. In this scheme uses EC-ElGamal to encrypt power consumption data and construct a virtual aggregation area for users with a certain degree of trust to shield the data of a single user. Guan et al. [11] proposed a flexible threshold for data aggregation based on the secret sharing scheme. This scheme adjust the aggregation threshold according to the energy consumption information and time period of each specific residential area to ensure the privacy of personal data during the aggregation process, while supporting fault tolerance. Karampour et al. [12] proposed use Paillier encryption system and AV net mask to realize the aggregation of privacy protection data in smart grid can effectively protect the privacy of user data without any security channel. Chen et al. [13] proposed a data aggregation scheme for smart meters based on homomorphic encryption algorithm and noise addition. In this scheme, each smart meter generates a random noise to disturb its power consumption, and then sends the random noise and power consumption data to the aggregator. Assume that the sum of random noise of all smart meters is zero. Guan et al. [14] proposed an anonymous privacy protection method based on the Paillier homomorphic scheme, which uses pseudonyms and bilinear pairing to achieve data aggregation. Okay et al. [15] proposed a privacy preserving data aggregation protocol based on Domino-Ferrer and Paillier schemes, which implements data aggregation on the fog layer. In [16], a dynamic member data aggregation scheme based on identity signature and homomorphic encryption algorithm is proposed. The operation center obtains the sum of power consumption data in the virtual aggregation area, but knows nothing about the single user's use data. This scheme reduces the complexity of new user joining and old user exiting. However, the above research methods do not consider the trusted environment.

To achieve a trusted environment, several studies used blockchain as privacy-preserving method for data aggregation. Guan et al. [17] proposed a privacy-preserving data aggregation scheme for power grid communications. The study divided users into different groups and each group has a private blockchain. The study uses multiple pseudonyms to hide users' identity. In this scheme, key management center (KMC) is used to generate multiple public and private keys for users, which does not realize decentralization.

Blockchain technology has attained significant attention recently and provides a number of ways for reliable processing and storage of data in a decentralized manner. Therefore, it is suitable for smart grid systems with multiple nodes. This paper proposes a decentralized data aggregation scheme for privacy-preservation based on blockchain, which is used to collect electricity consumption data without trust and reliability in smart grid.

The main contributions of this paper are as follows:

1) The leader election algorithm is proposed to select a smart meter from a residential area as a mining node to participate in the blockchain network.
2) A decentralized data aggregation scheme based on blockchain is proposed. The mining node uses Merkle hash tree to perform security authentication and data aggregation for smart meters in the residential area without any trusted third party.
3) Paillier encryption, Boneh-Lynn-Shacham Short Signature and SHA-256 function are applied to ensure the transparency of the blockchain data while achieving privacy protection.

The rest of this paper is organized as follows. In Sect. 2, Blockchain, bilinear pairing, Boneh-Lynn-Shacham Short Signature, and the Paillier cryptosystem are given. In Sect. 3, the proposed system model is presented, and our scheme is proposed in Sect. 4. The security analysis is shown in Sect. 5. In Sect. 6, the performance of our scheme is evaluated. The research is concluded in Sect. 7.

2 Preliminaries

In this section, we briefly introduce the necessary background.

2.1 Blockchain

Blockchain technology was first proposed in 2008 by Satoshi Nakamoto for Bitcoin [18]. Blockchain technology has been widely used in payment, Internet of things, healthcare, finance and so on [19]. Blockchain is a decentralized distributed ledger database maintained by network-wide nodes [20], which comprising a chain of different data blocks in a chronological order. All hash data added to the block is immutable. Blockchain is a new application mode of consensus mechanism, distributed data storage, encryption algorithm and so on. Its key technologies include block structure, Merkle tree, P2P network, hash function, timestamp, asymmetric encryption mechanism, etc. [21].

Blockchain is a new type of decentralized protocol, which has the characteristics of decentralization, anonymity, security, reliability, non-forgery, tamper resistance and so on. The miners are responsible for creating blocks, and each block in the blockchain is identified by a hash in the header. The hash is generated by the SHA-256 hash algorithm, which uses plaintext of any size and computes a 256-bit encrypted hash of fixed size. Each header contains the address of the previous block in the chain. The information in the block cannot be deleted or changed.

2.2 Boneh-Lynn-Shacham Short Signature

Boneh-Lynn-Shacham (BLS) Short Signature [22] scheme is a typical bilinear pairing scheme, which uses SHA-256 hash function $H_1 : \{0, 1\}^* \rightarrow G_1$ and g is a random generator of G_1, and a bilinear map $e : G_1 \times G_1 \rightarrow G_2$. The BLS signature scheme is divided into three phases: key generation, signature, and verification.

Key Generation. The secret key $x \in Z_q^*$, and compute the public key $PK = x \cdot g$.

Signature. The plaintext $m \in G_1$, compute the signature $\sigma = x \cdot H(m)$.

Verification. If $e(\sigma, g) = e(H(m), PK)$, then the signature is verified. Otherwise fails.

2.3 Paillier Cryptosystem

Paillier cryptosystem [23] is a probabilistic public-key cryptosystem that uses asymmetric encryption algorithm, which can effectively implement homomorphic properties. The encryption algorithm satisfies homomorphism of addition and multiplication, and can operates directly on the ciphertext without needing to know the corresponding plaintext. Therefore, it is widely used in many privacy protection applications. It includes three algorithms: key generation, encryption and decryption.

Key Generation. Randomly select two large primes p and q, where $|p| = |q| = |\kappa|$. Then calculate $\lambda = lcm(p - 1, q - 1)$. Defined a function $L(u) = \frac{u-1}{N}$, where $N = pq$. Choose a generator $g \in Z_{N^2}^*$, and calculate $\mu = (L(g^\lambda \bmod N^2))^{-1} \bmod N$. The public key is (N, g), and the corresponding private key is (λ, μ).

Encryption. Given a message $m \in Z_N$, choose a random number $r \in Z_N^*$. $\gcd(r, N) = 1$, The ciphertext is calculated as $C = Enc(m) = g^m \cdot r^N \bmod N^2$.

Decryption. Given the ciphertext $C \in Z_N$, The corresponding message is decrypted with the private key (λ, μ) as $m = Dec(C) = L(C^\lambda \bmod N^2) \cdot \mu \bmod N$.

3 System Model

3.1 Communication Model

The system model of our scheme consists of operation center (OC) and smart meter (SM) in the residential area (RA), which is demonstrated in Fig. 1. In our scheme, we mainly focus on remove the control center and the trusted third party while protecting the data privacy of the user's smart meter.

Operation Center (OC). The operation center reads the real-time power consumption data aggregated by the mining nodes of each block from the private blockchain for billing, power consumption trend analysis, adjustment of power generation plans, and dynamic pricing. To increase efficiency, each administrative district will establish its own OC. OC is vulnerable to attacks by external adversary. Therefore, OC is not assumed to be trusted.

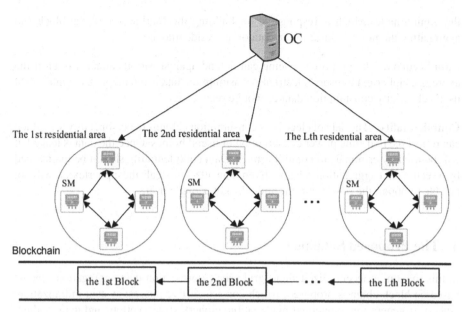

Fig. 1. System model

Smart Meter (SM). A SM is an electricity meter for each user's site in the residential area. The smart meter regularly and simultaneously (e.g. every 15 min) collects the power consumption data of each user's household electrical equipment. Peer-to-peer (P2P) communication is used between SMs. Each residential area uses leader election algorithm to select a smart meter from the smart meters as the mining node (MN), Then each residential area constructs a block through a MN. The MN is responsible for generating system parameters, authenticates the legitimacy of the data transmitted by the smart meter and aggregates the encrypted data. Then, SM encrypts all kinds of collected data and uploads it to the MN after a short period of time.SM is considered to be honest-but-curious, and it does not actively modify the received data. However, it may analyze the received data to infer some valuable information.

3.2 Design Goals

To solve the issues mentioned above, ensure the integrity and privacy of users' power consumption data while decentralizing or no relying on the trusted third parties, the design goals include four aspects.

Privacy-Preservation. Neither OC nor any other user has access to other user's data in the residential area. An external adversary cannot obtain the user's power consumption data, even if he knows the ciphertext. Even if the adversary and OC collude with each other, they can't get the power consumption data of a single user's smart meter.

Decentralizing. Our scheme does not need a trusted third party or a central authority. The leader election algorithm is used to select a smart meter in the residential area as the mining node, which is responsible for building the Merkle tree of the block and aggregating the power consumption data of the residential area.

Data Security. The proposed scheme can defend against various attacks. Even if the aggregate ciphertext of users' electricity consumption data is intercepted, the individual user's electricity consumption data cannot be recovered.

Confidentiality. The data of electricity consumption belongs to personal privacy, which can reflect the real-time power consumption of users' homes. Once the data is leaked, it will be used by criminals to commit crimes. Data confidentiality should be maintained by a secure data aggregation scheme. Even if an attacker steals the ciphertext, it will not be able to obtain the power consumption data of a single user.

4 The Proposed Scheme

In this section, a decentralized smart grid privacy protection data aggregation scheme based on block chain is proposed, which consists of five phases: system initialization, ciphertext generation, ciphertext aggregation, ciphertext decryption, and data reading. The notations are listed in Table 1.

Table 1. Notations.

Symbol	Definition
g_1, g_2	A generator of G
RA_j	The jth residential area
m_i	Power consumption data of the ith smart meter in RA_j
n	Number of smart meters in the jth residential area
H1	Hash functions: $H_1: \{0, 1\}^* \to G$
L	Number of residential areas
SM_i	Smart meter in jth residential area
MN_j	Mining node of the jth residential area
M_j	The aggregated electricity consumption data of the j-th residential areas
‖	Concatenation operation

Each smart meter in the system acts as a node, and each node has three states: follower, leader, and candidate. All nodes start from the follower state. Each term begins with an election in which one or more candidates try to become leaders. If a candidate wins the election, it will be the leader for the rest of its term. The state change of leader election algorithm is shown in Fig. 2.

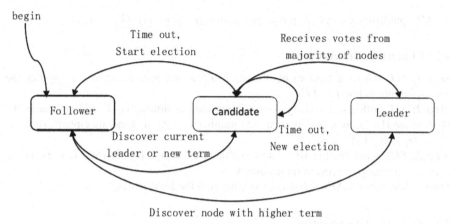

Fig. 2. State transition model of leader election algorithm

4.1 System Initialization

OC collects electricity consumption data of smart meters in L residential areas. There are n smart meters in RA_j. Through leader election algorithm, selects a SM as a mining node from the n SMs in RA_j, then constructs the *jth* block, where MN_j is the root of the Merkle tree in the *jth* block. The consumption data of SMs in RA_j is aggregated to MN_j through Merkle tree. The structure of Blockchain is shown in Fig. 3.

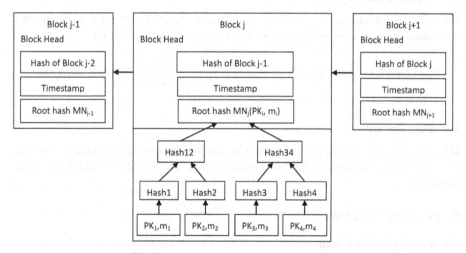

Fig. 3. Blockchain structure in our scheme.

MN_j runs Bilinear parameter generator $Gen(\kappa)$ to generate (q, g_1, G_1, G_2, e), and g_1 is a generator of G_1. MN_j calculates Paillier cryptosystem public key (N, g_2), corresponding private key (λ, μ), $g_2 \in Z_{N^2}^*$. MN_j choose a SHA-256 hash function H_1 and a secure cryptographic hash function H_2, where $H_1 : \{0, 1\}^* \rightarrow G_1, H_2 : \{0, 1\}^* \rightarrow \{0, 1\}^\kappa$.

MN_j publishes the system public parameter $\{q, g_1, g_2, G_1, G_2, e, N, H_1\}$.

4.2 Ciphertext Generation

Step 1: SM_i selects a random number $x_i \in Z_q^*$ as the private key and computes the corresponding public key $PK_i = x_i \cdot g_1$.

Step 2: SM_i collects electricity consumption data at timestamp T, and computes the Hash value $H_2(T)$, then selects a random number $r_i \in Z_N^*$ to generate ciphertext: $C_i = g_2^{m_i} \times (r_i \times H_2(T))^N \bmod N^2$.

Step 3: SM_i generates the BLS short signature $\sigma_i = x_i \cdot H_1(C_i\|PK_i\|Ts_i)$, Ts_i is the current timestamp to prevent replay attack.

Step 4: SM_i sends $C_i\|PK_i\|Ts_i\|\sigma_i$ to MN through the Merkle tree.

4.3 Ciphertext Aggregation

Step 1: After receives $C_i\|PK_i\|Ts_i\|\sigma_i$, MN_j verifies whether $e(\sigma_i, g_1) \overset{?}{=} e(H_1(C_i\|PK_i\|Ts_i), PK_i)$ hold, the signature is valid and MN_j will accept SM_i's ciphertext. In order to make the verification more efficient, MN_j adopts batch verification.

Step 2: MN_j aggregates the ciphertext.

$$C = Enc(m) = \prod_{i=1}^{n} C_i = \prod_{i=1}^{n} g_2 \cdot (r_i \cdot H_2(T))^N \bmod N^2 = g_2^{\sum_{i=1}^{n} m_i} \cdot \prod_{i=1}^{n} (r_i \cdot H_2(T))^N \bmod N^2$$

4.4 Ciphertext Decryption

MN_j uses the private key (λ, μ) to decrypt the aggregated ciphertext to obtain the aggregated electricity consumption data M_j of the *jth* residential district.

$$M_j = Dec(C) = L(C^\lambda \bmod N^2) \cdot \mu \bmod N = \frac{L(C^\lambda \bmod N^2)}{L(g_2^\lambda \bmod N^2)} \bmod N = \sum_{i=1}^{n} m_i$$

4.5 Data Reading

MN_j generates the $(j + 1)th$ block, and adds the *jth* block to the blockchain after the $(j - 1)th$ block. OC obtains the power consumption data through the public key read blockchain.

5 Security Analysis

5.1 Privacy-Preservation

When an external attacker invades a smart meter, only the ciphertext C_i sent by a smart meter can be obtained. Even if the malicious user intercepts the ciphertext C_i, because he/she does not know the decryption key λ of the Paillier encryption algorithm, he/she cannot decrypt the ciphertext C_i to obtain the power consumption data of a single user. The power consumption data of a single smart meter is not disclosed, so as to protect the privacy of users.

5.2 Decentralized

In our scheme, the blockchain can be implemented without a trusted third party or central authority, the availability and reliability of data is guaranteed by MN election. Any SM is not controlled or operated by other SMs and OC. P2P network is adopted among smart meters to realize decentralization. The whole process does not rely on a trusted third party to make our solution more reliable and convenient (Table 2).

Table 2. Comparison between proposed scheme and other related schemes.

Security requirements	[9]	[11]	[12]	Our scheme
Blockchain-based	No	No	No	Yes
Decentralization	No	No	No	Yes
Non-repudiation	No	Yes	No	Yes
Privacy	Yes	Yes	Yes	Yes
Confidentiality	Yes	Yes	Yes	Yes
Data integrity	Yes	Yes	Yes	Yes
Replay attack resistance	No	Yes	Yes	Yes
Data unforgeability	No	Yes	Yes	Yes

5.3 Data Security

The electricity consumption data of SM_i in RA_j is encrypted as $C_i = g_2^{m_i} \times (r_i \times H_2(T))^N \bmod N^2$, m_i is secure and privacy-preservation. Even if an adversary intercepts C_i, he/she cannot recover the power consumption data of a single smart meter. After MN collects all the smart meter power consumption data in the residential area through data aggregation, only the aggregated data can be obtained through decryption, and the plaintext of single smart meter power consumption data cannot be recovered.

5.4 Confidentiality

The power consumption data includes user privacy and business secrets. The usage data of the smart meters are encrypted by Paillier cryptosystem algorithm derived from [24]. After receiving the ciphertext of the smart meters in the residential area, only MN can decrypt the aggregated plaintext data. Since Theorem 1 of [24] represents confidentiality based on the DDH assumption, even if the adversary eavesdrops on the ciphertext of the smart meters in the residential area, the adversary still cannot infer any relevant information about usage data sent by the smart meters. The confidentiality of user power consumption data is guaranteed.

6 Performance Evaluation

The performance of our scheme is evaluated in this section, including the computation complexity of SM and OC, and the communication overhead.

6.1 Computation Complexity

Compared with multiplication operation and exponentiation operation, Leader election and Hash operation is negligible. In our scheme, the computations in the data aggregation process mainly include three phases, data encryption, batch verification and aggregation, decryption. We denote the computational cost of an exponentiation operation and a multiplication operation, by T_{exp}, T_{mul}, respectively. The computation complexities of the major entities in the system are as show in Table 3.

Table 3. Comparing computation complexity between the proposed scheme and other schemes.

Scheme Ref.	[9]	[11]	[12]	Our scheme
Overhead SM	$3T_{exp} + 4T_{mul}$	$4T_{exp} + 3\,T_{mul}$	$2T_{exp} + nT_{mul}$	$2T_{exp} + 4T_{mul}$
Overhead GW	nT_{mul}	$3T_{exp} + (2n + 1)\,T_{mul}$	nT_{mul}	–
Overhead CC	$T_{exp} + (4n + 3)T_{mul}$	$3T_{exp} + 2T_{mul}$	$T_{exp} + 3T_{mul}$	–
Overhead MN	–	–	–	$T_{exp} + (n + 1)\,T_{mul}$

6.2 Communication Overhead

The communication of our proposed scheme is only SM_i to MN_j, the power consumption data collected by SM_i is used to generate the report $(C_i \| PK_i \| Ts_i \| \sigma_i)$ and is sent to MN_j. The size of SM_i report is $S_z = |C_i| + |PK_i| + |Ts_i| + |\sigma_i|$. The maximum communication overhead is $S_{max} = n \cdot S_z = n \cdot (|C_i| + |PK_i| + |Ts_i| + |\sigma_i|)$. Suppose that SM_i generates a 2048-bit ciphertext C_i and chooses 160-bit Z_N^*, 160-bit G.

In PPMA and EFFECT scheme, the communication cost on SM-to-GW is 2048n bit, the communication cost on GW-to-CC is 2048 bit, the total communication overhead is 2048(n + 1) bit. In Karampour's scheme, the communication cost on SM-to-SM is n(2048(n − 1)) bit, the communication cost on SM-to-GW is 2048n bit, the communication cost on GW-to-CC is 2048 bit, the total communication overhead is 2048(n^2 + 1) bit.

In our scheme, the total communication overhead is 2048n bit. The comparison is shown in Table 4, the total communication cost of our scheme is less than the other schemes.

Table 4. Comparing communication cost between the proposed scheme and other schemes.

Scheme Ref.	[9]	[11]	[12]	Our scheme
SM-to-SM (bit)	–	–	$n(2048(n-1))$	–
SM-to-GW (bit)	2048n	2048n	2048n	–
GW-to-CC (bit)	2048	2048	2048	–
SM-to-MN(bit)	–	–	–	2048n

7 Conclusion

In this paper, a blockchain-based decentralized smart grid privacy-preserving data aggregation scheme was proposed, which does not rely on TTP or CA. The protocol proposes that smart meters in residential areas select a mining node through leader election algorithm, which records the data of smart meters into the blockchain. BLS signature and Paillier encryption are based on bilinear pairings, which are used to realize data authentication and data aggregation while ensuring the security and integrity of messages in the transmission process. Security analysis shows that our mechanism meets the requirements of privacy protection and security of smart meters. The performance evaluation shows that our scheme is superior to some popular data aggregation schemes in computational efficiency. Our scheme has low communication overhead and does not require any TTP or CA and secure channels. At present, we have decentralized the aggregation of one-dimensional power consumption data. In the future, we will work on the combination of blockchain and other algorithms to aggregate multidimensional electricity consumption data.

References

1. Fang, X., Misra, S., Xue, G., Yang, D.: Smart grid-the new and improved power grid: a survey. IEEE Commun. Surv. Tutor. **14**(4), 944–980 (2011)
2. Xue, K.P., Li, S.H., Hong, J.N., et al.: Two-cloud secure database for numeric-related SQL range queries with privacy preserving. IEEE Trans. Inf. Foren. Secur. **12**, 1596–1608 (2017)
3. Wu, J., Dong, M.X., Ota, K., et al.: Securing distributed storage for social internet of things using regenerating code and blom key agreement. Peer-to-Peer Netw. Appl. **8**, 1133–1142 (2015)
4. Guan, Z., Si, G., Du, X., Liu, P.: Protecting User Privacy Based on Secret Sharing with Error Tolerance for Big Data in Smart Grid. arXiv preprint arXiv:1811.06918 (2018)
5. Chen, J., Liu, G., Liu, Y.: Lightweight privacy-preserving raw data publishing scheme. IEEE Trans. Emerg. Top. Comput. (2020). https://doi.org/10.1109/tetc.2020.2974183
6. Liu, Y., Zhao, Q.: E-voting scheme using secret sharing and K-anonymity. World Wide Web: Internet Web Inf. Syst. **22**(4), 1657–1667 (2019)
7. Hassan, M.U., Rehmani, M.H., Kotagiri, R., Zhang, J., Chen, J.: Differential privacy for renewable energy resources based smart metering. J. Parallel Distrib. Comput. **131**, 69–80 (2019)

8. Piao, C., Shi, Y., Yan, J., Zhang, C., Liu, L.: Privacy-preserving governmental data publishing: a fog-computing-based differential privacy approach. Future Gener. Comput. Syst. **90**, 158–174 (2019)
9. Li, S., Xue, K., Yang, Q., Hong, P.: PPMA: privacy-preserving multisubset data aggregation in smart grid. IEEE Trans. Industr. Inf. **14**, 462–471 (2018)
10. Liu, Y., Guo, W., Fan, C., Chang, L., Cheng, C.: A practical privacy-preserving data aggregation (3PDA) scheme for smart grid. IEEE Trans. Industr. Inf. **15**(3), 1767–1774 (2018)
11. Guan, Z., Zhang, Y., Zhu, L., et al.: EFFECT: an efficient flexible privacy-preserving data aggregation scheme with authentication in smart grid. Sci. China Inf. Sci. **62**(3), 32103 (2019)
12. Karampour, A., Ashouri-Talouki, M., Ladani, B.T.: An efficient privacy-preserving data aggregation scheme in smart grid. In: 2019 27th Iranian Conference on Electrical Engineering (ICEE), pp. 1967–1971. IEEE (2019)
13. Chen, Y., Martínez, J.F., Castillejo, P., López, L.: A privacy-preserving noise addition data aggregation scheme for smart grid. Energies **11**(11), 2972 (2018)
14. Guan, Z., Zhang, Y., Wu, L., et al.: Appa: an anonymous and privacy preserving data aggregation scheme for fog-enhanced IoT. J. Netw. Comput. **125**, 82–92 (2019)
15. Song, J., Liu, Y., Shao, J., Tang, C.: A dynamic membership data aggregation (DMDA) protocol for smart grid. IEEE Syst. J. **14**(1), 900–908 (2020)
16. Okay, F.Y., Ozdemir, S., Xiao, Y.: Fog computing-based privacy preserving data aggregation protocols. Trans. Emerg. Telecommun. Technol. **31**(4), e3900 (2020)
17. Guan, Z.T., et al.: Privacy-preserving and efficient aggregation based on blockchain for power grid communications in smart communities. IEEE Commun. Mag. **56**(7), 82–88 (2018)
18. Nakamoto, S.: Bitcoin: a peer-to-peer electronic cash system. Consulted (2008)
19. Crosby, M., Pattanayak, P., Verma, S., Kalyanaraman, V.: Blockchain technology: beyond bitcoin. Appl. Innov. **2**(6–10), 71 (2016)
20. Yuan, Y., Wang, F.-Y.: Parallel blockchain: concept, methods and issues. Acta Autom. Sinica **43**(10), 1703–1712 (2017)
21. Xie, Q.H.: Research on blockchain technology and financial business innovation. Financ. Dev. Res. **5**, 77–82 (2017)
22. Boneh, D., Lynn, B., Shacham, H.: Short signatures from the weil pairing. In: Boyd, C. (ed.) ASIACRYPT 2001. LNCS, vol. 2248, pp. 514–532. Springer, Heidelberg (2001). https://doi.org/10.1007/3-540-45682-1_30
23. Paillier, P.: Public-key cryptosystems based on composite degree residuosity classes. In: Stern, J. (ed.) EUROCRYPT 1999. LNCS, vol. 1592, pp. 223–238. Springer, Heidelberg (1999). https://doi.org/10.1007/3-540-48910-X_16
24. Shi, E., Chan, H.T.H., Rieffel, E., Chow, R., Song, D.: Privacy-preserving aggregation of time-series data. In: Annual Network & Distributed System Security Symposium (NDSS), vol. 2, pp. 1–17 (2011)

Local Differential Privacy for Data Streams

Xianjin Fang, Qingkui Zeng(ORCID), and Gaoming Yang[✉]

School of Computer Science and Engineering,
Anhui University of Science and Technology, Huainan, China
gmyang@aust.edu.cn

Abstract. The dynamic change, huge data size, and complex structure of the data stream have made it very difficult to be analyzed and protected in real-time. Traditional privacy protection models such as differential privacy which need to rely on the trusted servers or companies, and this will increase the uncertainty of protecting streaming privacy. In this paper, we propose a new privacy protection protocol for data streams under local differential privacy and w-event privacy, which makes it possible to keep up-to-date statistics over time, and it is still available when the third parties are untrusted. We use sliding window to collect the data streams in real-time, finding out the occurrence of significant moves, capturing the latest data distribution trend, and releasing the perturbed data streams report in time. This protocol provides a provable privacy guarantee, reduces computation and storage costs, and provides valuable statistical information. The experimental results of real datasets show that the proposed method can protect the privacy of the data streams and provide available statistical data at the same time.

Keywords: Data streams · Local differential privacy · w-event privacy · Sliding window

1 Introduction

With the development of 5G technology, intelligent devices and sensors have produced more and more dynamic data, which we call the data stream. Real-time analysis of stream data can obtain valuable information to understand an important phenomenon [13], so it is widely used in various application fields, such as mobile crowd sensing [28], traffic service stream monitoring [19] and social network hotspot tracking [26]. The data service providers collect real-time data stream and publish real-time statistics, share and analyze [29] them with interested third-party to improve the service quality.

This work was supported by National Natural Science Foundation of China (61572034), Major Science and Technology Projects in Anhui Province (18030901025), Anhui Province University Natural Science Fund (KJ2019A0109).

© Springer Nature Singapore Pte Ltd. 2020
S. Yu et al. (Eds.): SPDE 2020, CCIS 1268, pp. 143–160, 2020.
https://doi.org/10.1007/978-981-15-9129-7_11

However, there are potential privacy risks in this process. On account of the joining of the untrusted third party, the attacker may query the original data of multiple timestamps of a single user through the differential attack to draw the user's data track and disclose the user's privacy information [20]. Recently research [4] has found that the user's mobile trajectory is highly unique from the user's mobile data obtained by mobile phone operators. Even if the desensitized dataset provides a small amount of anonymous information, it can still be linked to the designated user with relevant background knowledge. A series of similar findings reveal that the privacy of personal data stream is facing a huge risk, so it is of great significance to the research and development of data stream privacy collection and release mechanism, but in the real-time, irreversibility and large scale of data stream itself also bring challenges to the research.

Differential privacy (DP) [10] as a widely used privacy protection model provides strict privacy guarantee and theoretical proof, and it does not need to consider the attacker's background knowledge. One of the common methods of data publishing with differential privacy is to perturb the data before publishing and hide the sensitive information of individuals in the process of statistical analysis and data mining. At present, the research on the differential privacy model mainly focuses on the static scene, however the real-time data is collected and published all in the dynamic scene [5]. In the centralized interactive scene of differential privacy, the trusted curators collect sensitive data from different entities, carefully adding calibrated noise, and then sharing the final results with data analysts. The model is shown in Fig. 1. Dwork et al. [11] proposed two different privacy schemes for continuous data collection, namely event-level and user-level privacy. Event-level privacy protects user's privacy on a single timestamp in the data stream, but it does not protect user's privacy in the whole data stream; user-level privacy needs to add noise in the whole data stream, which will reduce the utility of data in the long run.

This model requires that the trusted data curator, however, if the curator is not trusted, there is a risk of the potential breach of privacy from a third party. And the attacker may obtain part of the original data of the data curator through repeated queries and infer the user's privacy. Local Differential Privacy (LDP) [21] is a distributed variant of differential privacy, which does not require a trusted data curator. Before sending individual privacy data, users perturb their data on the local device and send the perturbed privacy reports to resist privacy attacks under the centralized model. This model is shown in Fig. 2. At now, the research of the local differential privacy model is mainly focused on the release of single data [3], however, it's difficult for the LDP model to deal with complex real-time data. As the streaming evolves, the consumption of computing power and storage space will become larger, and the privacy budget will gradually decline.

Compared with the collection of traditional data, the length and content of the data streams change dynamically, the data size is huge, and the data type is complex. Aiming at the problem of how to protect streaming privacy under the local differential privacy model, we propose the locally differential

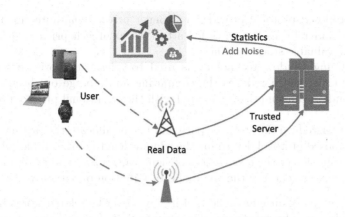

Fig. 1. Differential privacy protection model.

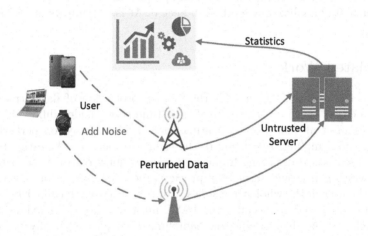

Fig. 2. Local differential privacy protection model.

private Streaming (LDPS) protocol based on local differential privacy and w-event privacy [22]. The LDPS protocol selects different algorithms to obtain the statistics according to the type of data streams. When the collected data streams are real-time numerical attributes such as temperature and humidity, longitude, latitude, and heart rate, etc., we calculate the value of mean [25]; for real-time classified attributes such as the user's default browser home page, search engine setting and most frequently emojis or words, etc. [27], we conduct the frequency estimation and find heavy hitters [2]. When data types are mixed, different protocols are used to process the data with different attributes identified. The main contributions are:

(1) Ensure that the individual user data never leaves the device by deploying the local differential privacy;

(2) The proposed protocol provides a stronger privacy guarantee for the data stream and reduces the ways for attackers to breach privacy, meanwhile, obtains valuable statistical data;

(3) The sliding window technology is used to release the private streaming in real-time, which reduces the computing and storage overhead and privacy budget consumption compared with the traditional privacy protection method;

(4) To further reduce the storage space and better allocate the privacy budget, the proposed protocol determine the window length of the stable sub-stream adaptively, detect the occurrences of significant moves and open a new window in time to capture the trend and distribution of data streams.

This paper is organized as follows. First, we describe related works in Sect. 2 and the background knowledge for this paper in Sect. 3. Then, we state the problem setting and methodology in Sect. 4 and propose our protocol in Sect. 5. Next, we evaluate and analyze our method in Sect. 6. At last, the work is summarized in Sect. 7.

2   Related Works

Recently, the research schemes for the privacy protection of data streams are mainly focused on the release of real-time time series under different privacy budgets. Fan et al. [15] propose a framework of FAST based on perturbation, filtering, and sampling. According to the error rate between the estimated and predicted statistical data, the framework releases noisy report at the sampling points, which can provide user-level privacy protection, i.e., to protect the privacy of the user in the whole time-series. However, their work cannot be applied to infinite data streams because the FAST must allocate the maximum number of releases in advance, and the sampling mechanism can only be applied if each timestamp has an equivalent budget. Kellaris et al. [22] propose a new model, w-event ϵ-differential privacy (w-event privacy for short), which combines the gap between event-level privacy and user-level privacy, they also give new mechanisms to implement the w-event privacy model.

Differential privacy has attracted much attention in the real-time release of streaming data [17] because of its advantages in mathematical proof and privacy protection. However, these mechanisms are based on trusted servers, which strictly limits their application in practice. Fan et al. [14] propose an adaptive system, which releases aggregate statistical information of real-time and spatio-temporal data streams under differential privacy model by sampling and filtering steps. Although this mechanism optimizes the budget allocation of numerical attributes, it applies only to finite data streams. Wang et al. [30] present the adaptive framework AdaPub, which can update the parameters with the data stream evolving. These researches extend the mechanism by considering the sliding window of the w timestamp and optimizing the budget allocation within the window. While these efforts provide good insight into publishing data streams under differential private guarantees, they rely on a trusted server that is not convenient to deploy in many real-world applications.

In order to solve the problem of untrusted servers, many scholars and researchers discuss the local differential privacy model, i.e., the individual raw data is perturbed before it is sent from the client. Duchi et al. [6–8] proposed the min-max mechanism of numerical attribute publication based on local differential privacy. Erlingsson et al. [12] developed a RAPPOR protocol for real-time publishing binary attributes, which is based on random response technology to limit the probability of inference of sensitive information. Wang et al. [12] improve the accuracy of numerical attributes of the min-max mechanism and extend it to publish binary and numerical attribute data. However, the proposed mechanism randomly selects k attributes for perturbation, which is not realistic in some practical application scenarios. Kim et al. [23] develop a mechanism for the health data stream by leveraging local differential privacy. In addition, these mechanisms cannot be used to distinguish between ordered and disordered attributes.

The mechanisms mentioned above carefully allocate the privacy budget on each timestamp. However, even in a relatively short period, repeated differential privacy computing will accumulate the privacy loss to a large value, so an adaptive compression mechanism is needed to reduce the loss of privacy budget. Recently, Joseph et al. [20] apply a compression technique to continuously release binary attributes under local differential privacy. For user clients with similar data distribution, this mechanism will consume the local privacy budget only when the distribution of users changes significantly. Soheila et al. [13] propose an adaptive dynamic compression method in the local differential privacy data stream mechanism, which adaptively adjusts the window length to reduce the consumption of the privacy budget. Wang et al. proposed a RescueDP protocol [29], which provides privacy protection statistical data distribution on infinite timestamps through adaptive sampling, adaptive budget allocation, dynamic grouping, perturbation, and filtering mechanisms.

3   Preliminaries

In this section, we introduce the local differential privacy and w-event privacy model, and some related techniques used in these models. The definitions used in this paper are given below.

Definition 1 *(w-neighboring). Let $S_t = \{D_1, D_2,..., D_t\}$ be a prefix stream of sequential data where at each timestamp i, a dataset D_i is collected with an arbitrary number of rows each corresponding to a unique user. For any positive integer w, two prefix streams S_t, S_t' are defined as w-neighboring if:*

(1) for each D_i, D_i', $i \in [1, t]$ and $D_i \neq D_i$' it holds that D_i , D_i' neighboring, and;
(2) for each $i_1 \in [1, t]$, $i_2 \in [1, t]$, $i_1 < i_2$, and $i_1 \neq i_2$, it holds that $i_2 - i_1 + 1 \leq w$.

The sliding window arranges tuples in streaming data according to their timestamps. The sliding window, with a fixed length w, always keeps the newest

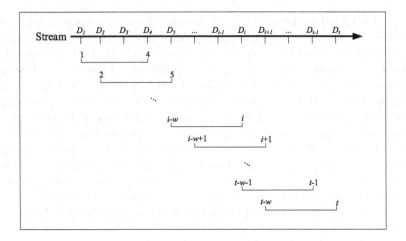

Fig. 3. Sliding window model.

$w - th$ tuples, while discarding old ones. Figure 3 shows the sliding window model with the window length of 4. w-event privacy is an extension of differential privacy for continuously publishing data streams. It provides a provable privacy guarantee for any sequence of events that occur in any sliding window of the w timestamp. The definition as follows:

Definition 2 *(w-event privacy).* *Let M be a random mechanism, and let D be the domain of all possible output M. M satisfies w-event ϵ-differential privacy when S_t and S_t' are w-neighboring, if it holds that:*

$$Pr[M(S_t) \in D] \le e^\epsilon \cdot Pr[M(S_t') \in D] \tag{1}$$

Definition 3 *(Stably sub-stream).* *Given a threshold $\delta > 0$, a sub-stream is stably from timestamp i to j, if and only if $d(S_t, S_i') \le \delta$, $\forall t, t' \in [i, j]$, where $d(\cdot)$ is a distance measurement method.*

The generation of a significant move denotes the outbreak of a new event or the occurrence of a new trend in the data stream. When the newly observed tuples maintain the stability of the current window, they can be added to the current window to form a stably sub-stream. Otherwise, a new window should be opened to capture new trends in the data stream.

Definition 4 *(Significant move).* *Let $S_{i,j}$ be a stably sub-stream in timestamp [i, j]. A newly observed tuple S_{j+1} is a significant move if the distance of S_j and S_{j+1} is greater than δ.*

Local differential privacy is a new privacy definition for individual privacy in clients and a special case of differential privacy, the perturbation process in LDP shifts from the server-side to the client-side. Under this definition, the modification between any two pieces of local data has little impact on the query results.

Even if a piece of data is known, an adversary cannot obtain accurate individual information by observing the query results because of data perturbations on the local client. Therefore, the risk of privacy disclosure between the two local data is in a very small and acceptable range. The definition as follows:

Definition 5 *(ε-local differential privacy). Where ε>0, a randomized mechanism A satisfies ε-local differential privacy if and only if, for any pairs of input tuples x and x', for any possible output x* (in the domain belonging to A), we have:*

$$Pr[A(x) = x^*] \le e^\epsilon \cdot Pr[A(x') = x^*] \tag{2}$$

Theorem 1 *(Sequential composition). Consider mechanism A that provides ϵ_i-local differential privacy. A sequence of mechanism A over a data stream S provides $\sum \epsilon_i$-local differential privacy.*

4 Problem Setting

In this section, we discuss the problem statement about the data stream under the local differential privacy model and propose some methods to solve these problems.

4.1 Problem Statement

We describe the data stream firstly. We consider an infinite source stream dataset S of d states and denote the stream that collected from the user set U_i in first timestamp i as S_i, $S_i = \{D_1, D_2, ..., D_i\}$, $i \in [1, t]$, D_i is the dataset sent by U_i's users at timestamp i. We set the data stream within the timestamp range i to j as $S_{i,j}$.

To protect the privacy of real-time data streams under the limited storage space and computing power of edge nodes, the client's data streams must be perturbed before being sent to the server to ensure privacy requirements. Therefore, our goal is to publish the infinite data streams in real-time, which can ensure the privacy of each client, maintain the data utility and provide valuable statistical information.

First, We need to prevent privacy breaches before the client transfers the data stream. Second, how to use the local differential privacy model to ensure the utility of data while providing privacy protection for the individual data and how to reduce the computing power and large overhead of storage space caused by the perturbed mechanism. Third, how to detect the concept drift of data streams to reduce errors. Last, how to meet the definition of w-event privacy and adjust the privacy budget allocation adaptively in real-time under the local differential privacy model.

4.2 Propose Solution

The individual raw data stream will never leave the devices through the deployment of the local differential privacy model. This will provide a powerful privacy guarantee and reduce how adversaries can breach privacy.

Our goal is to protect raw individual data and to publish the perturbed stream which satisfies w-event ϵ-differential privacy while providing valuable statistics. With the evolving of the data stream, the stable subseries and judges the significant points appear, we will sniff out new trends of the data streams in time and allocates the privacy budget adaptively. Therefore, this method can be applied to infinite data streams and reduce storage space and computing consumption.

The privacy protection of numerical attribute data streams consists of four steps: standardization, perturbation, adaptive allocation, and decoding. The first step is to standardize the numerical attribute data stream and encode the normalized data according to the corresponding mechanism. The second part is the perturbation, which implements the perturbed mechanism of the standardized data stream that satisfies the definition of local differential privacy. The third step is adaptive allocation, which determines the stably sub-stream and distinguishes the significant moves in time, and dynamically adaptively allocates the privacy budget. In the fourth step, data streams after the real-time perturbation are collected, and the value of mean is obtained after aggregation, and the mean value is normalized and restored.

The privacy protection process of categorical attribute data streams consists of four steps: encoding, perturbation, adaptive allocation, and decoding. The first step is to encode the data stream, such as a one-hot encoding or bloom filters. The second step is to deal with the perturbation of the encoded data stream which satisfies the definition of local differential privacy. The third step is to compare the data in the sliding window during the perturbation and allocate the privacy budget adaptively according to the data distribution of the sliding window to make it meet the definition of w-event privacy. The fourth step is to decode the aggregated data stream and get the frequency estimation of the classification attributes.

5 The Local Differentially Private Streaming Protocol

In this section, we describe our mechanism Local Differentially Private Streaming (LDPS) for publishing multi-variable data streams under local and w-event differential privacy.

5.1 Numerical Attributes

For numerical attributes, our goal is to estimate the mean value from the sanitized stream. We standardize the raw streams S, set the sliding window with the length of w, threshold t and privacy budget ϵ. The perturbation mechanism

Algorithm 1. The Local Differentially Private Streaming for numerical attributes

Input: the streams S; the window length w; the threshold t; and privacy budget ϵ_i;
Output: S_mean

```
 1: Normalize S;
 2: Initial Per = [], count = 0;
 3: for i = 0 to w do
 4:     Per.append(LDP(Sᵢ))
 5: end for
 6: for i = w to n do
 7:     if count = w then
 8:         count = 0
 9:         Per.append(LDP(Sᵢ))
10:         continue
11:     end if
12:     if count < w then
13:         if d(d(Sᵢ₋₂ - Sᵢ₋₁) - d(Sᵢ₋₁ - Sᵢ)) ≤ t then
14:             Per.append(Per[i - 1])
15:             count+ = 1
16:         else
17:             Per.append(LDP(Sᵢ))
18:             count = 0
19:         end if
20:     end if
21: end for
22: S_mean = Decode(Per);
23: Denormalize(S_mean);
24: return S_mean;
```

of the proposed method follows the typical LDP numerical attribute mechanism and parameters.

The LDP perturbation mechanism is conducted normally in initial w timestamps. After timestamp w, the sliding window will slide and allocate the privacy budget adaptively with the stream evolving. We calculate the l_1 distance between the real value of the current timestamp and the real value of the previous and subsequent timestamps respectively and set the threshold t to compare the difference between these two distances. If the difference is less than the threshold, then the perturbed report at the subsequent timestamp will be the same one in the current timestamp, and the stably sub-stream is formed; if the difference is greater than the threshold, we will continue the perturbation mechanism at the subsequent timestamp and denote this timestamp as a significant move. When a significant move occurs as shown in Fig. 4(a) or the length of stably sub-stream is greater than the sliding window length w as shown in Fig. 4(b), a new window is opened and the LDP perturbation steps are conducted for the next w timestamps.

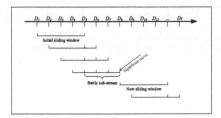   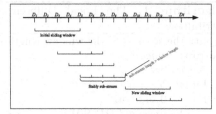

(a) The model when a significant point occurs.

(b) The model when the sub-stream length is greater than the window length.

Fig. 4. The Local differentially private streaming protocol for numerical attributes.

The server collects the perturbed report of sequence S and aggregates it, calculates all the perturb report mean value and reverses standardization to get the estimated mean value. Specific steps such as Algorithms 1.

5.2   Categorical Attributes

For categorical attributes, our goal is to estimate each value frequency from the sanitized stream. Given the input streams S and the sliding window length w, the perturbation mechanism of the proposed method follows the chosen LDP categorical attribute mechanism and parameters.

We conduct the LDP perturbed mechanism in initial w timestamps. In the next timestamp, the sliding window will begin to slide with the time-series S. If the real data of the subsequent timestamp has been released in its previous w timestamps sliding window, then the perturbed report will be the same one in the current timestamp. If the real data of the subsequent timestamp has not been released in the previous w timestamp, we will continue the perturbation mechanism at the subsequent timestamp and denote this timestamp as a significant move.

The server collects the perturbed report of sequence S and aggregates it. The sub-stream of perturbed data in the sliding window is w nearest neighbor data stream, which satisfies the definition of w-event privacy, conforms to the differential privacy combination theorem, and satisfies the definition of LDP between each two tuples. Specific steps such as Algorithms 2.

5.3   Privacy Analysis

We first prove the LDPS protocol satisfies the ϵ-local differential privacy, and then prove that it also satisfies the w-event privacy.

Let S_i be the current timestamp data stream and S_{i+1} be the last time release. To prove that the LDPS protocol satisfies w-event privacy, first, we need to prove that the perturbed report for every two timestamps satisfies the definition of ϵ_i-local differential privacy. Then, according to Theorem 1, we need to prove that the sum of the privacy budgets consumed by the LDPS within a window of length w does not exceed.

Algorithm 2. The Local Differentially Private Streaming for categorical attributes

Input: the streams S; the window length w; the perturbed mechanism parameters;
Output: $f(d_i), i \in (0, |D|)$
1: $InitialPer[]$;
2: **for** $i = 0$ to w **do**
3:     $Per.append(LDP(S_i))$
4: **end for**
5: **for** $i = w$ to n **do**
6:     **for** $j = i - w - 1; j > i - 1; j - -$ **do**
7:         **if then**$S_j = S_i$
8:             $Per.append(LDP(S_j))$
9:             **Break**
10:        **else**
11:            $Per.append(LDP(S_i))$
12:        **end if**
13:     **end for**
14: **end for**
15: $f(d_i) = Decode(Per)$;
16: **return** S_mean;

Theorem 2. *The Local Differentially Private Streaming protocol satisfies ϵ-local differential privacy.*

Proof. In the perturbation step of LDPS, we perturb the streaming on clients by the LDP's mechanism. So, we can ensure that the tuples in the neighboring timestamp are satisfied the ϵ-local differential privacy.

Theorem 3. *The Local Differentially Private Streaming protocol satisfies w-event privacy.*

Proof. Due to the allocation of privacy budget adaptively, we compress the privacy budget to 0 which using the same perturbation report as at the previous timestamp. Assume that the i-th data privacy budget is ϵ_i, we consider the definition of local differential privacy protection in two scenarios respectively. First, in the scenario that perturbation at both the current and previous timestamp, we use the same LDP perturb mechanism with the same parameters and therefore have the same privacy budget. In the timestamp i, by definition of ϵ-local differential privacy we have:

$$\frac{Pr[LDPS(S_i) = x^*]}{Pr[LDPS(S_{i-1}) = x^*]} \le e^{\epsilon_i} \tag{3}$$

Second, in the scenario that the current timestamp stream adopts the previous perturb report, the current privacy budget is adaptively compressed to 0, and the privacy guarantee begins to decline because of releasing repeatedly, we have:

$$\frac{Pr[LDPS(S_i) = x^*]}{Pr[LDPS(S_{i-1}) = x^*]} = 1 \le e^0 \tag{4}$$

So, the LDPS protocol satisfies the ϵ_i-local differential privacy in differential scenarios.

In the whole sliding window, there are also two scenarios: normal perturbation in the whole window and form stably sub-stream in the window. We set each tuple in the whole sliding window has itself privacy budget ϵ_i, even if the budget is 0. According to theorem 1, the data stream in the current sliding window satisfies $\sum \epsilon_i$-local differential privacy. So, we have a privacy budget of $\sum \epsilon_i$ for w-event $\sum \epsilon_i$ differential privacy, by definition of w-event privacy, there are:

$$\frac{Pr[LDPS(S_t) \in D]}{Pr[LDPS(S_i') \in D]} \le e^{\sum \epsilon_i} \tag{5}$$

6   Experiments

6.1   Experimental Setup

Datasets. We selected three public datasets as experimental datasets.

Table 1. Experimental datasets.

Dataset	IPUMS	Twitter daily activities	Gas sensor
Number of Instances	1000000	60093175	919438
Domain size/Mean value	78	635	27.1767, 57.5680

We choose the 2017 *Integrated Public Use Microdata Series* (IPUMS) [1] and selects the age attribute, which has 25 data categories; we extract 1% from the dataset and take the first million pieces of data as the experimental dataset for the categorical attribute. *Twitter daily activities* [24] is the Microsoft Research datasets of longitudinal, daily, per-county activity periods of aggregated Twitter users. We extract 500000 records and choose the per-country attribute as experimental datasets for the categorical attribute.

The *Gas-Sensor* dataset [18] has recordings of a gas sensor array composed of 8 MOX gas sensors, and a temperature and humidity sensor. We use the humidity and temperature attribute as the experimental datasets for the numerical attribute. The number of instances, domain sizes, or mean values of datasets are shown in Table 1.

Experimental Situation. These experiments were implemented in Python 3.7 with NumPy and xxhash libraries and were performed on a PC with Intel Core i7-7700hq CPU and 16 GB RAM. Each experiment was repeated 100 times to reduce the influence of contingency on the experimental results.

Parameter Setting. We consider varying the privacy budget parameter ϵ, the length of sliding window w and threshold t for mean value computing and varying the length of sliding window w for frequency estimation. In the mean estimation experiment, Duchi et al.'s method [9] and the Laplace mechanism [31] are chosen as the LDP perturbation mechanism. For convenience, respectively, they are abbreviated as Duchi and LM. In the frequency estimation experiment, RAPPOR [16] mechanism is chosen as the LDP perturbation mechanism. We adopt the same parameter settings and noise correction methods when using these typical LDP mechanisms.

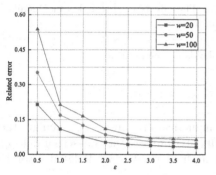 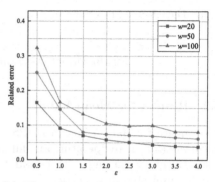

(a) The effects of privacy budgets in LM.   (b) The effects of privacy budgets in Duchi's method.

Fig. 5. The effects of privacy budgets on temperature.

Experimental Metrics. Related error is taken as the error measure of mean value calculation, and MAPE is taken as the error measure of frequency estimation. The related error is the absolute value of the predicted value minus the real value divided by the real value. The definition of related error is as follows:

$$Realtederror = \left| \frac{y_i - x_i}{x_i} \right| \times 100\% \tag{6}$$

And the MAPE is the absolute value between the estimated and true frequency, divide the absolute value by the true frequency, then cumulate these values and divide by the size of the data value domain. The definition of MAPE is as follows:

$$MAPE = \frac{\sum\limits_{i=1}^{|D|} \left| \frac{y_i - x_i}{x_i} \right|}{|D|} \times 100\% \tag{7}$$

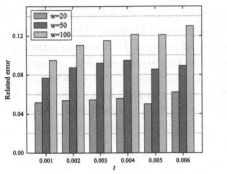

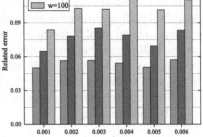

(a) The effects of thresholds in LM.

(b) The effects of thresholds in Duchi's method.

Fig. 6. The effects of thresholds on temperature.

6.2 Results for Mean Value

To evaluate the data utility of LDPS on numerical attributes, we calculate the mean value of the temperature and humidity attributes of the Gas-sensor dataset respectively by varying ϵ, threshold t, length of window w. Related error in Eq. (6) is selected as a metric.

We choose w to be 20, 50, 100, ϵ from 0.5 to 4.0, and t from 0.001 to 0.006. When we evaluate the effects of different ϵ values, make t 0.003; evaluate the effects of different t, make ϵ 2. Figure 5(a) shows the effects of ϵ and w on data utility when the Duchi's method is chosen as perturbing mechanism, and Fig. 5(B) shows the effects of ϵ and w on data utility when the Laplace mechanism is chosen as perturb mechanism. It can be seen that the data utility is higher

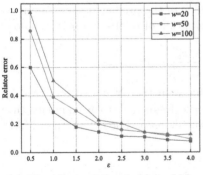

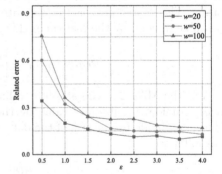

(a) The effects of thresholds in LM.

(b) The effects of privacy budgets in Duchi's method.

Fig. 7. The effects of privacy budgets on humidity.

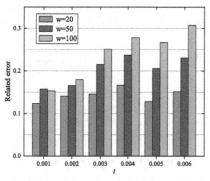

(a) The effects of thresholds in LM.

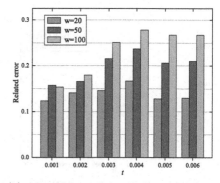

(b) The effects of thresholds in Duchi's method.

Fig. 8. The effects of thresholds on humidity.

when ϵ is large and w is small; the data utility is lower when ϵ is small and w is large, while the privacy guarantee level is on the contrary.

In Fig. 6, we can see the effects of t and w under the Duchi and LM perturb mechanism. As t value increases, data utility does not always decline, but increases first and then decreases. And the effects of window length is similar to the results in Fig. 5, The higher the w, the lower the data utility.

We verify the data utility of the same parameters on the humidity attribute dataset. The results are shown in Fig. 7 and Fig. 8, and we can get similar effects on data utility.

6.3 Results for Frequency Estimation

To evaluate the data utility of LDPS on categorical attributes, we estimate the frequency of each attribute value in the 'AGE' attribute of IPUMS and

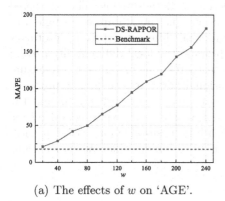

(a) The effects of w on 'AGE'.

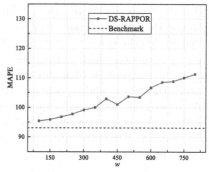

(b) The effects of w on 'CountryID'.

Fig. 9. The effects of w in frequency estimation.

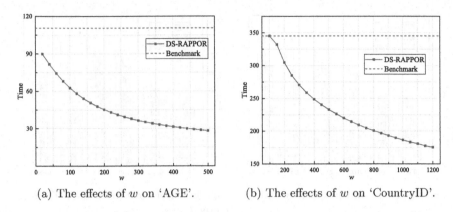

(a) The effects of w on 'AGE'.   (b) The effects of w on 'CountryID'.

Fig. 10. The effects of runtime in frequency estimation.

'CountryID' attribute of Twitter daily activities by varying the length of window w and choose MAPE in Eq. (7) as a metric. The parameters k, h, p, q and f of the perturbation mechanism RAPPOR are set to 256, 4, 0.5, 0.75, 0.5 on 'AGE' and 256, 8, 0.5, 0.75, 0.5 on 'CountryID', respectively.

We consider conducting experiments from the perspectives of data utility and runtime and choose RAPPOR protocol as the perturb mechanism. And we change the time-series streaming to normal data, adopt the RAPPOR to perturb these data as a benchmark. Figure 9 shows that the MAPE value increases with the increase of the window length w. On the contrary, Fig. 10 shows that the experimental runtime decreases with the increase of the window length w. So, we can see that varying the window length w affect data utility, privacy, and runtime.

7   Conclusion

This paper focuses on the privacy protection of data streams. The untrusted third parties may query the original data of multiple timestamps of a single user to breach the user's privacy while current local differential privacy protocols can hardly handle the data streams. We propose the local differentially private streaming protocol, which can not only protect streaming privacy but also ensure high utility, and less storage and computational power overhead. The proposed method utilizes the sliding window that satisfies w-event privacy to find the stably sub-stream and significant moves in real-time. The experimental results show that the proposed protocol has high utility, is suitable for both numerical and categorical attributes, and maintains its utility under different distributions and streaming sizes.

References

1. University of Minnesota: IPUMS USA. https://www.ipums.org
2. Bassily, R., Nissim, K., Stemmer, U., Thakurta, A.G.: Practical locally private heavy hitters. In: Advances in Neural Information Processing Systems, pp. 2288–2296 (2017)
3. Bassily, R., Smith, A.: Local, private, efficient protocols for succinct histograms. In: Proceedings of the Forty-Seventh Annual ACM Symposium on Theory of Computing, pp. 127–135 (2015)
4. De Montjoye, Y.A., Hidalgo, C.A., Verleysen, M., Blondel, V.D.: Unique in the crowd: the privacy bounds of human mobility. Sci. Rep. **3**, 1376 (2013)
5. Ding, B., Kulkarni, J., Yekhanin, S.: Collecting telemetry data privately. In: Advances in Neural Information Processing Systems, pp. 3571–3580 (2017)
6. Duchi, J., Wainwright, M.J., Jordan, M.I.: Local privacy and minimax bounds: sharp rates for probability estimation. In: Advances in Neural Information Processing Systems, pp. 1529–1537 (2013)
7. Duchi, J.C., Jordan, M.I., Wainwright, M.J.: Local privacy and statistical minimax rates. In: 2013 IEEE 54th Annual Symposium on Foundations of Computer Science, pp. 429–438. IEEE (2013)
8. Duchi, J.C., Jordan, M.I., Wainwright, M.J.: Local privacy, data processing inequalities, and statistical minimax rates. arXiv preprint arXiv:1302.3203 (2013)
9. Duchi, J.C., Jordan, M.I., Wainwright, M.J.: Minimax optimal procedures for locally private estimation. J. Am. Stat. Assoc. **113**(521), 182–201 (2018)
10. Dwork, Cynthia., McSherry, Frank., Nissim, Kobbi, Smith, Adam: Calibrating noise to sensitivity in private data analysis. In: Halevi, Shai, Rabin, Tal (eds.) TCC 2006. LNCS, vol. 3876, pp. 265–284. Springer, Heidelberg (2006). https://doi.org/10.1007/11681878_14
11. Dwork, C., Naor, M., Pitassi, T., Rothblum, G.N.: Differential privacy under continual observation. In: Proceedings of the Forty-Second ACM Symposium on Theory of Computing, pp. 715–724 (2010)
12. Erlingsson, Ú., Pihur, V., Korolova, A.: Rappor: randomized aggregatable privacy-preserving ordinal response. In: Proceedings of the 2014 ACM SIGSAC Conference on Computer and Communications Security, pp. 1054–1067 (2014)
13. Ezabadi, S.G., Jolfaei, A., Kulik, L., Kotagiri, R.: Differentially private streaming to untrusted edge servers in intelligent transportation system. In: 2019 18th IEEE International Conference on Trust, Security and Privacy in Computing and Communications/13th IEEE International Conference on Big Data Science and Engineering (TrustCom/BigDataSE), pp. 781–786. IEEE (2019)
14. Fan, L., Xiong, L.: An adaptive approach to real-time aggregate monitoring with differential privacy. IEEE Trans. Knowl. Data Eng. **26**(9), 2094–2106 (2013)
15. Fan, L., Xiong, L., Sunderam, V.: Fast: differentially private real-time aggregate monitor with filtering and adaptive sampling. In: Proceedings of the 2013 ACM SIGMOD International Conference on Management of Data, pp. 1065–1068 (2013)
16. Fanti, G., Pihur, V., Erlingsson, Ú.: Building a rappor with the unknown: privacy-preserving learning of associations and data dictionaries. Proc. Priv. Enhancing Technol. **2016**(3), 41–61 (2016)
17. Hassidim, A., Kaplan, H., Mansour, Y., Matias, Y., Stemmer, U.: Adversarially robust streaming algorithms via differential privacy. arXiv preprint arXiv:2004.05975 (2020)

18. Huerta, R., Mosqueiro, T., Fonollosa, J., Rulkov, N.F., Rodriguez-Lujan, I.: Online decorrelation of humidity and temperature in chemical sensors for continuous monitoring. Chemom. Intell. Lab. Syst. **157**, 169–176 (2016)
19. Jolfaei, A., Kant, K.: Privacy and security of connected vehicles in intelligent transportation system. In: 2019 49th Annual IEEE/IFIP International Conference on Dependable Systems and Networks-Supplemental Volume (DSN-S), pp. 9–10. IEEE (2019)
20. Joseph, M., Roth, A., Ullman, J., Waggoner, B.: Local differential privacy for evolving data. In: Advances in Neural Information Processing Systems, pp. 2375–2384 (2018)
21. Kasiviswanathan, S.P., Lee, H.K., Nissim, K., Raskhodnikova, S., Smith, A.: What can we learn privately? SIAM J. Comput. **40**(3), 793–826 (2011)
22. Kellaris, G., Papadopoulos, S., Xiao, X., Papadias, D.: Differentially private event sequences over infinite streams (2014)
23. Kim, J.W., Jang, B., Yoo, H.: Privacy-preserving aggregation of personal health-data streams. PloS One **13**(11) (2018)
24. Microsoft: Longitudinal, daily, per-county activity periods of aggregated Twitter users. https://www.microsoft.com/en-us/download/details.aspx?id=57387
25. Nguyên, T.T., Xiao, X., Yang, Y., Hui, S.C., Shin, H., Shin, J.: Collecting and analyzing data from smart device users with local differential privacy. arXiv preprint arXiv:1606.05053 (2016)
26. Sun, L., Ge, C., Huang, X., Wu, Y., Gao, Y.: Differentially private real-time streaming data publication based on sliding window under exponential decay. Comput. Mater. Continua **58**(1), 61–78 (2019)
27. Team, A., et al.: Learning with privacy at scale. Apple Mach. Learn. J. **1**(8) (2017)
28. Wang, Q., Zhang, Y., Lu, X., Wang, Z., Qin, Z., Ren, K.: Real-time and spatio-temporal crowd-sourced social network data publishing with differential privacy. IEEE Trans. Dependable Secure Comput. **15**(4), 591–606 (2016)
29. Wang, Q., Zhang, Y., Lu, X., Wang, Z., Qin, Z., Ren, K.: Rescuedp: real-time spatio-temporal crowd-sourced data publishing with differential privacy. In: IEEE INFOCOM 2016-The 35th Annual IEEE International Conference on Computer Communications, pp. 1–9. IEEE (2016)
30. Wang, T., Yang, X., Ren, X., Zhao, J., Lam, K.Y.: Adaptive differentially private data stream publishing in spatio-temporal monitoring of IoT. In: 2019 IEEE 38th International Performance Computing and Communications Conference (IPCCC), pp. 1–8. IEEE (2019)
31. Wang, Y., Wu, X., Hu, D.: Using randomized response for differential privacy preserving data collection. In: EDBT/ICDT Workshops, vol. 1558 (2016)

A Personalized Preservation Mechanism Satisfying Local Differential Privacy in Location-Based Services

Datong Wu[1], Xiaotong Wu[2(✉)], Jiaquan Gao[2], Genlin Ji[2], Xiaolong Xu[3], Lianyong Qi[4], and Wanchun Dou[5]

[1] Changzhou University, Changzhou, China
wudatong@cczu.edu.cn
[2] School of Computer Science and Technology, Nanjing Normal University, Nanjing, China
{wuxiaotong,73025,glji}@njnu.edu.cn
[3] School of Computer and Software,
Nanjing University of Information Science and Technology, Nanjing, China
njuxlxu@gmail.com
[4] School of Information, Science and Engineering, Qufu Normal University, Rizhao, China
lianyongqi@gmail.com
[5] The State Key Lab for Novel Software Technology, Nanjing University, Nanjing, China
douwc@nju.edu.cn

Abstract. With the wide application of location-based services, there is a huge amount of users' spatial data generated by mobile devices every day. However, the data is left from mobile users and faced with leakage risk from adversaries or untrusted data receivers. Therefore, spatial data should be perturbed to satisfy local differential privacy (LDP), which is a strong privacy metric in the local setting. In this paper, we study the problem of designing a personalized mechanism satisfying LDP for spatial data. We first construct attack and defense for privacy of spatial data and give a novel privacy definition with LDP and users' personalized requirements. We propose a personalized location privacy preservation mechanism for spatial data satisfying LDP. We demonstrate the optimal utility and privacy guarantee of our mechanism. We analyze the impact of the key parameters on data utility via the experiments over the real dataset.

Keywords: Local differential privacy · Local privacy · Randomized Response · Mobile network.

1 Introduction

With the explosive development of mobile communications and infrastructures, there are a large number of location-based applications and services in mobile

© Springer Nature Singapore Pte Ltd. 2020
S. Yu et al. (Eds.): SPDE 2020, CCIS 1268, pp. 161–175, 2020.
https://doi.org/10.1007/978-981-15-9129-7_12

devices (e.g., smart phones and wearable devices) to improve the quality of living of people from various fields [26, 27]. For example, mobile users utilize sport software on smart watch to record their trajectories and make a scientific plan. They also send their location information to the third party and get location-based services, including GPS navigation, shopping and takeaways. Although mobile users benefit from the convenient location-based services, their sensitive location information (i.e., home or work address) may be threatened by adversaries or the untrusted third party [24, 25]. It brings significant security risks for mobile users. To this end, it needs privacy preservation mechanisms to guarantee their location privacy.

In recent years, there have been a large number of works to design various metrics and mechanisms to protect location privacy of mobile users, including mix zone [7], k-anonymity [8], dummy location [21] and differential privacy (DP) [6, 22]. In detail, anonymization and perturbation techniques (e.g., mix zone, k-anonymity and dummy location) are to generate or modify users' trajectories by empirical analysis. It can't provide perfect location privacy preservation when auxiliary information of adversaries is enough. Differential privacy is a strong privacy preservation metric with rigorous mathematical definition. However, differential privacy is suited to the central setting, which assumes that the third party is trusted. However, in the real applications, mobile users even don't know who is the third party or control the usage of their location information. Therefore, all of the above metrics and mechanisms are not fully suited to mobile network with perfect privacy guarantee.

In order to overcome the disadvantages of the previous methods, Duchi et al. [5] proposed a novel privacy metric, named *local differential privacy* (LDP), which is suited to the local setting. It assumes that the third party is not trusted. LDP limits the probability of the difference between any two location points, instead of any two datasets in DP. In the definition of LDP, each mobile user only considers his/her own location information and doesn't care about others' privacy requirements. There have been a few of works to design a lot of LDP mechanisms for various scenes in mobile network, including heavy hitter identification [19], marginal release [2], graph data mining [15]. However, to the best of our knowledge, there are few works to design the proper mechanism for spatial data under local differential privacy. Therefore, the focus of the paper is on *designing a personalized location privacy preservation mechanism to satisfy local differential privacy.*

In order to solve the above problem, we propose a personalized preservation mechanism for spatial data satisfying location differential privacy. The mechanism makes full use of Randomized Response (RR) mechanism [20], which reports a random location point derived from some probability distribution. In addition, our proposed mechanism guarantees different privacy requirements for mobile users, i.e., personalized privacy. In summary, the main contributions of the paper can be listed as follows:

- We construct attack and defense of location privacy among the third party and mobile users. We also give a novel privacy definition, which satisfies local differential privacy and personalized privacy requirement.
- We propose a personalized preservation mechanism for spatial data satisfying location differential privacy. We also demonstrate our mechanism is optimal in terms of data utility by theoretical analysis.
- We utilize heat map to evaluate the impact of key parameters on the utility of perturbed location points for our proposed mechanism.

The remaining of the paper is organized as follows. Section 2 introduces the related work about privacy preservation techniques for mobile network. Section 3 presents the system model in mobile network and attack and defense for privacy. Section 4 proposes a novel location privacy approach satisfying our defined privacy metric. Section 5 evaluates the utility of our approach influenced by different parameters. Section 6 concludes the work of the paper.

2   Related Work

Location privacy is one of the most concerned problems for individuals and the society in various scenes, especially in mobile network. There have been a series of works to either set privacy standards or design privacy preservation algorithms for spatial data [3,9,16–18,29]. The common privacy techniques consist of mix zone [7], k-anonymity [8], dummy location [21] and differential privacy [6]. However, these techniques are not fully suitable to protect users' privacy in the local setting. To this end, local differential privacy has been proposed as a novel privacy metric [5]. In order to satisfy the requirement, most of preservation mechanisms utilize Randomized Response [20], in which the probability of an answer to a query is derived from some distribution. Based on RR, k-RR is designed for frequency estimation of categorical data [11]. For numerical data, the value is firstly encoded as a binary one and then perturbed by RR [4]. Spatial data is a special data structure, which is a combination of categorical and numerical data. It may be categorical data, including country, province, city, town, street. For this case, Chen et al. [1] designed a personalized count estimation protocol to satisfy local differential privacy. Zhao et al. [28] proposed a probabilistic top-down partitioning algorithm to generate a sanitized location-record data. It may be numerical data, including latitude, longitude, altitude and time. Xiong et al. [23] presented a generalized randomized response mechanism to achieve local differential privacy. However, to the best of our knowledge, there are few works to design a personalized preservation mechanism for spatial data satisfying local differential privacy.

3   Preliminaries

3.1   System Model

In mobile network, there are multiple key participants. Here, we assume that there is a constant region $\mathcal{R}$, in which there are a set of n mobile users

$\mathcal{U} = \{u_1, u_2, \cdots, u_n\}$ and one service provider $\mathcal{P}$. In regular, the latter receives trajectory information of the former and then offers the corresponding service. The set of trajectories from all users are defined as $\mathcal{T} = \{T_1, T_2, \cdots, T_n\}$. The trajectory information is defined as an ordered set of spatial-temporal 3D volumes $l_i = \langle x_i, y_i, t_i \rangle$, $i \in [m]$. In detail, (x_i, y_i) represents location information at time t_i. Suppose that the service provider $\mathcal{P}$ is untrusted, whose objective is to leverage his/her *side information* to connect the trajectory with the real identity of the user. Therefore, we also call $\mathcal{P}$ an adversary and will use them interchangeably in the following section.

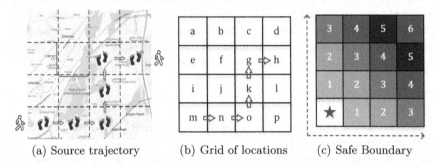

(a) Source trajectory   (b) Grid of locations   (c) Safe Boundary

Fig. 1. An example of grid of location

3.2   Grid of Locations

We introduce *the grid method* (e.g., Uniform Grid (UG) and Adaptive Grids (AG)) in [13] to split the map into multiple disjoint blocks. It is worthwhile to note that we have assumed that the region $\mathcal{R}$ is constant in Section 3.1. Here, we present the following example to illustrate the grid method shown in Fig. 1.

Example 1. Figure 1(a) shows the trajectory of some user u_i in the real map. It is obvious to observe that the user moves from the bottom left to the upper right corner. By the grid method, the region $\mathcal{R}$ is divided into 16 grids, which each is a rectangle with the area of α square meters and is labelled by a unique integer or character (e.g., character in Fig. 1(b)). It is noted that the area of α is dynamic. As a result, the trajectory of user u_i is changed to an ordered set of characters or integers. In Fig. 1(b), the trajectory is $\langle m, n, o, k, g, h \rangle$.

By the grid method, the region $\mathcal{R}$ is divided to multiple disjoint blocks, which each is labelled by a unique integer or character. That is, $\mathcal{R}$ is defined as a set of blocks $\mathcal{B} = \{B_1, B_2, \cdots, B_z\}$, in which z is the number of blocks. Therefore, the trajectory $\mathcal{T}_i$ of each user u_i is generalized as $\mathcal{I}_i = \langle \mathcal{I}_{i1}, \mathcal{I}_{i2}, \cdots, \mathcal{I}_{im} \rangle$, $\mathcal{I}_{ij} \in \mathcal{B}$. In detail, for any location record $l_j = \langle x_j, y_j, t_j \rangle$ of $\mathcal{T}_i$, it computes which block the location $\langle x_j, y_j \rangle$ belongs to. In particular, it is worthwhile to note that it is not necessary for mobile users to move two adjacent blocks. This is up to the time that mobile users report data.

3.3   Privacy Preservation

Differential privacy [6] is a strong privacy metric with rigorous mathematical definition in the central setting. That is, it usually supposes that data collectors are trusted. Thus, it is not suited for the local setting with untrusted collectors. To this end, local differential privacy is proposed as follows:

Definition 1 (ϵ-Local Differential Privacy [5]). *A sanitized mechanism $\mathcal{M}$ satisfies ϵ-local differential privacy if and only if for any pair of different values (v_i, v_j) and any output $O \in Range(\mathcal{M})$, we have*

$$\Pr[\mathcal{M}(v_i) \in O] \leq \exp(\epsilon) \cdot \Pr[\mathcal{M}(v_j) \in O], \tag{1}$$

in which $Range(\mathcal{M})$ is the domain of $\mathcal{M}$.

For local differential privacy, the domain of $\mathcal{M}$ is one of the key components. The size of the domain has an important influence on both privacy and utility of perturbed data. Meanwhile, we observe that the domain of $\mathcal{M}$ is correlated with safe boundary defined as follows:

Definition 2 (Safe Boundary). *A safe boundary τ for some user is a set of blocks, inside which the user feels comfortable to disclose.*

Here, we illustrate the safe boundary by the following example:

Example 2. At the beginning, a user u_i is in a block labelled by a red star in Fig. 1(c). The different safe boundary is labelled by different colours. If $\tau = 2$, the safe boundary are green blocks.

Once some user determines his/her safe boundary, The *safe region $\mathcal{SR}$* is defined as all blocks within the safe boundary except for user's current block. Based on safe region, personalized local differential privacy is defined as follows:

Definition 3 ((τ, ϵ)-Personalized Local Differential Privacy). *A sanitized mechanism $\mathcal{M}$ satisfies (τ, ϵ)-personalized local differential privacy (PLDP) if and only if any pair of different blocks $(v_i, v_j) \in \mathcal{SR}^2$ and any output $O \in Range(\mathcal{M})$, we have*

$$\Pr[\mathcal{M}(v_i)] \leq \exp(\epsilon) \cdot \Pr[\mathcal{M}(v_j)] \tag{2}$$

in which $Range(\mathcal{M})$ is the domain of $\mathcal{M}$.

Before any user sends his/her location information to service providers, he/she needs to perturb his/her data by some private mechanism, which satisfies (τ, ϵ)-personalized local differential privacy.

3.4   Threat Model

Assume that there is an attacker to get side information of users in some constant region $\mathcal{R}$. The side information is a set of the real identities and accurate locations or rough area of mobile users. It is defined as $\mathcal{S} = \{S_1, S_2, \cdots, S_k\}$, in which $S_i = \langle ID_i, l'_1, l'_2, \cdots, l'_m \rangle$ and ID_i is the real identity of some user. In order to get $\mathcal{S}$, the attacker takes various legal or illegal measures. For example, the attacker directly tracks some user within a certain time or implants malicious software on mobile devices to eavesdrop location information.

In general, the attacker utilizes side information to launch *inference attack* [21]. The attack consists of two key factors, including α and $\mathcal{S}$. On one hand, the smaller the area α, the more accurate the location is. On the other hand, the more the side information, the higher the probability to distinguish the real trajectory is. Different from [21], mobile users regularly report their perturbed block index rather than location information. Meanwhile, adversaries have accurate or rough location information of mobile users instead of blocks. Thus, it is a challenge to construct the threat model between different types of data.

For trajectory T_j of some user u_j, the attacker $\mathcal{A}$ compares each trajectory $S_i \in \mathcal{S}$ with it. The comparison is viewed as a probability problem in the paper. We assume that the prior knowledge is derived from the uniform distribution, i.e., $\Pr[T_j] = 1/n$. In addition, side information is independent on each user. According to the Bayesian theorem, the probability between T_j over S_i is

$$\Pr[T_j|S_i] = \frac{\Pr[S_i|T_j]\Pr[T_j]}{\Pr[S_i]} \propto \Pr[S_i|T_j]. \tag{3}$$

Therefore, once the attacker $\mathcal{A}$ receives perturbed trajectory from some user, he/she computes the probability with that in side information. In the previous literatures, they usually assume that the entries of a trajectory is independent with each other and the difference is derived from Gaussian distribution $N(0, \sigma^2)$. That is,

$$\Pr[S_i|T_j] = \prod_{k=1}^{m} \Pr[l'_k|l_k] = C \cdot \exp\left\{ -\frac{1}{2\sigma^2} \sum_{k=1}^{m} |l'_k - l_k|^2 \right\}, \tag{4}$$

in which C is a constant and $|l'_k - l_k|^2 = (l'_k.x - l_k.x)^2 + (l'_k.y - l_k.y)^2$. Since each user just reports his/her block B_i at some time, we adopt the central position as user's location. Therefore, Eq. (4) is changed to

$$\Pr[S_i|T_j] = C \cdot \exp\left\{ -\frac{1}{2\sigma^2} \sum_{k=1}^{m} |l'_k - B_{i_k}| \right\} \qquad B_{i_k} \in \mathcal{B}. \tag{5}$$

In Eq. (5), the area α has an important influence on $B_{i_k} \in \mathcal{B}$.

3.5   Problem Formulation

The focus of our paper is on how to design a proper mechanism satisfying local differential privacy in mobile network. To this end, we design an effective algorithm under LDP based on RR. In addition, according to the privacy preservation

---

Algorithm 1. Personalized Location Privacy Preservation PLPP

Input: personalized parameter τ, privacy parameter ϵ, unit rectangle's area α, the number of reports t, time interval v
Output: perturbed trajectory

1: $\mathcal{B} \leftarrow$ a set of blocks according to α for the grid of some region
2: $T \leftarrow t$-length integer array, initially 0
3: **for** $i \in [t]$ **do**
4:     generate current location (x, y)
5:     map location (x, y) to block b in $\mathcal{B}$
6:     $T[i] \leftarrow \mathsf{LRG}(\mathcal{B}, b, \tau, \epsilon)$
7:     wait for v seconds
8: **end for**
9: **return** T

Algorithm 2. Location Randomized Generator LRG

Input: blocks $\mathcal{B}$, block index b, personalized parameter τ, privacy parameter ϵ
Output: perturbed trajectory

1: $\mathcal{C} \leftarrow$ a set of blocks within safe boundary τ for b according to $\mathcal{B}$
2: $d \leftarrow |\mathcal{C}|$
3: generate y derived from the following probability at random

$$
y = \begin{cases} b & \text{w.p. } \frac{e^\epsilon}{e^\epsilon + d - 1} \\ !b & \text{w.p. } \frac{1}{e^\epsilon + d - 1} \end{cases} \tag{6}
$$

$!b$ represents an entry in $\mathcal{C}$
4: **return** y

---

metric in Sect. 3.3 and threat model in Sect. 3.4, there are three key parameters that have influence on the degree of privacy, including personalized parameter τ, privacy parameter ϵ and the area α. For mobile users, their objective is to get the maximum utility and satisfy PLDB, which decides the degree of privacy, i.e., $\Pr[S_i|T_j]$. According to Eq. (5), $\Pr[S_i|T_j]$ is up to the sum of $\left| l'_k - B_{i_k} \right|$. Therefore, it needs to maximize the utility for any location point with PLDB privacy guarantee.

4   Privacy Preservation Mechanism Satisfying PLDB

4.1   The Design of Privacy Mechanism

In this paper, we utilize the extended version namely k-RR [10] of randomized response to perturb location information of mobile users. That is, we construct a location randomized generator (LRG) to output a block at random. For a mobile user u_i, he/she needs to set proper values for key parameters $\alpha, \tau, p_0, p_1, \cdots, p_\tau$ to maximize utility, in which p_i is a probability of a block within safe boundary to be chosen. We assume that the distance between the perturbed and correct location points is inversely proportional to service quality. In other words, the greater the distance, the poorer the service quality is. The proportion of unit distance is $c/\alpha \in (0,1)$, in which $c > 0$ is constant and $\alpha > 1$. We also assume that it has the same probability in the same safe boundary. Suppose that the service quality is 1 in the current location, which has the maximal quality. In addition, the most important property is that our designed mechanism must satisfy (τ, ϵ)-personalized local differential privacy. Therefore, once user u_i chooses parameter τ, his/her expectation utility is derived as follows:

$$\mathrm{E}[U(\tau, p_0, p_1, \cdots, p_k)] = p_0 + \sum_{k=1}^{\tau} 4k \cdot p_k \cdot \left(\frac{c}{\alpha}\right)^k \tag{7}$$

$$\text{s.t.} \quad p_0 + \sum_{k=1}^{\tau} 4k \cdot p_k = 1 \tag{8}$$

$$\forall k \in [\tau], \; \frac{p_0}{p_k} \le \exp(\epsilon) \tag{9}$$

$$\alpha > 1 \tag{10}$$

$$\tau \in Z \tag{11}$$

$$p_k \in (0,1) \quad k = 0, 1, \cdots, \tau \tag{12}$$

in which p_k is the probability of selection for some block and p_0 is the probability of the current block.

For each mobile user, his/her objective is to maximize the expected utility. The challenge is to set proper probability for each block in the safe boundary when τ is constant. The existing works to implement local differential privacy usually consists of three components, including *encoding*, *perturbation* and *aggregation* [19]. In order to reduce processing time, we select direct encoding (DE) [14]. In other words, it doesn't adopt any encoding but directly perturbs data. Meanwhile, we utilize k-RR [14] mechanism to perturb the location information. The main mechanism namely PLPP is shown in Algorithm 1. For each mobile user, he/she reports perturbed location to the service provider t times. Every time, the user first gets current location by a mobile device and then maps it to a block in $\mathcal{B}$ (line 3-4). Next, he/she calls LRG to perturb the block and records the result. Therefore, the core of the mechanism is perturbation mechanism LRG. It is noted that all the operations are executed by the mobile user.

For LRG, a natural idea is to utilize the existing mechanism, i.e., k-RR. Algorithm 2 presents the detailed operations. It first computes the number d of blocks within safe boundary τ (line 1-2). For blocks except of the current block, they have the same probability, i.e., $1/(e^\epsilon + d + 1)$, while the current block has the probability $e^\epsilon/(e^\epsilon + d + 1)$. Compared to other blocks, the current block in LRG has the highest probability. Meanwhile, the time and space complexity of Algorithm 1 are $O(t \cdot \tau^2)$ and $O(t)$, respectively.

4.2 Utility and Privacy Analysis

We firstly discuss utility of mechanism PLPP. By the following theorem, we demonstrate that PLPP maximizes the utility.

Theorem 1. *When parameter τ is constant, mechanism PLPP maximizes the expected utility* $E[U]$.

Proof. By Eq. (8), the maximum problem of $E[U]$ is changed as:

$$E[U] = 1 - \sum_{k=1}^{\tau} 4k \cdot p_k + \sum_{k=1}^{\tau} 4k \cdot (\frac{c}{\alpha})^k \cdot p_k = 1 - \sum_{k=1}^{\tau} 4k \cdot p_k \cdot (1 - \beta^k). \quad (13)$$

It implies that the maximum problem is changed to a minimum problem as follows:

$$\max_{p_1,p_2,\cdots,p_\tau} E[U] \iff \min_{p_1,p_2,\cdots,p_\tau} \sum_{k=1}^{\tau} \underbrace{k \cdot (1 - \beta^k)}_{\triangle} \cdot p_k. \quad (14)$$

Since Eq. $\triangle$ is greater than 0, p_k should be smaller. It is best that each p_k has the smallest value. According to Eq. (9), $p_1 = p_2 = \cdots = p_\tau = \frac{p_0}{e^\epsilon}$. With Eq. (8), we have $p_0 = \frac{e^\epsilon}{e^\epsilon+d-1}$ and $p_k = \frac{1}{e^\epsilon+d-1}$, $k \in [\tau]$.

Theorem 2. *Our designed mechanism PLPP satisfies (τ, ϵ)-personalized local differential privacy.*

Proof. According to Eq. (6), it is obvious to derive

$$\frac{\Pr[y = x]}{\Pr[y \neq x]} = \frac{e^\epsilon/(e^\epsilon + d - 1)}{1/(e^\epsilon + d - 1)} \leq e^\epsilon,$$

in which x is the current block of mobile users.

5 Experimental Evaluation

In the section, the objective of experiments over the real-world dataset is to analyze the impact of different parameters on the utility of perturbed data.

5.1 Experimental Setting

The evaluation is performed on a desktop computer, which has 16G of RAM and AMD Ryzen 5 3550H with Radeon Vega Mobile Gfx 2.10GHz running Windows 10 operating system. All of algorithms are implemented by Python. All of testing datasets are real.

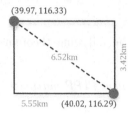

Fig. 2. Size of $\mathcal{R}$

Table 1. Four levels of grid for the map.

Level	Unit size (m^2)	# of Blocks
$L1$	4.438×3.417	1251×1000
$L2$	8.869×6.834	626×500
$L3$	13.313×10.262	471×333
$L4$	17.737×13.669	313×250

There are three key parameters that have the influence on utility and privacy of data. They are privacy parameter ϵ, the area of unit rectangle α and safe boundary τ. Here, we set their value range, i.e., $\epsilon \in [0.1, 10]$ and $\tau \in [1, 20]$. For the area of unit rectangle, its value is shown in Table 1. There are four different levels, i.e., $L1$-$L4$.

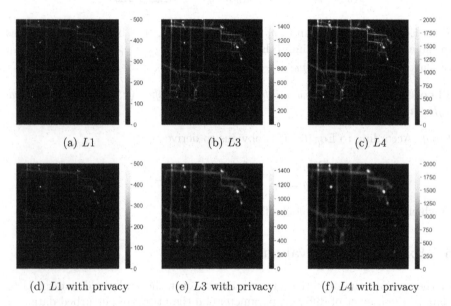

Fig. 3. Heat map for different α.

Dataset Setting. In the experiments, we select **Geolife** as our experimental dataset, which is collected by Microsoft Research Asia [12]. It is about GPS trajectories of 182 users from April 2007 to August 2012. Each trajectory consists of a large number of time-stamped points, each of which consists of the information of latitude, longitude and altitude. These trajectories have a variety of sampling rates, e.g., every 1-5 seconds or 5-10 meters per location. Since the source locations are loose, we don't select all the locations in **Geolife**. In the contrast, we first give a constant region to execute the experiments. As shown in Fig. 2, the latitude is from 39.97 to 40.02, while the longitude is from 116.29 to 116.33. Therefore, the area of the given region is about 18.981km^2. In the region, there are 4, 411, 983 location points of **Geolife**.

Evaluation Metrics. It is important to select a proper evaluation metric of data utility to evaluate the impact of different parameters. However, it is difficult to find a quantitative method to get the concrete utility. To this end, our experiments choose **heat map** to directly compare utility. In fact, heat map is widely applied in the location-based services, such as real-time monitoring of road traffic. Each block with a certain number of location points has a type of color.

5.2 Experimental Results

There are three key parameters that have an important influence on privacy and utility of data, including privacy ϵ, the area of the rectangle α and safe boundary τ. In the section, we give the detailed results one by one.

Impact of Parameter α. According to different sizes of each block, Table 1 shows four levels of grid for the given area, i.e., $L1$–$L4$. $L1$ has the minimum area of each block, while $L4$ has the maximum area. As a result, $L1$ has the maximum number of blocks and $L4$ has the minimum number. Figure 3(a)–(c) show the heat map for source data in different grids. It is obvious to see that when the size of a block is bigger, the number of location points is more. For $L4$ in Fig. 3(c), it has the brightest trajectories, which shows the most common routes of mobile users.

Meanwhile, we consider the influence of parameter α on data utility. We set privacy parameter $\epsilon = 1$ and safe boundary $\tau = 4$. The concrete results are shown in Fig. 3(d)–(f). We evaluate the utility of the same grids by comparing their heat map. $L4$ has the biggest difference of heat maps shown in Fig. 3(c) and (f), while $L1$ almost has no difference. It implies that α has an important influence on the data utility after perturbation. The greater parameter α, the more the negative influence on data utility is. The reason is that the greater value of α implies the greater area of perturbation for a location point causes the more difference.

Impact of Parameter ϵ. Privacy parameter ϵ is a key factor to decide the level of privacy preservation for source data. However, it is inevitable to cause the loss of data utility. In order to analyze the influence of ϵ on data utility, we take $L2$ to evaluate the effect. Meanwhile, we set the other parameters as $\epsilon \in [0.1, 1, 4, 8]$ and $\tau = 5$.

Figure 4 shows the heat maps of $L2$ for different privacy levels. It is obvious to see that with the increasement of ϵ, the loss of data utility is decreasing. This implies that the higher the level of privacy preservation, the more the loss of

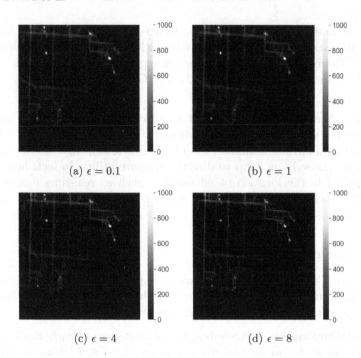

Fig. 4. Heat map of $L2$ for different privacy levels.

utility is. We also find that Fig. 4(a) and (b) are very similar. The reason is the perturbation mechanism, which is decided by Eq. (6). That is, the location point is in its source position, which is up to ϵ and the number of blocks within safe boundary. If the number of blocks within safe boundary is far greater than e^{ϵ}, ϵ should be as great as possible.

Impact of Parameter τ. τ decides the boundary, within which a source point can be set after perturbation. It is an important factor to influence the privacy and data utility. We take $L2$ to evaluate the effect. Meanwhile, we set the other parameters as $\tau \in [2,4,6,8]$ and $\epsilon = 1$.

In Fig. 5, we find that with the increasement of τ, the loss of data utility is increasing since the heat map is increasingly blurred. Relatively speaking, $\tau \leq 4$ is a good choice, in which the loss of data utility within tolerance. That is, the farthest distance to the source location point is about 36m. Therefore, it is a proper distance for mobile users. In addition, for different α, τ has different values. Generally speaking, the greater parameter α, the smaller parameter τ is.

In summary, α and τ have the negative influence and ϵ has the positive influence on the loss of data utility.

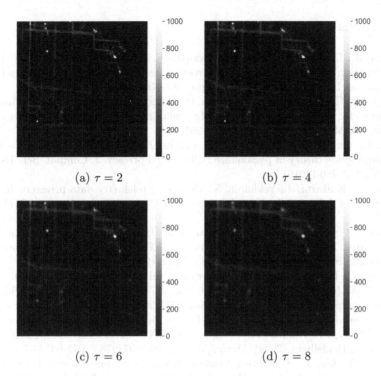

Fig. 5. Heat map of $L2$ for different safe boundaries.

6   Conclusion

The paper focuses on the design of a personalized mechanism for spatial data to satisfy local differential privacy. To this end, we have analyzed attack and defense for spatial data privacy between mobile users and the untrusted third party. We have given a novel definition for spatial data, i.e., personalized local differential privacy. We have proposed a personalized location preservation mechanism for spatial data satisfying local differential privacy. The mechanism satisfies the requirements of both privacy and personal preference. Experimental results show the impact of different parameters on data utility. We plan to consider the utility of the third party for various applications (e.g., frequency estimation, heavy hitter identification) in the future.

Acknowledgment. This research was partially supported by the National Key Research and Development Program of China (No. 2017YFB1400600).

References

1. Chen, R., Li, H., Qin, A.K., Kasiviswanathan, S.P., Jin, H.: Private spatial data aggregation in the local setting. In: Proceedings of 32nd IEEE International Conference on Data Engineering, ICDE, pp. 289–300. IEEE (2016)
2. Cormode, G., Kulkarni, T., Srivastava, D.: Marginal release under local differential privacy. In: Proceedings of the 2018 International Conference on Management of Data, SIGMOD, pp. 131–146. ACM (2018)
3. Cui, L., Qu, Y., Nosouhi, M.R., Yu, S., Niu, J., Xie, G.: Improving data utility through game theory in personalized differential privacy. J. Comput. Sci. Technol. **34**(2), 272–286 (2019)
4. Ding, B., Kulkarni, J., Yekhanin, S.: Collecting telemetry data privately. In: Proceedings of Advances in Neural Information Processing Systems, pp. 3571–3580 (2017)
5. Duchi, J.C., Jordan, M.I., Wainwright, M.J.: Local privacy and statistical minimax rates. In: Proceedings of 54th Annual IEEE Symposium on Foundations of Computer Science, FOCS, pp. 429–438. IEEE (2013)
6. Dwork, C.: Differential privacy: a survey of results. In: Agrawal, M., Du, D., Duan, Z., Li, A. (eds.) TAMC 2008. LNCS, vol. 4978, pp. 1–19. Springer, Heidelberg (2008). https://doi.org/10.1007/978-3-540-79228-4_1
7. Freudiger, J., Shokri, R., Hubaux, J.-P.: On the optimal placement of mix zones. In: Goldberg, I., Atallah, M.J. (eds.) PETS 2009. LNCS, vol. 5672, pp. 216–234. Springer, Heidelberg (2009). https://doi.org/10.1007/978-3-642-03168-7_13
8. Gedik, B., Liu, L.: Protecting location privacy with personalized k-anonymity: architecture and algorithms. IEEE Trans. Mob. Comput. **7**(1), 1–18 (2008)
9. Gu, B.S., Gao, L., Wang, X., Qu, Y., Jin, J., Yu, S.: Privacy on the edge: customizable privacy-preserving context sharing in hierarchical edge computing. IEEE Trans. Netw. Sci. Eng. (2019, in press). https://doi.org/10.1109/TNSE.2019.2933639
10. Kairouz, P., Oh, S., Viswanath, P.: Extremal mechanisms for local differential privacy. In: Proceedings of Annual Conference on Neural Information Processing Systems, pp. 2879–2887 (2014)
11. Kairouz, P., Oh, S., Viswanath, P.: Extremal mechanisms for local differential privacy. J. Mach. Learn. Res. **17**, 17:1–17:51 (2016)
12. Microsoft: GPS trajectory dataset of Geolife project. https://www.microsoft.com/en-us/download/details.aspx?id=52367
13. Qardaji, W.H., Yang, W., Li, N.: Differentially private grids for geospatial data. In: Proceedings of 29th International Conference on Data Engineering, ICDE, pp. 757–768. IEEE (2013)
14. Qin, Z., Yang, Y., Yu, T., Khalil, I., Xiao, X., Ren, K.: Heavy hitter estimation over set-valued data with local differential privacy. In: Proceedings of the 2016 SIGSAC Conference on Computer and Communications Security, CCS, pp. 192–203. ACM (2016)
15. Qin, Z., Yu, T., Yang, Y., Khalil, I., Xiao, X., Ren, K.: Generating synthetic decentralized social graphs with local differential privacy. In: Proceedings of the ACM SIGSAC Conference on Computer and Communications Security, CCS, pp. 425–438. ACM (2017)
16. Qu, Y., Yu, S., Gao, L., Zhou, W., Peng, S.: A hybrid privacy protection scheme in cyber-physical social networks. IEEE Trans. Comput. Soc. Syst. **5**(3), 773–784 (2018)

17. Qu, Y., Yu, S., Zhou, W., Peng, S., Wang, G., Xiao, K.: Privacy of things: emerging challenges and opportunities in wireless internet of things. IEEE Wirel. Commun. **25**(6), 91–97 (2018)
18. Qu, Y., Yu, S., Zhou, W., Tian, Y.: GAN-driven personalized spatial-temporal private data sharing in cyber-physical social systems. IEEE Trans. Netw. Sci. Eng. (2020, in press). https://doi.org/10.1109/TNSE.2020.3001061
19. Wang, T., Blocki, J., Li, N., Jha, S.: Locally differentially private protocols for frequency estimation. In: Proceedings of 26th USENIX Security Symposium, pp. 729–745. USENIX (2017)
20. Warner, S.L.: Randomized response: a survey technique for eliminating evasive answer bias. J. Am. Stat. Assoc. **60**(309), 63–69 (1965)
21. Wu, X., Li, S., Yang, J., Dou, W.: A cost sharing mechanism for location privacy preservation in big trajectory data. In: Proceedings of International Conference on Communications, ICC, pp. 1–6. IEEE (2017)
22. Wu, X., Wu, T., Khan, M., Ni, Q., Dou, W.: Game theory based correlated privacy preserving analysis in big data. IEEE Trans. Big Data 1 (2017, in press). https://doi.org/10.1109/TBDATA.2017.2701817
23. Xiong, X., Liu, S., Li, D., Wang, J., Niu, X.: Locally differentially private continuous location sharing with randomized response. IJDSN **15**(8), 1–13 (2019)
24. Xu, X., He, C., Xu, Z., Qi, L., Wan, S., Bhuiyan, Z.A.: Joint optimization of offloading utility and privacy for edge computing enabled IoT. IEEE Internet Things J. **7**(4), 2622–2629 (2019)
25. Xu, X., Liu, Q., Zhang, X., Zhang, J., Qi, L., Dou, W.: A blockchain-powered crowdsourcing method with privacy preservation in mobile environment. IEEE Trans. Comput. Soc. Syst. **6**(6), 1407–1419 (2019)
26. Xu, X., Liu, X., Xu, Z., Dai, F., Zhang, X., Qi, L.: Trust-oriented IoT service placement for smart cities in edge computing. IEEE Internet Things J. **7**(5), 4084–4091 (2019)
27. Yu, S.: Big privacy: challenges and opportunities of privacy study in the age of big data. IEEE Access **4**, 2751–2763 (2016)
28. Zhao, X., Li, Y., Yuan, Y., Bi, X., Wang, G.: Ldpart: effective location-record data publication via local differential privacy. IEEE Access **7**, 31435–31445 (2019)
29. Zhou, C., Fu, A., Yu, S., Yang, W., Wang, H., Zhang, Y.: Privacy-preserving federated learning in fog computing. IEEE Internet Things J. (2020, in press). https://doi.org/10.1109/JIOT.2020.2987958

Location-Aware Privacy Preserving Scheme in SDN-Enabled Fog Computing

Bruce Gu[1], Xiaodong Wang[1], Youyang Qu[1], Jiong Jin[2], Yong Xiang[1],
and Longxiang Gao[1(✉)]

[1] Deakin University, 221 Burwood Highway, Burwood, VIC, Australia
{bgu,xdwang,y.qu,yong.xiang}@deakin.edu.au
[2] Swinburne University of Technology, John Street, Hawthorn, VIC, Australia
jiongjin@swin.edu.au

Abstract. Fog computing, as a novel computing paradigm, aims at alleviating data loads of cloud computing and brings computing resources closer to end users. This is achieved through fog nodes such as access points, sensors, and fog servers. According to the fog computing location awareness capabilities, a large quantity of devices exists in the physical environment with a short cover range. This leads to location privacy exposure by the connection triggered. Adversaries can pry into more private data through the commodiously accessible location information. Although the existing privacy-preserving schemes can address some issues such as differential privacy, it cannot meet various privacy expectations in practice for fog computing variants. Motivated by this, we propose a location-aware dynamic dual ϵ-differential privacy preservation scheme to provide the ultimate protection. We start by establishing the first scheme by clustering fog nodes with SDN-enabled fog computing. In addition, we customize ϵ-differential privacy preservation scheme to tailor-made for the variant fog computing services. Furthermore, we employ a modified Laplacian mechanism to generate noise, with which we find the optimal trade-off. Extensive experimental results confirm the significance of the proposed model in terms of privacy protection level and data utility.

Keywords: Differential privacy · Fog computing · Software defined network

1 Introduction

With the rapid development of the fog computing [3], connectivity between fog nodes is becoming stronger and more ubiquitous. An increasing volume of entities are becoming intelligent and serving as fog nodes. They can perceive the surrounding environment, connect to the Internet, and receive commands remotely by their location information. The intelligence of these fog nodes is the result of data, analysis, and feedback from various systems or servers of different mobile devices. A large amount of the data leads to an increased possibility of privacy

S. Yu et al. (Eds.): SPDE 2020, CCIS 1268, pp. 176–190, 2020.
https://doi.org/10.1007/978-981-15-9129-7_13

issues such as location-aware privacy, sensitive context-aware privacy, etc. [7,8]. Therefore, it is necessary to protect the privacy between fog computing devices and users among the network infrastructure.

According to the fog computing reference model [4], location-based services have been widely used [24], for example, vehicular systems, smart grid, and smart city. Traditionally, end devices are required to connect to the best available fog node in order to improve user experience in a convenient way [16]. Location-aware privacy issues occur when the transmission has been confirmed [25]. Adversaries can easily detect and attack fog nodes in an appropriate manner. The main challenge for location-aware fog computing systems is how to securely and efficiently provide privacy-preserving methodologies among a large number of devices that contain sensitive location information [18].

Furthermore, with the growing demand for data, users' personal information can be disclosed against users' willing. However, with the potential threat of untrustworthy of the location service provider (fog node) and user sensitive information leakage, fog nodes containing the threat from users' privacy in the collection, distribution and use of location information [22]. Although some data privacy-preserving methods or algorithms are promoted, it is impractical for traditional privacy-preserving techniques to directly address the identified problem in an appropriate manner.

In this paper, in order to obtain an optimal tradeoff with high accuracy and efficiency, we propose a Dynamic Dual Scheme ϵ-Differential Privacy model (DDSDP) based on software-defined fog computing services. Software-defined fog computing provides the network with programmability and privacy protection in a flexible and dynamic way. In the proposed model, we use dual schemes to obtain tradeoff optimization. Firstly, we start from the fog nodes clustering approach. This approach brings the user into fog computing services by connecting with a group of fog nodes instead of one stable service provider, while it increases the difficulty when adversaries approach their collision attack. We customize ϵ-differential privacy based on the distance between clustered fog nodes. Moreover, we develop a QoS-based mapping function to measure data utilities and privacy protection level. Our extensive experiments indicate the efficiency and accuracy in a dynamic manner.

The main contributions of this work are summarized as follows.

- We propose a Dynamic Dual ϵ-Differential Privacy scheme (DDSDP) to preserve location-aware privacy. We consider a dynamic clustered connection for the fog nodes in the initial stage. This preserved direct attack from adaptable adversaries. According to customized Laplacian Mechanism differential privacy preservation setup, we customized protection levels and data utilities in order to achieve optimal protection.
- We analyze and modify the SDN-based fog computing control layer known as Dynamic Solution Layer (DSL). It dynamically customizing the clustering level to respond to different clustering situations. It protects from a stabilized system to a random variable system. Moreover, it increases the difficulty level for adversaries to analyze the real location of the user.

– We conduct experiments on a real-world dataset to demonstrate the proposed algorithms. The evaluation results show the significant performances in terms of data utility and privacy protection level regarding location-aware applications, respectively.

The remaining part of this paper is organized as follows. Section 2 introduces the related work and a literature review from the existing problems and solutions. We prompt the dynamic solution layer from modified SDN-based fog computing in Sect. 3. Followed by system modelling and analysis in Sect. 3. The system performance and evaluation are described in Sect. 4. Finally, we summarized and conclude this paper in Sect. 6.

2 Related Work

Fog computing brings data closer to the user instead of relying on communication with the data center [6]. One of the key benefits of fog computing is the dense geographical distribution that can be achieved by deploying fog nodes in different locations and connecting each of these nodes to end devices [20]. This geographical distribution enables more efficient communication between end users or devices and the server. The geographical distribution of the fog nodes also enables location-based mobility support for IoT devices such that traversal of the entire network is not necessary [22]. This is distinct from the situation in a cloud network, in which all data must be uploaded to the cloud side for computation and data packets must then be sent back to the end devices [12]. This delays the communication of data, especially in environments with real-time application requirements such as for the control of oil pump valves. Apart from all the beneficial location-aware features from fog computing, the leading problem appears. The protection of users' location privacy heave in sight.

According to the location-aware privacy preserving issues in fog computing, a few papers considered problem [14,22]. Approaches including k-anonymity based privacy preservation, t-Closeness and other variants. In addition, privacy-preserved pseudonym scheme proposed by J. Kang [10] has been discussed privacy issues in location based fog computing Internet vehicles. Qu et al. proposed a GAN-driven location privacy-preserving method by means of differential privacy [17,19]. Although these technologies provided well-performance results, they are more focusing on a stabilized network condition instead of dynamic and customized fog computing constrains.

SDN has been proved and widely applied on fog computing infrastructure [9, 11]. SDN is designed to solve the challenges within fog computing by decoupling data and control plane. The integration between SDN and fog computing can effectively improve the performance of the IoTs. Although the deployment of SDN with fog computing seems promising, the privacy issues can not be avoided [2].

Lyu [13] conducted deep research on the customized ϵ-differential privacy preserving methodology and successfully proven by Qu [15], Badsha [1] and Wang

[23]. These approaches have high effectiveness in social network, recommender system, and location-aware applications. They have solid theoretical foundations as well as providing high level privacy protections [21].

3   System Modelling and Analyze

In this section, we present our dynamic dual ϵ-differential privacy preserving (DDSP) scheme in SDN enabled fog computing service. This dynamic model focus on protecting location-aware privacy content occurred between users and fog nodes. We first introduce a modified control layer from SDN infrastructure, named as Dynamic Solution Layer (DSL). This new control layer aims to provide a dynamic clustering solution rely on the reality transmission. Each cluster creation is based on modified Affinity Propagation (AP) clustering method. In this approach, adversaries are not be able to determine the source of the initial connected fog node as the clusters are dynamically updated. Therefore, this clustering approach create fist privacy protection. Moreover, we present modified Laplacian Mechanism and add Laplacian Noise to increase the protection level. We use QoS mapping method to measure the distance between each cluster. Thus, the ultimate dual protection of the privacy in terms of privacy level and data utility has been created in SDN enable fog computing services.

3.1   Dynamic Solution Layer

In this section, we present the proposed innovative architecture that integrates the fog computing environment with SDN. As shown in Fig. 1, two main physical device component layers are proposed in our architecture: the control layer and the infrastructure layer.

In our proposed reference model, programmability is proposed to analyze the location information and user data to determine the quantity of fog nodes involved. Furthermore, in the clustering condition, two or more fog nodes are assigned to perform location aware analyze as well as providing fuzzification towards adversaries attack. Clustering method is a virtualized network based on geographically distributed fog nodes. In reality, all fog nodes are still physically located at their original locations, but nm virtually, they are clustered via SDN to improve their location fuzzification. For example, adversary aims to attack a user. In traditional methodology, user connect with the closest or best signal fog node. However, adversary will easily determine the exact location. Instead, when user first create transmission with fog computing network, they connect to the clustered fog nodes which contains two or more available. Adversary only be able to determine the clustered fog nodes instead of locating the exact fog node to obtain the true location information.

DSL also provide a dynamic feedback solution for end users to improve the protection level of privacy. All clustering updates and reunited with different fog nodes operate in this layer. In other word, the cluster for our proposed model is dynamic. Reunited and updates will be defined when connection capacity reach limitation. Each fog nodes has theoretic limitation, DSL also be responsible for QoS data utility measurement.

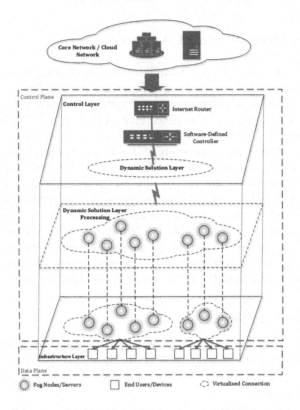

Fig. 1. Overview of the dynamic solution layer within SDN based fog computing.

3.2 Virtualized Fog Node Clustering

Virtualized clustering is our first scheme in terms of privacy preserving in our proposed model. First of all, we formulate the fog node location of Fog Computing as a clustering problem with multi constraints. The vitalization for the clustering organiszed by SDN controller demonstrates in Fig. 2.

Entropy Weight Method Based Cluster Triggering. The basic idea of the EWM is to determine objective weights based on the variability of certain indicators. In our scenario, the EWM is applied to calculate the weight of each element in each dimension. Generally, a smaller elemental entropy e^j indicates that an element is more meaningful, providing more information and related to more data in the fog network environment, and thus should be assigned a greater weight in the associated dimension. On the other hand, a larger entropy e^j indicates that an

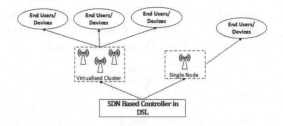

Fig. 2. Vitualized fog clustering by SDN controller.

element is of smaller value, provides less information, and plays a smaller role in the overall evaluation, and thus, it should have a smaller weight.

Unification Process and Weight Factors. For the overall network environment, the SDN controller collects and stores all fog node location identification numbers and specifications. Based on the historical data collected ahead of time, the SDN controller places all elements and factors into a matrix F, where the elements $F = F_1^1, F_2^1, F_3^1, F_\beta^1$ represent different factors of the same fog node and the elements $F = F_1^1, F_1^2, F_1^3, F_1^\alpha$ represent the same factor for different fog nodes.

$$F = \begin{bmatrix} F_1^1 & F_2^1 & F_3^1 & \dots & F_\beta^1 \\ F_1^2 & F_2^2 & F_3^2 & \dots & F_\beta^2 \\ \dots\dots\dots \\ F_1^\alpha & F_2^\alpha & F_3^\alpha & \dots & F_\beta^\alpha \end{bmatrix} \tag{1}$$

Since all factors have different indices, a unification process is required before the aggregate indicator can be calculated. More specifically, the absolute values must be converted to relative values to solve the problem of different absolute values for different indices. The matrix F after the unification process is denoted by F'.

$$F' = \begin{bmatrix} \frac{F_1^1}{\sum_{i=1}^\alpha F_1^i} & \frac{F_2^1}{\sum_{i=1}^\alpha F_2^i} & \frac{F_3^1}{\sum_{i=1}^\alpha F_3^i} & \cdots & \frac{F_\beta^1}{\sum_{i=1}^\alpha F_\beta^i} \\ \frac{F_1^2}{\sum_{i=1}^\alpha F_1^i} & \frac{F_2^2}{\sum_{i=1}^\alpha F_2^i} & \frac{F_3^2}{\sum_{i=1}^\alpha F_3^i} & \cdots & \frac{F_\beta^2}{\sum_{i=1}^\alpha F_\beta^i} \\ \dots\dots\dots\dots\dots\dots \\ \frac{F_1^\alpha}{\sum_{i=1}^\alpha F_1^i} & \frac{F_2^\alpha}{\sum_{i=1}^\alpha F_2^i} & \frac{F_3^\alpha}{\sum_{i=1}^\alpha F_3^i} & \cdots & \frac{F_\beta^\alpha}{\sum_{i=1}^\alpha F_\beta^i} \end{bmatrix} \tag{2}$$

Since the unification process has been applied, the weight factor must be calculated for each factor j in each dimension i, where $i = 1, 2, ..., n$ and $j = 1, 2, ..., m$.

$$p_{ij} = \frac{F'_{ij}}{\sum_{i=1}^n x_{ij}} \tag{3}$$

Once the weight factors have been calculated, the entropy value of each factor j must be calculated, where $j = 1, 2, ..., m$. Here, $k = 1/\ln(n) > 0$ and $e_j >= 0$.

$$e_j = -k \sum_{i=1}^n p_{ij} \ln p_{ij} \tag{4}$$

A redundancy rate is calculated to reduce the deviation during this process. For $j = 1, 2, ..., m$, the redundancy rate will be $d_j = 1 - e_j$. The weight factors after the redundancy correction are calculated as follows:

$$w_j = \frac{d_j}{\sum_{j=1}^{m} d_j} \tag{5}$$

Cluster Triggering Process. Since the weight factors for each element in each dimension have been determined, the clustering process is performed based on these weight factors. Suppose that t_{trig} is the threshold level for triggering clustering and depends on the environment of the fog network and that T_{trig} is the result of the triggering process and depends on each element and its calculated weight factor. The clustering result depends on the fog node factor that is associated with the maximum value.

$$T_{trig}^1 = \frac{F_1^1}{\sum_{i=1}^{\alpha} F_1^i} \times t_{trig}$$

$$T_{trig}^2 = \frac{F_2^1}{\sum_{i=1}^{\alpha} F_2^i} \times t_{trig}$$

$$\cdots$$

$$T_{trig}^{\beta} = \frac{F_{\beta}^1}{\sum_{i=1}^{\alpha} F_{\beta}^i} \times t_{trig}$$

$$T_{trig} = max(T_{trig}^1, T_{trig}^2, ..., T_{trig}^{\beta}) \tag{6}$$

3.3 Affinity Propagation Based Clustering

Affinity propagation (AP) is a semi-supervised clustering algorithm based on nearest neighbor propagation that was proposed by [5]. Unlike in other clustering methods, in AP, it is not necessary to specify the final number of clusters. The cluster centers are selected from among the existing location data points instead of being generated as new data points. The model of the AP clustering method is less sensitive to the initial input location data and does not require the data similarity matrix to be symmetric. In a fog network, the input data can be of different types due to the different selections made by our triggering process based on the weight factors. Therefore, the AP algorithm is most suitable for clustering the fog nodes.

Preference. The clustering center similarity, $sim(i, k)$, represents the similarity between data point i and data point k. This similarity is calculated using the Euclidean distance:

$$sim(i, k) = \sqrt{\sum_{r=1}^{n} (i - k)^2 \times T_{trig}} \tag{7}$$

Responsibility. In the responsibility matrix, $r(i, k)$ denotes the extent to which data point k is suitable for being designated as the cluster center for data point i and represents a message sent from i to k, where $k \in 1, 2, ..., N$ and $k \neq k'$.

$$r(i, k) = (s(i, j) - max \{a(i, k') + sim(i, k')\}) \times T_{trig} \qquad (8)$$

In the above equation, $a(i, k)$ is a value representing the availability of point i to a point other than k, and its initial value is 0. $s(i, k)$ denotes the responsibility of points other than k to point i, where points outside of i are competing for the ownership of i. $r(i, k)$ denotes the cumulative responsibility of k to become the cluster center for i. When $r(i, k) > 0$, this indicates a greater responsibility of k to become the cluster center.

Availability. The availability $a(i, k)$ denotes the likelihood that data point i will select data point k as its cluster center and represents a message sent from k to i.

$$a(i, k) = min \left\{ 0, r(k, k) + \sum_{k} \{max(0, r(i', k))\} \right\} \times T_{trig} \qquad (9)$$

$$a(k, k) = (\sum_{k} \{max(0, r(i', k))\}) \times T_{trig} \qquad (10)$$

Here, $r(i', k)$ denotes the responsibility value of point k as the cluster center for points other than i; all responsibility values that are greater than or equal to 0 are summed, and we also add the responsibility value of k as its own cluster center. Specifically, point k is supported by all data points with corresponding responsibility values greater than 0, and data point i selects k based on its cumulative value as a cluster center.

Damping Factor λ. As the algorithm iteratively updates the values of availability and responsibility, a damping factor is applied. The effect of this factor λ is to enable the AP algorithm to converge more efficiently. The damping factor takes on values between 0 and 1. During each iteration of the algorithm, λ acts on the responsibility and availability values to weight the update relative to the previous iteration.

$$r_n = (1 - \lambda) \times r_n + \lambda \times r_{n-1} \qquad (11)$$

$$a_n = (1 - \lambda) \times a_n + \lambda \times a_{n-1} \qquad (12)$$

3.4   Laplacian Mechanism and Laplacian Noise

We probabilistic the original single clustering query results to protect location privacy. In order to protect users' location-aware content privacy, we use Laplacian mechanism to change the real value by adding Laplacian noise to the original clustering result data, so that the differential privacy is satisfied before and after adding noise.

$$M(D) = f(D) + Y$$

s.t.

$$Lap(\alpha) = \frac{p_x(z)}{p_y(z)} = exp(\frac{\epsilon \cdot \| f(x) - f(y) \|}{\Delta f}) \tag{13}$$

where ϵ defines privacy budget, ϵ can be customized due to the clustering requirement in order to achieve better privacy budget result. Y determines Laplacian
distributed noise. $Lap(\alpha)$ defines the probability density of the mechanism while
α decides the size of the noise.

3.5   QoS Data Utility Mapping

In the DDSDP model, we have defined the distance between each cluster
$sim(i, k)$ in early paragraph, we use Softmax function to model QoS data utility
function and privacy protection level ϵ. The softmax function assigns decimal
probabilities to each class in a multiclass problem. It is also widely used to mapping the data utility and privacy protection level according to the QoS. The
mapping function illustrated as

$$QoS(\epsilon_i) = k \times \frac{\exp(\theta_i^t sim_{ik} \cdot x)}{\sum_{k=1}^{K} \exp(\theta_k^t sim_{ik} \cdot x)} \tag{14}$$

where $k \in K$ and defined as the parameter to adjust the maximum amplitude
value, θ is determined the steepness of the curve and x denotes the location.

3.6   Dynamic Dual Scheme Differential Privacy

In fog computing, each user publishes their sensitive location data upon the
connection created. However, these location information needs privacy protection
before been published. We have created first scheme to increase the difficulty level
when adversary aims to attack. Furthermore, our second scheme aims to provide
ultimate privacy protection to the users. We use ϵ-Customizable Differential
Privacy to obtain our goal. We formulated the mechanism when $M \to \Delta(\chi)$ is
considered to be ϵ-differentially privacy as

$$Pr[M(D) \in \Omega] = \exp(QoS(\epsilon_i)) \cdot Pr[M(D') \in \Omega]$$

$$= \exp(k \times \frac{\exp(\theta_i^t sim_{ik} \cdot x)}{\sum_{k=1}^{K} \exp(\theta_k^t sim_{ik} \cdot x)}) \cdot Pr[M(D') \in \Omega] \tag{15}$$

s.t.

$$\forall \Omega \subseteq \chi,$$

$$\forall (D, D') \subseteq \psi,$$

where χ denotes noisy outcome and D defines the space of the sensitive location
data, where $\epsilon \geq 0$, and $\psi \subseteq \forall (D, D') \subseteq \psi$ denotes proximal relation between the
data.

4   Performance Evaluation

In this section, we run a series of simulations to testify the performance of our proposed DDSDP model in serval ways. First, we evaluate the data utilities by sampling time slot with different location; then, we evaluate privacy protection level with different time slot by different locations. Third part of the experiment would evaluate the performance of the clustering approach including clustering results, transmission results, clustering distance, and loading performance for the overall fog nodes. In order to verify these results, we use latest version of the "VicFreeWiFi Access Point Locations" dataset, which contains 571 raw data of location information. This dataset is available in serval locations across 300 kms and it allows 250 MB per devices, per day. Within the dataset, it contains detailed location information for the access points, including 391 nodes recorded in city center, 44 nodes in northbound area, and 82 nodes west-northbound area. These location information leads the location-aware issues for adversaries to determine the users.

In the following experiments, we compare our model with different ϵ value in order to obtain the best performance and customization of the ϵ-differential privacy protection scheme. Moreover, we also evaluate the performance of the clustering efficiency as SDN-enabled fog computing should contains more customizations features without effect original performance. Respectively, the SDN enabled clustering results demonstrates better network performance.

4.1   Data Utilities Performance

Figure 3 shows the results of the data utilities according to our DDSDP model. This figure demonstrate the general trends of the QoS functionality. We selected three customized representative parameter values for the ϵ, which when $\epsilon = 1$, $\epsilon = 0.5$, and $\epsilon = 0.1$, by comparing with raw data value to observe our results, which makes it applicable to various scenarios. We start with clustering algorithm to choose 20 available clustered fog network, these clustered network based on QoS measurement from the clustering distances. Laplacian mechanism is responsible to generate noisy responses. As shown in the figure, smaller ϵ values leads better overall data utility performance value. For the particular dataset scenarios, when ϵ value equals to 0.1, we have achieve the peak value which is 1.7 with clustering time slot 5.

4.2   Privacy Protection Level Evaluation

We consider different clustering situations in terms of the performance for privacy protection level. In the initialization stage, we enabled three representative parameter value same with data utilities evaluation to setup the customized ϵ. The reason to choose three ϵ value aim to simulate the randomness of Laplacian mechanism which leads to different noisy responses. As shown in Fig. 4, privacy protection level comparison in term of customizable ϵ is based on cluster distance. Sampling time slot 7 with one of the cluster reach the maximum privacy

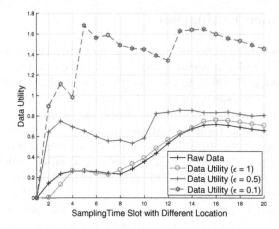

Fig. 3. Data utilities performance among three ϵ values.

protection level as 1.5, as well as the cluster in time slot 20 remain to the highest value along with other three values. Although the performance for three parameters retains different results from different cluster, it justifies the outstanding importance of the customization. For example, for time slot 4's cluster, we should select customized the ϵ value to 1, respectively.

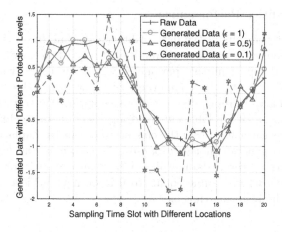

Fig. 4. Privacy levels with different locations.

4.3   Clustering Efficiency Performance

Figure 5 shows the node clustering results generated via the AP clustering method in the DSL. In these results, the estimated number of clusters is 16, and these clusters are formed from 517 available fog nodes. We tested three similarity values to evaluate the system performance. Among the results, the minimum similarity is $2.000000e^{-8}$, and the median and maximum similarity values are 0.017874 and 1.276488, respectively. The similarity is based on the longitudinal and latitudinal locations along with the connection speed. The homogeneity rate is 0.513, which indicates the extent to which nodes with the same properties are clustered. In this particular dataset, the rate is based predominantly on the connection speed. The completeness and V-measure results are 0.133 and 0.211, respectively, and the adjusted Rand index is 0.080. The clustering results were generated by the DSL system and show good performance.

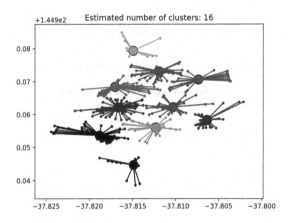

Fig. 5. Efficiently clustered results.

One of the key factors in testing the performance of the clustered network is the file transmission speed. As seen from our simulations, the standard fog network is better able to handle a small amount of data. However, as the file size grows, the performance of the resource-sharing clustered network becomes superior to that of the standard network, as shown in Fig. 6. In both simulations, the dataset was run from the same starting level of zero. As the file transmission time increases with increasing file size, the two systems perform almost the same in the range of 4000 MB to 5000 MB. However, when the file size is over 5000 MB, the speed gap becomes increasingly larger with increasing file size. This is because of the power of sharing computing capacities among the nodes, which enables the borrowing of other nodes to help with computations.

In Fig. 6, we conducted file loading times for videos downloaded from 200 different fog nodes, where the upper line is the video loading time in the clustered fog environment and the lower line is the result without clustering. Therefor, there are large time fluctuations in the non-clustered environment as the end device keeps trying to find a node that is available for downloading. By contrast, the upper line shows a significantly more stable loading time, reflecting an improved user experience.

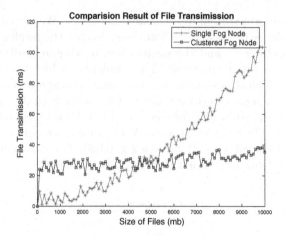

Fig. 6. Comparison of file transmission results.

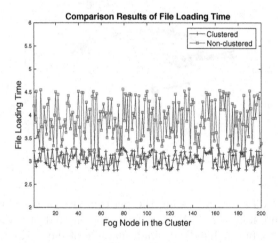

Fig. 7. Comparison of file loading time.

In conclusion, the proposed DDSDP model shows high quality dual scheme privacy protection level in terms of data utility and privacy protection level (Fig. 7).

References

1. Badsha, S., et al.: Privacy preserving location-aware personalized web service recommendations. IEEE Trans. Serv. Comput. 1 (2018). https://doi.org/10.1109/TSC.2018.2839587
2. Baktir, A.C., Ozgovde, A., Ersoy, C.: How can edge computing benefit from software-defined networking: a survey, use cases, and future directions. IEEE Commun. Surv. Tutor. **19**(4), 2359–2391 (2017). https://doi.org/10.1109/COMST.2017.2717482

3. Bonomi, F., Milito, R., Natarajan, P., Zhu, J.: Fog computing: a platform for internet of things and analytics. In: Bessis, N., Dobre, C. (eds.) Big Data and Internet of Things: A Roadmap for Smart Environments. SCI, vol. 546, pp. 169–186. Springer, Cham (2014). https://doi.org/10.1007/978-3-319-05029-4_7
4. Bonomi, F., Milito, R., Zhu, J., Addepalli, S.: Fog computing and its role in the internet of things. In: Proceedings of the First Edition of the MCC Workshop on Mobile Cloud Computing, MCC 2012, New York, NY, USA, pp. 13–16. ACM (2012). https://doi.org/10.1145/2342509.2342513. http://doi.acm.org/10.1145/2342509.2342513
5. Frey, B.J., Dueck, D.: Clustering by passing messages between data points. Science **315**(5814), 972–976 (2007). https://doi.org/10.1126/science.1136800. http://science.sciencemag.org/content/315/5814/972
6. Gao, L., Luan, T.H., Yu, S., Zhou, W., Liu, B.: FogRoute: DTN-based data dissemination model in fog computing. IEEE Internet of Things J. **4**(1), 225–235 (2017)
7. Gu, B., Wang, X., Qu, Y., Jin, J., Xiang, Y., Gao, L.: Context-aware privacy preservation in a hierarchical fog computing system. In: ICC 2019–2019 IEEE International Conference on Communications (ICC), pp. 1–6. IEEE (2019)
8. Gu, B.S., Gao, L., Wang, X., Qu, Y., Jin, J., Yu, S.: Privacy on the edge: Customizable privacy-preserving context sharing in hierarchical edge computing. IEEE Trans. Netw. Sci. Eng. (2019)
9. Kadhim, A.J., Hosseini Seno, S.A.: Maximizing the utilization of fog computing in internet of vehicle using SDN. IEEE Commun. Lett. **23**(1), 140–143 (2019)
10. Kang, J., Yu, R., Huang, X., Zhang, Y.: Privacy-preserved pseudonym scheme for fog computing supported internet of vehicles. IEEE Trans. Intell. Transp. Syst. **19**(8), 2627–2637 (2018)
11. Li, C., Qin, Z., Novak, E., Li, Q.: Securing SDN infrastructure of IoT? Fog networks from MITM attacks. IEEE Internet of Things J. **4**(5), 1156–1164 (2017)
12. Luan, T.H., Gao, L., Li, Z., Xiang, Y., Sun, L.: Fog computing: focusing on mobile users at the edge. CoRR abs/1502.01815 (2015). http://arxiv.org/abs/1502.01815
13. Lyu, L., Nandakumar, K., Rubinstein, B., Jin, J., Bedo, J., Palaniswami, M.: PPFA: privacy preserving fog-enabled aggregation in smart grid. IEEE Trans. Ind. Inf. **14**(8), 3733–3744 (2018). https://doi.org/10.1109/TII.2018.2803782
14. Ma, L., Liu, X., Pei, Q., Xiang, Y.: Privacy-preserving reputation management for edge computing enhanced mobile crowdsensing. IEEE Trans. Serv. Comput. 1 (2018). https://doi.org/10.1109/TSC.2018.2825986
15. Qu, Y., Yu, S., Gao, L., Zhou, W., Peng, S.: A hybrid privacy protection scheme in cyber-physical social networks. IEEE Trans. Comput. Soc. Syst. **5**(3), 773–784 (2018). https://doi.org/10.1109/TCSS.2018.2861775
16. Qu, Y., et al.: Decentralized privacy using blockchain-enabled federated learning in fog computing. IEEE Internet of Things J. (2020)
17. Qu, Y., Yu, S., Zhang, J., Binh, H.T.T., Gao, L., Zhou, W.: GAN-DP: generative adversarial net driven differentially privacy-preserving big data publishing. In: ICC 2019–2019 IEEE International Conference on Communications (ICC), pp. 1–6. IEEE (2019)
18. Qu, Y., Yu, S., Zhou, W., Peng, S., Wang, G., Xiao, K.: Privacy of things: emerging challenges and opportunities in wireless internet of things. IEEE Wireless Commun. **25**(6), 91–97 (2018). https://doi.org/10.1109/MWC.2017.1800112
19. Qu, Y., Yu, S., Zhou, W., Tian, Y.: GAN-driven personalized spatial-temporal private data sharing in cyber-physical social systems. IEEE Trans. Netw. Sci. Eng. (2020)

20. Stojmenovic, I., Wen, S.: The fog computing paradigm: scenarios and security issues. In: 2014 Federated Conference on Computer Science and Information Systems, pp. 1–8, September 2014. https://doi.org/10.15439/2014F503
21. Wang, Q., Chen, D., Zhang, N., Ding, Z., Qin, Z.: PCP: a privacy-preserving content-based publish? Subscribe scheme with differential privacy in fog computing. IEEE Access **5**, 17962–17974 (2017). https://doi.org/10.1109/ACCESS.2017.2748956
22. Wang, T., Zhou, J., Chen, X., Wang, G., Liu, A., Liu, Y.: A three-layer privacy preserving cloud storage scheme based on computational intelligence in fog computing. IEEE Trans. Emerg. Topics Comput. Intell. **2**(1), 3–12 (2018). https://doi.org/10.1109/TETCI.2017.2764109
23. Wang, W., Zhang, Q.: Privacy preservation for context sensing on smartphone. IEEE/ACM Trans. Netw. **24**(6), 3235–3247 (2016). https://doi.org/10.1109/TNET.2015.2512301
24. Yi, S., Hao, Z., Qin, Z., Li, Q.: Fog computing: platform and applications. In: 2015 Third IEEE Workshop on Hot Topics in Web Systems and Technologies (HotWeb), pp. 73–78, November 2015. https://doi.org/10.1109/HotWeb.2015.22
25. Qu, Y., Zhang, J., Li, R., Zhang, X., Zhai, X., Yu , S.: Generative adversarial networks enhanced location privacy in 5G networks. Sci. China Inf. Sci. (2020)

PLFG: A Privacy Attack Method Based on Gradients for Federated Learning

Feng Wu$^{(\boxtimes)}$

Yunnan University, Kunming, China
gzwf@mail.ynu.edu.com

Abstract. Privacy of machine learning becomes increasingly crucial, abundant emerging technologies have been spawned to solve privacy problem and federated learning (FL) is one of them. FL can replace data transmission through transmission gradient to prevent the leakage of data privacy. Recent researches indicated that privacy can be revealed through gradients and a little auxiliary information. To further verify the safety of gradient transmission mechanism, we propose a novel method called Privacy-leaks From Gradients (PLFG) to infer sensitive information through gradients only. To our knowledge, the weak assumption of this level is currently unique. PLFG uses the gradients obtained from victims in each iteration to build a special model, then updates initial noise through the model to fit victims' privacy data. Experimental results demonstrate that even if only gradients are leveraged, users' privacy can be disclosed, and current popular defense (gradient noise addition and gradient compression) cannot defend effectively. Furthermore, we discuss the limitations and feasible improvements of PLFG. We hope our attack can provide different ideas for future defense attempts to protect sensitive privacy.

Keywords: Federated learning · Privacy leakage · Gradients · Model

1 Introduction

Federated learning has been used in various applications and achieved excellent results, such as bank joint anti-money laundering modeling, credit risk control modeling. The radical reason why it could achieve such a merit is that it could solve the problem of data island and privacy leakage in machine learning [12,22]. In a quintessential FL system, the participants did not need to upload their private data but model parameters [8,10] or gradients [17] with the central server. This structure of FL protects the participants' privacy being leaked, hence it was considered a safe practice to exchange gradients.

Regrettably, recent studies substantiated that the gradient sharing mechanism might not be as safe as imagined. Privacy can also be leaked through the gradient [13]. This makes us reflect on "whether gradient exchange is safe?". Previous works have proposed numerous attack methods to reveal the private data

© Springer Nature Singapore Pte Ltd. 2020
S. Yu et al. (Eds.): SPDE 2020, CCIS 1268, pp. 191–204, 2020.
https://doi.org/10.1007/978-981-15-9129-7_14

[7,13,27]. These methods have one thing in common: they all need to know a few auxiliary information beyond the gradient to make inferences about privacy [2,7,13]. Here we consider a more challenging situation: only based on the gradient information to infer the victim's private data. Formally, clients delivered the gradient information ΔW of each iteration, can we restore the data information in the training set? In the past, the answer was impossible. In this article, we demonstrated that this is feasible.

This article proposed a method named PLFG to infer user privacy based solely on gradients. PLFG can infer the privacy of the victim through the gradient in each iteration with high confidence. In the whole process of inference, all participants are training normally, and the adversary does not need to get any additional information about target data set, so that PLFG will be more stealthy. Since less information is required to attack, PLFG is more challenging and realistic.

In summary, PLFG has two distinct benefits. (1) The adversary do not need any additional means to spy on any information regarding the training set makes the attack extremely simple and fast, and the risk of participants' privacy being leaked will be higher. (2) In a real scenario, it is tough for an adversary to realize any information concerning the training set, consequently PLFG is more in line with attack scenarios in the real world.

The main contributions of this study are summarized as follows:

(1) We proposed an inference attack method called PLFG to carry out privacy leakage attacks in FL tasks. Compared with previous work, PLFG requires fewer requirements when attacking, and it can also leak users' privacy data.
(2) We found a feasible range of initial noise required for the attack and conducted a theoretical analysis. Utilizing the traditional initial noise range can not get the users' privacy very well.
(3) We verified that gradient noise and gradient compression are not effective for our attack. Unlike numerous previous work gradient-based attacks, these defense methods cannot against PLFG effectively.

The rest of this paper is organized as follows. Related work is briefly listed in Sect. 2. We presented the attack means for leakage privacy in Sect. 3. Experiments were conducted to verify our approach in Sect. 4, and followed by a defense strategies discussion in Sect. 5. Finally, we summarized the paper and present future work in Sect. 6.

2   Related Work

To expand the training set to obtain a more utility model, data providers need to collaborate to "share" the data and collaboratively train the model. "Sharing" does not directly disclose data to other participants, on the contrary, each participant independently training its model on own data, then shares training results (e.g. gradients) with others, thereby protects the training data. Although this training mechanism seems safe, the model will unconsciously record certain data that involve participants' privacy, such as image texture, feature map, correlation et al., which makes the model vulnerable to dishonest participants, so that the private data of victims are stolen maliciously.

Previous researches [2,7,13] used generative adversarial networks (GAN) [5] to attack the collaborative distributed training. Any user participating in the training may become an adversary, generating infinite approximations with other participants' training data to steal the privacy of others. Furthermore, the study in [13] indicated that when process language tasks, only the words that appear in the training set will generate gradients in the embedded layer of the model, which leads to the risk of leakage of data information of other participants.

Above methods all infer privacy in the training stage. Whereas, in the prediction stage, the training data (part or all) or the statistical characteristics of the training data can also be extracted through a reverse attack. In 2014, Fredrikson et al. [4] combined the demographic information of patients in the task of drug dose prediction to restore the genomic information of patients. In 2015, Fredrikson et al. [3] reconstructed the face image data used in model training by observing the prediction results of the target model. Ateniese et al. [1] analyzed the model to determine whether its training data met specific statistical characteristics. In 2017, Shokri et al. [18] proposed membership inference attack, given a record to determine whether it is in the training set.

The most pioneering work is to infer pictures pixel-wise or infer text token-wise only through gradients [27]. Yet, this method is limited by the fact that it must know the gradient value calculated from the model for a single sample or the number of samples in the training set. In general, this is arduous to achieve in a real scenario.

These works are excellent, meanwhile, they all have one thing in common: the ability or knowledge of the adversary frequently exceeds the actual situation. The reality is that they are usually unable to manipulate the training set on a large scale and do not figure out the data information of the target commonly.

3   Privacy-Leaks from Gradients (PLFG)

3.1   Privacy Leakage Model

As exhibited in Fig. 1, both the normal participant and the victim are performing training tasks ordinarily, meanwhile, the server S isolates the victim (the victim does not know). After several iterations of training, S will obtain a model from the gradient uploaded by the victim. As a general rule, there is a high probability that this model will overfit (on the victim dataset). Note that in a quintessential FL system, the amount of training data of each participant is few. Hence the assumption of overfitting in this paper is entirely consistent with the real scenario. Overfitting models often contain a large amount of data information regarding the training set [6]. Our goal is to find out the private data in the training set based on the overfitting characteristics.   We demonstrated that it was feasible to steal data privacy through gradients only in FL. Our target is a

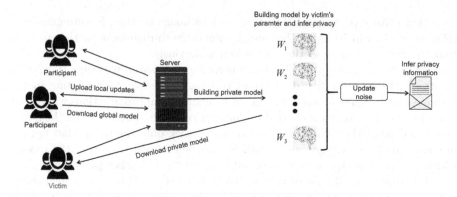

Fig. 1. Overview of attack: the parameter server needs to isolate a specific participant for training, and use the parameters\gradients uploaded by it to build a model F wholly trained by the victim. Noise is fed into model F, using traditional forward and backpropagation algorithms to update the noise instead of model parameters. In the end, the adversary can fit a sample similar to the private data. Obviously, the whole process does not need other information besides gradients.

FL system: at each iteration, each participant will be trained with their training data to calculate the gradient corresponding to their data as formula 1:

$$\nabla W_{t,i} = \frac{\partial \ell \left(F \left(\mathbf{x}_{t,i}, W_t \right), \mathbf{y}_{t,i} \right)}{\partial W_t} \tag{1}$$

After calculating the gradients, each participant will transfer them to the central server through the network. After receiving the gradients, the server calculates the corresponding global model according to the parameters\gradients (see 2). Repeat this process until the model converges, and then the training of federated learning is finished.

$$\nabla W_t = \sum_{j}^{C} \nabla W_{t,j}; \quad W_{t+1} = W_t - \eta \nabla W_t \tag{2}$$

Each iteration will produce a different set of gradients, and each of them represents the model in different periods. Our goal is to fit the corresponding training data through these models obtained by the gradients.

3.2   Model Design

Using the attack scheme 3.2, the adversary attempts training the victim individually to obtain the model trained by "specific data". Once the entire federated learning process is finished, the adversary will send the standard global model to the victim for two cardinal reasons: (1) destroying the efficiency of victim's model is not the target of the adversary; (2) the rewarding correct feedback to the victim can increase the concealment of the attack.

Theoretically, the loss obtained by feeding the training data to the overfitted model is 0. The addition of epsilon to loss function is to enhance the robustness of the algorithm (the loss of a small part of training data on the overfitting model is not necessarily 0).

Algorithm 1. Privacy leaks in federated learning

Input: $\mathcal{X}_{fake}$: The initial value is used to fit the original sample;
        W_i^v: The gradients of the victim in i-th round of training;
        $\mathcal{E}$: A constant with a value of (0,1);
Output: x_{fake}^*
1: **for** $i = 1$ to n **do**
2:     $W_i^v = W_{i-1}^v - \eta \Delta W_i^v$
3:     W_i^v add in W_{list}
4:     **if** $i = n$ **then**
5:         $W_{final}^v = W_i^v$
6:         $W_i^v = W_i^{globle}$
7: $x_{fake} = \text{trunc\_N}(0.01, 0.015)$
8: **for** W in W_{list} **do**
9:     **for** $i = 1$ to n **do**
10:         $loss_i = L\left(F\left(W, x_{fake,i}\right), y\right)$
11:         $D_{loss} = \|loss_i - \varepsilon\|^2$
12:         $\Delta W_i = \partial D_{loss}/\partial x_{fake,i}$
13:         $x_{fake,i+1} = x_{fake,i} - \mu \Delta W_i$
14:         **if** $i = n$ **then**
15:             $x_{fake,i+1}$ add in X_{fake}
16: Choose the best result x_{fake}^* in set X
17: **return** x_{fake}^*

3.3 Privacy Leaked by Model

To fit training data through the model, we need to randomly initialize an input x_{fake}, and feed it into the model. Then we will get a set of outputs, and minimize the distance between the output and the real output (see formula 3).

$$loss^\sim = L\left\{F\left(W_i, x_{fake}\right), y\right\} \tag{3}$$

where y is not a standard label value, a sea of cases it is more likely to be a set of one-hot encoding. Thus, the adversary does not need to know the exact label. Optimize x_{fake} to make $loss^\sim$ as minute as possible. At present, due to the particularity of the model, x_{fake} will be closer to the training data to a certain extent. The optimization process is as formula 4:

$$x_{fake}^* = \underset{x_{fake}}{\arg\min} \|loss^\sim - \varepsilon\|^2 = \underset{x_{fake}}{\arg\min} \|L\left\{F\left(W_i^v, x_{fake}\right) - y\right\} - \varepsilon\|^2 \tag{4}$$

The distance $\|loss^\sim - \varepsilon\|^2$ is differentiable w.r.t fake inputs x_{fake}, thus can be optimized using standard gradient-based methods.

4   Performance Evaluation

4.1   Experimental Setup

All experiments are performed on Windows10 and NVIDIA RTX2060 graphics cards, and the experimental platform is TensorFlow2.1. We conducted experiments using the fashion_mnist [21], mnist, and cifar10 datasets. We leveraged the Adam optimizer [27] for optimization with learning rate of 0.002, $\beta1$ of 0.5 and $\beta2$ of 0.999. More experimental details are described in the next section.

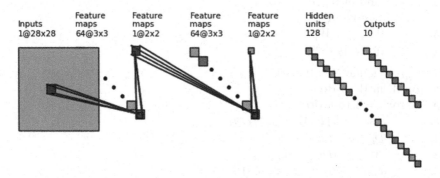

Fig. 2. Convolutional neural network structure used in the experiment. It includes two 64×3×3 convolutional layers, two 1×2×2 pooling layers and two fully connected layers.

4.2   Dataset

We used three different data sets to verify PLFG, and analyzed the results to judge its effect. The data sets used are:

mnist: It is a 28 28 grayscale image. Contains handwritten digits 0 to 9, which contains 60000 training samples and 10000 test samples.

Fashion_mnist: The dataset has all the external features of mnist [21]. It consists of 60,000 training data records and 10,000 records serving as test data. It consists of clothes images of digits ranging from 0 to 9.

Cifar10: CIFAR-10 is a colour image data set closer to pervasive objects. There are a total of 10 categories of RGB colour pictures, and the size of each picture is 32 32 3.

Since the pixel of all pictures are in the range of [0,255], to experiment better, we need to scale the pixel of each picture to the range of [0,1]. Because the goal is to train a classifier, we consider using softmax as the output layer. To more closely approximate the real scenario, the pictures in this article leverage colour pictures instead of grayscale images, therefore all data sets are not processed in grayscale.

4.3 Privacy Leaked

To more realistically simulate a typical federated learning scenario (the training set is small), we set the training set to 20 and include all type of labels. The model structure is manifested in Fig. 2.

We set the activation function of the output layer to softmax, accordingly the final output of the model is a set of probability distributions. The data leaked through the gradient is shown in Fig. 3. The leaked results may not seem satisfactory, but for the adversary, the latent space distribution of the source data has been revealed. Using the correct latent space will enhance GAN-based attacks and further leak privacy.

| Initial | M_1 | M_2 | M_3 | M_4 | M_5 | Original |

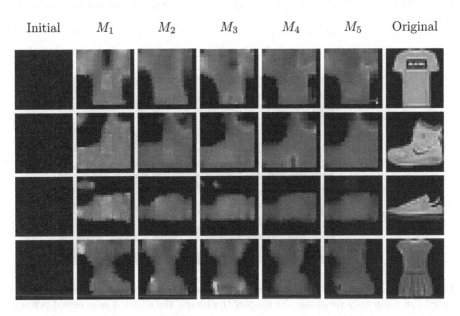

Fig. 3. Privacy leaked from gradients. Even if the restoration result is different from the original image, it is enough to infer a part of private information.

We originally planned to leverage standard normal distribution to generate a noise image for fitting. However, the image obtained after model optimization is indistinguishable for the naked eye. The results are shown in Fig. 4. Where M_i represents the model generated at a training stage i. There is a fascinating rule been found: PLFG(Privacy-leaks from Gradients) seems to prefer to leverage a specific monotonous color to infer the data, hence the private data of the original training set cannot be completely restored. Still, by inferring the outline, the adversary can effortlessly comprehend numerous crucial information of the original data (such as label, approximate style, etc.) based on his knowledge. This is fatal for participants who are unwilling to disclose any privacy.

It can be seen from the final result that when inferring user privacy data directly through gradients, even if the data obtained by the adversary is not perfect, the data may be sufficient for leaking privacy. The adversary may also make further attacks based on this inferred result, which the participants do not desire to see.

Initial M_1 M_2 M_3 M_4 M_5 Original

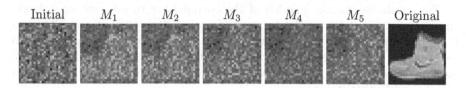

Fig. 4. The image obtained by fitting using the standard normal distribution as the initial value

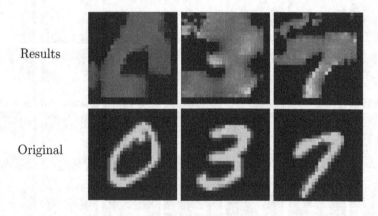

Fig. 5. Leakage results of handwritten digits. The leaked information is visible to the naked eye. Generally speaking, the simpler the image, the easier it is to reveal privacy.

Through analysis, we believed that the most possible reason is that owing to the non-centralized distribution of noise pixels, the optimal solution elements obtained by the loss function are not "centralized", hence the features of the image cannot be restored correctly. Therefore, we exploit the truncated normal distribution to make the generated random pixels located in the range [0.01, 0.015] to make them as concentrated as possible, to ensure that the obtained features are more concentrated, and are more able to restore the original features of training data.

Besides, we also performed experiments on mnist; the results are exhibited in Fig. 5. It is found that the restoration effect on mnist is better than fashion_mnist. Apart from the contours, numerous details have been restored, and the appearance of the data set can be easily determined with the naked eye even the adversary without any prior knowledge. The most likely reason is that the features of handwritten digits are much simpler than clothing [21], the fewer features the model abstracts from, the easier it is to recover.

In addition, we also found a fascinating phenomenon, as shown in Fig. 6. It is effortless to discover that the fitting effect does not get better as the model loses less on the training set. On the contrary, when the model loss is extremely minuscule, reaching 0.001, the fitting effect is not as pleasurable as the loss at 0.1. The reason for this is that the model training is a process of continually extracting and processing data features. In this case, when the model is exceedingly overfitting, the features extracted from the picture are already acutely abstract. The model can leverage these highly abstract features to generalize and improve its robustness on unknown data sets. Therefore, it is arduous for adversary to restore the image with these highly abstract features. We believe that the work of Andrew et al. [9] can explain this phenomenon to a certain extent.

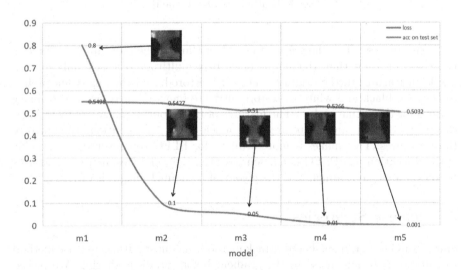

Fig. 6. Visualization of privacy leakage history. In the beginning, as the degree of fitting of the model is higher, the privacy leakage becomes more serious, but when the degree of fitting reaches certain threshold, the efficiency of leakage will decrease.

4.4 Limitations of PLFG

On fashion_mnist and mnist datasets, PLFG has been verified: In the federated learning task, we can infer a part of the data privacy that the user does not desire to disclose just by the gradient uploaded by the victim. If this method can also be used to infer data privacy on more intricate images? For this reason, we verified on the cifar10, and the results obtained are not satisfactory, as indicated in Table 7.

Results

Original

Fig. 7. Leakage results of cifar10

It can be seen that the effect of our algorithm on the more intricate images is far less pleasant than the simple ones. In a multitude of cases, only quiet a few local features of the original image are restored, and the algorithm prefers to leverage black and white to restore intricate images. There are two primary reasons for this situation: (1) The features of the colourful image are more intricate in the model, and there are often a sea of optimal solutions that involve those features. This makes it more arduous for PLFG to converge to a specific optimal solution. (2) PLFG is not sensitive to colour changes, hence it performs better on a single channel, and the colour of 3-channel images is often vibrant.

5   Defense Strategies

Since PLFG is a gradient-based attack method, the most natural defense method to think of is to add noise to the gradient before gradient sharing. We picked Gaussian noise and Laplacian noise (which are widely used in differential privacy researches) and set the mean to 0 for experiments. From Fig. 8(a) to 8(b), we observe that the impact of noise types on the defense effect is not as significant as magnitude of noise. When variance is at the scale of 10^{-4}, the noisy gradient is entirely unable to prevent any privacy leakage. For noise with variance 10^{-2}, privacy inference will be more arduous, but privacy can still be restored. Only when the variance is larger than 10^{-1}, PLFG cannot infer any effective privacy, but this comes at the expense of model convergence efficiency and model accuracy. It is worth noting that in Fig. 8(c), as the magnitude of the noise increases, the longer the convergence period of the model increases the attack cost. However, as long as the model eventually converges, then PLFG must infer certain privacy for the following reasons: (1) Different from DLG [27] directly uses gradients, PLFG based on the model created by the gradients, hence provided the final model converges correctly, private information must be included in the model. (2) Noise will reduce the information contained in gradients, though as the gradient aggregates, the information in it will continuously increase. In summary, adding noise to the gradient may postpone the attack to a certain extent, but it does not help against PLFG most of the time.

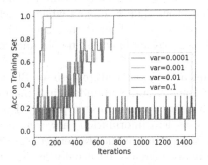
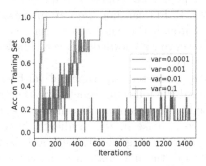

(a) Defend with different magnitude Laplace noise.

(b) Defend with different magnitude Gaussian noise.

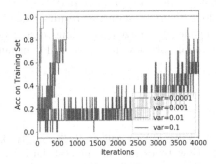
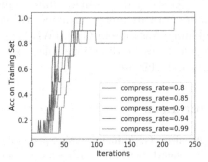

(c) Final iteration result when defend with different magnitude Laplace noise.

(d) Defend with gradient compress.

Fig. 8. The effectiveness of various defense strategies

We also experimented with gradient compression [11] and found that it can only slightly affect the model convergence efficiency. Previous work [11,20] indicated that gradients can be compressed by more than 300 times without losing accuracy. In this case, the sparsity is above 99% and still no impact on PLFG. As shown in Fig. 8(d), even the compress rate reaches 0.99, it still cannot play any preventive effect on attacks. The reason for this should be the same as what we analyzed in the previous paragraph. Considering the particularity of PLFG, perhaps the most feasible defense is to encrypt and aggregate the gradient (only the participants can decrypt, and the server only does operations). However, the effect of this method can only be verified based on the specific encryption algorithm, and we will continue to research it in the future.

6   Summary and Future Work

In this paper, we proposed an inference attack against federated learning named PLFG. PLFG can not use any information other than gradients when attacking. Through this very challenging assumption, we indicated that even when the adversary's knowledge is very limited, the privacy may still be obtained by adversary.

We conducted experimental verification and theoretical analysis of PLFG, obtained the following conclusion: the gradients contains abundant information related to the training data, hence the adversary can steal users' privacy. Even if there is noise in the gradients, it contains less information, however, in a particular training scenario such as federated learning, as the gradient constantly aggregate, the information in it will gradually increase, eventually leading to leakage. This indicates that gradient compression and noise have no effective against PLFG.

PLFG still requires many improvements, which can make it perform better on more intricate images. Enhance the colour diversity of output results. Such as combining Wasserstein GAN (WGAN) to generate images according to specific image features, to directional blast out possible privacy data. We will continue to research this area.

References

1. Ateniese, G., Mancini, L.V., Spognardi, A., Villani, A., Vitali, D., Felici, G.: Hacking smart machines with smarter ones: How to extract meaningful data from machine learning classifiers. Int. J. Secur. Networks **10**(3), 137–150 (2015)
2. Fredrikson, M., Jha, S., Ristenpart, T.: Model inversion attacks that exploit confidence information and basic countermeasures. In: Proceedings of the 22nd ACM SIGSAC Conference on Computer and Communications Security, CCS'2015, New York, NY, USA, pp. 1322–1333. Association for Computing Machinery (2015)
3. Fredrikson, M., Jha, S., Ristenpart, T.: Model inversion attacks that exploit confidence information and basic countermeasures. In: Proceedings of the 22nd ACM SIGSAC Conference on Computer and Communications Security, CCS'2015, New York, NY, USA, pp. 1322–1333. Association for Computing Machinery (2015)
4. Fredrikson, M., Lantz, E., Jha, S., Lin, S., Page, D., Ristenpart, T.: Privacy in pharmacogenetics: an end-to-end case study of personalized warfarin dosing. In: 23rd USENIX Security Symposium (USENIX Security 14), San Diego, CA, pp. 17–32. USENIX Association, August 2014

5. Goodfellow, I.J., et al.: Generative adversarial networks (2014)
6. Hawkins, D.M.: The problem of overfitting. J. Chem. Inf. Comput. Sci. **44**(1), 1–12 (2004). PMID: 14741005
7. Hitaj, B., Ateniese, G., Perez-Cruz, F.: Deep models under the GAN: information leakage from collaborative deep learning. In: Proceedings of the 2017 ACM SIGSAC Conference on Computer and Communications Security, CCS'2017, New York, NY, USA, pp. 603–618. Association for Computing Machinery (2017)
8. Iandola, F.N., Moskewicz, M.W., Ashraf, K., Keutzer, K.: Firecaffe: near-linear acceleration of deep neural network training on compute clusters. In: The IEEE Conference on Computer Vision and Pattern Recognition (CVPR), June 2016
9. Ilyas, A., Santurkar, S., Tsipras, D., Engstrom, L., Tran, B., Madry, A.: Adversarial examples are not bugs, they are features. In: Wallach, H., Larochelle, H., Beygelzimer, A., Fox, F.-B.E., Garnett, R. (eds.) Advances in Neural Information Processing Systems, vol. 32, pp. 125–136. Curran Associates Inc. (2019)
10. Li, M., et al.: Scaling distributed machine learning with the parameter server. In: 11th USENIX Symposium on Operating Systems Design and Implementation (OSDI 14), Broomfield, CO, pp. 583–598. USENIX Association, October 2014
11. Lin, Y., Han, S., Mao, H., Wang, Y., Dally, W.J.: Deep gradient compression: reducing the communication bandwidth for distributed training (2017)
12. McMahan, H.B., Ramage, D.: Federated learning: collaborative machine learning without centralized training data (2017)
13. Melis, L., Song, C., De Cristofaro, E., Shmatikov, V.: Exploiting unintended feature leakage in collaborative learning. In: 2019 IEEE Symposium on Security and Privacy (SP), pp. 691–706 (2019)
14. Qu, Y., et al.: Decentralized privacy using blockchain-enabled federated learning in fog computing. IEEE Internet Things J. **7**(6), 1 (2020)
15. Youyang, Q., Shui, Y., Gao, L., Zhou, W., Peng, S.: A hybrid privacy protection scheme in cyber-physical social networks. IEEE Trans. Comput. Soc. Syst. **5**(3), 773–784 (2018)
16. Youyang, Q., Shui, Y., Zhou, W., Peng, S., Wang, G., Xiao, K.: Privacy of things: emerging challenges and opportunities in wireless internet of things. IEEE Wirel. Commun. **25**(6), 91–97 (2018)
17. Elsevier SDOL. Journal of parallel and distributed computing (2009)
18. Shokri, R., Stronati, M., Song, C., Shmatikov, V.: Membership inference attacks against machine learning models. In: 2017 IEEE Symposium on Security and Privacy (SP), pp. 3–18 (2017)
19. Shui, Y.: Big privacy: challenges and opportunities of privacy study in the age of big data. IEEE Access **4**, 2751–2763 (2016)
20. Tsuzuku, Y., Imachi, H., Akiba, T.: Variance-based gradient compression for efficient distributed deep learning (2018)
21. Xiao, H., Rasul, K., Vollgraf, R.: Fashion-mnist: a novel image dataset for benchmarking machine learning algorithms (2017)
22. Yang, Q., Liu, Y., Chen, T., Tong, Y.: Federated machine learning: concept and applications. ACM Trans. Intell. Syst. Technol. **10**(2), 1–19 (2019)
23. Shui, Y., Liu, M., Dou, W., Liu, X., Zhou, S.: Networking for big data: a survey. IEEE Commun. Surv. Tutorials **19**(1), 531–549 (2017)
24. Zhang, J., Chen, B., Yu, S., Deng, S.: PEFL: a privacy-enhanced federated learning scheme for big data analytics (2019)
25. Zhang, J., Chen, J., Wu, D., Chen, B., Yu, S.: Poisoning attack in federated learning using generative adversarial nets, pp. 374–380 (2019)

26. Zhao, Y., Chen, J., Wu, D., Teng, J., Yu, S.: Multi-task network anomaly detection using federated learning, pp. 273–279 (2019)
27. Zhu, L., Liu, Z., Han, S.: Deep leakage from gradients. In: Wallach, H., Larochelle, H., Beygelzimer, A., Fox, F.-B.E., Garnett, R. (eds.) Advances in Neural Information Processing Systems, vol. 32, pp. 14774–14784. Curran Associates Inc. (2019)

A Survey of Game Theoretical Privacy Preservation for Data Sharing and Publishing

Datong Wu[1], Xiaotong Wu[2(✉)], Jiaquan Gao[2], Genlin Ji[2], Taotao Wu[3], Xuyun Zhang[4], and Wanchun Dou[5]

[1] Changzhou University, Changzhou, China
wudatong@cczu.edu.cn
[2] School of Computer Science and Technology, Nanjing Normal University,
Nanjing, China
{wuxiaotong,73025,glji}@njnu.edu.cn
[3] Huawei Company, Shenzhen, China
wutaotaoxpy@gmail.com
[4] Department of Computing, Macquarie University, Macquarie Park, Australia
xuyun.zhang@mq.edu.au
[5] The State Key Lab for Novel Software Technology, Nanjing University,
Nanjing, China
douwc@nju.edu.cn

Abstract. Privacy preservation has been one of the biggest concerns in data sharing and publishing. The wide-spread application of data sharing and publishing contributes to the utilization of data, but brings a severe risk of privacy leakage. Although the corresponding privacy preservation techniques have been proposed, it is inevitable to decrease the accuracy of data. More importantly, it is a challenge to analyze the behaviors and interactions among different participants, including data owners, collectors and adversaries. For data owners and collectors, they need to select proper privacy preservation mechanisms and parameters to maximize their utility under a certain amount of privacy guarantee. For data adversaries, their objective is to get the sensitive information by various attack measurements. In this paper, we survey the related work of game theory-based privacy preservation under data sharing and publishing. We also discuss the possible trends and challenges of the future research. Our survey provides a systematic and comprehensive understanding about privacy preservation problems under data sharing and publishing.

Keywords: Game theory · Data privacy · Nash equilibrium · Data sharing and publishing

1 Introduction

With the fast development of communications and infrastructures, there is a huge volume of data generated by various devices, including smart phones and

S. Yu et al. (Eds.): SPDE 2020, CCIS 1268, pp. 205–216, 2020.
https://doi.org/10.1007/978-981-15-9129-7_15

wearable devices [24]. Data sharing and publishing greatly improve the convenience of the daily life of peoples by data analysis techniques, such as service recommendation and data mining [5,9,19–23,44]. For example, some mobile user sends his/her health information collected by a smart watch to medical experts and gets a scientific sport plan. Mobile users also take advantage of their own data to get others' applications and services, such as GPS navigation, shopping and takeaway. The data collectors (e.g., hospitals) share medical data to disease prevention departments to predict possible infectious diseases (e.g., coronavirus disease 2019, COVID-19 [39]). Although users benefit from the applications and services, it brings a certain amount of leakage risk of their sensitive information. Since data sent to service providers is left from data owners (e.g., mobile users), they cannot control the usage of the data. The risk may cause monetary or reputation loss of users to hinder data sharing and publishing [38,40].

In recent years, there have been a series of research works to propose various private metrics and algorithms, including k-anonymity [31], ℓ-diversity [14], t-closeness [11], differential privacy (DP) [7,8,34], local differential privacy (LDP) [6]. k-anonymity requires that each record in a perturbed dataset at least $k-1$ same records. Differential privacy is a rigorous mathematical definition that uses a privacy parameter ϵ to limit the probability to distinguish any two datasets. Different from DP, LDP is an extended version, which is suited to the local setting. There are a lot of randomized mechanisms to satisfy DP and LDP, including the Laplace mechanism [8], the exponential mechanism [16], the Randomized Response mechanism [37]. Different private metrics and mechanisms are suitable to different scenes. Although these private metrics and mechanisms protect privacy of users, it decreases the accuracy of data and thus degrades the service quality of users.

Although there are a lot of effective private metrics and mechanisms, it is a challenge for users and data collectors (e.g., service providers) to choose proper private mechanisms and parameters and interact with the other key participants. On one hand, users and data collectors need to consider the balance between utility and privacy. On the other hand, they also analyze the influence of important factors, including attack strength of adversaries and the privacy degree of the other users and collectors. To this end, game theory is an efficient theoretical tool to research the behavior of various participants [17]. In actually, there have been a series of works to utilize game theory to analyze the interactions among multiple participants for privacy. Meanwhile, the game theoretical analysis contributes to improving efficiency of protection and reducing the cost of privacy.

However, to the best of our knowledge, there are few works to survey the related work about game theory-based privacy analysis for data sharing and publishing. In the previous surveys [4,15,18,25,42,43], most of them focus on the survey of information security rather than the game theory-based privacy analysis. For example, Manshaei et al. [15] and Pawlick et al. [18] mainly focus on game theory-based network security and privacy. Therefore, this paper tries to survey the game theory-based privacy in data sharing and publishing. We first introduce the preliminaries about scenes, privacy metrics, players and model of games. Then, we survey the existing works about privacy preservation in data sharing and publishing. Finally, we discuss the possible future research directions.

The remaining part of the paper is organized as follows. Section 2 introduces the preliminaries about the key elements based on game theory. Section 3 surveys the existing game theoretical works for privacy analysis. Section 4 discusses the existing works and present the possible future research directions. Section 5 concludes the main work of the paper.

2 Preliminaries

In this section, we introduce the preliminaries about scenes, privacy metrics, game players and models.

2.1 Scenes

In this paper, we focus on two scenes, including data sharing and data releasing [26]. In these two scenes, data can be used for monetary reward and for service. For the former, users send their data to the data collector and get the monetary reward (i.e., data trading). For the latter, users send their data to service providers and get corresponding services. In detail, they are listed as follows:

- **Data Sharing.** In order to get some service (e.g., location-based service, medical service), sensitive information (e.g., location, health information) of some user is shared to the third party.
- **Data Publishing.** The third party collects a huge volume of data from users. Meanwhile, he/she may publish or share the perturbed data to the public or the organization.

For data sharing, either users need to perturb their data so as to protect their privacy. For data publishing, data collectors (e.g., service providers) needs to prevent users' data from privacy leakage.

2.2 Privacy Metrics

There have been a series of privacy metrics and mechanisms to protect privacy, including $k-$anonymity [31], differential privacy [8] and local differential privacy [6]. Here, we present the definitions of the above privacy metrics as follows.

Definition 1 ($k-$anonymity [31]). *A perturbed mechanism $\mathcal{M}$ satisfies $k-$anonymity if after perturbation of some dataset D, each record has at least $k-1$ same records.*

Both DP and LDP are rigorous mathematical definitions and suitable to different scenes. DP is used for the central setting, while LDP is for the local setting.

Definition 2 (Differential Privacy [8]). *A randomized mechanism $\mathcal{M}$ satisfies ϵ-differential privacy if for any two datasets D_i and D_j which have at most one different record and the domain $\mathcal{O}$ of mechanism $\mathcal{M}$, the output should satisfy the following requirement:*

$$\Pr[\mathcal{M}(D_i) \in \mathcal{O}] \leq \exp(\epsilon) \cdot \Pr[\mathcal{M}(D_j) \in \mathcal{O}] \tag{1}$$

Definition 3 (Local Differential Privacy [6]). *A randomized mechanism $\mathcal{M}$ satisfies ϵ-local differential privacy if for any two value v_i and v_j and the domain $\mathcal{O}$ of mechanism $\mathcal{M}$, the output should satisfy the following requirement:*

$$\Pr[\mathcal{M}(v_i) \in \mathcal{O}] \leq \exp(\epsilon) \cdot \Pr[\mathcal{M}(v_j) \in \mathcal{O}] \tag{2}$$

2.3 Players

In the privacy games, there are three key participants listed as follows:

- **Data Owners (DO).** In order to get some service, the players share their personal information (e.g., trajectory, medical information) to data collectors. When the data collectors are untrusted, the owners should prevent their information from the leakage by some private mechanisms.
- **Data Collectors (DC).** The data collectors collect data from a large number of users. For trusted data collectors, they should protect users' data and avoid the possible leakage. For untrusted data collectors, they are adversaries.
- **Data Adversaries (DA).** The objective of data adversaries is to get sensitive information of data owners. On one hand, they get side information by illegal measurements (e.g., eavesdropping devices, tracking) to launch inference attack. On the other hand, they may be untrusted collectors and get perturbed data from users.

For DOs and trusted DCs, their objective is to protect data from leakage. For untrusted DCs and DAs, their objective is to get sensitive information of DOs.

2.4 Game Model

According to different participants, the existing works about game theory-based privacy analysis are classified into four types as follows:

- **Data Owner vs. Collector (DOC).** In this case, data collectors are not trusted, so that data owners need to adopt preservation mechanisms to protect their privacy. However, it brings a certain amount of utility loss, varying from privacy parameters. Therefore, the objective of data owners is to minimize the utility loss, while the objective of the latter is to get sensitive information as much as possible.

- **Data Owner vs. Owner (DOO).** In some privacy metric (e.g., k-anonymity), the privacy decision of some data owner influences his own privacy, but also the privacy of the others. That is, some data owner benefits from the other's privacy protection, which may lead to the unwillingness to protect privacy.
- **Data Collector vs. Adversary (DCA).** Data collectors get a huge volume of data from users and have the responsibility to prevent privacy leakage against the adversaries. Therefore, there is the defense and attack between data collectors and adversaries.
- **Data Collector vs. Collector (DCC).** Due to the privacy correlation of different datasets, the privacy degree of some dataset is influenced by its own privacy requirements and the others' privacy parameters. Therefore, there is the interactions between multiple data collectors.

3   Privacy Games in Data Sharing and Publishing

According to different game models in Sect. 2.4, we present the detailed works of DOC, DOO, DCA and DCC.

3.1   DOC

In order to get high-quality service, the data owners get the optimal utility under a privacy requirement.

Shokri [29] considers a common scene, in which data owners share their personal information to a untrusted third party (i.e., data collector). Under a joint guarantee of differential privacy and distortion privacy, the objective of data owners is to minimize their utility loss. As an adversary, the data collector attempts to find the data owners' secret by an inference attack. Therefore, it causes defense and attack between data owners and adversaries. In order to analyze the actions of different participants, Shokri [29] constructs a Stackelberg privacy game. In detail, the data owner first chooses a protection mechanism and then the adversary follows by designing an optimal inference attack. Shokri demonstrates that the optimal inference attack results in the same privacy for the data owner. In addition, it proposes linear program solutions for game analysis, in which each participant tries to get the optimal utility. The game result shows that the joint guarantee of differential privacy and distortion privacy is better than differential privacy and distortion privacy.

In order to get users' data, the data collector either provides some specified service or offers the payment to the data owner. Different from the previous scenes, Chessa et al. [3] propose a special case, in which the data collector take the results of data analysis as a public good. The authors construct a game theory-based model, in which each data owner contributes a part of or all of data at a self-chosen level of precision. The data collector controls the degree of data precision. Chessa et al. [3] discuss two cases, i.e., homogeneous and heterogeneous individuals. The authors demonstrate that the data collector can decrease the bound on the precision of the data to increase the population estimate's accuracy.

On the other hand, the data collector offers payments to incentivize data owners to report their real information.

Similar to [29], Wang et al. [36] consider the scheme of data for monetary reward. The data collector doesn't know the privacy cost of data owners and tries to design a payment strategy to spend the minimal payment to get the desired accurate objective. The authors construct a Bayesian game model and analyze Nash equilibrium points. Meanwhile, a sequence of mechanisms are designed to increase the number of data owners, who report their real information. More importantly, the designed mechanism is asymptotically optimal.

Wang et al. [35] considers a case, in which an untrusted data collector offers payments for noisy data due to privacy concerns of data owners. Although it protects privacy of data owners, it degrades the quality of data. Therefore, it causes an interaction between the data collector and data owners. In order to get a desired quality of noisy data, Wang et al. [35] construct a game model to design a payment mechanism. The privacy requirement of each data owner is controlled by privacy parameter ϵ in differential privacy. Meanwhile, the privacy parameter also influences the quality of perturbed data. The authors design a payment mechanism and analyze Nash equilibrium of the game. In the payment mechanism, for each data owner, the probability to report the real data as a best strategy is $\frac{e^\epsilon}{e^\epsilon+1}$. As a result, the payment mechanism satisfies ϵ-differential privacy due to $\frac{e^\epsilon}{e^\epsilon+1}/\frac{1}{e^\epsilon+1} = e^\epsilon$.

Sooksatra et al. [30] propose a novel challenge: how to design a scheme that benefits both data owners and collectors and promotes their cooperation to prevent data secondary use (e.g., data releasing). The purpose of the scheme is to make data owners report their accurate information and the data collector not resell data. The authors consider two cases, i.e., data for services and data for monetary reward. Sooksatra et al. [30] construct an iterated data trading game model with asymmetric incomplete information. Then, the authors reveal the data trading dilemma problem, including two aspects. The first one is whether or not data owners report their data and face a risk of data release by the data collector. The second one is whether or not the data collector resell data to the others. To this end, the authors propose a zero-determinant strategy to promote data owners and collectors to cooperate rather than defection.

In the above literatures, none of them consider the privacy correlation of data owners' data. Since the social correlation of data owners, it implies that their data is correlated. As a result, the privacy degree of some data owner is influenced by his/her and the other's privacy requirement. Liao et al. [13] construct a two-stage Stackelberg game, in which the data collector chooses a certain number of data owners that report their perturbed data. The authors derive that at Nash equilibrium, only one data owner considers the privacy correlation and the others send their real data. For the data collector, the authors present an optimal privacy protection mechanism.

Sfar et al. [28] discuss the privacy preservation problem in Internet of Things. The data owners (e.g., drivers and vehicles) send their data to the data collector (e.g., data requester). The authors construct a game model to analyze the behaviors of data owners to get the optimal privacy mechanism.

The mobile crowd sensing (MCS) system is one of the most common applications in data sharing. In the MCS system, noisy sensory data is sent to the data collector. In order to motive data owners to report their true data, Jin et al. [10] propose a payment mechanism and construct a Bayesian game model to analyze the behaviors between data collectors and owners. As a result, the authors propose a truth discovery algorithm to motive data owners to maximize their efforts. Meanwhile, the algorithm satisfies individual rationality and budget feasibility.

3.2 DOO

Kumari et al. [33] consider privacy game in data publishing, in which each data owner reports his/her real or dummy data to the data collector. Under the privacy requirement of k-anonymity, the privacy degree of each data owner is influenced by the others' privacy decision. The authors construct a cooperative privacy game (CoPG), in which each player considers a real value called cooperative value. At Nash equilibrium, the authors use information loss metric to evaluate the efficiency of anonymization process.

3.3 DCA

Chen et al. [2] propose an interesting problem: what is the behavior of a data owner to maximize his/her utility in a case with clear privacy costs? The authors construct an interaction game between a data owner and an adversary. The latter attempts to get the real value of the former's data. In detail, for each data owner, he/she has a value $v \in \{0, 1\}$ and then reports the randomized value v' to the data collector. The purpose of the data collector is to get the accurate value v. Since the data collector doesn't know the private value of the data owner, the authors construct a Bayesian game and analyze Bayesian Nash equilibrium. According to different payment functions, the authors discuss three cases and derive that the behavior of the data owner takes a randomized strategy.

Vakilinia et al. [32] consider a cyber threat information sharing scene to have proactive knowledge on the cybersecurity devices and improve the defense efficiency. Although the data collector gets the payment, they face the risk of privacy leakage. To this end, the authors construct a dynamic game model between the data collector and the adversary. In detail, the objective of the adversary is to maximize his/her utility by attacking, while the data collector needs to decide the amount of information. The authors propose 3-way game model with three main components, including CYBEX, data collectors and an adversary. They also derive an optimal strategy of how much sanitation an data collector choose to maximize his/her utility.

3.4 DCC

When there are multiple datasets, their privacy is correlated with each other. It implies that the privacy degree of some data collector is influenced by both his/her and the others' privacy protection. To this end, Wu et al. [41] firstly present a novel definition of correlated differential privacy to describe the privacy relationship between different datasets. Then, the authors construct a game model, in which each data collector publishes the dataset and decides the proper privacy parameter ϵ under differential privacy. They also analyze the existence and uniqueness of the pure Nash equilibrium.

For cybersecurity, multiple organizations share their network data to improve the defense of the whole network. Rawat et al. [27] introduce the idea of Blockchain concept to propose a novel information sharing system, i.e., iShare. The authors construct a Stackelberg game model to analyze the behaviors of organizations.

4 Discussion and Future Research Directions

In this section, we briefly discuss the privacy games in Sect. 3 and then present the possible research directions in the future.

4.1 Discussion

By the description in Sect. 3, we find that most of the existing works focus on DOC and DCA. In these two game models, they consists of three key participants, including data owners, collectors and adversaries. In particular, data collectors are the most important participants. A large number of works usually assume that the data collector is untrusted in a game model. The basic strategy is to take privacy as a commodity and evaluate its price. Then, the data collector offers a certain amount of payment or service as the compensation for privacy risk. When the data collector is trusted, the objective of data collectors is to maximize the utility of perturbed data under a certain amount of privacy guarantee. The brief description of privacy games under data sharing and publishing is shown in Table 1.

4.2 Future Research Directions

Game Model for Local Differential Privacy. Local differential privacy is a novel privacy metric in a local setting. In the previous works, there are few works to utilize local differential privacy to construct the privacy game models. It is interesting that some works (e.g., [35]) have been taken advantage of the similar idea of LDP to construct game models. In fact, with the fast development of Internet of Things and mobile cloud computing, a lot of efficient privacy mechanisms have been proposed to satisfy local differential privacy, including RR [37] and k-RR [1,12]. Therefore, it is a possible research direction to utilize these mechanisms to construct the game model in the local setting.

Table 1. Brief description of privacy games under data sharing and publishing

	Game Model	Privacy Problems	Classification	Technique
Shokri [29]	Stackelberg game	Data sharing	DOC	Differential privacy
Chessa et al. [3]	Non-cooperative game	Data sharing	DOC	–
Wang et al. [36]	Bayesian game	Data sharing	DOC	Differential privacy
Wang et al. [35]	Non-cooperative game	Data sharing	DOC	Differential privacy
Sooksatra et al. [30]	Non-cooperative game	Data publishing	DOC	–
Liao et al. [13]	Stackelberg game	Data sharing	DOC	Correlated differential privacy
Sfar et al. [28]	Non-cooperative game	Data sharing	DOC	–
Jin et al. [10]	Bayesian game	Data sharing	DOC	–
Kumari et al. [33]	Cooperative game	Data sharing	DOO	k-anonymity
Chen et al. [2]	Bayesian game	Data publishing	DCA	Differential privacy
Vakilinia et al. [32]	Non-cooperative game	Data publishing	DCA	Differential privacy
Wu et al. [41]	Non-cooperative game	Data publishing	DCC	Correlated differential privacy
Rawat et al. [27]	Stackelberg game	Data sharing	DOO	–

Game Analysis for DOO and DCC. Relatively speaking, there are few works about DOO and DCC for data sharing and publishing. At present, the condition to construct such privacy game is that there exists the privacy correlation between owners or collectors. The privacy correlation indicates two aspects: (i) some data owner/collector improves the degree of privacy preservation to increase the privacy degree of the others; and (ii) due to the correlation of data, the risk is higher with the addition of more data owners. It is a challenge to define a proper privacy metric to compute the correlation of privacy.

Multiple-Agents for Privacy Game. In the existing privacy games, there are usually two agents to interact with each other. However, in the real environments, there are more than two agents to participate in the game. For example, data collectors receive data from data owners and then sell them to the third party. It implies that the privacy model considers the interaction not only between data owners and collectors, but also between data collectors and the third party. It is more challenging to construct the privacy model and analyze Nash equilibrium points.

5   Conclusion

This paper surveys the related work about privacy games in data sharing and publishing. We have classified privacy games into four types, i.e., DOO, DOC, DCA and DCC. We have presented a certain number of literatures based on game theory to analyze the behaviors of different participants for data privacy. Our object is to help readers to understand the existing works and the possible future directions.

References

1. Bun, M., Nelson, J., Stemmer, U.: Heavy hitters and the structure of local privacy. ACM Trans. Algorithms **15**(4), 51:1–51:40 (2019)
2. Chen, Y., Sheffet, O., Vadhan, S.: Privacy games. In: Liu, T.-Y., Qi, Q., Ye, Y. (eds.) WINE 2014. LNCS, vol. 8877, pp. 371–385. Springer, Cham (2014). https://doi.org/10.1007/978-3-319-13129-0_30
3. Chessa, M., Grossklags, J., Loiseau, P.: A game-theoretic study on non-monetary incentives in data analytics projects with privacy implications. In: Proceedings of 28th Computer Security Foundations Symposium, CSF, pp. 90–104. IEEE (2015)
4. Do, C.T., et al.: Game theory for cyber security and privacy. ACM Comput. Surv. **50**(2), 30:1–30:37 (2017)
5. Dou, W., Qi, L., Zhang, X., Chen, J.: An evaluation method of outsourcing services for developing an elastic cloud platform. J. Supercomput. **63**(1), 1–23 (2013). https://doi.org/10.1007/s11227-010-0491-2
6. Duchi, J.C., Jordan, M.I., Wainwright, M.J.: Local privacy and statistical minimax rates. In: Proceedings of 54th Annual Symposium on Foundations of Computer Science, FOCS, pp. 429–438. IEEE (2013)
7. Dwork, C., McSherry, F., Nissim, K., Smith, A.: Calibrating noise to sensitivity in private data analysis. In: Halevi, S., Rabin, T. (eds.) TCC 2006. LNCS, vol. 3876, pp. 265–284. Springer, Heidelberg (2006). https://doi.org/10.1007/11681878_14
8. Dwork, C., McSherry, F., Nissim, K., Smith, A.D.: Calibrating noise to sensitivity in private data analysis. J. Priv. Confidentiality **7**(3), 17–51 (2016)
9. Fung, B.C.M., Wang, K., Chen, R., Yu, P.S.: Privacy-preserving data publishing: a survey of recent developments. ACM Comput. Surv. **42**(4), 14:1–14:53 (2010)
10. Jin, H., Su, L., Nahrstedt, K.: Theseus: Incentivizing truth discovery in mobile crowd sensing systems. In: Proceedings of the 18th ACM International Symposium on Mobile Ad Hoc Networking and Computing, Chennai, India, 10–14 July 2017, pp. 1:1–1:10. ACM (2017)
11. Li, N., Li, T., Venkatasubramanian, S.: t-closeness: Privacy beyond k-anonymity and l-diversity. In: Proceedings of the 23rd International Conference on Data Engineering, ICDE, pp. 106–115. IEEE (2007)
12. Li, N., Ye, Q.: Mobile data collection and analysis with local differential privacy. In: Proceedings of IEEE 20th International Conference on Mobile Data Management (MDM), pp. 4–7 (2019)
13. Liao, G., Chen, X., Huang, J.: Social-aware privacy-preserving correlated data collection. In: Proceedings of the Nineteenth ACM International Symposium on Mobile Ad Hoc Networking and Computing, MobiHoc 2018, Los Angeles, CA, USA, 26–29 June 2018, pp. 11–20. ACM (2018)
14. Machanavajjhala, A., Gehrke, J., Kifer, D., Venkitasubramaniam, M.: l-diversity: Privacy beyond k-anonymity. In: Proceedings of the 22nd International Conference on Data Engineering, ICDE, p. 24. IEEE (2006)
15. Manshaei, M.H., Zhu, Q., Alpcan, T., Basar, T., Hubaux, J.: Game theory meets network security and privacy. ACM Comput. Surv. **45**(3), 25:1–25:39 (2013)
16. McSherry, F., Talwar, K.: Mechanism design via differential privacy. In: Proceedings of 48th Annual Symposium on Foundations of Computer Science (FOCS), pp. 94–103. IEEE (2007)
17. Osborne, M.J., Rubinstein, A.: A Course in Game Theory. MIT Press, Cambridge (1994)

18. Pawlick, J., Colbert, E., Zhu, Q.: A game-theoretic taxonomy and survey of defensive deception for cybersecurity and privacy. ACM Comput. Surv. **52**(4), 82:1–82:28 (2019)
19. Qi, L., Dai, P., Yu, J., Zhou, Z., Xu, Y.: "time-location-frequency"-aware Internet of Things service selection based on historical records. IJDSN **13**(1), 1–9 (2017)
20. Qi, L., Xiang, H., Dou, W., Yang, C., Qin, Y., Zhang, X.: Privacy-preserving distributed service recommendation based on locality-sensitive hashing. In: Proceedings of International Conference on Web Services, ICWS, pp. 49–56. IEEE (2017)
21. Qi, L., Yu, J., Zhou, Z.: An invocation cost optimization method for web services in cloud environment. Sci. Program. **2017**, 4358536:1–4358536:9 (2017)
22. Qi, L., Zhou, Z., Yu, J., Liu, Q.: Data-sparsity tolerant web service recommendation approach based on improved collaborative filtering. IEICE Trans. Inf. Syst. **100**-**D**(9), 2092–2099 (2017)
23. Qu, Y., Gao, L., Luan, T.H., Xiang, Y., Yu, S., Li, B., Zheng, G.: Decentralized privacy using blockchain-enabled federated learning in fog computing. IEEE Internet Things J. **7**(6), 5171–5183 (2020)
24. Qu, Y., Yu, S., Gao, L., Zhou, W., Peng, S.: A hybrid privacy protection scheme in cyber-physical social networks. IEEE Trans. Comput. Soc. Syst. **5**(3), 773–784 (2018)
25. Qu, Y., Yu, S., Zhou, W., Peng, S., Wang, G., Xiao, K.: Privacy of things: emerging challenges and opportunities in wireless Internet of Things. IEEE Wirel. Commun. **25**(6), 91–97 (2018)
26. Qu, Y., Yu, S., Zhou, W., Tian, Y.: Gan-driven personalized spatial-temporal private data sharing in cyber-physical social systems. IEEE Trans. Netw. Sci. Eng. 1 (2020). https://doi.org/10.1109/TNSE.2020.3001061
27. Rawat, D.B., Njilla, L., Kwiat, K.A., Kamhoua, C.A.: ishare: blockchain-based privacy-aware multi-agent information sharing games for cybersecurity. In: Proceedings of International Conference on Computing, Networking and Communications, ICNC, pp. 425–431. IEEE Computer Society (2018)
28. Riahi, A., Challal, Y., Moyal, P., Natalizio, E.: A game theoretic approach for privacy preserving model in IoT-based transportation. IEEE Trans. Intell. Transp. Syst. **20**(12), 4405–4414 (2019)
29. Shokri, R.: Privacy games: optimal user-centric data obfuscation. PoPETs **2015**(2), 299–315 (2015)
30. Sooksatra, K., Li, W., Mei, B., Alrawais, A., Wang, S., Yu, J.: Solving data trading dilemma with asymmetric incomplete information using zero-determinant strategy. In: Chellappan, S., Cheng, W., Li, W. (eds.) WASA 2018. LNCS, vol. 10874, pp. 425–437. Springer, Cham (2018). https://doi.org/10.1007/978-3-319-94268-1_35
31. Sweeney, L.: k-anonymity: a model for protecting privacy. Int. J. Uncertainty Fuzziness Knowl. Syst. **10**(5), 557–570 (2002)
32. Vakilinia, I., Tosh, D.K., Sengupta, S.: 3-way game model for privacy-preserving cybersecurity information exchange framework. In: Proceedings of Military Communications Conference, MILCOM, pp. 829–834. IEEE (2017)
33. Kumari, V., Chakravarthy, S.: Cooperative privacy game: a novel strategy for preserving privacy in data publishing. Hum. Centric Comput. Inf. Sci. **6**(1), 1–20 (2016). https://doi.org/10.1186/s13673-016-0069-y
34. Wang, M., Xu, C., Chen, X., Hao, H., Zhong, L., Yu, S.: Differential privacy oriented distributed online learning for mobile social video prefetching. IEEE Trans. Multimedia **21**(3), 636–651 (2019)

35. Wang, W., Ying, L., Zhang, J.: A game-theoretic approach to quality control for collecting privacy-preserving data. In: Proceedings of 53rd Annual Allerton Conference on Communication, Control, and Computing, pp. 474–479. IEEE (2015)
36. Wang, W., Ying, L., Zhang, J.: Buying data from privacy-aware individuals: the effect of negative payments. In: Cai, Y., Vetta, A. (eds.) WINE 2016. LNCS, vol. 10123, pp. 87–101. Springer, Heidelberg (2016). https://doi.org/10.1007/978-3-662-54110-4_7
37. Warner, S.L.: Randomized response: a survey technique for eliminating evasive answer bias. J. Am. Stat. Assoc. **60**(309), 63–69 (1965)
38. Williams, M., Nurse, J.R.C., Creese, S.: Smartwatch games: encouraging privacy-protective behaviour in a longitudinal study. Comput. Hum. Behav. **99**, 38–54 (2019)
39. Wu, F., et al.: A new coronavirus associated with human respiratory disease in China. Nature **579**(7798), 265–269 (2020)
40. Wu, X., Li, S., Yang, J., Dou, W.: A cost sharing mechanism for location privacy preservation in big trajectory data. In: Proceedings of International Conference on Communications, ICC, pp. 1–6. IEEE (2017)
41. Wu, X., Wu, T., Khan, M., Ni, Q., Dou, W.: Game theory based correlated privacy preserving analysis in big data. IEEE Trans. Big Data (2017). https://doi.org/10.1109/TBDATA.2017.2701817
42. Yu, S.: Big privacy: challenges and opportunities of privacy study in the age of big data. IEEE Access **4**, 2751–2763 (2016)
43. Yu, S., Liu, M., Dou, W., Liu, X., Zhou, S.: Networking for big data: a survey. IEEE Commun. Surv. Tutorials **19**(1), 531–549 (2017)
44. Zhou, C., Fu, A., Yu, S., Yang, W., Wang, H., Zhang, Y.: Privacy-preserving federated learning in fog computing. IEEE Internet Things J. 1 (2020). https://doi.org/10.1109/JIOT.2020.2987958

Anomaly and Intrusion Detection

Network Anomaly Detection Using Federated Learning and Transfer Learning

Ying Zhao[1], Junjun Chen[1], Qianling Guo[2], Jian Teng[3(✉)], and Di Wu[4]

[1] College of Information Science and Technology,
Beijing University of Chemical Technology, Beijing 100029, China
{zhaoy,chenjj}@mail.buct.edu.cn
[2] Library, Beijing University of Chemical Technology, Beijing 100029, China
guoql@mail.buct.edu.cn
[3] Center for Information, Beijing University of Chemical Technology,
Beijing 100029, China
tengj@mail.buct.edu.cn
[4] School of Computer Science, University of Technology Sydney,
Sydney, NSW 2194, Australia
Di.Wu-16@student.uts.edu.au

Abstract. Since deep neural networks can learn data representation from training data automatically, deep learning methods are widely used in the network anomaly detection. However, challenges of deep learning-based anomaly detection methods still exist, the major of which is the training data scarcity problem. In this paper, we propose a novel network anomaly detection method (NAFT) using federated learning and transfer learning to overcome the data scarcity problem. In the first learning stage, a people or organization O_t, who intends to conduct a detection model for a specific attack, can join in the federated learning with a similar training task to learn basic knowledge from other participants' training data. In the second learning stage, O_t uses the transfer learning method to reconstruct and re-train the model to further improve the detection performance on the specific task. Experiments conducted on the UNSW-NB15 dataset show that the proposed method can achieve a better anomaly detection performance than other baseline methods when training data is scarce.

Keywords: Network traffic analysis · Federated learning · Transfer learning

1 Introduction

With the development of information technology, communication networks play a critical role in all facets of society and gradually changes the way people live. For example, paperless offices through computer networks can facilitate information sharing and save resources, and video communication can be done with network applications rather than telephone. Moreover, many novel technologies, such

© Springer Nature Singapore Pte Ltd. 2020
S. Yu et al. (Eds.): SPDE 2020, CCIS 1268, pp. 219–231, 2020.
https://doi.org/10.1007/978-981-15-9129-7_16

as the Internet of Things (IoT) and the Internet of Vehicles (IoV), are also based on communication networks. While bringing great convenience to people, computer networks are facing enormous security challenges. Cyber attacks are threatening the financial interests of business organizations and the privacy of individuals, such as ransomware [1], cryptojacking [2], DDoS attacks [3], and others. Therefore, it is necessary to ensure cybersecurity to retain the computer network's integrity and availability.

Researchers have proposed various methods to identify cyber attacks during the last ten years [4–6]. Network anomaly detection systems are widely used in the cyber security field. Network anomaly detection systems can be generally categorized into two groups, misused-based method and anomaly-based method [7]. The misused-based method focuses on existing network anomaly patterns and uses rule-based machine learning algorithms to identify network anomaly. However, misused-based method can only identify known anomalies. The anomaly-based method detects anomalies by matching the similarity of network traffic to benign network behavior so that this method can identify unknown anomalies. In the past decade, numerous network anomaly detection methods have been proposed. Among these approaches, deep learning-based methods achieve great success due to their ability to learn complex data patterns.

Although showing advanced detection performance, deep learning-based detection methods still face a significant challenge, namely data scarcity. Deep learning algorithms require a large dataset to optimize parameters of neural networks. However, in the real scenario, collecting training data of network anomaly detection is expensive. It will take massive computing resources and labor resources to label network traffic data.

To tackle the challenge of data scarcity, this paper proposes a novel two-stage network anomaly detection method using federated learning and transfer learning. In the first stage, we jointly train a detection model, which can learn basic knowledge from other participants' training data in federated learning. Federated learning [8,9] is a new type of distributed learning architecture. Different from the traditional distributed learning architecture where private training data needs to be shared with a central server, the participant of federated learning locally trains model with private data and only share model parameters to the central server to preserve data privacy. In the real scenario, network management organizations generally have their private network traffic data with labels. However, they are reluctant to share it with a third party because the network traffic data contains sensitive information such as user privacy. Furthermore, these labeled network traffic can be used to initiate cyber attacks [10–12]. Therefore, people or network management organizations are willing to join in the federated learning not only because of the data scarcity problem, but also the data privacy protection mechanism.

In the second stage, we introduce the transfer learning method to further improve the model detection performance on a specific anomaly detection task. Because of the diversity of network anomalies and the imbalance in the distribution of training data, the detection model trained by federated learning usually has a high accuracy for the overall anomaly detection, but may not be effective for a specific anomaly detection task. Therefore, we use the transfer learning approach to reconstruct and fine-tune the global detection model after federated learning. The contributions of this paper can be summarized as follows.

- We propose a novel two-stage network anomaly detection method using federated learning and transfer learning to overcome the challenge of training data scarcity. In the federated learning phase, the participant can learn basic knowledge from other participants' training data and can protect its data privacy because they do not need to upload their own training data to a third-party server.
- In the transfer learning stage, the global model trained by federated learning is reconstructed and re-trained to enhance the model detection performance on a specific task.
- Experiments conducted on the UNSW-NB15 dataset show that the proposed method can achieve a better anomaly detection performance than baseline methods when training data is scarce.

The rest of this paper is organized as follows. Section 2 introduces background knowledge about federated learning and transfer learning. Section 3 details the proposed anomaly detection method. The experimental setting and results are given in Sect. 4. In Sect. 5, we conclude this paper and introduce future works.

2   Background

2.1   Federated Learning

In the information age, one of the biggest concerns of cyber security is privacy [13,14]. Participants distribute their local training data to a central server to train a global model in the traditional collaborative learning. However, the data transfer from the participant to the central server may increase the risk of privacy leakage. As shown in Fig. 1, attackers can steal user data during data transfer or can steal data by hacking into the server. Moreover, the data-sharing strategy of the traditional collaborative learning increases network transmission time and increases the computational overhead of the central server, which slow down model training.

To protect data privacy and reduce server-side computing overhead, federated learning is proposed [8]. In federated learning, participants train model locally with their own dataset and only send the model parameters to the server; Then, the server averages model parameters to renew the global model. The objective function of federated learning can be formulated as Eq. 1.

$$\mathcal{L}(\omega) = \frac{1}{n} \sum_{i \in P_k} \mathcal{L}_i(\omega) \tag{1}$$

where n is the number of participants, P_k represents the local training data of k-th participant, $\mathcal{L}_i(\omega)$ indicates the loss function of the i-th sample, ω is the parameters.

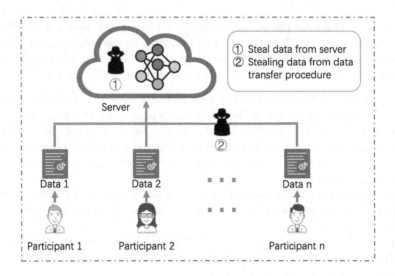

Fig. 1. Privacy leakage in the centralized collaborative learning.

To optimize the objective function of federated Learning, participants use the gradient descent algorithm to calculate the derivative of their loss function. At t-th round, participants send the derivative $G_{t,k}$ to the central server. Then, the server uses the uploaded $G_{t,k}$ to renew the global model. The model update equation is shown as Eq. 2.

$$M_{t+1} = M_t + \eta \frac{1}{n} \sum G_{t,k} \qquad (2)$$

where η is the update weight, M_{t+1} represents the global model at the $(t+1)$-th iteration.

Because federated learning can protect user privacy, some researchers used federated learning to analyze network traffic. Bakopoulou et al. [15] used federated learning to predict PII exposure or ad requests in HTTP packets. Zhao et al. [16] proposed a multi-task network anomaly detection method based on federated learning that allows participants to collaboratively train a detection model, without sharing private training data.

2.2 Transfer Learning

Transfer learning [17] is suitable for the scenario where a classifier trained with source domain data is used in a different target domain. In general, the source domain is not identical but related to the target domain. Following the definitions and notation as introduced in [18], a domain D is defined by $\mathcal{D} = \{\mathcal{X}, P(X)\}$, where $\mathcal{X}$ is a d-dimensional feature space and $P(X)$ is a marginal probability distribution. A task $\mathcal{T}$ is composed of a label space $\mathcal{Y}$ and the conditional probability distribution $P(Y|X)$. We can assume that there are two domains with their related tasks: a source domain $\mathcal{D}^s = \{\mathcal{X}^s, P(X^s)\}$ with $\mathcal{T}^s = \{\mathcal{Y}^s, P(Y^s|X^s)\}$ and a target domain $\mathcal{D}^t = \{\mathcal{X}^t, P(X^t)\}$ with $\mathcal{T}^t = \{\mathcal{Y}^t, P(Y^t|X^t)\}$. Accordingly, transfer learning can be used in the scenario where $\mathcal{Y}^s$ is similar to $\mathcal{Y}^t$ and $\mathcal{D}^s$ is different from $\mathcal{D}^t$.

Transfer learning methods are widely used in many fields, such as computer vision, health monitoring [19], and others. In the network anomaly detection field, Wu et al. [20] used transfer learning to learn knowledge from a source model to a target model, and Singla et al. [21] used the target dataset to re-train the source model to construct the target detection model. However, these methods do not consider how to obtain the source data to conduct the source model. To address the above problem, we use federated learning to build the source domain model in this paper.

3   Network Anomaly Detection

In this section, we introduce the proposed network anomaly detection framework. Figure 2 presents the detection model training procedure. In the proposed method, federated learning focuses on training a global model with multiple participants to learn basic knowledge from a related anomaly detection task, and the transfer learning transfers the knowledge from the source domain to the target domain.

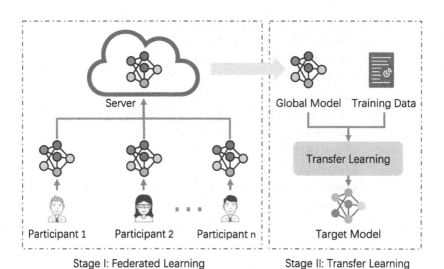

Fig. 2. Network anomaly detection framework.

3.1 Overall of Detection Model Training

The model training is divided into two stages: federated learning stage and transfer learning stage. In the federated learning stage, we jointly train a global model (*Net-S*) as the source model for next stage. In the transfer learning stage, we reconstruct the detection model (*Net-S*) by removing the output layer of *Net-S* and concatenate extra network layers (*Net-T*) to the remaining *Net-S*; Then, we re-train the new detection model. The detailed training process is described in Sects. 3.2, 3.3, respectively.

The network structures of the *Net-S* and *Net-T* are shown in Table 1. They are composed of linear layers and LeakyReLU (Leaky Rectified Linear Unit [22]) layers, Dropout layer, and Softmax layer, where *input_size* is the dimension of the input sample and *output_size* presents the output size. For the network anomaly detection, the data samples often come from network traffic and are presented in vectors; Therefore, linear layers are used to transform the input samples and the outputs of hidden layers. LeakyReLU is the activation function, which can avoid the "dying ReLU" problem [22] and allow a small, non-zero, constant gradient. Dropout is used to reduce overfitting that leads to degraded performance on the test dataset.

Table 1. Network structures

Net-S	*Net-T*
Linear(*input_size*, 256)	Linear(256, 128)
LeakyReLU()	LeakyReLU()
Linear(256, 512)	Dropout()
LeakyReLU()	Linear(128, 128))
Dropout()	LeakyReLU()
Linear(512, 1024)	Linear(128, *output_size*)
LeakyReLU()	Softmax()
Linear(1024, 256)	
LeakyReLU()	
Linear(256, *output_size*)	
Softmax()	

3.2 Stage I: Training Source Model Using Federated Learning

Federated learning can collaboratively train a neural network model in a decentralized learning strategy [23]. Instead of uploading private training data to the central server, participants train locally with their own data and only share model updates with the server. Because federated learning can overcome data scarcity and preserve data privacy, we use federated learning to train a model as the source model for the transfer learning stage.

The training procedure is shown in Algorithm 1. In our setting, each participant is a network management or research organization that has private labeled network traffic data. At first, all participants need to agree on the training protocol of federated learning, which includes model structure, loss function, and others [24]. For network anomaly detection, we use cross-entropy as the loss function $\mathcal{L}^k$ for each participant, which is given as Eq. 3.

$$\mathcal{L}^k = \sum_{\forall x \in X^k} y_i(x) log(\hat{y}_i(x)) \tag{3}$$

where X^k presents the private training dataset of participant k, $y_i(x)$ is the ground truth vector for sample x, and $\hat{y}_i(x)$ is the estimate value.

Algorithm 1: Model training using federated learning

Given K participants (indexed by k); ω_t^k indicates model parameters of k-th participant at round t; ω_t is global model parameters at round t; η is learning rate;

1 **for** *Iteration t* **do**
   /* Participant side: */
2   **for** *Participant k* **do**
3           $\omega_t^k = \omega_{t-1}$
4   **for** *Local epoch e* **do**
5              $\omega_{t+1}^k = \omega_t^k - \eta \frac{\partial}{\partial X^k} \mathcal{L}^k$
6   **end**
7   **end**
8   Send ω_t^k to the server;
   /* Server side: */
9       $\omega_t = \frac{1}{K} \sum_{k=1}^{K} \omega_t^k$;
10   Send ω_t to each participant;
11 **end**

At training round t, each participant train a local model to minimize the loss function with its own training data, and then send the model parameters ω_t^k to the server. In the server side, the FederatedAveraging Algorithm [8] is used to combine participant parameters and renew the global model. Then, the server delivers the new model parameters ω_t to each participant. After the training of federated learning, the global model can be used as the source model for transfer learning.

3.3   Stage II: Transfer Learning

Federated learning jointly trains a global model with all participants' private training data. Therefore, federated learning can overcome the data scarcity

problem in network anomaly detection. In the real scenario, different participants (network management organizations) may face different cyber attacks.
For example, participant A focuses on DDoS attacks, and other participants
focus on malware. Accordingly, we use the transfer learning method to improve
the detection performance for specific detection task further.

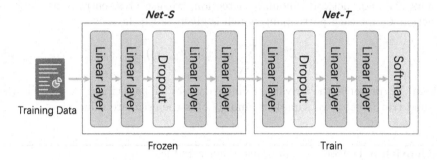

Fig. 3. Transfer learning process.

Figure 3 presents the process of transfer learning. After the federated learning
stage, a source model (Net-S) has been trained. Then the Net-T is added to the
Net-S that excludes the last linear layer and Softmax layer to reconstruct detection model for the transfer learning. In the training procedure, Net-S is frozen,
and only Net-T is trained on the target domain dataset. Once the detection
accuracy of the model is converged, the training ends.

4   Experiments

4.1   Dataset and Experimental Setting

In this paper, we used the UNSW-NB15 dataset [25] to test the proposed
anomaly detection method. The UNSW-NB15 dataset is a representative dataset
for intrusion detection evaluation, which is collected by the Australian Centre
for Cyber Security. This dataset provides about 31 hours labeled network traffic,
including benign and attacks traffic.

To evaluate the proposed method, we defined the following experimental scenario. One network management organization O_t intends to conduct a detection
model for the exploits attack, but its training samples are scarce. To solve this
problem, O_t engages in federated learning, where O_t and the other 9 participants
jointly train a model for a similar network anomaly detection task. As shown
in Table 2, based on the UNSW-NB15 dataset, two datasets are conducted for
O_t and other participants, respectively. The dataset D_o is the private dataset of
O_t, which contains only benign and exploits attack records. Other participants
split the dataset D_p equally as their private dataset in federated learning. The
D_p includes benign traffic, generic attack, fuzzers, DoS, reconnaissance, analysis

Table 2. Details of dataset

Dataset	Category	Number of records
D_o	Benign	10,000
	Exploits	10,000
D_p	Benign	90,000
	Generic Attack	33,400
	Fuzzers	24,000
	DDoS	15,000
	Reconnaissance	13,000
	Analysis Attack	2,600
	Backdoors	2,000

attack, and backdoors [25]. After the federated learning stage, O_t used transfer learning to further improve detection performance on the exploits attack with its dataset.

In the experimental procedure, 70% of the dataset was used for training, and the remaining 30% was used for testing. For each experiment, training data and test data were randomly selected in proportion. Experiments were repeated five times, and the average value was used as the experimental result.

4.2 Evaluation Metrics

We used three typical metrics, accuracy, precision, and recall, to evaluate the proposed method in this paper. The equations of accuracy, precision, and recall are shown as Eqs. 4, 5, and 6, respectively.

$$Accuracy = \frac{TP + TN}{TP + FP + TN + FN}. \tag{4}$$

$$Precision = \frac{TP}{TP + FP}. \tag{5}$$

$$Recall = \frac{TP}{TP + FN}. \tag{6}$$

where TP is true positive observations, FP indicates false positive observations, TN is true negative observations, and FN indicates false negative observations.

4.3 Experimental Results

In this section, we first compared the exploits attack detection performance of the proposed method (NAFT) with other machine learning algorithms, deep neural networks (DNN), logistic regression (LR), k-nearest neighbors (K-NN), and decision tree (DT). Note that the DNN and the proposed method have

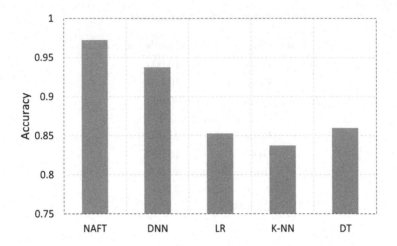

Fig. 4. Accuracy of different methods.

the same network structure (*Net-S+Net-T*). Then, we evaluated the impact of
the sample size on the accuracy of the proposed NAFT. All experiments were
performed by Keras [26] on an Ubuntu server with Nvidia GTX 1080Ti GPU.

Figure 4 shows the experimental results of exploits attack detection. The proposed NAFT achieves the best detection accuracy 97.23%, and the accuracies of
DNN, LR, K-NN, and DT are 93.74%, 85.27%, 83.72%, and 85.97%, respectively.
Compared to DNN, it improves accuracy by 3.49%. Compared to other machine
learning methods, NAFT also significantly improves the detection accuracy. Furthermore, from the above experimental results, it can be seen that neural network
methods generally have stronger detection performance than traditional machine
learning methods.

Table 3. Precision and recall of different methods

	NAFT	DNN	LR	k-NN	NB
Precision	0.9748	0.9437	0.8513	0.8316	0.8620
Recall	0.9696	0.9302	0.8546	0.8456	0.8564

As shown in Table 3, we compared the precision and recall of different methods. The NAFT gets the best detection performance on precision and recall.
The DNN ranks second, and the precision and recall of other methods are all
less than 90%. In summary, the proposed method does improve anomaly detection performance, especially in the case of small training samples.

Furthermore, we evaluate the effect of training data size on model accuracy.
In this experimental setting, we gradually decrease the number of training samples and do not change the number of testing samples. Figure 5 illustrates the

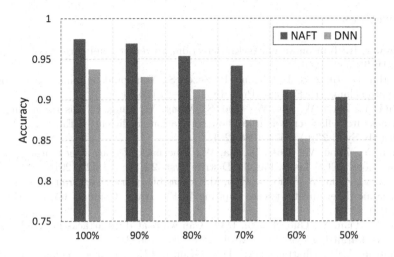

Fig. 5. Accuracy at different training dataset sizes.

detection accuracies of the NAFT and DNN method under different training dataset sizes. As the size of the training dataset decreases, the accuracies of both the NAFT and DNN decreases, and the accuracy of DNN decreases even more. When the size of the training dataset becomes 50%, the accuracy of NAFT is still higher than 90%, but the accuracy of the DNN reduces to 83.56%. The reason for the above phenomenon is that the proposed NAFT can learn related knowledge from a similar anomaly detection task using federated learning and use the transfer learning method to further improve the accuracy of the target task; Therefore, the proposed method can still maintain a high accuracy under a small training sample size.

5   Conclusion

In this paper, we propose a two-stage learning method (NAFT) based on federated learning and transfer learning to deal with the data scarcity problem in network anomaly detection. The NAFT comprises two learning stage. In the first stage, a people or organization O_t, who intends to conduct a network anomaly detection model, engages in federated learning to lean basic knowledge from other participants. In the second stage, O_t reconstructs the detection model trained by federated learning and uses its private training data to re-train the new model. Compared with DNN, LR, K-NN, and DT methods, the proposed method can achieve better detection performance when the training samples are scarce. For future work, we plan to introduce other transfer learning methods, such as adversarial discriminative domain adaptation [27], in our learning framework to improve the detection performance further.

References

1. Brewer, R.: Ransomware attacks: detection, prevention and cure. Network Secur. **2016**(9), 5–9 (2016)
2. Carlin, D., Burgess, J., O'Kane, P., Sezer, S.: You could be mine (d): the rise of cryptojacking. IEEE Secur. Priv. **18**(2), 16–22 (2019)
3. Shui, Y., Zhou, W., Jia, W., Guo, S., Xiang, Y., Tang, F.: Discriminating ddos attacks from flash crowds using flow correlation coefficient. IEEE Trans. Parallel Distrib. Syst. **23**(6), 1073–1080 (2011)
4. Shui, Y., Zhou, W., Doss, R., Jia, W.: Traceback of ddos attacks using entropy variations. IEEE Trans. Parallel Distrib. Syst. **22**(3), 412–425 (2010)
5. Shui, Y., Zhou, W., Guo, S., Guo, M.: A feasible ip traceback framework through dynamic deterministic packet marking. IEEE Trans. Comput. **65**(5), 1418–1427 (2015)
6. Yu, S., Tian, Y., Guo, S., Wu, D.O.: Can we beat ddos attacks in clouds? IEEE Trans. Parallel Distrib. Syst. **25**(9), 2245–2254 (2013)
7. Bhuyan, M.H., Bhattacharyya, D.K., Kalita, J.K.: Network anomaly detection: methods, systems and tools. IEEE Commun. Surv. Tutorials **16**(1), 303–336 (2013)
8. McMahan, HB., et al.: Communication-efficient learning of deep networks from decentralized data (2016). arXiv preprint arXiv:1602.05629
9. Konečný, J., McMahan, H.B., Yu, F.X., Richtárik, P., Suresh, A.T., Bacon, D.: Federated learning: Strategies for improving communication efficiency (2016). arXiv preprint arXiv:1610.05492
10. Lin, Z., Shi, Y., Xue, Z.: IDSGAN: Generative adversarial networks for attack generation against intrusion detection (2018). arXiv preprint arXiv:1809.02077
11. Usama, M., et al.: Generative adversarial networks for launching and thwarting adversarial attacks on network intrusion detection systems. In: 2019 15th International Wireless Communications and Mobile Computing Conference (IWCMC), pp. 78–83. IEEE (2019)
12. Shui, Y., Guo, S., Stojmenovic, I.: Fool me if you can: mimicking attacks and anti-attacks in cyberspace. IEEE Trans. Comput. **64**(1), 139–151 (2013)
13. Shui, Y.: Big privacy: challenges and opportunities of privacy study in the age of big data. IEEE Access **4**, 2751–2763 (2016)
14. Shui, Y., Liu, M., Dou, W., Liu, X., Zhou, S.: Networking for big data: a survey. IEEE Commun. Surv. Tutorials **19**(1), 531–549 (2016)
15. Bakopoulou, E., Tillman, B., Markopoulou, A.: A federated learning approach for mobile packet classification (2019). arXiv preprint arXiv:1907.13113
16. Zhao, Y., Chen, J., Wu, D., Teng, J., Yu, S.: Multi-task network anomaly detection using federated learning. In: Proceedings of the Tenth International Symposium on Information and Communication Technology, pp. 273–279 (2019)
17. Weiss, K., Khoshgoftaar, T.M., Wang, D.D.: A survey of transfer learning. J. Big Data **3**(1), 1–40 (2016). https://doi.org/10.1186/s40537-016-0043-6
18. Pan, S.J., Yang, Q., Sinno Jialin Pan and Qiang Yang: A survey on transfer learning. IEEE Transactions on knowledge and data engineering **22**(10), 1345–1359 (2009)
19. Chen, Y., Wang, J., Yu, C., Gao, W., Qin, X.: Fedhealth: A federated transfer learning framework for wearable healthcare (2019). arXiv preprint arXiv:1907.09173
20. Wu, P., Guo, H., Buckland, R.: A transfer learning approach for network intrusion detection. In: 2019 IEEE 4th International Conference on Big Data Analytics (ICBDA), pp. 281–285. IEEE (2019)

21. Singla, A., Bertino, E., Verma, D.: Overcoming the lack of labeled data: Training intrusion detection models using transfer learning. In: 2019 IEEE International Conference on Smart Computing (SMARTCOMP), pp. 69–74. IEEE (2019)
22. Maas, A.L., Hannun, A.Y., Ng, A.Y.: Rectifier nonlinearities improve neural network acoustic models. In: Proceedings of the International Conference on Machine Learning, vol. 30, p. 3 (2013)
23. Qu, Y., et al.: Decentralized privacy using blockchain-enabled federated learning in fog computing. IEEE Internet Things J. **7**, 6 (2020)
24. Yang, Q., Liu, Y., Chen, T., Tong, Y.: Federated machine learning: Concept and applications. ACM Trans. Intell. Syst. Technol. (TIST) **10**(2), 1–19 (2019)
25. Moustafa, N., Slay, J.: UNSW-NB15: a comprehensive data set for network intrusion detection systems (UNSW-NB15 network data set). In: 2015 Military Communications and Information Systems Conference (MilCIS), pp. 1–6. IEEE (2015)
26. Chollet, F., et al.: Keras (2015). https://github.com/fchollet/keras
27. Tzeng, E., Hoffman, J., Saenko, K., Darrell, T.: Adversarial discriminative domain adaptation. In: Proceedings of the IEEE Conference on Computer Vision and Pattern Recognition, pp. 7167–7176 (2017)

Variational Autoencoder Based Enhanced Behavior Characteristics Classification for Social Robot Detection

Xiaolong Deng[1]($\boxtimes$) (iD), Zhengge Dai[1], Mingdong Sun[2], and Tiejun Lv[1] (iD)

[1] Key Lab of Trustworthy Distributed Computing and Service of Education Ministry, Beijing University of Posts and Telecommunications, Beijing 100876, China
shannondeng@bup.edu.cn, {daizhengge,lvtiejun}@bupt.edu.cn
[2] BeiJing THUNI Soft Corporation Limited, Beijing 100084, China
sunmd@thunisoft.com

Abstract. With the development of Internet and online social communication tools, malicious social bots have become a problem which cannot be ignored. They are intentionally manipulated by some organizations or people and always disseminate malicious information on the Internet, which greatly impact network environment. As a result, the detection of malicious social bots has become a hot topic in machine learning and many kinds of classification methods are widely used to detect social bots. However, the current classification methods are limited by the unbalanced dataset in which the samples of human users always outnumber samples of social bots. Given by the nature of binary classification problem of detecting social bots, the imbalance of the dataset greatly impacted the classification accuracy of the social bots. Aiming to promote the classification accuracy, this article has proposed the use of Variational Autoencoder (VAE) to generate samples of social bots basing on existing samples and thus mitigate the problem of imbalance dataset before feeding the original dataset into classifiers. In this way, the classification accuracy of social bots and normal human users can be efficiently improved basing on selected six categories of user account features. In order to verify the advantage of VAE in generating social bot samples, other traditional oversampling algorithm named SMOTE and SMOTE based SVM are also used to generate samples of social bots and compared in the contrast experiments. The experimental results indicated that the proposed method in this article has achieved better classification accuracy compared with other scenarios using the same datasets.

Keywords: Malicious information · Social bots · Classification accuracy · Dataset training · Machine learning

1 Introduction

With the development of the Internet, social network has become a significant part of ours daily life. Generally speaking, every social network account corresponds to one user and this user uses his social network account to connect with others. However, there are a

© Springer Nature Singapore Pte Ltd. 2020
S. Yu et al. (Eds.): SPDE 2020, CCIS 1268, pp. 232–248, 2020.
https://doi.org/10.1007/978-981-15-9129-7_17

large number of social network accounts which are not used by real human beings. They are named social robots a.k.a. social bots. Social bots are usually manipulated by some software systems which are designed to control those social bots. The primary goals of maintaining these accounts are to disperse malicious information, which could be advertisement, malicious public opinion, fake news or even illegal contents. As a result, it is very important to identify these social bots in social network so that the service provider of social network can restrict the malicious behaviors of these social bots.

In this case, methods focus on detecting the social bots from a large dataset are proposed by researchers. Because the process of deciding whether a social network account is a robot or a human being is a binary classification problem, the final classification accuracy of these methods are largely depended on balance of the positive and negative samples of the dataset, which means the ratio of social bots and human users. However, the number of human being users often greatly outnumbers the one of social bots. In this scenario, this article proposes the use of Variational Autoencoder (VAE) to address the imbalance problem of the dataset.

The main contribution of this article is to use VAE to learn the statistical attribution of social bots in probability space and then uses these high-level features to generate new samples of social bots while given some random noise input. In this way, the imbalance of the dataset is mediated and the final classification accuracy of social bots' detection is improved. The whole process consists of the following operations: taking the minority classes from the Twitter user Dataset as the input of VAE; the encoder component of VAE taking the projecting the data into high dimension vector space; the decoder adding random noise to the features in high dimension space as initial value; the decoder uses these initial values to projecting them into Twitter social account data. In this way, some new social robots accounts data are generated. Then these data are added into the original dataset. In this article, a neural network technology was used as the classifier of the revised dataset. It will take the revised dataset, which include half social bots and half normal human twitter account, as training dataset. Then a random testing sub-dataset will be selected from the original dataset to test the effectiveness of the classifier. In order to prove the performance of this article, the classifier will also be trained on (1) original dataset with unbalanced human and social bots' samples (2) revised dataset which is added social bots samples generated by another popular oversampling algorithm. By proving the improvement of the neural network detection accuracy using VAE over the two scenarios as mentioned above, the effectivity of VAE can be proved.

The designed whole process of social bots detection can be found in Fig. 1. Variational Autoencoder is used to generate new social bots samples and built a balanced dataset before classifier training.

2 Related Work

The research on detecting online social bots basically began in 2010. At that time, the basic machine learning models and algorithms were used in it. For example, in 2010, Chu and Gianvecchio [1] firstly established a standard detection process to detect social bots with a set of measurements over 500,000 twitter accounts dataset. Their detection process including four parts: an entropy-based component calculating the latent regularity of the

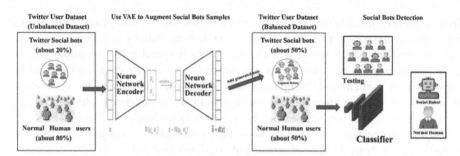

Fig. 1. Detection system design overview

twitter posted by a particular user, a machine-learning-based component classifying social bots from overall twitter dataset, an account properties component which can decide the personal information of an account, and a decision maker able to decide whether the input twitter account is a normal human. It also firstly used the features extracted from twitter user account to determine whether the account is a normal human user or a social bot. In 2011, Yang and Wilson [2] deployed the support vector machine (SVM) for uncovering social network social bots based on account data in the Renren Online Social Network. It utilized the user network features including average ratio of the number of incoming friend requests accepted and outgoing friend requests which are sent in one hour and collusion coefficient between different large groups. In this paper, Sybil graph and novel types of Sybil features were firstly applied to online social network.

From 2012, several papers focused on using social graph to depict the social network and using graph related algorithms to classify the social bots of online social network. For instance, in 2012, aiming to detect fake accounts in large scale social network, Cao and Sirivianos [3] designed a tool named SybilRank which marked impersonation possibilities of users by using social graph attributes. This social graph properties based algorithm will give each user a score according to their similarity of being sake and proved to be reliable under a large-scale data canter. In 2013, Beutel and Xu [4] focused on analyzing social graph between Facebook users and pages as well as the times at which the edges (links by other users) in the graph were established. They proposed two new algorithms to distinguishing the malicious behaviour according to graph structure and edge constraints.

From 2015, with the application of much more machine learning algorithms and mathematic models in this area, researchers transfers their researching focal point to the effectivity of detecting process by using less features of Twitter accounts. In 2015, Zafarani and Liu [5] derived a classification method with limited information given the realistic situation that the information of social bots may vary. It shows that lower to 10 bits data is sufficient to help decide whether an account is social bot. In this paper, the features of account are divided into five categories. The classification framework is proved to be robust under different datasets and algorithms. However, with the development of social bots on imitating normal human users and the increasing complexity of online social network, social bots are becoming more and more hidden and different to distinguish from normal human users. In 2016, Clark and Williams held the view that former detection methods which mainly based on user metadata cannot achieve great accuracy when facing social bots with powerful capacities [6]. They proposed to utilize the content of tweet as a main benchmark when classifying twitter accounts. Three linguistic features of a user's text are used in the detection process which including the average URL count per tweet, the average language dissimilarity between a user's tweeting, and the decay rate of text introduction of one user during different time-ordered tweets. In the same year, DARPA held a competition with the name of "The DARPA twitter bot challenge" [7], applying machine learning methods to identify social robots. During this competition, multiple teams compete on detecting a particular set of social bots of a certain topic including five features of twitter accounts: tweet syntax, cached real-time network statues, twitter semantics properties, cached behaviour features and user profile. Those teams who having achieved high detection accuracy have figured out the efficacious combinations of different features and applied specifically optimized machine learning methods to train on these features.

With the rise of deep learning, from 2016, researchers have employed more models in deep learning to this area. In 2016, Chavoshi [8] proposed a Twitter bot detection system called DeBot which utilized unsupervised machine learning algorithm to group up correlated users accounts in social network. The key technique they used to realize it is a novel lag-sensitive hash mapping algorithm based on synchronism properties of user accounts. Their final classification accuracy achieve up to 94% which can be validated on thousands of Twitter bots per day. In 2017, Cai and Li [9] used the combination of CNNs (convolutional neural networks) and LSTM (long short-term memory) model to extract and build connection between semantic information of user in twitters. It also built a latent timing model to take the textual features as well as behaviour features of users into detection process. Also, in 2017, Varol and Ferrara [9] made comprehensive conclusion on the existing research on social bots and applied new classification algorithms to detect social bots. They leveraged more than thousand features from public data and meta-data of social network users including such as friends, tweet content, sentiment patterns, network statues, activity time slots and so on. In their article, machine learning algorithms regarding random forest, decision trees, AdaBoost classifier and logistic regression are used to detect non-human twitter accounts while random forest is the best classifier for the accuracy criteria named the area under curve (AUC). Also, in 2017, Gilani and Farahbakhsh [11] collected large scale Twitter dataset and define various metrics based on metadata of users. Basing on these metrics, the twitter accounts were divided into four categories and then several questions are asked to distinguish certain relationships between the identity of these accounts (whether they are social bots are real human users) and their features including content view times, the source of twitter, account age, content viewed and account profile. In 2018, in order to extract more information from very limited data and improve the efficiency of detecting social bot, Kudugunta and Ferrara [12] used the sole twitter content to decide whether a twitter account is a social robot. They utilized LSTM to figure out the contextual information which takes the user metadata and twitter content as input. Another contribution point is that they devised a technique based on synthetic minority oversampling in order to produce large scale dataset. This measure highly improves the balanced level of the dataset by generating minority samples and thus increases the final classification accuracy. The proposed detection model achieved perfect precision up to 99% for the AUC and solved the negative effects brought by limited minority samples data. Last but not least, in 2018, B. Wu, L. Liu [13] applied Generative Adversarial Networks (GAN) to generate social bots samples and thus effectively improved the accuracy of social bots detection, which inspires this paper to dig deeper in using deep learning model to address the imbalance of social bots training dataset.

For the part of machine learning algorithm VAE, it was firstly proposed by Diederik and Max [14] in 2014. In this paper, VAE was used as inference and learning tool in directed probabilistic models to generate pictures based on MNIST dataset and VAE generates relatively ideal pictures. Although the original application of VAE is in the field of generating images, VAE also presents promising potentiality as generation model in other fields. The application of VAE in generating textual data is rising in recent years. Because the previous standard RNNLM (recurrent neural network language model) can generate sentences one word at a time and does not produce an explicit semantic representation of the sentence. In 2016, Vinyals and M [15] proposed VAE generation model based on RNN, which can create the potential semantic representation information at the sentence level by just sampling from the priors yields well-structured and diverse sentences. In 2019, Shen and Celikyilmaz [16] proposed various multi-level network structures for VAE (the ML-VAE model), which are expected to make use of high-level semantic features (themes and emotions) and fine-grained semantic features (specific word selection) in order to generate globally coherent long text sequences. In their project, hierarchical RNN decoder was proposed as a generation network to take advantage of the expression of sentence level and word level. Moreover, the author also found that it is better to transmit hidden variables to RNN decoder at high level and to output a mesh to RNN decoder at lower level to generate word than to directly transmit hidden variables to RNN decoder. Shen and Celikyilmaz also evaluated ML-VAE with language model for unconditional and conditional text generation tasks. The complexity of language modeling and the quality of the generated examples are greatly improved over some of the baseline levels. Additionally, in 2019, Zhang and Yang proposed a syntax-infused VAE which is able to integrate grammar trees with language sentences increase the performance of generating sentences. An unsupervised machine learning model based on SIVAE-i is proposed and presents syntactically controlled sentences production. The model of the system of Zhang and Yang was tested on real human words trees dataset and produced satisfied results for producing sentences with greater loss and little grammar mistakes. As a result, We can find that it is feasible to apply VAE to generate natural language information and twitter account information in textual format and the generated VAE social bots dataset may promote our detecting accuracy.

3   Designed Framework and Implementation

3.1   Twitter Account Features Selection

A twitter account has many features. For example, features that normal users can percept, including the number of friends and followers, the content of tweets produced by the users, profile description and user settings etc. Also, there are other implicit features which involving personal emotion and social network connection in the back-end dataset.

These features have already been thoroughly analyzed and categorized. Generally, these features are divided into following six categories which can be found in Table 1. In our project, eleven features having better classification effect for social bots are selected from these six categories which presented in Table 1.

Table 1. Features and their categories.

Category	Features used
User-based features	Number of favorite topics, most frequent words used in twitter, the punctuation using habit, the length of the twitter, number of forwarding other twitters
Friends features	Number of the ratio of followers and followed other accounts
Network features	Number of URL linkage, the resource of the tweets
Temporal features	Number of mentions of other users
Content and language features	Topic tags
Sentiment features	The sentiment similarity of twitters

Number of Favorite Topics: this feature represents how many topics a twitter user interested in. Normally, a human user is interested in several specific topics and keeps following these topics by posting their own comments, interacting with other twitter users under the same topic or thumbing up other twitters. Yet for twitter social bots, their main job is to extend their influence and target topics that they are designed to. Thus, their favorite topics may remain the same and unrelated to each other.

Most Frequent Words Used in Twitter: When normal human users post twitters, they have their own typing style and language usage habit. Some words and expression will be more frequent used by a particular human user. However, because the content of social robots is generated by system, their language habit is usually more random and uncertain.

The Punctuation Using Habit: The reason using this feature is the same as the most frequent words used in twitter. It is defined as follows:

$$d_n = \Sigma_{i=1}^{N} v_i \tag{1}$$

Where v_i denotes the variance of the happening of a specific word's usage.

The Variance of the Length of the Twitter: The length of twitter posted by normal human users normally fluctuates a lot. It depends on what the users what to express and how intense of their felling. This feature not likely exists in social bots account for they focus on one topic and act as a particular role. It is defined as follows:

$$\sigma = \frac{\Sigma \left(d_n - \overline{d_n} \right)^2}{N}, \; \overline{d_n} = \frac{\Sigma d_n}{N} \tag{2}$$

Where $\overline{d_n}$ means the average of the twitter length, N stands for the total number of the twitter account and d_n is the numerical value of the nth twitter's length.

Number of the Ratio of Followers and Followed Other Accounts: For normal users, they have limited time so they don't follow too many other twitter accounts. In this case, the ratio of followers and followed other accounts is normally no larger than 10. But for a social robot it is normal that they follow a large crowd of people in order to disperse their influence in larger people set.

Number of URL Linkage: This feature represents the average number of URL linkage in a twitter account. For normal human, their main intention of using social network is to communicate with other people and express their own opinions and posting an external URL is not a common operation for them. Social bots are always intended to direct other normal users to other sources, for example inducing others to fishing website, selling illegal sources or posting fake advertisements. So the frequency of using extra URL is larger than normal users.

The Resource of the Tweets: It represents the average ratio of twitters that pushed from other sources of the total twitters of the user. One main task of social network for human users is providing a good place to share their actions on other applications (for instance, sharing one's favorite song from Spotify). So, some tweets from normal users are from external resource, which uses official interface provided by Twitter. On the contrary, social bots is unlikely to share this information from other legal external applications. Even if they do, it is highly possible that they use illegal interface.

Number of Mentions of Other Users: This feature represents the average number of mention of other users in a user' twitter. The form is used as "@name" in twitter. Because the social bots need to influence more normal users, generally they mention more users than human being.

Topic Tags: This feature represents the average number of tag usage for a user. Each tweet can be selected to correlate with a topic by using the symbol "#topic". Generally normal human user will not use this tag frequently or use more than one tag. Yet in order to expand their influence, social bots are more inclined to use more tags which could be a good feature to distinguish normal users from bots.

Number of Forwarding Other Twitters: It represents the average ratio of the number of retweeting and self-edited tweet. Normally, twitters forwarded by human users are high correlated with their interested topics with their comments. While for social bots, they tend to retweet more frequently without their own opinions so that to disperse them more quickly.

The Sentiment Similarity of Twitters: This feature represents the latent sentiment and semantic similarity of one user's twitter. This feature is realized by using "Vector Semantic Space" (VSS), which can analyze the potential relatedness between words and documents. The similarity of the distribution of words between two documents a and b can be calculated as follows:

$$s = \frac{\Sigma_{i=1}^{N}(a_i \times b_i)}{\sqrt{\sum_{i=1}^{N}(a_i)^2} \times \sqrt{\sum_{i=1}^{N}(b_i)^2}} \tag{3}$$

Where a and b denote the row vector of document of word A and word B, they can be expressed as a $= \{a_1, a_2, \ldots, a_n\}$ and b $= \{b_1, b_2, \ldots, b_n\}$. The closer the value of s. 1, the more similar the word A and B is. Human users usually have a common sentiment pattern when posting twitters with a larger value of s close to 1. However, social bots post sentiment dissimilar twitters with lower value s which is close to 0.

3.2 VAE

Variational Autoencoder was firstly proposed in 2014 as a generated model and the main target of VAE is to construct a function using the latent variable to generate the target data. More specifically, it tries to map the original data into latent variables and supposes the latent variables obey a certain type of distribution (for example normal distribution in this case). Then it uses the latent variables to generate new data with random noise added. As the results, the ultimate goal of this algorithm is to better make the generated distribution close to the real distribution of the dataset. The goal of VAE is to better make the generated distribution close to the real distribution of the dataset. In order to realize it, what VAE do is to make transformations between different distributions using neural network. What VAE trying to build this is: supposing there is a N dimension vector, which stands for N features that are used to solely determining one twitter user account. For each feature, there is a distribution of it. And what the VAE do is to sampling from these distributions and use a deep neural network to rebuild a simulated twitter account.

The structure of VAE consists of an encoder, a decoder, and a loss function which can be found in Fig. 2. The encoder takes the twitter account data as input and mapping every input data into latent attributes. Because these latent variables obey normal distribution, each of them has two attributes including mean value and variance. The decoder uses the latent value to regenerate twitter account information. In order to use VAE to generate new samples, the latent attributes will be modified each time in generating a new account. In order to generate new samples which possess original accounts' properties but not totally the same, before directly takes the mean value attribute as its input, the decoder adds random noise to the variance attribute and then adds the revised variance to the mean value. That being said the latent attributes will be modified each time when generating a new account. In this project, the latent attributes are assigned random noise to make sure it can generate different and thorough twitter social bots accounts. Specifically, the mathematic deduction is as follows: suppose the input data samples denote as $\{X_1, X_2, \ldots, X_n\}$ with the distribution p(X). However, we cannot directly calculate this distribution. Then we look into the latent variable p(Z), which is mapped by the encoder from the p(X). Now we can suppose p(Z|X) is the exclusive posterior probability distribution of X_n and p(Z|X) obeys normal distribution. The decoder can recover the twitter account data by sampling from p(Z|X). Formula (4) is used to calculate the distribution of Z:

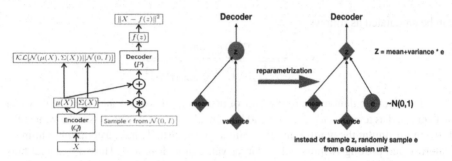

Fig. 2. The structure of VAE   **Fig. 3.** Flow of reparameterization

$$p(Z) = \sum_X p(Z|X)p(X) = \sum_X \mathcal{N}(0, I) * p(X) = \mathcal{N}(0, I) \sum_X p(X) = \mathcal{N}(0, I) \quad (4)$$

In this way, the distribution of Z can be kept in standard normal distribution whose mean value is denoted as $\mu(X)$ and variance is denoted as $\Sigma(X)$. Then random noise (in this case realized by sample a value from $\mathcal{N}(0, I)$) is added into $\Sigma(X)$ and the revised $\Sigma(X)$ is added to $\mu(X)$ as the final input of decoder. In this way, the decoder is able to continually generate new bots' samples. Finally, the model is trained multiple epochs based on the loss function which has two parts: (1) Kullback–Leibler divergence, also known as KL divergence, between the distribution of $\mathcal{N}(\mu(X), \Sigma(X))$ and $\mathcal{N}(0, I)$ (2) Mean-square error, also known as MSE, between the input data X and the output data $f(z)$. Finally, the flow chart of VAE is shown in Fig. 2.

In formula (4), for the reason that Z is a random variable, in the process of calculating the back propagation in neural networks, Z will be an undifferentiated variable. And a method named reparameterization will be used to calculate the back information of Z. The basic idea of this method is to introduce a Gaussian distribution ε, which can transform Z to a fixed value which can be found in Fig. 3 while circles represent random variables and squares represent variables.

3.3   Social Robot Classification Method

The problem of detecting social bots is defined as follows: $D = \{d_1, d_2, \ldots, d_n\}$ represents the information of a single twitter account where d_1 to d_n represents the N key features of this account. The dataset $W = \{D_1, D_2, \ldots, D_m\}$ consists of M accounts while each account is either a normal human user or a robot. The category R consists of two parts: R_r (robots) and R_h (human). The essence of this problem is to decide whether a twitter account D belongs to R_r or R_r. What this project done is to improve the performance of a function which can mapping a twitter account D based on its N features d_1 to d_n to the correct categories R_r or R_h. The definition of this mapping is as follows ($\varphi(A_n)$ represents the mapping function):

$$\varphi(A_n) = \begin{cases} 0 & A_n \in R_r \\ 1 & A_n \in R_h \end{cases}, \text{ where } R = \{R_r, R_h\} \quad (5)$$

In fact, this process is simplified as a binary classification problem. Considering the binary decision problem on pure numeral dataset is very mature and holds high recognition accuracy, we select the most common and accurate method– simple neural network. So, what limited the performance of the final classification accuracy of this neural network is the balance and abundance of the training dataset. In the following sections, we will focus on how to address the imbalance problem of dataset.

3.4   The Overall System Design

Figure 4 shows the overall system design of this project. Firstly, eleven key and highly-discriminative features are selected and extracted from the original dataset. Then they are transformed into pure numeral data to facilitate the training and classification process. Secondly, the dataset are split into two parts: testing and training dataset under the ratio of 1:4. In each sub-dataset, social bots accounts and human user account are separated (the ratio of social bots accounts and human users is about 1:4. Thirdly, the VAE takes the social bots accounts of the training dataset as input and output generated more social bots accounts. The newly generated social bots accounts are added to the previous training dataset to solve the imbalance problem. Fourthly, the neural network classifier uses the revised training dataset as its training dataset and the final classification accuracy will be tested by the testing dataset.

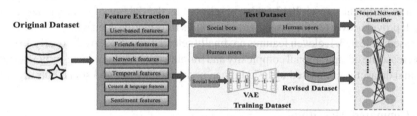

Fig. 4. Overall system design

3.5   Detection Algorithm Process

The flow chart of the detection process is shown in Fig. 5. The main process can be listed as the following steps:

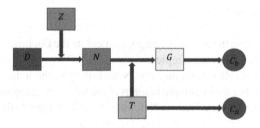

Fig. 5. Detection process

1. Divide the original dataset into training dataset T and testing dataset E. The twitter account neural network classier C_a is trained on the training dataset T.
2. Divide the training dataset into two parts: pure social bot dataset B and pure human user dataset H. The VAE model is trained on B to generate new social bots accounts.
3. The decoder D and the encoder N could generate new twitter account with given random noise Z, which is added to the input of N.
4. Add G into the training dataset T and used the revised dataset to train a new neural network classifier C_b.
5. Compared the performance of C_a and C_b.

4 Results and Discussion

4.1 Dataset

Because detection of social bots has become a hot topic these years, a number of public datasets are available online and bot repository is selected by us as the original dataset resource. Bot repository (https://botometer.iuni.iu.edu/data/index.html) is a centralized website to share annotated datasets of Twitter social bots and normal human users. It provides dataset of different magnitude, crawled from twitter website in different years. In our experiment, cresci-2017 folder is selected as the dataset of training and testing data. It provides over ten thousand twitter accounts information each with 23 features. As discussed in Sect. 3.1, eleven features are finally selected and used. Additionally, in order to decrease the computational complexity and training time while keeping sufficient data, the final dataset is composed of 1970 human user accounts and 463 social bots account.

4.2 Compared Algorithm

In order to prove the performance of VAE in generating social bots accounts, traditional over-sampling algorithm named Synthetic Minority Over-sampling Technique (SMOTE) is selected as the compared algorithm. SMOTE algorithm is a revised scheme of random oversampling while random oversampling simply copies samples randomly to add new samples into the original dataset. SMOTE algorithm is design to solve the over fitting problem of the classification model so that the information the model learns become too specific rather than general. To solve this, SMOTE algorithm analyses the minority samples and composites new samples according to original samples. The SMOTE process is as follows:

(1) For every samples in the minority category, calculate the Euclidean distance between it and every other minority samples;
(2) Define parameter called sampling rate N according to the unbalanced level of the original dataset. For every sample belongs to the minority category, randomly select several samplings using k-Nearest Neighbor algorithm. Denote the neighbor sample selected as X_n;
(3) For every selected the neighbor sample X_n, using formula (6) below to generated new samples:

$$x = x + rand(0, 1) * (\widetilde{x} - x) \tag{6}$$

The compared algorithm is realized by Imblearn Python library (https://pypi.org/pro ject/imblearn/). Same as VAE, SMOTE algorithm also takes the training dataset as input data. The new samples generated by SMOTE are also added into the original dataset. The augmented dataset will be used to train the simple neural network classifier and final accuracy will be calculated using the testing dataset.

4.3 Experimental Process and Results Analysis

Parameter Settings: After designing basic structure of VAE, selecting appropriate parameters is also a vital part in constructing neural network. In machine learning, these parameters are called hyperparameters. Hyperparameters includes a set of settings includes the layer of the neural network, the number of the neuron of each layer, the learning rate, the coefficient of regression, etc. And these hyperparameters should be revised continuously during the training time until the neural network can achieve optimal results. In this paper, the selection of these hyperparameters including layers, learning rate, number of the neurons referenced the settings in previous work [13] which utilized GAN to generate social bots samples. The settings of the neural network used in this article are listed below:

1) Layers: According to related research focus on make prediction based on pure data, two to four layers is the common settings. After testing and optimizing, each neural network component including encoder, decoder and our classifier used three layers in this article.
2) Activation function: activation function performs as the role of processing function between each previous layer and later layer of neural network. In this project, two activation functions were used:
   Sigmod function: $f(x) = \max(0, x)$ and ReLU function: $\sigma(x) = \frac{1}{1+e^{-x}}$.
   In this case, Sigmod function is the ideal function for activation function before the last layer output. For the input layers, because the final equivalent function of neural network is highly possible non-linear, ReLU is the ideal non-linear function.
3) Optimization function: Machine learning algorithm is always focus on optimization model and optimize the loss function (the optimized objective function). According to the original VAE algorithm and open source research projects about using VAE to generate text data, Adam algorithm is selected as optimization algorithm of encoder and the classical SGD (Stochastic Gradient Descent) algorithm is selected as optimization algorithm of both decoder and neural network classifier.
4) Learning rate: To get accurate predictions, a learning algorithm called gradient descent updates the weights as it moves back from the output to the input in neural network. The gradient descent optimizer estimates the good value of the model weight in multiple iterations by minimizing a loss function (L), and this is where the learning rate comes into play. It controls the speed at which the model learns.

$$L = -\left[y \log(\hat{y}) + (1 - y) \log(1 - \hat{y})\right] \tag{6}$$

Where y denotes expected output and $y^\wedge$ is the actual output of the neural network. According to the original VAE algorithm and other researched using VAE to generate text data, our learning rate in VAE and neural network classifier is between 0.0001 to 0.0005 which can help to reach the most optimal learning effect.

5) Number of neurons: In this project, according the settings of the neurons in related researches and continuous optimization of the parameters during the practical experiments, the number of the neurons of each layer can be determined. For the first layer of the encoder, the number of the neurons should be equal to the input data's dimension. For the last layer of the decoder, the number of the neurons should also equal to the dimension of the twitter account data. Besides, the number of the neurons of other layers ranges from 10 to 30 depends on the nature and final performance of experiments. For the decode, the function of it is to learn the latent features of the twitter accounts which means data compression, so the neurons of it are set between 10 to 25. For the decoder and neural network classifier, the function of them is to regenerate the data and accurately decided whether an account is a social bot. In this case, the neurons are set between 20 and 30 for better distinguishing performance.

Experimental Results and Analysis: Firstly, the VAE should be trained on the social bots samples of the original dataset. The encoder would use the neural network to convert the input twitter samples data into low-dimension vector and then the decoder should add random noise to the features extracted and regenerate high-dimension twitter account data. Then the output data would be calculated its loss between input real account data using SGD algorithm. Thus, the loss function of the decoder, encoder in this project is a logarithm function. After 2000 epochs training, the final curve of the loss function and the variance of the loss function are presented in Fig. 6.

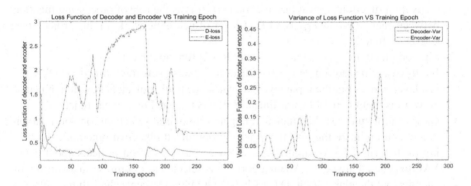

(a) loss function curve for decoder and encoder   (b) variance of the loss function

Fig. 6. Loss function of VAE components in training process

The loss function fluctuates a lot at the beginning of the whole training process. For the reason that the encoder has not learnt the basic features of the incoming social bots samples in the lack of training epochs, in the front 225 epochs, the VAE is adjusting its internal neural network to conform its distribution to the social bots. Also, in the training process, the loss of encoder changed more violently and keeps higher value than the decoder. It represents that the beginning statue of encoder could be further than decoder and takes more dramatically change to the final state. After about 260 training rounds, the loss function of both decoder and encoder declined to be smooth, which means that the features have been basically extracted and incorporated in VAE's neural network.

Additionally, the total training time is also recorded in the experiment. The time of training each epoch is recorded and the accumulative training time is also recorded in Fig. 7. As the result presented in the graph, it takes much longer time to train the encoder than the decoder, which also proves the early speculation that the encoder is more time-consuming to train according to the dramatically change of loss function.

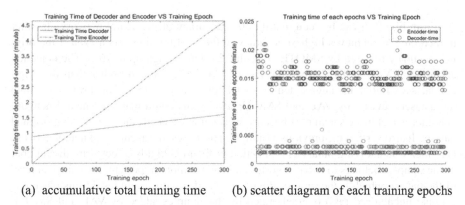

(a) accumulative total training time   (b) scatter diagram of each training epochs

Fig. 7. Training time of VAE components in training process

In order to prove the effectivity of VAE in learning the latent features of social bots tweets and generating new samples, we need to test the dataset mixed with the samples VAE generated on the neural network classifier. If the final detection accuracy increases compared to neural network classifier trained on original dataset, it can prove that the VAE is effective. Furthermore, if the final detection accuracy increases compared to the same structure classifier trained on dataset mixed with twitter bots samples generated by other oversampling method which in this project refers to SMOTE algorithm, we can draw the conclusion that VAE is more effective than the traditional oversampling method. For the experiment design of this project, in order to control variables, the same dataset and minority samples are used when training the VAE and SMOTE model and the neural network classifier used the same hyperparameters when trained on augmented dataset generated by VAE and SMOTE algorithm. Additionally, the same test set is used as the criteria of final accuracy of the classifier.

The VAE, SMOTE and SMOTE based SVM algorithms will generate some social bots until the number of social bot samples is equal to the normal human user samples. Then the neural network classifier will train on according revised dataset. The result diagram can be found in Fig. 8.

Fig. 8. Accuracy comparation of classifiers

From Fig. 8, it can be seen that the final accuracy of the neural network classifier trained on VAE achieves highest accuracy in the final training epoch even if the original accuracy realized by SMOTE algorithm is high enough up to 76%. The detection accuracy of VAE is higher than the one of SMOTE 1.5% and higher than the original dataset without any augmented on social bots' samples 15%. This proves that both the datasets revised by VAE and SMOTE algorithms could make the neural network classifier detect more social bots because its accuracy exceeds the one of using original dataset. It also verifies the previous assumption proposes: the accuracy of neural network classifier when solving binary classification problem is highly affected by the number of the samples belongs to two categories and what is more important, the balanced level of the dataset which is the ratio of the positive and negative samples. In this place, the original unbalanced ratio is ameliorated by the samples added by VAE and SMOTE accordingly. The result shows that if the ratio is closer to 1, the accuracy of the classifier will better be assured. Additionally, the result presents that the accuracy improvement made by VAE overpasses the accuracy made by SMOTE algorithm by 1.5 per cent and closed to which of SMOTE based SVM algorithm. It demonstrates that compared to SMOTE algorithm, the VAE can better help the neural network classifier to learn the features of social bots' samples and thus improves its detection ability. This is brought up by the strong capability of VAE in extracting the latent properties of social bots and VAE is better in imitating these samples. In fact, it is decided by the nature of VAE which used neural network model which can better extract features from existing dataset while SMOTE algorithm which realized oversampling on a simple and too random method.

5   Conclusions and Future Work

This article aims at using VAE to solve the problem of unbalanced data between normal human users and social bots by generating social bot samples. In order to prove the effectiveness of VAE in generating new samples, two compared experiments are conducted including training the classifier on original dataset and training the classifier on dataset added with new social bots generated by SMOTE algorithm. The experimental result shows that dataset revised by using the social bot data generated from VAE effectively improves the accuracy compared to the compared algorithms.

However, there are some problems existing in the usage of VAE. Firstly, for the accuracy improvement with the increase of the training epochs, the result reached by VAE presents fluctuation compared to the smooth result curve of the compared experiments and it may be caused by the mean square error between the generated data and the original data by VAE. This will cause the uncertain ambiguity of the generated data which will affect the accuracy when training the classifier in some epochs. Secondly, the accuracy improved by VAE over traditional oversampling SMOTE algorithm is obvious and close to the better algorithm of SMOTE based SVM. It may because the total number of the original dataset is not large enough so the advantage of VAE cannot be fully presented in this case. In future work, in order to overcome the problem of the uncertain ambiguity of the generated data, adversarial nets can be combined with VAE which means to apply adversarial nets to train it while keeping the basic structure of VAE. Moreover, the VAE can be deployed in large scale dataset to better present its advantage over traditional oversampling algorithm.

Thanks to the support of National Key Research and Development Program of China under Grant (NO. 2017YFC0820603, NO. 2018YFC0831301 and NO. 2018YFC0831302).

References

1. Chu, Z., Gianvecchio, S., Wang, H., Jajodia, S.: Who is tweeting on twitter: human, bot, or cyborg?. In: Proceedings of the 26th Annual Computer Security Applications Conference, pp. 21–30, 6-10 December 2010
2. Yang, Z., Wilson, C., Wang, X., Gao, T., Zhao, B.Y., Dai, Y.: Uncovering social network sybils in the wild. In: Proceedings of the 2011 ACM SIGCOMM Conference on Internet Measurement Conference, pp. 259–268, 2–4 November 2011
3. Cao, Q., Sirivianos, M., Yang, X., Pregueiro, T.: Aiding the detection of fake accounts in large scale social online services. In: Proceedings of the 10th USENIX Symposium on Networked Systems Design and Implementation, p. 15, 25–27 April 2012
4. Beutel, A., Xu, W., Guruswami, V., Palow, C., Faloutsos, C.: "CopyCatch: stopping group attacks by spotting lockstep behavior in social networks. In: Proceedings of the 22nd International Conference on World Wide Web, pp. 119–130, 13-17 May 2013
5. Zafarani, R., Liu, H.: 10 bits of surprise: detecting malicious users with minimum information. In: Proceedings of the 24th ACM International on Conference on Information and Knowledge Management, pp. 423–431, 18-23 October 2015
6. Clark, E.M., Williams, J.R., Galbraith, R.A., Jones, C.A., Danforth, C.M., Dodds, P.S.: Sifting robotic from organic text: a natural language approach for detecting automation on twitter. J. Comput. Sci. **16**, 1–7 (2016)
7. Subrahmanian, V.S., et al.: The darpa Twitter bot challenge. Computer **49**(6), 38–46 (2016)
8. Chavoshi, N., Hamooni, H., Mueen, A.: DeBot: Twitter bot detection via warped correlation. In: Proceedings of the 16th IEEE International Conference on Data Mining, pp. 817–822, 12-15 December 2016
9. Cai, C., Li, L., Zengi, D.: Behavior enhanced deep bot detection in social media. In: Proceedings of IEEE International Conference on Intelligence and Security Informatics, pp. 128–130, 22-24 July 2017
10. Varol, O., Ferrara, E., Davis, C.A., Menczer, F., Flammini, A.: Online human-bot interactions: detection, estimation, and characterization. In: Proceedings of the Eleventh International AAAI Conference on Web and Social Media, pp. 280–289, 15-18 May 2017

11. Gilani, Z., Farahbakhsh, R., Tyson, G., Wang, L., Crowcroft, J.: Of bots and humans (on Twitter). In: Proceedings of the 2017 IEEE/ACM International Conference on Advances in Social Networks Analysis and Mining, pp. 349–354, 31 July–3 August 2017
12. Kudugunta, S., Ferrara, E.: Deep neural networks for bot detection. Inf. Sci. **467**, 312–322 (2018)
13. Wu, B., Liu, L., Dai, Z., Wang, X., Zheng, K.: Detecting malicious social robots with generative adversarial networks. KSII Trans. Internet Inf. Syst. **13**(11), 5515–5594 (2019). https://doi.org/10.3837/tiis.2019.11.018
14. Kingma, D.P.: Max welling, "auto-encoding variational Bayes". In: The 2nd International Conference on Learning Representations (ICLR2014), p. 14 (2014)
15. Vinyals, O., Dai, A.M., Jozefowicz, R., Bengio, S.: Generating sentences from a continuous space. Comput. Sci. (2015)
16. Shen, D., Celikyilmaz, A., Zhang, Y., Chen, L., Wang, X., Gao, J., et al.: Towards generating long and coherent text with multi-level latent variable models (2019)
17. Zhang, X., Yang, Y., Yuan, S., Shen, D., Carin, L.: Syntax-infused variational autoencoder for text generation (2019)

A Decentralized Weighted Vote Traffic Congestion Detection Framework for ITS

Yang Song, Zhuzhu Wang$^{(\boxtimes)}$, Junwei Zhang$^{(\boxtimes)}$, Zhuo Ma, and Jianfeng Ma

Department of Cyber Engineering, Xidian University, Xi'an 710071, China
zzwang_2@stu.xidian.edu.cn, jwzhang@xidian.edu.cn

Abstract. With the rapid development of Internet of Vehicles (IoV), the applications of traffic congestion detection based on Intelligent Traffic System (ITS) are proposed and widely used. However, location privacy leakage has become a serious problem in traffic congestion detection based on traffic voting, because vehicles will upload traffic congestion information and their own locations to the traffic management server. In this paper, we propose a decentralized weighted vote traffic congestion detection framework, which allows vehicles can safely participate in the traffic voting, under location privacy protection, and accurately obtain the traffic congestion status of the road. Specifically, we introduce blockchain technology into traffic congestion detection, and apply smart contract to replace the traditional trusted third party. We propose a weighted voting scheme, and set the weight of votes depending on the distance between the vehicle's current position and the location of congestion. The security analysis result shows that our framework can satisfy the above requirements. Finally, the experiment results demonstrate that our framework is efficient and practical.

Keywords: Traffic congestion detection · Weighted vote · Blockchain · Location privacy protection

1 Introduction

In recent years, Intelligent Traffic System (ITS) has attracted wide attention due to the rapid development of Internet of Vehicles (IOV), which is aiming to establish a large, functional, real-time, accurate, efficient traffic management system [1]. Meanwhile, as an important part of ITS, traffic congestion detection has been widely studied. Traffic congestion is due to unbalanced traffic flow or insufficient traffic infrastructure. Analysis and detection of traffic congestion can improve the use efficiency of roads and reduce the costs of traffic congestion [6]. At present, traffic congestion detection has been widely used in ITS, such as intelligent traffic signal light management [21], traffic monitoring [2].

The traffic congestion detection based on traditional ITS requires participating vehicles to upload their location and current traffic condition information to the server of the traffic management department. Klein et al. [11] propose

© Springer Nature Singapore Pte Ltd. 2020
S. Yu et al. (Eds.): SPDE 2020, CCIS 1268, pp. 249–262, 2020.
https://doi.org/10.1007/978-981-15-9129-7_18

the concept of vehicles' cooperation with the traffic management department to manage traffic congestion by voting. In protocol vehicles must trust the central authority. However, the server may collect vehicles' location information, infer their travel chain, expose movement path, and cause serious privacy problems. At the same time, for the traffic congestion of a road section, most schemes do not take into consideration the impact of the distance between the vehicle's location and the location of the congestion on the final result. This strategy will bring a lag effect and fail to provide real-time information about each route to road users [13].

In recent years, several related schemes and approaches have been proposed to cope with the location privacy protection and anonymity issue for using traffic voting in traffic congestion detection problem in ITS [3,5]. For example, the vehicle provides encrypted segment-based route information to a road side unit (RSU), and uses homomorphic encryption to collect data for all segments by a single message [20]. The data in above protocols are handled by the TTP (trusted third party), which undoubtedly increases the risk of data being used privately and leaked. How to use blockchain to guarantee the privacy of location and data security while accurately obtaining the traffic congestion status of the road through traffic voting is a challenging problem.

In this paper, to address the above issue, we propose a decentralized weighted vote traffic congestion detection framework for ITS, which can protect the privacy of the vehicle's location, and set the voting weight according to the vehicle's location to make the voting result more accurate and more consistent with the real traffic congestion status. We introduce blockchain which can solve the abuse and disclosure of vehicles' private data which stored in the TTP. At the same time, the use of weighted vote can get accurate traffic congestion, and our weighted vote protocol can prevent privacy disclosure. To summarize, our protocol can achieve the following requirements:

1. *Decentralization:* In this paper, we introduce the blockchain technology instead of using traditional TTP to manage data and ballots, so as to eliminate the risk of data and votes being used privately and leaked. The blockchain network is constructed by roadside units (RSUs) that vehicles complete the interaction with the blockchain by submitting and receiving data to the nearby RSU.
2. *Privacy of location and confidentiality of location strategy:* Our framework use ECC encryption to ensure the confidentiality of the location strategy and privacy of the vehicle's location. No one can use the ballot information to get the voting information of a vehicle, and the confidentiality of the location strategy also guarantees that the vehicle will not adjust location parameters according to the location strategy.
3. *Weighted voting:* Traffic management set Location strategy based on the road to be scored. The corresponding weight is calculated by using the location parameter of the vehicle. When the vehicle is close to the road to be scored, the corresponding voting weight is high and the voting result has a significant influence on the result of road congestion score. On the contrary,

the voting weight is low, and the impact of the voting on the result of road congestion score can be ignored.

The remaining parts of this paper are organized as follows. Section 2 shows the related work associated with our framework. Then, Sect. 3 presents some preliminary background and Sect. 4 describes the problem formulations which includes system model, threat model and security requirements. Our scheme is presented in Sect. 5, followed by Sect. 6 which gives the security analysis. Later on, Sect. 7 shows the performance analysis. Finally, the concluding remark of this whole paper is summarized in Sect. 8.

2   Related Work

Pan et al. [17] propose a traffic collision detection system based on crowd voting. Lin et al. [14] propose Highway Voting System (HVS) would allow vehicles to vote to provide traffic management with information about traffic congestion. Chen et al. [5] come up with Traffic Voting System (TVS), a system that allows travelers and drivers to actively share information about their location and road conditions and form travel chains to improve overall traffic efficiency. But in TVS and HVS systems, data on the vehicle's ballot and location information is stored in TTP, where vehicles' private data and location tracks can be compromised and abused illegally.

It is well known that location privacy protection [9,22,23] as an important issue in traffic congestion detection has been widely studied [8]. Brown et al. [3] propose that vehicles send a fuzzy encrypted data and add noise to the statistics to protect the privacy of each vehicle. It relies on the trusted-third-party to process and store the data, which in reality is unreliable. Padron et al. [16] use the distributed vehicular ad hoc network to transmit data instead of the TTP, and also assumes that congestion information can only be obtained when the vehicle is close to the traffic congestion, making the final congestion information more accurate. However, it must be adopted by a large number of vehicles, the feasibility is not strong.

Blockchain is a peer-to-peer decentralized network with the property of open consensus, non-tamperability, and traceability. In recent years, the research and design of decentralized voting based on Blockchain has become a research hotspot. McCorry et al. [15] propose the first implementation of a decentralised and self-tallying internet voting protocol with maximum voter privacy using the Blockchain. Khoury et al. [10] propose a decentralized trustless voting platform that relies on Blockchain technology. Pawlak et al. [18] introduce a Blockchain voting system that can be audited.

Normally, every eligible voter can vote, and only one at a time. However, in fact, the ballots of some voters should be weighted against the ballots of others. For instance, in traffic congestion voting, the weight of vehicles should be related to the distance between vehicles and the traffic congestion, so as to accurately reflect the traffic congestion. A voting system is supporting weight is developed [7] which based on REVS propose the specific requirements that should be satisfied in the weight of the right to vote. The disadvantage of this method is that multiple rounds of key generation methods need to be run in the election generation stage, and the administrator also needs to store a list of keys corresponding to different weights, which will reduce the system operational efficiency.

3   Preliminaries

3.1   Hash Commitment

The commitment scheme is a cryptographic primitive that permits one to commit to a chosen value while keeping it hidden to others, with the ability to reveal the committed value later. Commitment schemes are designed so that a party cannot change the value or statement after they have committed to it, that is, commitment schemes are binding. The hash commitment scheme usually has two steps, namely commitment phase and verify phase [19].

$$(com, key) := commmit(msg) \tag{1}$$

$$match := verify(com, key, msg) \tag{2}$$

We require that the hash commitment satisfies the following standard security guarantees:

1. **Hiding.** When given com, it is infeasible to find the msg which corresponds to the com.
2. **Binding.** It is infeasible to find a msg which satisfies $msg \neq msg'$ such that $verify(commit(msg), msg') == true$. That means, once a commitment is made, it cannot be changed. Mathematically, there are not any two different messages with the same commitment and key.

3.2   EC-ELGamal

The encryption process using EC-ElGamal [12] encryption consists of three parts: KGen,Enc,Dec.

KGen: $(P_k, S_k) \longleftarrow (G)$. This algorithm outputs the key pair(P_k, S_k) on select elliptic curve $Ep(a, b)$ and its base point G.

Enc: $(C_1, C_2) \longleftarrow (P_k, M)$. This algorithm outputs the encryption ciphertext pair (c_1, c_2) on inputting the public key P_k and the point M which encoded by the plaintext m.

Dec: $M \longleftarrow (S_k, C_1, C_2)$. This algorithm outputs the decryption result M, then decode the M to plaintext m.

3.3 Smart Contract

Smart contract is a special protocol that runs on a blockchain with the specified running logic. Our voting protocol is implemented in a smart contract based on Ethereum [4], and the user on the blockchain can check the contract code at any time to know the functions of a smart contract. Because contract deployments and invocations are verified and broadcasted by the miners and stored in a new block state in the blockchain, so it cannot be changed or retrieved by the publishers or users themselves. Using smart contract ensures data consistency and the complete and correct execution of the election process.

4 Problem Formulations

4.1 System Model

As shown in Fig. 1, the participants in the system model include traffic management server(TMS), vehicles, and smart contract.

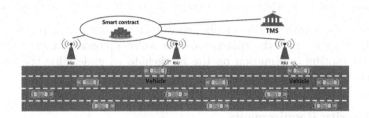

Fig. 1. System model

RSU. RSUs are distributed around the road and are connected to the blockchain as network nodes. The vehicle sends the ballot to the blockchain via a nearby RSU. At the same time, vehicle can also accept the message in the blockchain from the RSU to complete the voting process.

TMS. TMS is the initiator of the election and generates the location strategy for the election and two key pairs to encrypt the vehicle's score and ballot, then the location strategy and two key pairs are uploaded to smart contract through the RSU.

Vehicle. Vehicles observe the election published by TMS by receiving the RSU's message, and then calculate the voting location parameters with their own position, and score the current traffic jam. By uploading their ballots to the smart contract of blockchain through the RSU, vehicles can participate in voting.

Smart contract. The smart contract is to accept the location parameters, commitment and the ballot of vehicle through the data uploaded to the blockchain by the RSU, then calculate the voting weight of each vehicle, then generate the proof of each vehicle's ballot. Finally calculate and publish the final voting result.

4.2 Threat Model

The entities in decentralized weighted vote traffic congestion detection framework have the possibility to play the role of the attackers.

Vehicle. Vehicle is semi-honest and curious. In the election, Vehicle may have following adversarial behaviors: First, when submitting ballots, the vehicle may be curious about the location of other vehicle and contents of their ballots. That is, the vehicle may launch the privacy disclosure attack. Second, once the vehicle knows the content in the location strategy published by TMS, vehicle can adjust his or her location to increase the voting weight by uploading a ballot which location parameter is closer to the location strategy. Thus, it's possible for the vehicle to launch the known-strategy attack.

TMS. TMS is honest but curious. During the election, TMS may have following adversarial behaviors: Because TMS has the key pair for the election, and may be curious about the location parameters uploaded by vehicles and decrypt by using the private key to obtain it. That is, TMS may launch a location privacy attack. In addition, the TMS may be able to link the ballot to a vehicle depending on the voting weight. In other words, TMS may launch a weight analysis attack.

Outsiders. There may be some malicious outsiders in the whole process of election, who tries to infer the contents of the ballot uploaded by the vehicles or modify the voting information on the blockchain to undermine the successful completion of the voting process.

4.3 Security Requirements

1) *Privacy of location and confidentiality of location strategy.* The real location of a vehicle cannot be obtained from the location parameter in the vehicle's ballot. In addition, vehicle cannot know the content of the location strategy and adjust location to make their voting weight become higher.
2) *Fairness.* Vehicle do not know how many ballots the current road received until the ballots are counted. At the same time, the voting weight is related to the distance between the vehicle and the location strategy, so that the vehicle close to the location strategy have a higher voting weight.
3) *Privacy of weighted vote.* Traffic management server or vehicles cannot use the voting weight to link any ballot with the vehicle who cast it.

5 The Proposed Framework

In Fig. 2, we give a general description of the framework at various phases. Voting protocol contains the following three entities: the traffic management server(TMS), the vehicle, the smart contract, and consists of following phases: voting preparation phase, commitment phase, voting phase, tally phase.

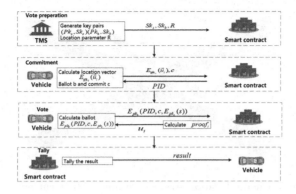

Fig. 2. Voting process

5.1 Overview

At the beginning of the election, TMS generates two pairs of encryption keys for election, and generates location strategy and weight equation. Then TMS sends the two private keys, location strategy and weight equation to the smart contract, and the public keys are published.

When the election begins, during the $Time_{commit}$, the vehicle v_i sends the commitment and location parameter to the smart contract, then smart contract stores them and sends PID_i to v_i.

When in $Time_{vote}$, the vehicle v_i sends the ballot to the smart contract, then the smart contract generates proof of the ballot.

Finally, smart contract removes the illegal ballots, then decrypts and calculates to get the weight of each vehicle, and finally uses weight to calculate the final voting result.

5.2 Voting Preparation

*Step*1: TMS first generates the EC-ELGamal public/private key pair (Pk_s, Sk_s) to encrypt vehicle's score, and key pair (Pk_b, Sk_b) to encrypt the vehicle's ballot. Then TMS generates the location strategy $\vec{v} = (x_e + y_e)$ based on the road location and encrypts the $\vec{v}$ by Pk_s to get the $\mathbb{P} = Enc_{Pk_s}(\vec{v})$.

*Step*2: As Fig. 3 shown. The location strategy parameter R is set according to the road that needs to be scored. When vehicles located in [0, R], the voting weight is high, and the score of these vehicles have a great influence on the final tally result. For vehicles in [R,5R], we believe that they are gradually far away from the current road or on other roads, the weight of these vehicles decreases exponentially, and the impact of the vehicles' score on the final tally result is very small so that it can be ignored. Then TMS generates the weight equation.

$$F(x) = (\frac{x}{R} - 1)e^{(\frac{x}{R}-1)} + \frac{e+1}{e} \qquad (3)$$

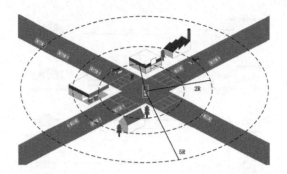

Fig. 3. Choose location strategy parameter R in current road

*Step*3: TMS sends Sk_s Sk_b $\mathbb{P}$ R and $F(x)$to smart contract via a secure channel, and publishes the public key Pk_s Pk_b and $\mathbb{P}$.

5.3   Commitment

*Step*1: During the $Time_{commit}$, vehicle v_i use its current location parameter $\overrightarrow{u_i} = (x + y)$ to calculate $Enc_{Pk_s}(\overrightarrow{u_i})$.

*Step*2: Vehicle v_i scorse current road traffic jam conditions and gets the score s, the range of the score is $[1, 2, 3, \cdots, 10]$ the bigger the number, the better the road traffic status is. Then v_i encrypts it with the public key Pk_s gets the $Enc_{Pk_s}(s_i)$, and calculates the commitment c_i, where $c_i = H_c(Enc_{Pk_s}(s_i))$. Finally v_i sends $Enc_{Pk_s}(\overrightarrow{u_i})$ and c_i to the smart contract.

*Step*3: When smart contract receive the $Enc_{Pk_s}(\overrightarrow{u_i})$ and c_i, then generates a unique PID_i for each legal vehicle and store the tuple $(Enc_{Pk_s}(\overrightarrow{u_i}), c_i, PID_i)$, and sends the PID_i to the v_i. After $Time_{commit}$, smart contract will no longer accept any $Enc_{Pk_s}(d_i)$ and c_i from v_i.

5.4   Voting

*Step*1: When $Time_{vote}$ start, v_i submits the ballot b_i and encryps it with the public key Pk_b, where $b_i = Enc_{pk_b}(Enc_{pk_s}(s_i), c_i, PID_i)$.

*Step*2: Until the end of $Time_{vote}$, when receiving b_i, smart contract decrypt b_i using private key Sk_b to obtain $Enc_{pk_s}(s_i)$, c_i and PID_i. Then smart contract will check if the PID_i is legal and haven't voted yet, if yes, smart contract records the PID_i and marks PID_i as voted in the PID_{list}. The smart contract reveals c_i, if satisfies then generates $proof_i$ where $proof_i = c^* = u_i \cdot c_i$, u_i is a random number.

*Step*3: The smart contract sends u_i to v_i, and published $proof_i$ in the blockchain.

5.5 Tally

*Step*1: First, smart contract gets the $\vec{u_i}$ and $\vec{v}$ by decrypting $Enc_{Pk_s}(\vec{u_i})$ and $Enc_{Pk_s}(\vec{v})$ using the private key Sk_s and calculates the voting weight $w_i = F(|\vec{u_i} - \vec{v}|)$.

*Step*2: Smart contract gets the total n of all the legal ballots and calculates the voting weight of each vehicle, then gets s_i decrypt $Enc_{Pk_b}(s_i)$ by using private key Sk_s.

*Step*3: Smart contract calculates the final result and sends it to the blockchain. TMS and vehicles can get traffic congestion detection result through blockchain.

$$result = \frac{\sum_{i=1}^{n} \frac{s_i}{w_i}}{\sum_{i=1}^{n} \frac{1}{w_i}} \tag{4}$$

6 Security Analysis

6.1 Privacy of Location and Confidentiality of Location Strategy

Our protocol guarantees that during the voting process, the location parameter $\vec{u_i} = (x + y)$ of vehicle and location strategy $\vec{v}$ will not be disclosed.

Here we denote an adversary A who is aming to get the privacy of vehicle's location $\mathbb{L}$ and location strategy $\mathbb{L}_s$. When the adversary A could access network. There are two possible cases.

Case 1. In order to get the vehicle's location, A has to decrypt $E_{Pk_s}(\vec{u_i})$ based on Sk_s derived by Pk_s, there is

$$Pr[S'_k \leftarrow KGen(G); M' \leftarrow A(Dec(Enc_p k_s.Sk_s)) : Verify(Enc_p k, Sk, M)$$
$$= Verify(Enc'_p k, Sk', M') = 1] < v(k) \tag{5}$$

which leads to the difficulty in calculating elliptic discrete logarithms. Therefore, A could not be able to get the private key and Case 1 can only occur with a negligible probability. As a result, the information in the $E_{Pk_s}(\vec{u_i})$ can not be calculated by A.

Case 2. Assuming there is an adversary A who is able to calculate the private key and get the $\vec{u_i}$ and $\vec{v}$, then the A get the location $\mathbb{L}'$ of vehicle from the $\vec{u_i}$, and location strategy $\mathbb{L}'_s$ from the $\vec{v}$, there is

$$Pr[\mathbb{L}' \leftarrow \vec{u_i}, \mathbb{L}'_s \leftarrow \vec{v}; Verify(\mathbb{L}, \mathbb{L}_s) = Verify(\mathbb{L}', \mathbb{L}'_s)] < v(k) \tag{6}$$

Therefore, it is computationally infeasible for the A to find the real location $\mathbb{L}$ of vehicle and the location strategy $\mathbb{L}'_s$.

6.2 Fairness

Our protocol is using the commitment to ensure that the ballot before the voting phase is not leaked to resist the ballot privacy disclosure attack. If the dishonest vehicle V intends to change his ballot, and the adversary A intends to get the ballot from commitment c, there is case.

Case. The dishonest vehicle V generates a new ballot $\mathbb{Q}$ or The adversary A intends to search the ballot $\mathbb{Q}$ instead of the original one $\mathbb{B}$ and expects the same output c, there is

$$Pr[c \leftarrow H_c(\mathbb{B}); c \leftarrow \mathbb{Q}, \mathbb{Q} \neq \mathbb{B}] < v(k) \tag{7}$$

Therefore, it is computationally infeasible to find a new ballot which is different from the original one for the dishonest vehicle or adversary.

Each vehicle will correct calculate the real location parameter, so their ballot will be counted by the real voting weight, and the weight will be high when vehicle close to the traffic jam, so as to get accurate voting results. The level of weight is related to the distance between the vehicle and the location strategy set by TMS. The closer the vehicle is to the road to be scored, the higher voting weight will be.

6.3 Privacy of Weighted Vote

In the protocol we proposed, the voting weight is calculated by the smart contract, and the vehicles do not know their voting weights before voting. If the dishonest vehicle V intends to change his ballot to get higher voting weight W_v according to the location strategy $\mathbb{L}$, and the adversary A intends to get the ballot from voting weight W_v, there is case.

Case 1. The dishonest vehicle V generates a new ballot $\mathbb{Q}$ according to Location Strategy $\mathbb{L}$ and get high voting weights W_s, there is

$$Pr[W_v' \leftarrow F(\mathbb{Q}), W_v \leftarrow F(\mathbb{B}); \mathbb{Q} \leftarrow \mathbb{L}, W_v' > W_v] < v(k) \tag{8}$$

Therefore, it is infeasible for the dishonest vehicle to find a ballot according to the location strategy $\mathbb{L}$ which makes the voting weight higher.

Case 2. Assuming there is an adversary A who intends to get the ballot $\mathbb{Q}$ from the voting weight W_v, there is

$$Pr[\mathbb{Q} \leftarrow W_v, W_v \leftarrow \mathbb{B}; Verify(\mathbb{Q}) = Verify(\mathbb{B}) = 1] < v(k) \tag{9}$$

Therefore, it is computationally infeasible to find the real ballot from the voting weight for adversary, so it cannot be linked to the vehicle according to the voting weight.

7   Performance Evaluation

The blockchain platform we used is Ethereum, and the network is private chain configured by Geth client running on a PC(CPU:Intel(R)Core(TM) i5-3317U CPU @ 1.70 GHz, RAM:8G, OS:Ubuntu 16.04 LTS). The smart contract is programmed using Solidity language which version is v0.5.7, using the remix compiler, and then we use Truffle, which is a development environment, testing framework and asset pipeline for Ethereum to deploy our smart contract to the private chain network.

We use ethereum nodes to represent each vehicle, which is consistent with the actual hardware environment of the vehicle. Then we send a number of transactions on the contract and test 30 vehicles' voting, with gas consumption per step interacting with the smart contract as shown in Table. 1. T represents TMS's deployment of smart contract and the operation that interact with it. V is for operations that vehicles interact with smart contract during the voting.

Table 1. Deploy smart contract gas used

Role	Transaction	Gas costed	Cost in $
T	Contract deployment voting contract	2598937	2.4157
	Contract deployment library	737922	0.6859
	Voting preparation	22488	0.0153
	Tally	2335549	2.1709
V	Commitment	334457	0.3108
	Voting	1232499	1.1456

The voting contract contains our voting logic code and ECC decryption code. The deployed library contains a data structure for voting. The total Gas used by TMS when deploying the smart contract is 3336859 gas.

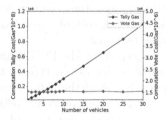

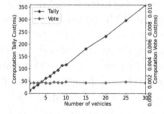

Fig. 4. Voting gas used in different number of vehicles

Fig. 5. Voting time used in different number of vehicles

For the whole voting process, the relationship between gas consumption and the number of voting participants is shown in Fig. 4. It can be seen that the gas

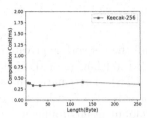

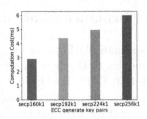

Fig. 6. Computation cost of Keccak-256 hash function in different length of the plaintext

Fig. 7. Computation cost of EC-ElGamal generate key pair under different curves

consumption of vote counting is in direct proportion to the number of vehicles participant.

In Fig. 5, we show the relationship between counting expenses and the number of vehicles. The calculation cost of the time of a single vehicle's ballot remains basically the same, since the vehicle's PID, ciphertext and encrypted ballot's commitment are only validated during the voting phase, so the computational overhead is roughly the same.

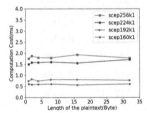

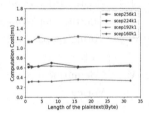

Fig. 8. Computation cost of encrypt in different length of the plaintext under different curves

Fig. 9. Computation cost of decrypt in different length of the plaintext under different curves

We used the Keccak-256 hash function in our experiment to promise the vehicles' encrypted ballots, because this algorithm is also the common hash function in Ethereum. Figure 6 shows the computational cost of the Keccak-256 we generated to encrypt votes in different open text spaces.

During the voting phase, vehicles' ballots are encrypted by the EC-ElGamal algorithm. Figure 7 shows the computational cost of generating encryption key pairs of different lengths under different elliptic curves. And the computation time is positively correlated with the finite domain of elliptic space. Therefore, as the size of finite field of elliptic curve increases, the generation time of key pair increases correspondingly.

As shown in Fig. 8 and Fig. 9, the computation time cost has little relation with the change of plaintext size, but is positively correlated with the choice of curve and the size of private key pair.

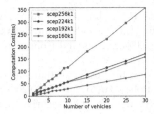

Fig. 10. Computation cost of decrypt in different number of vehicles

Figure 10 shows the computational overhead relationship between the use of different elliptic curves and the number of vehicles during the tally stage of decryption. It can be seen that the computational time cost is positively correlated with the size of finite field of elliptic curve.

8   Conclusion

In this paper, we propose a decentralized weighted vote traffic congestion detection Framework for ITS, which achieves that the vehicle can perform traffic congestion voting without a trusted-third-party while ensuring the vehicle's location privacy. In addition, we propose a weighted vote protocol, that is, the voting weights of the vehicles change with the distance from the traffic congestion center. The security analysis shows that our protocol is able to resist the privacy disclosure attack, known-strategy attack and weight analysis attack. Finally, the experiment results show that the usage weighted vote in our protocol can get the traffic jam condition efficiently and accurately, and is also feasible in real life.

Acknowledgements. This work was supported by the National Natural Science Foundation of China (Grant No. 61872283, U1764263, 61702105, U1804263, U1708262).

References

1. An, S., Lee, B.-H., Shin, D.-R.: A survey of intelligent transportation systems. In: 2011 Third International Conference on Computational Intelligence, Communication Systems and Networks, pp. 332–337. IEEE (2011)
2. Baiocchi, A., Cuomo, F., De Felice, M., Fusco, G.: Vehicular ad-hoc networks sampling protocols for traffic monitoring and incident detection in intelligent transportation systems. Transp. Res. Part C Emerg. Technol. **56**, 177–194 (2015)
3. Brown, J.W.S., Ohrimenko, O., Tamassia, R.: Haze: privacy-preserving real-time traffic statistics. In: Proceedings of the 21st ACM SIGSPATIAL International Conference on Advances in Geographic Information Systems, pp. 540–543 (2013)
4. Buterin, V., et al.: A next-generation smart contract and decentralized application platform. White paper, **3**(37) (2014)
5. Chen, W., Zhang, K., Li, Z.: Traffic voting system to achieve the balance between privacy and trip chain data acquisition. In: 2018 IEEE International Conference on Industrial Engineering and Engineering Management (IEEM), pp. 1101–1105. IEEE (2018)

6. de Souza, A.M., Yokoyama, R.S., Maia, G., Loureiro, A., Villas, L.: Real-time path planning to prevent traffic jam through an intelligent transportation system. In: 2016 IEEE Symposium on Computers and Communication (ISCC), pp. 726–731. IEEE (2016)
7. Eliasson, C., et al.: An electronic voting system supporting vote weights. Internet Res. Electr. Netw. Appl. Policy **16**(5), 507–518 (2006)
8. Hubaux, J.-P., Capkun, S., Luo, J.: The security and privacy of smart vehicles. IEEE Secur. Privacy **2**(3), 49–55 (2004)
9. Ji, Y., Zhang, J., Ma, J., Yang, C., Yao, X.: BMPLS: blockchain-based multi-level privacy-preserving location sharing scheme for telecare medical information systems. J. Med. Syst. **42**(8), 147 (2018)
10. Khoury, D., Kfoury, E.F., Kassem, A., Harb, H.: Decentralized voting platform based on ethereum blockchain. In: 2018 IEEE International Multidisciplinary Conference on Engineering Technology (IMCET), pp. 1–6. IEEE (2018)
11. Klein, I., Ben-Elia, E.: Emergence of cooperation in congested road networks using ICT and future and emerging technologies: a game-based review. Transp. Res. Part C Emerg. Technol. **72**, 10–28 (2016)
12. Koblitz, N.: A course in number theory and cryptography, vol. 114. Springer, New York (1994). https://doi.org/10.1007/978-1-4419-8592-7
13. Lee, K., Hui, P.M., Wang, B.-H., Johnson, N.F.: Effects of announcing global information in a two-route traffic flow model. J. Phys. Soc. Japan **70**(12), 3507–3510 (2001)
14. Lin, W.-H., Lo, H.K.: Highway voting system: embracing a possible paradigm shift in traffic data acquisition. Transp. Res. Part C Emerg. Technol. **56**, 149–160 (2015)
15. McCorry, P., Shahandashti, S.F., Hao, F.: A smart contract for boardroom voting with maximum voter privacy. In: Kiayias, A. (ed.) FC 2017. LNCS, vol. 10322, pp. 357–375. Springer, Cham (2017). https://doi.org/10.1007/978-3-319-70972-7_20
16. Padron, F.M., Mahgoub, I., Rathod, M.: Vanet-based privacy preserving scheme for detecting traffic congestion. In: High Capacity Optical Networks and Emerging/Enabling Technologies, pp. 066–071. IEEE (2012)
17. Pan, Y.-R., Chen, B.-H., Lin, Z.-Y., Cbeng, H.-Y.: Traffic collision detection using crowd voting. In: 2017 International Conference on Information, Communication and Engineering (ICICE), pp. 274–277. IEEE (2017)
18. Pawlak, M., Guziur, J., Poniszewska-Marańda, A.: Voting process with blockchain technology: auditable blockchain voting system. In: Xhafa, F., Barolli, L., Greguš, M. (eds.) INCoS 2018. LNDECT, vol. 23, pp. 233–244. Springer, Cham (2019). https://doi.org/10.1007/978-3-319-98557-2_21
19. Preneel, B.: Analysis and design of cryptographic hash functions. PhD thesis, Katholieke Universiteit te Leuven (1993)
20. Rabieh, K., Mahmoud, M.M., Younis, M.: Privacy-preserving route reporting scheme for traffic management in vanets. In: 2015 IEEE International Conference on Communications (ICC), pp. 7286–7291. IEEE (2015)
21. Younes, M.B., Boukerche, A.: Intelligent traffic light controlling algorithms using vehicular networks. IEEE Trans. Veh. Technol. **65**(8), 5887–5899 (2015)
22. Shui, Yu.: Big privacy: Challenges and opportunities of privacy study in the age of big data. IEEE access **4**, 2751–2763 (2016)
23. Zhang, J., Zong, Y., Yang, C., Miao, Y., Guo, J.: Lboa: Location-based secure outsourced aggregation in IoT. IEEE Access, p. 1 (2019)

CVNNs-IDS: Complex-Valued Neural Network Based In-Vehicle Intrusion Detection System

Mu Han$^{(\boxtimes)}$, Pengzhou Cheng, and Shidian Ma

Jiangsu University, Zhenjiang 212013, China
{hanmu,masd}@ujs.edu.cn, 1056225295@qq.com

Abstract. The bus of the Controller area Network (CAN) in the vehicle is frequently attacked under the environment of efficient communication. This paper explores ways to hide features of the intrusion detection system (IDS) and obtain a high-precision during an attack on the Internet of vehicle (IoV). To protect the privacy features of the hidden layer with regard to anomaly detection, we proposed the CVNNs-IDS. The system converts the data into an image in real-time using the encoder and then maps it into the complex domain whiles it rotates it to reconstruct the real features to achieve the purpose of system protection. Available researches show that features from random angles are obtained by attackers, making it impossible to distinguish between the real or fake feature. The accuracy of the proposed method CVNNs-IDS is 98%. Results obtained represents that our proposed method performed better than the traditional techniques with regard to performance and security.

Keywords: In-vehicle security · IDS · CAN · CVNNs · Privacy protection

1 Introduction

Although the current rapid development of 5G communication technology has provided sufficient in-vehicle communication guarantee for the development of auto-pilot, the Internet of vehicle (IoV) and cloud service platform connection, however, it has limitations with the maturity of the technology. Without the support of V2X, which ensures communication between exterior devices such as mobiles, vehicles, the Internet, etc., the maturity of the technology cannot be achieved [1]. Hence, it is with regard to the communication process with external devices that the security of IoV is threatened. Hackers employ the use of the Internet attacks(e.g., dos attack, fuzzy attack, malfunction attack, etc.)

Supported by the Innovation Plan for Postgraduate Research of Jiangsu Province in 2014 under Grant KYLX1057.
National Science Foundation of China under Grant 61902156.
Natural Science Foundation of Jiangsu Province under Grant BK20180860.

© Springer Nature Singapore Pte Ltd. 2020
S. Yu et al. (Eds.): SPDE 2020, CCIS 1268, pp. 263–277, 2020.
https://doi.org/10.1007/978-981-15-9129-7_19

to attack the electronic control units (ECUs) of the vehicle. It is within the ECUs that various ways of protecting the CAN bus are applied, including the most effective one intrusion detection. Apart from identifying malicious attacks with high accuracy, it also reduces the computational cost as compared to other methods.

Most of the existing methods will need to improve the physical layer or generate MAC authentication message based on cryptography or modify the CAN controller in order to be able to protect the security of the CAN bus. However, the existing method increases the cost and computational complexity of the process or experiment. Research available indicates that IDS based on deep learning (DL) is one of the best in detecting an anomaly because it forms a security barrier between the external devices and the internal CAN bus by placing it at the gateway. This helps to monitor the in-vehicle system continuously. However, the most important function of IDS is to determine whether the CAN packet is abnormal. Currently, researches available with regard to IDS indicates an improvement in that area.

Research by Golovko et al. presented neural network ensembles for intrusion detection [2], and research by Buczak et al. proposed a survey of data mining and deep learning methods for cybersecurity intrusion detection [3]. The development of data science is bound to be accompanied by privacy problems. However, the two main types of privacy problems under deep learning are well elaborated in [1]. Research by Meng et al. also proposes a direct disclose as a result of massive data collection [4]. In [5], the studies introduced direct privacy leakage caused by insufficient generalization ability of models. Individual privacy is becoming more challenging due to the rapid technological growth in areas like the Internet, big data, deep learning and artificial intelligence due to the large-scale data collection. Therefore, private information protection with regard to IoV is becoming a critical area which has a direct impact on the driver. The privacy protection concerning DL is in three main parts and deeply discussed in [6] by Liu Junxu. Recent research by Xiang et al. in [7] employs an interpretable complex-valued neural network to boost the challenge of inferring input attributes from features.

Although the classification model established by DL can effectively detect abnormal data, it is also faced with limitations such as features are not protected or secured during the training process and the leakage of privacy. Attackers can retrieve the features by employing reverse engineering and build models to avoid being easily detected [7]. Hence, we propose CVNNs-IDS (Complex-valued Neural Network-based Intrusion Detection System) with an embedded local decoder to help address the limitations that have been stated above. The function of the local encoder is to convert CAN data into CAN image, and extract shallow features to hide into the random phase of complex features. The role of the local encoder effectively addresses the problem with features being leaked in the hidden layer. The proposed model can detect anomalies and send the results to the local decoder for decoding. Finally, the result obtained from the experiment will determine whether or not the CAN bus will transmit the data frame. The proposed model CVNNs-IDS is able to identify multiple types of attacks by generating a lot of unknown attack images during the training process of GAN at the preliminary stage of the work, hence improving the anomaly detection rate. The proposed scheme has the following advantages:

- Higher accuracy: the CVNNs-IDS can identify unknown and known attacks at the same time.
- Better security: with regard to the security of the CVNNs-IDS model, more of the attack packets are detected.
- More excellent scalability: the effect of the CVNNs-IDS model on different cars indicates a higher detection rate and can be updated in time according to the network changes.

1.1 Organization of This Paper

This study introduces the convenience brought by 5G, IDS for in-vehicle, and the security risk based on deep learning. The remainder of this paper is organized as follows: In Sect. 2 we deal with the related works of the research, and explains the practical proposal for protecting the privacy feature from being disclosed and the proposed scheme CVNNs-IDS is discussed in Sect. sec3, and in Sect. 4, the experiment and results are presented. Finally, the conclusion is presented in Sect. 5.

2 Related Works

The limitation associated with the CAN bus is that it can transmit instructions regardless of the data frame generated by the ECUs. The difficult part is to determine whether it is a standard or malicious message. To address the problems associated with malicious attacks, Muter et al. proposed an entropy-based anomaly detection for in-vehicle networks [8]. However, it was difficult to distinguish between the change in information entropy caused by the injection of a small number of messages and the change in information entropy caused by task-triggered signals. Hence, affecting their accuracy. Research by [9] also proposed an intrusion detection mechanism that takes advantage of Bloom filtering to test the data frame periodically based on message identifiers and parts of the data-field. This helps to facilitate the detection of potential replay or modification attacks. Presently, deep learning (DL) is attracting much attention in the research arena of IDS. Current research by Taylor et al. in [10] proposed a long short-term memory network method to detect anomaly messages with CAN. Their approach uses RNN to predict the next symbol in the sequence.

Anomalies are flagged when the error between real and predicted values is high. Kang et al. presented a method in [11] to detect abnormality by using DNN that initializes the parameters through the unsupervised pre-training of deep belief networks (DBN), thereby improving the detection accuracy. Yu et al. in [12] proposed an anomaly detection method for in-vehicle CAN bus based on random forest. Researches claim their approach reduced the false-positive rate.

Hyun et al. in their current study, developed IDS for in-vehicle based on Generative Adversarial Nets (GAN). This was a novel approach that converts CAN ID into images by one-hot encoding, which was able to detect known and unknown attacks [13]. Jichici et al. also proposed a deep Neural network approach with an excellent performance to detect both the replay and injection attack of the CAN bus [14]. Although the various studies stated above used DL to detect anomaly data in IoV, they had limitations in addressing attacks that are direct to the model or invades the CAN controller. Therefore we propose CVNNs-IDS, which covert the CAN ID images to complex-valued data through the native encoder. The processor module is then established to build a complex neural network which is then used for the classification. The results are decoded by the local decoder to achieve the purpose of the detection. Results from the experiment show that the proposed scheme improves the safety of the model, directly protects the privacy and the safety of drivers without reducing the accuracy of the detection is achieved.

3   CVNNs-IDS: Complex-Valued Neural Network Based IDS

3.1   The Workflow of the CVNNs-IDS System

The proposed model based on a complex-valued neural network discussed in this article includes a local encoder, a detection model of the complex-valued neural network, and a local decoder. The flow chart for the CVNNs-IDS is shown in Fig. 1.

1. The local encoder G extracts the CAN message, which are encoded the images in real-time. It then transforms the features of the images encoded by the heat vector to the complex domain.
2. The image features are rotated by $\theta \in (0, 2\pi)$ through GAN local decoder. All features are sent to the processing module, and then it identifies the complex-valued images to the prediction of the result.
3. The local decoder decodes the predicted results from the second step and informs the CAN bus whether it is abnormal.
4. However, when the vehicle enters an unfamiliar network environment, the characteristics adopted by the encoder and the false images generated by WGAN will be sent to the cloud processing module to train a more accurate model to update the local CVNNs-IDS.

All three modules are simultaneously trained to form the intrusion detection system presented in this paper. This helps to ensure that the CAN bus completes a secure communication between the ECUs.

3.2   The Local Encoder Model

The ECUs communicate in real-time with the CAN bus. Available research shows that about 2000 CAN message frames are generated every second. Hence our

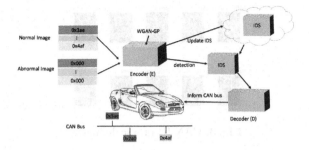

Fig. 1. The detection flow chart for the CVNNs-IDS

proposed system is designed to ensure security in real-time. Since the ID field of the CAN packet is an identification for the ECUs, features can be encoded into complex-values images whether the CAN packet is accepted or rejected after which anomaly detection is done by employing the complex-valued neural network. Analysis of the data frame shows that the ID field of each standard data frame is encoded in hexadecimal. Hence, each element of the CAN ID is converted into a binary form with 16 digits. The binary form of each element of the CAN IDs are then encoded into one-hot-vector, Which then generates a 3 * 16 image. It is done by converting the first digit of 0×123 to 1000...000, the second converted to 0100...000, and the third digit converted to 0010...000. Figure 2(a) [13] below shows the encoding process of a CAN ID and a 64 CAN ID. Figure 2(b) shows a sample image that converts 64 consecutive CAN Ids into images. The dataset and the model established in the experimental part of this research are based on standard data frames. However, the anomalous extended frame can still be safely detected by re-training the model since the entire process employs the same theory.

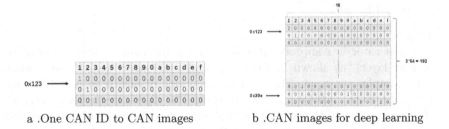

a .One CAN ID to CAN images   b .CAN images for deep learning

Fig. 2. CAN data covert to one-hot encoding

Since CAN ID is converted into a grayscale image, which is a matrix of 0 or 1 as shown in Fig. 3, consequently introduce the local encoder G to extract the features of the CAN image. And two parameters include θ and b that were generated randomly to construct complex features to hide real features, are also introduced.

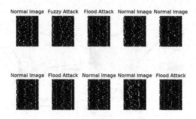

Fig. 3. CAN ID grayscale image

Let (i,y)⊆ D supply input, and it is then labelled in the training dataset. Given the input i to the encoder G, the features are computed as follows:

$$a = G(i) \tag{1}$$

However, our model rejects to forward real features to the CVNNs-IDS directly. After introducing the deceptive b matrix with the same real features, the real features are hidden in the complex number domain as follows:

$$x = \exp(i\theta)[a + b * i] \tag{2}$$

The complex feature is then rotated through the parameter θ, and the veritable features are then protected from disclosure again.

This section of the analysis introduces a local encoder based on the WGAN training model [15]. Inspired by references [7] and [16], we define the generator as a feature extractor that is trained with a range of $\Delta\theta'$ s and b′ s to hide the real characteristics in a random phase. Letting D represent the discriminator, and we train it to distinguish the generated feature from the original feature. This is an efficient way to protect the characteristics of the CAN data, which increases the difficulty for attackers to obtain the features, crack the model, and even realize the invasion. The composition of the proposed model is as follows, as shown in Fig. 4(c):

– Design the generator
  The generator is composed of a deconvolutional neural network consisted of four layers, as shown in Fig. 4(a), and can extract real features when train samples are input. The activation function of each layer is ReLU, with exception to the last layer, which is Tanh. The discriminator then identifies the generated characteristics. This improves the authenticity of the generated image, after the backpropagation of the calculated cost function.
– Design the discriminator
  The discriminator consists of five layers of CNN, as shown in Fig. 4(b), LeakyReLU is also used by the activation function of each layer, and sigmoid is used as a function activation of the last layer. The discriminator is trained iteratively to distinguish real features from confused-features. The discriminator then opposes the generator to improve its recognition rate.

However, literature [7] proposed that when an ideal encoder is decoded, the features attacker gained should be sufficiently confused with the actual characteristics. Hence, Let $\alpha' = \Re[x * exp(-i\theta')] = \Re[(a+bi)\ exp\ (i\theta - i\theta')] = \Re\ [(a+bi)\ exp\ (i\Delta\theta)]$ that has the same distribution with α. The encoder E extract the CAN image and chooses between b and θ secretly to transform it to complex-valued type. To simplify the calculation, we define some fixed values for b. The training loss function of the model is as follows.

$$D = argmax\mathbb{E}_{I \sim pI, \Delta\theta \sim U(0,\pi), b \neq G(I)}[D(G(I)) - D(\Re[(G(I)+bi)e^{i\Delta\theta}])] \quad (3)$$

$$G = argmin\mathbb{E}_{I \sim pI, \Delta\theta \sim U(0,\pi), b \neq\ G(I)}[D(\Re[(G(I)+bi)e^{i\Delta\theta}])] \quad (4)$$

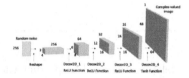

a .The generator model base on WGAN

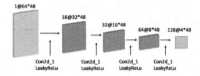

b .The discriminator model base on WGAN

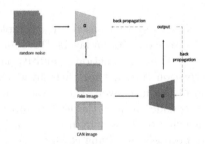

c .The encoder G base on WGAN

d .Images are generated by encoder G

Fig. 4. The design and function figure for local encoder

In Fig. 4(d), Our encoder processes the raw data and get four kinds of images of 3 stages that are the CAN imagesshallow feature images, and the features of the complex-valued. The encoder trained based on Algorithm 1.

3.3   The Detection Model of the Complex-Valued Neural Network

The CVNNs-IDS system is designed to guarantee not only the accuracy of real-time verification but also the security of the model itself. Since we converted CAN message into images, CNN [17] is more suitable for extracting features of images, which is still operated to identify abnormal messages in Fig. 5.

Algorithm 1. local encoder, our proposed algorithm. All experiments in the paper used the default values $\alpha = 0.00005$, $c = 0.01$, $m = 64$, $n_{critic} = 5$. $CANimagesize = 64 * 48$, $epochs = 30000$.

Require: :α, the learning rate. c, the clipping parameter. m, the batch size. n_{critic}, the number of iterations of the critic per generator iteration.
Require: :w_0, initial critic parameters. θ_0, initial generator's parameters.
1: **while** θ has not converged **do**
2:     **for** $t = 0, ..., n_{critic}$ **do**
3:         $Sample_{CANImages}$ $\{x^{(i)}\}_1^m \sim \mathbb{P}_r$ a batch from the real data.
4:         $Sample_{CANImages}$ $\{z^{(i)}\}_{p_1}^m \sim p(z)$ a batch of prior samples.
5:         $g_w \leftarrow \nabla_w \{argmax\mathbb{E}_{I \sim pI, \Delta\theta \sim U(0,\pi), b \neq G(I)}[D(G(I)) - D(\Re[(G(I) + bi)e^{i\Delta\theta}])]\}$
6:         $w \leftarrow w + \alpha \cdot RMSProp(w, g_w)$
7:         $w \leftarrow clip(w, -c, c)$
8:     **end for**
9:     $Sample_{CANimages}$ $\{z^{(i)}\}_{p_1}^m \sim p(z)$ a batch of prior samples.
10:     $g_\theta \{argmin\mathbb{E}_{I \sim pI, \Delta\theta \sim U(0,\pi), b \neq G(I)}[D(\Re[(G(I) + bi)e^{i\Delta\theta}])]\}$
11:     $\theta \leftarrow \theta - \alpha \cdot RMSProp(\theta, g_\theta)$
12: **end while**

A Convolutional Neural Network(CNN) model (Φ) was used to predict the results as follows:

$$h = \Phi(x) \tag{5}$$

In this chapter, we designed the CVNNs-IDS system based on a complex convolution neural network that consists of three convolution layers, three max-pooling layers, and one fully connected layer. The loss function is multivariate cross-entropy. ReLU is adopted as an activation function for each layer, and softmax is used as the activation function of the last layer. The whole model shown in Fig. 5. However, Since the GAN encoder rotates the feature after it has been extracted, all the subsequent processing of the feature needs to satisfy the formula which comes from the recently proposed by Xiang et al. [7].

$$\Phi(f^\theta) = e^{i\theta}\Phi(f) \tag{6}$$

In other words, every layer of processing module shall satisfy the following recursion, which has been proved.

$$\Phi_j(f_{j-1}^{(\theta)}) = e^{i\theta}\Phi_j(f_{j-1}), \forall j \in [2, ...n], \forall \theta \subseteq [0, 2\pi] \tag{7}$$

To satisfy Eq. 7, For the convolution layer, there is the need to remove the bias parameter and gain the $Conv(f) = w \otimes f$. Hence, we modify the ReLU activation function with the following non-linear layers [17]:

$$\delta(f_{ijk}) = \frac{\|f_{ijk}\|}{max\{\|f_{ijk}\|, c\}} * f_{ijk} \tag{8}$$

where k in f_{iik} is defined as nerve activation at neuron (i, j), and c is a constant.

In the same way, we continue to modify the max-pooling layer in order to obtain the feature with the maximum norm, which ensures the rotated θ invariance. Also, this research we also improves the other layer to adapt to the complex neural network. The design for CVNNs-IDS is shown in Fig. 5, and the algorithm is presented as follows.

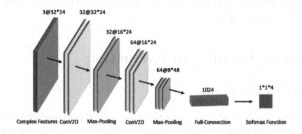

Fig. 5. The CVNNs-IDS based on complex neural network

Algorithm 2. CVNNs, our proposed algorithm. All experiments in the paper used the default values CVNNs-features = 32*24, Adam = RMSprop, a = 0.00005, $bach_size$ = 64, $epochs$ = 50.

Require: :, the learning rate, the batch size, epochs, Adam, loss, Activation function = ReLU(we modified), $loss = categorical_crossentropy$,Complex-valued features $D = (x_k, y_k)_{k=1}^m$

1: Randomly initialize all connection weights and thresholds in the complex-valued convolutional neural network in the range of 0 to 1
2: **for all** $(x_k, y_k) \in D$ **do**
3:     $(x_k, y_k) \leftarrow complex - valued\ convolutional\ of\ first\ layer$
4:     $(x_k, y_k) \leftarrow MaxPooling2D$
5:     $(x_k, y_k) \leftarrow complex - valued\ convolutional\ of\ second\ layer$
6:     $(x_k, y_k) \leftarrow MaxPooling2D$
7:     $(x_k, y_k) \leftarrow complex - valued\ convolutional\ of\ third\ layer$
8:     $(x_k, y_k) \leftarrow MaxPooling2D$
9:     $(x_k, y_k) \leftarrow Fullyconnectedlayer$
10:    $Adam = RMSprop(lr = 0.00005)$
11: **end for**
12: **return** the accuracy and loss of the CVNNs model we trained.

The function of the decoder is to decode the results predicted by CVNNs. After sending the prediction result to the decoder D, decoder D produces the actual consequence $\hat{y}$ to notify the CAN bus whether the data is abnormal:

$$\hat{y} = d(\Re[h \cdot \exp(-i\theta)]) \tag{9}$$

Where $\Re$ supplies the operation with the real part of the extract of the complex-valued [7], the whole complex-valued neural network is applied to the convolutional neural network.

In summary, this chapter theoretically expounds on the safety and high precision accuracy of CVNNs-IDS. IDS dose not only protect the extracted features but also detects known attacks and unknown attacks through complex-valued neural networks. Therefore, ensuring the security of the CAN bus, which is the privacy and safety of each driver.

4   Experiment Result and Evaluation

4.1   Experiment Environment

We accelerate three reference parameters that are abnormal detection rate, normal detection rate, and false-positive rate to verify our model. Table 1 show that the hardware environment of the model we trained. Otherwise, Fig. 6 exhibit that the process of collecting the data, which are applied in the second of the experiment to detect the scalability of the system we investigated.

- Abnormal detection rate is the proportion of the number of abnormal tests in the total abnormal data.
- The normal detection rate is the proportion of normal messages detected in the total standard message.
- The false-positive rate of a critical parameter is the so-called error rate, which is directly related to the safety of the driver.

Table 1. Experiment environment for CVNNs-IDS.

Hardware	Parameter
CPU:	Intel(R) Core(TM) i5
RAM:	32GB
GPU:	NVIDIA GeForce GTX 1650

4.2   Dataset of the Normal and Abnormal

The entire dataset in Table 2 was extracted from three different brands of cars, which includes the standard driving dataset, the fuzzy attack dataset, the flood attack dataset, the malfunction attack dataset, and the replay attack dataset.

- Fuzzy attack: Researchers injected some messages of spoofed random CAN ID and data values to the CAN bus every two milliseconds.
- Flood attack: Some high-priority CAN ID (e.g. "0 × 000" CAN ID packet) are injected to train IDS to detect high-traffic types of attacks.

Fig. 6. Data collected via OBD port on our laboratory car for CVNNs-IDS test

- Malfunction attack: The aim of injecting some malfunction message frames is to improve IDS identification of abnormal traffic attacks caused by faults after ECU attacks.
- Replay attack: The same message was sent to the CAN packet of the steering and handbrake every five milliseconds. We injected about 100,000 such attack data to improve the accuracy of IDS detection of replay attacks.
- Unkonwn attack: Apart from these datasets, we train a generator over the WGAN [15] according to the normal CAN images, which have a function that produces more fake images for our unknown attack dataset.

Table 2. Experiment environment for CVNNs-IDS

Data-Type	Normal message	Abnormal message
Free-Driving	988987	N/A
Flood-Attack	149547	32422
Fuzzy-Attack	3347013	491847
Malfunction-Attack	1326510	139080
Replay-Attack	424287	101543
Unknown-Attack	N/A	136666

4.3 Experiment Evaluation

In the section of system testing, we mainly did an aggressive test to check the security of the CVNNs-IDS model. Accurate testing was employed to detect the capability to protect the CAN bus, and contradistinctive testing was also done to demonstrate the advantages of the CVNNs-IDS that was investigated.

In this experiment, we simulated the attacker to intercept feature images when the features are being transmitted to the CVNNs-IDS module. However, the random angle was chosen to reconstruct the real feature after obtaining complex characteristics. Finally, the reconstructed CAN images are different from the inputted images significantly, which make it difficult for us to get real features and increased the difficulty of our attack. We present that the difference of these CAN image in Fig. 7(a). This includes four types of images rotated by six different random angles to get a feature map that is very different from the original image, indicating the safety of our encoder.

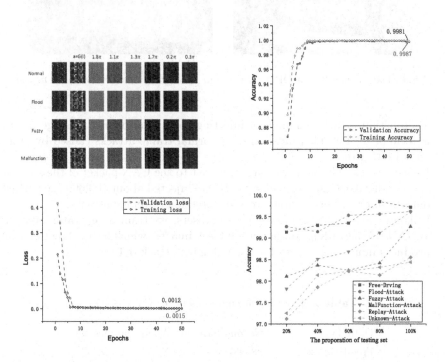

Fig. 7. The results of each part of the experiment: (a)feature reconstruction images in complex-valued neural network; (b) the training accuracy for CVNNs-IDS model; (c) the training loss for CVNNs-IDS model; (d) the testing accuracy for CVNNs-IDS model.

Despite the surety of the security of the model, we cannot ignore the accuracy of the IDS system. Therefore, the detection experiment is divided into two parts: The first part ensures the security and robustness of the model through the accuracy of a test data, while as the second part applies the model to the SAIC Roewe marvel x, which is an essential test of the system's scalability. Figure 7(b) and Fig. 7(c) show that the accuracy and loss of the CVNNs-IDS. The result obtained proves that the accuracy rate on the test set reaches 99.95% after 50 iterations. It does not only guarantee the security of the model but also increases the detection rate. From Fig. 7(d), the normal detection rate that was set-up is 99% averagely on the whole test data. It was also be deduced from the same Fig. 7(d) that the abnormal detection rate obtained 99% except for unknown attacks. However, the detection rate of unknown attacks was not less than 98%, as indicated in the results. Hence, the accuracy of the proposed CVNNs-IDS is guaranteed.

In the second part of the experiment, the driving data of another car brand was re-selected to test the model. The results are shown in Table 3 below. The result shows that the detection rate is also very stable, proving that the model has good scalability.

Table 3. Experiment environment for CVNNs-IDS

Training set	Normal detection rate	Abnormal detection rate	False-positive detection rate
Normal messages	99.7%	N/A	0.32%
Flood attack	N/A	99.6%	0.41%
Fuzzy attack	N/A	99.9%	0.13%
Malfunction attack	N/A	99.8%	0.22%
Unknown attack	N/A	98.1%	1.93%

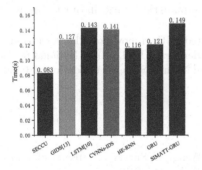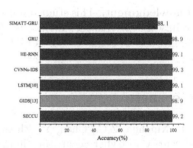

Fig. 8. The comparison experiment: (a) the calculation cost of CVNNs-IDS with other IDS, (b) the comparation of accuracy on investigated CVNNs-IDS.

A comparative experiment was carried out. Research by Hyun et al. improved the CAN data encoding based on GIDS; hence, a specific comparison with IDS based on deep learning in previous studies in terms of detection time and accuracy [18] was performed. The results show that the detected precision does not decrease under the condition that we guarantee the security of the model. However, only the calculation cost increases slightly. As shown in Fig. 8, the accuracy rate of 99.3% obtained by the proposed model is the best as compared to other existing IDS models that are based on deep learning techniques.

5 Conclusion

In this paper, we investigated the CVNNs-IDS model based on deep learning for the in-vehicle network, which guarantees the security of the model only when the accuracy rate of the detection does not decrease. We proposed encoding 64 continuous CAN messages by the one-hot vector, and two random parameters ware selected to hide the real feature through the encoder, based on the GAN model. Hence, the CVNNs-IDS module, which can detect the unknown and known attack processes the rotated complex features, and returns the results to the decoder. Also, when the vehicle driving environment changes, the cloud detection model will be updated continuously. From the experimental results above, the accuracy rate still keeps on 98%, which is better than the performance of the existing models.

This research, therefore, presents that the CVNNs-IDS model, with three major characteristics: a stable rate of accuracy, higher security, and scalability, is very suitable for the Internet of vehicle.

A deep learning-based anomaly detector is currently one of the best methods to verify the CAN bus, but the attack data of most anomalous detected models are simulated employing custom injection. To accurately identify the attack by the model, we intend to acquire the dataset and train the high-precision anomalous detected model in the case of the realistic attack, in our future work.

Acknowledgment. This studied was supported by the Innovation Plan for Postgraduate Research of Jiangsu Province in 2014 under Grant KYLX1057, National Science Foundation of China under Grant 61902156 and Natural Science Foundation of Jiangsu Province under Grant BK20180860 .

References

1. Li Xinghua, Z.C., Chen, Y., Zhang, H., Weng, J.: Survey of internet of vehicles security. J. Cyber Secur. (in Chinese), **4**(3), 17–33 (2019)
2. Golovko, V., Kachurka, P., Vaitsekhovich, L.: Neural network ensembles for intrusion detection. In: 2007 4th IEEE Workshop on Intelligent Data Acquisition and Advanced Computing Systems: Technology and Applications, pp. 578–583 (2007)
3. Buczak, A., Guven, E.: A survey of data mining and machine learning methods for cyber security intrusion detection. IEEE Commun. Surv. Tutorials **18**(2), 1153–1176 (2015)
4. Xiaojian, M.X.Z.: Big data privacy management. Comput. Res. Dev. **52**(2), 265–281 (2015)
5. Yeom, S., Giacomelli, I., Fredrikson, M., Jha, S.: Privacy risk in machine learning: analyzing the connection to overfitting. In: 2018 IEEE 31st Computer Security Foundations Symposium (CSF), pp. 268–282 (2018)
6. Liu Junxu, M.X.: Survey on privacy-preserving machine learning. Comput. Res. Dev. (in Chinese), **57**(2), 346–362 (2020)
7. Xiang, L., Ma, H., Zhang, H., Zhang, Y., Ren, J., Zhang, Q.: Interpretable complex-valued neural networks for privacy protection. arXiv preprint arXiv:1901.09546 (2019)

8. Mter, M., Asaj, N.: Entropy-based anomaly detection for in-vehicle networks. In: 2011 IEEE Intelligent Vehicles Symposium (IV), pp. 1110–1115 (2011)
9. Groza, B., Murvay, P.: Efficient intrusion detection with bloom filtering in controller area networks. IEEE Trans. Inf. Forensics Secur. **14**(4), 1037–1051 (2019)
10. Taylor, A., Leblanc, S., Japkowicz, N.: Anomaly detection in automobile control network data with long short-term memory networks. In: 2016 IEEE International Conference on Data Science and Advanced Analytics (DSAA), pp. 130–139 (2016)
11. Kang, M.J., Kang, J.W.: Intrusion detection system using deep neural network for in-vehicle network security. PLoS ONE **11**(6), e0155781 (2016)
12. Wu, Q.G.L., Yu, H.: Anomaly detection method of vehicle-mounted CAN bus based on random forest. J. Jilin Univ. (Sci. Sci. Edn.) **56**(3), 663–668 (2018). (in Chinese)
13. Seo, E., Song, H.M., Kim, H.K.: GIDS: GAN based Intrusion Detection System for In-Vehicle Network. In: Conference on Privacy (2018)
14. Jichici, C., Groza, B., Murvay, P.-S.: Examining the use of neural networks for intrusion detection in controller area networks. In: International Conference on Security for Information Technology and Communications, pp. 109–125 (2018)
15. Arjovsky, M., Chintala, S., Bottou, L.: Wasserstein GAN. arXiv preprint arXiv:1701.07875 (2017)
16. Su, J.: O-GAN: extremely concise approach for auto-encoding generative adversarial networks. arXiv preprint arXiv:1903.01931 (2019)
17. Simonyan, K., Zisserman, A.: Very deep convolutional networks for large-scale image recognition. arXiv preprint arXiv:1409.1556 (2014)
18. Xiao, J., Wu, H., Li, X.: Internet of things meets vehicles: sheltering in-vehicle network through lightweight machine learning. Symmetry **11**(11), 1388 (2019)

Intrusion Detection Scheme
for Autonomous Driving Vehicles

Weidong Zhai and Zhou Su$^{(\boxtimes)}$

School of Cyber Science and Engineering, Xi'an Jiaotong University, Xi'an, China
384914432@qq.com, zhousu@ieee.org

Abstract. With the recent breakthroughs, autonomous driving vehicles (ADVs) are promising to bring transformative changes to our transportation systems. However, recent hacks have demonstrated numerous vulnerabilities in these emerging systems from software to control. Safety is becoming one of the major barriers for the wider adoption of ADVs. ADVs connect to vehicular ad-hoc networks (VANETs) to communicate with each other. However, malicious nodes can falsify information and threaten the safety of passengers and other vehicles with catastrophic consequences. In this work, we present a novel reputation-based intrusion detection scheme to detect malicious ADVs through dynamic credit and reputation evaluation. To further encourage user's participation, an incentive mechanism is also built for ADVs in the intrusion detection system. We demonstrate the feasibility and effectiveness of our proposed system through extensive simulation, compared with current representative approaches. Simulation results show that our proposed scheme can acquire better intrusion detection results, reduced false positive ratio, and improved user participation.

Keywords: Autonomous driving vehicles · Credit · Dynamic threshold · Intrusion detection · Incentive model

1 Introduction

With the rapid development of the automobile industry, many believe that autonomous driving vehicles (ADVs) will bring transformative changes to our society. As a networked cyber-physical system, ADVs will greatly improve the current traffic environment and bring convenience to people's travel. A number of leading carmakers, including Toyota and Volkswagen, have announced their plain to commercialize self-driving cars to the general public in the next five years. As reported in [1], 25% of the vehicles on the road will be ADVs by 2035.

ADVs communicate with each other through vehicular ad-hoc network (VANET), which can be broadly considered as a mobile ad-hoc network on the road tailored for automobiles [2]. For example, ADVs can share information about current road conditions to help others plan their routes. Apart from vehicle-to-vehicle communication, ADVs can also communicate with Roadside

© Springer Nature Singapore Pte Ltd. 2020
S. Yu et al. (Eds.): SPDE 2020, CCIS 1268, pp. 278–291, 2020.
https://doi.org/10.1007/978-981-15-9129-7_20

Units (RSUs) to obtain desired information. All transmitted data which ADVs rely heavily on for safe driving should be protected by the security mechanisms [3]. Existing security approached mainly focus on cryptographic mechanisms. Although cryptographic mechanisms can protect the confidentiality and integrity of data, they cannot cope with the insider attackers well. When there are malicious nodes inside the VANET, they can manipulate data and connection to sabotage the network. For example, some ADVs will release a lot of false news (such as traffic accidents, road congestion, etc.), and these false news may cause chaotic traffic and accidents [4]. Besides, there are many new attack surfaces in the VANET, such as selfish attack, black hole attack, sybil attack and so on [5].

To cope with these issues, Intrusion Detection System (IDS) has been a primary instrument to detect the presence of attackers for many organizations and governments during the past decade. Existing works on leveraging IDS to augment communication security often attempts to address denial of service (DOS) external network [6] and unauthorized access from remote machine (R2L), while internal attacks are not handled well. In [7], the detection is based on voting among randomly selected clusters. This approach makes a strong assumption that cluster head can be trusted, and this is often not true when under attack.

In this paper, distinguished from the current paradigm, we explore mechanisms to incentivize mutual inspection among the peers in the VANET. ADVs can accumulate credits by contributing community-vetted information to the network, and falsified information can be detected using a jointly computed SVM among all the peers. More specifically, we first let ADVs evaluate neighboring vehicles' behaviors and filter these evaluation value, and then derive the credit value of each vehicle. Next, we established the intrusion detection mechanism by calculating the dynamic threshold and setting rules based on SVM. In order to encourage ADVs to take part in network activities, we develop an incentive model based on bargaining game. We conduct extensive experiments and simulations to demonstrate the feasibility and efficiency of our scheme by comparing with the conventional intrusion detection schemes in VANETs.

The structure of this paper is organized as follows. In the second part, we review the related work. The third part provides the system model for VANET, and the forth part describes the intrusion detection scheme. The fifth part shows our incentive model. In order to demonstrate the effectiveness of our scheme, the sixth part shows our simulation results. In the last part, we conclude the paper.

2   Related Work

In this section, we briefly review the researches on security of VANET, including IDS and the credibility mechanism. IDS is one of the most reliable methods to protect VANET from being attacked [8]. The research on external attacks has been relatively mature, so the recent work mainly focuses on how to deal with attacks launched by internal malicious nodes in VANET. Zhang et al. [9] present a cluster-based intrusion detection method. It no longer requires each node to conduct monitoring, but chooses a cluster head among a group of nodes to be an intrusion detection agent. The agent carries out detection by collecting information in real time. Amiri *et al.* [10] combines neural network and clustering algorithm to propose a multi-agent-based intrusion detection method, which greatly saves energy consumption in the VANET. Bismeyer *et al.* [11] introduces an IDS based on the ideas of existing position and movement verification approaches. Their schemes are effective against the fake congestion attack and the denial of congestion attack. In [12,13], the authors propose IDS based on rule matching to detect malicious vehicles. Although they have high detection rate, they can only detect specified attacks and ignore other unknown attacks. However, this is different from our approach which is extensible in attack scenarios.

There are increasing security schemes of VANET using the credibility mechanism. Initial credibility schemes were deployed based on centralized or decentralized infrastructure, such as [14,15], but this approach proved difficult to adapt to the rapidly changing nature of VANET. Xu *et al.* [16] present a credit evaluation scheme consisting of direct evaluation and indirect evaluation, which is used to evaluate the reliability of edge nodes in mobile social networks. Hu *et al.* [17] propose a recommendation scheme for a group of vehicles, that is, a node with high credibility is voted on each group as the cluster head. The head node evaluates group's credibility based on feedback back from other vehicles in the group. These schemes will undoubtedly result in substantial resource savings. However, some selfish nodes in the network have not been well handled, and these vehicles will not have the enthusiasm to share and forward information to save their own network resources.

3   System Model

3.1   Traffic Model

In our work, the entire traffic model is composed of the Credit Center, RSUs and ADVs. The RSUs are scattered on both sides of the road. ADVs travels on the road, and each car will pass at least one RSU signal coverage. We assume that the width of each road in the entire traffic is the same.

According to Little's Law, which states that the long-term average number of customers is equal to the long-term effective arrival rate multiplied by the average waiting time of customers in this stable system, the traffic flow μ of each RSU (the number of ADVs arriving per unit time) can be calculated as

$$\mu = \frac{\bar{C}}{\bar{t}}, \tag{1}$$

where $\bar{C}$ is the average number of ADVs covered by a RSU, and $\bar{t}$ is the average time that takes a car to travel this distance. We have

$$\bar{t} = \frac{l}{\bar{v}}, \tag{2}$$

where l is the length of the road covered by the RSU and $\bar{v}$ is the average speed of the ADV. Therefore, the traffic flow can be expressed as:

$$\mu = \frac{\bar{C}}{l} \times \bar{v}. \tag{3}$$

$\bar{v}$ is affected by the degree of traffic congestion, which can be expressed as

$$\bar{v} = \max \left\{ v_{\max} \times \left(1 - \frac{\bar{C}}{C_{\max}} \right), v_{\min} \right\}. \tag{4}$$

According to [18], in free and steady-state traffic flow, the speed of vehicles follows a normal distribution, that is

$$f(v) = \frac{1}{\sigma\sqrt{2\pi}} e^{-\left(\frac{v-\bar{v}}{\sigma\sqrt{2}}\right)^2}, \tag{5}$$

where $\sigma = \alpha\bar{v}$, and $v_{\min} = \bar{v} - \beta\sigma$. (α, β) is determined according to the constantly changing traffic conditions on the road section. In order to guarantee $v_{\min} \leq v \leq v_{\max}$, we need to find a truncated normal distribution of v. It can be formulated as

$$f(v, \bar{v}, \sigma, v_{\min}, v_{\max}) = \frac{2f(v)}{erf\left(\frac{v_{\max}-\bar{v}}{\sigma\sqrt{2}}\right) - erf\left(\frac{v_{\min}-\bar{v}}{\sigma\sqrt{2}}\right)}, \tag{6}$$

and

$$erf(x) = \sqrt{\frac{2}{\pi}} \int_0^x e^{-\eta^2} d\eta. \tag{7}$$

3.2 Attack Model

Selfish Attack. Selfish attack refers to that some ADVs in VANET don't respond to the communication request of other nodes in order to save its network resources and storage space, or intentionally discards the packets that other nodes wish to forward, so that some important information in the network cannot be conveyed. It is conceivable that if there is an accident on a road, and the message cannot be transmitted because of the selfish attack, it will lead to traffic congestion and even more serious accidents. The packet loss rate of these nodes is usually much higher than that of nearby nodes.

On-Off Attack. Malicious ADVs in the network behave normally from time to time and carry out some attacks. Such nodes usually use a certain period of normal performance to accumulate the credit of other nodes, and then launch malicious attacks to consume this value. But they always keep themselves in the trusted range to ensure that they will not be excluded the network.

Hostile Attack. It mainly includes data packet replication and resource exhaustion attacks. Their common feature is that malicious nodes will send a large number of unwanted data packets to overload the network and waste bandwidth. Therefore, when a malicious vehicle performs such an attack, its message replication rate or packet transmission rate will be higher, respectively.

4 Intrusion Detection Scheme

4.1 Global Credit Model

Firstly, we need to calculate the direct trust value between the ADVs. After each ADV interacts with another ADV, it needs to evaluate the satisfaction of the other. We define the satisfaction of ADV i to ADV j at the k-th interaction as

$$S_{i,j}^k = \begin{cases} 0, dissatisfaction \\ 1, satisfaction \\ t \in (0,1), \ otherwise \end{cases}. \tag{8}$$

ADV i will calculate the direct trust to ADV j in combination with the satisfaction obtained from previous interactions, and as the time goes by, the proportion of satisfaction in past periods should be reduced. The time decay function is defined as follows

$$h_k = e^{\xi(k-K)}, \xi > 0, h_k \in (0,1], \tag{9}$$

where K is the total number of evaluations, and ξ is the adjustment parameter. The evaluation value of ADV i to ADV j can be expressed as

$$DT_{i,j} = \frac{\sum_{k=1}^{K} S_{i,j}^k h_k}{\sum_{k=1}^{K} h_k}. \tag{10}$$

According to [19], ADVs that continuously provided low-quality information should be penalized. The penalty function can be shown as

$$P_{i,j} = \delta \left(\sum_{k=1}^{k} h_k - DT_{i,j} \right). \tag{11}$$

Therefore, the direct trust value that ADV i evaluates ADV j can be obtained by

$$ET_{i,j} = \frac{DT_{i,j}}{DT_{i,j} + P_{i,j}}. \tag{12}$$

Then, we will calculate the global credit of ADVs. ADVs should periodically send RSU its own collection of direct trust values about other ADVs. The RSU will send credit center these data to calculate the global credit. The direct trust values of all ADVs for ADV i can be regarded as a set of variables with independent and identical distribution, so this set of values satisfies the central limit theorem, and we denote it as $ET_i = \{ET_{1,i}, ET_{2,i}, ..., ET_{k,i}, ..., ET_{n,i}\}$. We have

$$\mu_i = E(ET_{i,j}) = \frac{1}{n-1} \sum_{k=1, k \neq i}^{n} ET_{k,i}, \tag{13}$$

$$\sigma_i = \sqrt{D\left(ET_{i,j}\right)} = \sqrt{\frac{1}{n-1} \sum_{k=1,k\neq i}^{n} \left(ET_{k,i} - \mu_i\right)^2}, \tag{14}$$

where μ_i is the mathematical expectation of the set of values, and σ_i is the standard deviation. We use these two parameters to filter this set of values so that it satisfies $ET_{k,i} \in [\mu_i - \varepsilon\sigma_i, \mu_i + \varepsilon\sigma_i]$, where ε is the regulator, and its size is positively correlated with σ_i.

The behavior of node i in the most recent period can be quantified as

$$\bar{\mu}_i = \frac{1}{m} \sum_{k \in S} ET_{k,i}, \tag{15}$$

where S is the set of direct trust values satisfying the condition and m is the number of elements in the set. Combined with past credit values, the global credit value of the i-th period can be calculated by

$$T_{i,n} = T_{i,n-1} + \frac{\bar{\mu}_i - T_{i,n-1}}{|\bar{\mu}_i - T_{i,n-1}|}\theta. \tag{16}$$

4.2 Dynamic Credit Threshold

When a vehicle's credit value falls below a threshold, it is marked as a malicious node. The traditional credit scheme gives a fixed threshold to determine, which results in on-off attack. In order to accurately identify malicious nodes in the process of frequent credit changes, we propose to set a dynamic global credibility threshold.

We use $\mathcal{T} = \{T_1, T_2, ..., T_k, ..., T_n\}$ to represent the current credit of all ADVs. Assuming that $T_1 < T_2 < ... < T_k < ... < T_n$, we have

$$\widehat{T} = (1-p)\left(T_1 + T_2 + ... + T_k + ... + T_n\right), \tag{17}$$

where p is the proportion of normal nodes in the VANET. According to [20], it is easy to prove that there must be a value T_k in the set $\mathcal{T}$ that satisfies

$$\begin{cases} T_1 + T_2 + ... + T_{k-1} < \widehat{T} \\ T_1 + T_2 + ... + T_{k-1} + T_k \geq \widehat{T} \end{cases}. \tag{18}$$

Then, the critical value to judge the credit state of ADVs in the n-th cycle can be expressed as $S_n = T_n$. Finally, considering the critical value calculated in the previous period and combining with the time attenuation function, we calculated the threshold value of credit detection in the current vehicle network as

$$S = \frac{\sum_{k=0}^{n} S_k \times h_k}{\sum_{k=0}^{n} h_k}. \tag{19}$$

Only the ADV with credit value above S are considered to be trustworthy and thus able to participate in network activities normally.

4.3   Intrusion Detection

Combined with the credibility model designed above, this section proposes an scheme to identify malicious nodes in VANET. ADVs on the road are required to monitor the network attributes of their neighbors and calculate related monitoring indicators, including packet loss rate (PLR), packet transmission rate (PTR), and message repetition rate (MRR) during this period [7]. Each node needs to determine whether its neighbors are malicious according to the following rules:

- If $PLR > TH_1$, it is marked as the malicious node that launched the Selfish Attack.
- If $PTR > TH_2$, and the value is significantly higher than others, We tagged it as the malicious node that launched the Resource Depletion Attack.
- If $MRR > TH_3$, this ADV should be marked as the malicious node which launched the Packet Replication Attack.

Here, TH_1, TH_2, TH_3 are thresholds set in advance.

In addition to the rule-based judgment method mentioned above, the ADVs also need to incorporate a detection method based on machine learning. We use the Support Vector Machine (SVM) algorithm. Compared with other traditional machine learning methods, such as neural networks, SVM's training time is shorter, and it occupies less memory. We only need to save the support vector. The algorithm includes training and classification processes.

During the training process, the ADVs will continuously collect the network features (PLR, PTR, MRR) of its nearby nodes, and then use these features as the input vector of the training algorithm. The purpose of training is to calculate a set of feature values called support vectors. This set of vectors allows the data to be separated into two sides, namely normal and abnormal (binary classification). The detailed content of the algorithm is not repeated in this solution.

In the classification process, each vehicle node will make abnormal judgments on the newly collected data according to the training model. If a vehicle is judged as a malicious node, it will be recorded. Subsequently, the monitoring node will make the final decision according to the following rules:

- If both the SVM and the rule-based judgment method determine that the ADV is a malicious node, the monitoring node should send an intrusion report to the nearby RSU, including its network characteristics and ID, and update the experience trust for the malicious node according to the penalty function in the experience trust.
- If the SVM determines that the ADV is a malicious node, and the rule determines that the node is a normal node, then the rule needs to be updated, and its threshold (PLR, PTR, MRR) is replaced by the current features (such as support vectors) provided by the SVM.

The ADVs must perform anomaly detection on their current neighbor nodes and send monitoring reports to nearby RSUs. When a ADV is suspected of being a malicious node, the RSU needs to make a decision based on the credit values of the judgment nodes. Suppose RSU receives an intrusion report about node i, let $\mathcal{M} = \{1, 2, ..., m, ..., M\}$ denote the set of vehicles in neighboring nodes that consider i to be a malicious node, and $\mathcal{N} = \{1, 2, ..., n, ..., N\}$ denote the set of vehicles that consider i to be a normal node. Then, We calculate the judgement value as:

$$C_i = \frac{\sum_{m \in \mathcal{M}} (\max T_m \times T_m) - \sum_{n \in \mathcal{N}} (\max T_n \times T_n)}{\sum_{m \in \mathcal{M}} T_m + \sum_{n \in \mathcal{N}} T_n}. \tag{20}$$

We compare C_i to the predefined threshold A. If $C_i > A$, we consider node i as a malicious node and reduce its credibility to an untrusted state.

5 Incentive Model

The Credit Center needs to increase ADVs' credit value based on their activity level. Let the activity level of ADV i in k-th cycle be a_i^k and $a_i^k \in [0,I]$. I is the highest activity level. The formula for calculating the credit rewards is

$$R_i\left(a_i^k\right) = \frac{a_i^k \left(1 - \widehat{T}_i^{k-1}\right)\theta}{I+1}, \tag{21}$$

where θ is the weight parameter. $\widehat{T}_i^{k-1}$ is the new credit value in the $(k-1)$-th cycle, and it can be updated by

$$\widehat{T}_i^k = \begin{cases} T_i & k = 0, \\ T_i^{k-1} + R_i & \widehat{T}_i^k < 1, \\ 1 & other, \end{cases} \tag{22}$$

We regard the credit center as the buyer A, and R_i is the highest price the buyer is willing to pay.

According to the activity level, we quantified the resource consumption of ADV i. It can be expressed by

$$E_i\left(a_i^k\right) = \psi \log_2 \left(1 + e^{1 - \frac{I+1}{a_i^k}}\right), \tag{23}$$

where ψ is the weight parameter. We regard ADV i as the seller B, and E_i is the lowest price that seller can accept.

Depending on the reward value and the amount of resource consumption, we consider the following three cases:

- $R_i < E_i$: This situation means that the highest price offered by the buyer is lower than the lowest price acceptable to the seller, so the transaction fails, and the vehicle will be unwilling to remain active and participate in activities on the network.
- $R_i = E_i$: In this case, we default to normal transaction.

– $R_i > E_i$: This means that the highest price offered by the buyer is higher than the lowest price accepted by the seller, that is, the two parties have not reached a consensus on the transaction price. Due to the selfishness of the two parties in the game, the seller will pursue the maximization of benefits, while the buyer wants to reduce the payment.

Let's just consider the case of $R_i > E_i$. We use the bargaining game to solve the optimal transaction price. The cake C can be denoted by

$$C = R_i \left(a_i^k \right) - E_i \left(a_i^k \right). \tag{24}$$

Let χ_A and χ_B be the return functions of A and B, respectively, we have

$$\chi_A \left(\gamma_A \right) = \gamma_A C, \chi_B \left(\gamma_B \right) = \gamma_B C, \tag{25}$$

$$\gamma_A + \gamma_B = 1, \gamma_A \geq 0, \gamma_B \geq 0. \tag{26}$$

The bargaining model is a process in which two parties take turns to make offers until one party's allocation is accepted by the other. Each round of bidding will have a certain cost for both parties, that is, both parties have their own patience value, which we will call the discounted value here. Considering the relationship between the discounted values of A and B and the activity of the other, according to [21], we can define the discounter value of A is

$$\delta_A = 1 - \frac{e^{v\theta} - e^{-v\theta}}{e^{v\theta} + e^{-v\theta}}, \theta = \frac{I-1}{a_i}, \tag{27}$$

and the discounter value of B is

$$\delta_B = \frac{e^{v\theta'} - e^{-v\theta'}}{e^{v\theta'} + e^{-v\theta'}}, \theta' = \frac{I}{a_i}. \tag{28}$$

So, we can get the sub-game Nash equilibrium of the game

$$\gamma_A^* = \frac{1 - \delta_B}{1 - \delta_A \delta_B}, \gamma_B^* = \frac{\delta_B - \delta_A \delta_B}{1 - \delta_A \delta_B}. \tag{29}$$

At this point, we can get the transaction price of both parties in the case which can be formulized by

$$R_i^* = E_i + \frac{1 - \delta_B}{1 - \delta_A \delta_B} C \tag{30}$$

6 Simulation Experiment

In this section, we present relevant simulation setup and results of the proposed scheme.

6.1 Setup

We use Network Simulator version 2 (NS2) combined with Simulation of Urban Mobility (SUMO) to carry out the simulation experiment of the proposed scheme. NS2 is an object-oriented network simulator, which provides various protocols and programming interfaces for researchers to use. SUMO is a traffic system simulation software that can realize microscopic control of traffic flow, including specifying the number, speed, behavior of vehicles and setting the type and conditions of roads. In the experiment, SUMO generates tracking files for the movement of ADVs, and NS2 loads these files and runs the intrusion detection scheme we propose.

Table 1. The main parameters of the traffic model.

Parameter name	Value
Number of ADVs	100
Simulation area	$5\,\mathrm{km}^2$
Maximum speed	$80\,\mathrm{km/h}$
Wireless communication protocol	802.11p
Transmission range	500 m
Simulation time	2 min
Detection period	10 s
μ	50
C_i	0.8
TH_1, TH_2, TH_3	0.85

Table 1 summarizes the main parameters of the simulation. To facilitate the experiment, we initialize the global credit value of each ADV according to normal distribution, and the value is between 80 and 100. We consider two metrics to verify the practicability of our intrusion detection scheme, including detection ratio (DR) and false positive ratio (FPR). The DR means the percentage of the number of correctly identified malicious nodes in the experiment, and the FPR refers to the percentage of the number of malicious nodes misreported in the experiment to the number of normal nodes. We set the DR of both schemes to be 100 when the malicious nodes in the network do not exist, and FPR to be 0 when the normal nodes do not exist.

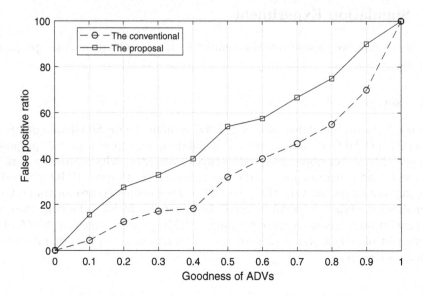

Fig. 1. Comparison of success rate of intrusion detection under different ratio of trusted ADV.

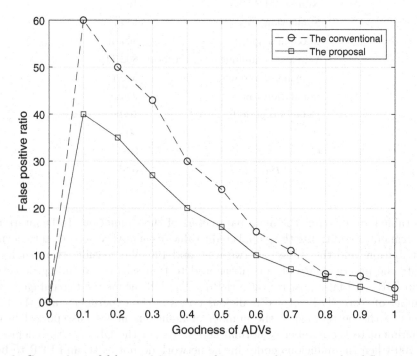

Fig. 2. Comparison of false positive ratio of intrusion detection under different ratio of trusted ADV.

6.2   Results

We compare the proposed detection scheme with the conventional neural network. Figure 1 shows the comparison of the success rates of intrusion detection of the two schemes under different trusted ADV ratios. It can be seen that the effect of the proposed scheme in this paper is significantly better than that of neural network. This is because the rule setting in the scheme of this paper adds a comparison with the network attributes of surrounding nodes. The topological structure of the vehicle-mounted network changes frequently. When the ADVs' density of some road sections is large, the relevant indicators generated by it will increase or decrease significantly. The neural network cannot adapt well to this scenario. Figure 2 shows that the FPR of our scheme is lower than that of the traditional scheme. When the number of trusted ADVs in the network is lower, the FPR is obviously higher. This is because the collusion attack launched by a large number of malicious nodes will greatly affect the evaluation of normal ADVs' credit values. Although such a situation is rarely encountered in future reality, it cannot be ignored.

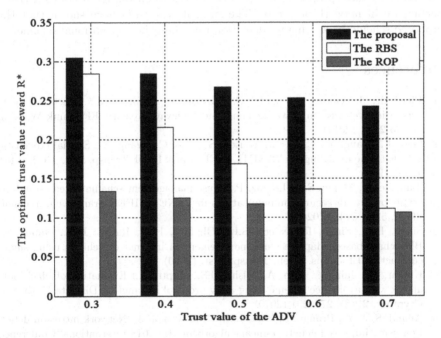

Fig. 3. The optimal credibility reward obtained by ADV with different trust value in the two-round game

In addition, we also simulate the incentive model in the scheme. Figure 3 shows the optimal trust value rewards given by our scheme under different trust value. As it is shown that ADVs with less trust value can get the better rewards, which can motivate it to behave more positively. We considered two traditional schemes for comparison, i.e., Reputation-Based Scheme (RBS) and Random Offer Price (ROP). In the RBS, the quotes of buyer and seller are only related to their credibility, and the reward value decreases too much with the increase of trust value, which will cause the ADVs with high credit degree lose the motivation to keep active. In the ROP, the buyer and seller quote at random, and the reward value is too low to encourage ADVs to participate in the VANET activities. In contrast, our scheme can give different ADVs appropriate incentive values to ensure the stability of the VANET.

7   Conclusion

In this paper, we have proposed an intrusion detection scheme based on the credit of ADVs and SVM. The credit value of each ADV is calculated by their assessment and center limit theorem. Based on the credit values, we have presented a method to calculate the dynamic credibility threshold which forms the basis for an intrusion detection scheme by combining the SVM algorithm. Furthermore, we have proposed an incentive model to encourage users to actively participate in network activities. The simulation results have shown that the proposed scheme have a higher detection rate than the conventional scheme.

References

1. Bierstedt, J., Gooze, A., Gray, C., Raykin, L., Walters, J.: Effects of next-generation vehicles on travel demand and highway capacity. FP Think Working Group **2**, 11 (2014)
2. Guo, J., Zhang, Y., Chen, X., Yousefi, S., Guo, C., Wang, Y.: Spatial stochastic vehicle traffic modeling for VANETs. IEEE Trans. Intell. Transp. Syst. **19**(2), 416–425 (2018)
3. Tangade, S., Manvi, S.S., Lorenz, P.: Trust management scheme based on hybrid cryptography for secure communications in VANETs. IEEE Trans. Veh. Technol. **69**(5), 5232–5243 (2020)
4. Singh, P.K., Singh, R., Nandi, S.K., Ghafoor, K.Z., Rawat, D.B., Nandi, S.: Blockchain-based adaptive trust management in internet of vehicles using smart contract. IEEE Trans. Intell. Transp. Syst. (2020)
5. Kumar, M., Jain, V., Jain, A., Bisht, U.S., Gupta, N.: Evaluation of black hole attack with avoidance scheme using aodv protocol in vanet. J. Discrete Math. Sci. Cryptogr. **22**(2), 277–291 (2019)
6. Anand, S. J. V., Pranav, I., Neetish, M., Narayanan, J.: Network intrusion detection using improved genetic k-means algorithm. In: 2018 International Conference on Advances in Computing, Communications and Informatics (ICACCI), pp. 2441–2446, Bangalore (2018). https://doi.org/10.1109/ICACCI.2018.8554710
7. Sedjelmaci, H., Senouci, S. M.: A new intrusion detection framework for vehicular networks. In: IEEE International Conference on Communications (ICC), Sydney, NSW, pp. 538–543 (2014). https://doi.org/10.1109/ICC.2014.6883374
8. Sedjelmaci, H., Senouci, S.M., Feham, M.: An efficient intrusion detection framework in cluster-based wireless sensor networks. Secur. Commun. Netw. **6**(10), 1211–1224 (2013)

9. Zhang, Y., Lee, W., Huang, Y.A.: Intrusion detection techniques for mobile wireless networks. Wireless Netw. **9**(5), 545–556 (2003)
10. Amiri, E., Keshavarz, H., Heidari, H., Mohamadi, E., Moradzadeh, H.: Intrusion detection systems in MANET: a review. In: International Conference on Innovation (2014)
11. Bismeyer, N., Stresing, C., Bayarou, K. M.: Intrusion detection in VANETs through verification of vehicle movement data (2010)
12. Sedjelmaci, H., Bouali, T., Senouci, S.M.: Detection and prevention from misbehaving intruders in vehicular networks. In: IEEE Global Communications Conference, vol. 2, pp. 39–44 (2015)
13. Nguyen, A., Mokdad, L., Othman, J.: DJAVAN: detecting jamming attacks in vehicle ad hoc networks. Perform. Eval. **87**, 405–410 (2013)
14. Patwardhan, A., Joshi, A., Finin, T., Yesha, Y.: A data intensive reputation management scheme for vehicular ad hoc networks. In: 2006 Third Annual International Conference on Mobile and Ubiquitous Systems: Networking and Services, San Jose, CA, pp. 1–8 (2006). https://doi.org/10.1109/MOBIQ.2006.340422
15. Minhas, U.F., Zhang, J., Tran, T., Cohen, R.: Towards expanded trust management for agents in vehicular ad-hoc networks. Int. J. Comput. Intell.: Theory Pract. (IJCITP) **5**(1), 1–8 (2006)
16. Xu, Q.Y., Su, Z., Wang, Y.T., Dai, M.H.: A trustworthy content caching and bandwidth allocation scheme with edge computing for smart campus. IEEE Access **6**, 63868–63879 (2018)
17. Hu, H., Lu, R., Zhang, Z., Shao, J.: Replace: a reliable trust-based platoon service recommendation scheme in vanet. IEEE Trans. Veh. Technol. **66**(2), 1–1 (2016)
18. Khabbaz, M.J., Fawaz, W.F., Assi, C.M.: A simple free-flow traffific model for vehicular intermittently connected networks. IEEE Trans. Intell. Transp. Syst. **13**(3), 1312–1326 (2012)
19. Xing, R., Su, Z., Zhang, N.: Trust-evaluation-based intrusion detection and reinforcement learning in autonomous driving. IEEE Netw. **33**(5), 54–60 (2019)
20. Gingold, H., Xue, F.: On asymptotic summation of potentially oscillatory difference systems. J. Math. Anal. Appl. **330**(2), 1068–1092 (2007)
21. Le, V., Lin, Y.W., Wang, X.M., Feng, Z.Y., Zhang, P.: A cell based dynamic spectrum management scheme with interference mitigation for cognitive networks. In: VTC Spring 2008 - IEEE Vehicular Technology Conference, pp. 1594–1598 (2008)

Hyperparameter Optimization of ICS Intrusion Detection Classifier Based on Improved Hybrid Algorithm

Chenjun Tang[1], Hai Liang[1], Yong Ding[1,2(✉)], Yujue Wang[1], and Shijie Tang[1,3]

[1] Guangxi Key Laboratory of Cryptography and Information Security,
School of Computer Science and Information Security,
Guilin University of Electronic Technology, Guilin 541004, China
stone_dingy@126.com
[2] Cyberspace Security Research Center, Peng Cheng Laboratory,
Shenzhen 518055, China
[3] School of Electronic Engineering and Automation,
Guilin University of Electronic Technology, Guilin 541004, China

Abstract. In recent years, machine learning methods have become commonly used in industrial control networks for anomalous intrusion detection. In order to get better detection results, the performance of the intrusion detection classifier needs to be optimized. In the process of machine learning model optimization, hyperparameter optimization of the model is an important part of the process. At present, traditional hyperparameter optimization method has shortcomings such as low efficiency and too much reliance on experience, which requires a common and efficient algorithm for hyperparameter optimization under different conditions. To solve this problem, this paper improves the gird search algorithm and the adaptive cuckoo algorithm respectively, and proposes Adaptive Cuckoo and Grid Search (AC-GS) algorithm based on the two improved algorithms. The AC-GS algorithm can update search range and adjusts the step size equal-proportionally according to the distribution of the current local optimal solution during the grid search phase. The experimental results show that compared with existing hyperparametric tuning methods, the proposed algorithm is more versatile. When the target function is monotonic or complex, this algorithm can achieve higher optimization efficiency. This algorithm trains an intrusion detection classifier to better recognize cyber attacks.

Keywords: Hyperparameter optimization · Grid search · Adaptive cuckoo algorithm

This article is supported in part by the National Natural Science Foundation of China under projects 61772150, 61862012 and 61962012, the Guangxi Key R&D Program under project AB17195025, the Guangxi Natural Science Foundation under grants 2018GXNSFDA281054, 2018GXNSFAA281232, 2019GXNSFFA245015, 2019GXNS-FGA245004 and AD19245048, and the Peng Cheng Laboratory Project of Guangdong Province PCL2018KP004.

S. Yu et al. (Eds.): SPDE 2020, CCIS 1268, pp. 292–305, 2020.
https://doi.org/10.1007/978-981-15-9129-7_21

1 Introduction

Industrial manufacturing is gradually becoming networked and informatized, and Industrial Control System (ICS) has become an important part of the national industrial infrastructure. Attacks against ICS are becoming more frequent worldwide. In 2017, the WannaCry virus wreaked worldwide destruction on a large scale, with the main target being computer equipment in industrial, educational, and medical systems, controlling the devices to encrypt large amounts of data, seriously affecting the normal operation of the system as well as the productive lives of users [1]. Thus, how to quickly identify the types of attacks on industrial control networks and the sources of attacks is particularly important.

Intrusion detection technology serves as an important early warning measure for industrial control systems, which can detect cyber attacks and benefit the protection of industrial control systems [2]. According to the types of attacks that may be encountered, there are two types of industrial network intrusion detection methods, namely, detection methods for variant attacks and detection methods for covert process attacks. In variant attack detection methods, anomalous intrusion detection techniques can be used for large variant attacks. At this phase, anomalous intrusion detection is usually implemented with the help of machine learning algorithms such as support vector machine, random forest, multilayer perceptron, etc. By simulating an intrusion into an industrial control network, capturing data from network traffic and industrial production environments, datasets can be generated to train machine learning models for intrusion detection and obtain classifiers for detecting malicious traffic.

In order to obtain better detection results, the detection accuracy of the classifier needs to be improved, and one feasible approach is to adjust the hyperparameters of the model before training the intrusion detection model. Currently, the most widely used adjustment method for hyperparameters is the grid search [3] or random search algorithm [4], which determines the optimal value by pre-determining the hyperparameter search range and exhausting all points in the search space within the range. However, when the scope of the search is large, the time overhead for that search solution is significant.

In practice, larger steps are typically used first in the grid search method to find the current global optimum and the position of the solution in the search space, and then gradually reduces the search scope and step length to find a more accurate optimal value. This operational scheme could reduce time overhead of search, but there is no unified strategy for narrowing the scope of search and it relies entirely on the personal experience of experimentalists. Especially if the objective function of optimization is non-convex, so it is likely to miss the global optimal value. Another method is meta-heuristic search algorithm. It gives a set of feasible solutions to hyperparameter optimization problems with low time cost and strong global search capability, but has low accuracy for some convex optimization problems. As a result, there is a lack of efficient, high-precision hyperparameter optimization algorithms for different optimization scenarios.

This paper investigates the problem of hyperparameter optimization of intrusion detection models based on machine learning methods and solves the problem of low efficiency and insufficient accuracy of traditional hyperparameter optimization methods. We made the following three contributions.

(1) An improved grid search algorithm is proposed. The improved algorithm can automatically update the search range according to the current local optimal solution distribution, thus the search accuracy is improved.
(2) An improved adaptive cuckoo algorithm is proposed, a new mathematical model is constructed, and the step-factor computer system of the adaptive cuckoo algorithm is improved to increase the convergence speed of the algorithm while ensuring search accuracy.
(3) Based on the above two improved algorithms, the AC-GS algorithm is proposed, which can automatically reduce the search range in the grid search phase based on the distribution of the most valuable values searched at the current step, and generate meta-heuristic search boundaries based on two different range selection strategies. In meta-heuristic search phase, this algorithm is able to search based on the search range generated in the grid search phase.

The hyperparameter optimization experiment on intrusion detection classifier shows that AC-GS algorithm can improve the hyperparameter optimization efficiency and the optimization accuracy more effectively than the existing algorithm.

The remainder of this paper is organized as follows. Section 2 introduces the current status of domestic and international research in this field. Section 3 introduces the preparatory knowledge of this paper. Section 4 describes this hybrid algorithm in detail. Section 5 presents the results of simulation experiments and verification of algorithms. Finally, Sect. 6 concludes the paper.

2 Related Works

2.1 Anomalous Intrusion Detection Methods

Anomaly intrusion detection is an important method to detect attack variants, which can establish the normal behavior of the target system. Anomalous intrusion detection techniques based on statistical methods had been applied earlier and were more mature [5]. In recent years, intrusion detection methods based on machine learning have a great development. Anomaly intrusion detection is usually realized by support vector machine, random forest, multilayer perceptron and other machine learning algorithms.

For supervisory control and data acquisition system (SCADA) attack, Almalawi et al. [6] proposed an unsupervised anomaly detection method, which used the density factor of k-nearest neighbor to calculate the inconsistent score, and extended the traditional fixed width clustering technology to extract similar detection rules. The real data set and simulation data set were used for experimental verification, which can significantly improve the accuracy of intrusion detection. Wu, Chen and Li [7] proposed a novel network intrusion detection model utilizing convolutional neural networks. Wu and Feng [8] used ANN as the classifier of industrial control intrusion detection. Firstly, independent component analysis was used to obtain the main features of the original industrial control network data, so as to reduce the structural complexity of ANN, and then PSO was used to optimize the structural parameters of ANN. Finally, based on the original data of industrial system, experiments were carried out to verify that the proposed intrusion detection method can be used in the actual industrial control system. Deng et al. [9] proposed a multi protocol intrusion detection method based on support vector machine, which can deal with the complexity of industrial control system communication network and perform well in security protection. Yu, Guo and Stojmenovic [10] developed semi-Markov models for detecting web browsing behavior and use second order statistical metrics to distinguish large-scale legitimate access behavior from attacks that simulate legitimate access.

Among the various anomalous intrusion detection methods based on machine learning, random forests are constantly being used in intrusion detection systems due to their strong generalization capabilities. In recent years, there has been a significant increase in the number of schemes using random forests as classifiers. Jiang et al. [11] proposed a hybrid model for network intrusion detection that combines improved rough set theory and random forest algorithms. Anton, Sinha and Schotten [12] used SVM and random forests for intrusion detection in industrial control systems and found that random forests performed slightly better than SVM by analyzing the correlation between individual features for downscaling. Buczak and Guven [13] also found that random forest-based intrusion detection systems have lower detection time complexity compared to SVM-based intrusion detection systems.

2.2 Optimization Methods Based on Meta-heuristics

In order to ensure better intrusion detection, the learning model training process requires constant tuning of the model, especially the hyperparameters of the model, which determine the complexity, learning ability and generalization ability of the model. They are usually not available directly from the training set and need to be set up on their own before training. The purpose of hyperparameter optimization is to find a better set of hyperparameter configurations for an algorithmic model so that the model has high robustness and generalization capability. A common optimization method is to find the best hyperparameters in the model using a meta-heuristic prime search method [14].

Meta-heuristic Algorithm (MA) is a class of algorithms that use meta-heuristic information from target problem to guide the search. Compared with deterministic search methods, meta-heuristic search algorithms converge faster and can effectively reduce the search scope and target problem complexity [15]. Mishra et al. [16] provided a detailed survey and analysis of various machine learning techniques and point out that group intelligence optimization in meta-heuristic algorithms helps in solving the problem of nonlinear optimization in machine learning. Li et al. [17] proposed a hyperparameter optimization method based on improved particle swarm algorithm for synthetic aperture radar images. In the experiment, the search results of this method were better than the traditional genetic algorithm and the model stability obtained by optimization is better. Gu et al. [18] proposed an optimization method based on support vector machine and improved artificial swarm algorithm and forbidden search. They proposed a synchronous optimization strategy for feature selection and parameter calculation to solve the problems of network data redundancy and insufficient model parameters.

Cuckoo search (CS) algorithm is a novel biogenic heuristic algorithm with simple structure, less set parameters than genetic algorithm, particle swarm algorithm and other biogenic heuristics [19], which is more efficient in solving practical problems such as industrial system optimization and engineering optimization. However, CS algorithm has limited applicability. The CS algorithm has a higher optimization efficiency when the optimization objective function is a multi-peak function. For the single-peak function, CS algorithm is not as efficient as the deterministic algorithm in finding the optimality [20]. Based on CUDA and Cuckoo Search algorithm, weaknesses of CS algorithm such as low optimization accuracy and slow convergence speed are solved, but the applicability of CS algorithm is not extended.

3   Preliminaries

3.1   Cuckoo Search Algorithm

Cuckoo search is a meta-heuristic algorithm based on biological habits, which simulates the breeding phenomenon of cuckoos breeding in the nests of other birds and their flight patterns when searching for nests. It is able to search for optimal solutions to complex optimization problems quickly and efficiently. There is evidence that the flight paths of both cuckoos and parasitic birds obey Lévy's flight patterns [21]. The implementation of cuckoo search is based on the following three ideal rules:

(1) Each cuckoo lays only one egg at a time, and randomly selects a nest for placement.
(2) The bird's nest corresponding to the highest quality egg will be retained for the next generation.
(3) The total number of available host bird nests is fixed, and parasitic eggs have a probability to be discovered by the host. This probability is a parameter. If the parasitic egg is found by the host, it will be pushed out of the bird's nest.

In the above rules, each egg corresponds to a feasible solution, and the global update formula to define the position of the bird's nest is [22]:

$$X_i^{t+1} = X_i^t + \alpha \left(X_i^t - X_b^t \right) \frac{\mu}{|v|^{1/\beta}} \tag{1}$$

Among them, X_i^{t+1} represents the position of the i-th nest in the $t+1$ generation; X_b^t denotes the bird nest with the best adaptation after this update; α is the step size factor; β is the index value in the power law formula, usually $\beta \in [1,2]$. μ, v follow the normal distribution, $\mu \sim N\left(0, \sigma_\mu^2\right)$, $v \sim N\left(0, \sigma_\mu^2\right)$, where σ_μ, σ_v are:

$$\sigma_\mu = \left[\frac{\Gamma(1+\beta)\sin\left(\frac{\pi\beta}{2}\right)}{2^{(\beta-1)/2}\Gamma\left(\frac{1+\beta}{2}\right)\beta} \right]^{1/\beta}, \sigma_v = 1 \qquad (2)$$

Because the variance of Lévy flight increases faster than Brown random walk process, in an uncertain environment, Lévy flight can maximize the search efficiency.

The parasitic eggs laid by cuckoos in the nests of other birds have a certain probability of being found. The probability of being found is p_a, $p_a \in (0,1)$. The nests being discovered will be abandoned. Once the nest is abandoned, cuckoo will search for a new solution near the nest, and this flight path can be represented as a random walk process:

$$\begin{cases} X_i^{t+1} = X_i^t + vH\left(p_a - \varepsilon\right)\left(X_j^t - X_k^t\right) \\ H\left(p_a - \varepsilon\right) = \begin{cases} 0, p_a - \varepsilon < 0 \\ 1, p_a - \varepsilon > 0 \end{cases} \end{cases} \qquad (3)$$

In formula (3), X_i^t and X_k^t represent two randomly selected solutions in the t-th generation solution set, the compression factor v and another random value ε are uniformly distributed numbers on $[0, 1]$.

3.2 Cuckoo Algorithm with Adaptive Step

The performance of the CS algorithm is affected by the step length factor α and compression factor v, where α determines the global search capability of the algorithm and v affects the local search capability of the algorithm. And in the actual optimization problem, the values of the two variables need to be adjusted several times according to experience to achieve equilibrium, the larger value of α can improve the global convergence speed of the algorithm, but this will sacrifice the search accuracy, the smaller value of α will bring the opposite consequences. In the local search process, the larger value of v is prone to suboptimal solution, while the smaller value of v may make the results fall into the local optimum. In order to solve the above problems, Chen, Wang and Yan [23] proposed an adaptive cuckoo algorithm (ACS).

Based on the original algorithm, the ACS algorithm was improved in two points:

(1) Change the fixed α in CS to an adaptive value related to the adaptation degree of the nest, this makes the algorithm can dynamically adjust the step size according to the adaptation degree of each individual in the process of running, which is helpful to improve the search accuracy, α can be expressed as the following equation.

$$\alpha = e^{-\left|\frac{bestfit(t)+\Delta}{bestfit(t)-fit_i(t)+\Delta}\right|} \tag{4}$$

In formula (4), $bestfit(t)$ denotes the optimal fit of generation t (i.e., the optimal value currently obtained by the objective function). Δ denotes a small constant that serves to avoid 0 divided by 0. From this equation, it can be seen that the further away from the region of the current optimal solution in the search space, the greater the step length of Lévy's flight. This feature enables the ACS algorithm to converge faster to the region where the optimal solution is located in the search space, and maintain the search accuracy of the local range, so as to achieve a better balance between global and local search.

(2) Dynamic inertial weights are used instead of compression factor v. Inertial weights are introduced to improve the search capability of the algorithm, balancing the relationship between global search and local search as follows.

$$v = e^{\frac{-t}{2nI}} \tag{5}$$

In formula (5), t indicates the number of current iterations of the algorithm; I indicates the total number of iterations. Obviously, as the number of iterations increases, the optimization space of the algorithm gradually decreases and the range of local random wandering should also be appropriately reduced to prevent the new values generated after the current optimal solution is discarded without excessive bias.

Combining formulas (1), (3), (4) and (5), the improved cuckoo algorithm can be obtained as follows.

$$X_i^{t+1} = X_i^t + e^{-\left|\frac{bestfit(t)+\Delta}{bestfit(t)-fit_t(t)+\Delta}\right|} \times \left(X_i^t - X_b^t\right) \frac{\mu}{|v|^{1/\beta}} \tag{6}$$

$$\begin{cases} X_i^{t+1} = X_i^t + e^{\frac{-t}{2nI}} H\left(p_a - \varepsilon\right)\left(X_j^t - X_k^t\right) \\ H\left(p_a - \varepsilon\right) = \begin{cases} 0, p_a - \varepsilon < 0 \\ 1, p_a - \varepsilon > 0 \end{cases} \end{cases} \tag{7}$$

4   Proposed Method

This paper adopts a hybrid algorithm that combines an improved grid search method with an improved ACS algorithm. The algorithm can be divided into two execution phases, namely, grid search phase and meta-heuristic search phase. The grid search phase uses an improved grid search algorithm that gradually approximates the optimal solution of the objective function by iteratively narrowing the search range, and switches to the second phase (meta-heuristic search phase) if it is found that the current search range may have more than one extreme value point. The meta-heuristic search uses an improved ACS algorithm. Based on the ACS algorithm, this algorithm improves the step size adjustment mechanism and convergence speed. Finally, when the standard deviation of multiple optimization results is below a certain value and the optimization results no longer get better, the algorithm terminates and outputs the current optimization solution and optimization value.

The following is a detailed description of the various parts of this mixing algorithm.

4.1 Improvements in the Grid Search Phase

In the conventional Grid Search (GS) method, the hyperparameter search process is one-time. After all the specified search elements are calculated in the model, it is needed to analyze the performance of the model under different hyperparameters, and then manually select the next hyperparameter search range based on the analysis results. Repeat this process several times until model performance is optimal. In the improved algorithm proposed in this paper, the iteration process is automated. With each iteration, the algorithm automatically adjusts the search range for the next iteration based on the distribution of feasible solutions obtained in that iteration, similar to the idea of a greedy algorithm.

Take a binary function as an example. If the objective function $z = f(x, y)$ and the optimization objective is the minimum value of z, the number of iterations of the algorithm is i and the number of extreme points currently searched is num_p. The entire search process is as follows, and the pseudocode is shown in Algorithm 1.

Algorithm 1: Improved Grid Search

Parameters: $d, U_i, L_i, K, num_{max}, time_{max}$;
Initialization: $i = 0$;
while $num_p < num_{\max}$ **do**
    Generate feasible solution set T_i
    Calculate $z = f(x^*, y^*), \exists \forall (x^*, y^*) \in T_i$
    Update U_i, L_i, num_p
    if $time_f >= time_{max}$ **then**
        Generate upper boundary according to greedy strategy
        Generate lower boundary according to greedy strategy
    end
    else
        Generate upper boundary according to non-greedy strategy
        Generate lower boundary according to non-greedy strategy
    end
    Perform ACS algorithm
end

---

(1) Initialize the key parameters of the algorithm, including the initial upper boundary set U_0, the initial lower boundary set L_0, the dimension d, the set of aliquots constants K and so on for each hyperparameter of the search.

(2) Generate the current feasible solution set T_i based on the current constraint boundary of the optimization problem.

(3) The set of feasible solutions is substituted into the calculation of the objective function to find all the local optimal solutions that exist in the current set of feasible solutions.

(4) Before reaching the stop condition of the first phase, the algorithm jumps to step (2) to continue the iteration and update the search scope.

(5) When the algorithm reaches the stop condition of the first phase, it stops the iterative grid search and generates new search regions based on the upper and lower bound sets at this time, entering the meta-heuristic search phase proposed in this paper. In this paper, the termination condition is determined by the number of current extreme value points num_p and the number of extreme value points upper limit num_{max}, where num_{max} is set manually before the algorithm execution. The iterative grid search is stopped if the number of extremely small value points generated by the n-th iteration $mum_p > mum_{max}$.

The feasible domain of the second phase of the algorithm (i.e., the meta-heuristic search phase) is generated based on the local optimal solution distribution at the end of the first phase. There are two strategies for the generation of feasible domains, namely, greedy and non-greedy strategies. Under the greedy strategy, the region around the global optimal solution obtained in the grid search phase is the feasible domain. Under the non-greedy strategy, the feasible domain is expanded. In the set of local optimal solutions obtained in the grid search phase, the concatenation of the regions surrounding each local optimal solution constitutes the feasible domain. The hybrid algorithm controls the strategy for generating the search range through the parameter $time_{max}$. When the target function performs an operation in a single time greater than $time_{max}$, a non-greedy strategy is used, and conversely a greedy strategy is used.

4.2 Improvements to the Adaptive Cuckoo Search Algorithm

In the meta-heuristic search phase of the hybrid algorithm, this paper uses the improved ACS algorithm. The core of the original ACS algorithm is the Lévy flight's step factor regulation mechanism. As shown in formula (4), the closer the target function $fit_i(t)$ to the optimal $bestfit(t)$ of the t-th iteration, the smaller the step factor α of the levy flight. In [24], the given step length formula also conforms to this law, which makes the new optimal solution for the next iteration of the Lévy flight not deviate too much from the optimal solution for the t-th iteration. Thus, the accuracy of the search is improved. In areas farther away from the optimal solution in search space, the Lévy flight has a larger step and is more conducive to global search. Therefore, in order to improve the convergence speed of the adaptive cuckoo algorithm, the value of α can be increased appropriately without changing the above rules. Based on this assumption, an inequality is introduced:

$$e^x \le \frac{1}{1-x}(x < 1) \tag{8}$$

Let $x = -\left|\frac{bestfit(t)+\Delta}{bestfit(t)-fit_i(t)+\Delta}\right|$, we get:

$$e^{-\left|\frac{bestfit(t)}{bestfit(t)-fit_i(t)}\right|} \leq 1 - \frac{1}{\left|1 - \frac{fit_i(t)}{bestfit(t)}\right| + 1} \qquad (9)$$

Similarly, the improved adaptive cuckoo algorithm takes $fit_i(t)$ and $bestfit(t)$ as independent variables and α^* as dependent variable to construct a new mathematical relationship:

$$\alpha^* = 1 - \frac{1}{\left|1 - \frac{fit_i(t)}{bestfit(t)}\right| + 1} \qquad (10)$$

Obviously, the closer the target function value $fit_i(t)$ is to the optimal value $bestfit(t)$ for that iteration on the t-th iteration, the smaller the step factor α^* will be. Typically, $\alpha^* > \alpha$, which guarantees a larger search area away from the optimal nest (the current optimal solution), is more favorable for searching the global optimal solution. The convergence speed of the algorithm has also been increased. And in the local random search phase, the new adaptive cuckoo algorithm is consistent with the original algorithm mechanism. The second phase of the algorithm is essentially the same as the execution process of the original ACS algorithm. The pseudocode is shown in Algorithm 2, and the execution process is as follows:

(1) According to the search range given in the first stage of the AC-GS algorithm, n feasible solutions are randomly generated within the search range.
(2) Calculate the corresponding value for each feasible solution one by one and save the feasible solution and its corresponding adaptation value.
(3) If the algorithm does not reach the stop condition, the step factor of the Lévy flight is calculated according to the value corresponding to each feasible solution, and the Lévy flight is executed. Otherwise, jump to step (5).
(4) Determine which new feasible solutions are discarded according to a predetermined probability, and if a solution is discarded, a random wander function is executed to find a new solution near the discarded solution. Then jump to step (2).
(5) Based on the current distribution of the feasible solutions, find the optimal solution and its fit value and output it.

Algorithm 2: Improved Adaptive Cuckoo Search

Input parameters and the objective function
Generate feasible solutions randomly
Calculate fitness according to the objective function
while !*stopcriterion* **do**

    Calculate step size factor according to fitness
    Get a cuckoo randomly by Lévy flights
    Abandon some feasible solutions
    Generate a new solution near the abandoned solution
    Calculate fitness according to the objective function

end
Output optimal solution and fitness

---

5 Hyperparameter Optimization Experiment

5.1 Dataset of Industrial Control Network

In the experiment, an intrusion detection learner for industrial control system was built using a random forest algorithm and the hyperparameters of the random forest were optimized. The training set data were generated using the Mississippi State University (MSU) natural gas pipeline control system intrusion detection standard data set, which is generated from network data from the SCADA system of natural gas pipelines, numerically processed and characterized by extraction. The raw network traffic includes attack traffic and normal traffic. The dataset divides the attack types into four categories, namely, response injection, denial of service (DoS), reconnaissance, and command injection, which can be further broken down into seven subcategories. The correspondence between the tag values in the dataset and the type of attack is shown in Table 1.

Table 1. Network traffic classification

Attack type	Description	Label value
Normal	Instance not part of an attack	0
NMRI	Naive malicious response injection attack	1
CMRI	Complex malicious response injection attack	2
MSCI	Malicious state command injection attack	3
MPCI	Malicious parameter command injection attack	4
MFCI	Malicious function command injection attack	5
DOS	Denial-of-service	6
Reconnaissance	Reconnaissance attack	7

5.2 Experiment Process

In the simulation experiments, grid search, ACS, AC-GS algorithms were used to optimize the maximum impurity (hyperparameter $min\_impurity\_decrease$) of the random forest classifier to achieve as high an accuracy as possible for invasion detection. The random forest estimator was used as the optimization objective function of the algorithm, and the median accuracy value obtained from 51 runs and 2-fold cross-validation was used as the fit value, and the parameter optimization space was $[0, 0.01]$.

Since the operating mechanisms of the three algorithms are very different, in order to facilitate comparison, the graph shows the operating time of the algorithm (AC-GS algorithm statistics the sum of the time cost of the two phases) as the horizontal coordinate, and the intrusion detection accuracy as the vertical coordinate to plot the relationship between the three algorithms to compare the hyperparameter optimization efficiency. As can be seen in Fig. 1, the curve of the ACS algorithm produces an oscillation before about 100 s due to the randomness of the lévy flight. Over time, at about 60 s, the AC-GS algorithm outperformed the grid search algorithm in terms of optimization. After 300 s, the results of each algorithm stabilize, while the results of the ACS algorithm deteriorate slightly, apparently 30 iterations are not enough for the meta-heuristic algorithms. Due to the deterministic nature of both GS and AC-GS algorithms, there is a clear advantage when the objective function is not a multi-peak function. The iterative optimization features of AC-GS allow the results of the algorithm to be closer to the optimal value faster than the GS algorithm. Record the best

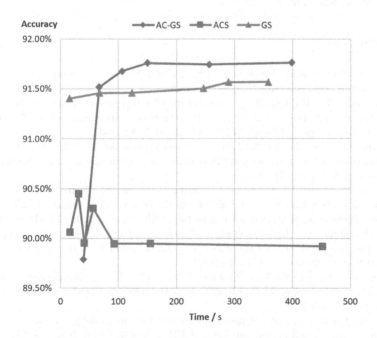

Fig. 1. Accuracy of each algorithm - time trend line

Table 2. Comparison of the optimization accuracy of each algorithm

Algorithm	Accuracy rate
GS	91.5683
ACS	90.4501
AC-GS	91.7633

accuracy achieved by each algorithm in this process, as shown in Table 2, the AC-GS algorithm is better than ACS and grid search in finding the best results.

6   Conclusion

At present, the security problems of industrial control networks are becoming more and more prominent, which places higher demands on the reliability of intrusion detection systems. To deal with the problem that traditional optimization methods are slow and not effective enough on intrusion detection classifiers, a hybrid algorithm based on improved grid search and improved adaptive cuckoo search is proposed in this paper. This algorithm has better versatility and higher search speed. In simulation experiments, we used this algorithm to optimize the hyperparameters of industrial control system intrusion detection classifier and compared this hybrid algorithm with other optimization algorithms. The results showed that the random forest classifier, which is optimized by this algorithm, has a higher detection accuracy.

References

1. Sun, Z., Strang, K.D., Pambel, F.: Privacy and security in the big data paradigm. J. Comput. Inf. Syst. **60**(2), 146–155 (2020)
2. Benisha, R.B., Raja Ratna, S.: Detection of interruption attack in the wireless networked closed loop industrial control systems. Telecommun. Syst. **73**(3), 359–370 (2019). https://doi.org/10.1007/s11235-019-00614-3
3. Wang, X., Gong, G., Li, N., Qiu, S.: Detection analysis of epileptic EEG using a novel random forest model combined with grid search optimization. Front. Hum. Neurosci. **13**(2), 52–64 (2019)
4. Javeed, A., Zhou, S., Yongjian, L., Qasim, I., Noor, A., Nour, R.: An intelligent learning system based on random search algorithm and optimized random forest model for improved heart disease detection. IEEE Access **7**, 180235–180243 (2019)
5. Yu, S., Zhou, W., Jia, W., Guo, S., Xiang, Y., Tang, F.: Discriminating DDoS attacks from flash crowds using flow correlation coefficient. IEEE Trans. Parallel Distrib. Syst. **23**(6), 1073–1080 (2012)
6. Almalawi, A., Yu, X., Tari, Z., Fahad, A., Khalil, I.: An unsupervised anomaly-based detection approach for integrity attacks on SCADA systems. Comput. Secur. **46**, 94–110 (2014)
7. Wu, K., Chen, Z., Li, W.: A novel intrusion detection model for a massive network using convolutional neural networks. IEEE Access **6**, 50850–50859 (2018)

8. Wu, F.: Information fusion and intelligent pattern recognition for network intrusion in industrial network systems based on ICA and PSO-ANN. In: Yang, Y., Ma, M. (eds.) Green Communications and Networks. LNEE, vol. 113, pp. 1247–1254. Springer, Dordrecht (2012). https://doi.org/10.1007/978-94-007-2169-2_146

9. Deng, L., Peng, Y., Liu, C., Xin, X., Xie, Y.: Intrusion detection method based on support vector machine access of modbus TCP protocol. IEEE Smart Data **2015**, 380–383 (2017)

10. Yu, S., Guo, S., Stojmenovic, I.: Fool me if you can: mimicking attacks and anti-attacks in cyberspace. IEEE Trans. Comput. **64**(1), 139–151 (2015)

11. Jiang, J., Wang, Q., Shi, Z., Lv, B., Qi, B.: RST-RF: a hybrid model based on rough set theory and random forest for network intrusion detection. In: ACM International Conference Proceeding Series, pp. 77–81 (2018)

12. Anton, S.D., Sinha, S., Dieter Schotten, H.: Anomaly-based intrusion detection in industrial data with SVM and random forests. In: 2019 27th International Conference on Software, Telecommunications and Computer Networks, SoftCOM 2019, pp. 10–15 (2019)

13. Buczak, A.L., Guven, E.: A survey of data mining and machine learning methods for cyber security intrusion detection. IEEE Commun. Surv. Tutor. **18**(2), 1153–1176 (2016)

14. Golilarz, N.A., Addeh, A., Gao, H., Ali, L., Roshandeh, A.M., Mudassir Munir, H., Khan, R.U.: A new automatic method for control chart patterns recognition based on convnet and harris hawks meta heuristic optimization algorithm. IEEE Access **7**, 149398–149405 (2019)

15. Wang, C.F., Liu, S.Y., Zheng, G.Z.: A branch-and-reduce approach for solving generalized linear multiplicative programming. Math. Probl. Eng. **2011** (2011)

16. Mishra, P., Varadharajan, V., Tupakula, U., Pilli, E.S.: A detailed investigation and analysis of using machine learning techniques for intrusion detection. IEEE Commun. Surv. Tutor. **21**(1), 686–728 (2019)

17. Li, Y., Liu, G., Li, T., Jiao, L., Lu, G., Marturi, N.: Application of data driven optimization for change detection in synthetic aperture radar images. IEEE Access **8**, 11426–11436 (2020)

18. Gu, T., Chen, H., Chang, L., Li, L.: Intrusion detection system based on improved abc algorithm with tabu search. IEEJ Trans. Electr. Electron. Eng. **14**(11), 1652–1660 (2019)

19. Yang, X.S., Deb, S.: Engineering optimisation by cuckoo search. Int. J. Math. Modell. Numer. Optim. **1**(4), 330–343 (2010)

20. Yang, X.S., Deb, S.: Cuckoo search via Lévy flights. In: 2009 World Congress on Nature and Biologically Inspired Computing, NABIC 2009, pp. 210–214 (2009)

21. Yang, X.S.: From swarm intelligence to metaheuristics: nature-inspired optimization algorithms. Computer **49**(9), 52–59 (2016)

22. Huang, X., Xie, Z., Huang, X.: Fault location of distribution network base on improved cuckoo search algorithm. IEEE Access **8**, 2272–2283 (2020)

23. Chen, H., Wang, H., Yan, B.: Application of CUDA and cuckoo algorithm based SVM in industrial control system intrusion detection (in Chinese). J. East China Univ. Sci. Technol. **45**(1), 8–16 (2019)

24. Naik, M.K., Panda, R.: A novel adaptive cuckoo search algorithm for intrinsic discriminant analysis based face recognition. Appl. Soft Comput. J. **38**, 661–675 (2016)

Trust Computation and Forensics

Bitcoin-Based Anti-collusion Fair Payments for Outsourcing Computations in Cloud Computing

Duo Zhang[1,2], Xiaodong Zhang[3], Sheng Gao[4], and Youliang Tian[1(✉)]

[1] State Key Laboratory of Public Big Data,
College of Computer Science and Technology, Guizhou University, GuiYang, China
youliangtian@163.com
[2] School of Mathematics and Statistics, Guizhou University, GuiYang, China
[3] College of Mathematics and Computer Science, Liupanshui Normal College,
Liupanshui, China
[4] School of Information, Central University of Finance and Economics, Beijing, China

Abstract. As an attractive cloud computing model, outsourcing computation often has a fair payment issues. In cloud computing, resource-constrained users outsource tasks and pay for them. However, the traditional outsourcing computation model can hardly resist the threat of collusion between calculators. In this paper, we propose a new scheme of Bitcoin-based anti-collusion fair payments for outsourcing computations (BAPay), give the architecture of BAPay, security requirements, and describe the design details. Besides, the scheme guarantees that an honest calculator will be paid for doing the calculations, regardless of the outsourcer's behaviour. In addition, the security analysis shows that BAPay achieves completeness and fairness.

Keywords: Cloud computing · Outsourcing computation · Bitcoin · Anti-collusion · Fair payments

1 Introduction

As a promising computing paradigm, cloud computing has many attractive advantages. With the rapid development of cloud computing technology, more and more individuals and businesses to upload all kinds of data to a third party cloud platforms, to facilitate sharing or cost savings [1]. In cloud computing, as

This work is supported by the Key Projects of the Joint Fund of the National Natural Science Foundation of China (No. U1836205); the National Natural Science Foundation of China (No. 61662009, No. 61772008); the Guizhou Province Science and Technology Major Special Plan (No. 20183001); the Research on Key Technologies of Blockchain for Big Data Applications (No. [2019]1098); the Foundation of Postgraduate of Guizhou Province (No. YJSCXJH2019015).

S. Yu et al. (Eds.): SPDE 2020, CCIS 1268, pp. 309–321, 2020.
https://doi.org/10.1007/978-981-15-9129-7_22

end users are usually resource-constrained, they often need to outsource computing services, which brings great impetus to the development of cloud computing [2]. Although cloud computing provides users with flexible and efficient outsourcing services, the security, completeness and reliability of data remain the main concerns of users [3–5]. For example, in outsourcing computation, users are not willing to pay for services if the results returned by the outsourcing service provider are incorrect.

Recently, great efforts have been made to verifiable outsourcing computation [6]. Although these technologies can guarantee the security of data storage and the correctness of computing, they cannot solve all security threats in cloud computing. Because in an outsourcing computation, the calculators want to get the service reward before returning the calculation result to the outsourcer. However, the outsourcer expects to get and check the results, and then pays for the service if the calculations are correct. Therefore, if the outsourcer and the calculators do not trust each other, the payment issue can be extremely challenging for an outsourcing computation that considers fairness.

In fact, to address the issues of payment, the payment mechanism of most existing scheme still adopts the traditional, relies on the trusted third party [7]. However, in the cloud, the traditional payment need a bank generates payment token, which has some disadvantages. Recently, technologies such as Bitcoin and Blockchain have received a lot of attention, because they can operate without either party's control. Therefore, we divide the calculation task into smaller tasks and assign them to different calculators. After each calculator completes the corresponding calculation task, the calculation results are sent to the outsourcer. Establish a fair payment protocol based on Bitcoin between the outsourcer and the calculators so that cryptocurrency can be transferred between them without the need for a third party. To the best of our knowledge, Bitcoin technologys are rarely widely and fairly used in payments for the outsourcing computation.

1.1   Our Contribution

In this paper, we propose a Bitcoin-based anti-collusion fair payment framework (BAPay) for outsourcing computations of cloud computing, and eliminate the third-party, trusted or not, while ensuring the fairness of payment against malicious outsourcer (O) and calculators (C). In our proposed protocol, we use the idea of Bitcoin contract to guarantee that no matter how a malicious O behaves, C will be paid if they are honest. The contributions of this paper are three-fold:

- Firstly, the system architecture, specification and security requirements of BAPay system are proposed, and its design details are described. We demonstrate that BAPay enjoys completeness and fairness where means that the resistance to colluding attacks does not depend on any third party.
- Secondly, in the protocol, it is ensured that the calculators either earns the service fee and gets his guaranty back simultaneously or pays a penalty in the form of deposit to the outsourcer. The proposed protocol enables an automatic penalty to calculators if the outsourcer does not pay as he promised.

- Finally, taking advantage of the anonymity of Bitcoin, we solve the collusion problem of calculators in the outsourcing computation. Our system architecture can be used for general calculations in the outsourcing computation. Besides, the security analysis shows that BAPay achieves completeness and fairness.

1.2 Related Work

In recent years, Bitcoin has attracted widespread attention in recent years because of its anonymity. Bitcoin, an early and successful use of Blockchain technology, is issued under the pseudonym Satoshi Nakamoto [8]. To expand the potential uses of Bitcoin technologies, Ethereum, Smart contracts and related technologies have been proposed. Bonneau et al. [9] first systematically described Bitcoin and cryptocurrencies. Andrychowicz et al. [10,11] constructed a time limit commitment scheme, and also proposed a secure multi-party lottery protocol based on Bitcoin. Similarly, Bentov and Kumaresan [12] showed how to use Bitcoin systems to design fair and secure computing protocols. Note that the research work of these schemes mainly includes two aspects: outsourcing storage and outsourcing computation.

As for outsourcing computation, a number of solutions have been presented recently. There are different validation solutions for different computing tasks. In order to protect the rights and interests of the honest participants, Golle et al. [13,14] proposed a distributed computing outsourcing security model, which used repeated computation to verify the correctness of the calculated results. Szajda et al. [15], Sarmenta et al. [16], proposed a probabilistic verification mechanism for detecting cheaters, but the computational cost was high. In order to improve efficiency, Du et al. [17] proposed a promise-based scheme to prevent server spoofing. Monrose et al. [18] used computational proofs to ensure proper server behavior. Gennaro et al. [19] proposed a verifiable outsourcing computation scheme that protects the privacy of inputs and outputs. Carbunar et al. [20] first considered the payment problem in the outsourcing computation scenario and proposed a fair payment scheme. Chen et al. [21] further proposed a conditional electronic payment system based on restricted partial blind signature scheme.

Note that existing solutions in outsourcing computation payment schemes seem to require trusted third parties to achieve fair payment. For example, banks. However, if the transaction costs in the system are too high, banks are reluctant to implement them. To solve these problems, Dong et al. [22] proposed a protocol for checking the correctness of computing in cloud computing based on game theory and the Ethereum smart contract. Huang et al. [23] proposed a Blockchain-based outsourcing solution that still requires a trusted third party. Chen [24] proposed a Bitcoin-based fair payments for outsourcing computations of fog devices, but this scheme could not really realize decentralized outsourcing services based on Blockchain. While ensuring fairness of payment against malicious outsourcers and calculators, Zhang et al. [25] introduce an outsourcing service payment framework based on Blockchain in cloud computing. In this paper, we propose an anti-collusion payment protocol based on Bitcoin that can solve the collusive threat of the calculators and ensure the correct execution of the service.

1.3 Organization

The rest of the paper is organized as follows: in Sect. 2, we present the system architecture, definition and security requirements. We propose a Bitcoin-based anti-collusion fair payment framework (BAPay) in Sect. 3. Security analysis is given in Sect. 4. Finally, we give a brief conclusion.

2 System Architecture, Definition and Security Requirements

In this section, we first present the system architecture and definition of BAPay. Then, the security requirements are described in detail.

2.1 System Architecture of BAPay

The main process of our protocol is depicted in Fig. 1, and it involves an outsourcer (i.e., resource-ronstraint user), calculators (i.e., cloud service providers) and a Bitcoin Network [26, 27]. The outsourcer come to an agreement with calculators through Bitcoin Network system. Suppose O plans to subscribe an outsourcing service sv from C. The details are given as follows:

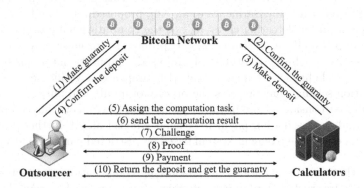

Fig. 1. An example of transaction

2.2 Definition of BAPay

BAPay consists of five phases: the system setup phase, the service implementation phase, the establish payment phase, the service verification phase, and the service redeem phase. The first four phases are compulsory and the service redeem phase is performed by O only if C fails to provide a valid service implementation proof.

System Setup Phase. O and C initialize some parameters such as unredeemed transactions to be used in the subsequent phases.

Service Implementation Phase. sv is implemented based on three procedures: service subscription, service enforcement and preliminary service confirmation, which are sequentially performed as below.

- *Service Subscription*: O subscribes sv from C by sending service-related data to C.
- *Service Enforcement:* In this procedure, sv is enforced by C. Upon receiving the subscription data from O, C enforces sv.
- *Preliminary Service Confirmation:* After obtaining the signature from C, O thinks that sv has been preliminarily implemented, where *preliminarily* means that the sv implementation will be checked by O before the payment.

Establish Payment Phase. In this phase, O and C jointly initiate the service checking and specify the service requirements. A payment protocol is established between O and C to ensure the smooth operation of the outsourcing computation task. At the same time, in order to prevent collusion, O also sets the corresponding anti-collusion mechanism to ensure the real effectiveness of the calculation results.

Service Verification Phase. This phase is performed by C to earn the (partial) service fee from C by proving that the (partial) sv implementation meets the (partial) requirements. Certainly, O can ensure that the (partial) service fee is paid to C only if the (partial) sv implementation is what is expected.

Service Redeem Phase. Only if C fails to prove that the (partial) sv implementation meets the (partial) requirements of O before a specific time, BAPay comes to the service redeem phase. In this phase, O can claim enough deposits from C no matter how C behaves.

2.3   Security Requirements

In BAPay, both O and C are of mutual distrust and they can be malicious. Concretely, the malicious O aims to enjoy sv provided by C without paying the service fee, and the malicious C wants to get the service fee from O without implementing sv as specified in the requirements of O. The malicious C may collude with others to cheat O. Hence, for an efficient outsourcing system, it should be satisfy the properties of completeness, fairness and anti-collusion.

- *Completeness:* If both O and C are honest, then O can obtain the required service implementation and C can gain the corresponding service fee.

- **Fairness:** The fairness for C means that it is infeasible for the malicious O to enjoy valid sv provided by C without paying the service fee. In the case of the malicious C, the fairness for O means that it is infeasible for C to get the service fee paid by O without providing a valid sv implementation proof in terms of the requirements of O before a specific time. Particularly, if a malicious C fails to provide such a proof, O is able to get enough compensation or penalty from C.
- **Anti-collusion:** If C is honest, then C doesn't know what the real intentions of O. If C is honest but curious, then between two or more C's collusion gain the full result to the private data for O, and O's data security will face a huge challenge.

3 BAPay: Bitcoin-Based Anti-collusion Fair Payment Framework

3.1 Main Idea

When a resource-constrained outsourcer O wants to obtain certain results, the corresponding calculation task is sent to multiple calculators C, and after receiving the correct return results for all the tasks, it calculates the desired results through the returned results. For C, BAPay requires that there is no collusion between the calculators. If all the C receive the computing task collude and share the computing task of the O, they can recover the true intention of the outsourcer O. According to the security requirements, the main challenges to design BAPay include fairness and anti-collusion. This paper attempts to prevent collusion from the perspective of interests, and proposes a Bitcoin script based anti-collusion payment protocol, in which most C participating in collusion will suffer economic losses, so they will not choose to collude with other C.

3.2 Design Details of BAPay

As we know, the Bitcoin script is simple, stack-based and purposefully not Turing-complete. In order to achieve easy understanding and keep the exposition simple, we present a BAPay following the style of Bitcoin transactions.

System Setup Phase. Let H be a cryptographic hash function, such as SHA-256. A secure symmetric encryption algorithm should be chosen for specified services if necessary. O and C choose their own ECDSA public-secret key pairs, denoted by (pk_o, sk_o) and (pk_c, sk_c), respectively. All the parties have come to an agreement on a public key used in receiving Bitcoin.

Service Implementation Phase. The outsourcer O prepares the outsourcing instance F_i. Through a special transaction in Bitcoin system, O creates a Bitcoin contract to form agreements with C. The outsourcing service sv is implemented based on the following three procedures.

- **Service Subscription:** O preprocesses service-related local $(q_1, ..., q_n)$ and sends the result $(m_1, ..., m_n)$ to C for sub-scribing sv. Note that the preprocessing is specified by concrete outsourcing services. Meanwhile, O also generates a random number R and sends it to each C.
- **Service Enforcement:** In this procedure, upon receiving the subscription $(m_1, ..., m_n)$ from O, C is first based on $(m_1, ..., m_n)$ to compute $(r_1, ..., r_n)$ then return it to the O and finish sv. Finally, C generates a digital signature according to the enforcement of sv, because the transaction Tx can only be redeemed through the signature of C private key sk_c.
- **Preliminary Service Confirmation:** After obtaining $(r_1, ..., r_n)$, O considers that sv has been preliminarily implemented, where preliminarily means that sv implementation will be checked by O before the payment.

Establish Payment Phase. This phase is performed by C to earn the service fee from O by proving that the sv implementation meets the requirements. Specifically speaking, O builds a Bitcoin transaction to pay for outsourcing services sv. For each C, O creates a transaction Pay_i of value $d\mathbf{B}$, the structure of the transaction Pay_i is shown in Fig. 2.

TxPay$_i$ (in: Tx)
in-script: sig$_v$ (TxPay$_i$)
out-script $(body, \sigma_1, \cdots, \sigma_n, \sigma_U, \sigma_B, \sigma_{S_i})$: $(\mathrm{ver}_{m_1}(body, \sigma_1) \wedge \cdots \wedge \mathrm{ver}_{m_n}(body, \sigma_n)$ $\wedge \mathrm{ver}_B(body, \sigma_B)) \vee$ $(\mathrm{ver}_{S_i}(body, \sigma_{S_i}) \wedge \mathrm{ver}_U(body, \sigma_U))$
val: $d\,\mathbf{B}$

Fig. 2. The structure of the transaction Pay_i

There are two ways to cash in Pay_i. Under normal circumstances, the transaction will be cashed by $Charge_i$ after time t, which corresponds to the way it is cashed after the symbol $\vee$ in the output script. The structure of the transaction $Charge_i$ is shown in Fig. 3. Note that the transaction body $Charge_i$ is created by O, which then generates a signature about the transaction and sends it to the corresponding C.

Service Verification Phase. C generates a signature about the transaction after checking the transaction $Charge_i$ sent by O. Note that the transaction $Charge_i$ can only be redeemed through the signature of C private key sk_c. Based on $(m_1, ..., m_n)$, C computes $(r_1, ..., r_n)$ and returns it to O. Afterwards, C receives service fees by publishing and cashing in transactions $Charge_i$ after time t.

Of course, the transaction Pay_i can also be cashed in through another the transaction $Collude_i$, which requires collusion between the calculators C because a signature of a set of private keys $(sk_{m_1}, ..., sk_{m_n}, sk_B)$ (i.e. (pk_B, sk_B) is a shared key pair) is required. The structure of the transaction $Collude$ is shown in Fig. 4.

Because the keys are generated by messages m_i, the calculators C who know the messages m_i can compute the corresponding private keys. If the calculators C know exactly what O wants, the best route to collude with each other C and must share the messages m_i freely. Therefore, if a C knows all the messages m_i, as well as the private keys sk_B, then he can cash in the transaction Pay_i. Furthermore, O restores the final result based on the result returned by the calculators C.

$TxCharge_i$ **(in: TxPay$_i$)**
in-script: $\varnothing, \cdots, \varnothing$, sig$_U$ (TxCharge$_i$), $\varnothing$, sig$_{s_i}$ (TxCharge$_i$)
out-script $(body, \sigma_1)$: ver$_{s_i}(body, \sigma_1)$
val: $d\,\textrm{B}$
tlock: t

Fig. 3. The structure of the transaction $Charge_i$

$TxCollude$ **(in: TxPay$_i$)**
in-script: sig$_{m_1}$ (TxCollude), $\cdots$, sig$_{m_n}$ (TxCollude), $\varnothing$, sig$_B$ (TxCollude), $\varnothing$
out-script $(body, \sigma_1)$: ver$_{s_i}(body, \sigma_1)$
val: $d\,\textrm{B}$

Fig. 4. The structure of the transaction $Collude$

Service Redeem Phase. Although the payment protocol above somewhat inhibits collusion, there is still a issue. The co-conspirators may avoid loss of interest by sharing their results r_i rather than their messages m_i. If they have all the results, they can still get the outsourcer's true intentions. Therefore, the payment protocol must be modified to solve the collusion issue.

Assuming that the calculation returned by the calculators C are $(r_1, ..., r_n)$, according to the previous method of generating sk_{m_i}, the O generates a set of private keys $(sk_{r_1}, ..., sk_{r_n})$ using r_i and R. By swapping the private key of the cashing condition in the previous transaction Pay_i from the private key generated by the $(m_1, ..., m_n)$ for the private key generated by the calculation result $(r_1, ..., r_n)$, then the calculation result can be prevented from being shared by the calculators C. Therefore, we need to convert the transaction Pay_i into a new transaction Pay_i'.

To implement this transformation, the O needs to generate a new transaction Pay'_i instead of the previous transaction Pay_i. The output scripts for Pay'_i and Pay_i is similar, and the transaction structure of Pay'_i is shown in Fig. 5.

To implement Pay_i, the O needs the signature of the private key, so the O sends the transaction Pay_i to either calculators C for the signature. The case where the calculators C does not sign this transaction Pay_i will be discussed in the security analysis. Similarly, there are two ways to implement the transaction Pay'_i. The first way is the same as $Charge$, and the second way is similar to $Collude$, replacing sk_{r_i} with the private key sk_{m_i}. The transaction structure of $Collude'_i$ is shown in Fig. 6. In this case, if a C has enough r_i, he can implement the transaction Pay'_i.

Note that this protocol applies to payment agreements that can tolerate collusion by $n-1$ calculators C, that is, if not all calculators collude, they will not be able to recover the outsourcer O true results. In addition, it is also possible to set tolerable $l-1$ calculators collusion based on the idea of threshold, which is a case for further discussion.

TxPay$'_i$ (in: Tx)
in-script: sig_{m_1} (TxPay$'_i$), $\cdots$,sig_{m_n} (TxPay$'_i$), sig_B (TxPay$'_i$)
out-script $(body, \sigma_1, \cdots, \sigma_n, \sigma_U, \sigma_B, \sigma_{S_l})$: $(\text{ver}_{r_1}(body, \sigma_1) \wedge \cdots \wedge \text{ver}_{r_n}(body, \sigma_n)$ $\wedge \text{ver}_B(body, \sigma_B)) \vee$ $(\text{ver}_{S_l}(body, \sigma_{S_l}) \wedge \text{ver}_U(body, \sigma_U))$
val: d ฿

Fig. 5. The structure of the transaction Pay'_i

TxCollude$'$ (in: TxPay$'_i$)
in-script: sig_{r_1} (TxCollude$'$), $\cdots$, sig_{r_n} (TxCollude$'$),Ø,sig_B (TxCollude$'$),Ø
out-script $(body, \sigma_1)$: $\text{ver}_{S_l}(body, \sigma_1)$
val: d ฿

Fig. 6. The structure of the transaction $Collude'_i$

In this paper, the BAPay protocol based on Bitcoin mainly takes advantage of the anonymity of Bitcoin, which makes it impossible for calculators of the collusion to distinguish which a calculator has cashed in the transaction and taken away all the service fees. In other words, if the calculators collude, only one C will cash in on the transaction and take the fees, and all other calculators will lose the corresponding fees. From the perspective of interests, these calculators will not collude.

4   Security Analysis

Theorem 1. *The proposed Bitcoin-based anti-collusion fair payments protocol (BAPay) satisfies the security requirement of completeness.*

Proof. Completeness refers to the completeness of the structure of the protocol, which can achieve the purpose of the protocol. In other words, the O can not only obtain the calculations, but also guarantees their privacy. At the same time, the calculators C can get the corresponding service fee.

In normal case, both O and C follow the protocol process. O sends the outsourcing tasks and corresponding parameters to the C, and publishes the transaction on the Bitcoin network. According to the requirements of the outsourcing task, C calculates and returns the calculations to O. After t time, C will exchange the transaction $Charge$ for the transaction Pay'_i, and all C will obtain corresponding Bitcoin from O for his reward, and O will get back his deposit. At last, O gets the correct return result and restores the desired result.

Theorem 2. *Based on the anonymity of Bitcoin, Bitcoin-based anti-collusion fair payments protocol (BAPay) satisfies the the security requirement of fairness.*

Proof. We use Bitcoin script transactions to achieve fairness. If either O or C does not follow the normal process of the protocol, it will suffer the loss of interests or terminate the protocol to protect the interests of the participants.

Assuming that O does not collude with C, C will honestly return the correct results. But they are curious, and may collude with each other to obtain C private information. Both participants may not follow the normal procedures of the protocol. Two cases should be taken into account:

- *Case* 1. O does not follow the normal flow of the protocol.
  - If O does not build the payment protocol Pay for a payment, then C will not provide an outsourcing service and the protocol terminates $\perp$.
  - If O does not implement in the transaction Pay, it will be converted to the transaction Pay'. However, in order to prevent the disclosure of O privacy and prevent C from sharing the calculation results. Generally speaking, O chooses to convert the transaction Pay into Pay'. Otherwise, the protocol terminates $\perp$. At the same time, C can still get the reward, the privacy of O can no longer be guaranteed.
- *Case* 2. C does not follow the normal flow of the protocol. In the protocol, O sends the signature $Charge'$ to C, which signs the transaction and publishes it. If C does not sign the transaction, the agreement terminates $\perp$. Of course, C does not obtain the service reward.
  - If C chooses to collude and share the received message m_i, then one of C can redeem all transactions Pay paid to each C through the transaction $Charge$, thus the other C will lose their due service reward. From the perspective the interests of the individual, all of C do not choose collusion.
  - If C chooses to collude and share the received message r_i, similarity, one of C can redeem all transactions Pay' paid to each computing party through the transaction $Charge'$, thus the other C will lose their due service reward. As discussed earlier, when C converts the transaction Pay to the transaction Pay', the signature of the private key sk_c is required. If neither C signs the transaction as required by the protocol and shares the results, they still seem to know the results of O calculations and obtain the service reward. But says in practical terms, the C who knows all the returned results can still cash in the fees payable to other C. From the perspective the interests of the individual, C also does not choose collusion.

- If C negotiates in advance to avoid one C withdrawing the reward due to other C. Because of the anonymity of Bitcoin, they could not tell which of the co-conspirators cashed in. So it's hard to use a deposit or any other way to prevent one of the calculators from taking away the reward.

According to the above proof, the collusion C will lose its reward. Furthermore, from the perspective the interests of the individual, C does not collude. Therefore, it is reasonable to restrain collusion through interests in the protocol.

5 Conclusion

In this paper, we propose an anti-collusion fair payments framework based on Bitcoin. To be specific, we introduce the architecture of BAPay and describe the design details of BAPay. Under our protocol, the resource-constraint user pays the service fee through the Bitcoin, and the transaction can be exchanged under different conditions. In addition, by taking advantage of the excellent characteristics of Bitcoin and combining with the multi-signature scheme, we have solved the issue of the calculators collusion in the outsourcing computation. Our security analysis indicate that BAPay achieves completeness and fairness. In the future, it is interesting to address the issue of payment equity based on Bitcoin, Blockchain and Smart contract technologies in more complex cloud.

References

1. Zhang, Y.H., Deng, R., Liu, X.M., Zhang, D.: Blockchain based efficient and robust fair payment for outsourcing services in cloud computing. Inf. Sci. **462**, 262–277 (2018)
2. Armbrust, M., et al.: A view of cloud computing. Commun. ACM **53**(4), 50–58 (2010)
3. Huang, Z., Liu, S., Mao, X., Chen, K., Li, J.: Insight of the protection for data security under selective opening attacks. Inf. Sci. **412**, 223–241 (2017)
4. Li, J., Zhang, Y., Chen, X., Xiang, Y.: Secure attribute-based data sharing for resource-limited users in cloud computing. Comput. Secur. **72**, 1–12 (2018)
5. Zhang, Y., Li, J., Chen, X., Li, H.: Anonymous attribute-based proxy reencryption for access control in cloud computing. Secur. Commun. Netw. **9**(14), 2397–2411 (2016)
6. Ateniese, G., et al.: Provable data possession at untrusted stores. In: Proceedings of the 14th ACM Conference on Computer and Communications Security (CCS)2007, pp. 598–609. ACM (2007). https://doi.org/10.1007/978-1-59593-703-2/07/0011
7. Chen, X., Li, J., Huang, X., Ma, J., Lou, W.: New publicly verifiable databases with efficient updates. IEEE Trans. Dependable Secure Comput. **12**(5), 546–556 (2015)
8. Nakamoto, S.: Bitcoin: a peer-to-peer electronic cash system (2008)
9. Bonneau, J., Miller, A., Clark, J., Narayanan, A., Kroll, J. A., Felten, E.W.: SoK: research perspectives and challenges for bitcoin and cryptocurrencies. In: IEEE Symposium on Security and Privacy 2015, San Jose, USA, pp. 104–121 (2015). https://doi.org/10.1109/SP.2015.14

10. Andrychowicz, M., Dziembowski, S., Malinowski, D., Mazurek, L.: Secure multiparty computations on bitcoin. In: IEEE Symposium on Security and Privacy(SP)2014, San Jose, USA, pp. 443–458 (2014). https://doi.org/10.1109/SP.2014.35

11. Andrychowicz, M., Dziembowski, S., Malinowski, D., Mazurek, L.: Fair two-party computations via bitcoin deposits. In: Böhme, R., Brenner, M., Moore, T., Smith, M. (eds.) FC 2014. LNCS, vol. 8438, pp. 105–121. Springer, Heidelberg (2014). https://doi.org/10.1007/978-3-662-44774-1_8

12. Bentov, I., Kumaresan, R.: How to use bitcoin to design fair protocols. In: Garay, J.A., Gennaro, R. (eds.) CRYPTO 2014. LNCS, vol. 8617, pp. 421–439. Springer, Heidelberg (2014). https://doi.org/10.1007/978-3-662-44381-1_24

13. Golle, P., Stubblebine, S.: Secure distributed computing in a commercial environment. In: Syverson, P. (ed.) FC 2001. LNCS, vol. 2339, pp. 289–304. Springer, Heidelberg (2002). https://doi.org/10.1007/3-540-46088-8_23

14. Golle, P., Mironov, I.: Uncheatable distributed computations. In: Naccache, D. (ed.) CT-RSA 2001. LNCS, vol. 2020, pp. 425–440. Springer, Heidelberg (2001). https://doi.org/10.1007/3-540-45353-9_31

15. Szajda, D., Lawson, B., Owen, J.: Hardening functions for large scale distributed computations. In: Symposium on Security and Privacy 2003, Berkeley, USA, pp. 216–224 (2003). https://doi.org/10.1109/SECPRI.2003.1199338

16. Sarmenta, L.F.G.: Sabotage-tolerance mechanisms for volunteer computing systems. Future Gener. Comput. Syst. 18(4), 561–572 (2002)

17. Du, W., Jia, J., Mangal, M., Murugesan, M.: Uncheatable grid computing. In: Proceedings of the 24th International Conference on Distributed Computing, Systems, ICDCS 2004, pp. 4–11. IEEE Computer Society (2004). https://doi.org/10.1109/ICDCS.2004.1281562

18. Monrose, F., Wyckoff, P., Rubin, A. D.: Distributed execution with remote audit. In: Proceedings of the 1999 ISOC Network and Distributed System Security Symposium (NDSS) 1999, San Diego, pp. 103–113 (1999)

19. Gennaro, R., Gentry, C., Parno, B.: Non-interactive verifiable computing: outsourcing computation to untrusted workers. In: Rabin, T. (ed.) CRYPTO 2010. LNCS, vol. 6223, pp. 465–482. Springer, Heidelberg (2010). https://doi.org/10.1007/978-3-642-14623-7_25

20. Carbunar, B., Tripunitara, M.V.: Payments for outsourced computations. IEEE Trans. Parallel Distrib. Syst. 23(2), 313–320 (2012)

21. Chen, X., Li, J., Susilo, W.: Efficient fair conditional payments for outsourcing computations. IEEE Trans. Inf. Forensics Secur. 7(6), 1687–1694 (2012)

22. Dong, C., Wang, Y., Aldweesh, A., McCorry, P., Moorsel, A.: Betrayal, distrust, and rationality: Smart counter-collusion contracts for verifiable cloud computing. In: Proceedings of the ACM SIGSAC Conference on Computer and Communications Security (CCS) 2017, pp. 211–227. ACM (2001). arXiv:1708.01171v4

23. Huang, H., Chen, X., Wu, Q., Huang, X., Shen, J.: Bitcoin-based fair payments for outsourcing computations of fog devices. Future Gener. Comput. Syst. 78, 850–858 (2018)

24. Chen, X., Li, J., Ma, J., Lou, W., Wong, D.S.: New and efficient conditional e-payment systems with transferability. Future Gener. Comput. Syst. 37, 252–258 (2014)

25. Zhang, Y., Deng, R., Liu, X., Zheng, D.: Outsourcing service fair payment based on blockchain and its applications in cloud computing. IEEE Trans. Serv. Comput. 8(7), 1–14 (2018)

26. Ding, J., Yu, N., Lin, X., Zhang, W.: A private information retrieval and payment protocol based on bitcoin. Inf. Secur. **4**(06), 1–9 (2019)
27. Quick, D., Choo, K.R.: Digital droplets: microsoft skydrive forensic data remnants. Future Gener. Comput. Syst. **29**(6), 1378–1394 (2013)

Rational Delegation of Computation Based on Reputation and Contract Theory in the UC Framework

Xiaoxia Jiang and Youliang Tian[✉️][iD]

State Key Laboratory of Public Big Data,
College of Computer Science and Technology, Guizhou University,
Guiyang 550025, China
15650751086@163.com, yltian@gzu.edu.cn

Abstract. The previous schemes for rational delegation of computation resorting to game theory focus on what is the possible equilibrium results. However, they seem to ignore how to design an optimal incentive mechanism scientifically and effectively so that the final result meets designer's expectations when a information structure is given. More importantly, there is an open question that whether the designed rational delegation of computation protocol is still secure in the UC framework. To address these challenges, in this paper, we first construct a reputation model leveraging Gompertz model to ensure that client can choose high-quality computing parties. Secondly, we design an optimal mechanism resorting to contract theory in the case of information asymmetry. Then we construct an ideal functionality for rational delegation of computation based on reputation and contract theory. In addition, we design a protocol for rational delegation of computation based on reputation and contract theory to securely realize the functionality. In the end, we prove that the proposed protocol is still secure in the UC framework.

Keywords: Rational delegation of computation · Universally composable · Reputation · Contract theory

1 Introduction

The core idea of delegation of computation is that the computing-constrained client outsources a calculation task to a powerful computing party. The key issue

Supported by the National Natural Science Foundation of China under Grant Nos. 61662009 and 61772008; Science and Technology Major Support Program of Guizhou Province under Grant No. 20183001; Ministry of Education-China Mobile Research Fund Project under Grant No. MCM20170401; Key Program of the National Natural Science Union Foundation of China under Grant No. U1836205; Science and Technology Program of Guizhou Province under Grant No. [2019]1098; Project of High-level Innovative Talents of Guizhou Province under Grant No. [2020]6008; Innovative talent team of Guizhou ordinary colleges and Universitie(Guizhou-Education-Talent-Team[2013]09).

© Springer Nature Singapore Pte Ltd. 2020
S. Yu et al. (Eds.): SPDE 2020, CCIS 1268, pp. 322–335, 2020.
https://doi.org/10.1007/978-981-15-9129-7_23

in this process is how to ensure the privacy of the data and the correctness of the results. In order to be more in line with the real situation, rational delegation of computation which introduces game theory into delegation of computation is proposed, in which the players are regarded as rational players who always act in their own interests to maximize own utilities.

There are some researches on rational delegation of computation resorting to game theory. An incentivizing outsourced computation scheme was proposed in [1], the authors incentivized rational contractors to work honestly by a reputation or credit system. Then Kupcu [9] constructed an incentivized outsourced computation scheme resistant to malicious contractors since he pointed out that the literature [1] could neither resist malicious contractors nor provide fair payment for participants. Dong et al. [4] utilized the game theory and smart contracts to incentivize clouds behave honestly, which also avoided heavy cryptographic protocols. Tian et al. [11] discussed the attack and defense limitation of players in the rational delegation of computation by resorting to information theory. A incentive protocol based on social norms in crowdsourcing applications was proposed in [13]. Ma et al. [10] presented a reputation-based incentive game model for crowdsourcing service in the light of evolutionary game theory.

The focus of the aforementioned researches is that what is the possible equilibrium result given a information structure. However, they seem to ignore how to design an optimal incentive mechanism for the given information structure so that the final result is consistent with our expectations. In recent years, it has been popular to use contract theory to design optimal incentive mechanisms in various research areas. For instance, Zeng et al. [12] proposed an incentive mechanism design for computation offloading in heterogeneous fog computing. In addition, Zhou et al. [14] designed the efficient incentive and task assignment mechanisms based on the contract theory and matching theory to address the issues of computation resource allocation and task assignment optimization in vehicular fog computing. Kang et al. employed contract theory to design incentive mechanisms for Internet of Vehicles in [7] and federal learning in [6], respectively.

More importantly, whether the rational delegation of computation protocol with designed incentive mechanism is still secure in the universally composable (UC) framework is an open question, where the UC framework provides strong security guarantees for cryptographic protocols.

Furthermore, on the basis of the specific analysis in the scenario of delegated computation, the client often faces the following major problems because of information asymmetry: 1) how the client selects the high-quality computing party; 2) how the client judges the ability of the computing party; 3) how the client constrains the behavior of the computing party so that the computing party can act as he wishes.

Our Contributions. To address these aforementioned challenges, in this paper, we investigate rational delegation of computation based on reputation and contract theory in the UC framework, our concrete contributions are shown below.

1. We construct a reputation model by introducing Gompertz model to evaluate the computing party's reputation, such that the client can select the computing parties according to his requirements.
2. Based on the information screening model and the moral hazard of hidden action model in contract theory, the optimal contract is designed in the case of information asymmetry between the client and the computing party.
3. We propose an ideal functionality $\mathcal{F}_{RDC-RCT}$ for rational delegation of computation based on reputation and contract theory in the ideal world, as well as a protocol $\pi_{RDC-RCT}$ to realize the ideal functionality $\mathcal{F}_{RDC-RCT}$ in the real world.
4. We prove that the proposed protocol $\pi_{RDC-RCT}$ is secure in the UC framework, that is, the protocol $\pi_{RDC-RCT}$ securely realizes the ideal functionality $\mathcal{F}_{RDC-RCT}$.

Organization. The rest of this paper is organized as follows: In Sect. 2, we describe our system overview. Then we construct a reputation model in Sect. 3. In Sect. 4, we design an efficient incentive mechanism based on contract theory. In Sect. 5, we present the ideal functionality for rational delegated computation based on reputation and contract theory. Then in Sect. 6, we design a protocol for rational delegation of computation to realize the ideal functionality. In Sect. 7, we provide the protocol analysis. The conclusion is given in Sect. 8.

2 System Overview

2.1 System Model

The system model considered in our construction comprises one client denoted by P_D and multiple computing parties denoted by $\{P_1, \ldots, P_M\}$ - see Fig. 1.

First of all, the client broadcasts the calculation task to the computing parties, and the interested computing parties return the response information to indicate that they are willing to accept the task. In the face of numerous response information, the client selects the computing parties according to their respective reputations (reputation evaluation model is given in Sect. 3), and it is required that only the computing party whose reputation is not less than a certain threshold is qualified to participate in the calculation task. Since the client does not know the types of the computing parties, the client provides different contracts (more details about contracts design are given in Sect. 4) to the qualified computing parties. Each computing party selects the most suitable contract according to its type and signs it, and then submits a deposit specified in the contract to the client. Then the client assigns the subtask for each computing party, after each computing party executes the computing task and sends the calculation result to the client, the client judges whether the computing parties have correctly performed the task based on the observable results and makes the corresponding fee payment. Finally, the client updates each computing party's interaction assessment based on his own performance this time.

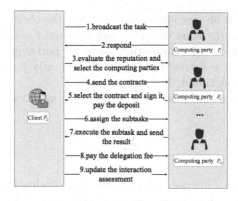

Fig. 1. System model

2.2 Adversary Model

There are some of the following potential adversarial behaviors in our model. On the one hand, the malicious computing party may disguise as a player with other types to sign a contract that does not belong to his own type. On the other hand, the malicious computing party may take the action that does not meet the expectation of the client after signing the contract.

3 Reputation Model

We adopt the Gompertz model [8] to construct the reputation model for the reason that the reputation evaluation of human interaction conforms to the general development law described by the Gompertz model. The formal definition of the reputation model is as follows:

$$R_{i,t}(r_{i,t}) = se^{ue^{vr_{i,t}}} \tag{1}$$

Where s, u and v are model parameters, s specifies the maximum value of the reputation, u controls the displacement along the X-axis, and v adjusts the growth rate of the reputation model. The output of the model $R_{i,t}$ denotes the reputation evaluation of client on the computing party P_i at time t, where $t \in [0,\ldots,T]$. The input of reputation model $r_{i,t}$ should reflect the historical interaction between the client and the computing party, and the closer the interaction is, the greater the impact it should have on the credibility evaluation at time t.

Let $\beta_{i,t}$ be the client's interaction evaluation to the computing party P_i at time t, in order to reward the computing party who performed well during the task execution, and at the same time punish the computing party who failed to complete the task as required, we improve the setting in [10], as below:

$$\beta_{i,t} = \begin{cases} 0, & Ver_{i,t} = null \\ 1, & Ver_{i,t} = active \\ -2, & Ver_{i,t} = negative \end{cases} \tag{2}$$

If and only if there is no any interaction between the client and the computing party P_i, $Ver_{i,t} = null$. Apparently, for any P_i when $t = 0$, $Ver_{i,0} = null$ then $\beta_{i,0} = 0$. If and only if the computing party P_i performs the delegated task well at time t, $Ver_{i,t} = active$. Conversely, If and only if the computing party behaves dishonestly at time t, $Ver_{i,t} = negative$.

The input of reputation model $r_{i,t}$ is presented as follows [5]:

$$r_{i,t} = \sum_{t'=0}^{t} \lambda^{t-t'} \beta_{i,t'} \tag{3}$$

where, $\lambda \in [0, 1]$ is the influence factor of interactive evaluation, and $\lambda^{t-t'}$ reduces the influence degree of historical interactive evaluation. The input $r_{i,t}$ contains the aggregate information of interaction evaluation by the client to the computing party P_i before time t. In particular, when $t = 0$, that is, when the client has not interacted with any P_i, the client cannot evaluate the computing parties' reputation based on past interaction information. At this time, $r_{i,0} = 0$, then the corresponding reputation assessment is $R_{i,0}(r_{i,0}) = se^u$, for any computing party P_i. Consider that the client allows computing parties that have never interacted to participate in the task execution. Therefore, the reputation threshold should be set to be $R_{th} = R_{i,0}(r_{i,0}) = se^u$, that is, only the computing party whose reputation is not less than the prescribed reputation threshold R_{th} can be allowed to interact with the client and participate in the computing task.

4   Incentive Mechanism

There are the following asymmetric information between the client and the computing party in light of the specific analysis: 1) The client does not know the type (i.e. ability) of the computing party before completing the signing of contract. 2) The client is unaware of the computing party's specific actions (i.e. selected strategy) after signing the contract with the computing party. Therefore, we will resort to the information screening model and the moral hazard with hidden action model in contract theory [2] to design an efficient incentive mechanism for rational delegation of computation.

4.1   Model Definition

It is assumed that there are N computing parties whose reputation meet the prescribed requirement after reputation evaluation in accordance with Sect. 4. Let $\mathcal{G}_i = (\mathcal{P}_i, \mathcal{T}_i, a_i, o_i, Con_i, SR_i, U_i)$ denote the interaction between the client P_D and each computing party P_i, respectively, where $i = 1, \ldots, N$.

- $\mathcal{P}_i = \{P_D, P_i\}$ is the set of players in the rational delegation of computation, including the client and the i-th computing party.

- $\mathcal{T}_i = \{\theta_{iH}, \theta_{iL}\}$ is the type space of the computing party P_i. Each computing party has a type $\theta_i \in \mathcal{T}_i$, and $\theta_i \in [0,1]$. Note that the type in this article refers specifically to the private information about the ability of the computing party, where θ_{iH} and θ_{iL} mean the high capacity and the low capacity, respectively. Intuitively, $\theta_{iH} > \theta_{iL}$.
- $a_i \in [0,1]$ is the of action chosen by the computing party who has singed the contract, and refers specifically to the effort of the computing party in this paper.
- $o_i \in \{0, Q\}$ is the output, namely the observable result determined jointly by the type and the action of the computing party. Specifically, it represents the profit obtained by the client ultimately in this paper.
- $Con_i = \{con_{iH} = (d_{iH}, f_{iH}), con_{iL} = (d_{iL}, f_{iL})\}$ is the set of contracts designed by the client, which contains the contracts for all different types of computing parties. d_i denotes the deposit required by the computing party P_i specified in the contract $con_i = (d_i, f_i) \in Con_i$ to the client in advance, $d_i \in \{d_{iH}, d_{iL}\}$. f_i denotes the delegation fee specified in the contract $con_i = (d_i, f_i) \in Con_i$ to be paid by the client to the computing party P_i, $f_i \in \{f_{iH}, f_{iL}\}$. In particular, only if $o_i = Q$ will the client pay f_i to the computing party, and $Q \geq f_i \geq 0$.
- $SR_i : \theta_i \rightarrow con_i$ is a selection rule of the computing party P_i, namely the computing party with type θ_i chooses the corresponding contract $con_i = (d_i, f_i)$ from the set of contracts Con_i received from the client.
- $U_i = (u_i, u_{Di})$ is the set of utilities for the computing party P_i and the client, where u_i denotes the computing party's utility, and u_{Di} denotes the utility of the client interacting with P_i. Let u_D denote the total utility of the client interacting with N computing parties.

4.2 Utility Function of Players

we will discuss the utility function of the computing party and the client respectively in this part.

Utility Function of the Computing Party. Suppose the computing party P_i selects a contract $con_i = (d_i, f_i)$ after receiving a set of contracts Con_i from the client. Furthermore, it is assumed that P_i with type θ_i (i.e. his ability) is able to produce the output Q with probability $\theta_i a_i$ after taking action a_i (i.e. his effort). P_i will hence get the fee f_i with probability $\theta_i a_i$ and definitely lose his deposit d_i. Generally, let the calculation cost of the action a_i taken by the computing party d_i be: $\psi(a_i) = \frac{1}{2}ca_i^2$, where c is the cost coefficient. The utility function of the computing party P_i is as follows:

$$u_i = \theta_i a_i f_i - d_i - \frac{1}{2}ca_i^2 \tag{4}$$

Utility Function of the Client. Since the client does not know the type of computing party in advance, we assume that his prior distribution of the computing party's capability is: the probability that the computing party with high capability is α, and the probability that the computing party with low capability is $1 - \alpha$. Moreover, Q is completely related to f_i, and only when the user gets the profit Q will he pay the fee f_i to the computing party. The total utility function of the client interacting with P_i is as follows:

$$u_{Di} = \alpha[\theta_{iH}a_{iH}(Q - f_{iH}) + d_{iH}] + (1 - \alpha)[\theta_{iL}a_{iL}(Q - f_{iL}) + d_{iL}] \quad (5)$$

And then the total utility of the client interacting with N computing parties is:

$$u_D = \sum_{i=1}^{N} u_{Di} = \sum_{i=1}^{N} \alpha[\theta_{iH}a_{iH}(Q-f_{iH})+d_{iH}]+(1-\alpha)[\theta_{iL}a_{iL}(Q-f_{iL})+d_{iL}] \quad (6)$$

4.3   Optimal Contract Design

The computing party P_i is always eager to maximum his own utility by choosing the contract and action, i.e. $\max_{(a_i,(d_i,f_i))} u_i$. For a given contract $con_i = (d_i, f_i)$, the optimal action choice of P_i that satisfies the first-order condition is as follows,

$$a_i^* = \frac{\theta_i f_i}{c} \quad (7)$$

Hence the maximum utility of P_i in the contract $con_i = (d_i, f_i)$ is as follows:

$$\frac{\theta_i^2 f_i^2}{2c} - d_i \quad (8)$$

We observe that the utility of the computing party decreases with the increase of the deposit d_i and increases with the increase of the delegation fee f_i. At the same time, the optimal action choice of the computing party is independent of the deposit d_i, but it increases with the increase of the delegation fee f_i, indicating that the higher the delegation fee, the more incentive for the computing party to make more efforts.

Due to the information asymmetry between the client and the computing party, the client faces two constraints from the computing party: 1) individual rationality; 2) incentive compatibility. Each contract must satisfy these two constraint requirements in order to motivate different types of computing parties to help the client complete the calculating tasks.

Definition 1 (Individual Rationality). *The expected utility obtained by each computing party accepting the contract shall not be less than the maximum expected utility obtained by the computing party not accepting the contract. Where, the maximum expected utility obtained by the computing party not accepting the contract is called the reserved utility. In this paper, assume that the reserved utility is 0, then*

$$u_i = \frac{\theta_{ik}^2 f_{ik}^2}{2c} - d_{ik} \geq 0, \forall i \in \{1, ..., N\}, \forall k \in \{L, H\} \quad (9)$$

Definition 2 *(Incentive Compatibility). Each computing party can only get the maximum utility by selecting its own type θ_{ik} of contract (d_{ik}, f_{ik}), rather than other type θ_{im} of contract (d_{im}, f_{im}), i.e.*

$$\frac{\theta_{ik}^2 f_{ik}^2}{2c} - d_{ik} \geq \frac{\theta_{ik}^2 f_{im}^2}{2c} - d_{im}, \forall i \in \{1, \ldots, N\}, \forall k, m \in \{L, H\}, k \neq m \quad (10)$$

At this time, let $k = L, H$, the maximum utility problem of the client can be formulated as follows:

$$\max_{(d_{ik}, f_{ik})} \{\sum_{i=1}^{N} \alpha[\theta_{iH} a_{iH}(Q - f_{iH}) + d_{iH}] + (1 - \alpha)[\theta_{iL} a_{iL}(Q - f_{iL}) + d_{iL}]\}$$

$$s.t. \quad \frac{\theta_{iH}^2 f_{iH}^2}{2c} - d_{iH} \geq \frac{\theta_{iH}^2 f_{iL}^2}{2c} - d_{iL}, \forall i \in \{1, \ldots, N\} \quad (ICH) \quad (11)$$
$$\frac{\theta_{iL}^2 f_{iL}^2}{2c} - d_{iL} \geq \frac{\theta_{iL}^2 f_{iH}^2}{2c} - d_{iH}, \forall i \in \{1, \ldots, N\} \quad (ICL)$$
$$\frac{\theta_{iH}^2 f_{iH}^2}{2c} - d_{iH} \geq 0, \forall i \in \{1, \ldots, N\} \quad (IRH)$$
$$\frac{\theta_{iL}^2 f_{iL}^2}{2c} - d_{iL} \geq 0, \forall i \in \{1, \ldots, N\} \quad (IRL)$$

Intuitively, we remark that the individual rationality constraint of high-type computing party (IRH) is not tight at the optimal point, besides, the inequality constraint (ICL) must hence hold at the optimal point (because of space limitation, the detailed proof process is omitted). After removing the inequalities (IRH) and (ICL), it is easy to find that the remained constraints (ICH) and (IRL) are both tight at the optimal point. And then the maximum utility problem of the client can be further formulated as follows:

$$\max_{(d_{ik}, f_{ik})} \{\sum_{i=1}^{N} \alpha[\theta_{iH} a_{iH}(Q - f_{iH}) + d_{iH}] + (1 - \alpha)[\theta_{iL} a_{iL}(Q - f_{iL}) + d_{iL}]\}$$

$$(12)$$

$$s.t. \quad \frac{\theta_{iH}^2 f_{iH}^2}{2c} - d_{iH} \geq \frac{\theta_{iH}^2 f_{iL}^2}{2c} - d_{iL}, \forall i \in \{1, \ldots, N\} \quad (ICH)$$
$$\frac{\theta_{iL}^2 f_{iL}^2}{2c} - d_{iL} \geq 0, \forall i \in \{1, \ldots, N\} \quad (IRL)$$

Finally, the results of optimal contract parameters are calculated as follows:

$$f_{iH}^* = Q$$
$$f_{iL}^* = \frac{(\alpha - 1)\theta_{iL}^2 Q}{(2\alpha - 1)\theta_{iL}^2 - \theta_{iH}^2}$$
$$d_{iL}^* = \frac{(\alpha - 1)^2 \theta_{iL}^6 Q^2}{2c[(2\alpha - 1)\theta_{iL}^2 - \theta_{iH}^2]^2} \quad (13)$$
$$d_{iH}^* = \frac{\theta_{iH}^2 Q^2[(2\alpha - 1)\theta_{iL}^2 - \theta_{iH}^2]^2 + (-\theta_{iH}^2 + \theta_{iL}^2)(\alpha - 1)^2 \theta_{iL}^4 Q^2}{2c[(2\alpha - 1)\theta_{iL}^2 - \theta_{iH}^2]^2}$$

According to the above analysis, a set of contracts designed for different types can be obtained, namely $\{con_{iH}^* = (d_{iH}^*, f_{iH}^*), con_{iL}^* = (d_{iL}^*, f_{iL}^*)\}$.

5   Ideal Functionality $\mathcal{F}_{RDC-RCT}$

As pointed out in [3], the universally composable (UC) framework provides strong security guarantees for cryptographic protocols. In this section, we will define the ideal functionality $\mathcal{F}_{RDC-RCT}$ for rational delegation of computation based on the reputation and contract theory to capture the security requirements and tasks of the cryptographic protocols.

We denote the adversary in the ideal world by $\mathcal{S}$. Let D_{ini} denote the set containing all computing parties, D_{res} denote the set of computing parties responding to the broadcast information, D_{sel} denote the set of computing parties that meet the reputation requirements of the client, respectively.

Functionality $\mathcal{F}_{RDC-RCT}$

$\mathcal{F}_{RDC}$ handles at time t as follows, where $t \in \{1, \dots, T\}$.

Setup:
- Initialize the sets as $D_{ini} = \{P_1, \dots, P_M\}$, $D_{res} = \phi$, $D_{sel} = \phi$, respectively.
- Execute $Setup(1^m) \rightarrow (\theta_{ik})$, where m is the security parameter and θ_{ik} is the type of P_i, then send (sid_t, θ_{ik}) to P_i.

Broadcast:
- Upon receiving $(Broadcast, P_D, P_i, sid_t, task)$ from P_D, broadcast the information $(Broadcast, P_D, sid_t, task)$ to each $P_i \in D_{ini}$.
- Upon receiving $(Broadcast, P_i, P_D, sid_t, ok)$ from P_i, send $(Broadcast, P_i, sid_t, ok)$ to P_D, and set $D_{res} := D_{res} \cup P_i$. Otherwise, send $(Broadcast, P_i, sid_t, \perp)$ to P_D.

Select:
- Evaluate the reputation for each $P_i \in D_{res}$ at time $t-1$, i.e. $R_{i,t-1}$.
- Send $(Select, P_D, sid_t, ok)$ to P_i and P_i is added to D_{sel} (i.e. $D_{sel} := D_{sel} \cup P_i$) if $R_{i,t-1} \geq R_{th}$. Otherwise, send $(Select, P_D, sid_t, \perp)$ to P_i.

Sign (information screening model):
- Send $(Sign, sid_t, (con_{iH}^*, con_{iL}^*)$ to each $P_i \in D_{sel}$ and P_D.
- Send $(Signed, sid_t, con_{ik}^*)$ to corresponding P_i and P_D. Then receive $(Signed, P_i, sid_t, deposit(d_{ik}^*))$ from P_i and $(Signed, P_D, sid_t, deposit(f_{ik}^*))$ from P_D.

Execute (moral hazard with hidden action model):
- The task is divided into $|D_{sel}|$ subtasks. Send $(Execute, P_D, sid_t, task_i)$ to P_i, where $task_i = (F_i, x_i^*)$ denotes a subtask, and x_i^* is an obscured input to ensure the privacy of the original data x_i.
- Send (sid_t, a_{ik}^*) to P_i. Send $(Executed, P_i, sid_t, result_i)$ to P_D, where $result_i$ denotes an obscured calculation result.

Verify: Send $(Verify, sid_t, Ver_{i,t} = active, payoff(f_{ik}^*))$ to P_i, and record $(Verify, sid_t, Ver_{i,t} = active)$. Send $(Verify, sid_t, y_i)$ to P_D.

Update: Update the interaction opinion $\beta_{i,t}$ at time t for each $P_i \in D_{ini}$. Send $(Update, sid_t, \beta_{i,t})$ to P_D and record $(Update, sid_t, \beta_{i,t})$.

Corrupt (adversary model):
- Upon receiving $(Corrupt, sid_t, P_i)$ from $\mathcal{S}$, record $(sid_t, Corrupted(P_i))$ and send $(Corrupt, sid_t, \perp)$ to $\mathcal{S}$.
- Upon receiving $(Signed, sid_t, con_{il}^*)$ from $\mathcal{S}$, send $(Signed, sid_t, con_{il}^*)$ to P_i and P_D, respectively, and receive $(Signed, P_i, P_D, sid_t, deposit(d_{il}^*))$ from P_i, where $l \neq k$.
- Upon receiving $(Executed, sid_t, a_{il}, result_i')$ from $\mathcal{S}$, send (sid_t, a_{il}) to P_i, $(Executed, sid_t, result_i')$ to P_D, respectively.
- Send $(Verify, sid_t, Ver_{i,t} = negative, payoff(0))$ to P_i, and record $(Verify, sid_t, Ver_{i,t} = negative)$.

Fig. 2. Functionality $\mathcal{F}_{RDC-RCT}$

The ideal functionality is formalized in Fig. 2. Roughly speaking, *Setup* presents the initialization process, the type of each computing party can be obtained according to it; *Broadcast* describes the process of broadcasting the task; *Select* can select the qualified computing parties on the basis of reputation evaluation; *Sign* formalizes the information screening model, which contains the interactions of designing the optimal contracts and signing the contracts among the client and the computing parties; *Execute* defines the moral hazard with hidden action model, which shows the process of choosing the action and performing the tasks; *Verify* contains the process of results verification and payoff; *Update* shows the client's interaction opinion of the computing parties. In addition, *Corrupt* defines the adversary model which captures the attack behaviors by the adversary.

6   Protocol $\pi_{RDC-RCT}$

Note that the definitions and initializations of these notations like P_D, P_i, D_{ini}, D_{res}, D_{sel} are the same as in Sect. 5. The protocol $\pi_{RDC-RCT}$ at time t is as follows, where $t \in \{1, \dots, T\}$.

Setup

- "Nature" assigns the type $\theta_{ik} \in D_{ini}$ for each P_i according to the probability distribution over $\mathcal{T}_i$, and sends (sid_t, θ_{ik}) to P_i.
- P_D and all $P_i \in D_{ini}$ perform $Setup(1^m) \to (param = (g, h), (pk, sk))$, where *param* contains all public parameters of Pedersen commitment, and (pk, sk) is a pair of keys for homomorphic encryption and decryption.

Broadcast the Task. When receiving $(Broadcast, sid_t, P_D)$:

- P_D broadcasts $(Broadcast, P_D, P_i, sid_t, task)$ to all $P_i \in D_{ini}$.
- P_i who is interested in it sends the response $(Broadcast, P_i, P_D, sid_t, ok)$ to P_D, and then $D_{res} := D_{res} \cup P_i$.

Select the Computing Parties. When receiving $(Select, sid_t, P_D)$:

- P_D evaluates the reputation $R_{i,t-1}$ of each $P_i \in D_{res}$ according to the reputation model in Sect. 4.
- If $R_{i,t-1} \geq R_{th}$, P_D sends $(Select, P_D, P_i, sid_t, ok)$ to P_i and sets $D_{sel} := D_{sel} \cup P_i$. Otherwise, send $(Select, P_D, P_i, sid_t, \perp)$ to P_i.

Sign the Contract. When receiving $(Sign, sid_t, P_D, P_i \in D_{sel})$:

- P_D designs optimal contracts (see Sect. 5) for different types and sends $(Sign, P_D, P_i, sid_t, (con_{iH}^*, con_{iL}^*))$ to each $P_i \in D_{sel}$.

- If P_i with type θ_{ik} chooses to sign the contract con_{ik}^*, P_i will send $(Signed, P_i, P_D, sid_t, con_{ik}^*, deposit(f_{ik}^*))$ to P_D. If P_i with type θ_{ik} chooses to sign the contract con_{il}^*, P_i will send $(Signed, P_i, P_D, sid_t, con_{il}^*, deposit(f_{il}^*))$ to P_D.

Execute the Task. When receiving $(Execute, sid_t, P_D, P_i \in D_{sel})$:

- P_D splits the task into $|D_{sel}|$ subtasks and sends $(Execute, P_D, P_i, sid_t, task_i)$ to P_i, where $task_i = (F_i, x_i^*)$, $x_i^* = Enc(x_i, pk)$.
- If P_i with type θ_{ik} chooses the action a_{ik}^*, P_i will send $(Executed, P_i, P_D, sid_t, com_{y_i^*}, dec_{y_i^*})$ to P_D, where $com_{y_i^*}$ is a commitment to the encrypted computation result y_i^*, and $dec_{y_i^*}$ denotes the decommitment information of $com_{y_i^*}$.
- If P_i with type θ_{ik} chooses the action a_{il}, he will send $(Executed, P_i, P_D, sid_t, com_i, dec_i)$ to P_D.

Verify the Result. When receiving $(Verify, sid_t, P_D)$:

- P_D attempts to open the commitment using $dec_{y_i^*}$, if he fails to open it, P_D will send $(Verify, P_D, P_i, sid_t, Ver_{i,t} = negative, payoff(0))$ to P_i, and then record $(Verify, sid_t, Ver_{i,t} = negative)$.
- Otherwise, P_D can further obtain the unencrypted result, i.e. $y_i = Dec(y_i^*, sk)$.
- If P_D can observe the output $o_i = Q$, he will send $(Verify, P_D, P_i, sid_t, Ver_{i,t} = active, payoff(f_{ik}^*))$ to P_i and record $(Verify, sid_t, Ver_{i,t} = active)$. Otherwise, P_D sends $(Verify, P_D, P_i, sid_t, Ver_{i,t} = negative, payoff(0))$ to P_i, and then record $(Verify, sid_t, Ver_{i,t} = negative)$.
- If there is no interaction between $P_i \in D_{ini} \backslash D_{sel}$ and P_D, P_D will send $(Verify, P_D, P_i, sid_t, Ver_{i,t} = null)$ to $P_i \in D_{ini} \backslash D_{sel}$, and then record $(Verify, sid_t, Ver_{i,t} = null)$.

Update the Interaction Opinion. When receiving $(Update, sid_t, P_D)$:

P_D updates the interaction evaluation on each $P_i \in D_{ini}$ according to the performance of P_i at time t on the basis of the reputation model in Sect. 3.

7 Protocol Analysis

In this section, we will show that the proposed protocol $\pi_{RDC-RCT}$ securely realizes the ideal functionality $\mathcal{F}_{RDC-RCT}$ the UC framework. Informally, in order to prove the security of the protocol, it is always required to show that any adversary's behaviors in the real world can be simulated in the ideal world.

Theorem 1. *The protocol* $\pi_{RDC-RCT}$ *securely realizes the ideal functionality* $\mathcal{F}_{RDC-RCT}$.

Proof. Let $\mathcal{A}$ be an adversary that interacts with parties running the protocol $\pi_{RDC-RCT}$ in the real world. We will build a simulator $\mathcal{S}$ such that any environment $\mathcal{Z}$ can not distinguish with a non-negligible probability between the interaction in the real world and the interaction in the ideal world. $\mathcal{S}$ runs an internal embedded copy of $\mathcal{A}$ denoted $\tilde{\mathcal{A}}$. Any input from the environment $\mathcal{Z}$ is passed to the adversary $\tilde{\mathcal{A}}$, and any output from $\tilde{\mathcal{A}}$ is copied to $\mathcal{S}$ as its output. $\mathcal{S}$ responds as follows to the various events that occur during the execution when P_i is corrupted.

Setup: (i) Upon receiving $(Corrupt, sid_t, P_i)$ from $\tilde{\mathcal{A}}$, forward this message to $\mathcal{F}_{RDC-RCT}$. (ii) Upon receiving $(Corrupt, sid_t, \perp)$ from $\mathcal{F}_{RDC-RCT}$, forward this message to $\tilde{\mathcal{A}}$.

Broadcast: (i) Upon receiving $(Broadcast, P_D, sid_t, task)$ from $\mathcal{F}_{RDC-RCT}$, forward this message to $\tilde{\mathcal{A}}$. (ii) Upon receiving any message from $\tilde{\mathcal{A}}$, forward it to $\mathcal{F}_{RDC-RCT}$.

Select: Upon receiving any message from $\mathcal{F}_{RDC-RCT}$, forward it to $\tilde{\mathcal{A}}$.

Sign: (i) Upon receiving $(Sign, sid_t, (con^*_{iH}, con^*_{iL}))$ from $\mathcal{F}_{RDC-RCT}$, forward it to $\tilde{\mathcal{A}}$. (ii) Upon receiving $(Signed, sid_t, con^*_{il})$ from $\tilde{\mathcal{A}}$, forward it to $\mathcal{F}_{RDC-RCT}$. (iii) Upon receiving $(Signed, sid_t, d^*_{il})$ from $\tilde{\mathcal{A}}$, forward it to $\mathcal{F}_{RDC-RCT}$.

Execute: (i) Upon receiving $(Execute, P_D, sid_t, task_i)$ from $\mathcal{F}_{RDC-RCT}$, forward it to $\tilde{\mathcal{A}}$. (ii) Upon receiving $(Executed, sid_t, com_i, dec_i)$ from $\tilde{\mathcal{A}}$, forward it to $\mathcal{F}_{RDC-RCT}$.

Verify: Upon receiving any message from $\mathcal{F}_{RDC-RCT}$, forward it to $\tilde{\mathcal{A}}$.

Update: The functionality is executed as $\mathcal{F}_{RDC-RCT}.Update$.

Indistinguishability. On the one hand, $\mathcal{S}$ accesses the embedded copy of the real adversary $\mathcal{A}$ (i.e. $\tilde{\mathcal{A}}$) to learn about the various attack behaviors of the real-world adversary, and forwards all the messages from $\tilde{\mathcal{A}}$ to the ideal functionality $\mathcal{F}_{RDC-RCT}$ to reproduce the real adversary's attack behaviors. On the other hand, $\mathcal{S}$ learns the feedbacks in the ideal world by interacting with $\mathcal{F}_{RDC-RCT}$, and likewise, completely forwards the message from the ideal function to the $\tilde{\mathcal{A}}$. In addition, no matter in the ideal world or the real world, the selection of the computing party's type is based on the same probability distribution over T_i. Moreover, the random numbers (i.e. com_i, dec_i) selected by the adversary as the disguised result information are also subject to the same uniform distribution both in the real world and in the ideal world. Therefore, the simulator $\mathcal{S}$ perfectly simulates any behavior of a real-world adversary, which means that for every real-world adversary $\mathcal{A}$ there is a simulator $\mathcal{S}$ such that for all environment $\mathcal{Z}$, the probability that $\mathcal{Z}$ can distinguish the interaction with $\mathcal{A}$ and real-world parties running the protocol $\pi_{RDC-RCT}$ and the interaction with $\mathcal{S}$ and "dummy" parties running the ideal functionality $\mathcal{F}_{RDC-RCT}$ is at most a negligible probability. The protocol $\pi_{RDC-RCT}$ hence securely realizes the $\mathcal{F}_{RDC-RCT}$ in the UC framework.

8 Conclusion

In this paper, we focus on rational delegation of computation based on reputation and contract theory in the UC framework. Instead of emphasizing the possible outcomes, we are more inclined to investigate how to design an optimal mechanism to make the equilibrium result as we wish. Specifically, we firstly introduce a reputation model so that the client can choose the high-quality computing parties. Then we resort to contract theory to design a efficient incentive mechanism in the case of information asymmetry. Furthermore, we construct an ideal functionality $\mathcal{F}_{RDC-RCT}$ for rational delegation of computation based on reputation and contract theory. In addition, we design a protocol $\pi_{RDC-RCT}$ for rational delegation of computation based on reputation and contract theory to securely realize the functionality $\mathcal{F}_{RDC-RCT}$. Last of all, the proposed protocol $\pi_{RDC-RCT}$ is proven to satisfy the UC security according to the protocol analysis.

Although this solution considers the interaction between a client and multiple computing parties, there is currently no incentive for cooperation or competition between computing parties, and their respective actions are independent of each other. Our next step is to consider the cooperative or competitive relationship between the computing parties, that is, their respective utility is related to the actions of others, and the more complex interaction will be our future work.

Acknowledgments. We would like to thank the anonymous reviewers for their valuable comments and helpful suggestions.

References

1. Belenkiy, M., Chase, M., Erway, C.C., Jannotti, J., Küpçü, A., Lysyanskaya, A.: Incentivizing outsourced computation. In: Feigenbaum, J., Yang, Y.R. (eds.) NetEcon 2008, pp. 85–90. ACM, New York (2008). https://doi.org/10.1145/1403027.1403046
2. Bolton, P., Dewatripont, M.: Contract Theory. The MIT Press, Cambridge (2005)
3. Canetti, R.: Universally composable security: a new paradigm for cryptographic protocols. In: FOCS 2001, pp. 136–145. IEEE (2001). https://doi.org/10.1109/SFCS.2001.959888
4. Dong, C., Wang, Y., Aldweesh, A., McCorry, P., van Moorsel, A.: Betrayal, distrust, and rationality: smart counter-collusion contracts for verifiable cloud computing. In: Thuraisingham, B.M., Evans, D., Malkin, T., Xu, D. (eds.) CCS 2017, pp. 211–227. ACM, New York (2017). https://doi.org/10.1145/3133956.3134032
5. Huang, K.L., Kanhere, S.S., Hu, W.: On the need for a reputation system in mobile phone based sensing. Ad Hoc Netw. **12**, 130–149 (2014)
6. Kang, J., Xiong, Z., Niyato, D., Xie, S., Zhang, J.: Incentive mechanism for reliable federated learning: a joint optimization approach to combining reputation and contract theory. IEEE Internet Things J. **6**(6), 10700–10714 (2019)
7. Kang, J., Xiong, Z., Niyato, D., Ye, D., Kim, D.I., Zhao, J.: Toward secure blockchain-enabled internet of vehicles: optimizing consensus management using reputation and contract theory. IEEE Trans. Veh. Technol. **68**(3), 2906–2920 (2019)

8. Kenney, J.F., Keeping, E.S.: Mathematics of statistics-part one (1954)
9. Küpçü, A.: Incentivized outsourced computation resistant to malicious contractors. IEEE Trans. Dependable Secur. Comput. **14**(6), 633–649 (2017)
10. Ma, X., Ma, J., Hui, L., Qi, J., Sheng, G.: RTRC: a reputation-based incentive game model for trustworthy crowdsourcing service. Commun. China **13**(12), 199–215 (2016)
11. Tian, Y., Guo, J., Wu, Y., Lin, H.: Towards attack and defense views of rational delegation of computation. IEEE Access **7**, 44037–44049 (2019)
12. Zeng, M., Li, Y., Zhang, K., Waqas, M., Jin, D.: Incentive mechanism design for computation offloading in heterogeneous fog computing: a contract-based approach. In: ICC 2018, pp. 1–6. IEEE (2018). https://doi.org/10.1109/ICC.2018.8422684
13. Zhang, Y., van der Schaar, M.: Reputation-based incentive protocols in crowdsourcing applications. In: Greenberg, A.G., Sohraby, K. (eds.) INFOCOM 2012, pp. 2140–2148. IEEE (2012). https://doi.org/10.1109/INFCOM.2012.6195597
14. Zhou, Z., Liu, P., Feng, J., Zhang, Y., Mumtaz, S., Rodriguez, J.: Computation resource allocation and task assignment optimization in vehicular fog computing: a contract-matching approach. IEEE Trans. Veh. Technol. **68**(4), 3113–3125 (2019)

A PBFT Consensus Scheme with Reputation Value Voting Based on Dynamic Clustering

Shenchen Zhu[1], Ziyan Zhang[1], Liquan Chen[1,2(✉)], Hui Chen[1], and Yanbo Wang[1]

[1] School of Cyber Science and Engineering, Southeast University, Nanjing 211100, Jiangsu, China
lqchen@seu.edu.cn
[2] Purple Mountain Laboratories for Network and Communication Security, Nanjing 211111, Jiangsu, China

Abstract. At present, the consensus algorithm based on reputation voting generally has the problem of credit value accumulation caused by Matthew effect, which will lead to the risk of system centralization. Therefore, we propose a new blockchain consensus scheme based on PBFT mechanism, which divides the nodes into three categories: production node, upper node and common node, and the first two types are generated by node selection algorithm and replaced regularly. In the node selection algorithm, random parameters are introduced to make the reputation value no longer the only standard. In addition, in order to solve the problems of high message complexity and poor scalability shortcomings in PBFT, we use ISODATA algorithm to segment the nodes in the system, and simplify the consensus process of these existing PBFT algorithm, which greatly reduces the message complexity of the consensus processing without compromising the fault-tolerant performance of the system.

Keywords: Blockchain · PBFT · Dynamic clustering · Reputation model

1 Introduction

As the underlying core technology of Bitcoin, blockchain is essentially considered as a decentralized distributed ledger. With the core advantages of decentralization, blockchain has huge development potential in the fields of finance, IoT, healthcare, privacy data management and so on [1–3]. Consensus mechanism is an important part of blockchain technology, and its quality directly affect the performance of the system. Although public blockchain algorithms such as Pow [4], PoS [5], and DPoS [6] have good security, they still have some problems including high time-delay and low throughput capacity. Paxos [7] and Raft [8] are traditional representative distributed consensus algorithms, which are mainly oriented to databases, logs and other underlying storage areas however, the Byzantine-fault-tolerance problem was not considered in these algorithms. The PBFT algorithm [9] solves the Byzantine-fault-tolerance problem well, but the nodes cannot dynamically join the system while PBFT is running, and its scalability needs to be improved. Scalability will be one of the biggest challenges in the application

© Springer Nature Singapore Pte Ltd. 2020
S. Yu et al. (Eds.): SPDE 2020, CCIS 1268, pp. 336–354, 2020.
https://doi.org/10.1007/978-981-15-9129-7_24

of blockchain technology [10]. Although there are some problems with the PBFT algorithm, due to its advantages of low time-delay, low energy consumption, no bifurcation, and resolution of Byzantine-fault-tolerance, PBFT has a better overall performance and is more suitable for most customized application scenarios [11].

Among the related researches on the improvement of the PBFT algorithm, the research based on credit and voting has a relatively good performance in balance of the scalability, security and decentralization. However, the following two problems still exist:

1) *Problem of centralization tendency caused by time accumulation*: When the system continues running for a long period of time, some nodes increase their reputation value by holding positions with functions such as voting and production. As the reputation value is improved, these nodes will have an advantage in the next election. The repetition of this process will continuously speed up the improvement of the reputation value of these nodes, and eventually lead to the centralization of the entire system. The CDBFT [12] algorithm proposed by Y. Wang et al. establishes a privilege classification mechanism for nodes, which effectively prevents "Expected" nodes from being elected as master nodes. "Normal" nodes can be elected as primary nodes only after all "Credible" nodes have been elected or are not eligible for vote [12]. It is difficult for "Normal" nodes to obtain equal voting rights; therefore, the centralization trend of the system is inevitable. The CPBFT [13] algorithm proposed by Y. Wang and Z. Song et al. divides nodes by the credit rating and assigns corresponding credit coefficients to different levels of nodes. The election of the master node will continue to favor the "A" node. Other algorithms [14, 15] based on credit and voting also have this problem.

2) *Problem of overall efficiency*: In the existing related research, the system often defines an overly complicated role system and election mechanism. The VPBFT [16] algorithm defines four roles of nodes: production node, voting node, ordinary node, and candidate node. The number of nodes in all roles changes dynamically in real time. The system will consume a lot of unnecessary resources in role allocation, role switching and role statistics. The vBFT algorithm [17] simplifies the roles: only defines three roles of master, client, and slave. However, the global voting mechanism and the design of the global data pool still restrict the scalability. The CoT algorithm [14] is based on P2P architecture. By generating a credit graph and a credit matrix, the credit value of nodes is calculated to select "delegated" nodes and perform PBFT consensus between "delegated" nodes. The cost of iterative calculation of credit values and consensus stage of "delegated" nodes is relatively large.

In order to solve the above problems, we put random factors in the election process. Voting is randomly conducted to select some candidate nodes, of which the node with the highest reputation value can be selected. Combined with the mechanism of reputation value update, each node has an equal opportunity to be elected, and the malicious nodes are limited. Therefore, a decentralized fair election that is not affected by running time is realized. In addition, in order to reduce the overall complexity of the system, we will use dynamic clustering as the basis to limit the voting and election activities within the group, and conduct production voting activities only in the entire network.

By combining the POV mechanism [18] with the PBFT algorithm, this paper proposes a PBFT consensus mechanism (RC-VPBFT) based on dynamic clustering and reputation value voting. RC-VPBFT will adopt the idea of POV mechanism, simply divide nodes into three roles, establish a reputation value evaluation system, and design a new election algorithm so that the reputation value is no longer the only criterion for node selection, which avoid the centralization tendency of system with time accumulation. In addition, the RC-VPBFT mechanism will use the network delay between nodes as the "node distance", cluster the nodes dynamically, and simplify the traditional PBFT algorithm. Therefore, without reducing the fault-tolerance performance of the system, the message complexity of the achieving consensus is greatly reduced. Finally, we also design a new network extension protocol to support the dynamic joining and exiting of nodes in RC-VPBFT.

2   RC-VPBFT Mechanism Model

In order to improve the operating efficiency of the system, the RC-VPBFT mechanism uses dynamic clustering algorithms to group nodes, and each group is called a "consensus cluster". Production activities are performed on a global scale, and reputation value updates and node elections activities are performed within the consensus cluster.

2.1   Roles for Nodes

The topology of the RC-VPBFT mechanism is shown in Fig. 1. There are three types of nodes in each consensus cluster. Different kinds of nodes supervise and restrict each other, jointly maintain balance of the system:

1) *Ordinary node*: The Ordinary node is responsible for selecting the superior node, accepting and responding to queries from the production node, as well as impeaching the superior node and production node which has malicious behavior. All network nodes joining the system have the identity of ordinary node.
2) *Superior node*: The superior node is responsible for not only selecting production nodes but also accepting and responding to queries from production nodes. The superior nodes are selected by a mechanism that combines the random recommendation of ordinary nodes and the comparison of reputation values.
3) *Production node*: The production node is responsible for confirming transactions, packaging blocks, and extending the blockchain. It is selected by a mechanism that combines the random recommendation of superior nodes and the comparison of reputation values.

2.2   Running Framework

The algorithm flow of the RC-VPBFT mechanism is shown in Fig. 2. RC-VPBFT takes "round" as the unit during the execution process, and the complete process from the preparation stage to the end stage is called a round. Each consensus cluster generates a block after a round. As shown in Fig. 2, each round of execution process is divided into three stages:

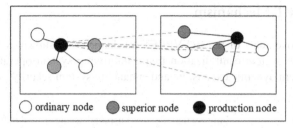

Fig. 1. Topological structure of consensus mechanism

1) *Preparation stage*: Firstly, group the nodes to determine whether the ISODATA algorithm needs to be executed at this time. If necessary, execute the ISODATA algorithm, otherwise proceed to the next step. Then determine whether superior node recommendation is needed at this time. If needed, the superior node recommendation algorithm will be executed, otherwise the next step will be taken. Finally, determine whether production node recommendation is needed at this time. If there is a need, the production node recommendation algorithm should be executed, otherwise it will enter the consensus stage.

2) *Consensus stage*: To start with, according to the improved PBFT algorithm, verify the transactions in the consensus cluster by voting. Then package all the verified transactions and generate a block after the number of transactions verified by voting is greater than the set value, or after the runtime is greater than the set value.

3) *Final stage*: In the first instance, verify the survival of all nodes in the cluster. Then process the join request of the new node in this round. If there is no join request, skip this stage and enter a new round.

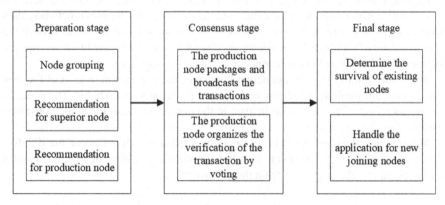

Fig. 2. Block diagram of algorithm flow

3   RC-VPBFT Mechanism

The main improvements of the RC-VPBFT mechanism are shown in Fig. 3, including reducing the system centralization trend, improving system operating efficiency, supporting system dynamic expansion, and enhancing system security performance.

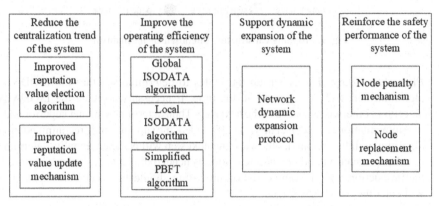

Fig. 3. Main improvements of RC-VPBFT

3.1   Network Dynamic Expansion Protocol

Dynamic Join of Nodes
When a new node (called A) tries to join a running blockchain network, it needs to know the IP information of at least one running node (called B) in the network, then Node A sends a join request to node B. After receiving A's request, B feeds back the IP information of all nodes in the consensus cluster where B is located to A. A uses the obtained IP information to issue connection requests in sequence.

When the running node in the network receives the connection request of the new node, it puts information of the new node IP into the temporary node list. The nodes in the temporary node list do not participate in the consensus behavior in the consensus cluster.

When nodes in a consensus cluster run to the final stage, all nodes add the IP information in the temporary node list to the official node list, and these newly joined nodes will participate in the consensus from the next round.

3.2   ISODATA Dynamic Clustering Algorithm

Global ISODATA Dynamic Clustering Algorithm
PBFT consensus enables transaction verification. In order to ensure the security of the system, the PBFT consensus must be maintained globally. However, node activities such as reputation value update, node election, and node replacement do not require

the consensus throughout the network. Therefore, the consensus mechanism proposed in this paper uses the ISODATA algorithm [19] to group the nodes, which transfer the reputation value update, node election and node replacement activities from the entire system to each group. That can reduce the complexity of the election activities and improve performance of the system.

Since the number of nodes in the system changes dynamically, the number of groups is not fixed, so ISODATA is more suitable for blockchain environment than the K-means algorithm [20] and K-medoids algorithm [21], which needs to determine the number of groups in advance.

In actual operation, RC-VPBFT uses the number of nodes as the dimension and the round-trip time returned by ping as the distance to perform clustering operations, divides the nodes with lower time delay of mutual communication into a group to improve the communication efficiency as much as possible.

Improved Local ISODATA Dynamic Clustering Algorithm
Although ISODATA dynamic clustering algorithm has good grouping performance, it is too complicated, and the overhead of continuous calculation is too large. The dynamic clustering algorithm is only introduced for node grouping in this paper, the accuracy of grouping does always not need to maintain. In this regard, this paper proposes an improved local ISODATA dynamic clustering algorithm for single group splitting. The specific algorithm is designed as follows:

a) Groups with a long network delay or large number of nodes are likely to cause congestion, which slows down the operation of the entire system. Therefore, these groups need to be split to improve efficiency. Groups with lower network delay or fewer nodes have some waste of resources but does not affect the overall operation of the system. Therefore, there is no need to constantly control the size of these groups through merging. In summary, the main purpose of the local algorithm is to split the single group that have an adverse effect on system efficiency.

b) The distance in the global algorithm is the network delay between each node, and the dimension is represented by the number of nodes. For the reason of the local algorithm needs to be executed in real time, the definition of this distance cannot meet the real-time requirements. In the steps such as standard deviation calculation, only the distance from the given node to the central node is used, so the multidimensional vector can be simplified to one dimension. Therefore, the distance in the local algorithm is defined as the network delay from the node to the central node, and the central node is defined as the node with the smallest total network delay.

c) On account of the basis of clustering is the network delay time, the standard deviation vector of a single group reflects the communication quality within the group to a certain extent and can be used to split a single group with a long network delay and a large number of nodes.

d) When the average time for the nodes in the group to reach consensus over a period exceeds the threshold, the system is decided to be in an inefficient state, and a local ISODATA algorithm will be triggered.

Through the above design, the local ISODATA dynamic clustering algorithm maintains a good bipartite splitting effect, while achieving vector mapping from multi-dimensional to one-dimensional, greatly improving the efficiency of local clustering. The specific algorithm is as follows:

Step 1. Initialization
The initialization parameters is set as Table 1:

Table 1. Initialization parameters of local ISODATA algorithm

Parameter	Description
θ_N	Minimum sample size in each cluster that affect merging
N	Number of samples in current group
α	Weight of network delay that affects splitting
z_j	Center sample of group j
T_l	Seconds of greenwich mean time of the last global algorithm
T	Current seconds of greenwich mean time

Step 2. Global Judgment
If $T - T_1 \geq 604800$, set T_1 to T, jump out, and go to the global ISODATA algorithm; Otherwise, continue execution.

Step 3. Preliminary Judgment
If $N \leq 2\theta_N$, the group does not have the conditions for splitting, jump to step 8;

Step 4. Standard Deviation Calculate
For group j, calculate the standard deviation of the group: $\sigma_j = \sqrt{\frac{1}{N} \sum_{y_k \in S_j} y_{ki}^2}$, where S_j is a set of single group, y_k is the i-th component of the k-th sample in the j-th category, and i is the serial number of sample in z_j.

Step 5. Merge/Split Judgment
If $N \geq \frac{\alpha \theta_N}{\sigma_j}$,continue execution; Otherwise, skip to step 8;

Step 6. Split
Split S_j into two groups, the center of which is z_{j+} and z_{j-}. the calculation methods of z_{j+} and z_{j-} are as follows: given a value of k, $0 < k < 1$, let $r_j = k\sigma_j$; then $z_{j+} = z_j + r_j$, $z_{j-} = z_j - r_j$, where the value of k should make the distance different from the samples in Sj to z_{j+} and z_{j-}. Meanwhile, k needs to make the samples in S_j still in the split new sample class.

Step 7. Parameter Update

Update the number of samples N in the group.

Update the single group center z_j through calculation $z_j = \max_{y_k \in S_j} \left\{ \sum_{i=1}^{N} y_{ki} \right\}$.

Step 8. Termination Judgment

Over a period, monitor the average time for nodes in the group to reach consensus. If the trigger condition is still met, return to step 4 and obtain a second splitting opportunity for group with samples smaller than the minimum sample size;

Otherwise, the algorithm ends.

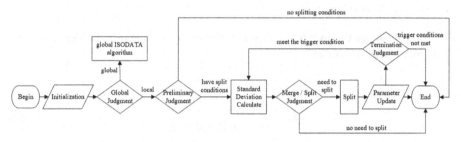

Fig. 4. Local ISODATA algorithm flowchart

The overall structure of the local ISODATA algorithm is shown in Fig. 4. The global judgment avoids the repeated operation of the global algorithm and the local algorithm. The preliminary judgment completes the pre-pruning in most cases, and the termination judgment guarantees the efficiency of the algorithm in extreme cases where the delay is too large.

Through the execution of the above steps, RC-VPBFT uses the local ISODATA algorithm to split the consensus cluster during normal operation; uses the global ISODATA algorithm occasionally to obtain the best division scheme for the consensus cluster. It not only avoids the huge overhead and improves the operating efficiency of the system, but also ensures the rationality of node grouping to a certain extent.

3.3 Mechanism of Reputation Value Update

The mechanism of reputation value update can effectively reduce the adverse effects of malicious nodes on the system and encourage nodes to comply with system regulations [22]. the reputation value is set to update before the superior node election. The nodes in the group send out a list which contains the reputation value of whole group, and each node updates the reputation value of the nodes according to most of the received messages.

Definition 1. The reputation value of newly added node is 1.

Definition 2. The node with a non-positive reputation value is regarded as a malicious node, and it will be actively driven away from the system.

Definition 3. After the generation of a valid block is completed, the reputation value of all nodes increases, and the increasing can be represented by:

$$R_{i+1} = lg(10^{R_i} + p) \tag{1}$$

where p is the growth factor, which can be set to 10. the logarithmic model is chosen to make the growth rate of reputation value faster in the early stage, while gradually decreases in the later stage.

Definition 4. When the node has malicious behavior, the reputation value decreases, and the reduction can be written as:

$$R_{i+1} = \begin{cases} R_i - q_1 & R_i \leq \lambda \\ q_2 R_i & R_i > \lambda \end{cases} \tag{2}$$

The definition of malicious behavior is shown in Table 2, where q_1 is the low-speed deceleration factor, q_2 is the high-speed degeneration factor, and λ is the deceleration limit. In this paper, q_1 is set to 0.1, while q_2 is set to 0.5, and λ is set to 2.

Table 2. Definition of malicious behavior

Node type	Malicious behavior
Production node	Data verification and packaging not completed within the specified time Tampering with verification results
Superior node	Publish fake voting results Initiate incorrect impeachment of the production node
Ordinary node	The judgment is inconsistent with the final voting result Initiate incorrect impeachment of the production node or superior node

With a piecewise linear regression model, RPBFT can instantly adjust the reputation value of nodes according to their behavior. We run a network with 200 nodes in which there are 16 evil nodes and we record the fluctuations of reputation as Fig. 5. It can be seen from the experiment that the decline of the reputation value is much faster than the rise of the reputation value, furthermore, the rising trend of reputation value gradually slowed. Under this mechanism, the increase of reputation value is a long-term process, but the reduction of reputation value is very easy, which makes each node cherish its own reputation value and take cautious actions.

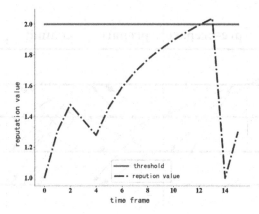

Fig. 5. Change of node reputation value

3.4 Simplified PBFT Algorithm

The traditional PBFT algorithm consists of five steps. When there are n nodes in the system, the number of messages required to reach a consensus is approximately equal to $2n^2$. As the number of nodes in the system increases, the number of messages required to reach a consensus will increase in square order. The explosive increase in the number of messages will greatly extend the time it takes to reach consensus, thereby becoming a bottleneck in system performance and limiting the size of the system.

In order to solve this problem, this paper simplifies the traditional PBFT algorithm as shown in Fig. 6, node 0 is the master node and nodes 1 to 3 are slave nodes.

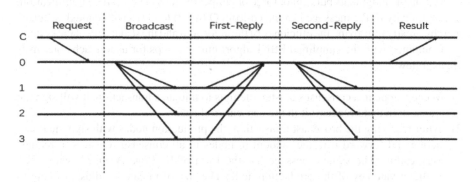

Fig. 6. Simplified PBFT consensus flow chart

Compared with the PBFT algorithm (Fig. 7), we have eliminated the complex message broadcasting in the PERPARE phase and the COMMIT phase. Each node makes its own judgment, and the master node summarizes all the judgments and makes a final decision.

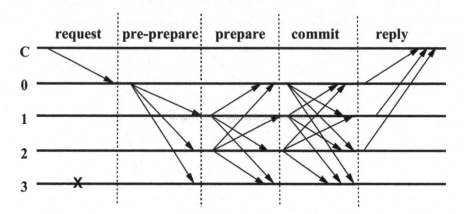

Fig. 7. PBFT consensus flow chart

Overall, the Simplified PBFT algorithm mainly includes the following two steps.

1) Each slave node signs its own judgment and sends it directly to the master node.
2) The master node summarizes all the judgments, makes a final judgment by majority rule, and broadcasts the following content to all slave nodes.

    a) The judgment of each node
    b) Final decision.

Since the judgment of each slave node has been signed by itself, the master node can only count the judgments but cannot forge or tamper the judgments. After simplification, the complexity of the message is reduced from $O(n^2)$ to $O(n)$ with enough security, thereby greatly improving the efficiency of the algorithm and the scalability of the system.

Combined with the simplified PBFT algorithm, the steps for us to reach consensus are as follows:

1) When a node in a consensus cluster attempts to initiate a transaction, it will sign the transaction and broadcast it in the consensus cluster.
2) After receiving the broadcast transaction, the production nodes with sign the transaction and forward it to the random m nodes in all consensus clusters to request verification. The signed message has the form of $K_{P_i}\langle timestamp, T\rangle$, where K_{P_i} is the private key of the production node. The size of m can be adjusted freely to meet different requirements for system security. The security of the system increases with the increase of m, and accordingly, the time required to reach consensus also increases with the increase of m.
3) After receiving the message from the production node, the m nodes in step 2 make their own judgments on the transactions contained in the message, and sign the judgments then send them back to the production node. The signed message has the form of $K_{N_i}\langle timestamp, T, judgement\rangle$, where K_{N_i} is the private key of the node.

4) When the production node receives more than or equal top judgments that agree with the transaction, the transaction is deemed to have passed verification, and the system reaches consensus on this message. The size of p can be adjusted freely to meet different requirements for system security.

When the number of verified transactions stored in the production node reaches a certain number, the production node must package these transactions and broadcast it to all nodes in the system.

Since the block contains the judgment records of all nodes, the node received the broadcast block can use these records to verify whether each transaction in the block has passed the verification, or the block will be treated as an illegal block. The node that received the illegal block will reject the block, broadcast the illegal block in the consensus cluster, and initiate impeachment on the production node; otherwise, the node will add the block to the local blockchain.

3.5 Node Election Mechanism

Superior Node Election
Assume that k superior nodes need to be elected.

The election process of the superior node is as follows: first, each node randomly generates k node numbers as its own "referral target" and sends the numbers to all other nodes. After receiving the "referral targets" from all other nodes, each node summarizes and arranges them in descending order, then selects the first 2 k nodes as candidate nodes. If multiple nodes have the same number of votes, select the node that joined the network early.

Production Node Election
Each superior node randomly generates a node number as "referral target" and sends the numbers to other superior node. After receiving the "referral targets" from other superior node, each superior node summarizes and selects the node with the highest reputation value as the production node. If multiple nodes have the same reputation value, select the node that joined the network early.

3.6 Node Replacement Mechanism

According to our design, there are three types of nodes in the system, of which production nodes and superior nodes have more permissions than ordinary nodes. In order to avoid the risk of the production node or the upper node being occupied by the same node for a long time, we introduced a node replacement mechanism, which aims to regularly replace the production nodes and the superior node, reducing the degree of centralization and risks of the system

The node replacement mechanism is improved from the PBFT's view switching mechanism, focusing on strengthening the supervision of production nodes and superior nodes. Normally, node replacement occurs in the following three situations:

1) A node ends its term
2) A node was found to be dereliction of duty;
3) A node has malicious behavior.

When the production node or the upper node is replaced due to the end of the term, the ordinary node will reselect the production node or the superior node according to the normal process, and the reputation value of the old production node or the old superior node will not be affected. When the production node or the superior node is replaced due to malicious behavior or malfeasance, the ordinary node will initiate impeachment against the former. If the impeachment is successful, the former will be punished by the reduction of the reputation value, and the authority of the superior node/production node will be cancelled immediately. The ordinary node will then select a new superior node/production node.

In general, in the RC-VPBFT algorithm, ordinary nodes elect and supervise superior nodes, while superior nodes elect and supervise production nodes (as shown in Fig. 8). Through this mechanism, the ordinary node, the superior node, and the production node form a mutual check and balance to ensure the safety of the system.

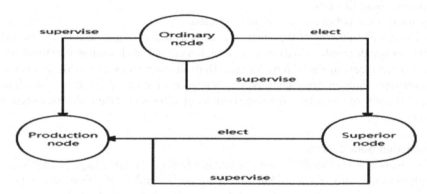

Fig. 8. Mutual supervision of nodes

Production Node Replacement

The production node is replaced when the following situation occurs:

The number of blocks packed by the production node reaches the threshold

The initiator of the replacement is the superior node. The superior node is responsible for recording the number of blocks packed by the current production node. By limiting the workload of production nodes, the system is prevented from tending to be centralized.

The production node did not package the transaction and generate new block within the specified time.

The initiator of the replacement is the sender of the transaction.

Suppose A is the sender of a transaction. If A does not receive a valid block containing this transaction within a specified time, A broadcasts a query in the cluster. If other nodes receive a valid block containing this transaction, A synchronizes this block from other nodes. Otherwise, A initiate's impeachment of the production node and attaches the transaction to the impeachment as evidence.

The production node maliciously tampers with the verification results of single or multiple transactions in the block.

The exchange initiator can be any node. Every transaction in the block should be verified by voting, and every node participating in the voting will leave their signature on the voting result. If the node receiving the block finds that there are traces of forgery or tampering in the voting result, it should Initiate impeachment of the production node, and attach the tampered block to the impeachment as evidence.

The replacement of the production node includes the following steps:First, a node initiates impeachment, requesting the replacement of the production node. Then, the other nodes decide whether to approve the impeachment based on the sufficiency of the impeachment information and send their decision with signature to the superior node. Finally, the superior node broadcasts the voting results to all notes. When the number of yes-votes is greater than two thirds of the total number of nodes, the production node will be replaced, namely, a new production node election will be performed.

Superior Node Replacement

The superior node is replaced when the following situation occurs:

a) The term of the superior node ends.
b) The superior node maliciously initiated the replacement of the production node.

When most other nodes object to the replacement, the replacement is considered illegal, and the superior node that initiated the replacement will be punished.

c) Publish fake voting results.

Due to the lack of valid signatures of other nodes in the forged voting results, this behavior will not affect the normal production node election. The upper node that issued the voting result will be impeached, and the fake voting result will be attached to the impeachment information as evidence.

The replacement of the superior node includes the following steps: First, a certain node initiates impeachment, requesting a superior node replacement; then, other nodes check the evidence in the impeachment information to decide whether to support the impeachment, and send their judgment with signature to other nodes. If more than two-thirds of the nodes support the impeachment, the impeached node loses the status of the superior node. A new superior node will be elected.

3.7 Node Penalty Mechanism

In Sect. 3.6, we listed the malfeasance and malicious behavior of the superior node/ production node and formulated the corresponding supervision and punishment mechanism. In addition to the superior node/ production node, ordinary nodes will also be punished when the following behaviors occur:

1) During the transaction confirmation process, the judgment is inconsistent with the final voting result.
2) During the election process, the judgment is inconsistent with the final voting result.

The reputation value of punished nodes will be reduced according to the rules described in Sect. 3.3, which will reduce their chances of becoming superior nodes/production nodes in the election. Nodes with a reputation value less than 0 after being punished will be forced to move out of the network.

4 Experiment Analysis

4.1 Fault Tolerance

The fault tolerance performance of a consensus mechanism can be measured by the ratio of the number of malicious nodes allowed to normal nodes when the system is running normally. In the RC-VPBFT algorithm, the maximum number of malicious nodes that can be tolerated is:

$$\frac{m}{2} - 1, m \leq N \tag{3}$$

where N is the total number of nodes in the system, and m is the number of nodes participating in verification in each consensus, which is an adjustable variable. In practical applications, when the security requirements of the system are high, the maximum value of m can be set to N, at this time, the number of tolerable failure nodes in the system reaches the maximum value is:

$$\frac{N}{2} - 1 \tag{4}$$

In other words, when the number of malicious nodes in the system is f, the total number of nodes can be restricted as:

$$N \geq 2 * f + 1 \tag{5}$$

In the traditional PBFT algorithm, when the number of malicious nodes in the system is f, the total number of nodes in the system is not less than [9]:

$$N \geq 3 * f + 1 \tag{6}$$

Through comparison, it can be found that when the number of malicious nodes in the system is the same, the RC-VPBFT algorithm requires fewer total nodes in the system than the PBFT algorithm, that is, the RC-VPBFT algorithm has better fault tolerance performance.

4.2 Message Complexity

In the blockchain network, every broadcast message needs to consume a certain amount of network bandwidth, causing time delays. The number of messages required in a complete consensus process using RC-VPBFT algorithm can be expressed as:

$$T = 1 + N + N + N \tag{7}$$

where, N is the number of nodes currently participating in the consensus. As can be seen from the (7), with the increase of N, the number of messages required for a single consensus process in the network increases linearly.

In the PBFT algorithm, broadcast messages exist in the three stages of pre-preparation, preparation and confirmation, and the number of messages is N, N^2 and N^2, respectively. The number of messages required in a complete consensus process in the PBFT algorithm can be written as:

$$T = 1 + N + N^2 + N^2 + N \tag{8}$$

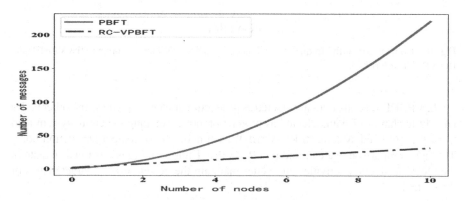

Fig. 9. Comparison of message complexity

As shown in Fig. 9, the number of messages required to reach consensus in the RC-VPBFT algorithm is much less than the PBFT algorithm.

4.3 System Centralization Trend

The core advantage of blockchain is decentralization, so it is necessary to consider the impact of consensus algorithms on the degree of system decentralization. According to the VPBFT algorithm [8] and the RC-VPBFT algorithm, we simulated 50 votes in a 200-node system. the times that each node is elected as a production node is shown in Fig. 10:

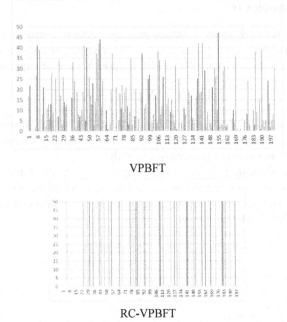

Fig. 10. Comparison of the frequency each node becomes a production node in the VPBFT and RC-VPBFT algorithms

In VPBFT, several nodes are elected as production nodes in 50 votes, and other nodes have little chance of being elected as production nodes, making the entire system tend to be a centralized system. In RC-VPBFT, each node can become a production node. Through comparison, we can find that RC-VPBFT allows more nodes to participate in the block production activities and better maintain the decentralized characteristics of the system.

5   Conclusion

In this paper, we propose a PBFT consensus mechanism based on dynamic clustering reputation value voting. By introducing random parameters in the node recommendation algorithm, the reputation value is no longer used as the only criterion for node recommendation, which avoids the problem of the accumulation of the reputation value existing in some nodes caused by the Matthew effect and the tendency of the system to be centralized due to this problem. By introducing the ISODATA algorithm and simplifying the PBFT algorithm, the complexity of the message is reduced from $O(n^2)$ to $O(n)$ with enough security, so that the system can accommodate more nodes under the same hardware and network condition, which improve the security of the system. By designing the network dynamic expansion protocol, the dynamic joining and exiting of nodes are partially realized, new nodes can join in existing network freely.

References

1. Khan, F.A., Asif, M., Ahmad, A., et al.: Blockchain technology, improvement suggestions, security challenges on smart grid and its application in healthcare for sustainable development. Sustain. Cities Soc. **55**, 102018 (2020)
2. Casino, F., Dasaklis, T., Patsakis, C.: A systematic literature review of blockchain-based applications: current status, classification and open issues. Telemat. Inf. **36**, 55–81 (2019)
3. Frizzo-Barker, J., Chow-White, P.A., Adams, P.R., et al.: Blockchain as a disruptive technology for business: a systematic review. Int.J. Inf. Manag. **51** (2020)
4. Xue, T., Yuan, Y., Ahmed, Z., et al.: Proof of contribution: a modification of proof of work to increase mining efficiency. In: 2018 IEEE 42nd Annual Computer Software and Applications Conference (COMPSAC), pp. 636–644 (2018)
5. King, S., Nadal, S.: PPcoin: peer-to-peer crypto-currency with proof-of-stake. Engineering (2012)
6. Nguyen, C.T., Hoang, D.T., Nguyen, D.N., et al.: Proof-of-stake consensus mechanisms for future blockchain networks: fundamentals, applications and opportunities. IEEE Access **7**, 85727–85745 (2019)
7. Lamport, L.: Brief announcement: leaderless byzantine paxos. In: Peleg, D. (ed.) DISC 2011. LNCS, vol. 6950, pp. 141–142. Springer, Heidelberg (2011). https://doi.org/10.1007/978-3-642-24100-0_10
8. Ongaro, D., Ousterhout, J.: In search of an understandable consensus algorithm. In: USENIX, pp. 305–320 (2014)
9. Castro, M., Liskov, B.: Practical Byzantine fault tolerance. In: Proceedings of the Third USENIX Symposium on Operating Systems Design and Implementation (OSDI), pp. 173–186 (1999)
10. Bugday, A., Ozsoy, A., Öztaner, S.M., et al.: Creating consensus group using online learning-based reputation in blockchain networks. Pervasive Mob. Comput. **59** (2019)
11. Vincent, G.: From blockchain consensus back to Byzantine consensus. Future Gener. Comput. Syst. **107**, 760–769 (2020)
12. Wang, Y., et al.: Study of blockchains's consensus mechanism based on credit. IEEE Access **7**, 10224–10231 (2019)
13. Wang, Y., Song, Z., Cheng, T.: Improvement research of PBFT consensus algorithm based on credit. In: Zheng, Z., Dai, H.-N., Tang, M., Chen, X. (eds.) BlockSys 2019. CCIS, vol. 1156, pp. 47–59. Springer, Singapore (2020). https://doi.org/10.1007/978-981-15-2777-7_4
14. Lv, S., Li, H., Wang, H., Wang, X.: CoT: a secure consensus of trust with delegation mechanism in blockchains. In: Si, X., Jin, H., Sun, Y., Zhu, J., Zhu, L., Song, X., Lu, Z. (eds.) CBCC 2019. CCIS, vol. 1176, pp. 104–120. Springer, Singapore (2020). https://doi.org/10.1007/978-981-15-3278-8_7
15. Veronese, G.S., Correia, M., Bessani, A.N., et al.: Efficient byzantine fault-tolerance. IEEE Trans. Comput. **62**(1), 16–30 (2013)
16. Wang, H., Guo, K., Pan, Q.: Byzantine fault tolerance consensus algorithm based on voting mechanism. J. Comput. Appl. **39**(06), 1766–1771 (2019)
17. Wang, H., Guo, K.: Byzantine fault tolerant algorithm based on vote. In: 2019 International Conference on Cyber-Enabled Distributed Computing and Knowledge Discovery (CyberC), Guilin, China, pp. 190–196 (2019)
18. Li, K., Li, H., Wang, H., et al.: PoV: an efficient voting-based consensus algorithm for consortium blockchains. Front. Blockchain **3**, 11 (2020)
19. Ball, G.H., Hall, D.J.A.: Clustering technique for summarizing multivariate data. Syst. Res. Behave Sci. **12**(2), 153–155 (1967)

20. Likas, A., Vlassis, M., Verbeek, J.: The global K-means clusteringalgorithm. Pattern Recogn. **36**(2), 451–461 (2003)
21. Pattabiraman, V., Parvathi, R., Nedunchezian, R., et al.: A novel spatial clustering with obstacles and facilitators constraint based on edge detection and K-medoids. In: International Conference on Computer Technology and Development, pp. 402–406 (2009)
22. Tang, C., Wu, L., Wen, G., et al.: Incentivizing honest mining in blockchain networks: a reputation approach. IEEE Trans. Circ. Syst. II: Express Brief. **67**(1), 117–121 (2020)

Multi-user Dynamic Symmetric Searchable Encryption for Attribute-Value Type Database in Cloud Storage

Shanshan Li$^{(\boxtimes)}$, Chunxiang Xu$^{(\boxtimes)}$, Yuan Zhang, and Xinsheng Wen

School of Computer Science and Engineering, University of Electronic Science
and Technology of China, Chengdu 611731, China
ershineli@126.com, chxxu@uestc.edu.cn, zy_loye@126.com, wen_xinsheng@163.com

Abstract. Cloud storage services allow a data owner to share their data
with each other as a group. Typically, the data owner outsources files to
the cloud server, and some authorized users can access and edit the files
subsequently. In reality, the most widely-used format of files in such a
cloud-based collaboration system is attribute-value type one, e.g., an excel
spreadsheet, where each file corresponds to an item and multiple attribute
values. Each attribute value can be considered as a keyword, and a type
of attribute values "describes" an attribute. The database generated by
such files is called the attribute-value type database. Authorized users can
search outsourced files by either keywords or attributes such that they
can access the files flexibly. However, due to the sensitivity of the outsourced files, the data owner always encrypts the file before outsourcing,
which precludes users from searching target files. This problem could be
mitigated by utilizing DSSE, but it only supports searching over ciphertexts by keywords, and thereby is unsatisfactory for the attribute-value
database. Furthermore, DSSE schemes built on a single-user setting are
out of alignment with the practical applications. In this paper, we propose a multi-user DSSE scheme for attribute-value type database based on
blind storage, dubbed MDSSE, such that authorized users can search over
files by either keywords or attributes, while the confidentiality of the files
is ensured. We analyze MDSSE in terms of security and efficiency, which
proves that MDSSE is secure against various attacks with high efficiency
in terms of communication and computation costs.

Keywords: Dynamic symmetric searchable encryption · Blind
storage · Attribute-value type database · Cloud storage

1 Introduction

With the booming development of cloud storage [1–8], data sharing service has
been the most featured services in cloud storage systems and has deeply impacted
on people's daily life [9,10]. The typical application of the data sharing service is

© Springer Nature Singapore Pte Ltd. 2020
S. Yu et al. (Eds.): SPDE 2020, CCIS 1268, pp. 355–368, 2020.
https://doi.org/10.1007/978-981-15-9129-7_25

a cloud-based collaboration system [11], which has been widely applied in current companies to reduce office costs and significantly improve office efficiency. In such a cloud-based collaboration system, files to be shared are always formatted, and the typical format is the attribute-value one, where a file corresponds to a data item (which can be considered as the file identifier) and has several attributes, and there is an attribute value (which can be considered as a keyword) corresponding to an attribute for the file. The database generated by such a file format is called the attribute-value type database [12,13]. Generally, a file is generated by the data owner and is outsourced to the cloud server who stores the file into attribute-value type database. Subsequently, each authorized user can search files by either attributes or keywords and can execute operations (i.e., addition, deletion, update) to accomplish online collaborative work.

While users enjoy the convenience of the cloud-based collaboration system, it also raises concerns about the security of outsourced data. Since the uncontrollability of the cloud server in cloud storage, once the cloud server is compromised, the contents of the outsourced data would be leaked [14,15]. Therefore, to guarantee data confidentiality, users always encrypt their data before data outsourcing. However, the encryption operation precludes users from performing fine-grained access on the encrypted database, especially users who want to search files by keywords over an encrypted database.

To resolve this tension, a cryptographic primitive, dynamic symmetric searchable encryption (DSSE), extended from SSE schemes [16,17], firstly was proposed and formalized in [19–21] to support search files by keywords and update operations over the encrypted database. However, existing DSSE schemes [22–25] are applicable to the general database, where each file only has multiple keywords without considering attributes. Thus, in the general database, authorized users can only search files by keywords, not by attributes. Due to the incompatibility between the general database and the attribute-value type database, traditional DSSE schemes cannot be directly applied to the attribute-value type database. Furthermore, DSSE schemes [26–28] are built on a single-user setting, which only allow the data owner herself/himself to submit search queries to a keyword. Actually, the attribute-value type databases serve multiple users simultaneously for the outsourced data, instead of only one user. Thus, the single-user setting is out of alignment with the practical applications.

In this paper, we propose a multi-user DSSE scheme for attribute-value type database, dubbed MDSSE. Specifically, the contributions of this paper are summarized as follows.

- We propose a triple dictionary structure for the attribute-value type database, compared with the dual dictionary in existing DSSE schemes [26,30], it not only builds indexes for keywords and files, namely inverted index and forward index, but also generates the index for attributes. The triple dictionary consists of three types of indexes: the file index-based, the attribute index-based, and the keyword index-based.
- Based on the triple dictionary, we present a multi-user DSSE scheme using the blind storage structure that stores the counters' information for

keywords, dubbed MDSSE. Compared with existing DSSE schemes, MDSSE supports the efficient operations and multi-user setting for attribute-value type database.
- We analyze the security of MDSSE to prove that it can resist against various attacks. We also conduct comprehensive experiments showing that MDSSE is efficient for practical application.

2 Preliminaries

2.1 Technical Background

Attribute-Value Type Database. As shown in Table 1, we depict the attribute-value type database. There are m files, n attributes, and each attribute has multiple keywords. For the file ind_2, it has several attributes, for example, the attribute at_1 with the keyword value $W_{1,2}$ respectively, however, the file ind_2 does not have the attribute at_2 which denotes by $\perp$. Different files may have the same value under an attribute.

Table 1. Attribute-value type database

FileValueAttribute	at_1	at_2	at_3	$\cdots$	at_{n-1}	at_n
ind_1	$W_{1,1}$	$W_{2,1}$	$\perp$	$\cdots$	$W_{n-1,1}$	$W_{n,1}$
ind_2	$W_{1,2}$	$\perp$	$W_{3,2}$	$\cdots$	$W_{n-1,2}$	$\perp$
$\cdots$	$\cdots$	$\cdots$	$\cdots$	$\cdots$	$\cdots$	$\cdots$
ind_m	$\perp$	$W_{2,r}$	$W_{3,t}$	$\cdots$	$\perp$	$W_{n,v}$

Pseudorandomness Functions. Let $F : \{0,1\}^* \times \{0,1\}^* \to \{0,1\}^*$ be an efficient, length-preserving, keyed function. F is a pseudorandom function if for all probabilistic polynomial-time distinguishers D, there is a negligible function $negl$ such that :

$$|\Pr[D^{F_k(\cdot)}(1^\lambda) = 1] - \Pr[D^{f(\cdot)}(1^\lambda) = 1]| \leq negl(\lambda), \tag{1}$$

where the first probability is taken over uniform choice of $k \in \{0,1\}^\lambda$ and the randomness of D, and the second probability is taken over uniform choice of $f \in F$ and the randomness of D.

Blind Storage. Blind storage firstly was proposed by Muhammad Naveed et al. [29], which allows the users to outsource information in the cloud server and guarantees the cloud server does not learn the details of the information. While the users retrieving the information, the cloud server just learns about its existence of the information but the contents are not revealed. Furthermore, blind storage supports operations such as addition, update, and deletion.

In blind storage, the information is divided into fixed-size blocks, which are indexed by a sequence of random integers generated by the information-related seed. Besides, the cloud server only recognizes blocks uploaded and downloaded, which reflects that blind storage leaks little information to the cloud server.

2.2 System Model

The system model is shown in Fig. 1. There are three entities in MDSSE: the data owner, the search user and the cloud server.

Data owner: the data owner has a collection of files to be outsourced, where each file contains multiple attributes and each attribute corresponds to a keyword. Moreover, the data owner outsources the encrypted data to the cloud server without local backup. Additionally, while executing addition and deletion operation, the data owner updates the counters' information for each keyword which is stored on the cloud server through the blind storage structure.

Search user: while searching a keyword, the search user generates the search token and sends it to the cloud server to request the list of file identity containing a keyword or an attribute.

The cloud server: the cloud server provides the cloud storage service for the data owner. It is responsible for the triple dictionary structure for the encrypted database, performs blind storage for the counters' information of each keyword. Furthermore, the cloud server is required to support both for keyword searches and data updates.

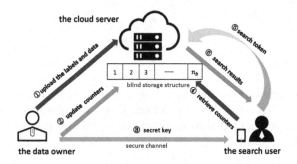

Fig. 1. System model

2.3 Security Model

Adversary Model. In the security model, we consider two types of attacks from the semi-trusted cloud server. The details are described as follows:

- Type I attack: The semi-trusted cloud server wants to retrieve the outsourced data from the encrypted data.
- Type II attack: The semi-trusted cloud server wants to know the exact searching keywords or attributes and wants to determine whether the keyword has been searched before when a new file is added.

2.4   Design Goals

In this paper, we aim to design a multi-user dynamic symmetric searchable encryption scheme using the blind storage structure based on the attribute-value type database, in which several challenging problems exist.

- How to build a practical structure for the attribute-value type database. In [26], Kim et al. have constructed a dual dictionary that takes advantage of both the inverted and the forward indexes at the same time. For the attribute-value type database, it includes the attributes additionally, therefore, how to extend the dual dictionary making it suitable for this type of database has been the key point.
- How to avoid updating all entries regarding to this keyword after each search. In [26], when users search a keyword, the cloud server would use a new key to reconstruct the dual dictionary to guarantee security, which causes the huge computation overhead for the cloud server. As such, this is a problem that requires urgent attention.
- How to resist the leakage of the number of keywords stored in the blind storage structure. In order to support multi-user searching, we adopt a blind storage structure to store the counters' information on each keyword. However, since the size of counters information for keywords is relatively small, therefore, different counters for different keywords would contain the same number of blocks. Thus, the cloud server can determine the number of existing keywords that have been stored in the blind storage structure. Hence, how to solve the problem mentioned above raises great concern.

To design a multi-user DSSE scheme using the blind storage structure based on the attribute-value type database, MDSSE should satisfy the requirements as follows:

- Security. The data owner should encrypt the data before outsourced, which guarantees the cloud server or an adversary is unable to acquire the content of the outsourced data; When the data owner adds a file to the cloud server, the cloud server cannot learn that the added file whether matches a previous search query.
- Functionality. The scheme should support the keyword search for multi-user other than a single-user, and also supports the outsourced data update (eg. addition, deletion) for the attribute-value type database.
- Efficiency. The scheme should be efficient and conveniently implement.

3   Construction of MDSSE

MDSSE consists of three entities: the data owner($\mathcal{O}$), the search user ($\mathcal{S}$), the cloud server ($\mathcal{CS}$). The details of MDSSE are described as follows.

Setup. Under the system security parameter λ, the public parameter is $PP = \{\lambda, H_0, H_1, H_2, \psi, \Gamma, G_{key}(\cdot), \alpha, \kappa\}$. H_0 is a hash function $H_0 : \{0,1\}^* \to \{0,1\}^{192}$, H_i is a hash function $H_i : \{0,1\}^* \times \{0,1\}^* \to \{0,1\}^\lambda, i = 1, 2$, ψ is a pseudorandom function, and $\psi : \{0,1\}^\lambda \times \{0,1\}^* \to \{0,1\}^\lambda$, Γ is a pseudorandom generator, $G_{key}(\cdot)$ is a pseudorandom function, α is used as the expansion parameters in blind storage system ($\alpha > 1$), κ denotes the minimum number of blocks in a communication. $\mathcal{O}$ constructs the blind storage structure for the keyword counters' information $KeyCounter$, which consists of n_b blocks of λ bits each. At the beginning, the blocks are initialized with 0. $\mathcal{CS}$ initializes an empty map $DictW$ and a triple dictionary data structure $Dict$ consisting of $Dict_1, Dict_2, Dict_3$.

$\mathcal{O}$ constructs and outsources $KeyCounter$ to $\mathcal{CS}$. The details are as follows.

- $\mathcal{O}$ randomly chooses $key_{prf} \leftarrow \{0,1\}^\lambda$ and randomly selects K_ψ for pseudorandom function ψ.
- The blind storage structure consists of n_b blocks of λ bits each. In the beginning, we initialize n_b blocks with 0. This phase takes into a large collection of information about the keywords w under the corresponding attributes at, where each keyword under the attribute has a unique id denoted as $id_{at||w} = H_0(at||w)$. The information of each keyword w consists of the counter information $cnt^{(w)}$ that represents the number of files containing w. For each keyword w, the data owner pads the corresponding information to q blocks of λ bits each, where $q \in [2, n_b]$. Thus, each keyword w contains q blocks of λ bits each, and the header of each block contains the id of the keyword $id_{at||w}$. Additionally, the header of the first block of the keyword w indicates the size of the counter's information q. For each keyword w, we construct the blind storage as follows.
  - $\mathcal{O}$ computes the seed $\sigma = \psi_{K_\psi}(id_{at||w})$ as the input of the pseudorandom generator Γ. The pseudorandom generator Γ generates a sufficiently long bit-number using σ and parses it as a sequence of integers in the range $[n_b]$. $\pi[\sigma, l]$ denotes the first l integers of this sequence. $\mathcal{O}$ generates a set $S_f = \pi[\sigma, \max(\lceil \alpha * q \rceil, \kappa)]$.
  - Let $S_f^0 = \pi[\sigma, \kappa]$, then check if the following conditions hold. If either of the above two does not hold, the system aborts.
    * Exist q free blocks indexed by the integers in the set S_f.
    * Exist one free block indexed by the integers in the set S_f^0.
  - $\mathcal{O}$ picks a subset $S_f' \subset S_f$ that contains q integers, and ensures that the q blocks indexed by these integers in the subset S_f' are free. The q integers in the set S_f are in a random order. We pick the first q integers indexing free blocks and make these from the subset S_f'. We mark the q blocks as unfree, and then we write $cnt^{(w)}$ in order. The header of all q blocks contain $id_{at||w}$, and the header of the first block of the keyword w indicates the size of counter's information q.

Addition. $\mathcal{O}$ interacts with $\mathcal{CS}$ to add a file F to the cloud server. The details are as follows.

- $\mathcal{O}$ generates the secret key $key^{(ind)} \leftarrow \psi(key_{prf}, ind)$, and then computes $label^{(ind)} \leftarrow H_1(key^{(ind)}, cnt^{(ind)})$, where ind is the identity of F, $cnt^{(ind)}$ is the order of the attribute.

- For each attribute $at \in DB(ind)$, where $DB(ind)$ is the set of attributes of ind, $\mathcal{O}$ generates a secret key as $key^{(at)} \leftarrow \psi(key_{prf}, at)$. $\mathcal{O}$ computes $label^{(at)} \leftarrow H_2(key^{(at)}, cnt^{(at)})$, in which $cnt^{(at)}$ reflects the order of w under at. w is the corresponding keyword of ind under the attribute at.
- For the keyword w, $\mathcal{O}$ generates a key as $key_{at}^{(w)} \leftarrow \psi(key_{prf}, at||w)$.
- $\mathcal{O}$ retrieves the information of keyword w under the attribute at, which stores via blind storage. The details are as follow.
  - $\mathcal{O}$ computes $\sigma = \psi_{K_\psi}(id_{at||w})$, and defines the set S_f^0 of size κ.
  - $\mathcal{O}$ retrieves the blocks indexed by S_f^0 from B, searches the blocks in the order they appear in $S_f^0 = \pi[\sigma, \kappa]$ until a block which is marked as belonging to $id_{at||w}$ is encountered.
  - If no such block is encountered, the keyword information is not appeared in the system, $\mathcal{O}$ initialized $cnt^{(w)} = 0$. Otherwise, if the block is encountered, this is the first block of the information about the keyword w, $\mathcal{O}$ recovers q from the header of this block, which is the size of the information for the keyword w.
  - $\mathcal{O}$ computes $S_f = \pi[\sigma, \max(\lceil \alpha * q \rceil, \kappa)]$, and retrieves the blocks indexed by $S_f \backslash S_f^0$.
  - $\mathcal{O}$ obtains the secret key $key_{at}^{(w)}$ and counter's information $cnt^{(w)}$.
- $\mathcal{O}$ sets $cnt^{(w)} \leftarrow cnt^{(w)} + 1$, computes the label $label_{at}^{(w)} \leftarrow G_{key_{at}^{(w)}}(w, cnt^{(w)}||0)$ and $data \leftarrow ind \oplus at \oplus label^{(at)} \oplus label^{(ind)} \oplus G_{key_{at}^{(w)}}(w, cnt^{(w)}||1)$.
- $\mathcal{O}$ sends $\{label_{at}^{(w)}, label^{(at)}, label^{(ind)}, data\}$ to $\mathcal{CS}$.
- $\mathcal{CS}$ adds $\{label^{(ind)}, label^{(at)}\}$ to $Dict_1$, adds $\{label^{(at)}, label_{at}^{(w)}\}$ to $Dict_2$, and adds $\{label_{at}^{(w)}, (label^{(at)}, label^{(ind)})\}$ to $Dict_3$. Furthermore, $\mathcal{CS}$ adds $data$ to $DictW$ with the location $label_{at}^{(w)}$.
- $\mathcal{O}$ updates the information of the keyword w via blind storage described above.

Deletion. $\mathcal{O}$ deletes a file F from the database. The details are as follows.

- $\mathcal{O}$ computes $key^{(ind)} \leftarrow \psi(key_{prf}, ind)$, and generates labels as $label^{(ind)} \leftarrow H_1(key^{(ind)}, cnt^{(ind)})$;
- $\mathcal{O}$ sends the set $\{label^{(ind)}\}$ to $\mathcal{CS}$;
- For each $label^{(ind)}$, $\mathcal{CS}$ searches $label^{(ind)}$ through $Dict_1$, obtains $label^{(at)}$, and deletes $\{label^{(ind)}, label^{(at)}\}$ from $Dict_1$;
- For each $label^{(at)}$, $\mathcal{CS}$ searches $label^{(at)}$ through $Dict_2$, obtains $label_{at}^{(w)}$, and deletes $\{label^{(at)}, label_{at}^{(w)}\}$ from $Dict_2$;
- $\mathcal{CS}$ searches each $label_{at}^{(w)}$ through $Dict_3$, obtains $(label^{(at)}, label^{(ind)})$ from $Dict_3$. Then $\mathcal{CS}$ deletes $\{label_{at}^{(w)}, (label^{(at)}, label^{(ind)})\}$ from $Dict_3$ and $data$ from $DictW[label_{at}^{(w)}]$.
- For all keywords $w \in DB(at)$ where $at \in DB(ind)$, $\mathcal{O}$ updates $cnt^{(w)}$ through blind storage structure.

SearchKeyword. $\mathcal{S}$ searches to find the identity of files containing a keyword w under the attribute at. The details are as follows.

- $\mathcal{O}$ computes $\sigma = \psi_{K_\psi}(id_{at||w})$ and $key_{at}^{(w)} \leftarrow \psi(key_{prf}, at||w)$, sends σ and $key_{at}^{(w)}$ to $\mathcal{S}$ using a secure channel.
- $\mathcal{S}$ defines the set S_f^0 of size κ, retrieves the blocks indexed by S_f^0 from B, searches the blocks in the order they appear in $S_f^0 = \pi[\sigma, \kappa]$ until a block which is marked as belonging to $id_{at||w}$ is encountered.
- If no such block is encountered, the keyword information is not appeared in the system. Otherwise, if the block is encountered, this is the first block of the information about the keyword w, $\mathcal{S}$ recovers q from the header of this block, which is the size of the information for the keyword w.
- $\mathcal{S}$ computes $S_f = \pi[\sigma, \max(\lceil \alpha * q \rceil, \kappa)]$, and retrieves the blocks indexed by $S_f \backslash S_f^0$. The first block is the counter information $cnt^{(w)}$.
- For $i \in [1, cnt^{(w)}]$, $\mathcal{S}$ computes $label_{at}^{(w)} \leftarrow G_{key_{at}^{(w)}}(w, i||0)$, and sends the labels set $\{label_{at}^{(w)}\}$ to $\mathcal{CS}$.
- For each $label_{at}^{(w)}$, $\mathcal{CS}$ retrieves the corresponding encrypted data $data$ from $DictW$ and $(label^{(at)}, label^{(ind)})$ from $Dict_3$. $\mathcal{CS}$ sends back the set $\{data\}$ and $\{label^{(at)}, label^{(ind)}\}$ to $\mathcal{S}$.
- While receiving the two sets, for $i \in [1, cnt^{(w)}]$, $\mathcal{S}$ computes $ind \leftarrow data \oplus at \oplus label^{(at)} \oplus label^{(ind)} \oplus G_{key_{at}^{(w)}}(w, i||1)$, and acquires the identity of files.

SearchAttribute. $\mathcal{S}$ searches database to find the identity of files containing an attribute at. The details are as follows.

- For each $w \in DB(at)$, $\mathcal{O}$ computes $\sigma = \psi_{K_\psi}(id_{at||w})$ and $key_{at}^{(w)} \leftarrow \psi(key_{prf}, at||w)$. $\mathcal{O}$ sends two sets $\{\sigma\}$ and $\{key_{at}^{(w)}\}$ to $\mathcal{S}$ via a secure channel.
- For each keyword $w \in DB(at)$, $\mathcal{S}$ requires the counter's information as follows:
  - $\mathcal{S}$ retrieves $\sigma = \psi_{K_\psi}(id_{at||w})$, and defines the set S_f^0 of size κ.
  - $\mathcal{S}$ retrieves the blocks indexed by S_f^0 from B, searches the blocks in the order they appear in $S_f^0 = \pi[\sigma, \kappa]$ until a block which is marked as belonging to $id_{at||w}$ is encountered.
  - If no such block is encountered, the keyword information is not appeared in the system. Otherwise, if the block is encountered, this is the first block of the information about the keyword w, $\mathcal{S}$ recovers q from the header of this block, which is the size of the information for the keyword w.
  - $\mathcal{S}$ computes $S_f = \pi[\sigma, \max(\lceil \alpha * q \rceil, \kappa)]$, and retrieves the blocks indexed by $S_f \backslash S_f^0$.
  - $\mathcal{S}$ obtains the keyword counters' information $cnt^{(w)}$.
- For each keyword $w \in DB(at)$, $\mathcal{S}$ requires the identity of files as follow:
  - For $i \in [1, cnt^{(w)}]$, $\mathcal{S}$ computes $label_{at}^{(w)} \leftarrow G_{key_{at}^{(w)}}(w, i||0)$, and sends the labels set $\{label_{at}^{(w)}\}$ to $\mathcal{CS}$.

- For each $label_{at}^{(w)}$, $\mathcal{CS}$ retrieves the corresponding encrypted data $data$ from $DictW$ and $(label^{(at)}, label^{(ind)})$ from $Dict_3$. $\mathcal{CS}$ sends back the set $\{data\}$ and $\{label^{(at)}, label^{(ind)}\}$ to $\mathcal{S}$.
- While receiving the two sets, for $i \in [1, cnt^{(w)}]$, $\mathcal{S}$ computes $ind \leftarrow data \oplus at \oplus label^{(at)} \oplus label^{(ind)} \oplus G_{key_{at}^{(w)}}(w, i\|1)$, and acquires the identity of files.

4   Security Analysis

In this section, we address the security of MDSSE with respect to the adversary model described in Sect. 2.3.

4.1   Type I Attack

While the data owner outsources data to the cloud server, it is imperative to encrypt the outsourced data. The encrypted data can resist against the cloud server spying on the content of the outsourced data and prevent adversaries from obtaining the content of the outsourced data if the cloud server is corrupted.

Theorem 1. *In MDSSE, if an adversary $\mathcal{A}$ corrupts the cloud server, he cannot retrieve the outsourced data in plaintext.*

Proof. During the **Addition** phase, the data owner wants to outsource a file F to the cloud server. Firstly, he computes the labels for the file by $label^{(ind)} \leftarrow H_1(key^{(ind)}, cnt^{(ind)})$, in which $cnt^{(ind)}$ is the order of attributes, where the number of file labels is proportional to the number of attributes of the file. Secondly, he computes the labels for the attributes by $label^{(at)} \leftarrow H_2(key^{(at)}, cnt^{(at)})$ where $cnt^{(at)}$ is the order of keyword w under the attribute at, namely, for F, each attribute corresponds to an attribute label. Thirdly, the data owner computes the labels for the keyword w under the attribute at by $label_{at}^{(w)} \leftarrow G_{key_{at}^{(w)}}(w, cnt^{(w)}\|0)$, where the input of the pseudorandomness function is the keyword w, the order of newly added files in all files containing keyword w $(cnt^{(w)})$ connecting 0. Finally, he computes the encrypted data with $data \leftarrow ind \oplus at \oplus label^{(at)} \oplus label^{(ind)} \oplus G_{key_{at}^{(w)}}(w, cnt^{(w)}\|1)$. $label_{at}^{(w)}$ is used as the location in which the encrypted data $data$ will be stored at the dictionary $DictW$.

If an adversary $\mathcal{A}$ compromises the cloud server, he can obtain the triple dictionary $Dict$, the map $DictW$ and the blind storage $KeyCounter$. We assume that $\mathcal{A}$ wants to search a keyword w under an attribute at. First, he has to know the counter of files containing w which is stored blindly in $KeyCounter$. Since different keyword occupies different number of blocks, it is infeasible for $\mathcal{A}$ to guess the blocks storing the counter of w and retrieves the counter information. Furthermore, we assume $\mathcal{A}$ randomly guesses the counter and sets it as $cnt^{(w)'}$, he would retrieve the locations $label_{at}^{(w)}$ from $Dict_3$, and gain the encrypted data $data$ with $label_{at}^{(w)}$. If $\mathcal{A}$ wants to obtain the identity of files containing w, he needs to compute $ind \leftarrow data \oplus at \oplus label^{(at)} \oplus label^{(ind)} \oplus G_{key_{at}^{(w)}}(w, i||1)$.

However, $key_{at}^{(w)}$ securely transfers via a secure channel, it is computationally infeasible to recover it from the leaked information. Thus, $\mathcal{A}$ cannot retrieve the outsourced data in plaintext even he compromises the cloud server.

4.2   Type II Attack

When users upload a new file, the addition query does not leak any keyword information about the file.

Theorem 2. *In MDSSE, the cloud server or an adversary $\mathcal{A}$ cannot learn the keywords of the added file whether to match a previous search query.*

Proof. During **Addition** phase, the data owner computes the file label $label^{(ind)} \leftarrow H_1(key^{(ind)}, cnt^{(ind)})$, the attribute label $label^{(at)} \leftarrow H_2(key^{(at)}, cnt^{(at)})$, the keyword label $label_{at}^{(w)} \leftarrow G_{key_{at}^{(w)}}(w, cnt^{(w)}||0)$, the data $data \leftarrow ind \oplus at \oplus G_{key_{at}^{(w)}}(w, cnt^{(w)}||1) \oplus label^{(at)} \oplus label^{(ind)}$. While computing the keyword label, the data owner acquires the counter of the keyword $cnt^{(w)}$ from the blind storage structure and sets $cnt^{(w)} \leftarrow cnt^{(w)}+1$. After that, the data owner outsources the labels $\{label^{(ind)}, (label^{(at)}, label_{at}^{(w)}, data)\}$ to the cloud server. Upon receiving the labels, $\mathcal{CS}$ adds $\{label^{(ind)}, label^{(at)}\}$ to $Dict_1$, adds $\{label^{(at)}, label_{at}^{(w)}\}$ to $Dict_2$, adds $\{label_{at}^{(w)}, (label^{(at)}, label^{(ind)})\}$ to $Dict_3$ and updates the dictionary $DictW$. The data owner updates the counter dictionary $KeyCounter$.

During **SearchKeyword** phase, the search user acquires the counter's information from $KeyCounter$ and computes the search labels as $label_{at}^{(w)} \leftarrow G_{key_{at}^{(w)}}(w, i||0)$, where $i \in [1, cnt^{(w)}]$. The cloud server retrieves $data$ and $(label^{(at)}, label^{(ind)})$ for each $label_{at}^{(w)}$, and sends back two sets $\{data\}$, $\{label^{(at)}, label^{(ind)}\}$ to the search user. Upon receiving these two sets, the search user recovers the file identities by computing $ind \leftarrow data \oplus at \oplus label^{(at)} \oplus label^{(ind)} \oplus G_{key_{at}^{(w)}}(w, i||1)$, where $i \in [1, cnt^{(w)}]$, and gets the identity of files.

If the cloud server or an adversary $\mathcal{A}$ wants to learn the adding file F whether including the keyword w having been searched before, the adding file must be related to the previously searched keywords. As described before, the newly adding file is unlinkable with the queried keyword due to the indistinguishability between the pseudorandomness function G and a random function. Therefore, the cloud server or an adversary $\mathcal{A}$ cannot learn the keywords of the adding data whether to match a previous search query, which guarantees security.

5   Performance Evaluation

We implement our scheme in JAVA with MRICAL using the computer with a single Intel Core i7 4790 K 4.00 GHz CPU, 16 GB of RAM. Our evaluations

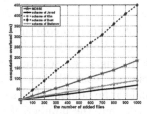

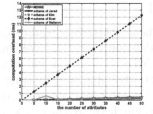

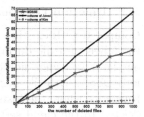

Fig. 2. Computation cost in addition (a)

Fig. 3. Computation cost in addition (b)

Fig. 4. Computation cost in deletion (a)

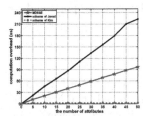

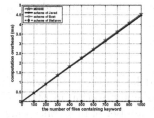

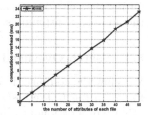

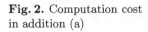

Fig. 5. Computation cost in deletion (b)

Fig. 6. Computation cost in search (a)

Fig. 7. Computation cost in search (b)

focus on the performance of each operation, including computation overhead and communication overhead.

5.1 Addition Overhead

Compared with existing schemes, MDSSE requires the data owner to compute the labels for attributes during addition operation. The costs of generating all attribute labels are the same as the identity labels' cost, where the number of total attribute labels is the same as the identity labels. We show the computation delay on the data owner side of MDSSE in Fig. 2 and Fig. 3. In Fig. 2, we set that, in MDSSE, each file has 20 attributes, in other schemes, each file has 15 keywords, where the costs of computation are proportional to the number of files added to the cloud server. Furthermore, in Fig. 3, we set that the number of attributes is the same as the number of keywords, the computation overhead is a linear positive correlation with the number of attributes(keywords). According to the analysis, we can see that the data owner can generate the labels for about 6000 files in 1 s if the number of attributes is 20. Additionally, during the addition operation, the communication complexity is proportional to the number of attributes.

5.2 Deletion Overhead

Compared with existing schemes, MDSSE requires the data owner to compute the labels of a file during deletion operation. We show the computation delay on the data owner side of MDSSE in Fig. 4 and Fig. 5. In Fig. 4, we set that, in MDSSE, each file has 20 attributes, and in other schemes, each file has 15 keywords, where the costs of computation are proportional to the number of files deleted to the cloud server. Furthermore, in Fig. 5, we set that the number of attributes is the same as the number of keywords, the computation overhead is a linear positive correlation with the number of attributes(keywords). According to the analysis, we can see that the data owner can generate the labels for about 24000 files in 1 s if the number of attributes is 20. Additionally, in MDSSE, during the deletion operation, the communication complexity is proportional to the number of attributes.

5.3 Search Overhead

We show the computation delay on the data owner side of MDSSE in Fig. 6 and Fig. 7. In Fig. 6, the costs of computation in MDSSE and Javad et al.'s scheme [27] are proportional to the number of files containing the keyword. However, for Bost et al.'s scheme [28] and Stefanov et al.'s scheme [25], the costs of computation are unrelated to those numbers. In MDSSE, when a search user searches an attribute, the computation costs are proportional to the number of keywords that the attribute contains, which has shown in Fig. 7. If an attribute has 30 keywords, the search user can get the results in 15 ms, which is tolerable to the search user. During the **Search** phase, the cloud server has to update the encrypted data with a new key in Kim et al.'s scheme [26], which causes huge computation overhead. Compared with Kim et al.'s scheme [26], in MDSSE, we overcome the disadvantages and the computation cost in cloud server side is much less than Kim et al.'s scheme [26]. Additionally, we evaluate the communication complexity of MDSSE and other schemes [25–28], the experiment results show that the communication complexity is proportional to the number of files containing the keyword.

6 Conclusion

In this paper, we have proposed a multi-user DSSE scheme for attribute-value type database, where we have designed a triple dictionary for the attribute-value type database and employ the blind storage structure to free users from the huge storage overhead. We prove that MDSSE can resist against the semi-trusted cloud server to guarantee security. We also have implemented the experiment and the result shows that MDSSE is practical and efficient.

Acknowledgments. This work is supported by the National Key R&D Program of China under Grant 2017YFB0802000, the National Nature Science Foundation of China under Grant 61872060, and the National Natural Science Foundation of China under Grant 61830203.

References

1. Lei, Z., Anmin, F., Shui, Y., Mang, S., Boyu, K.: Data integrity verification of the outsourced big data in the cloud environment: a survey. J. Network Comput. Appl. **122**, 1–15 (2018)
2. Zhang, Y., Xu, C., Li, H., Yang, K., Cheng, N., Shen, X.S.: PROTECT: Efficient password-based threshold single-sign-on authentication for mobile users against perpetual leakage. IEEE Trans. Mobile Comput. (2020)
3. Shui, Y.: Big privacy: challenges and opportunities of privacy study in the age of big data. IEEE Access **4**, 2751–2763 (2016)
4. Yu, S., Liu, M., Dou, W., Liu, X., Zhou, S.: Networking for big data: a survey. IEEE Commun. Surv. Tutorials **19**(1), 531–549 (2017)
5. Zhang, Y., Xu, C., Cheng, N., Li, H., Shen, X.S.: Chronos$^+$+: an accurate blockchain-based time-stamping scheme for cloud storage. IEEE Trans. Serv. Comput. **13**(2), 216–229 (2020)
6. Kamara, S., Lauter, K.: Cryptographic cloud storage. In: Sion, R., et al. (eds.) FC 2010. LNCS, vol. 6054, pp. 136–149. Springer, Heidelberg (2010). https://doi.org/10.1007/978-3-642-14992-4_13
7. Shanshan, L., Chunxiang, X., Yuan, Z.: CSED: client-side encrypted deduplication scheme based on proofs of ownership for cloud storage. J. Inf. Secur. Appl. **46**, 250–258 (2019)
8. Yuan, Z., Chunxiang, X., Hongwei, L., Kan, Y., Jianying, Z., Xiaodong, L.: HealthDep: an efficient and secure deduplication scheme for cloud-assisted eHealth systems. IEEE Trans. Industr. Inf. **14**(9), 4101–4112 (2018)
9. Yuan, Z., Chunxiang, X., Jining, Z., Xiaojun, Z., Junwei, W.: Cryptanalysis of an integrity checking scheme for cloud data sharing. J. Inf. Secur. Appl. **23**, 68–73 (2015)
10. Zhang, Y., Xu, C., Ni, J., Li, H., Shen, X.S.: Blockchain-assisted public-key encryption with keyword search against keyword guessing attacks for cloud storage. IEEE Trans. Cloud Comput. (2019)
11. Google doc. https://www:google:cn/intl/zh--cnall/docs/about/
12. Nadkarni, P.M., Brandt, C.M., Marenco, L.: WebEAV: automatic metadata-driven generation of web interfaces to entity-attribute-value databases. J. Am. Med. Inf. Assoc. **7**(4), 343–356 (2000)
13. Nadkarni, P.M., Brandt, C.: Data extraction and ad hoc query of an entity-attribute-value database. J. Am. Med. Inf. Assoc. **5**(6), 511–527 (1998)
14. Böjosep, A.D., Katz, R., Konwinski, A., Gunho, L., Patterson, D., Rabkin, A.: A view of cloud computing. Commun. ACM **53**(4), 50–58 (2010)
15. Zhang, Y., Xu, C., Lin, X., Shen, X.S.: Blockchain-based public integrity verification for cloud storage against procrastinating auditors. IEEE Trans. Cloud Comput. (2019)
16. Song, D.X., Wagner, D., Perrig, A.: Practical techniques for searches on encrypted data. In: 21th International Proceedings on S and P, Berkeley, CA, USA, pp. 44–55. IEEE (2000)
17. Goh, E.-J.: Secure indexes. GIACR Cryptol. ePrint Archive **2003**, 216 (2003)
18. Reza, C., Juan, G., Seny, K., Rafail, O.: Searchable symmetric encryption: improved definitions and efficient constructions. J. Comput. Secur. **19**(5), 895–934 (2011)

19. Chang, Y.-C., Mitzenmacher, M.: Privacy preserving keyword searches on remote encrypted data. In: Ioannidis, J., Keromytis, A., Yung, M. (eds.) ACNS 2005. LNCS, vol. 3531, pp. 442–455. Springer, Heidelberg (2005). https://doi.org/10. 1007/11496137_30

20. Kamara, S., Papamanthou, C., Roeder, T.: Dynamic searchable symmetric encryption. In: International Proceedings on CCS, Raleigh, North Carolina, USA, pp. 965–976. ACM (2012)

21. Kamara, S., Papamanthou, C.: Parallel and dynamic searchable symmetric encryption. In: Sadeghi, A.-R. (ed.) FC 2013. LNCS, vol. 7859, pp. 258–274. Springer, Heidelberg (2013). https://doi.org/10.1007/978-3-642-39884-1_22

22. Cash, D., Grubbs, P., Perry, J., Ristenpart, T.: Leakage-abuse attacks against searchable encryption. In: 22th International Proceedings on CCS, Denver, Colorado, USA, pp. 668–679. ACM (2015)

23. Islam, M.S., Kuzu, M., Kantarcioglu, M.: Access pattern disclosure on searchable encryption: ramification, attack and mitigation. In: 19th International Proceedings on NDSS, San Diego, CA, USA, pp. 1–12. ISOC (2012)

24. Zhang, Y., Katz, J., Papamanthou, C.: All your queries are belong to us: the power of file-injection attacks on searchable encryption. In: 25th International Proceedings on USENIX Security, Vancouver, BC, Canada. pp. 707–720. USENIX Association (2016)

25. Emil, C., Papamanthou, C., Shi, E.: Practical dynamic searchable encryption with small leakage. In: 21th International Proceedings on NDSS, San Diego, CA, USA, pp. 72–75. ISOC (2014)

26. Kim, K.S., Kim, M., Lee, D., Park, J.H., Kim, W.-H.: Forward secure dynamic searchable symmetric encryption with efficient updates. In: 24th International Proceedings on CCS, New York, NY, USA, pp. 1449–1463. ACM (2017)

27. Ghareh Chamani, J., Papadopoulos, D., Papamanthou, C., Jalili, R.: New constructions for forward and backward private symmetric searchable encryption. In: 25th International Proceedings on CCS, New York, NY, USA, pp. 1038–1055. ACM (2018)

28. Bost, R.: $\varphi o\varsigma$: Forward secure searchable encryption. In: 23th International Proceedings on CCS, New York, NY, USA, pp. 1143–1154. ACM (2016)

29. Naveed, M., Prabhakaran, M., Gunter, C.A.: Dynamic searchable encryption via blind storage. In: 35th International Proceedings on S and P, San Jose, CA, USA, pp. 639–654. IEEE (2014)

30. Hahn, F., Kerschbaum, F.: Searchable encryption with secure and efficient updates. In: 21th International Proceedings on CCS, New York, NY, USA, pp. 310–320. ACM (2014)

Revocable Attribute-Based Encryption Scheme with Arithmetic Span Program for Cloud-Assisted IoT

Hu Xiong$^{(\boxtimes)}$, Jinhao Chen$^{(\boxtimes)}$, Minghao Yang$^{(\boxtimes)}$, and Xin Huang$^{(\boxtimes)}$

School of Information and Software Engineering,
University of Electronic Science and Technology of China, Chengdu, China
xionghu.uestc@gmail.com, jinhaochen.cloud@gmail.com,
yangminghao1205@gmail.com, huangxin90427@gmail.com

Abstract. Efficient user revocation and description of the access policy are essential to enhance the practicality of attribute-based encryption (ABE) in real-life scenarios, such as cloud-assisted IoT. Nevertheless, existing ABE works fail to balance the two vital indicators. Motivated by this, in this paper, we present a revocable ciphertext-policy attribute-based encryption with arithmetic span programs (R-CPABE-ASP) for cloud-assisted IoT. For the first time, the presented R-CPABE-ASP achieves efficient user revocation and expressive description of access policy simultaneously. In R-CPABE-ASP, each attribute involved in access policy is merely used once to check whether a user owns access to shared data. Hence, the R-CPABE-ASP work enables efficient data encryption compared with existing revocable ABE works by reducing unnecessary cost for defining access policy. Meanwhile, as shown in the outsourced version of R-CPABE-ASP, the costly part for users to decrypt the data is outsourced to powerful cloud servers. Therefore, users in our R-CPABE-ASP can access their data in a more efficient way by merely one exponential operation. Finally, we carry out detailed theoretical analysis and experimental simulations to evaluate the performance of our work. The results fairly show that our proposed work is efficient and feasible in cloud-assisted IoT.

Keywords: Cloud-assisted IoT · Attribute-based encryption · Arithmetic span program · Revocation

1 Introduction

The Internet of Things (IoT) is a complex heterogeneous network. It connects various smart devices through communication and information technology to achieve intelligent identification, positioning, tracking, supervising and so on [1]. At present, IoT applications have been widely used in different fields such as smart cities, e-health, and intelligent transportation systems. However, with the increase of smart devices, more resources are required to manage and process the large amount of data generated by numerous smart devices in the IoT [2–6].

© Springer Nature Singapore Pte Ltd. 2020
S. Yu et al. (Eds.): SPDE 2020, CCIS 1268, pp. 369–383, 2020.
https://doi.org/10.1007/978-981-15-9129-7_26

For example, medical systems and traffic monitoring systems generate giga-level high-definition images and videos per minute [7]. It is hard for ordinary users or smart devices in the traditional IoT to undertake the heavy burden in both storage and calculation. Fortunately, cloud-assisted IoT provides a promising solution for solving the kind of data explosion problem under the constraints of individual object capabilities. As a powerful platform, cloud computing empowers users with on-demand services [8] for storing, accessing, and processing data.

Although cloud computing brings immense benefits to IoT, it also takes unprecedented security risks due to its openness. Specifically, the data collected by the smart devices may contain the user's private information [9,10]. The curious cloud servers and the unauthorized users may make the endeavors to obtain user's personal information for financial gains. For this reason, keeping the confidentiality of user's data is vital of importance. Meanwhile, out of the needs of efficient data sharing in cloud-assisted IoT, it is desirable to design an effective mechanism that enables flexible access control. Due to the advantages in ensuring data confidentiality and realzing fine-grained access control, the primitive of attribute-based encryption (ABE) [11] was widely explored in cloud-assisted IoT. In the ABE schemes [11–14], both the ciphertext and the key are related to a set of attributes. The encrypter can formulate an encryption strategy consisting of attributes according to the sensitive content and the receiver's characteristic information. With this method, the resulting ciphertext can only be decrypted by users whose attributes meet the encryption strategy. In this way, not only the confidentiality of the sensitive data is assured but also the access control is achieved in a flexible and fine-grained way. While a series of ABE schemes followed [15,16], nonetheless, the potential user revocation [17] in cloud-assisted IoT is also challenging to the conventional ABE work.

For enhancing the practicality of ABE, the conception of revocable ABE was subsequently presented. The methods applied in the revocable ABE works for achieving user revocation can be typically divided into two categories: direct revocation and indirect revocation. In directly revocable ABE works [18,19], the data encryptors need to maintain a revocation list delivered by the trusted authority and keep it up-to-date. Obviously, the communication overhead for requesting the latest revocation list from the trusted authority is burdensome for data encryptors. To avoid the heavy overhead for maintaining the revocation list, various ABE works that supports indirection user revocation were proposed [20–23]. In an ABE work that supports indirect revocation, each non-revoked user will receive an extra key update material from the trusted authority for generating a complete decryption key. It is effectively guaranteed that the revoked users without key update materials have no access to the shared data. Despite of this, existing revocable ABE works is still insufficient to handle the complicated access policy in a large-scale cloud-assisted IoT system. In these works, the attributes involved in the access policy will be multiply used to establish a fine-grained access control of the sensitive data. It indeed causes extra overheads for embedding the access policy into a ciphertext.

Motivated by this, in this paper, we present a revocable ciphertext-policy attribute-based encryption scheme with arithmetic span program [24–27] (R-CPABE-ASP) for cloud-assisted IoT environment. The presented R-CPABE-ASP not only achieves fine-grained access control and necessary user revocation but also enables efficient access policy description. Thanks to the expressive ASP access structure and decryption outsourcing, our R-CPABE-ASP obtains high efficiency in the phases of encryption and decryption. In detail, our main contributions are listed below:

- We propose the first R-CPABE-ASP scheme that achieves user revocation and ASP access structure simultaneously. The presented R-CPABE-ASP can effectively address the potential changes in user's access right to shared data thanks to the introduction of user revocation.
- Compared with existing revocable ABE works where the attributes will be multiply required to establish an access policy, each attribute in access policy of our R-CPABE-ASP scheme is merely used once. Hence, the R-CPABE-ASP owns higher efficiency in data encryption for embedding the access policy into a ciphertext. Furthermore, an outsourced version of R-CPABE-ASP (OR-CPABE-ASP) is given, in which the overhead for data decryption is reduced to one exponential operation. Thus, even light weight users can efficiently access the data in cloud-assisted IoT environment.
- Our proposed R-CPABE-ASP is proved to be adaptively secure under the $MDDH_{k,l}^m$ assumption by using dual system encryption technology [28]. Finally, the detailed theoretical analysis and experimental simulations demonstrate that the presented R-CPABE-ASP is secure, efficient and feasible in cloud-assisted IoT.

1.1 Organizations

The rest of this paper is conducted as follows: Sect. 3 gives some basic notations and structures. The concrete construction of R-CPABE-ASP is contributed in Sect. 4. The performance evaluation is carried out in Sect. 5. Finally, this paper is concluded in Sect. 6.

2 Related Work

Attribute-based encryption (ABE) has been well explored in two branches of key-policy ABE and ciphertext-policy ABE since its seminal proposal [11]. Goyal et al. [12] presented a key-policy attribute-based work, in which each user's secret key is bound to a tree-access structure. Kaaniche and Laurent [13] presented a privacy-preserving ABE scheme. In their scheme, the general tree access structure is adopted to prevent the sensitive data from being deciphered without authorization. Li et al. [14] proposed a secure cloud data storage system for cloud IoT environment by utilizing ABE with AND-gate access structure. Nevertheless, the normal access structures adopted in these works suffer from heavy overheads to define the access policy of the sensitive data. The fatal reason is that existing access structures establish access control to sensitive data by enumerating all the attribute permutations that meet the access policy. It inevitably causes extra expenses for defining the access policy during the phase of data encryption since the same attribute is used multiple times. Subsequently, the proposal of the arithmetic span program (ASP) [24] contributes a feasible solution for describing the access policy in an efficient manner. By adopting the notion of ASP, the access policy can be defined as an arithmetic expression of the attributes involved [26]. Even for a complicated access policy, the same attribute is merely required once. For this reason, the overhead for defining the access policy is significantly reduced. Inspired by this, Chen et al. [25] constructed the first KP-ABE for ASP. Ma et al. [27] presented the first CP-ABE for ASP recently. Nevertheless, the above mentioned works can hardly handle the challenging user revocation issue caused by the change of the user's permission in real-life scenarios.

For heightening the feasibility of conventional ABE works in real-life scenarios, measures for realizing user revocation have been well studied in the context of ABE. Zhang et al. [18] proposed a directly revocable ABE work with constant-size ciphertext. In their work, the user revocation is realized by the revocation list embedded into the ciphertext during data encryption. However, each the encrypter needs to continuously request the latest revocation list from the trusted authority. Fairly, encrypters in their work will confront heavy communication burden for keeping the revocation list up-to-date. This issue also threatens all ABE works that support direct user revocation. For eliminating this issue, Qin et al. [20] proposed indirect revocable ABE work. In their work, the trusted authority periodically broadcasts the key update materials to each non-revoked user. Only the users who generate a complete decryption key with the key update materials have access to the data. In this way, the procedure of user revocation will not put any extra burden on the encrypter. Thereafter, Xu et al. [21] constructed a secure IoT cloud storage system that achieves fine-grained access control by LSSS access structure. Wei et al. [23] contributed a revocable storage system for ensuring the security of e-Health records in public cloud scenarios.

Obviously, both efficient access structure and user revocation are essential to make a practical and robust ABE work in cloud-assisted IoT. What a pity, to the best of our knowledge, the ABE work that supports ASP access structure and user revocation simultaneously has not been well discussed.

3   Preliminaries

In this section, some basic knowledge that will be used in the following part of this paper is given.

3.1   Mathematical Notations

For a prime order asymmetric bilinear pairing $(e, \mathbb{G}, \mathbb{H}, \mathbb{G}_T, g, h)$, $\mathbb{G}, \mathbb{H}, \mathbb{G}_T$ are prime order groups, e is a map from $\mathbb{G} \times \mathbb{H}$ to $\mathbb{G}_T$, g and h are the generators of $\mathbb{G}$ and $\mathbb{H}$, respectively. With the basis, some operations can be defined as:

◇ Given a vector $\mathbf{A} = (g^{a_1}, g^{a_2})^{\top}$ and a matrix $\mathbf{B} \in \mathbb{Z}_p^{3 \times 2}$, $\mathbf{A^B} = g^{\mathbf{B}(a_1, a_2)^{\top}}$, where $a_1, a_2 \in \mathbb{Z}_p$.

◇ Given a matrix $g^{\mathbf{C}_1^{\top}}$, where $\mathbf{C}_1 = (c_{11}, c_{21}, c_{31}) \leftarrow_R \mathbb{Z}_p^3$, $\boldsymbol{\lambda} \leftarrow_R \mathbb{Z}_p^{2 \times 1}$, the result of $g^{\boldsymbol{\lambda} \cdot \mathbf{C}_1^{\top}}$ can be easily obtained as:

$$
g^{\boldsymbol{\lambda} \cdot \mathbf{C}_1^{\top}} = g^{\begin{bmatrix} \lambda_{11} \\ \lambda_{21} \end{bmatrix} \cdot [c_{11}\ c_{21}\ c_{31}]} = g^{\begin{bmatrix} \lambda_{11} \cdot c_{11}\ \lambda_{11} \cdot c_{21}\ \lambda_{11} \cdot c_{31} \\ \lambda_{21} \cdot c_{11}\ \lambda_{21} \cdot c_{21}\ \lambda_{21} \cdot c_{31} \end{bmatrix}}
$$

$$
= \begin{bmatrix} (g^{c_{11}})^{\lambda_{11}}\ (g^{c_{21}})^{\lambda_{11}}\ (g^{c_{31}})^{\lambda_{11}} \\ (g^{c_{11}})^{\lambda_{21}}\ (g^{c_{21}})^{\lambda_{21}}\ (g^{c_{31}})^{\lambda_{21}} \end{bmatrix},
$$

where $g^{c_{11}}, g^{c_{21}}, g^{c_{31}}$ can be gained from the matrix $g^{\mathbf{C}_1^{\top}}$.

◇ Given a matrix $g^{\mathbf{C}_1^{\top}}$ with unknown $\mathbf{C}_1 \leftarrow_R \mathbb{Z}_p^3$ and a matrix $\boldsymbol{\vartheta} \leftarrow_R \mathbb{Z}_p^{3 \times 2}$, the value of matrix $g^{\mathbf{C}_1^{\top} \cdot \boldsymbol{\vartheta}}$ can be easily obtained following the above-mentioned steps.

3.2   Basis Structure

To simulate the composite-order groups with three primes- order subgroups. We first choose $l_1, l_2, l_3, l_w \geq 1$, and pick $\mathbf{W}_1 \leftarrow_R \mathbb{Z}_p^{l \times l_1}, \mathbf{W}_2 \leftarrow_R \mathbb{Z}_p^{l \times l_2}, \mathbf{W}_3 \leftarrow_R \mathbb{Z}_p^{l \times l_3}$, where $l = l_1 + l_2 + l_3$. $(\mathbf{W}_1^* | \mathbf{W}_2^* | \mathbf{W}_3^*)^{\top}$ is defined as the inverse of $(\mathbf{W}_1 | \mathbf{W}_2 | \mathbf{W}_3)$. It is clear that $\mathbf{W}_i^{\top} \mathbf{W}_i^* = \mathbf{I}$, and $\mathbf{W}_i^{\top} \mathbf{W}_j^* = \mathbf{0}$ $(i \neq j)$, where $\mathbf{I}$ is the identity matrix. And for any $\mathbf{T} \leftarrow_R \mathbb{Z}_p^{l \times l_w}$, there's always $\mathbf{T} = \mathbf{B}^{(1)} + \mathbf{B}^{(2)} + \mathbf{B}^{(3)}$, where $\mathbf{B}^{(1)} \leftarrow_R \mathsf{span}^{l_w}(\mathbf{W}_1^*), \mathbf{B}^{(2)} \leftarrow_R \mathsf{span}^{l_w}(\mathbf{W}_2^*), \mathbf{B}^{(3)} \leftarrow_R \mathsf{span}^{l_w}(\mathbf{W}_3^*)$.

Theorem 1. Given matrices $\mathbf{W}_1, \mathbf{W}_2, \mathbf{W}_3, \mathbf{W}_1^*, \mathbf{W}_2^*, \mathbf{W}_3^*, \mathbf{T}$ mentioned in the basis structure, the following two distributions $\{\mathbf{W}_1^{\top}\mathbf{T}, \mathbf{W}_3^{\top}\mathbf{T}, \mathbf{T}\}$ and $\{\mathbf{W}_1^{\top}\mathbf{T}, \mathbf{W}_3^{\top}\mathbf{T}, \mathbf{T} + \mathbf{P}^{(2)}\}$ are statistically identical with the probability $1 - 1/p$, where $\mathbf{P}^{(2)} \leftarrow_R \mathsf{span}^{l_w}(\mathbf{W}_2^*)$.

3.3   MDDH$_{k,l}^m$ Assumption

For any PPT adversary $\mathcal{A}$, $\mathsf{Adv}_{\mathcal{A}}^{\mathrm{MDDH}_{k,l}^m}(\lambda) = |\Pr[\mathcal{A}(\mathbb{G}, g^{\mathbf{M}}, g^{\mathbf{MS}}) = 1] - \Pr[\mathcal{A}(\mathbb{G}, g^{\mathbf{M}}, g^{\mathbf{S}'}) = 1]|$ is negligible for a security parameter λ, in which g is the generator of $\mathbb{G}$, $\mathbf{M} \leftarrow_R \mathbb{Z}_p^{l \times k}$, $\mathbf{S} \leftarrow_R \mathbb{Z}_p^{k \times m}$, $\mathbf{S}' \leftarrow_R \mathbb{Z}_p^{l \times m}$ $(m \geq 1$ and $l > k \geq 1)$. According to [29], the MDDH$_{k,l}^m$ assumption is equivalent to the well-known k-Linear assumption [29]. For convenience, we denote MDDH$_{k,k+1}^1$ by MDDH$_k$ in the remainder part of this paper.

3.4   Arithmetic Span Program

The ASP access policy is formed with a vector set $\mathcal{V} = \{\mathbf{y}_i, \mathbf{z}_i\}_{i \in [n]}$ and a map $\pi : [n] \rightarrow A$, where A is an attribute set and $n = |A|$. If there is an attribute vector $\mathbf{x} = (x_{\pi(1)}, x_{\pi(2)}, \cdots, x_{\pi(n)}) \in \mathbb{Z}_p^n$ which satisfies the ASP $(\mathcal{V}, \pi)$, it is able to get $\gamma_1, \cdots, \gamma_n \in \mathbb{Z}_p$ such that $\sum_{i=1}^{n} \gamma_i(\mathbf{y}_i + x_{\pi(i)}\mathbf{z}_i) = (1, 0, \cdots, 0)$.

Theorem 2. For any attribute set S that is not satisfied with $\mathcal{V} = \{(\mathbf{y}_j, \mathbf{z}_j)\}_{j \in S}$, the distributions

$$\{s, \mathbf{y}_j \left(\begin{smallmatrix} l_0 s \\ \mathbf{L} \end{smallmatrix}\right) + r_j p_j, \mathbf{z}_j \left(\begin{smallmatrix} l_0 s \\ \mathbf{L} \end{smallmatrix}\right) + r_j p_j', s_j\}_{j \in S}, (\{\alpha + r l_0, r, r p_j\})_{j \in S} \text{ perfectly hide}$$

α, where $p_j, p_j', l_0, s, r, s_j \leftarrow_R \mathbb{Z}_p, \mathbf{L} \leftarrow_R \mathbb{Z}_p^{l'-1}$, and $r_j \neq 0$.

One-Use Restriction. Similar to the ideas of [25, 30], for $\forall (\mathbf{y}_i, \mathbf{z}_i), (\mathbf{y}_j, \mathbf{z}_j) \in \mathcal{V}$, if $i \neq j$, then these two pairs of vectors correspond to different attributes.

4   Revocable CP-ABE for Arithmetic Span Programs for Cloud-Assisted IoT

4.1   System and Threat Models

The responsibility of each entity involved is described as below:

- **Key generate center** is the manager of the whole system. It is responsible for generating long-term key materials for each users and broadcast key update information to non-revoked users.
- **Smart devices** are data collectors. They can be various wearable devices or personal health monitor. Each smart devices will continuously gather the personal information and uploaded the encrypted data to the cloud server.
- **Cloud server** is a powerful third-party entity for mitigating the heavy burden of data storage and management for data users.
- **Data user** is the entity that is authorized to access the shared data. Each non-revoked data user can periodically receive the key update information from key generate center to synthesize a complete decryption key.

In the R-ABE-ASP scheme, the cloud servers that are responsible for storing the user's data may curious-but-honest. It may snoop user's personal information while honestly response for user's request. Besides, the users whose attributes mismatch the access policy or has been revoked may also make efforts to eavesdrop user's sensitive data.

4.2   Design Goals

In this paper, we plan to design a secure R-CPABE-ASP scheme that can not only achieve user revocation but also enable the efficient description of access policy. For this purpose, the R-CPABE-ASP should achieve the following goals.

- Data confidentiality: The data stored on the cloud servers can only be decrypted by authorized users. It should be inaccessible to the adversary defined in the threat model.
- Efficiency: The data is supposed to be stored and shared in an efficient manner. The overhead for smart devices to encrypt the sensitive data and the cost for data users to access corresponding data should be carried out in a low-cost manner.
- Reliable access control: Considering the complex application scenarios in cloud-assisted IoT, the user revocation mechanism is also necessary except for fine-grained access control to sensitive data.

4.3 Outline of the R-CPABE-ASP

Different from the CP-ABE scheme with other access structures like LSSS, an attribute vector $\mathbf{x}$ corresponding to the attribute set S is needed in the R-CPABE-ASP scheme, which controls the various relationship between attributes and access structure. And now, we show the outline of a R-CPABE-ASP scheme that is formed with seven algorithms as below.

Setup(λ): This algorithm is executed by the key generate center to initialize the system. Taking a security parameter λ as input, the algorithm outputs the public parameter pp and the master secret key msk.

AttrKeyGen(st, pp, msk, S, $\mathbf{x}$, ID): This algorithm is executed by the key generate center to generate the attribute related key for data users. Taking the state information st, public parameter pp, the master secret key msk, an attribute set S, an attribute vector $\mathbf{x}$ and unique credential ID of a user as input, this algorithm outputs the corresponding attribute key AK_{ID}.

KeyUpdate(st, msk, t, REL): This algorithm is executed by the key generate center to produce the key update materials for each non-revoked user. Taking the state information st, the master secret key msk, current time period t and revocation list REL as input, this algorithm outputs the key update information KU_t.

KeyGen(pp, AK_{ID}, KU_t): This algorithm is executed by each users to produce the complete decryption key. Taking the public parameter pp, the attribute key AK_{ID} of a user and the key update information UK_t as input, this algorithm outputs the whole secret key sk_t.

Encrypt(pp, $(\mathcal{V}, \pi)$, msg, t): This algorithm is executed by various smart devices. Taking the public parameter pp, an arithmetic span program $(\mathcal{V}, \pi)$, a message msg and current time period t as input, the algorithm outputs the ciphertext ct_t under time period t.

Decrypt(ct_t, $sk_{t'}$, $(\mathcal{V}, \pi)$): This algorithm is carried out by the authorized data users to access the shared data. Taking a ciphertext ct_t, the secret key $sk_{t'}$ and an arithmetic span program $(\mathcal{V}, \pi)$, the algorithm outputs the message msg or a symbol $\perp$ for a failure decryption.

Revoke(REL, ID, t): This algorithm is carried out by key generate center to revoke the compromised users. Taking the revocation list REL, the credential ID of a user and current time period t, this algorithm updates the REL by adding a tuple (ID, t).

4.4 Construction

The detailed description of the proposed puncturable ciphertext-policy attribute-based encryption scheme for arithmetic span program is presented as below.

- Setup(λ, ℓ, N): On input a security parameter λ, the maximum length of the time period ℓ and the maximum users of the system N, this algorithm sets a bilinear group generator $\mathcal{G}$ and computes $(\mathbb{G}, \mathbb{H}, \mathbb{G}_T, e, g, h) \leftarrow \mathcal{G}(\lambda)$. In the tuple $(\mathbb{G}, \mathbb{H}, \mathbb{G}_T, e, g, h)$, there exists a map $e : \mathbb{G} \times \mathbb{H} \rightarrow \mathbb{G}_T$, and g, h are the generators of $\mathbb{G}$ and $\mathbb{H}$, respectively. In addition, this algorithm selects a hash function $H : \{0,1\}^* \rightarrow \mathbb{Z}_p$ and some parameters $\mathbf{C}_1 \leftarrow_R \mathbb{Z}_p^3, \mathbf{D} \leftarrow_R \mathbb{Z}_p^2, \mathbf{K}, \mathbf{K}_0, \mathbf{K}_1, \mathbf{K}', \mathbf{K}_0', \mathbf{K}_1', \mathbf{L}_0, \vartheta_1, \cdots, \vartheta_\ell \leftarrow_R \mathbb{Z}_p^{3\times 2}, \alpha_1, \alpha_2 \leftarrow_R \mathbb{Z}_p^3$ randomly. Then, this algorithm picks a binary tree BT with N leaf nodes that are used to store the information of users and initialize an empty list REL to record the revoked user's credential, as well as the state information $\mathsf{st} = \mathsf{BT}$. Finally, this algorithm outputs the public parameter as $pp = (g, h, H, g^{\mathbf{C}_1^\top}, g^{\mathbf{C}_1^\top \mathbf{K}}, g^{\mathbf{C}_1^\top \mathbf{K}_0}, g^{\mathbf{C}_1^\top \mathbf{K}_1}, g^{\mathbf{C}_1^\top \mathbf{K}'}, g^{\mathbf{C}_1^\top \mathbf{K}_0'}, g^{\mathbf{C}_1^\top \mathbf{K}_1'}, g^{\mathbf{C}_1^\top \mathbf{L}_0}, e(g^{\mathbf{C}_1^\top}, h^{\alpha_1}), e(g^{\mathbf{C}_1^\top}, h^{\alpha_2}), \vartheta_1, \cdots, \vartheta_\ell)$ and the master secret key as $msk = (\mathbf{C}_1, \mathbf{D}, \mathbf{K}, \mathbf{K}_0, \mathbf{K}_1, \mathbf{K}', \mathbf{K}_0', \mathbf{K}_1', \mathbf{L}_0, \alpha_1, \alpha_2)$.
- AttrKeyGen($\mathsf{st}, pp, msk, S, \mathbf{x}, \mathsf{ID}$): On input the state information st, public parameter pp, the master secret key msk, an attribute set S, an attribute vector x and the unique credential ID of the user that generated by the system when the user joins for the first time, this algorithm arbitrarily assigns an unused leaf node δ of BT to store the information of this user. After that, for each node $\varrho \in \mathsf{Path}(\delta)$, this algorithm picks an random vector $\boldsymbol{\xi}_\varrho$ and stores it in this node. Then, this algorithm further calculates $IK_\varrho = h^{\boldsymbol{\xi}_\varrho}$. Subsequently, this algorithm samples $\mathbf{b}, \{\mathbf{b}_y, \mathbf{b}_y'\}_{y \in S} \leftarrow_R \mathsf{span}(\mathbf{D})$ and then computes

$$K_0 = h^{\mathbf{b}}, \{K_{0,y} = h^{\mathbf{b}_y}, K_{0,y}' = h^{\mathbf{b}_y'}\}_{y \in S},$$

$$\{K_{1,y} = h^{(\mathbf{K}+x_y \mathbf{K}')\mathbf{b} + (\mathbf{K}_0 + H(y)\mathbf{K}_1)\mathbf{b}_y + x_y(\mathbf{K}_0' + H(y)\mathbf{K}_1')\mathbf{b}_y'}\}_{y \in S}, K_2 = h^{\alpha_1 - \mathbf{L}_0 \mathbf{b}}.$$

Finally, this algorithm outputs the attribute key $AK_{\mathsf{ID}} = \{K, IK_\varrho\}_{\varrho \in \mathsf{Path}(\delta)}$ where $K = (K_0, \{K_{0,y}, K_{0,y}', K_{1,y}\}_{y \in S}, K_2)$.
- KeyUpdate($\mathsf{st}, msk, t, \mathsf{REL}$): For each node $\varrho \in \mathsf{KUNodes}(\mathsf{BT}, \mathsf{RL}, t)$, this algorithm retrieves the random vector $\boldsymbol{\xi}_\varrho$ stored from the node ϱ. After that, it generates the key update information as follows:

$$KU_{\varrho,0} = h^{\alpha_2 - \boldsymbol{\xi}_\varrho} \cdot h^{\sum\limits_{k \in \Upsilon} \vartheta_k \cdot \tau_{\varrho,1}}, KU_{\varrho,1} = h^{\tau_{\varrho,1}},$$

where $\Upsilon = \{k | t(k) = 0\}$ and $\tau_{\varrho,1} \leftarrow_R \mathbb{Z}_p^{2\times 1}$ is randomly picked. Finally, this algorithm outputs key update information $KU_t = \{\varrho, KU_{\varrho,0}, KU_{\varrho,1}\}_{\varrho \in \mathsf{KUNodes}(\mathsf{BT}, \mathsf{RL}, t)}$.
- Keygen($pp, AK_{\mathsf{ID}, KU_t}$): For each node $\varrho \in \mathsf{Path}(\delta) \cap \mathsf{KUNodes}(\mathsf{BT}, \mathsf{RL}, t)$, this algorithm picks $\tau_1 \leftarrow_R \mathbb{Z}_p^{2\times 1}$ and calculates the time-related decryption key

$$K_{\mathsf{ID}, t} = (IK_\varrho \cdot KU_{\varrho,0} \cdot h^{\sum\limits_{k \in \Upsilon} \vartheta_k \cdot \tau_1}, KU_{\varrho,1} \cdot h^{\tau_1}),$$

where $\varUpsilon = \{k|t(k) = 0\}$. Finally, this algorithm outputs the whole decryption key $sk_t = (K_0, \{K_{0,y}, K'_{0,y}, K_{1,y}\}_{y\in S}, K_2, K_{\mathsf{ID},t})$.

- Encrypt$(pp, (\mathcal{V}, \pi), msg, t)$: Note that, $\mathcal{V} = (\mathbf{y}_j, \mathbf{z}_j)_{j\in[n]}$, and π is a map from $(\mathbf{y}_j, \mathbf{z}_j)$ to A. Let l denote the length of the vectors in $(\mathcal{V}, \pi)$. After receiving the public parameter pp, an arithmetic span program $(\mathcal{V}, \pi)$ satisfying with an attribute set A and a message $msg \in \mathbb{G}_T$, this algorithm performs below. This algorithm samples $\mathbf{L} \leftarrow_R \mathbb{Z}_p^{(l-1)\times 2}$, $s, \{s_j\}_{j\in[n]}$, $s_t \leftarrow_R \mathbb{Z}_p$ and then computes

$$C_0 = g^{s\mathbf{C}_1^\top}, C_{0,j} = g^{s_j\mathbf{C}_1^\top}, C_{1,j} = g^{\mathbf{y}_j\left(s\mathbf{C}_1^\top \mathbf{L}_0 \mathbf{L}\right)+s_j\mathbf{C}_1^\top \mathbf{K}},$$

$$C'_{1,j} = g^{\mathbf{z}_j\left(\begin{smallmatrix}s\mathbf{C}_1^\top \mathbf{L}_0\\\mathbf{L}\end{smallmatrix}\right)+s_j\mathbf{C}_1^\top \mathbf{K}'}, C_{2,j} = g^{s_j\mathbf{C}_1^\top(\mathbf{K}_0+H(\pi(j))\cdot\mathbf{K}_1)},$$

$$C'_{2,j} = g^{s_j\mathbf{C}_1^\top(\mathbf{K}'_0+H(\pi(j))\cdot\mathbf{K}'_1)}, C_3 = msg \cdot e(g,h)^{s\mathbf{C}_1^\top \alpha_1} \cdot e(g,h)^{s_t\mathbf{C}_1^\top \alpha_2},$$

$$C_4 = g^{-s_t\cdot\mathbf{C}_1^\top}, C_5 = g^{\mathbf{C}_1^\top \sum_{k\in\varUpsilon} \vartheta_k \cdot s_t}, \varUpsilon \in \{k|t(k) = 0\}.$$

Finally, this algorithm outputs the ciphertext $ct_t = (C_0, \{C_{0,j}, C_{1,j}, C_{2,j}, C'_{1,j}, C'_{2,j}\}_{j\in[n]}, C_3, C_4, C_5)$ under time period t.

- Decrypt$(ct_t, sk_{t'}, (\mathcal{V}, \pi))$: This algorithm aborts as $t' < t$. Or else, if the attribute vector $\mathbf{x}$ satisfies the arithmetic span program $(\mathcal{V}, \pi)$, this algorithm computes $\gamma_1, \gamma_2, \cdots \in \mathbb{Z}_p$ such that $\sum_{j\in[n]} \gamma_j(\mathbf{y}_j+x_{\pi(j)}\mathbf{z}_j) = (1, 0, \cdots, 0)$. On input a ciphertext associated and a secret key sk, this algorithm computes

$$Y_j = e(C_{1,j} \cdot C'^{x_{\pi(j)}}_{1,j}, K_0) \cdot e(C_{2,j}, K_{0,\pi(j)}) \cdot$$

$$e(C'^{x_{\pi(j)}}_{2,j}, K'_{0,\pi(j)}) \cdot e(C_{0,j}, K_{1,\pi(j)})^{-1}$$

$$A = e(C_0, K_2) \cdot \prod_{j\in[n]} Y_j^{\gamma_j}, B = e(C_4, K_{\mathsf{ID},t',1}) \cdot e(C_5, K_{\mathsf{ID},t',2}), \varUpsilon = \{k|t(k) = 0\},$$

and recovers the message as $msg = \frac{C_3 \cdot B}{A}$.

- Revoke$(\mathsf{REL}, \mathsf{ID}, t)$: After receiving a tuple (ID, t), this algorithm updates REL by inserting this tuple to revocation list and outputs updated list REL.

Limited by the space, the detailed security proof of R-CPABE-ASP is given in the full version of our paper [31], and omitted here.

4.5 Outsourced Version of R-CPABE-ASP Scheme

In this section, a outsourced R-CPABE-ASP (OR-CPABE-ASP) scheme is proposed. The OR-CPABE-ASP scheme consists the following 8 algorithms:

The Setup, AttrKeyGen, Keygen, Encrypt and Revoke algorithms are the same as R-CPABE-ASP scheme. The only difference is the outsourced R-CPABE-ASP scheme has following three algorithms:

Keygen.rand(sk_t): The algorithm samples $\tau \in \mathbb{Z}_p$ and computes $\bar{K}_0 = K_0^\tau, \{\bar{K}_{0,y} = K_{0,y}^\tau, \bar{K}'_{0,y} = K_{0,y}'^\tau, \bar{K}_{1,y} = K_{1,y}^\tau\}_{y \in S}, \bar{K}_2 = K_2^\tau, \bar{K}_{\mathsf{ID},t} = K_{\mathsf{ID},t}^\tau$. Finally, it sets $\bar{sk}_t = \{\bar{K}_0, \{\bar{K}_{0,y}, \bar{K}'_{0,y}, \bar{K}_{1,y}\}_{y \in S}, \bar{K}_2, \bar{K}_{\mathsf{ID},t}\}$ as the conversion key and outputs $(\bar{sk}_t, \tau)$ as the retrieval key.

Decrypt.out($ct_t, \bar{sk}_{t'}, (\mathcal{V}, \pi)$): This algorithm aborts as $t' < t$. Or else, if the attribute vector $\mathbf{x}$ satisfies the arithmetic span program $(\mathcal{V}, \pi)$, this algorithm computes $\gamma_1, \gamma_2, \cdots \in \mathbb{Z}_p$ such that $\sum_{j \in [n]} \gamma_j(\mathbf{y}_j + x_{\pi(j)}\mathbf{z}_j) = (1, 0, \cdots, 0)$. On input a ciphertext associated and a secret key sk, this algorithm computes

$$A = e(C_0, \bar{K}_2) \cdot \prod_{j \in [n]} \left[(e(C_{1,j} \cdot C_{1,j}'^{x_{\pi(j)}}, \bar{K}_0) \cdot e(C_{2,j}, \bar{K}_{0,\pi(j)}) \right]^{\gamma_j}$$
$$\cdot \left[e(C_{2,j}'^{x_{\pi(j)}}, \bar{K}'_{0,\pi(j)}) \cdot e(C_{0,j}, \bar{K}_{1,\pi(j)})^{-1}) \right]^{\gamma_j},$$

$$B = e(C_4, \bar{K}_{\mathsf{ID},t',1}) \cdot e(C_5, \bar{K}_{\mathsf{ID},t',2}), \Upsilon = \{k | \tilde{t}(k) = 0\}, \bar{C}_3 = C_3, \bar{C}' = \frac{B}{A}$$

and outputs $\bar{ct} = (\bar{C}_3, \bar{C}')$

Decrypt.user($\bar{ct}, \tau$): The algorithm recover the message as $msg = (\bar{C}_3/\bar{C})'^{-\tau}$.

4.6 Rationales Discuss

- Data confidentiality: according to the detailed security analysis displayed in the full version of our paper [31], our R-CPABE-ASP is adaptively secure against an adversary who has no corresponding attribution set or was revoked in the prior time period. Thereby, the presented R-CPABE-ASP scheme meets the requirement of data confidentiality.
- Efficiency: because of the introduction of ASP access structure, the access policy involved in the encryption phase can be defined in a more efficient way than the works adopting normal access structure. Hence, encryption efficiency is significantly improved by reducing the redundant description of the access policy. Meanwhile, as shown in the outsourced version of the R-CPABE-ASP, the decryption cost for data users is merely one exponential operation. By considering this, both the encryption efficiency and decryption efficiency are effectively assured in R-CPABE-ASP.
- Reliable access control: the compromised user can be efficiently revoked in the R-CPABE-ASP since the adoption of the user revocation mechanism. Hence, the reliability of data access is assured in R-CPABE-ASP.

5 Performance Evaluation

After the concrete construction of our OR-CPABE-ASP, an outsourced version of the OR-CPABE-ASP is given to mitigate the heavy decryption burden for users in our scheme. In this part, we mainly consider the OR-CPABE-ASP version for meeting the requirement of efficiency in cloud-assisted IoT scenarios. For making

Table 1. Properties and efficiency comparison among the works

Scheme	QZZC [20]	XYML [21]	CDLQ [22]	OR-CPABE-ASP
Revocation model	Indirect	Indirect	Indirect	Indirect
Security	Selective	Selective	Selective	Adaptive
Decryption key size	$(2\|S\|+5)\|\mathbb{G}\|$	$(2\|S\|+3)\|\mathbb{G}\|$	$(2\|S\|+3)\|\mathbb{G}\|$	$(10+7\|S\|)\|\mathbb{H}\|$
Ciphertext size	$\|\mathbb{G}\|+(3\|A\|+2)\|\mathbb{G}\|$	$\|\mathbb{G}_T\|+(3\|A\|+\|V\|+2)\|\mathbb{G}\|$	$\|\mathbb{G}_T\|+(3\|A\|+2)\|\mathbb{G}\|$	$9(1+\|A\|)\|\mathbb{G}\|$
Update key size	$2\|\mathbb{G}\|$	$2\|\mathbb{G}\|$	$2\|\mathbb{G}\|$	$5\|\mathbb{G}\|$
Encryption cost	$E_T+(4\|A\|+2)E_G$	$E_T+(5\|A\|+\|V\|+2)E_G$	$E_T+(4\|A\|+2)E_G$	$2E_T+(11\|A\|+8)E_G$
Decryption cost	$2P$	$(3\|A\|+2)P+\|A\|E_T$	E_T	E_T
Key update cost	$2E_G$	$(\|S\|+4)E_G$	$2E_G$	$5E_H$

an overall performance evaluation in terms of our OR-CPABE-ASP and the state-of-the-art works[1], both theoretical analysis and experimental simulations are carried out.

5.1 Theoretical Analysis

The detailed comparisons in terms of essential properties, communication and computation efficiency are summarized in Table 1. In this table, $|S|$ represents the number of attributes held by the user; $|A|$ is the size of attributes involved in the access policy; $|V|$ is the size of bits with the value of 0 in a time period string; $|\mathbb{G}|$, $|\mathbb{H}|$ and $|\mathbb{G}_T|$ denote the size of one element in group $\mathbb{G}$, $\mathbb{H}$ and $\mathbb{G}_T$; $E_{\mathbb{G}}$, $E_{\mathbb{H}}$ and E_T present one exponential operations in groups $\mathbb{G}$, $\mathbb{H}$ and $\mathbb{G}_T$, separately.

From the results of Table 1, all the works of QZZC [20], XYML [21], CDLQ [22] and ours adopt the indirect model to achieve user revocation. According to the results displayed in Table 1, it is fair to make a summary that both the works of QZZC [20] and CDLQ [22] outperform our OR-CPABE-ASP work in decryption key size, ciphertext size, update key size, data encryption efficiency and key update efficiency. Nonetheless, the works of QZZC [20] and CDLQ [22] only achieves selective security, which is too strict to handle the real-life security threats. Furthermore, our OR-CPABE-ASP scheme is more efficient in terms of data decryption than that in work of QZZC [20]. In QZZC [20], users need to carry out two heavy pairing operations to access the data stored on the cloud servers. While the cost for users to access the data is merely one exponential operation in our work. On the other hand, it is straightforward to see that the OR-CPABE-ASP scheme performs well in terms of security, ciphertext size, encryption efficiency and key update efficiency compared with XYML [21]. In XYML [21], the overhead for data encryption is affected by the value of current time period. The time period in their work is re-encoded as a binary string. During the phase of data encryption, the bits with a value of 0 in the time period string will induce extra exponential operations. In the worst case that all

---

[1] Denote the works of Qin *et al.* [20], Xu *et al.* [21] and Cui *et al.* [22] by QZZC, XYML and CDLQ, respectively.

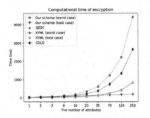
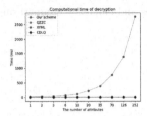
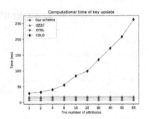

Fig. 1. Encryption cost   **Fig. 2.** Decryption cost   **Fig. 3.** Key update cost

bits of the time period string are with the value of 0, the resulting overheads for data encryption and ciphertext delivery will come to an unacceptably high level. By considering this, only our proposed OR-CPABE-ASP work is secure, efficient and feasible in the complex real-life cloud-assisted IoT scenarios.

5.2   Experimental Simulations

To discuss the feasibility and efficiency of the OR-CPABE-ASP work in a more comprehensive manner, the simulations for testing the computation efficiency are conducted in this section. We implement all the works with the PBC library on a Win 10 operation system installed with an Core i7-7700 @3.60 GHz processor and 8 G RAM. The results of simulations are shown in Fig. 1, Fig. 2 and Fig. 3.

The data encryption efficiency comparison among the works is shown in Fig. 1. In particular, we simulate XYML [21] and our OR-CPABE-ASP work under the extreme conditions. In XYML [21], data encryption cost is related to the length of bits with value of 0 in the current time period string. In this way, as all the bits are with value of 1, their work enjoy the best efficiency in terms of data encryption. On the contrary, if all the bits are with value of 0, the cost for data encryption is at ist maximum. Since the more expressive ASP access structure is introduced in our proposed work, hence there are also two cases in the data encryption phase of OR-CPABE-ASP work. The reason is that our OR-CPABE-ASP work is a ciphertext-policy variant of ABE. The data encryption cost will be affected by the expressiveness of the access structure. For instance, the access structure specifies that the user who has the 5 of 10 attributes is able to access the data. In traditional access structure, such as LSSS, all the possible attribute combinations are traversed to test whether a user owns the corresponding attributes (the worst case of our OR-CPABE-ASP work). However, in ASP access structure, the access policy can be easily described as the arithmetic expression results of these attributes. In other words, the involved attributes are merely required once such that the cost for defining the access policy is significantly reduced (the best cast of our work). Obviously, the OR-CPABE-ASP work is more efficient in data encryption than the state-of-the-art works [20–22] according to Fig. 1. It is easy to see that our OR-CPABE-ASP work is almost unaffected by the number of attributes involved in access policy.

Compared with the existing works [20–22] where the encryption overhead increases dramatically with the growth of the attribute's number, the OR-CPABE-ASP scheme is more applicable to the cloud-assisted IoT scenarios where the access policy for ciphertext may be complicated.

The cost for data decryption is shown in Fig. 2. From the details displayed in Fig. 2, the cost for data decryption in XYML [21] is affected by the number of attributes involved. In a sharp contrary, QZZC [20], CDLQ [22] and the OR-CPABE-ASP work keep a low and constant overhead in data decryption. A similar trend is also demonstrated during the phase of key update as shown in Fig. 3. It is worth noting that the OR-CPABE-ASP scheme owns the best efficiency in terms of the key update for each non-revoked user.

As described above, our proposed OR-CPABE-ASP work outperforms the state-of-the-art works in both the efficiency of encryption and decryption, which makes the possibility of fast data storage and convenient data access in our work. Taking into this account, our work is expected to achieve efficient data storage and sharing in cloud-assisted IoT environments compared with the state-of-the-art works utilizing similar underlying primitive.

6   Conclusion

In this paper, we construct the first revocable CP-ABE for arithmetic span programs (R-CPABE-ASP) for cloud-assisted IoT. Compared with existing revocable ABE works, the proposed R-CPABE-ASP scheme has the ability to describe the complicated access policy in an easier manner by adopting arithmetic span programs access structure. Hence, the data encryption efficiency in the R-CPABE-ASP work can be significantly enhanced. Meanwhile, we also show how to mitigate the heavy data decryption burden for users by giving an outsourced version of the R-CPABE-ASP scheme. Finally, the detailed theoretical analysis and experimental simulations demonstrate that our R-CPABE-ASP is secure and efficient in cloud-assisted IoT.

Acknowledgement. This work was supported in part by the Natural Science Foundation of China under Grant U1936101 and the 13th Five-Year Plan of National Cryptography Development Fund for Cryptographic Theory of China under Grant MMJJ20170204.

References

1. Farhan, M., et al.: IoT-based students interaction framework using attention-scoring assessment in elearning. Future Gener. Comput. Syst. **79**, 909–919 (2018)
2. Yu, S.: Big privacy: challenges and opportunities of privacy study in the age of big data. IEEE Access **4**, 2751–2763 (2016)
3. Yu, S., Liu, M., Dou, W., Liu, X., Zhou, S.: Networking for big data: a survey. IEEE Commun. Surv. Tutorials **19**(1), 531–549 (2016)

4. Xiong, H., et al.: Heterogeneous signcryption with equality test for IIoT environment. IEEE Internet Things J. (2020). https://doi.org/10.1109/JIOT.2020.3008955

5. Xiong, H., Bao, Y., Nie, X., Asoor, Y.I.: Server-aided attribute-based signature supporting expressive access structures for industrial Internet of Things. IEEE Trans. Ind. Inform. **16**(2), 1013–1023 (2019)

6. Xiong, H., Wu, Y., Jin, C., Kumari, S.: Efficient and privacy-preserving authentication protocol for heterogeneous systems in IIoT. IEEE Internet of Things J. (2020). https://doi.org/10.1109/JIOT.2020.2999510

7. Belguith, S., Kaaniche, N., Russello, G.: PU-ABE: lightweight attribute-based encryption supporting access policy update for cloud assisted IoT. In: 11th IEEE International Conference on Cloud Computing, CLOUD 2018, San Francisco, CA, USA, 2–7 July 2018, pp. 924–927. IEEE Computer Society (2018)

8. Lee, C., Chung, P., Hwang, M.: A survey on attribute-based encryption schemes of access control in cloud environments. I. J. Netw. Secur. **15**(4), 231–240 (2013)

9. Fu, A., Yu, S., Zhang, Y., Wang, H., Huang, C.: NPP: a new privacy-aware public auditing scheme for cloud data sharing with group users. IEEE Trans. Big Data (2017). https://doi.org/10.1109/TBDATA.2017.2701347

10. Mei, Q., Xiong, H., Chen, J., Yang, M., Kumari, S., Khan, M.K.: Efficient certificateless aggregate signature with conditional privacy preservation in IoV. IEEE Syst. J. (2020). https://doi.org/10.1109/JSYST.2020.2966526

11. Sahai, A., Waters, B.: Fuzzy identity based encryption. IACR Cryptology ePrint Archive, vol. 2004, p. 86 (2004)

12. Goyal, V., Pandey, O., Sahai, A., Waters, B.: Attribute-based encryption for fine-grained access control of encrypted data. In: Proceedings of the 13th ACM Conference on Computer and Communications Security (CCS 2006), pp. 89–98 (2006)

13. Kaaniche, N., Laurent, M.: Privacy-preserving multi-user encrypted access control scheme for cloud-assisted IoT applications. In: 2018 IEEE 11th International Conference on Cloud Computing (CLOUD), pp. 590–597. IEEE (2018)

14. Li, J., Zhang, Y., Ning, J., Huang, X., Poh, G.S., Wang, D.: Attribute based encryption with privacy protection and accountability for cloudIoT. IEEE Trans. Cloud Comput. (2020). https://doi.org/10.1109/TCC.2020.2975184

15. Goyal, V., Pandey, O., Sahai, A., Waters, B.: Attribute-based encryption for fine-grained access control of encrypted data. IACR Cryptology ePrint Archive vol. 2006, p. 309 (2006)

16. Ostrovsky, R., Sahai, A., Waters, B.: Attribute-based encryption with non-monotonic access structures. In: Ning, P., di Vimercati, S.D.C., Syverson, P.F., (eds.) Proceedings of the 2007 ACM Conference on Computer and Communications Security, CCS 2007, Alexandria, Virginia, USA, 28–31 October 2007, pp. 195–203. ACM (2007)

17. Xiong, H., Choo, K.-K.R., Vasilakos, A.V.: Revocable identity-based access control for big data with verifiable outsourced computing. IEEE Trans. Big Data (2017). https://doi.org/10.1109/TBDATA.2017.2697448

18. Zhang, Y., Chen, X., Li, J., Li, H., Li, F.: FDR-ABE: attribute-based encryption with flexible and direct revocation. In: 2013 5th International Conference on Intelligent Networking and Collaborative Systems, pp. 38–45. IEEE (2013)

19. Wu, A., Zheng, D., Zhang, Y., Yang, M.: Hidden policy attribute-based data sharing with direct revocation and keyword search in cloud computing. Sensors **18**(7), 2158 (2018)

20. Qin, B., Zhao, Q., Zheng, D., Cui, H.: (dual) server-aided revocable attribute-based encryption with decryption key exposure resistance. Inf. Sci. **490**, 74–92 (2019)

21. Xu, S., Yang, G., Mu, Y., Liu, X.: A secure IoT cloud storage system with fine-grained access control and decryption key exposure resistance. Future Gen. Comput. Syst. **97**, 284–294 (2019)
22. Cui, H., Deng, R.H., Li, Y., Qin, B.: Server-aided revocable attribute-based encryption. In: Askoxylakis, I., Ioannidis, S., Katsikas, S., Meadows, C. (eds.) ESORICS 2016. LNCS, vol. 9879, pp. 570–587. Springer, Cham (2016). https://doi.org/10. 1007/978-3-319-45741-3_29
23. Wei, J., Chen, X., Huang, X., Hu, X., Susilo, W.: RS-HABE: revocable-storage and hierarchical attribute-based access scheme for secure sharing of e-health records in public cloud. IEEE Trans. Dependable Secur. Comput. (2019). https://doi.org/10. 1109/TDSC.2019.2947920
24. Attrapadung, N., Hanaoka, G., Yamada, S.: Conversions among several classes of predicate encryption and applications to ABE with various compactness tradeoffs. In: Iwata, T., Cheon, J.H. (eds.) ASIACRYPT 2015. LNCS, vol. 9452, pp. 575–601. Springer, Heidelberg (2015). https://doi.org/10.1007/978-3-662-48797-6_24
25. Chen, J., Gong, J., Kowalczyk, L., Wee, H.: Unbounded ABE via bilinear entropy expansion, revisited. In: Nielsen, J.B., Rijmen, V. (eds.) EUROCRYPT 2018. LNCS, vol. 10820, pp. 503–534. Springer, Cham (2018). https://doi.org/10.1007/ 978-3-319-78381-9_19
26. Ishai, Y., Wee, H.: Partial garbling schemes and their applications. In: Esparza, J., Fraigniaud, P., Husfeldt, T., Koutsoupias, E. (eds.) ICALP 2014. LNCS, vol. 8572, pp. 650–662. Springer, Heidelberg (2014). https://doi.org/10.1007/978-3-662-43948-7_54
27. Ma, C., Gao, H., Wei, D.: A CP-ABE scheme supporting arithmetic span programs. Secur. Commun. Netw. **2020**, 1–16 (2020)
28. Attrapadung, N.: Dual system encryption via doubly selective security: framework, fully secure functional encryption for regular languages, and more. In: Nguyen, P.Q., Oswald, E. (eds.) EUROCRYPT 2014. LNCS, vol. 8441, pp. 557–577. Springer, Heidelberg (2014). https://doi.org/10.1007/978-3-642-55220-5_31
29. Escala, A., Herold, G., Kiltz, E., Rafols, C., Villar, J.: An algebraic framework for Diffie-Hellman assumptions. J. Crypto. **30**(1), 242–288 (2017)
30. Chen, J., Gay, R., Wee, H.: Improved dual system ABE in prime-order groups via predicate encodings. In: Oswald, E., Fischlin, M. (eds.) EUROCRYPT 2015. LNCS, vol. 9057, pp. 595–624. Springer, Heidelberg (2015). https://doi.org/10. 1007/978-3-662-46803-6_20
31. Xiong, H., Chen, J., Yang, M., Huang, X.: Revocable attribute-based encryption scheme with arithmetic span program for cloud-assisted IoT. IACR Cryptology ePrint Archive, 2020:553 **2020**, 553 (2020)

A Multi-data Collaborative Encryption in Concealed Data Aggregation for WSNs

Li Ma, Jia Geng[✉], Dongchao Ma, Yingxun Fu, and Ailing Xiao

School of Information Science and Technology, North China University of Technology,
Beijing 100144, China
1083092784@qq.com

Abstract. With the rapid development of the collection devices connected to the Internet of Things, data security has become more important. The sensor node located at the original location of the sensing data is often at the risk of various attacks, because it not only is a data source but also has limited computing power and shortage of energy. As a way to effectively improve the existing problems, secure data aggregation can reduce the energy of wireless sensor network transmission, and how to ensure network security has become a hot spot in research. Through analysis, a concealed data aggregation method suitable for multi-data collaborative encryption is proposed. Its main advantage is that it can simultaneously encrypt n kinds of heterogeneous data, and the base station at the receiving end can completely reconstruct it and separate it effectively and correctly. This method encrypts different types of data at the bottom node at one time, the calculation overhead and resource occupation are relatively small. It is suitable for resource-constrained nodes to ensure the safe use of data. Through simulation experiments and comparison with RCDA-HOMO and Sham Share, the results show that the proposed method is in a reasonable range of energy consumption and processing time on the basis of ensuring the encryption of multiple types of data. It is an effective multi-data aggregation scheme, which has the value of popularization and application on the nodes with limited computing power and resources.

Keywords: Data aggregation · Multi-data · Collaborative · WSN

1 Introduction

Wireless sensor networks (WSNs) composed of thousands of sensor nodes with limited power, computation, bandwidth and memory are often deployed in areas that are not suitable for human activities to carry out military surveillance, disaster monitoring, weather forecast, etc. [1] Due to the fact that there is no one on duty to replace the battery or charge [2], extending the life cycle of the node has become a hot spot in research. It has been found through research that the energy consumed by data during transmission is a thousand times more than that consumed during data processing. Therefore, reducing the energy consumption of sensors in data transmission is a feasible way to prolong the life cycle of WSNs [3].

S. Yu et al. (Eds.): SPDE 2020, CCIS 1268, pp. 384–398, 2020.
https://doi.org/10.1007/978-981-15-9129-7_27

Data aggregation [4], as one of the technologies to help minimize the energy consumption of sensors, refers to the process of collecting data and presenting data in summary form. By using this technology, data perceived by multiple member nodes can be aggregated into one data. The communication cost is reduced and the lifetime of WSNs is prolonged [5]. With the deepening of research and the continuous advancement of technology, WSNs have been applied to areas close to human life, such as health monitoring, drug management, and smart home [6], which leads to explosive growth of data [7]. But what comes with it is people's privacy has been threatened. During transmission, data carrying important sensitive information may faces different kinds of attacks, such as DDoS [8–10] and if the data is intercepted or illegally tampered with, it will cause serious property damage or personal threat [11]. Facing the threat of privacy disclosure, signature authentication and encryption algorithms are introduced into the process of data aggregation.

Secure data aggregation can be divided into hop-by-hop encryption and end-to-end encryption [12]. During hop-by-hop encryption, the encrypted data is decrypted first and then aggregated at each hop, and the operation is repeated until the data is transmitted to the base station. In this process, if the aggregator compromises, the intruder will get the data, which brings security risks to WSNs. While during end-to-end encryption, the sensor nodes transmit the encrypted data to the aggregation node which directly aggregates the cipher text and sends it to the base station. The base station uniformly decrypts and obtains the cipher text. Compared with hop by hop encryption, end-to-end encryption has higher security performance and less computing energy consumption.

Many end-to-end secure data aggregation schemes have been proposed. The scheme proposed in [13] is based on the modification of [14] public-key PH encryption system. A concealed data aggregation scheme is proposed, which can aggregate the data sensed by different types of sensors without confusing them. It also provides a method to extract the correct aggregation value of a specific application. CDAMA generates multiple points with different order for every application. Keys are generated for each application by using elliptic cryptography and this set of points. So that the base station can extract the aggregated result of different application with appropriate combination of point orders. In [15], a method based on additive homomorphic and elliptic curve cryptography is proposed, which can aggregate multiple queries into a single packet so as to reduce the communication cost. Each query with a unique ID is distributed by the base station to the sensor node, the public key is sent as well. By using improved elliptic curve based additive homomorphic encryption, a method to aggregate data encrypted with different keys is proposed in [16]. The entire network terrain is divided into different areas, and each area is assigned with a separate public key, which is used to encrypt the data detected.

These schemes have shown good performance, but they all can only encrypt one data at a time. However, most sensors now can sense two or more types of data at the same time, such as temperature, humidity, light intensity, etc. Based on this, if the scheme of the above-mentioned article is used, it will be necessary to encrypt the several data with the same algorithm and transmit it separately, which not only increases communication cost but also reduces the security performance. Using this feature of the sensor, this paper proposes a new concealed data aggregation scheme that is suitable for encrypting n kinds of heterogeneous data simultaneously, and the base station at the receiving end can completely reconstruct it and separate it effectively and correctly.

In this paper, we proposed a multi-data collaborative encryption in concealed data aggregation for WSNs. First, polynomial is used to mix data of which the purpose is that when the sensor can only perceive two types of data, if it is directly multiplied with a two-dimensional full rank matrix, the data will be too easy to crack. As said, we use the matrix multiplied by the encrypted vector to encrypt and mix multiple data again for the purpose of improving the security of this method and recovering data completely. Finally, multiple data are aggregated into one attached with a random number avoiding replay attack to reduce energy consumption. Boneh et al.'s signature scheme is also used in this method to achieve end-to-end security authentication. The simulation results show that the proposed method is reliable and effective on the basis of ensuring the encryption of multiple types of data. The contributions of this article are:

1 A new concealed data aggregation scheme for multi-data cooperative encryption (namely MCEDA) is proposed.
2 Data can be completely reconstructed and separated effectively and correctly.
3 The method can effectively resist monitoring, tampering and replay attacks.

The rest of the article is arranged as follows: Sect. 2 discusses the related work. Section 3 introduces Boneh et al.'s signature scheme, attack model and variables used in this method. In Sect. 4, we propose a data aggregation method: A Multi-data Collaborative Encryption in Concealed Data Aggregation for WSNs. Section 5 discusses the safety of this method. The simulation results and analysis are given in Sect. 6. Section 7 summarizes the article.

2 Related Work

Kyung-ah Shim proposes a data aggregation method [17] based on an additive homomorphic encryption scheme and an identity-based signature scheme, which also uses batch verification techniques to reduce verification costs for multiple signatures. By applying binary quick search (BQS) to the batch verification technique, the method supports fast multiple signature verifications at the CHs for filtering injected false data. It also reveals security weaknesses of RCDA themes proposed in [18], in which the author proposes RCDA-HOMO, RCDA-HETE, and Naive RCDA-HETE.

Homomorphic encryption is widely used to protect end-to-end confidentiality, but it has the disadvantages of malleability, unauthorized aggregation, and limited aggregation functions. So Hong Zhong et al. [19] propose an efficient and secure wireless sensor network recoverable data aggregation scheme to solve the above problems by combining homomorphic encryption technology with a signature scheme which ensures that the base station can recover the original sensor data and filter the false data in the network, so as to achieve the purpose of energy saving.

A symmetric additive homomorphic encryption scheme [20] based on Rao-Nam scheme is proposed to provide data confidentiality during data aggregation in WSN. Through channel decoding problem by embedding security in encoding matrix and error vector, the scheme possesses the ability to correct errors present in the aggregated data, which is secure against all attacks reported against private-key encryption schemes based on error correcting codes.

Vimal Kumar [21] mention that elliptic curve is often used for end to end data aggregation which is feasible on a base station to decrypt but inefficient on ordinary sensors. To solve this problem, a secure data aggregation algorithm based on bilinear pairing is proposed by using the homomorphic elliptic curve encryption method.

In [22], a new multi-functional secure data aggregation scheme (MODA), is proposed to help some statistics compute efficiently in a distributed mode by encoding raw data into well-defined vectors and adopting a homomorphic encryption scheme. In addition, two enhanced and complementary schemes are proposed based on MODA, namely, RODA and CODA. RODA can significantly reduce the communication cost at the expense of slightly lower but acceptable security on a leaf node, while CODA can dramatically reduce communication cost with the lower aggregation accuracy.

In [23], a lightweight and integrity-protecting oriented data aggregation scheme which has lightweight, secure and easy operability to preserve data privacy and integrity during data aggregation in WSN is proposed. By applying an additive homomorphic encryption, this method can encrypt the complex number formed by raw data and privacy factor without any decryption when aggregating data. Moreover, a distance-based formation scheme of network topology is presented to balance the energy consumption of cluster heads.

The authors of [24] propose a method using pseudonyms mechanism with anonymous communication by hiding source node identification and apply symmetric homomorphic encryption technique to protect data. Two different data sending scheme are proposed too.

These above methods are all improved on the basis of homomorphic encryption. Although homomorphic encryption is often used in secure data aggregation, it consumes too much energy compared with lightweight encryption, which affects the whole network life cycle.

Mohamed Elhoseny et al. [25] propose a novel encryption method for wireless sensor network based on dynamic sensor clusters which leverages elliptic curve cryptography algorithm to generate binary strings for every sensor. The proposed method combines with node ID, distance to the cluster head, and the index of transmission round to form unique 176-bit encryption keys. Thus, it can overcome many security attacks including brute-force attack, HELLO flood attack, selective forwarding attack, and compromised cluster head attack.

Numbers of method based on slice mixing technology are proposed, but the authors in [26] think them are not energy-efficient enough to be suitable for WSNs. So Simin Hu et al. propose an energy-efficient and privacy-preserving data aggregation algorithm by utilizing the data slicing technology and fake fragments to confuse the adversaries, which also can resist the untrusted aggregator.

Pengwei Hua et al. [27] present an energy-efficient adaptive slice-based security data aggregation scheme in which plenty of aggregation functions, such as max, min, and average deduced from the additive aggregation function are more focused on.

A malleability resilient concealed data aggregation protocol is proposed in [28] which uses a symmetric-key based MAC and a homomorphic MAC against outsider adversaries and active insider adversaries as well as insider and outsider adversaries. It simultaneously realizes the conflicting objectives like privacy at intermediate nodes, end-to-end integrity, replay protection, and en route aggregation.

Wael Alghamdi et al. [29] propose two novel schemes for concealed data aggregation in WSNs based on secret sharing and signature which are robust against both forwarding and modification attacks. Moreover, a novel method for malicious aggregator detection using homomorphic MAC, which helps verify the integrity of aggregated data is proposed too.

The previous methods can only encrypt one at a time, but most of today's sensors can sense more than two kinds of data at the same time. Based on this, a new concealed data aggregation scheme that is suitable for encrypting n kinds of heterogeneous data simultaneously is proposed.

3 Preliminaries

Boneh et al.'s Signature Scheme [30] is used in this scheme, which can verify the authenticity of the message on the basis of reducing communication cost by the aggregation signature. It is an excellent and widely used aggregation signature scheme. In addition, this part also introduces the network model and variable meaning in the scheme.

3.1 Network Model

WSNs are composed of thousands of sensor nodes which are divided into several clusters to form a star network, as shown in Fig. 1. The sensor nodes located at the original location directly connect to the cluster head nodes which are responsible for aggregating data and sending aggregated data to the base station (Table 1).

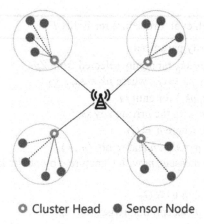

○ Cluster Head   ● Sensor Node

Fig. 1. Cluster topology

Table 1. Notations used in this article

Notion	Meaning
pki	Public Key
ski	Secret Key
x_i	Original Data
C	No.
A	Full Rank Matrix
Q	Aggregated Data
Sig	Signature
b	Cipher Text

3.2 Attack Model

The following three cases are enumerated to simulate the situation that the proposed method is attacked by the enemy:

- The adversary obtains or modifies the data transmitted in the channel by eavesdropping or tampering attacks.
- If the adversary compromises the leaf sensor node, the adversary can obtain the key of the node and make the false data to be transmitted in the network.
- If the adversary compromises the cluster head node, and the adversary can copy the aggregated content and send it to the base station.

3.3 Boneh et al.'s Signature Scheme

The scheme [30] consists of five steps: key generation, signature, verification, aggregation and verification aggregation. The specific process is as follows:

ALGORITHM 1: Boneh et al. Procedure for Entity i

·KeyGen(τ): τ is a security parameter.

   1 generate private key sk_i, randomly selected from Zp.

   2 generate public key $pk_i \in G_2$, where $pk_i = sk_i \times g_2$.

   3 output key pair (sk_i, pk_i) for entity i.

·Signx_i: sign message m with the private key sk_i :

   1 compute $h = H(m)$, where $h \in G_1$.

   2 generate signature $\sigma = sk_i \times h$ and return (m, σ).

·Verify$_{vi}(m,\sigma)$: verify message m with signature σ by public key pk_i .

   1 compute $h = H(m)$.

   2 compute $e_n(\sigma, g_2)$, $e_n(h,v_i) \in G_T$.

   3 if $e_n(\sigma, g_2) = e_n(h,v_i)$, accept; otherwise, reject.

·Agg$_k$ (δ, M): aggregate k signatures where message set $M = \{m_1, ..., m_k\}$; m_i for entity i and $\delta = \{\sigma_1, ...\sigma_k\}$; σ_i is the signature of m_i.

   1 produce aggregated signature $\sigma = \sigma_1 + \cdots + \sigma_k = \sum_{i=1}^{k} \sigma_k$, where $\sigma, \sigma_1, \cdots, \sigma_k \in G_1$.

·Agg-Verify$_\vartheta$ (σ, M): verify the aggregated signature. σ is the aggregated signature of message set M, where $M = \{m_1, \cdots, m_k\}$; m_i from entity i, and public key set $\vartheta = \{pu_1, ..., pu_k\}$; $pu_i \in U_i$.

   1 compute $h_i = H(m_i)$, for $1 \leq i \leq k$.

   2 accept if $e(\sigma, g_2) = \prod_{i=1}^{k} e(h_i, pu_i)$, where $e(\sigma, g_2), e(h_i, pu_i) \in G_T$; otherwise, reject.

---

4   The Proposed Protocol

In our method, different types of data sensed by a sensor node are encrypted together and sent to the cluster head. After the cluster head node receives all the messages from other members in the cluster, the cipher text is aggregated and sent to the base station, which verifies the authenticity of the messages and reconstructs the data.

Setup Phase

The base station prepares a pair of keys (pk_i, sk_i) used in the signature method proposed by Boneh et al. [30] for each sensor node, where pk_i is stored in the base station as a public key, and the private key ski and hash algorithm h are loaded into every sensor node. In addition, several n-dimensional full rank matrices generated by the base station will also be loaded into the node.

Signature- Encryption

When a sensor node v_i senses the change of physical environment and is ready to transmit a group of sensed data $(x_1, x_2,..., x_n)$ to the aggregation node, it will go through the following steps:

- Sensor node v_i encrypts data first:

(1) Construct the following polynomials to encrypt data.

$$f(x_1) = n * x_1$$

$$f(x_n) = f(x_{n-1}) + 1 * x_n \qquad (1)$$

(2) Generate a random number C, C is between 0 and n. The greater the n, the higher the security performance.
(3) The full rank matrix numbered C is used for mixing n kinds of data. It must be a full rank matrix to ensure that the solution to the equations is the only one, so that the data can be completely reconstructed.

$$A \cdot F(x) = b \qquad (2)$$

(4) $(b_1, b_2, \cdots, b_n)$ are calculated as follows and integrated into one data.

$$Q_i = 10^n * b_1 + 10^{n-1} * b_2 + \cdots + 10 * b_n \qquad (3)$$

(5) Generate a random number and synthesize a data M_i with Q_i.

- Sign as follows:

$$H_i = H(Q_i) \qquad (4)$$

$$Sig = pr_{vi} * h_i \qquad (5)$$

- Send (M_i, Sig_i, c_i) to cluster head.

Aggregation

When the cluster head receives messages from its cluster members, it does the following operations:

- The cluster node collects messages $(M_1, Sig_1, c_1), (M_2, Sig_2, c_2) \cdots (M_w, Sig_w, c_w)$ from its members.
- Aggregate signatures as follows:

$$s = \sum_{i=1}^{w} sig_i \qquad (6)$$

- Send the aggregated signature and the aggregated cipher text as a matrix.

$$\begin{bmatrix} S, w \\ M_1, c_0 \\ M_2, c_1 \\ \cdots \\ M_w, c_w \end{bmatrix} \tag{7}$$

Reconstruction-Verification Phase. When the base station receives the data sent from aggregation node, it starts to recover the data.

- Separate the random number, compare the new random number with the old random numbers, if equals, it has encountered a replay attack, reject.
- Reconstruction original data by the following equation.

$$\begin{bmatrix} b_{11} & b_{21} & \cdots & b_{n1} \\ b_{12} & b_{22} & \cdots & b_{n2} \\ & \cdots & \\ b_{1w} & b_{2w} & \cdots & b_{nw} \end{bmatrix} = \begin{bmatrix} Q_1/10^n (Q_1 \bmod 10^n)/10^{n-1} \cdots Q_1 \bmod 10 \\ Q_2/10^n (Q_2 \bmod 10^n)/10^{n-1} \cdots Q_2 \bmod 10 \\ \cdots \\ Q_w/10^n (Q_w \bmod 10^n)/10^{n-1} \cdots Q_w \bmod 10 \end{bmatrix} \tag{8}$$

- Solve inhomogeneous linear equations and get $f(x_1) f(x_2) \cdots f(x_n)$ by using C.

$$F(x) = A^{-1} \cdot b \tag{9}$$

- Decrypt according to the following formula to get the original data $(x_1, x_2, \cdots, x_n)$.

$$\begin{cases} x_n = f(x_n) - f(x_{n-1}) \\ x_{n-1} = (f(x_{n-1}) - f(x_{n-2}))/2 \\ \cdots \\ x_1 = f(x_1)/n \end{cases} \tag{10}$$

4.1   A Concrete Example

Now we give an example to demonstrate how MCEDA works. Suppose the data types that node1 perceives are humidity, temperature and wind speed, and their values are (*1, 3, 6*) respectively.

(1) Mix data.

$$f(x_1) = 3 * 1 = 3 f(x_2) = 9 f(x_3) = 15$$

(2) Select a full rank matrix in node randomly.

$$\begin{bmatrix} 1 & 1 & 1 \\ 1 & 0 & 1 \\ 0 & 0 & 1 \end{bmatrix} \cdot \begin{bmatrix} 1 \\ 9 \\ 15 \end{bmatrix} = b$$

(3) Aggregate data in vector b into one data.

$$27 * 10^3 + 18 * 10 + 3 = Q$$

(4) Generate a random number combined with Q to form M and Send (M, C, sig) to its cluster head.

After the cluster head gathers all the cipher text sent from its member, it sends aggregated data to BS. Once the base station receives packets, it de-aggregates the signature and verifies the data after reconstructing the original data.

(1) According to the second step of the Reconstruction-Verification Phase, use that formula to calculate the vector b.

$$b = \begin{bmatrix} 27 \\ 18 \\ 3 \end{bmatrix}$$

(2) Solve inhomogeneous linear equations.

$$\begin{bmatrix} f(x_1) \\ f(x_2) \\ f(x_3) \end{bmatrix} = \begin{bmatrix} 0 & 0 & 1 \\ 0 & -1 & 0 \\ 0 & 1 & -1 \end{bmatrix} \cdot \begin{bmatrix} 27 \\ 18 \\ 3 \end{bmatrix}$$

$$f(x_1) = 3 \quad f(x_2) = 9 \quad f(x_3) = 15$$

(3) Reconstruct to get the original data.

$$\begin{cases} x_3 = (15 - 9)/1 = 6 \\ x_2 = (9 - 3)/2 = 3 \\ x_1 = 3/3 = 1 \end{cases}$$

5 Security Analysis

This part is divided into two parts. The first part is to prove our method is safe by analyzing the three attack models mentioned in Sect. 3.2. Second, it is proved by analyzing the factors [31] that security data aggregation should ensure.

When the adversary wants to monitor or tamper with the data in the network, the real data first will become an incomprehensible form to transmit in the network after encryption, and the adversary cannot directly get the real data detected. In addition, the adversary can't sign correctly because the adversary cannot get a private key stored in the node. Once the false signature is transmitted, it will be found. In this case our approach is safe.

When the adversary compromises the sensor nodes, who does not know the encryption algorithm. While the cipher text has a fixed length basically, so the forged data will be found out if its length does not match. Even if the data forged by the opponent is of normal length, the data that is not in the reasonable range will be obtained after data reconstruction, the compromised node will also be found. In addition, no matter the adversary wants to send false data or modify data, it has to go through signature, so our method is very safe for this situation.

When the adversary compromises a cluster head, the data received by the cluster head is encrypted, so the adversary cannot get the original data directly. In addition, many cluster head election protocols have been proposed, and it turns out that dynamically changing the cluster head can extend the life cycle of the network. When the cluster head changes, the opponent can no longer use that cluster head to attack. So it seems that the proposed method is still safe in this case.

Analysis about the elements that should be satisfied by a secure data aggregation is given as following:

- Data confidentiality: Every data transmitted in the network is encrypted, so the intruder cannot directly get the original data detected by the sensors.
- Data integrity: Boneh et al.'s signature method is used. Once the data is modified, it cannot be verified, and the tampered data will be found out.
- Data freshness: Replay attack means that the attacker sends a packet that the base station has received to achieve the purpose of spoofing the system of. In MCEDA, random number matching mechanism is added to resist replay attack.
- Data availability: The proposed approach ensures that information in the network can be accessed when needed, and checks whether the system is active by eliminating the damaged nodes.
- Data accuracy: A dataset SURF_CLI_CHN_MUL_DAY_CES is used, and the relevant data of temperature, humidity and wind speed in July 2010 is selected, all of which are integers.

6   Simulation/Experimental Results

In order to verify the effectiveness of our proposed method, the following experiments are designed.

- processing time: the time from sensing data to preparing its packet.
- energy consumption: the average energy consumption on encryption and signature.
- delay: the time from sensing data to the completion of data reconstruction by the base station.
- lifetime: time until the first sensor node depletes its energy.

The simulation platform used is OMNeT++ 5.5.1. Six groups of experiments from 50 to 300 in increments of 50 is recorded. The nodes are deployed in a space of 500 m^2 × 500 m^2 with 100 J initial energy to record the process from the start to the end of the WSNs. The energy consumption for 1 bit of data for transmission is 0.66 mJ, 0.3 mJ for receiving 1bit of data, and 0.22 μJ for 1bit of data to process.

Two secure data aggregation methods are chosen to compare with MCEDA to evaluate the effectiveness of the proposed method. RCDA-HOMO is a very classical recoverable secure data aggregation method which uses a network model similar to MCEDA

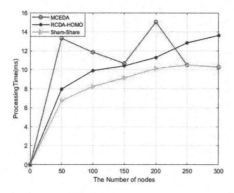

Fig. 2. Processing time

and Boneh et al.'s signature method. Although Sham-Share uses a different network model, it is a very excellent method recently proposed by Wael Alghamdi et al.

Figure 2 shows the average processing time of the three methods. It can be seen from the figure that the processing time of MCEDA is slightly longer than that of RCDA-HOMO and Sham-Share. In the case of 50 and 200 nodes, the processing time of MCEDA is 13.320095 ms and 15.031303 ms, respectively, 167.35% and 133.23% of RCDA-HOMO. Although the performance of MCEDA in processing time is not very good, it is worth noting, taking our simulation experiment as an example, that the processing time of MCEDA counts the time of encrypting three kinds of data at the same time, while The remaining two methods can only encrypt one data once.

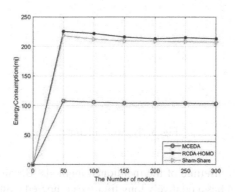

Fig. 3. Energy consumption

As shown in Fig. 3, it can be seen that the average energy consumption of MCEDA is significantly lower than that of RCDA-HOMO and Sham-Share, which are 104.716 mJ, 217.263 mJ and 210.573 mJ, respectively. This is because Sham-Share uses the method of secret sharing that has to send data twice, which leads to high energy consumption. The energy consumption of RCDA-HOMO is due to asymmetric encryption.

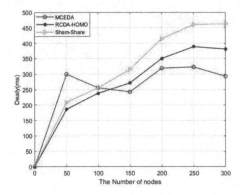

Fig. 4. Delay

As shown in Fig. 4, the delay of RCDA-HOMO and Sham-Share is basically increasing in proportion, while the delay of MCEDA at the beginning is slightly larger than that of the other two methods, which is lower than that of the other two methods with the increasement of nodes. The average delay of MCEDA, RCDA-HOMO and Sham-Share are 288.8039 ms, 302.74779 ms and 353.01136 ms, respectively.

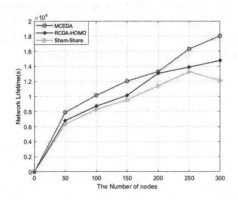

Fig. 5. Network lifetime

Figure 5 shows the lifetime of the mentioned methods. Because MCEDA has less energy consumption, it has a relatively long lifetime compared with the other two methods. The average lifetime of MCEDA, RCDA-HOMO and Sham-Share were 12934.33 s, 11220.5 s and 10146 s, respectively.

7 Conclusion

In this paper, we mainly introduce a new secure data aggregation method which is suitable for multi-data cooperative encryption. Its main advantage is it can simultaneously encrypt n kinds of heterogeneous data, and the base station at the receiving end can completely reconstruct it and separate it effectively and correctly. This method encrypts different types of data at the bottom node at one time, the calculation overhead and resource occupation are relatively small. Although we add signature scheme that consumes extra energy, the simulation results show that our method is suitable for wireless sensor networks.

Acknowledgements. This work was supported by National Key R&D Program of China (2018YFB1800302), Natural Science Foundation of China (61702013), Beijing Natural Science Foundation (KZ201810009011), Science and Technology Innovation Project of North China University of Technology (19XN108).

References

1. Cui, J., Shao, L., Zhong, H., Xu, Y., Liu, L.: Data aggregation with end-to-end confidentiality and integrity for large-scale wireless sensor networks. Peer-to-Peer Netw. Appl. 11(5), 1–16 (2017). https://doi.org/10.1007/s12083-017-0581-5
2. Singh, V.K., Singh, V.K., Kumar, M.: In-network data processing based on compressed sensing in WSN: a survey. Wireless Pers. Commun. 96(2), 2087–2124 (2017). https://doi.org/10.1007/s11277-017-4288-y
3. Zhang, J., Lin, Z., Tsai, P.-W., Xu, L.: Entropy-driven data aggregation method for energy-efficient wireless sensor networks. Inf. Fusion 59, 103–113 (2019)
4. Bharat, B., Sandeep, V., Amit, K.R.: A secure concealed data aggregation for multiple applications in wireless sensor networks. Int. J. Eng. Res. Manage. (IJERM) 2, 239–243 (2015)
5. Fang, W., Zhang, W., Zhao, Q., Ji, X., Chen, W., Biruk, A.: Comprehensive analysis of secure data aggregation scheme for industrial wireless sensor network. CMC-Comput. Mater. Continua 61(2), 583–599 (2019)
6. Jindal, A., Kumar, N., Singh, M.: Internet of energy-based demand response management scheme for smart homes and PHEVs using SVM. Future Gen. Comput. Syst. 108, 1058–1068 (2018)
7. Yu, S., Liu, M., Dou, W.C., Liu, X.T., Zhou, S.M.: Networking for big data: a survey. IEEE Commun. Surv. Tutorials 19(1), 531–549 (2017)
8. Yu, S., Zhou, W.L., Guo, S., Guo, M.Y.: A feasible IP traceback framework through dynamic deterministic packet marking. IEEE Trans. Comput. 65(5), 1418–1427 (2016)
9. Yu, S., Wang, G., Zhou, W.: Modeling malicious activities in cyber space. IEEE Netw. 29(6), 83–87 (2015)
10. Yu, S., Tian, Y., Guo, S., Wu, D.O.: Can we beat DDoS attacks in clouds? IEEE Trans. Parallel Distrib. Syst. 25(9), 2245–2254 (2014)
11. Yu, S., Gu, G., Barnawi, A., Guo, S., Stojmenovic, I.: Malware propagation in large-scale networks. IEEE Trans. Knowl. Data Eng. 27(1), 170–179 (2015)
12. Vinodha, D., Mary Anita, E.A.: Secure data aggregation techniques for wireless sensor networks: a review. Arch. Comput. Meth. Eng. 26(4), 1007–1027 (2018). https://doi.org/10.1007/s11831-018-9267-2
13. Lin, Y.H., Chang, S.Y., Sun, H.M.: CDAMA: concealed data aggregation scheme for multiple applications in wireless sensor networks. IEEE Trans. Knowl. Data Eng. 25(7), 1471–1483 (2013)
14. Boneh, D., Goh, E., Nissim, K.: Evaluating 2-DNF formulason ciphertexts. Proc Second Int'l Conf Theor. Cryptogr (TCC) 3378, 325–341 (2005)

15. Prathima, E.G., Prakash, T.S., Venugopal, K.R., Iyengar, S.S., Patnaik, L.M.: SDAMQ: secure data aggregation for multiple queries in wireless sensor networks. Procedia Comput. Sci. **89**, 283–292 (2016)
16. Ozdemir, S., Xiao, Y.: Integrity protecting hierarchical concealed data aggregation for wireless sensor networks. Comput. Netw. **55**(8), 1735–1746 (2011)
17. Shim, K.A., Park, C.M.: A secure data aggregation scheme based on appropriate cryptographic primitives in heterogeneous wireless sensor networks. IEEE Trans. Parallel Distrib. Syst. **26**(8), 2128–2139 (2015)
18. Chen, C.M., Lin, Y.H., Lin, Y.C., Sun, H.M.: RCDA: recoverable concealed data aggregation for data integrity in wireless sensor networks. IEEE Trans. Parallel Distrib. Syst. **23**(4), 727–734 (2012)
19. Zhong, H., Shao, L., Cui, J., Xu, Y.: An efficient and secure recoverable data aggregation scheme for heterogeneous wireless sensor networks. J. Parallel Distrib. Comput. **111**, 1–12 (2018)
20. Lakshmi, V.S., Deepthi, P.P.: A secure channel code-based scheme for privacy preserving data aggregation in wireless sensor networks. Int. J. Commun. Syst. **32**(1), e3832 (2018)
21. Kumar, V.: A bilinear pairing based secure data aggregation scheme for WSNs. In: 2019 15th International Wireless Communications and Mobile Computing Conference (IWCMC) (2019)
22. Zhang, P., Wang, J., Guo, K., Wu, F., Min, G.: Multi-functional secure data aggregation schemes for WSNs. Ad Hoc Netw. **69**, 86–99 (2018)
23. Zhao, X., Zhu, J., Liang, X., Jiang, S., Chen, Q.: Lightweight and integrity-protecting oriented data aggregation scheme for wireless sensor networks. IET Inf. Secur. **11**(2), 82–88 (2017)
24. Zhang, K., Han, Q., Cai, Z., Yin, G.: RiPPAS: a ring-based privacy-preserving aggregation scheme in wireless sensor networks. Sensors **17**(2), 300 (2017)
25. Elhoseny, M., Yuan, X., El-Minir, H.K., Riad, A.M.: An energy efficient encryption method for secure dynamic WSN. Secur. Commun. Netw. **9**(13), 2024–2031 (2016)
26. Hu, S., Liu, L., Fang, L., Zhou, F., Ye, R.: A novel energy-efficient and privacy-preserving data aggregation for WSNs. IEEE Access **8**, 802–813 (2020)
27. Hua, P., Liu, X., Yu, J., Dang, N., Zhang, X.: Energy-efficient adaptive slice-based secure data aggregation scheme in WSN. Procedia Comput. Sci. **129**, 188–193 (2018)
28. Parmar, K., Jinwala, D.C.: Malleability resilient concealed data aggregation in wireless sensor networks. Wireless Pers. Commun. **87**(3), 971–993 (2015). https://doi.org/10.1007/s11277-015-2633-6
29. Alghamdi, W., Rezvani, M., Wu, H., Kanhere, S.S.: Routing-aware and malicious node detection in a concealed data aggregation for WSNs. ACM Trans. Sensor Netw. **15**(2), 1–20 (2019)
30. Boneh, D., Gentry, C., Lynn, B., Shacham, H.: Aggregate and verifiably encrypted signatures from bilinear maps. In: Biham, Eli (ed.) EUROCRYPT 2003. LNCS, vol. 2656, pp. 416–432. Springer, Heidelberg (2003). https://doi.org/10.1007/3-540-39200-9_26
31. Rezvani, M., Ignjatovic, A., Bertino, E., Jha, S.: Secure data aggregation technique for wireless sensor networks in the presence of collusion attacks. IEEE Trans. Dependable Secure Comput. **12**(1), 98–110 (2015)

Multi-owner Encrypted Ranked Keyword Search Using Machine Learning Techniques

Laila Tul Badar[1] ⓘ, Chungen Xu[1](✉) ⓘ, and Ali Zakir[2] ⓘ

[1] School of Science, Nanjing University of Science and Technology, Nanjing, China
{lailatulbadar,xuchung}@njust.edu.cn
[2] School of Computer Science and Engineering, NJUST, Nanjing, China
alizakir@njust.edu.cn

Abstract. In the present era, the prevalence of network technology and cloud computing capabilities for multiple owner model has drawn much attention. Data owners outsource their data to the cloud and enjoy convenient services. However, extending single owner model into multiple owner model still have some issues, such as dimension reduction issue, high communication overhead, and efficient search in Searchable Symmetric Encryption (SSE) remain a challenging task. Integration of machine learning methods with the framework of searchable Encryption (SE) is a diverse way to solve these problems. In this paper, we developed Multi-owner encrypted ranked keyword search using Machine learning techniques(MERS-ML). Our Scheme utilized principal component Analysis (PCA) model to reduce high-dimensional data into low-dimensional codes and enabled low-overhead system maintenance. K-means clustering approach is used to solve the problem of the quality of different document of multiple owner model. To achieve fast query and efficient search relatively close to $O(log N)$, we designed search balanced index tree. Besides, attribute-based encryption is used to achieve convenient key management as well as authorized access control. Compared with previous work, our scheme provide adequate privacy protection, improved search efficiency, and introduce low overhead on computation and storage.

Keywords: Searchable encryption · Ranked keyword search · Multi owner model · Binary index tree · Principle component analysis

1 Introduction

Background. As a promising computing paragon, cloud computing has become a hot topic for research and industrial communities. It brings huge benefits to data owner such as, provide inclusiveness, flexibility, scalability, and rapid retrieval of data. Due to its highly desirable features, organizations, as well as individuals, are influenced to outsource their data onto the cloud server to accomplish ease and low management cost. Unfortunately, cloud computing is facing many problems and challenges during the transaction and storage of the outsourced data. Outsourced data onto the cloud contain sensitive information such as medical records, organization's financial records etc. Illegitimate use of client personal information or reveal any sort of private data is

© Springer Nature Singapore Pte Ltd. 2020
S. Yu et al. (Eds.): SPDE 2020, CCIS 1268, pp. 399–412, 2020.
https://doi.org/10.1007/978-981-15-9129-7_28

seemingly occur as data is stored in third-party cloud server. For the safety, security, and privacy of data, researchers have been paid much attention to the growing security incidents in cloud computing. To solve these issues, data must be encrypted before outsourced into the cloud server.

Related work and Challenges. Song et al. [1] proposed the Searchable Symmetric Encryption (SSE) model that supported effective keyword search over encrypted data along with the assurance of security and privacy of data. Curtmola et al. [2] provided security against adaptive and non-adaptive chosen-keyword attacks. Boneh et al. [3] proposed public-key encryption system with a keyword search. Xia et al. [4], proposed a balanced binary tree to build the index by using Greedy Depth First Search (GDFS) algorithm. Sun et al. [5] proposed TF * IDF keyword weight generation algorithm for better search accuracy, single keyword ranked search [6], fuzzy keyword search [7, 8], Dynamic keyword search [4], and Multi keyword ranked search [9] are the different flavor of public-key encryption that have been published with better security efficiency and query experiences. To achieve sublinear search time, Cao et al. [9] first proposed Multi keyword Ranked Search over Encrypted cloud data (MRSE) for single data owners and establish strict privacy requirements. However, due to high computation of matrix operations the performance of the model is decreased. Ranked keyword search scheme enhanced system usability by returning the most relevant documents in ranking order. So, users only need to decrypt a small number of ciphertext to achieve the desired documents. Though, these schemes only support searchable encryption for the "Single Owner" model. Owing to the diverse demand of application scenarios, users wanted to share their data on a cloud having multiple characteristics and host a large number of documents outsourced by Multiple Owners Model [10–13]. Multiple owner model is still facing some unsettled issues related to secure keys. It is difficult to design secure keyword search for multiple owner model because it uses their self-chosen secret keys and not share it with any other data owner which brings some major unresolved problem. These problems are, **(1)** Dimension disaster in the system overhead during index construction, trapdoor generation, and query execution is mostly determined by matrix multiplication. In other words large number of data from different data owners because high dimensionality issues leads to a results that searchable encryption cannot put into use in real world scenarios. **(2)** Data users need to generate multiple trapdoors for multiple data owners even for the same query. That's why SSE is still incompetent to satisfy user requirements. To solve these shortcomings, we need to examine the roots of the problems and find best conceivable solutions. Machine learning is so far the current popular technique that only supports the plain texts and didn't support the encrypted datasets. So, it is necessary to discuss both the problems and come up with high efficiency into SE model. Gou et al. [10] define multi-keyword ranked search scheme for multiple data owner model (MRSE-MO), and then design a keyword document and owners (KDO) weight generation algorithm. Experimental results showed that (KDO) weight generation algorithm is better than the traditional TF * IDF algorithm. When user wants to search for multiple owner model, the quality of different document from different owners are not same even if they are about the same area. In that situation, the operation of calculating similarity face dimensionality problem which bound the accessibility of the system. Last but foremost, it ignores the security and privacy in known Background Model (threat model, try to reveal the private data in SE system) [9].

In this paper, we focused on principle component analysis (PCA) [14] one of the lightweight unsupervised machine learning algorithm to solve the curse of dimensionality issue. It has been widely used in different fields of digital signal processing, robotic sensor data, and image processing. PCA applies a linear transformation to the data that allow variance within the data to be expressed in term of orthogonal eigenvectors. We used K-means clustering [15] algorithm, to solve the problem of quality of different documents in multiple owner model. To obtain high search efficiency, we proposed a balanced binary index tree and the Greedy Depth-first search (GFDS) algorithm generated by probabilistic learning. We performed random searches and get the sum of the relevant score of each index and after that sort it according to the score from high to low. Secure k-nearest neighbor (KNN) [16] algorithm is constructed to encrypt query and index vectors and ensure the security between the index and query vectors.

1.1 Our Contributions

The major contribution of our system are manifold:

- PCA algorithm is used to reduce the dimension of query and index vector in Multi Owner Model to enhance user experience and reduce system overhead.
- We construct binary index tree structure that followed the bottom-up Greedy-Depth-First-Search (GDFS) approach, and sorted the node by maximum probability. The complexity of the binary index tree are closed to $O(log\ N)$, proved that the query speed is faster and more stable than the previous work [9, 10].
- We proposed a K-means clustering approach, to solve the problem of document quality differences between different data owners.
- The extensive experiments on real-world dataset further shows that our scheme is indeed efficient and achieve effectiveness.

1.2 Organization

The rest of the paper is organized as follows. In Sect. 2, some basic notations, system model, threat models, and design goal of scheme is introduced. Brief construction of scheme is given in Sect. 3. Experiments and performance analysis is given in Sect. 4 and 5. In Sect. 6 we describe the conclusion of this paper.

2 Notation of Problem Formulation

Table 1. Introduced some important notations for understanding formulation and statement in this paper.

Table 1. Notations and Description

Notations	Description
DO	Represent Data Owners. It consists of n number of Data Owners such as $DO = (DO_1, DO_2 \ldots \ldots DO_n)$.
F	The collection of plaintext documents owned by DO_i is denoted as $F = (F1, F2 \ldots Fn)$ and the sequence of keywords is considered as $F_{i,j}$
C	The encrypted document collection F_i that store in the cloud server and expressed as $C = (C1, C2 \ldots Cn)$.
D	The dictionary specifically the set of keywords denoted as $(d_1, d_2 \ldots d_m)$ where D is used as a public list shared by all participants in our scheme. And M is the size of the dictionary
P_i	The n-length popularity vector associated with C.
I	The collection of index vector set of documents $F_{i,j}$ where t^{th} a bit of I means that $I[t] = 1$ the document has the keyword else $I[t] = 0$.
$\tilde{I}_{i,j}$	The update weighted index vector of documents after standardized processing
τ	Plaintext form of a balanced binary tree for the document of all data owners.
$\tilde{\tau}$	The encrypted form of a balanced binary tree for the document of all data owners.
Q	Weight query vector generated based on query request and represented as $Q = (Q_1 \ldots \ldots Q_m)$.
TD	The trapdoor which is the encrypted form of Q and calculated by data users.

2.1 Proposed Framework

There are three major entities involved in our proposed framework which are Data Owners *(DO)*, Data Users *(DU)*, and Cloud Server *(CS)* as illustrated in Fig. 1.

- *DO* has aspired to outsource the collection of documents D to a cloud server. But before that they need to encrypt the documents D to the encrypted form of C, and outsourced encrypted searchable index C to the cloud server.
- *DU* wants to access the files in which he/she are interested in the cloud data provided by all *DO*. *DU* generate the trapdoor and number k to search over encrypted data on cloud server, and retrieve *top-k* relevant documents. The retrieved Encrypted documents are decrypted with the secret keys.

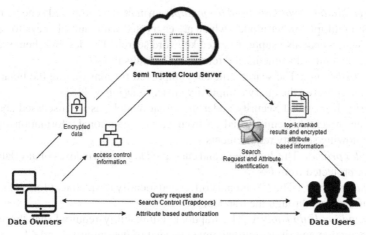

Fig. 1. The basic architecture of (MERS_ML)

- CS store the encrypted documents C and an encrypted searchable index for data owners, Based on request query from DU, it provide encrypted data with the most relevant *top-k* documents.

2.2 Threat Model

A cloud server is considered "honest-but-Curious" in SE, it is semi-trusted threat entity [13] Specifically, CS works honestly and correctly and executes the commands in the delegated protocol. However it is curious to infer and analyze received data (including index), and try to identify private information of encrypted data and carry out an attack. Depending on what information the cloud server knows, there are two threat models, which are discussed below;

- *Known ciphertext model.* In this model, the CS only knows the encrypted document collection, the searchable index outsourced by DO, trapdoors, and number k outsourced by DU. CS conducts ciphertext only attack (COA) [17] and try to destroy the privacy of DO and DU.
- *Known background model.* This model is stronger than Known ciphertext model. CS knows more statistical information about dataset such as encrypted documents size, encrypted index, trapdoors and their corresponding search results. CS try to learn the location of newly added entries as they are stored in lexicographical order in indexes.

2.3 Design Goals and Security Definitions

To ensure the correctness completeness and efficiency of ranked multi keyword scheme over encrypted cloud data outsourced by DO our system aim to achieve the following security goals:

1. *Ranked Multi keyword retrieval for multiple owners.* The proposed scheme not only support multiple owner model (which are encrypted with multiple keys for multiple data owners) but also support ranked keyword search. The design scheme retrieved all the matching documents and return *top-k* results to *DU*.
2. *Search efficiency.* The search efficiency improved by constructing the binary index tree and achieved the query complexity closer to $O(log\ N)$ [18]
3. *Security.* It provided Security under the threat models, as we discussed above, the scheme prevent the semi-trusted *CS* from learning additional information and fulfill the following security requirements
   - *Index privacy.* The documents and encrypted keywords indexes of any data owner are protected from *CS*
   - *Query privacy.* The *CS* did not collect and identify the plaintext form of keyword information through the trapdoor
   - *Trapdoor Unlinkability.* The trapdoor unlinkability required that the trapdoor generation algorithm are randomize instead of deterministic and *CS* recognized whether two trapdoor quires generated form the same search request.

3   The Design of MERS-ML

In this section, we describe (MERS-ML) framework by using secure (KNN) [16] model, consist of 5 probabilistic-polynomial-time algorithms (PPT) are discussed below,

$K \leftarrow keyGen$: It is a probabilistic index generation algorithm run by data owners. *DO* generate the secret key (*SK*), where $SK' = \{S', M_1', M_2'\}.M_1$ and M_2 are two invertible matrices their dimensions are $(n \otimes n)$ and S is a random $n - length$ vector.

$Updated - KeyGen(SK', \ell)$: For updating the keyword list and adding the new keyword ℓ into the dictionary *D*. DO_i generate new. $SK' = \{S', M_1', M_2'\}.M_1'$ and M_2' are two invertible matrices their dimensions are $(n + \ell) \otimes (n + \ell)$ and S' are a random $(n + \ell) - length$ vector. This support dynamic operations into the scheme.

$I \leftarrow Buildindex(F, SK)$: *DO* generate the searchable indexes for documents and add random noise into the weighted index vector *I* to obtain security under known background model [14]. The weighted index *I* and *SK* build an encrypted index tree $\tilde{\tau}$ based on the dataset *F*. Finally DO_i send the encrypted index tree $\tilde{\tau}$ to *CS*.

$TD \leftarrow GenTrapdoor(Q, SK)$: *DU* send query request to *DO*. *DO* generate a query $Q = \{Q_1....Q_n\}$ build the *TD* using *SK* and send Trapdoor *TD* to *CS*.

$Q \leftarrow Query(TD, K, I)$: *DO* send the trapdoor information and query instruction to *CS*. When the *CS* received query request, it perform ranked search on the index *I* with the help of *TD* and finally return *top-k* documents to *DU*.

3.1   Secure and Efficient MERS-ML Details

Plaintext form of binary index vector generation. According to the Keywords of documents and dictionary *D*, the *DO* build the index vector *I* of the binary form for his/her document. Then send the index vector to *CS*. It is also the classical expression of the vector space model (VSM) [19].

Index dimension reduction. Dimension disaster exacerbates redundancy in document vector, and cause computational burden on the system. As the number of data increases in multi-owner model, the data features become very sparse, which made keyword dictionary for index construction very large and leads to dimensionality issues in computing for all index vector form different owners. We used PCA [14] to overcome these issues which improve low query efficiency and increase the search efficiency of the scheme.

(1) We have a dataset X, $i = \{1, 2 \ldots .. m\}$, in the first step we need to preprocess the data. We normalized the data by calculating the mean $\bar{x}$ and subtracting the mean $\bar{x}$ from each of the data point x_i

$$xi - \bar{x} \tag{1}$$

(2) Calculated the covariance matrix that is symbolized with C.

$$Cij = \frac{\sum\limits_{i=1}^{n} (xi - \bar{x})\,(xi - \bar{x})}{(n-1)} \tag{2}$$

(3) Determine the eigenvalues and the corresponding eigenvectors of the covariance matrix to identify the principal components. C is the symmetric matrix so a positive real number λ and a non-zero vector v can be found such that

$$Cv = \lambda v \tag{3}$$

Where λ is a scalar value called the eigenvalue, and v is the eigenvector of C. To find non-zero v apply the singular value decomposition (SVD) method to solve the equation $|C - \lambda I| = 0$. If C is $m \times m$ matrix of full rank, n eigenvalues can be found $\lambda 1, \lambda 2 \ldots \lambda n$, and using $|C - \lambda I|v = 0$ all the corresponding eigenvectors found.

(4) After the eigenvectors obtained, we ranked it in decreasing order of eigenvalues, small eigenvalues mean that there components are less important, So we ignored them without losing important information and choose the first k (number of components).
Eigenvectors yielded the new k dimensions. Finally, obtain a new feature vector consisting of the eigenvector of principle component.

(5) In a final step, we need to modify our samples by re-orientating data from original one to the ones representing by principle components.

$$ReduceData = FeatureVector \times ScaledData \tag{4}$$

Here *FeatureVector* is matrix with the eigenvectors in the column transposed, so the eigenvectors now in rows. *Scaled Data* is the mean-adjusted data transposed and *Reduce Data* is the final dataset. After dimension reduction, we clustered the documents by using k-means approach and perform the clustering on all *DO* index vectors. We divided the keyword dictionary into multiple sub-dictionaries and in this sense large number of high similarity index vectors found, which solve the problem of document quality between different data owners. After getting the final data the length of index vectors become shorter than before and *DO* obtain a new binary index $\hat{I} = \{\hat{I}1 \ldots \ldots \hat{I}s\}$ with lower dimension size.

Secure Weight index generation. **(1)** *Correlativity matrix generation.* To construct the secure weight index for new binary index vector $\hat{I}$, and calculate the keyword weight precisely, it is compulsory to consider the semantic relationship between keywords that access the degree of influence among different keywords. We used the corpus to find the relevance between different keywords. We represented relevance between the keywords by obtaining the correlativity matrix $S_{M \times M}$ (symmetric matrix). **(2)** *Weight generation.* After obtaining the Correlativity matrix S, we use KDO [15] weight generation algorithm designed for constructing the weight of different data owners about different keywords and design average keyword popularity (AKP) about different DO. The AKP for single owner DO_i is computed as $AKP = (P_i \cdot I_i) \otimes \alpha_i$. Where $\alpha_i(\alpha_{i,1}, \alpha_{i,2} \ldots \alpha_{i,n})$ is an n-length (n is the size of dictionary),Pi is the n-length vectors (where n represent the number of document in F), I_i indicate the index vector of document $F_{i,j}$ and the operator $\otimes$ represent the product of two vectors corresponding elements, as if $L_i(d_t)| \neq 0$ then $\alpha_{i,t} = \frac{1}{|L_i(d_t)|}$ else $\alpha_{i,t} = 0$. Where $L_i(d_t)|$ is the number of document containing d_t. Based on correlation assumptions calculate the raw weight information for data owner DO_i is denoted as $W_i^{raw} = S \cdot AKP_i$ where $W_i^{raw} = (w_{i,1}^{raw}, w_{i,2}^{raw} \ldots \ldots w_{i,m}^{raw})$ **(3)** *Normalized weight.* All the keywords in dictionary are important, it is compulsory to normalized keyword weight. The maximum raw weight of every keyword among different owners are recorded as n-length list denoted as W_{max} where $W_{max} = (w_{i,1}^{raw}, w_{i,2}^{raw} \ldots \ldots)$ based on the vector W_{max} the normalized weight can be calculated as $W_{i,t} = \frac{W_{i,t}^{raw}}{W_{max[j]}}$ **(4)** *Weight index generation.* DO obtain a secure weight index vector as $\tilde{I}i.j = Ii.j \otimes Wi$ with high privacy protection strength. Where $\tilde{I}i.j$ denoted as weight index vector of the document $Fi.j = (j \in 1, 2 \ldots n)$.

Balanced index tree (BIT) construction. BIT is a binary index tree structure used to construct index for efficient search in a system. We design a BIT-tree based on a secure weighted index $\tilde{I}i.j$ and generate query vectors Q randomly. We used the "Greedy" method and bottom up strategy to pair similar nodes together. Based on probabilistic learning DO performs random searches to get the sum of matching scores for index and query vectors and sort the index according to descending order. The data structure of our index tree node i has 5 attributes: $\{ID, FID, Dv, Lch, Rch\}$ where ID stores the unique identifier for the node i. FID is the identifier of node i. If i is non-leaf node $FID = None$. D_v is the n-length vector of node i. Lch and Rch store the reference of left and right child node of i. We invoke the traditional algorithm to build BIT- tree on top of all document $di(i = 1, 2 \ldots m)$ and generate a unique identifiers $fFID$ of leaf node. If i is a leaf node it store document vector $\vec{D}di$ according to keyword dictionary and each dimension $i.\vec{D}$ is normalized as weighted index. If node i is the internal node and number of nodes is even,i. e., $2h$, assume that node i has t child nodes $(i1 \ldots it)$ then the vector is computed as $i.\vec{D}[v] = \max\{i1.\vec{D}[v], \ldots, it.\vec{D}[v]\}$ where $i = 1, \ldots, m$. if the number of input nodes is odd, i.e., $2h + 1$, create a parent node i_l for hth pair node, and then create a parent node i for i_l and the single node i_2. Finally, we obtain a binary index tree where the query complexity is close to $O(logN)$ [18]

Build an Encrypted Index. After obtaining plaintext weighted indexes DO_i encrypt weight index tree τ with the secret key SK. where $SK = \{S, M_1, M_2\}$ to get an encrypted index tree $\tilde{\tau}$. The index vector D_v of each node in a tree is split into two random vectors

$\{Dv'_1, Dv''_2\}$. Specifically if $S[j] = 0$, $Dv'_1[j]$ and $Dv''_2[j]$ will be equal to $Dv[j]$; else if $S[j] = 1$, $Dv'_1[j]$ is a random value $Dv''_2[j] = Dv[j] - Dv'_1[j]$ then each node encrypted index tree $\tilde{\tau}$ contains two vector as follow $\overline{D}_v = \{M_1^T Dv'_1, M_2^T Dv''_2\}$. After encrypted, the vectors in all tree nodes DO_i send the encrypted index tree $\tilde{\tau}$ to the CS. The construction of an encrypted index tree is completed. As the index tree is characterized by a set of nodes and set of pointers that specify all parent-child relationships, so the DO_i only encrypt the vector D_v carry in each node i, but it keeps all pointer constant. Therefore the encrypted and unencrypted index tree is isomorphic ($\tau \cong \tilde{\tau}$).

Trapdoor Generation. To avoid the outflow of private information, the DU evaluated the trapdoors according to the search keyword set, which is also the encrypted form of a search request. When DU wanted to search the documents, they only needed to send the query request to the CS. DO_i generate query Q where $Q = (Q_1 \ldots\ldots Q_m)$ and build the TD using SK and send TD to DU. The same process is utilized to split Q into two random vectors $\{Q'_1, Q''_2\}$ the difference if $S[j] = 0$, $Q'_1[j]$ is a random value and $Q''_2[j] = Q[j] - Q'_1[j]$ else if $S[j] = 1$, $Q'_1[j] = Q''_2[j] = Q[j]$ where $j \in \{1, 2 \ldots .m\}$ Finally DO_i return encrypted Q as $TD = \{M_1^{-1}Q'_1, M_2^{-1}Q''_2\}$ and send TD to CS.

Search process of MERS-ML. (1) *Query preparation.* DU sends the query request to the CS. DO_i check whether the query is valid if yes then DO_i generate the TD and initiate search queries to the CS. If access control passes CS use the encrypted index tree $\tilde{\tau}$ to search for index vectors that match the query vectors, and calculate the relevance score of an encrypted index vector in each tree node and trapdoor TD.CS return encrypted *top-k* documents to DU based on Rscore(2) *Calculate the relevance score.*

$$
\begin{aligned}
&= Score : (D_v.TD) \\
&= \{M_1^T D'_{v_1}, M_2^T D''_{v_2}\}.\{M_1^{-1}Q'_1 M_2^{-1}Q''_2\} \\
&= (M_1^T D'_{v_1})^T.(M_1^{-1}Q'_1) + (M_2^T D''_{v_2})^T.(M_2^{-1}Q''_2) \\
&= D'^T_{v1} M_1 M_1^{-1}Q'_1 + D''^T_{v2} M_2 M_2^{-1}Q''_2 \\
&= D'_{v1}.Q'_1 + D''_{v2}.Q''_2 \\
&= RScore(D_v.Q)
\end{aligned} \tag{5}
$$

The relevance score calculates from D_v and TD is exactly equal to that from D_v and this causes privacy leakage under known background model. To protect the trapdoors and keyword search under the known background model we should prevent the server from calculating the exact value by padding random noise into D_v and TD. To disturb the relevance score calculation during their generation. We generate random invertible matrix $(n + \ell) \otimes (n + \ell)$ the document vector will be extended to $(n + \ell)$ dimensions where ℓ is the random noise. We generated the index vector D_v of BIT-tree D_v is extended to $(n + \ell)$ dimension and the extended term $D_v[n + i]$, $i = 1 \ldots .\ell$ is set to a random number εi. Similarly, the query is also extended to $(n+\ell)$ dimensions and the elements are randomly set to 1 or 0. Thus the relevance score between query trapdoor and document vector is equal to $D_v \cdot Q + \sum \varepsilon j$ where $j \in \{i|Q[n + i] = 1\}$. The randomness of $\Sigma \varepsilon j$ ensures security under known background model. (3) *Search process of BIT-Tree.* BIT-tree used (GDFS) algorithm that can be executed to perform search on the index with high efficiency. The search algorithm is give below,

Algorithm 1 Search process of BIT-tree

Input:Root node of index tree r and query Q
Output:The $Result - list$ which contain $top - k$ documents with corresponding $RScore$
1: if the node i is not a leaf node then
2:    if Rscore $(D_v . Q) > kth$ score then
3:       GDFS $(i \ . \ high - relevance - child)$
4:       GDFS $(i \ . \ low - relevance - child)$
5:    else
6:       return
7:    end if
8: else
9:    if Rscore $(D_v . Q) > kth$ score then
10:       Update $Result - list$ and kth score
11:    end if
12:    return
13: end if

4 Security Analysis

Data security. We use the symmetric encryption technique such as advanced encryption standard (AES) to encrypt the outsourced data. As long as the encryption key is not exposed the privacy of outsourced data is also guaranteed.

Index and query confidentiality. In the MERS-ML scheme the weight index vector and binary index tree is generated, So that it cannot leak any private information. In our tree index query vectors are generated randomly and search queries only return the secure inner products [9]. In our scheme, every data owner has their own encrypted keys and the ciphertexts is completely different for the same keyword in different data files while keeping searchable ability. More precisely the security of other data owners will not be compromised if the adversary cooperates with any DO_i and leak his important data content. Moreover, the security is further enhanced as the padding random noise [16] into data is difficult to figure the transformed matrices.

Trapdoor security. Introducing random noise in the query will generate different query vectors and receive different relevance score distribution with the same search request. [4, 20] The existence of random noise in query and data vector making it impossible for CS to distinguish two TD generated by any one query. The scheme ensured the unlinkability of TD in known background model.

Keyword search. In (MERS-ML) the document key is implemented with Attribute-based encryption (ABE) so that the adversary cannot gather any statistical information of keyword and documents. DO use the access control information to encrypt the documents and then store the encrypted documents in the CS, and CS not decrypt the encrypted ciphertext to obtain the document key. Moreover the weight of one keyword for different owners not the same, the adversary not determined that the two documents contain same keyword according to relevance score. In this manner, the security and privacy of key management is ensured.

5 Experimental Analysis

We implement the proposed scheme using Python in Window 10 operating system with Intel Core i5-7200U processor 2.50 GHz, 8 GB RAM and evaluated its efficiency on real-world dataset and compare it with MKRS-MO [10] EDMRS [4] we used the academic papers provided by Elsevier, http://elsevier.com/, including 30,000 papers and 90,000 different keywords, 600 academic conferences selected as data owners involving multiple domains All results represent the average of 1000 trails.

Index Tree Construction. After receiving binary index vectors DO construct a searchable binary index tree encrypt it and send it to the cloud server. The encryption process mainly depends on two multiplication of matrix and n dimension vector. For the construction of the tree, we used random searches in probabilistic and statistical sense. Since the BIT-tree is a balanced binary tree so the height of the tree is proportional to $log\ N$, and the search complexity is $O(logN)$ (Where n is the number of nodes in the tree) which is used to retrieve top-k documents. Figure 2(a) shows that the time cost of generating an index tree is almost linear to the size of documents D when the size of keyword set is fixed. Figure 2(b) demonstrates that the size of keyword dictionary has great impact on the time cost of building index tree. Our scheme consumes less time than other existing scheme and is even more lightweight due to dimension reduction. Also, the time cost of construction is not ignorable overhead for the data owners it is one-time operation before data outsourcing.

Trapdoor Generation. Our scheme utilize the encryption process for the generation of trapdoors which follow vector splitting operation and two multiplication of $n \otimes n$ matrix. The time of generating trapdoors is extremely affected by the dimension of vector, and the time of generation of trapdoors (MERS-ML) is less than other schemes due to dimensions of the different vector. Figure 3(a) shows that the time of generating trapdoor is highly affected by the size of the dictionary. Figure 3(b) shows the number of keywords in the query request hardly influences the overhead of trapdoor generation, because the dimension of Matrices and size of dictionary is always fixed.

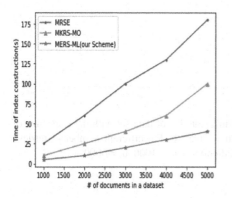 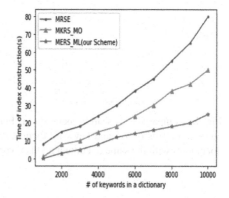

Fig. 2. Time cost of building index tree (a) For different size of dataset with the fixed dictionary u = 5000 (b) the fixed document dataset with different size of keyword dictionary n = 1000.

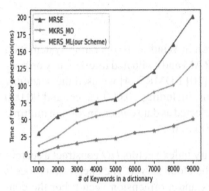
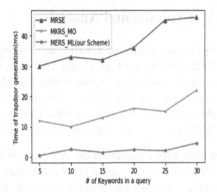

Fig. 3. Time cost of generating trapdoor (a) The same 5 query keywords within the different size of keyword dictionary (b) The Different number of query keywords within the same keywords dictionary, u = 5000.

Search Efficiency. This part of the experiment reveal the search efficiency of our scheme. The experiments on real-world dataset show that our results achieve near binary search and is superior to other comparison schemes. *DO* perform 10,000 random searches and get the sum of the matching scores of each index and all random query vectors. From Fig 4(a) we can see that the search efficiency of all the scheme increased with number of documents increases but our scheme achieve lower search time. Fig 4(b) shows the cost and search efficiency is improved by 5 times than the other comparison schemes in a different number of keyword search. By comparing the results we presume that when the size of the dataset increases the data features become sparser.

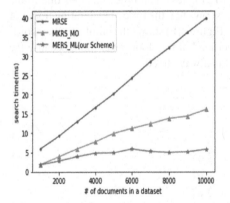
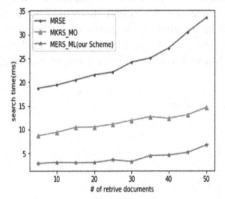

Fig. 4. Comparison of search operation (a) For different size of data set with the same size of query keywords q = 5 and keyword dictionary u = 5000 (b) For different number of retrieve documents with the same document and keyword dictionary n = 1000, u = 5000.

Moreover, the similarity between index and query vectors is mostly close to or equal to zero due to the sparseness of data features, which bring plenty of complications, and the construction of index tree is not a global order, so it is compulsory to traverse many nodes in the search, which show the limitation of the grouped balanced binary tree (MERS-ML).also the closer the number of random searches into infinity the higher the search efficiency of the index tree. Moreover, the maintenance cost of scheme based on BIT-tree is much lower than the other schemes. When data owner wants to add a new document into the *CS* we need to update the index tree by adding a new index leaf node in the index tree accordingly, and the search complexity of index tree is at least $O(logN)$ times and for data updates it is at least $O(logN)$ times, so that the total cost is $2O(logN)$ [21] (where N is the number of node that index tree contained). Also, the update on an index is based on documents identifies, and no access to the content of documents required.

6   Conclusion

In this paper, we introduced secure and efficient (MERS-ML) scheme and conduct deep security and experimental analysis by combining Machine learning techniques. To solve the problem of the quality of deferent documents of multiple owner model we cluster index vectors into multiple indexes and divide the keyword dictionary into multiple sub-dictionaries by using k-means clustering approach. Besides, our Scheme proposes principle component analysis (PCA) to avoid the curse of dimensionality, caused by big data sparsity and reduce the dimensions of index vector which improve the efficiency of secure (KNN) algorithm. Last but not least, we constructed a balanced index tree (BIT-tree) generated by sufficient amount of random searches and follow Greedy depth first algorithm to obtain better computational complexity close to $O(logN)$.The experiments on real world dataset show that our scheme is secure against threat models and prove the flexibility and efficiency of the system.

Acknowledgment. This work is partially supported by the Fundamental research Funds for the Central Universities (NO. 30918012204).

References

1. Song, D.X., Wagner, D., Perrig, A.: Practical techniques for searches on encrypted data. In: Proceeding 2000 IEEE Symposium on Security and Privacy. S & P 2000, pp. 44–55 (2000)
2. Curtmola, R., Garay, J., Kamara, S., Ostrovsky, R.: Searchable symmetric encryption: improved definitions and efficient constructions. J. Comput. Secur. **19**, 895–934 (2011)
3. Boneh, D., Di Crescenzo, G., Ostrovsky, R., Persiano, G.: Public key encryption with keyword search. In: Cachin, C., Camenisch, J.L. (eds.) EUROCRYPT 2004. LNCS, vol. 3027, pp. 506–522. Springer, Heidelberg (2004). https://doi.org/10.1007/978-3-540-24676-3_30
4. Xia, Z., Wang, X., Sun, X., Wang, Q.: A secure and dynamic multi-keyword ranked search scheme over encrypted cloud data. IEEE Trans. Parallel Distrib. Syst. **27**, 340–352 (2015)

5. Sun, W., et al.: Privacy-preserving multi-keyword text search in the cloud supporting similarity-based ranking. In: Proceedings of the 8th ACM SIGSAC Symposium on Information, Computer and Communications Security, pp. 71–82 (2013)
6. Wang, C., Cao, N., Li, J., Ren, K., Lou, W.: Secure ranked keyword search over encrypted cloud data. In: 2010 IEEE 30th International Conference on Distributed Computing Systems, pp. 253–262 (2010)
7. Fu, Z., Wu, X., Guan, C., Sun, X., Ren, K.: Toward efficient multi-keyword fuzzy search over encrypted outsourced data with accuracy improvement. IEEE Trans. Inf. Forensics Secur. **11**, 2706–2716 (2016)
8. Li, J., Wang, Q., Wang, C., Cao, N., Ren, K., Lou, W.: Fuzzy keyword search over encrypted data in cloud computing. In: 2010 Proceedings IEEE INFOCOM, pp. 1–5 (2010)
9. Cao, N., Wang, C., Li, M., Ren, K., Lou, W.: Privacy-preserving multi-keyword ranked search over encrypted cloud data. IEEE Trans. Parallel Distrib. Syst. **25**, 222–233 (2013)
10. Guo, Z., Zhang, H., Sun, C., Wen, Q., Li, W.: Secure multi-keyword ranked search over encrypted cloud data for multiple data owners. J. Syst. Softw. **137**, 380–395 (2018)
11. Zhang, W., Xiao, S., Lin, Y., Zhou, T., Zhou, S.: Secure ranked multi-keyword search for multiple data owners in cloud computing. In: 2014 44th Annual IEEE/IFIP International Conference on Dependable Systems and Networks, pp. 276–286 (2014)
12. Miao, Y., et al.: VCKSM: Verifiable conjunctive keyword search over mobile e-health cloud in shared multi-owner settings. Pervasive Mob. Comput. **40**, 205–219 (2017)
13. Li, J., Lin, Y., Wen, M., Gu, C., Yin, B.: Secure and verifiable multi-owner ranked-keyword search in cloud computing. In: Xu, K., Zhu, H. (eds.) WASA 2015. LNCS, vol. 9204, pp. 325–334. Springer, Cham (2015). https://doi.org/10.1007/978-3-319-21837-3_32
14. Smith, L.I.: A tutorial on principal components analysis (2002)
15. Peng, C.: Distributed K-Means clustering algorithm based on fisher discriminant ratio. j. Jiangsu Univ. Natl. Sci. Ed. **35**, 422–427 (2014)
16. Wong, W.K., Cheung, D. W.-l., Kao, B., Mamoulis, N.: Secure kNN computation on encrypted databases. In: Proceedings of the 2009 ACM SIGMOD International Conference on Management of data, pp. 139–152 (2009)
17. Delf, H., Knebl, H.: Introduction to Cryptography: Principles and Applications. Springer, Berlin (2007)
18. Knuth, D.: The Art of Computer programming, Vol 3: sorting and searching, 2nd edn. Addison-Wesley Publ. Co, Boston (1998)
19. Salton, G., Wong, A., Yang, C.-S.: A vector space model for automatic indexing. Commun. ACM **18**, 613–620 (1975)
20. Ballard, L., Kamara, S., Monrose, F.: Achieving efficient conjunctive keyword searches over encrypted data. In: Qing, S., Mao, W., López, J., Wang, G. (eds.) ICICS 2005. LNCS, vol. 3783, pp. 414–426. Springer, Heidelberg (2005). https://doi.org/10.1007/11602897_35
21. Chen, K., Lin, Z., Wan, J., Xu, L., Xu, C.: Multi-owner secure encrypted search using searching adversarial networks. In: Mu, Y., Deng, R.H., Huang, X. (eds.) CANS 2019. LNCS, vol. 11829, pp. 184–195. Springer, Cham (2019). https://doi.org/10.1007/978-3-030-31578-8_10

Attacks and Countermeasures

Detection of Various Speech Forgery Operations Based on Recurrent Neural Network

Diqun Yan$^{(\boxtimes)}$ ⓘ and Tingting Wu ⓘ

College of Information Science and Engineering, Ningbo University, Ningbo 315211, China
yandiqun@nbu.edu.cn

Abstract. Most existed algorithms of speech forensics have been proposed to detect specific forgery operations. In realistic scenes, however, it is difficult to predict the type of the forgery. Since the suspicious speech might have been processed by some unknown forgery operation, it will give a confusing result based on a classifier for a specific forgery operation. To this end, a forensic algorithm based on recurrent neural network (RNN) and linear frequency cepstrum coefficients (LFCC) is proposed to detect four common forgery operations. The LFCC with its derivative coefficients is determined as the forensic feature. An RNN frame with two-layer LSTM is designed with preliminary experiments. Extensive experiments on TIMIT and UME databases show that the detection accuracy for the intra-database evaluation can achieve about 99%, and the detection accuracy for the cross-database can achieve higher than 88%. Finally, compared with the previous algorithm, better performance is obtained by the proposed algorithm.

Keywords: Forensics · Forgery operations · Recurrent neural network

1 Introduction

Nowadays, speech recording can be easily forged by some audio software. It will cause a huge threat if we cannot make sure the speech is natural or maliciously modified. Specifically, it will bring an inestimable impact on society when the forged speech is used for news report, court evidence and other fields.

In the past decades, digital speech forensics plays a crucial role on identifying the authenticity and integrity of speech recordings. Lots of works have been proposed. In order to detect the compression history of AMR audio, Luo [1] proposed a Stack Autoencoder (SAE) network for extracting the deep representations to classify the double compressed audios with a UBM-GMM classifier. Jing [2] present a detection method based on adaptive least squares and periodicity in the second derivative of an audio signal as a classification feature. For protecting text-dependent speaker verification systems from the spoofing attacks, Jakub [3] proposed an algorithm for detecting the replay attack audio. In [4], Galina use a high-level feature with a GMM classifier to against the synthetize audio in ASVspoof challenge. To detect the electronic disguised speech, Huang [5] proposed a forensic algorithm that adopted the SVM model with the Mel-frequency Cepstral Coefficients (MFCC) statistical vectors as acoustic features, including the MFCC and its mean value and correlation coefficients. The experimental results

© Springer Nature Singapore Pte Ltd. 2020
S. Yu et al. (Eds.): SPDE 2020, CCIS 1268, pp. 415–426, 2020.
https://doi.org/10.1007/978-981-15-9129-7_29

show that their algorithm can achieve a high detection accuracy about 90%. In [6], Wang combined Linear Frequency Cepstrum Coefficient (LFCC) statistical moment and formant statistical moment as input features to detect electronic disguised audio in adding different SNR and different types of background noise.

Most of those forensic methods have achieved a good performance on detecting the modified speech with a specific forgery operation. However, they will be failed to detect the unknown forgery operation. For example, the electronic disguised classifier can identify whether the testing speech has undergone disguising processing. If the testing speech was only processed with noise-adding, the classifier will not give the correct result.

In recent years, some researchers start to focus on the forensics of various forgery operations. In [7], Jeong proposed a method to detect various image operations by a statistical feature. Luo [8] used the statistical features derived from image residuals to build an identifications of various image operations. The traditional features like MFCC are adopted as the acoustic feature in most existing forensic methods. However, with the fast development of deep learning, we can obtain a more powerful discrimination ability classifier based on deep learning techniques such as CNN and RNN [10–13]. In [9], Chen designed a convolutional neural network (CNN) with a fixed prior layer to classify different audio operations. The result shows that the CNN based method can achieved a better accuracy than the traditional forensic methods.

In this paper, we present an RNN to detect various speech forgery operations with the traditional feature MFCC and LFCC. We have made extensive experiments to verify the suitable feature and the architecture of RNN. The results show that the proposed method can detect the kinds of forgery operations, and outperforms better than the other detection works.

The rest of the paper is organized as follows. Section 2 introduces input of the network and feature extraction. Section 3 describes the proposed network architecture and some important hyper parameters. Section 4 presents comparative results for the detection of various forgery operation. Finally, the concluding remarks of this paper are given in Sect. 5.

2   Feature Extraction

The cepstrum coefficients which are the representation of the spectrum of speech signal in the setting window frame, have been commonly applied as a classificational feature to present the difference between original speech and the forged speech. The experimental results show that the forgery operations will cause the cepstrum coefficients of operated speech different from the original speech. In this section, we will give a briefly introduction of MFCC and LFCC, which are two of most used cepstrum coefficients.

2.1   Mel-Frequency Cepstrum Coefficient

MFCC is a beneficial speech feature based on human auditory perception characteristics, which are widely used for speech recognition [14]. Figure 1 shows the procedure for extracting the MFCC statistical moments.

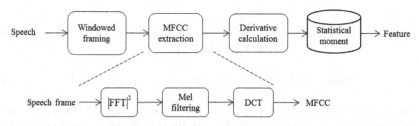

Fig. 1. Extraction procedure of MFCC statistical moment.

The MFCC focuses on the non-linear frequency characteristic and the size of Mel frequency corresponds to the relation of the logarithmic distribution of linear frequency and accords with the human ears' characteristic. The relationship between Mel frequency and linear frequency is shown as,

$$Mel(f) = 2595\lg(1 + f/700) \tag{1}$$

where f is linear frequency.

At first, the speech signal $x(n)$ is divided into N frames, and the Hamming window $H(n)$ is adopted to obtain the windowed frame from the raw speech signal, as shown,

$$H(n) = 0.54 - 0.46cos\frac{2\pi n}{Z-1}, n = 0, 1, \cdots, Z-1 \tag{2}$$

where Z is the total number of the frames in a speech sample.

Then the frequency spectrum $F(\omega)$ of the i-th frame $x_i(n)$ is calculated through a Fast Fourier Transform (FFT). The power spectrum $|F(\omega)|^2$ is process by a Mel-filter bank B_{Mel} which consist of M triangular band-pass filters. Then the power P_m of the m-th Mel-filter $B_m(\omega)$ is denoted as,

$$P_m = \int_{f_{lm}}^{f_{um}} B_m(\omega)|F(\omega)|^2 d\omega, m = 1, 2, \cdots, M \tag{3}$$

where f_{um} and f_{lm} present the upper and lower cut-off frequencies of $B_m(\omega)$.

Then pre-emphasize the i-th frame $x_i(n)$ and transform it through Fast Fourier Transform and gain the L-dimensional MFCC of $x_i(n)$ through discrete cosine transform. The calculative formula is defined as,

$$C_l = \sum_{m=1}^{M} \left[\log P_m \cdot \cos\frac{l(m-0.5)\pi}{M} \right], l = 1, 2, \ldots L \tag{4}$$

where C_l is the l-th MFCC composition, L is less than the number of Mel filters.

We also calculate the dynamic cepstrum coefficients derivatives ($\Delta MFCC$ and $\Delta MFCC$). Assume that v_{ij} is the j-th component of the MFCC vector of the i-th frame, and V_j is the set of all j-th components. The average value E_j of each component set V_j and the correlation coefficient $CR_{jj'}$ between different component sets V_j and $V_{j'}$ are obtained by Eq. 5 and Eq. 6, respectively.

$$E_j = E(V_j) = E(\{v_{1j}, v_{2j}, \cdots, v_{Nj}\}), j = 1, 2, \cdots L \tag{5}$$

$$CR_{jj'} = \frac{cov(V_j, V_{j'})}{\sqrt{VAR(V_j)}\sqrt{VAR(V_{j'})}}, 1 \le j \le j' \le L \tag{6}$$

$$W_{MFCC} = [E_1, E_2, \cdots, E_L, CR_{12}, CR_{13}, \cdots, CR_{L-1L}] \tag{7}$$

The E_j and $CR_{jj'}$ are combined to form the statistical moment W_{MFCC} of the L-dimensional MFCC vector by Eq. 7. In this way, the statistical moment $W_{\Delta MFCC}$ of the $\Delta MFCC$ vector and the statistical moment $W_{\Delta\Delta MFCC}$ of the $\Delta\Delta MFCC$ vector will also be obtained.

2.2   Linear Frequency Cepstral Coefficients

LFCC is an average distribution from low frequency to high frequency bandpass filters [14]. The extraction procedure of LFCC statistical moment is shown in Fig. 2.

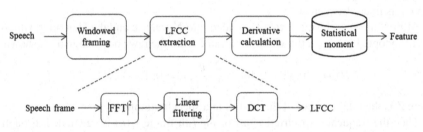

Fig. 2. Extraction procedure of LFCC statistical moment.

As shown in Fig. 2, the speech will firstly through the pre-process, and then the spectral energy can be obtained through the FFT, the calculative formula is shown as,

$$X_i(k) = \sum_{n=0}^{N-1} x_i(m)e^{-j2\pi/N}, 0 \le k \le N \tag{8}$$

$$E(i, k) = [X_i(k)]^2 \tag{9}$$

where $x_i(m)$ is the speech signal data of the i-th frame, N is the number of Fourier.

Then the spectral energy will be processed through the bank filter group which including L bank filters with the center frequency $f(m), m = 1, 2, \ldots L$. The frequency response of triangular band-pass filter is shown as,

$$H_l(k) = \begin{cases} 0, k < f(l-1) \\ \frac{k-f(l-1)}{f(l)-f(l-1)}, f(l-1) \le k \le f(l) \\ \frac{f(l-1)-k}{f(l+1)-f(l)}, f(l) \le k \le f(l+1) \\ 0, k > f(l+1) \end{cases} \tag{10}$$

And the filtering spectral energy processed by bank filter group is denoted as,

$$S(i, l) = \sum_{k=0}^{N-1} [X_i(k)]^2 H_l(k), 0 \leq l \leq L \qquad (11)$$

where l denote the i-th triangular band-pass filter.

Then the DCT is applied to calculate the cepstrum coefficients of the output of the bank filters, the calculated formula is denoted as,

$$lfcc(i, n) = \sqrt{\frac{2}{L}} \sum_{l=0}^{L-1} \ln[S(i, l)] cos\left(\frac{\pi n(2l-1)}{2L}\right) \qquad (12)$$

where n represents the spectrum after the DCT of the i-th frame,

As the same process of MFCC, we also calculate the first-order difference ΔLFCC of LFCC and second-order difference $\Delta\Delta$LFCC. The concrete calculative formula is shown as,

$$LFCC = \begin{vmatrix} x_{1,1} & \cdots & x_{1,n} \\ \cdots & \cdots & \cdots \\ x_{s,1} & \cdots & x_{s,n} \end{vmatrix} \qquad (13)$$

$$\Delta x_{i,j} = \frac{1}{3} \sum_{u=-2}^{2} u x_{i+u,j}, 3 \leq i \leq s-2, 1 \leq j \leq s \qquad (14)$$

3   Detection Method Based on RNN

In this section, we will give a general description of the proposed framework for detecting four forgery operations based on RNN.

3.1   Framework

Recently, many deep learning approaches have been applied as the classifier especially the CNN which can capture the highly complex feature from a raw sample significantly [15]. It is obvious that, the CNN structure can effectively extract deep high-level features and obtain a good detection result in image forensics. However, it is not suitable for speech forensic task because the CNN structure cannot capture the sequential connection well. Recently, RNN have been widely used for applications processing temporal sequences such as speech recognition, which can capture the correlation between the frames [16]. Hence, we apply the RNN model in our task of classify the various forgery operations.

The proposed framework is shown in Fig. 3. The traditional feature is extracted from raw waveform, then fed into the RNN. In this work, we choose the statistical moments of MFCC and LFCC cepstrum coefficients as the features mentioned in Sect. 2.1.

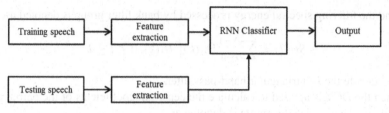

Fig. 3. Proposed classification framework.

Due to the gradient vanishing and exploding issues in training a single-layer RNN, most of the existing RNN architectures only consist of several layers (1, 2 or 3), although the deeper network will capture more useful information. Hence, in this work, to find the better architecture of RNN, three networks have been designed. The network configurations are shown in Fig. 4. Meanwhile, we set the *tanh* activation function to improve the performance of the model, and set the value of the Dropout function to 0.5, which can help the network reduce the overfitting in training procedure. And a Softmax layer is followed to output the probability.

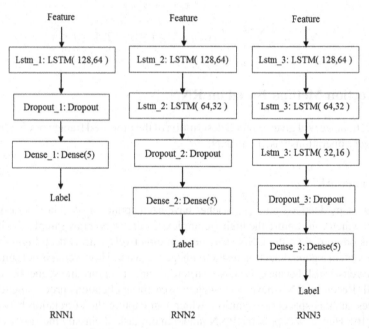

Fig. 4. Three proposed recurrent neural networks.

In the experimental stage, the RNN with two-layers of LSTM layers temporarily selected as the baseline network to find the best features among MFCC and LFCC for detect forgery operations. Then the selected features are used to determine the architecture of RNN.

3.2 Training Strategy

The training strategy of the proposed method includes two stages: training and testing. Before the training, we process the original speech by selecting a parameter for each forgery operation randomly. The training procedure is performed according to the process shown in Fig. 3. The classification feature will be firstly extracted from the original speech and the forged speech which through the disguising, noise-adding, high-pass filtering and low-pass filtering, and then the features will be used for training the RNN. In the testing, we frozen the parameters of RNN model, and choose a part of the original speech and forged speech as the test database, then the final detection result from the output of the Softmax layer will be obtained. Finally, the accuracy is taken as the evaluation metric, and we perform the confusion matrix by making a comparison of the predict labels of testing database and its true labels.

4 Experimental Results and Analysis

In this section, we first present the experimental data and then compare the proposed method with other existing methods.

4.1 Experiment Setup

We create four forgery databases based on the TIMIT speech database [17] and the UME speech database [18], including disguising, low-pass filtering, high-pass filtering and noise-adding. Specifically, we use the Audition CS 6 to build the electric disguised database, and the MATLAB is applied to build the other three forgery database. As shown in Table 1, for each forgery operation, we choose four different operational parameters. And we use the Gaussian white noise as the added noise. And the sample splicing of train setting and test setting of TIMIT and UME are shown in Table 2.

Table 1. Parameters processed by different forgery operations.

Operation	Parameter
Noise-adding	SNR (dB): 5, 10, 15, 20
Disguising	Modification degree: +4, +8, −4, −8
Low-pass filtering	Pass-band cut-off frequency (Hz): 500, 750, 1000, 1250
High-pass filtering	Pass-band cut-off frequency (Hz): 1750, 2000, 2250, 2500

Forged speech databases are built by selecting the forgery speech from those forgery databases. Then, a 4 NVIDIA GTX1080Ti GPUs with 11 GB graphic memory is used for the RNN training.

Table 2. Specific database for multiple operations (Natural/Operated).

Database	TIMIT		UME	
	Training	Testing	Training	Testing
TIMIT	4000/64000	2300/36800	6300/100800	4040/64640
UME	4040/64640	6300/100800	3200/51200	840/13400

4.2   Experimental Results

First, we choose a two-layer RNN architecture for selecting a suitable forensic feature from the acoustic features, including MFCC, LFCC and its first and second derivative called ΔMFCC, $\Delta\Delta$MFCC and ΔLFCC, $\Delta\Delta$LFCC. Then 6 well-trained two-layer RNN models are obtained for each feature and the sample for testing on TIMIT and UME are fed into the 6 models to compare the forensic capability of 6 acoustic features. Table 3 shows the detection accuracy of 6 traditional acoustic features. The MFCC with its first and second derivative features ΔMFCC, $\Delta\Delta$MFCC is better than the other features for classifying the various forged samples in the intra-database, the average accuracy is about 99%. But it is perform a lower accuracy in cross-database (testing the UME samples while the model was trained by TIMIT database), approximately 80%, which means the MFCC features may not be universal and robust.

Table 3. Average detection accuracy of six features in a two-layer RNN (%).

Training	Feature	Testing	
		TIMIT	UME
TIMIT	LFCC	99.17	98.43
	LFCC + ΔLFCC	99.69	87.90
	LFCC + ΔLFCC + $\Delta\Delta$LFCC	95.14	90.25
	MFCC	99.95	100
	MFCC + ΔMFCC	99.93	100
	MFCC + ΔMFCC + $\Delta\Delta$MFCC	100	100
UME	LFCC	88.95	97.92
	LFCC + ΔLFCC	87.90	98.28
	LFCC + ΔLFCC + $\Delta\Delta$LFCC	78.56	89.78
	MFCC	82.67	99.9
	MFCC + ΔMFCC	79.47	99.9
	MFCC + ΔMFCC + $\Delta\Delta$MFCC	77.67	99.92

Different from MFCC, the LFCC feature have a better performance in the forensic task of detect the various operations. As shown in Table 3, the LFCC and its first and second derivative features ΔLFCC, $\Delta\Delta$LFCC have achieved a detection accuracy about 88% in cross-database while maintaining a good performance in intra-database.

Compared with the results shown in Table 3, the MFCC features is not well performance the difference between the original samples and the four forged samples. It indicates that MFCC features is not robustness enough. Although the LFCC and its first and second derivate features is slightly reduced in the intra-database, it is also still in the acceptable range better than the MFCC in cross-database. Hence, the LFCCs is selected as the suitable acoustic feature considering.

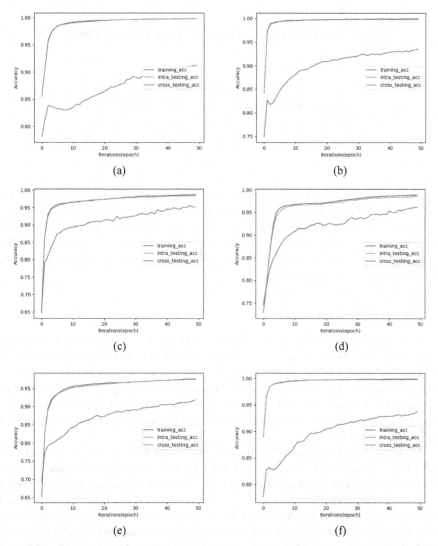

Fig. 5. Detection accuracy of three RNN networks among training process in TIMIT and UME database. (a) and (b) are the detection performance of RNN1 model. (c) and (d) are the detection performance of RNN2 model. (e) and (f) are the detection performance of RNN3 model. (a) (c) (e) are trained by TIMIT database and (b) (d) (f) are trained by UME database.

The structure of the RNN has play an important role in affecting the classification result. We design three structures for RNN in Fig. 4 to explore the impact of the specific network structures. Then, the selected features LFCCs are extracted from the original database and forgery databases for training the three RNN models. Finally, the classification probability will be obtained by the Softmax layer. The detection accuracy of three models based on TIMIT and UME databases in training process are shown in Fig. 5 (a–f). And the comparison results of three models are shown in Table 4.

Table 4. Average detection accuracy of different structures of RNN (%).

Structure	Testing					
	RNN1		RNN2		RNN3	
Training	TIMIT	UME	TIMIT	UME	TIMIT	UME
TIMIT	98.63	97.85	99.11	98.43	99.08	98.68
UME	87.07	96.93	88.95	97.92	88.90	97.85

As shown in the second and third rows, the testing results have an excellent accuracy (above 97%). And the RNN2 model achieved a better detection accuracy about 88% in detecting the cross-database. Results show that the detection ability of the RNN2 structure and the RNN3 network structure are similar. Hence, we choose the RNN2 model as the final structure for the detection of various forgery operations considering the complexity of the experiment.

4.3 Comparative Experiment

We make a comparative experiment of the detection performance between this work based on RNN and our previous work based on CNN [19]. In our previous work, we proposed a forensic method for identifying the four kinds of forgery operations. First, a fixed convolutional layer is used to obtain the residuals of the speech sample, and then the residual signals are classified by a set of convolutional layer group. The comparative experiment shows that the method proposed in this paper has greatly improved the classification accuracy.

As shown in Sect. 4.2, the RNN2 is determined as the final recurrent neural network with LFCCs as the acoustic feature in this work. Results show that the average detection accuracy of its classification result is about 90%. In order to compare with the existing work, we repeated the experiments in [19] with the original and forged databases, and the experimental results are shown in Table 5. As shown in the second and third rows, the test results all have excellent accuracy (above 96%) in the intra-database. Even the results of the CNN are slightly better than RNN. However, the test results all have a certain decline in the cross-database, and the detection rate of RNN can be maintained above 87%. Some of the multiclassification results given in this paper are comparable with the CNN model in [19], and some detection accuracy are significantly better than the detection method based on CNN.

Table 5. Classification capability of the proposed RNN compared with CNN model (%).

Classifier	Training	Testing	
		TIMIT	UME
CNN [19]	TIMIT	99.77	84.33
	UME	76.59	99.82
RNN	TIMIT	98.63	97.85
	UME	87.07	96.93

5 Conclusion

In this paper, we carefully design a speech forensic method based on RNN for the detection of various forgery operations, and provide extensive results to show that the proposed method can effectively identify forgery operations. In the future, we will extend the proposed model and explore the deep features extracted by the neural network to identify unknown forgery operations.

References

1. Luo, D., Yang, R., Li, B., et al.: Detection of double compressed AMR audio using stacked autoencoder. IEEE Trans. Inf. Forensics Secur. **12**(2), 432–444 (2017)
2. Jing, X.U., Xia, J.: Digital audio resampling detection based on sparse representation classifier and periodicity of second derivative. J. Digit. Inf. Manag. **13**(2), 101–109 (2015)
3. Gaka, J., Grzywacz, M., Samborski, R.: Playback attack detection for text-dependent speaker verification over telephone channels. Speech Commun. **67**, 143–153 (2015)
4. Lavrentyeva, G., Novoselov, S., Malykh, E., Kozlov, A., Kudashev, O., Shchemelinin, V.: Audio-replay attack detection countermeasures. In: Karpov, A., Potapova, R., Mporas, I. (eds.) SPECOM 2017. LNCS (LNAI), vol. 10458, pp. 171–181. Springer, Cham (2017). https://doi.org/10.1007/978-3-319-66429-3_16
5. Wu, H., Wang, Y., Huang, J.: Identification of electronic disguised speech. IEEE Trans. Inf. Forensics Secur. **9**(3), 489–500 (2014)
6. Cao, W., Wang, H., Zhao, H., Qian, Q., Abdullahi, S.M.: Identification of electronic disguised voices in the noisy environment. In: Shi, Y.Q., Kim, H.J., Perez-Gonzalez, F., Liu, F. (eds.) IWDW 2016. LNCS, vol. 10082, pp. 75–87. Springer, Cham (2017). https://doi.org/10.1007/978-3-319-53465-7_6
7. Jeong, B.G., Moon, Y.H., Eom, I.K.: Blind identification of image manipulation type using mixed statistical moments. J. Electron. Imaging **24**(1), 013029 (2015)
8. Li, H., Luo, W., Qiu, X., et al.: Identification of various image operations using residual-based features. IEEE Trans. Circuits Syst. Video Technol. **28**(1), 31–45 (2018)
9. Chen, Q., Luo, W., Luo, D.: Identification of audio processing operations based on convolutional neural network. In: ACM Workshop on Information Hiding and Multimedia Security, Innsbruck, pp. 73–77 (2018)
10. Szegedy, C., Liu, W., Jia, Y., et al.: Going deeper with convolutions. In: Proceedings of the IEEE Conference on Computer Vision and Pattern Recognition, Boston, pp. 1–9. IEEE (2015)
11. Liu, Y., Qian, Y., Chen, N., et al.: Deep feature for text-dependent speaker verification. Speech Commun. **73**, 1–13 (2015)

12. Tian, X., Wu, Z., Xiao, X., et al.: Spoofing detection from a feature representation perspective. In: 2016 IEEE International Conference on Acoustics, Speech and Signal Processing, Shanghai, pp. 2119–2123. IEEE (2016)
13. Variani, E., Lei, X., Mcdermott, E., et al.: Deep neural networks for small footprint text-dependent speaker verification. In: IEEE International Conference on Acoustics, Speech and Signal Processing, Florence, pp. 4052–4056. IEEE (2014)
14. Rana, M., Miglani, S.: Performance analysis of MFCC and LPCC techniques in automatic speech recognition. Int. J. Eng. Comput. Sci. 3(8), 7727–7732 (2014)
15. Chen, B., Luo, W., Li, H.: Audio steganalysis with convolutional neural network. In: Conference: the 5th ACM Workshop, Philadelphia, pp. 85–90 (2017)
16. Sak, H., Senior, A., Rao, K., et al.: Learning acoustic frame labeling for speech recognition with recurrent neural networks. In: 2015 IEEE International Conference on Acoustics, Speech and Signal Processing, Brisbane, pp. 4280–4284. IEEE (2015)
17. Timit Acoustic-Phonetic Continuous Speech Corpus. https://catalog.ldc.upenn.edu/LDC 93S1. Accessed 20 Feb 2017
18. Advanced Utilization of Multimedia to Promote Higher Education Reform Speech Database. http://research.nii.ac.jp/src/en/UME-ERJ.html. Accessed 27 Feb 2017
19. Wu, T.: Digital speech forensics algorithm for multiple forgery operations. Wirel. Commun. Technol. 28(3), 37–44 (2019). (in Chinese)

Robust, Imperceptible and End-to-End Audio Steganography Based on CNN

Jie Wang, Rangding Wang$^{(\boxtimes)}$, Li Dong, and Diqun Yan

College of Information Science and Engineering, Ningbo University, Zhejiang, China
wangrangding@nbu.edu.cn

Abstract. Recently, deep learning-based steganography emerges, where the end-to-end steganography is a promising direction. However, most of the existing approaches are developed for the image which are not suitable for the audio. In this paper, we design a CNN-based end-to-end framework that consists of an encoder and a decoder. The encoder achieves encoding the secret message into the audio cover and the corresponding decoder is used to extract the message. Specifically, a derivative-based distortion function is adopted as the loss function of the encoder. Besides, instead of directly generating the stego audios, the encoder in our framework generates the modification vector of the audio sampling value. In this way, the distortion incurred by message embedding can be further reduced. The experiment results show that, compared with the existing approach based on generative adversarial network (GAN), even without an adversarial steganalytic network, stego audios perform relatively more imperceptible. In addition, considering some possible pollution of stego audios in the transmission, we further improve the robustness of our approach by introducing noise simulation layers into the framework.

Keywords: End-to-end steganography · Deep learning · Minimal-distortion

1 Introduction

Nowadays, the problems of information security and privacy protection are ever-increasingly serious, information protection techniques [19,24,28] gain extensive attention. Steganography is an information hiding technique. It embeds secret message into public digital cover in an imperceptive fashion. Conversely, steganalysis aims to expose the existence of steganography. In the game of confrontation, the progress of steganography will promote the development of steganalysis, and vice versa.

Audio, as a common digital medium, is often used as the steganographic cover. Thus, lots of efforts have been made to design more advanced audio steganography. Traditional audio steganography hides messages in the redundancy of human perception. Take the example of LSB (Least Significant Bit)

© Springer Nature Singapore Pte Ltd. 2020
S. Yu et al. (Eds.): SPDE 2020, CCIS 1268, pp. 427–442, 2020.
https://doi.org/10.1007/978-981-15-9129-7_30

matching [17], message embedding is realized by changing the least significant bits of the audio sampling value. In this period, steganalysis is mainly based on hand-crafted features and some traditional machine learning techniques. In the work [13] and [14], Liu et al. proposed the features of Mel-Frequency Cepstrum Coefficient (MFCC) and Markov transition based on the second-order derivative of the audio signal, respectively. After feature extraction, Support Vector Machine (SVM) is employed for classification. After that, Luo et al. [15] further combines multiple improved features and puts them into the ensemble classifier to make the final decision.

With the advent of distortion minimization framework [5], steganography has entered a new stage. Under this framework, the advanced content-adaptive audio steganography design sophisticated distortion cost functions and then employ Syndrome-Trellis Codes (STCs) [4] to perform message embedding. According to the residual between original audio and reconstructed AAC audio, Luo et al. [16] designed an AAC-based distortion function. Recently, et al. [3] utilized derivative filters to calculate the complexity of the audio and combined the amplitude, then presented the derivative-based (DFR) distortion. Comparatively, deep learning has profoundly reformed the steganalysis field. Chen et al. [2] first proposed a Convolutional Neural Network (CNN) based steganalysis framework for the audio signal and surpass most traditional steganalysis methods. In another work, Lin et al. [11] further improved the detection performance by employing the High-Pass Filter (HPF) and the Truncated Linear Unit (TLU) activation function. Until now, these deep learning-based audio steganalysis [2,10–12] have seriously threatened the security of steganography.

The deep learning-based steganalysis impels the researchers that *whether the deep learning technique can be used for steganography?* With the awareness that both the adversarial training of GAN [6] and the confrontation between steganography and steganalysis can be formulated as min-max game, some pioneering GAN-based works have emerged. SSGAN [22] is the first to propose to introduce a steganalytic network into the GAN framework and synthesize cover image, which is more suitable for subsequent steganography. Under the framework of minimal-distortion, the purpose of ASDL-GAN [23] and UT-6HPF-GAN [25] were to learn the modification map through adversarial training with the steganalytic network. To address the problem that the embedding process is nondifferentiable, they proposed the TES and Double Tanh activation function, respectively. Although these approaches have achieved good results, the implementations are still inseparable from the participation of the prior steganography. In HayersGAN [7], HIDDeN [29] and SteganoGAN [26], the authors presented a more attractive conception, which is end-to-end embedding and extraction. In their GAN-based framework, the encoder is used to convert the original cover image and the message into the stego image, and the decoder aims to extract the message. While the steganalytic network used to encourage the encoder to produce less distortion on the cover image. In addition, there are some other works, e.g., ISGAN [27] and ChenGAN [1], considered to end-to-end hide and extract an entire secret image. Nowadays, GAN attracts lots of attention and it has been adopted to some fields of computer vision, speech synthesis, and privacy-preserving [20].

Arguably, steganography based on GAN is becoming one of the hot spots of research, especially the end-to-end steganography. As far as we know, however, the relevant research is quite limited in the audio field. We find that the performance of the aforementioned end-to-end steganography in the image field can not be generalized to the audio field. In this paper, we design a CNN-based end-to-end framework for audio steganography. In order to constrain the distortion after message embedding, our approach does not generate the stego audio directly, but the modification vector of audio sampling value. In addition, we make full use of the distortion function, which is designed for the framework of distortion minimalization as the optimization objective. The main contributions of our work are summarized as follows:

- A CNN-based framework for realizing end-to-end audio steganography is proposed, which output the modification vector of audio sampling value to constrain the distortion.
- The concept of minimal-distortion is introduced into our framework. We explore the possibility of using a distortion function as the loss function. Compared with the existing solutions in the image field, our approach has better imperceptibility at the same embedding rate.
- In order to improve the robustness to resist real-world interference, the specially designed noise simulation layers are employed in the training process.

The rest of this paper is organized as follows. Section 2 briefly reviews the related work. Section 3 describes our proposed framework, accompanied by model architecture and loss function. Section 4 presents the experimental results, and the final conclusion are given in Sect. 5.

2 Related Work

In this section, we briefly review some related work of minimal-distortion steganography and GAN-based end-to-end image steganography in detail, which lay the foundational concepts for our approach.

2.1 Minimal-Distortion Steganography

The framework of distortion minimization first proposed by [5] and becomes one of the widely-used steganographic model. Let $\mathbf{X}$ and $\mathbf{Y}$ be the cover and stego audio, $x_i \in \mathbf{X}$ and $y_i \in \mathbf{Y}$ denotes the sampling value, respectively. The additive distortion between the cover and stego audio can be express as

$$D(\mathbf{X}, \mathbf{Y}) = \sum_{i=1}^{n} \rho_i |x_i - y_i|, \tag{1}$$

where ρ_i is the cost of changing sampling value x_i to y_i. For a given distortion function, a steganographer can use STCs [4] to embed the message. Hence, the

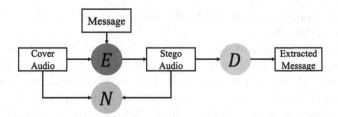

Fig. 1. The diagram of GAN-based end-to-end steganography. The framework contains three networks: an encoder E, a decoder D and a steganalytic network N. In the training process, the encoder E used to synthesize stego audio and the decoder D tries to extract the message from the synthesized stego audio. The adversarial training is realized by the participation of the steganalytic network N.

essential task of the steganographer is to design a heuristical distortion function with high undetectability. In the audio field, the AAC-based [16] and DFR [3] distortion are such two typical minimal-distortion schemes in which DFR distortion had achieved state-of-art performance. Because of the complexity and the large-amplitude of audio are suitable for the message hiding, DFR distortion takes these rules into account. First, the derivative filter residual is used to represent the complexity of the audio signal. For a given audio signal x, the derivative filter residual r_f is obtained by

$$r_f = x \otimes f, \tag{2}$$

where f can be any high-order filter. Next, DFR distortion will be inversely proportional to the sum of the derivative filter residual and amplitude. Mathematically, DFR distortion is calculated

$$\rho^+ = \rho^- = \frac{1}{|r_f| + |x| + \theta}, \tag{3}$$

where $|x|$ denotes the amplitude of audio sampling value and θ is a stabilizing constant introduced to avoid dividing by zero. In the implementation, it is proved that the message will not be embedded into the relatively flat regions via minimizing the expectation of DFR distortion.

2.2 GAN-Based End-to-End Image Steganography

In current literature, HayersGAN [7], HIDDeN [29], and SteganoGAN [26] are the three typical representatives that training a GAN-based framework to realize end-to-end image steganography. The paradigm of their GAN-based framework is shown in Fig. 1. It consists of three components, namely, an encoder E, a decoder D and a steganalytic network N. In practical application, the steganographer will feed cover images and the binary messages to the framework for training. In the training stage, the encoder receives the input data and outputs the stego image. The decoder aims to extract the message from the stego image. While the task of the steganalytic network is trying to distinguish the difference between the stego image and cover image. The existence of the steganalytic network N enables the framework to conduct adversarial training. The loss function of the framework also includes three parts: the loss of cover image distortion, the loss of message extraction and the adversarial loss. Once the training reaches equilibrium and no longer converges, the steganographer uses the encoder E to construct the stego image and send it to the receiver, while the receiver uses the corresponding decoder D to extract the message. The differences between the three frameworks are: HayersGAN [7] is a fully connected network; HIDDeN [29] applies convolutional network and noise layers to enhance the quality and the robustness of the stego image; SteganoGAN [26] adopts a DenseNet [8]-based structure, further improving the capacity and quality. Moreover, SteganoGAN [26] could handle big size images.

However, these methods are not directly fit the audio signal and can not achieve good security performance. In this paper, we integrate the characteristics of minimal-distortion steganography and GAN-based end-to-end steganography. In our proposed CNN-based framework, we introduce the distortion function as the loss function to conduct training. To characterize the changing value between the cover audio and stego audio, the encoder generates the modification vector. Experimental results show that our approach has better imperceptibility. In the next section, we will discuss our approach in detail.

3 End-to-End Audio Steganography Based on CNN

In this section, we describe our proposed CNN-based framework, including the network structure, the loss function, and the noise simulation layer.

3.1 Overview of the Basic Framework

As illustrated in Fig. 2, our proposed basic framework only contains two networks, i.e., the encoder E and the decoder D. Let $\mathbf{C} = (c)^{l \times 1}$ and $\mathbf{S} = (s)^{l \times 1}$ be the cover and stego audios of l samples, respectively. While $\mathbf{M} = (m)^{l \times 1}$ be the vectors of the original binary messages (note that when the length of message less than l, fill it with 0). Specifically, the encoder E receives the cover audios $\mathbf{C}$ and the binary messages $\mathbf{M}$, outputs the modification vectors $\mathbf{V} = (v)^{l \times 1}$. Then add the modification vectors $\mathbf{V}$ to the cover audios $\mathbf{C}$ to construct the stego audios $\mathbf{S}$. The reason why the encoder E does not generate the stego audios directly but the modification vectors is that the modification vectors can better constrain the distortion. Moreover, the modification vectors $\mathbf{V}$ are also the preparation for the subsequent derivative-based loss function. Finally, the stego audios $\mathbf{S}$ are send to the decoder D and output extracted messages $\widetilde{\mathbf{M}} = (\widetilde{m})^{l \times 1}$.

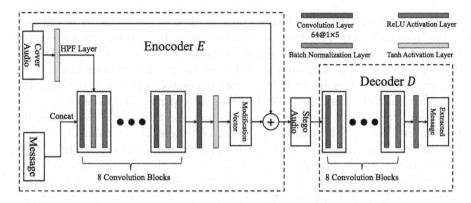

Fig. 2. The basic framework of our CNN-based approach. It consists of the encoder E and the decoder D. The rectangles labeled in different colors are used to represent different types of network layer. The text under the "Convolution layer" (i.e., 64@1×5) represents the number of output channels and the kernel size. The notation "+" denotes add the modification vector to the cover audio to construct stego audio.

3.2   Network Architecture

The details of the structure of the two networks are shown in Fig. 2. In the following, we first describe the encoder. On steganalysis side, it shall preprocess the input data using derivative filters to magnify the impacts of message embedding. While for steganography, it is expected to embed the message into the complex region. Thus, in order for the encoder E to focus on the complex region, a higher-order filter is fixed as the first HPF layer of E to calculate the residual maps. Then, concatenate the message vectors $\mathbf{M}$ to the residual maps and fed to 7 convolution blocks. Each convolution block consecutively consists of a 1×5 convolution layer with 32 channels, a batch normalization (BN) layer and a rectified linear unit (ReLU) activation layer. Having been processed by 7 convolution blocks, the feature maps are input into a 1×1 convolution layer and end with a hyperbolic tangent activation function (Tanh) activation layer. Hence, the final output $\mathbf{V}$ is constrained to $(-1, 1)$.

The structure of the decode D is similar to that of the encoder E. The difference is that the convolution block in the decode D only composed of a convolution layer and a ReLU activation layer. In addition, there is no Tanh activation layer and the fixed high-order filter in D.

3.3   Loss Functions

To meet end-to-end steganography, we define two loss functions to optimize. First, the decoder D aims to extract the message from the stego audio. Therefore, the loss $\mathcal{L}_D$ for training the decoder D, we calculate the cross-entropy loss between the original message $\mathbf{M}$ and the extracted message $\widetilde{\mathbf{M}}$. More formally, $\mathcal{L}_D$ is given as

$$\mathcal{L}_D = -\mathbb{E}_{\widetilde{\mathbf{M}},\mathbf{M}}[\mathbf{M}\log(\widetilde{\mathbf{M}}) + (1 - \mathbf{M})\log(1 - \widetilde{\mathbf{M}})]. \tag{4}$$

The mean square error (MSE) loss is employed by HayerGAN [7] and HIDDEN [29] to measure the extraction accuracy. However, we find that using the cross-entropy loss function makes the training converges faster.

Next, to evaluate the loss caused by message embedding, we suggest to use a derivative-based loss. In many GAN-based steganography methods, it is necessary to add a steganalytic network for impelling the encoder to produce less or imperceptible distortion on the cover. In practice, because the steganalytic network is too strong or weak, it may be difficult to balance the adversarial training. Inspired by minimal-distortion steganography [5], we introduce the empirical knowledge of steganographers. Specifically, we take the distortion function of the distortion minimization framework as the optimization objective and call it *distortion loss function*. When the encoder tries to optimize the distortion loss function, it can closely achieve the effect of adversarial training. Therefore, there is no need for a steganalytic network. Here, DRF distortion function [3] is chose to be distortion loss function, it can be defined as:

$$\mathcal{L}_e = \mathbb{E}_{\mathbf{C}} \left[\frac{\alpha \mathbf{V}}{|\mathbf{C} \otimes f| + |\mathbf{C}| + \theta} \right], \tag{5}$$

where the high-order filter f is identical to the fixed higher-order filter (HPF layer) of the encoder E and the stabilizing constant θ set to 1×10^{-5}. In our experiments, because the output of the encoder E is constrained to $(-1, 1)$, the modifiable space is small, which may cause the decoder D to be unable to extract the message. Thus, an empirical coefficient α is added to amplify the value of $\mathbf{V}$. In addition, α can prevent too much modification on a single sampling value.

Finally, the loss for training the encoder E is the sum of $\mathcal{L}_e$ and $\mathcal{L}_D$, i.e.,

$$\mathcal{L}_E = \mathcal{L}_D + \beta \mathcal{L}_e, \tag{6}$$

where the hyperparameter β control the relative importances among the above two losses. Such design is for the reason that the encoder E should predispose take to the message extraction into account. Otherwise, it is difficult for the decoder D to extract the message.

3.4 Enhance Robustness with Noise Simulation Layer

In the real-world, the stego audio may be polluted by the channel noise or steganalyzer's attack, resulting in the extracted message being distorted. Therefore, outstanding steganography should have certain robustness to resist noise. Driven by the success of HIDDeN [29] and ChenGAN [1], we introduce some noise simulation layers to the basic framework. As shown in Fig. 3, the noise simulation layers contain four types of noise in which the Gaussian Noise layer essentially adds gaussian noise with a standard deviation of σ to the stego audio.

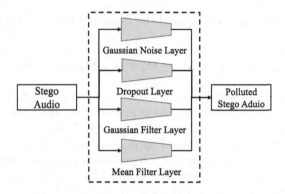

Fig. 3. The noise simulation layers. In the training stage, the select noise simulation layers will be fixed into the framework and pollute the stego audios.

The Dropout layer randomly modifies δ percent sampling values of the stego audio back to the original value. The rest types of noise layers, i.e., the Gaussian Filter layer and Mean Filter layer, are implemented the gaussian kernel with deviation ϱ and mean kernel to blur the stego audio.

In the training stage, one or more types of noise simulation layers will be placed after the stego audio to produce the polluted stego audio. Then, send the polluted stego audios $\mathbf{S}$ to the decoder D. Let P_i denotes the i-th noise layer, the loss function $\mathcal{L}_{PD}$ of the decoder D under noise converts to

$$\mathcal{L}_{PD} = -\frac{1}{k+1}\{\sum_{i=1}^{k}\mathbb{E}_{\mathbf{S},\mathbf{M}}[\mathbf{M}\log(D(P_i(\mathbf{S}))) + (1-\mathbf{M})\log(1-D(P_i(\mathbf{S})))] + \mathcal{L}_D\}. \tag{7}$$

Where k represents the number of noise layers used in the framework.

4   Experiment Results

In this section, we introduce the experimental setup. Then, the results are given from the following three aspects: investigation on derivative filter and loss weight, performance under the noisy scenario, and comparison with a competing method.

4.1   Experimental Setup

Our approach is evaluated on the TIMIT dataset[1]. This dataset contains 6300 audios with the sampling rate of 16 kHz. Note that each audio is of a different duration. To eliminate the impact of the input size, we randomly cut one-second (16000 sampling points) audio segments from the provided audio. We collect 15000 audio clips as the original cover audios in which 10000 cover audios are used for training the framework and the rest 5000 are used for testing. To verify the performance of our approach, we will give three evaluation metrics:

---

[1] https://github.com/philipperemy/timit.

Table 1. Performance of our proposed approach at 1 bps in the different setups.

β	1×10^{-3}			1×10^{-4}			1×10^{-5}			1×10^{-6}		
f	ACC	PESQ	MAE	ACC	PESQ	MAE	ACC	PESQ	MAE	ACC	PESQ	MAE
1-th	81.77	3.810	56.65	94.87	4.270	23.30	98.12	3.875	34.98	98.68	3.143	53.97
2-th	81.03	3.870	48.88	95.07	4.266	22.15	98.29	3.784	43.43	98.80	3.376	40.63
3-th	92.51	3.679	33.61	97.49	4.033	34.62	98.60	3.363	51.37	99.14	3.194	40.08
4-th	93.65	3.816	31.67	97.31	4.115	22.95	98.46	3.460	44.30	99.18	3.209	58.63
5-th	95.90	4.034	30.30	97.82	4.004	24.39	98.73	3.525	36.40	99.14	2.801	77.79
6-th	96.61	4.029	32.07	98.33	3.993	24.40	98.87	3.458	35.72	99.41	3.045	77.73

1) Accuracy of message extraction (ACC). It shows the proportion of the message that the decoder D can extract successfully. For an orginal message vector m and extracted message vector $\tilde{m}$, ACC can be express as:

$$ACC = \frac{1}{l} \sum_{i}^{l} (m_i \odot \tilde{m}_i). \tag{8}$$

where the symbol $\odot$ denotes exclusive nor.

2) Perceptual evaluation of speech quality (PESQ) [21]. It represents the perceptibility and the mean opinion scores (MOS) after the message embedding, whose scale ranges from -0.5 (bad) to 4.5 (excellent).

3) Mean absolute error (MAE). It means the magnitude of the average modification per sampling point and reflects the content difference between the cover audio c and the stego audio s, it defines as:

$$MAE = \frac{1}{l} \sum_{i}^{l} |c_i - s_i|. \tag{9}$$

The training procedure of the framework is iteratively optimizing the loss of the encoder E and the decoder D. Before the training, all parameters of the encoder E and the decoder D are initialized from a Glorot initialization. At the training stage, the number of training epochs set to 300, both networks use a batch-size of 16 and the Adam [9] optimizer with a learning rate of 1×10^{-4}. For the coefficient α in the Eq. (5), after some trials and errors, we empirically set to 200 in our experiment which can get acceptable performance. Our proposed CNN-based framework is implemented with Pytorch [18] and train on four NVIDIA GTX1080Ti GPUs with 11 GB memory.

4.2 Investigation on Derivative Filter and Loss Weight

In the original DFR distortion function [3], the authors stated that the high-order filter f influence its security performance. Therefore, in our experiments, we take six kinds of common derivative filters as following into account too:

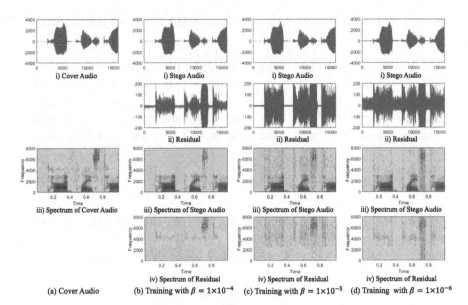

Fig. 4. Visual illustration of the cover and stego audio. (a) represents cover audio. (b), (c) and (d) represents stego audios and residual difference obtained after training with $\beta = 1 \times 10^{-4}$, $\beta = 1 \times 10^{-5}$, $\beta = 1 \times 10^{-6}$, respectively. From the sampling value of the residual difference, the distortion caused by the encoder is heavily focused on the area of large-amplitude and complexity. From the side of the spectrum, the difference between the cover audio and stego audio is the high-frequency region. In addition, comparing the sampling value and spectrum of the residual in the different training settings, it is found that with the value of β decrease, distortion starts to be less constrained.

$$f_1 = [-1, 1, 0], f_2 = [-1, 2, -1],$$
$$f_3 = [1, -3, 3, -1, 0], f_4 = [-1, 4, -6, 4, -1], \tag{10}$$
$$f_5 = [-1, 5, -10, 10, -5, 1, 0], f_6 = [-1, 6, -15, 20, -15, 6, -1].$$

where padding zero is to make the data size after convolution operation stays the same. Besides, the hyper-parameter β (please refer to (6)) balances the importances between distortion and accuracy of message extraction. As a result, we both investigate the impact of the derivative filter f and the hyper-parameter β. The experimental results at the embedding rate of 1 bps are reported in Table 1.

From Table 1, the following conclusions can be obtained:

1) Under a fixed derivative filter, with the value of the parameter β decrease, the accuracy of message extraction rises gradually to more than 99% and the score of PESQ shows a downward trend. On the contrary, it is obvious that the higher orders of the filter under the same β value brings the same trend.

2) It can be observed that even under 99% accuracy of message extraction, the score of PESQ hovers 3 which indicates the stego audio sounds the same as the cover audio. When the accuracy of message extraction is nearly 98% or less, the

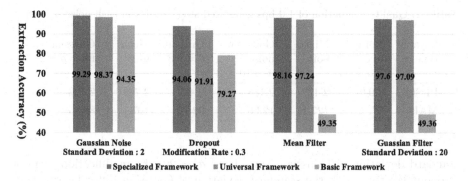

Fig. 5. Extraction accuracy under the noise scenario. The blue column represents the specialized framework, which means the noise layer in the training and test stage is the same. The orange column represents the universal framework, which means four types of noise layers are taken into account in the training stage. Finally, the grey column represents the basic framework without any noise layer. (Color figure online)

score of PESQ close to 4. This observation suggests that, under the guarantee of message extraction accuracy, our approach has good imperceptibility.

3) To visualize the effect of the distortion loss function intuitively, we illustrate the sampling value and spectrum of a randomly selected cover audio, the corresponding stego audios and residual with the 2-th order f_2. From Fig. 4-(b), when $\beta = 1 \times 10^{-4}$, the produced distortion in sampling value is mainly in the imperceptible area, i.e., the complexity and large-amplitude region. Besides, the differences between the cover audio and stego audio are mainly distributed in the high-frequency area. This phenomenon implies that the distortion loss function can supervise the encoder to hide the message into the imperceptible position of the audio cover. When $\beta = 1 \times 10^{-5}$, the distortion becomes more than before. Finally, the distortion from Fig. 4-(d) is difficult to be constrained and spread to the whole frequency band in $\beta = 1 \times 10^{-6}$.

4) Larger MAE does not mean lower PESQ score. For example, when $\beta = 1 \times 10^{-6}$, the score of PESQ with the 4-th order f_4 is higher than that with the 3-th order f_3. It can be explained by the same fact as 3) that, by optimizing the distortion loss function, the message is not only bounded in a less way but also embedded into the more imperceptible area.

4.3 Performance Under Noisy Environment

In this part, we would like to show the performance of our approach under the noise environment. To resist the inference of different noise, we add the corresponding or mixed noise simulation layer to the framework in the training stage. Considering that the noise has a great impact on extraction accuracy, therefore, we set f to 6-th and β to 1×10^{-6} according to the configuration with the highest extraction accuracy. In particular, within each noise layer, the

Table 2. Quality evaluation of 1.0 bps generated stego audios in each noise scenario.

Layer type	Noise free	Mixed noise	Gaussian noise $\sigma = 10$	Dropout $\delta = 0.3$	Mean filter	Gaussian filter $\varrho = 2$
PESQ	3.045	2.477	2.188	2.449	2.763	2.403
MAE	77.73	127.1	123.6	92.76	107.1	88.85

standard deviation of Gaussian Noise layer $\sigma = 20$, the modification ratio of Dropout layer $\delta = 0.3$, the standard deviation of Gaussian Filter layer $\varrho = 2$, kernel size of Gaussian Filter layer and Mean Filter layer set to 3. In this part of the experiment, similarly, we take 1 bps as the embedding rate.

First, Fig. 5 shows the extraction accuracy of the decoder D under different scenarios. Specifically, the specialized framework represents that a single noise simulation layer is added to the training stage, which is the same as the test stage; the universal framework represents that all noise simulation layers are mixed into the framework at the same time during the training. Obviously, the introduction of the noise layer greatly enhances the robustness of the method. The Specialized has a strong resistance to prescribe noise, while the Universal sacrifices a certain accuracy but has a higher generalization.

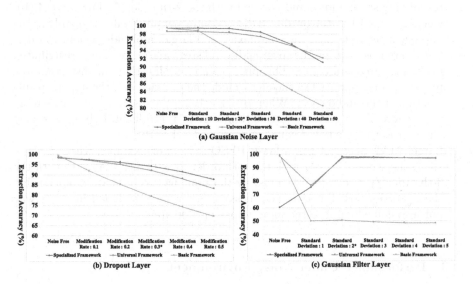

Fig. 6. Extraction accuracy under the different setups of noise layers. The notation "*" denotes the variable setting during the training stage.

Next, in Table 2, we give the quality evaluation results of stego audios generated by adding the noise simulation layers to the training. Note that these

Table 3. Results of comparative experiment with different embedding rates.

Embedding rate	1.0bps			0.5bps			0.1bps		
Steganography approach	ACC	PESQ	MAE	ACC	PESQ	MAE	ACC	PESQ	MAE
SteganoGAN [26] Using in audio	99.25	2.768	79.10	99.61	3.066	74.75	99.75	3.509	**43.35**
Proposed approach	**99.41**	**3.045**	**77.73**	**99.64**	**3.477**	**55.91**	**99.90**	**3.525**	56.05

stego audios are evaluated before pollution. Finally, we further investigate the impact of variable σ, δ and ϱ in the Gaussian Noise, Dropout and Gaussian Filter layer. The results are shown in Fig. 6. As can be seen, although each specialized framework is trained under the fixed variable of the noise layer, it also has a certain resistance to other situations. In conclusion, the universal framework has stronger robustness in various noisy environments.

4.4 Comparative Experiments with Different Embedding Rates

In this subsection, we compare our proposed approach with a similar technique. As far as we know, however, there is no relevant research in the audio field. To handle this problem, we consider choosing SteganoGAN [26] as the comparison approach and using it in the audio field. Compared with HayersGAN [7] and HIDDEN [29], the network structure of SteganoGAN [26] is more suitable for migrating to the audio signal and is the latest research. In order to the comparison at the approximate extraction accuracy, our approach chooses the relative satisfied performance setting getting from the previous subsection, that is, f is 6-th filter, β is 1×10^{-6}.

The comparative results in the setting of different embedding rates are shown in Table 3. As can be seen, in comparison, our approach is slightly higher than SteganoGAN [26] in the extraction accuracy. But there is a significant improvement in imperceptibility. The results demonstrate that even there is no steganalytic network for adversarial training, the imperceptible effect can be obtained by combining the distortion function of the prior knowledge of the steganographer. Moreover, the structure of our network is composed of common convolution blocks, while SteganoGAN [26] is a variant of DenseNet [8]. It is reasonable to conclude that when a more advanced network structure is adopted, the performance of our approach can be further improved.

5   Discussion and Future Work

In this paper, we design a CNN-based end-to-end audio steganography framework. Unlike the existing GAN-based schemes, we suggest to use the empirical designed distortion function as the loss function for training the network. Extensive experiments are conducted to find a practical setup of the loss functions.

Compared with the similar scheme using in the audio field, our approach has a significant improvement in the imperceptibility of the stego audio. Motivated by enhancing the robustness, in the last, the noise simulation layers are drawn into the training stage and make our approach more practical.

Although the performance of our approach is better than SteganoGAN [26] in the audio field, we shall note that our approach is far from the security of other non-end-to-end steganography algorithms. The main possible reason for this is that the range of audio sampling values (0–65536) is wider than that of image sampling values (0–255). It is difficult for the decoder to extract the message due to the weak change of sampling value, so more disturbance is needed. Furthermore, we also find SteganoGAN [26] has good resistance to steganalysis in the color image dataset, but not in the grey image dataset. The possible reason for this phenomenon can be explained by the three channels in the color image which provide more space for hiding messages. In reaction to the problem of low security, in future work, we plan to improve our approach by introducing more advanced network structures.

Acknowledgement. This work was supported by the National Natural Science Foundation of China (Grant No. U1736215, 61672302, 61901237), Zhejiang Natural Science Foundation (Grant No. LY20F020010, LY17F020010) and K.C. Wong Magna Fund in Ningbo University.

References

1. Chen, B., Wang, J., Chen, Y., Jin, Z., Shim, H.J., Shi, Y.Q.: High-capacity robust image steganography via adversarial network. KSII Trans. Internet Inf. Syst. **14**(1) (2020)
2. Chen, B., Luo, W., Li, H.: Audio steganalysis with convolutional neural network. In: Proceedings of the 5th ACM Workshop on Information Hiding and Multimedia Security, pp. 85–90. ACM (2017)
3. Chen, K., Zhou, H., Li, W., Yang, K., Zhang, W., Yu, N.: Derivative-based steganographic distortion and its non-additive extensions for audio. IEEE Trans. Circuits Syst. Video Technol. (2019)
4. Filler, T., Judas, J., Fridrich, J.: Minimizing additive distortion in steganography using syndrome-trellis codes. IEEE Trans. Inf. Forensics Secur. **6**(3), 920–935 (2011)
5. Fridrich, J., Filler, T.: Practical methods for minimizing embedding impact in steganography. In: Security, Steganography, and Watermarking of Multimedia Contents IX, vol. 6505, p. 650502. International Society for Optics and Photonics (2007)
6. Goodfellow, I., et al.: Generative adversarial nets. In: Advances in Neural Information Processing Systems, pp. 2672–2680 (2014)
7. Hayes, J., Danezis, G.: Generating steganographic images via adversarial training. In: Advances in Neural Information Processing Systems, pp. 1954–1963 (2017)
8. Huang, G., Liu, Z., Van Der Maaten, L., Weinberger, K.Q.: Densely connected convolutional networks. In: Proceedings of the IEEE Conference on Computer Vision and Pattern Recognition, pp. 4700–4708 (2017)
9. Kingma, D.P., Ba, J.: Adam: a method for stochastic optimization. arXiv preprint arXiv:1412.6980 (2014)

10. Lee, D., Oh, T.W., Kim, K.: Deep audio steganalysis in time domain. In: Proceedings of the 2020 ACM Workshop on Information Hiding and Multimedia Security, pp. 11–21. ACM (2020)
11. Lin, Y., Wang, R., Yan, D., Dong, L., Zhang, X.: Audio steganalysis with improved convolutional neural network. In: Proceedings of the ACM Workshop on Information Hiding and Multimedia Security, pp. 210–215. ACM (2019)
12. Lin, Z., Huang, Y., Wang, J.: RNN-SM: fast steganalysis of VoIP streams using recurrent neural network. IEEE Trans. Inf. Forensics Secur. **13**(7), 1854–1868 (2018)
13. Liu, Q., Sung, A.H., Qiao, M.: Temporal derivative-based spectrum and melcepstrum audio steganalysis. IEEE Trans. Inf. Forensics Secur. **4**(3), 359–368 (2009)
14. Liu, Q., Sung, A.H., Qiao, M.: Derivative-based audio steganalysis. ACM Trans. Multimedia Comput. Commun. Appl. (TOMM) **7**(3), 18 (2011)
15. Luo, W., Li, H., Yan, Q., Yang, R., Huang, J.: Improved audio steganalytic feature and its applications in audio forensics. ACM Trans. Multimedia Comput. Commun. Appl. (TOMM) **14**(2), 43 (2018)
16. Luo, W., Zhang, Y., Li, H.: Adaptive audio steganography based on advanced audio coding and syndrome-trellis coding. In: Kraetzer, C., Shi, Y.-Q., Dittmann, J., Kim, H.J. (eds.) IWDW 2017. LNCS, vol. 10431, pp. 177–186. Springer, Cham (2017). https://doi.org/10.1007/978-3-319-64185-0_14
17. Mielikainen, J.: LSB matching revisited. IEEE Signal Process. Lett. **13**(5), 285–287 (2006)
18. Paszke, A., et al.: Automatic differentiation in pytorch (2017)
19. Qu, Y., et al.: Decentralized privacy using blockchain-enabled federated learning in fog computing. IEEE Internet Things J. (2020)
20. Qu, Y., Yu, S., Zhou, W., Tian, Y.: GAN-driven personalized spatial-temporal private data sharing in cyber-physical social systems. IEEE Trans. Netw. Sci. Eng. (2020)
21. Rix, A.W., Beerends, J.G., Hollier, M.P., Hekstra, A.P.: Perceptual evaluation of speech quality (PESQ)-a new method for speech quality assessment of telephone networks and codecs. In: 2001 IEEE International Conference on Acoustics, Speech, and Signal Processing. Proceedings (Cat. No. 01CH37221), vol. 2, pp. 749–752. IEEE (2001)
22. Shi, H., Dong, J., Wang, W., Qian, Y., Zhang, X.: SSGAN: secure steganography based on generative adversarial networks. In: Zeng, B., Huang, Q., El Saddik, A., Li, H., Jiang, S., Fan, X. (eds.) PCM 2017. LNCS, vol. 10735, pp. 534–544. Springer, Cham (2018). https://doi.org/10.1007/978-3-319-77380-3_51
23. Tang, W., Tan, S., Li, B., Huang, J.: Automatic steganographic distortion learning using a generative adversarial network. IEEE Signal Process. Lett. **24**(10), 1547–1551 (2017)
24. Wang, M., Xu, C., Chen, X., Hao, H., Zhong, L., Yu, S.: Differential privacy oriented distributed online learning for mobile social video prefetching. IEEE Trans. Multimedia **21**(3), 636–651 (2019)
25. Yang, J., Ruan, D., Huang, J., Kang, X., Shi, Y.Q.: An embedding cost learning framework using GAN. IEEE Trans. Inf. Forensics Secur. **15**, 839–851 (2019)
26. Zhang, K.A., Cuesta-Infante, A., Xu, L., Veeramachaneni, K.: SteganoGAN: high capacity image steganography with GANs. arXiv preprint arXiv:1901.03892 (2019)
27. Zhang, R., Dong, S., Liu, J.: Invisible steganography via generative adversarial networks. Multimedia Tools Appl. **78**(7), 8559–8575 (2018). https://doi.org/10.1007/s11042-018-6951-z

28. Zhou, C., Fu, A., Yu, S., Yang, W., Wang, H., Zhang, Y.: Privacy-preserving federated learning in fog computing. IEEE Internet Things J. (2020)
29. Zhu, J., Kaplan, R., Johnson, J., Fei-Fei, L.: Hidden: hiding data with deep networks. In: Proceedings of the European Conference on Computer Vision (ECCV), pp. 657–672 (2018)

Adversarial Examples Attack and Countermeasure for Speech Recognition System: A Survey

Donghua Wang, Rangding Wang[✉], Li Dong, Diqun Yan, Xueyuan Zhang, and Yongkang Gong

Ningbo University, Ningbo, China
{wangrangding,dongli,yandiqun}@nbu.edu.cn

Abstract. Speech recognition technology is affecting and changing the current human-computer interaction profoundly. Due to the remarkable progress of deep learning, the performance of the Automatic Speech Recognition (ASR) system has also increased significantly. As the core component of the speech assistant in the smartphone or other smart devices, ASR receives speech and responds accordingly, which allows us to control and interact with those devices remotely. However, speech adversarial samples where crafted by adding tiny perturbation to original speech, which can make the ASR system to generate malicious instructions while imperceptual to humans. This new attack brings several potential severe security risks to the deep-learning-based ASR system. In this paper, we provide a systematic survey on the speech adversarial examples. We first proposed a taxonomy of existing adversarial examples. Next, we give a brief introduction of existing adversarial examples for the acoustic system, especially for the ASR system, and summarize several major methods of generating the speech adversarial examples. Finally, after elaborating on the existing countermeasures of adversarial examples, we discuss the current challenges and countermeasures against speech adversarial examples. We also give several promising research directions on both making the attack constructing more realistic and the acoustic system more robust, respectively.

Keywords: Speech adversarial examples · Speech recognition systems · Adversarial defense · Deep learning

1 Introduction

Deep learning has significantly improved the speech recognition system, which makes the end-to-end ASR system more achievable. ASR system receives the speech and interprets it to the corresponding command, which allows people to

Supported by the National Natural Science Foundation of China (Grant No. U1736215, 61672302, 61901237), Zhejiang Natural Science Foundation (Grant No. LY20F020010, LY17F020010), K.C. Wong Magna Fund in Ningbo University.

S. Yu et al. (Eds.): SPDE 2020, CCIS 1268, pp. 443–468, 2020.
https://doi.org/10.1007/978-981-15-9129-7_31

control the systems remotely. With the convenience and feasibility, the ASR systems have been extensively applied in various smartphone and home equipment. Smart devices are affecting and changing the human-machine interaction way, i.e., people control the smart home equipment via speaking remotely.

Despite its convenience and development, the ASR system have been found that existing potential security risks yet. Recently, the deep neural networks (DNNs) based ASR systems has been demonstrated that vulnerability to adversarial example, crafting carefully by adding peculiar noise to normal speech. However, adversarial attacks have been extensively investigated in the image domain, i.e., image classification, image segmentation, object detection, etc. In contrast, there are fewer investigations for the speech adversarial attack.

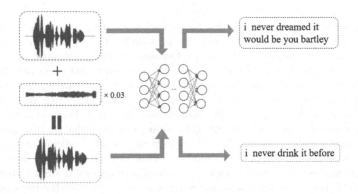

Fig. 1. An illustration of the adversarial attack: adding a small noise to the benign input makes ASR transcript the wrong result.

The goal of the adversary is to generate adversarial perturbation. The perturbation could mislead the ASR to make the wrong transcription but indistinguishable to humans. Figure 1 illustrates the original speech and its counterpart adversarial example generation. Vaidya et al. [1] first proposed an adversarial attack method on the ASR system. Carlini et al. [2] improved it and achieved more powerful attack. However, they aimed to synthesize new unrecognizable speech by exploits the feature process of ASR vulnerabilities instead of modifying existing recognizable speech. We will review existing adversarial attacks and countermeasures for acoustic system. Through our review, the current challenges and countermeasures against speech adversarial example will be discussed.

In this paper, we discuss and summarize the approaches for generating speech adversarial examples and the corresponding countermeasures. Compared with the existing review [3], we proposed a more detailed taxonomy and introduced the latest work. Our main contributions of this work: 1) We present a taxonomy for speech adversarial examples with respect to the threat model, perturbation, and benchmark. 2) We introduce the development of adversarial example in the acoustic system through briefly review the existing works. 3) we discuss the challenge in the speech adversarial example and propose several promising research directions in the future.

The rest of the paper is organized as follows: we introduce the state-of-the-art ASR systems and the principle of adversarial examples in Sect. 2. Followed by a taxonomy of the existing attacks will be described in Sect. 3, existing attacks and its countermeasures will be briefly reviewed separately in Sect. 4 and 5. The challenges of adversarial attack and countermeasures will be discussed in Sect. 6. We conclude our work in Sect. 7.

2 Background

In this section, we first review the speech recognition techniques in two state-of-the-art ASR systems. The general speech adversarial examples generation process is then thoroughly discussed.

2.1 ASR Overview

Considering of popularity and accessibility, we mainly introduce two state-of-the-art ASR systems: Kaldi and DeepSpeech. Note that these two ASR contains extensively advanced techniques that applied to commercial applications, which makes them suitable as victim models for adversarial examples investigate in the speech domain.

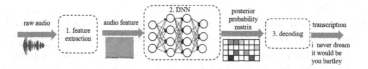

Fig. 2. An overview of the Kaldi system with the main components of the ASR system: (1) feature extraction of the raw audio, (2) calculating the posterior probability matrix with a DNN, (3) the decoding, which returns the transcription.

2.1.1 Kaldi

Kaldi [6] is a very popular and accessible open-source speech recognition toolkit, a DNN-HMM based model, which provides an extensive range of state-of-the-art algorithms for ASR, which has more than 8600 stars in the Github repository. The toolkit is written in C++ and is continuously being updated in Github [7]. Several kinds of researches have shown that Kaldi is extensively applied in commercials, i.e., Amazon Echo [8], IBM [4], and Microsoft [5]. Figure 2 illustrates the overview of the majority system components, which consisting of three steps: feature exaction, DNN, and decoding. As described in Fig. 2, the first step is to extract acoustic features like MFCC or Perceptual Linear Predictive (PLP) from raw audio. Those features are then taken as input to the pre-trained DNN to compute the posterior probability matrix. Finally, the static decoding graph is used to decode the posterior probability matrix, and the most probable word sequence from the raw audio will be found.

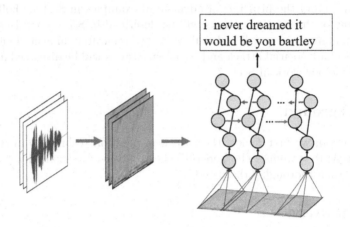

i never dreamed it would be you bartley

Fig. 3. The architecture of the DeepSpeech. The system first converts the raw speech to the acoustic feature (e.g., MFCC), then feeds the acoustic feature into the RNN-based model.

2.1.2 DeepSpeech

DeepSpeech [9] is an open-source speech-to-text engine, using a model trained by machine learning techniques based on Mozilla's implementation [10], which has more than 13600 stars in the Github repository. The developers of Deep-Speech claimed that Baidu would integrate DeepSpeech into the automatic car, CoolBox, and wearable devices in the future [11]. Figure 3 illustrates an overview of the main system processes, including feature extraction and model inference. The input of DeepSpeech is the acoustic features (e.g., MFCC), which extracted from the input raw audio. The acoustic features were fed into a multi-layer bi-directional model that uses the Connectionist Temporal Classification (CTC) loss [12], and produces a character level probability for each frame in acoustic features. Finally, the model output is decoded to a phrase.

2.2 Speech Adversarial Example

Adversarial examples have been intensely investigated in the image domain [13–17]. Recently, the adversarial example has increasingly been noticed in the speech domain. Adversarial examples in the ASR system task can be described as follows. Using a trained ASR system, a user inputs one speech to obtain the transcription result. Adversarial speeches are origin speech with tiny perturbation, often barely perceptual by humans. However, such perturbation misleads the ASR system to make the wrong transcription. Given a trained ASR system f and an original speech sample x, generating an adversarial example x' can generally be described as a constrained optimization problem

$$\min_{x'} \|x' - x\|$$
$$\text{s.t.} \quad f(x') = t'$$
$$f(x) = t \tag{1}$$
$$t \neq t'$$

Where $\| \cdot \|$ denotes the distance measurement, i.e., ℓ_0, ℓ_2 and ℓ_∞. t and t' denotes the transcription result of x and x', respectively. Let $\delta = x' - x$ be the perturbation added on x. Note that, in the rest of the paper, we will use the above symbol definition if not specified. This optimization problem minimizes the perturbation while misinterpreting the input speech. In the rest of this paper, we will present a taxonomy of speech adversarial example, and then discuss the existing perturbation generates methods and its countermeasures in detail.

3   Taxonomy of Adversarial Examples

To systematically review the existing attacks, we will discuss the speech adversarial examples methods from the following three aspects: threat model, perturbation and benchmark.

3.1   Threat Model

According to different scenarios, assumptions, and quality requirements, we divide the threat model into two aspects: adversarial knowledge and adversarial specificity.

1) Adversarial knowledge
   a) *White-box* attacks assume the adversary can get access to the target network, which allows the adversary to use the information about the target model, including training data, model architecture, hyperparameters and model weights, etc.
   b) *Black-box* attacks assume the adversary can not access to the target network. The adversarial, acting like a regular user, only knows the output of the target model.
2) Adversarial specificity
   a) *Non-Targeted* attacks do not assign a specific class to the network output. The class of output can be arbitrary except the original one. Therefore it has more options and spaces to mislead the output. This type of attack usually maximizes the edit distance of transcription result between generated examples and original samples.

b) *Targeted* attacks mislead the acoustic system to output a specific target assigned by the adversary. The targeted attack is more realistic and more challenging, especially in the ASR attack. This kind of attack usually minimizes the edit distance of transcription result between generated examples and original samples.

3.2   Perturbation

The small exquisitely designed perturbation is an essential premise for adversarial example. Adversarial examples are devised to be close to the original samples but imperceptible to humans, which could cause performance degradation of networks compared with that of a human. In light of different perturbation generation methods, we analyzes the perturbation from the following aspects: perturbation generation, perturbation range, perturbation scope, and perturbation measurement.

1) Perturbation generation
    a) *Gradient sign* based method first presents in image adversarial examples then be proved effective in speech adversarial examples. This type of attack allows the adversary to utilize the gradient information to generate adversarial examples. Concerning the input speech, the gradients of the loss are regarded as the perturbation and added to the input.
    b) *Optimization* based method sets the perturbation generation as an optimization problem, which aims to minimize the objective function concerning the perturbation.
    c) *Evolutionary algorithm* based method treats adversarial examples generation as a task to find the best fitness individual from a population of candidate adversarial example through continuous iteration. The most significant advantage of these methods is free gradient, which makes it possible to realize the over-the-air attack.
2) Perturbation scope
    a) *Individual* attacks generate perturbation independently for each input.
    b) *Universal* attacks only generate one universal perturbation for the whole data set, which can be added to arbitrary benign input speech.
    Most of the existing attacks focus on individual attacks. However, the universal perturbation can be applied to arbitrary speech input. That characteristic makes them easier deployment in the real world due to the adversary do not change the perturbation when changing the input.
3) Perturbation objective
    a) *Acoustic features perturbation* sets the acoustic features as the perturb objective, i.e., MFCCs. The perturbations are added to acoustic features, and then reconstruct to speech waveform.
    b) *Raw speech perturbation* sets the raw speech signal as the perturb objective. The perturbation is added to raw speech signal directly.

4) Perturbation measurement
   a) Statistical measurement can be divided into attack performance measurement and speech distortion measurement. Attack performance, i.e., edit distance, Character Error Rate (CER), Word Error Rate (WER), attack success rate (Success_rate). Distortion measurement, i.e., the Signal-to-Noise (SNR) and Perceptual Evaluation of Speech Quality (PESQ).
   b) Physical perception measures the quality of speech perceptual against adversarial perturbation, namely human study, i.e., Amazon Mechanical Turk (AMT), ABX test, etc.
   c) Over-the-air measures whether the adversarial examples can maintain the performance when played by the recorder or speaker, which is the significant assessment of the robust and practicality of the attack.

3.3 Benchmark

Adversary evaluates the effectiveness of their method on various data sets and target models, which result in difficult to assess the effectiveness of these methods and the robustness of acoustic models. The advanced ASR system and sentence-level speech data sets make the adversary hard to achieve high attack performance. Therefore, it is necessary to discuss the victim models and data sets used in the existing attacks.

1) *Victim models*: The popular and accessible acoustic models are usually selected as the target model. The acoustic model can be divided into the classification model and the recognition model. The classification model is briefly classified as the CNN-based model. The recognition models include DeepSpeech, Kaldi, and Lingvo [31], etc. Moreover, some researchers focus on attacking the online acoustic system (i.e., Google Voice), which is classified as other categories.
2) *Data sets*: Depending on different target model, the public and extensively used data sets are selected to evaluate the attack performance. Including but not limited to following: Mozilla Common Voice Dataset (MCVD) [18], Speech Command dataset (SCD) [19], Librispeech [20], IEMOCAP [21], etc.

4 Methods for Generating Speech Adversarial Examples

In this section, we will review the existing attacks with respect to the perturbation generate methods under the proposed taxonomy: the optimization-based method, the evolutionary algorithm based method, and the gradient sign-based method. Although several attacks are invalid under the later countermeasures, we present these methods to show the effectiveness at that time and explore possible research directions in the future.

Table 1 summaries the method for generating adversarial examples based on the taxonomy present in Sect. 3.

Table 1. Taxonomy of the speech adversarial examples

Threat model	Adversarial's knowledge	White-box		$[1,2,8,11,22–24,26,28,30,32–37,39–41]$
		Black-box		$[1,2,11,23,24,27,29,42–44]$
	Adversarial specifity	Target		$[1,2,8,11,22,23,26–30,32–36,40–44]$
		Non-target		$[24,36,37,39,44]$
Perturbation	Perturbation generate	Gradient sign		$[26,40,41]$
		Evolutionary scope		$[11,42–44]$
		Optimization		$[8,22–24,27–30,32–37,39]$
		Others		$[1,2]$
	Perturbation scope	Individual		$[1,2,8,11,22–24,26–30,32–35,40–44]$
		Universal		$[36,37,39]$
	Perturbation objective	Acoustic feature		$[1,2,24,26,41]$
		Raw speech		$[8,11,22,23,27–30,32–36,39,42,44]$
	Perturbation measurement	Success_rate		$[11,22,23,27,29,34–37,39–42]$
		SNR		$[8,11,23,29,32–34,36]$
		WER		$[8,24,30,32–34,44]$
		CER		$[24,39]$
		PESQ		$[33]$
		Edit distance		$[1,2,26,43]$
		AMT		$[1,2,23,29,30]$
		ABX test		$[24,41]$
		Over-the-air	Yes	$[1,2,22–24,27,29,30,32,33]$
			No	$[8,11,26,28,34–36,39–44]$
Benchmark	Victim models	CNN-based		$[11,36,37,40–42]$
		WaveNet		$[26]$
		DeepSpeech		$[11,28,29,33–35,39,43,44]$
		Kaldi		$[8,23,32,44]$
		Lingvo		$[30]$
		Others		$[1,2,11,22,24,27]$
	Data sets	MCVD		$[28,34,35,39,43,44]$
		SPE		$[11,37,42]$
		Librispeech		$[24,27,30]$
		IEMOCAP		$[11,40]$
		Others		$[8,11,26,27,36,41]$
		None		$[1,2,22,23,29,32]$

4.1 Optimization-Based Method

The essential idea of the optimization-based method is to devise an objective function. The objective function usually consisting of two parts: lower magnitude perturbation and higher attack success rate. In this section, we analyze the existing optimization-based method with respect to individual perturbation and universal perturbation.

4.1.1   Individual Perturbation

The individual perturbation method is the main research direction, which generates the perturbation for each input independently. Existing optimization-based, gradient sign-based as well as evolutionary-based works on speech adversarial examples are mainly concentrated in this category.

Vaidya et al. [1] proposed the first method to generate speech adversarial examples. They generated adversarial examples through fine-tuning the parameters of MFCC extraction until misinterpreted by ASR system, then reconstruct the MFCC features back to speech waveform. Carlini et al. [2] extend the Vaidya's work, they proposed *Hidden Voice Command*, which improves the efficiency and practicality of Vaidya's attack by taking account of more practical setting and background noise. However, the perturbation in reconstructed examples usually is regarded as random noise by humans.

To solve the issue of worse speech perceptual quality of *Hidden Voice Command*, Zhang et al. [22] presented *DolphinAttack*, exploiting the microphone vulnerability to modulate speech commands on ultrasound. They evaluate their attack on several ASR systems (i.e., Siri and Google Now) in the physical world. The result shows that the adversarial example generated by their method could successfully attack the ASR system, and the modulated speech command is inaudible to humans. However, they focus on the characteristic of the hardware rather than directly modify the raw speech, which makes their method uneasy to re-implemented.

Different from modulating inaudible voice commands to ultrasonic [22], Yuan et al. [23] presented *CommanderSong*, injecting malicious commands to more common carrier—song. They proposed a pdf-id sequence matching algorithm to solving the adversarial adversarial generation

$$\arg\min_{\delta} \|g\left(x + \delta\right) - b\|_1 \qquad (2)$$

Where $g(\cdot)$ represents the DNN's predictions that output the most likely pdf-ids. x is the original song, b represents a sequence of pdf-id of the malicious command, $\|\cdot\|_1$ denotes the L_1 distance of the sequence of pdf-id between the original song and adversarial sample. To find suitable δ, they utilized the iterative optimization algorithm to find the minimum perturbation. In addition, they introduced the hardware device noise to adversarial examples by a noise model, which makes their method realized the over-the-air attack. Experimental results showed that their method could achieve 100% attack success rate against the Kaldi, and the effectiveness of the noise model is verified. However, the noise model used in their approach is only valid on specific devices, and the experiments were conducted in a short distance.

Cisse et al. [24] presented a flexible method named *Houdini*. *Houdini* could attack different applications, i.e., speech recognition, pose estimation, and semantic segmentation. To attack the speech recognition system, they required to get the loss between target and current predict and then use the forward-backwards algorithm to find the adversarial example. Their approach successfully makes DeepSpeech2 [25] misinterpret the adversarial speech with 12% Word

Error Rate and 1.5% Character Error Rate on Librispeech dataset. They could successfully attack Google Voice with adversarial speech generated by Deep-Speech2. However, the exactly generated perturbation was not investigated.

Abdullah [27] proposed a novel attack method by exploiting knowledge of the signal processing algorithms. They design a Perturbation Engine (PE) that generate four classes perturbation, which can use to generate adversarial examples with selected parameters, i.e., contain audio speech, high-frequency intensity, and window size. They evaluate their attack on 12 machine learning models consists of the online and offline acoustic model (i.e., Google Speech Ai, DeepSpeech, et al.). However, the parameters selection strategy to generate adversarial examples was not given. Despite their method can successfully attack the target model, the acoustic perceptual quality of generated adversarial examples is not well.

Carlini et al. [28] demonstrated that targeted adversarial examples could be realized through directly modifying raw speech waveforms. They generated adversarial examples by solving the following optimization problem

$$
\begin{aligned}
\text{minimize} \quad & |\delta|_2^2 + c \cdot \ell(x + \delta, t^{'}) \\
\text{such that} \quad & dB(\delta) - dB(x) < \tau
\end{aligned}
\tag{3}
$$

Where c trades off the relative importance of being adversarial and remaining close to the original example. They measure distortion in Decibels (dB): $dB(x) = \max_i 20 \cdot \log_{10}(x_i)$, τ is the constant that constrains the perturbation. They proposed a novel approach to differentiate through the entire ASR system, which could reach faster convergence and lower perturbation magnitude. Experimental results showed that the adversarial speech is 99% similarity with the original one and has a 100% success rate against DeepSpeech. However, assuming the adversary access to target model is unreasonable, and whether their method could realize the over-the-air attack was not investigated.

To realize the over-the-air attack, Yakura et al. [29] proposed a novel physical attack method. They integrate transformations caused by playback and recording in the physical world into the generation process to gets a more robust adversarial example. The presented techniques are following

a) Band-pass filter

$$
\begin{aligned}
\underset{\delta}{\text{argmin}} \, \underset{f}{Loss}(MFCC(x^{'}), t^{'}) + \epsilon||\delta|| \\
where \ x^{'} = x + \underset{1000 \sim 4000 Hz}{BPF}(\delta)
\end{aligned}
\tag{4}
$$

Where $MFCC(\cdot)$ denotes the MFCC extraction process. $Loss_f$ is a loss function that measures the distance between model f prediction on $(MFCC(x^{'}))$ and given target label t. ϵ indicates the magnitude of the perturbation. BPF denotes the band of band-filter. In this way, generated adversarial examples could maintain robustness when frequency bands are cut by a speaker or microphone.

b) Impulse response

$$\underset{\delta}{\text{argmin}}\, \mathbb{E}_{h\sim\mathcal{H}}[\underset{f}{Loss}(MFCC(x'),t') + \epsilon||\delta||]$$

$$where\ x' = \underset{h}{Conv}(x + \underset{1000\sim4000Hz}{BPF}(\delta)) \tag{5}$$

Where $\mathcal{H}$ is a set of impulse responses and $Conv_h$ is the convolution using impulse response. In this way, generated adversarial examples could resist the reverberations produced in the environment in which they are played and recorded.

c) White Gaussian noise

$$\underset{\delta}{\text{argmin}}\, \mathbb{E}_{h\sim\mathcal{H},w\sim\mathcal{N}(0,\sigma)}[\underset{f}{Loss}(MFCC(x'),t') + \epsilon||\delta||]$$

$$where\ x' = \underset{h}{Conv}(x + \underset{1000\sim4000Hz}{BPF}(\delta)) + w \tag{6}$$

Where $w \sim \mathcal{N}(0,\sigma)$ denotes the White Gaussian noise. In this way, generated adversarial examples could acquire robustness to noise caused by recording equipment and the environment.

Through the above ways, the generated adversarial example could realize over-the-air attack. Experimental results showed that they could achieve 100% attack success rate in the over-the-air attack. However, the computational efficiency of constructing single adversarial examples is relatively low. Moreover, the validity of the method should be investigated under different speech data and the arbitrary target text.

To construct the over-the-air attack, Schönherr et al. [8,32] introduce a novel approach based on psychoacoustic to generate adversarial examples against Kaldi. In [8], they limit the adversarial perturbation under the hearing thresholds of the original speech and utilize the backpropagation algorithm to find minimal perturbation, which ensures the least noise is introduced to adversarial examples

$$\nabla X^*(i,k) = \begin{pmatrix} 2 \cdot Re(X(i,k)) \\ 2 \cdot Im(X(i,k)) \end{pmatrix} \cdot \widetilde{\phi}(i,k) \cdot \widetilde{H}(i,k), \quad \forall i,k \tag{7}$$

Where $\nabla X^*(i,k)$ denotes the generated perturbation, $X(i,k)$ denotes the frequency of i frame and k frequency after the Discrete Fourier Transform (DFT). $Re(\cdot)$ and $Im(\cdot)$ represents the real and imaginary of X. $\widetilde{\phi}$ denotes the time-frequency matrix of scale factors, $\widetilde{H}$ is the hearing threshold matrix. In this way, the generated adversarial example could counteract the noise during the over-the-air attack. In expand experiment, they found that the choice of the original speech example (i.e., speech, music) has greatly influenced the performance of the adversarial examples, for example, music and other unsuspicious audio samples are a better choice than others. In their later work [32], they combined the psychoacoustics and room impulse response (RIR) simulator to generate robust adversarial examples

$$x^{'} = \arg\max_{\widetilde{x}} \quad \mathbb{E}_{h \sim H_\theta} \left[P(t^{'}|\widetilde{x}_h) \right] \qquad (8)$$

Where $P(y|x)$ denotes mapping operation in ASR that mapping audio signal x to most likely transcription y. $\widetilde{x}$ represents the result of the signal x convolved with the room's impulse h. H_θ is a set of RIRs with parameter θ. Adversarial examples could resist diversity of room characteristics with different θ. Compared to existing play over-the-air works [2,8,28,30], which proved only effective on one specific static room setup or failed to attack physical ASR system in a different environment, the author utilized an RIR generator to maintain effectiveness on different room setups. However, the magnitude of perturbation was not investigated, and assuming that they can get information about the target network is unrealistic in practice.

Inspired by [8], Carlini's team [30] utilized the principle of auditory masking to generate adversarial examples. The section under auditory masking was selected to perturb to make perturbation is insensitivity to human. They divided their optimization into two stages: the first stage is to find a perturbation to fool the target network, and the second stage optimizes the perturbation to ensure imperceptible to humans

$$\delta \leftarrow \delta - lr \cdot \nabla_x[\ell_{net}(f(t(x + \delta), y)) + \alpha \cdot \ell_\theta(x, \delta)] \qquad (9)$$

Where lr is the learning rate, α is a weight that balances the importance of the robustness and the imperceptibility. ℓ_{net} represents the cross-entropy loss function of victim model. ℓ_θ is the imperceptibility loss. $t(\cdot)$ represents the reverberation function. Note that, auditory masking was contained in $t(\cdot)$. In this way, adversarial examples could be more imperceptible and robust. The generated adversarial examples achieved 100% attack success rate on arbitrary length target text against the Lingvo [31] classifier, a state-of-the-art sequence-to-sequence ASR model. However, assuming they could get access to the target network is unrealistic in practice.

At the same time, inspired by [8,30], Szurley et al. [33] proposed a similar psychoacoustic based optimization method to generate robust adversarial examples through design a psychoacoustic-property-based loss function and automated generation of room impulse responses. The projected gradient descent (PGD) method was used to solve the optimization. Experimental results showed their approach achieved 100% attack success rate. However, the transferability of their attack is not investigated.

In the latest work on attack ASR, Liu et al. [34] presented an improved adversarial attack method consisting of sampling perturbation technology (SPT) and weighted perturbation technology (WPT). The SPT reduces the perturbed number in the audio signal, which could reduce the computation resources and time costs during the generating process. The critical idea of WPT is that they introduce a weights vector α to δ, where adversarial example could be expressed as

$$x^{'} = x + \alpha \cdot \delta \qquad (10)$$

They utilized the Audio Sequence Location (ASL) model to find key points that have bigger weights and then used the iterative gradient method to find the exact perturbation. Moreover, they proposed a novel Total Variation Denoising (TVD) based loss, which could make the generated adversarial examples reaches higher performance, i.e., 100% attack success rate, and 31.9 dB SNR. However, whether the effect of their method on the over-the-air attack was not investigated.

Considering the realistic scenario, i.e., adversarial examples used to fool the enemy wiretapping device while correctly interpreted by friendly wiretapping device in the military scenario. Kwon et al. [35] presented selective audio adversarial examples

$$\arg \min_{x^*} L(x, x^*)$$
$$s.t. \quad f^p(x^*) = t \qquad (11)$$
$$f^v(x^*) = t^{'}$$

Where x^* denotes the selected adversarial example, f^p and f^v represent the protected ASR and victim ASR, respectively. They utilized decibel level loss to measure the speech distortion. The generated selected audio adversarial examples achieve 91.67% attack success rate and 85.67% protected accuracy on the advanced DeepSpeech system. Noted that, the victim ASR and protected ASR are the same architecture with different parameters. However, the architecture of the victim ASR and the protected ASR used in the evaluation is the same. The performance of their method on different architecture between the victim ASR and the protected ASR may need to investigate further (Fig. 4).

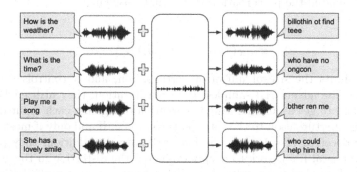

Fig. 4. Universal adversarial examples fool the ASR system. Left speech waveform: original normal speech. Center speech waveform: universal perturbation. Right speech waveforms: perturbed speech with wrong transcription results [39].

4.1.2   Universarial Perturbation

Recently, universal perturbation has been gradually investigated in the speech domain. However, there are few works on this aspect.

Abdoli et al. [36] first proposed the universal adversarial perturbation method for acoustic systems. They presented two methods to generate universal perturbation. Inspired by the image universal adversarial examples, they first generated a universal perturbation vector with an iterative greedy algorithm. The second method, they designed a novel penalty formulation as follow

$$minimize \quad SPL(\delta) + \max\{\max_{j \neq t}\{g(x+\delta)_j\} - g(x+\delta)_t, -k\}$$

$$s.t. \quad y_t = \arg\max_{y} f(y|x+\delta, \theta) \tag{12}$$

$$and \quad 0 \leq x + \delta \leq 1$$

Where SPL is sound pressure level (SPL), $SPL(\delta) = 20\log_{10} P(\delta)$. $g(\cdot)_j$ denotes the output of the pre-softmax layer of classifier f for j, c is the penalty coefficient, $c > 0$. k controls the confidence level of sample misclassification. y_t is the target class, θ denotes the parameters of classifier f. By solving the above optimization, they could find a universal perturbation. They evaluated their method on the 1D CNN based acoustic model, achieving 85.4% and 83.1% attack success rate for the targeted and untargeted attacks, respectively. However, their attack only evaluated on the classification model, and the universal perturbation audio does not perform well when played over-the-air.

Different from Abdoli [36], Vadillo et al. [37] exploited image adversarial perturbation generated method [15,38] to generate speech universal perturbation to against speech command classifier. They reformulated the algorithm in [15] and accumulated the perturbation vector that satisfying

$$||\delta||_p < \xi$$
$$\mathbb{P}_{x \in X}(f(x) \neq f(x+\delta)) > 1 - \alpha \tag{13}$$

where ξ limits the size of universal perturbation, and α controls the failure rate of all the adversarial samples. For each iteration, they utilized DeepFool [38] method to get a minimal sample perturbation against each input data and update the perturbation to the total perturbation δ. If and only if most samples data are deceived ($\mathbb{P} < 1 - \alpha$), the loop will stop. In addition, they proposed an experimental framework to deeply evaluated the distortion in the generated examples. Experimental results showed that their universal perturbation could make the perturbed audio misclassified to another class except the original. However, whether their perturbation method can achieve target attack was not investigated.

Compared to generate universal perturbation for speech classification-based model [36,37], Neekhara [39] proposed a universal adversarial perturbation to attack the recognition system that more challenge than classification models.

They found the universal perturbation vector as following

$$r_0 = \overleftarrow{0}$$
$$r_{N+1} = \texttt{Clip}_{r+\delta,\epsilon}\{r_N - \alpha sign(\nabla_{r_N} J(r_N))\} \tag{14}$$

Where $\texttt{Clip}_{r+\delta,\epsilon}\{\cdot\}$ limits the change of the generated adversarial speech in each iteration. Then universal perturbation δ was updated with r after multiple iterations. The universal perturbations were shown well performance on DeepSpeech, and it could reach 89.06% attack success rate. However, assuming the successful attack when the CER less than 0.5 rather than 0 means that their attack can not achieve the targeted attack.

4.2 Gradient Sign-Based Method

In this category approach, the adversary can exploit the information of the target model, which allows them to utilize the target model information to generate speech adversarial examples. For an input speech, the gradients of the loss function with respect to the input speech are treated as the perturbation that added to the input. The most significant advantage of this kind of method is that it can faster generate adversarial examples.

Iter et al. [26] utilized a pre-trained model WaveNet to generate adversarial examples through perturbing the MFCC features. Their perturbation can be expressed as

$$\delta = \epsilon sign(\nabla J(\theta, MFCC(x), t^{'})) \tag{15}$$

Where ϵ is the magnitude of the perturbation, $J(\cdot)$ denotes the loss function of the target model with parameters θ. They utilized the Fast Gradient Sign Method (FGSM) to find perturbation for MFCC features, and then the perturbed MFCC was reconstructed back to speech waveform. They demonstrated that despite the MFCC reconstruction is lossy, the coherence of the resulting audio.

Gong et al. [40] first proposed gradient sign-based method to generate speech adversarial examples

$$\delta = \epsilon sign(\nabla_x J(\theta, x, t^{'})) \tag{16}$$

Where ϵ is the magnitude of the perturbation. Giving the network's gradient go to zero when process long input sequences with RNN, they solved this problem by replacing the recurrent layers with convolutional layers. Evaluation results over three different speech paralinguistic model showed that the recognition error rate increases by about 30% with a perturbation factor of 0.032. However, assuming the adversary knows the target model is unrealistic in practices and the transferability of adversarial examples was not investigated.

Compared to the speech-to-text system, Kreuk et al. [41] presented a method to attack the speaker verification system. They utilized gradient sign to perturb the acoustic features (e.g., MFCC) and then reconstruct the acoustic features to speech waveform to generate adversarial examples. Attack performance is evaluated by increasing the false positive rate to nearly 90%. However, assuming the adversary has full knowledge about the target network, which is unrealistic in practice and the magnitude of perturbation was not investigated.

4.3 Evolutionary-Based Method

Compared to the previous two categories, the evolutionary algorithm based methods are gradient-free method. This kind of method does not require the information of the target model, which makes it possible to apply black-box attacks on ASR. Gradient-free is an excellent advantage of these methods.

Alzantot et al. [42] proposed the first genetic algorithm-based method to generate speech adversarial examples. They first initialize a population of candidate adversarial examples by adding noise only to least-significant bits of given speech clip, then compute the fitness score for each candidate, the candidates with high scores are more likely to next generation by selection, crossover and mutation. Their attack achieves 87% attack success rate on the target model, and 89% of the participant of human study not sensitive to the added noise. However, their method was only effective in the single words speech and on a CNN based speech classification network. Whether it is effective on attack ASR system needs further investigation.

Compared to attack speech classification over single word data sets [42], Taori et al. [43] extended Alzantot's method [42] to attack the speech recognition system. Combining the genetic algorithm and gradient estimation, they proposed an improved attack. They used a genetic algorithm to explore suitable examples on populations of candidates and utilized gradient estimation to find more peculiar noise when the adversarial examples are nearing its target. By replacing the traditional mutation with momentum mutation, they could achieve faster convergence. The generated adversarial speech is 89.25% similarity with the original one. However, their method only reaches 35% attack success rate on attacking the DeepSpeech model.

Khare et al. [44] proposed a multi-objective evolutionary algorithm based method to generate adversarial examples. The objectives contain achieve a higher error of the ASR system and lower magnitude of the perturbation. They solved this problem by minimizing the Euclidean distance of MFCC features and reducing the edit distance of transcription. They initialize populations by adding random uniform noise to the original speech signal, then the fitness score is calculated with two objectives for each population candidate. Those with higher scores are more like to be selected to crossover and mutation. Adversarial examples increase the Word Error Rate (WER) of DeepSpeech and Kaldi. The acoustic similarity between original and generated examples is maintained well (0.98,0.97, respectively). However, whether generated adversarial examples could successfully be transcribed to target text was not investigated.

At the same time, Du et al. [11] presented a novel approach based on particle swarm optimization (PSO), which called *SirenAttack*. In the white-box attack scenario, they utilized the PSO algorithm to search a coarse-grained noise and used the fooling gradient method to find exact adversarial noise by slightly revising coarse-grained noise. While in the black-box setting, they only used the

PSO algorithm to find the exact adversarial noise. Several state-of-the-art deep learning-based acoustic systems were evaluated, the result showed that their method achieves 99.45% attack success rate on the IEMOCAP dataset against the ResNet18 [45] model. Moreover, generated adversarial examples also fool the online ASR system (i.e., Google Cloud Speech). However, they only evaluated the effectiveness of the black-box attack on the single word speech, whether the effectiveness of their method against the ASR system over long sentence speech was not investigated (Table 2).

Table 2. Summary of countermeasures for speech adversarial examples

	Defense strategies	Representative Studies
Reactive	Adversarial detecting	[49,54]
	Network verification	[47,50–53]
Proactive	Adversarial retraining	[46]
	Model robustifying	[48,55,58,59]

5   Countermeasures for Speech Adversarial Examples

In this section, we will discuss the existing countermeasures for speech adversarial examples. The discussion from the following two aspects

1) *Reactive*: detect the generated adversarial examples after the acoustic systems are built. Existing works could further be subdivided into adversarial detecting, input reconstruction, and network verification.
2) *Proactive*: make the acoustic system more robustness to the potential adversarial attack. Depending on different strategies, proactive countermeasures could be further divided into adversarial (re)training and acoustic model robustifying.

5.1   Reactive Countermeasures

Reactive countermeasures focus on detecting the adversarial examples after the acoustic systems are built. According to the different characteristics of defense strategies, we will review the reactive countermeasures from adversarial detecting, input reconstruction, and network verification.

5.1.1   Adversarial Detecting

Adversarial detection can be regarded as a binary classification task. The goal is to perform binary classification on generated adversarial examples and normal samples. In general, this kind of defense approach designed a classifier, which makes classification on the acoustic feature or speech waveform. The advantage of these strategies is that the detection accuracy is relatively high. However, the shortcoming is that it needs to train a new classification.

To defend against the adversarial attack presented by Alzantot et al. [42], Rajaratnam et al. [49] proposed an adversarial detecting method. They utilized several kinds of audio preprocessing methods (i.e., compressions, speech coding, filtering, etc.) independently to detect the adversarial examples. Moreover, considering the adversary may aware of the preprocessing defense, they used different ensemble strategies to combine these methods. Evaluation results showed that their methods could achieve 93.5% precision and 91.2% recall. However, whether the effectiveness of their defense on more advanced adversarial examples was not investigated.

Samizade et al. [51] treated the adversarial detection task as a classification problem. They designed a CNN based classification neural network with 2D cepstral features input. The detection accuracy could achieve nearly 100% on detecting the attack proposed by Carlini et al. [28] and Alzantot et al. [42]. Moreover, their method can detect unknown attacks.

5.1.2 Network Verification

The difference examples is commonly explored to detecting adversarial attacks. Network verification utilizes this difference in detect adversarial examples, for example, the transcription difference on different ASR, the output difference after adding tiny noise to input, etc. This kind of defense method is a promising solution to defense adversarial examples due to it may detect the unseen attacks.

Inspired by the multi-version programming principle, Zeng et al. [47] proposed a novel method for detecting speech adversarial examples. Based on the fact that the transcription results of a normal speech by different ASR systems should be the same, they calculated the similarity score of output between every two ASR systems in several ASR systems in parallel. The similarity score of examples lower than the threshold is classified as adversarial examples. The detection accuracy could achieve 98.6% on attack proposed by [2, 43].

Inspired by the fact that speech classifiers are relatively robust to natural noise, Rajaratnam et al. [50] proposed a novel method to defense against adversarial attacks. Different from utilized audio preprocessing to detect adversarial examples, they added the random noise to the particular frequency band, then find a threshold by calculating the flooding scores of adversarial and benign examples in the training dataset. Test samples with flooding scores less than the threshold are regarded as adversarial examples. Moreover, to make the defense method more robust, they utilized the ensemble method to combined flooding scores under various configurations. The evaluation result shows that their detection method achieves 91.8% precision and 93.5% recall.

According to the difference of transcription results after added a low-level distortion to input through audio modification, Kwon et al. [53] utilized that difference to detect adversarial examples. Different transcription result is regarded as adversarial examples. Experimental results showed that their method could successfully detect the adversarial examples generated with Carlini et al. [28].

However, their detection method requires the original examples and its counterpart adversarial examples, which is unrealistic in practice because the defender cannot simultaneously obtain both two examples.

By analyzing audio characteristics, Yang [52] proposed a novel detection method using temporal dependency. They first utilized several basic input transformations on audio adversarial examples, i.e., quantization, local smoothing, downsampling, and autoencoder. Then, depending on the temporal dependency of the audio sequence, they calculated the consistency between the transcription result of the first k portion of the whole sequence and the first k portion transcription result of the whole sequence. In general, the transcription result of k portion is the same in clean examples while different in adversarial examples. Experimental results showed that their method could detect the adversarial examples generated by Alzantot et al. [42], Yuan et al. [23], and Carlini et al. [28]. Their method gives a novel idea to investigate adversarial examples and countermeasures.

Similar to Yang et al. [52], Ma et al. [54] proposed a novel efficient and straightforward detection method based on the temporal correlation between audio and video stream. Depending on the association between audio and video in adversarial examples lower than normal examples, they utilized the synchronization confidence score as a threshold for audio-video correlation, the score below the threshold will be regarded as adversarial examples. Experimental results showed that their method could successfully detect the adversarial examples generated by Carlini et al. [28].

5.2 Proactive Defense

Proactive defense methods focus on making the acoustic system more robustness to the potential adversarial attacks. Depending on different techniques, we will review the proactive defense from the following two aspects: adversarial training and model robustifying.

5.2.1 Adversarial Training

Adversarial training is a common defense method to resist adversarial examples. The principle of these methods is to make the network robust to attacks by retraining the network with adversarial examples. Although it can withstand the existing adversarial examples, the retrained network may be defeat by more advanced attacks.

Sun et al. [46] proposed a dynamic adversarial training method to make the ASR more robust. They dynamic integrate the adversarial examples generated by FGSM to the training set to substitute the clean input to retrain the speech recognition model. Moreover, they utilize teacher-student training to make their method more robust. Their adversarial training method achieves 23% relative Word Error Rate (WER) reduction. However, They did not evaluate the existing attack methods in the ASR systems.

5.2.2 Model Robustifying

The model robustifying defense methods have been widely explored, which focuses on eliminating the adversarial perturbation. Giving the adversarial perturbation is small, this kind of methods are usually effective to resist adversarial examples.

Latif [48] proposed a generative adversarial network (GAN) [56] based defense method. They utilized the generator to eliminate the adversarial perturbation. The evaluation result on data set consisting of adversarial examples generated by their own method (add the diversity of environment noise to benign samples) and benign samples shows that their method could mitigate the perturbation in generated adversarial examples.

Esmaeilpour et al. [55] proposed a novel defense approach against the adversarial attack. They combined the advantage of convolutional denoising of deep learning and the classification performance of support vector machines (SVM). They utilized the neural networks to smooth the spectrograms, which may reduce the influence introduced by adversarial perturbation. The smoothed spectrograms were processes by dynamic zoning and grid shifting, followed by extracting the speeded up robust feature (SURF) and finally fed into SVM. Experimental results showed that their method could mitigate the perturbation introduce by *BackDoor* [57] and *DolphineAttack* [22]. Furthermore, their method could make a good tradeoff between accuracy and resilience of deep learning models and SVM.

Similar to compared the transcription results of different ASR in Zeng et al. [47], Tamura et al. [58] compared the transcription results of different input of ASR, they proposed a sandbox based defense method to protect ASR system. They first utilized perturbation eliminating techniques (i.e., dynamic downsampling and denoising) to eliminating perturbation in adversarial examples, followed by comparing the CER of transcription results of DeepSpeech, the examples with CER larger than the threshold is regarded as adversarial examples. The evaluation result on the dataset constructed by different dataset shows that their method can successful defense the adversarial attack. However, they did not assigned the specific attack used in the evaluation, which can not evaluate the effectiveness of their defense on existing attacks.

Yang et al. [59] proposed a novel U-Net based attention model, $UNet_{At}$, to make the ASR system robust to the adversarial attacks. Inspired by speech enhancement based on U-Net, they integrate the attention gate into upsampling blocks to extract high-level feature representation from the input, which maintains the audio characteristic. Finally, the output of the U-Net is the enhanced audio and adversarial noise. Experimental results showed that their method could eliminate the perturbation introduce by Khare et al. [44] and Yakura et al. [29].

6 Challenges and Discussion

In this section, we discuss the current challenges and the potential solutions for adversarial examples on the ASR system. Although many attacks and countermeasures have been proposed recently, the challenges of constructing more strict and realistic attack methods and defense more advanced attacks need to be addressed. In addition, the fundamental reason for the existence of adversarial examples in the acoustic system also needs to be investigated. Moreover, exploring the audio characteristic may benefit to construct more robust countermeasures. In the following part, we first discuss the challenges and research direction of adversarial examples then discuss the countermeasures.

6.1 Augmentation Adversarial Examples

Despite the fact that a lot of adversarial attacks have been proposed, existing several difficult problems need to be addressed. We will discuss the current challenges and future research direction in the following two aspects: construct strict attack and transferability.

6.1.1 Construct Strict Attack

In the white-box scenario, Liu et al. [34] proposed method could set arbitrary long sentence as the target, and the perceptual speech quality of generated adversarial examples can maintain well. Although the method can achieve state-of-the-art performance, assuming the adversary have full knowledge about the target model is unrealistic in practices. In order to get rid of that limitation, Alzantot et al. [42] proposed a gradient-free method to generate adversarial examples but only effective for speech classification networks. Therefore, Taori et al. [43] extended [42] to attack the ASR system, but the author set only the phrase-level as the target rather than the sentence-level. Moreover, they need the logit output of the target model, which is unrealistic in over-the-air attack. Thus, we come up with a more realistic attack through defining a stricter black-box setting: the adversary can only get the transcription result from the target ASR system. Under this definition, how to design a strict black-box attack that satisfying adversary can set arbitrary long sentence as the target and achieving over-the-air attack needs further investigation in the future.

6.1.2 Transferability

The transferability of adversarial examples is that adversarial examples generated for model A not only can attack model A but also can attack unknown model B, where model A and model B have different architecture. In the image domain, researchers exploit the ensemble method to make adversarial examples have a certain transferability. However, relevant research is far less in speech adversarial examples. Cisse et al. [24] method showed adversarial examples generated with a DeepSpeech2 system are effective for Google Voice. Kruek et al. [41] method show that adversarial examples can maintain transferability between two models trained on different datasets with the same architecture. Vadillo et al. [37] demonstrated that universal adversarial examples for classification networks have better transferability with a large number of classes, but the corresponding conclusion can not apply to the ASR system. Therefore, constructing more transferable adversarial examples can be considered from the following two aspects: on the one hand, deeply exploring universal adversarial examples of the ASR system. On the other hand, investigating the theory of existence adversarial examples in the ASR system might help to find generalization perturbation.

6.2   Improving Countermeasures

The reason for the existence of adversarial examples is still an open question, how to ensure the security of ASR is a significant challenge. In this section, we will discuss some feasible defense strategies from two aspects: reactive defense and proactive defense.

6.2.1   Reactive Defense

Although several adversarial defense works have been proposed recently, there are existing promising research directions due to the variety of audio detection methods. For classification networks, despite existing several defense methods [49,50] exploits various audio preprocessing to detect adversarial examples. In addition, the acoustic feature and its higher-order version in audio detection tasks (i.e., steganalysis), as well as diversities ensemble methods can be used to detect adversarial examples. For the recognition system, Zeng et al. [47] utilized the different transcription results from diversity ASR to detect adversarial examples, while Kwon et al. [53] utilized the different transcription results of perturbed examples and normal examples from ASR. Moreover, some attack [8,43] selected the insensitive areas of the human as the perturbed areas. In the future, this area of speech should be emphasis analyzed. Thus, exploring insight and characteristics of perturbation will help to detect adversarial examples.

6.2.2   Proactive Defense

The goal of this strategy is to make the acoustic system robust to adversarial examples. The adversarial (re)training and eliminate adversarial perturbation are two main research directions. Adversarial (re)training has shown effective in improving the robustness of the network in the image domain. In speech adversarial examples, Sun et al. [46] proposed dynamic adversarial training to improve the robustness of the speech classification network. However, the adversarial training has not been proposed to make the ASR system robust. Thus, adversarial (re)train over with the latest adversarial examples is a promising method for improving the robustness of the ASR system. In addition, exploiting speech enhancement and denoising method to preprocess the input of ASR system is a promising method to resist adversarial examples, for example, Latif et al. [48] used GAN to eliminate the adversarial perturbation and Yang et al. [59] used UNet based model to eliminate the adversarial perturbation. Moreover, exploring the audio characteristic is also a promising method to resist the adversarial examples.

7   Conclusion

Recent researches have suggested that the DNN-based acoustic systems are vulnerable to speech adversarial examples. In this paper, we review the existing adversarial examples in the acoustic system. We propose a detailed taxonomy method, and then we make classification on speech existing adversarial attacks. Through reviewing existing adversarial attacks and countermeasures, the development of adversarial examples in the speech domain is discussed. Finally, we introduce the potential challenges in speech adversarial examples and its countermeasure and giving promising future research directions.

References

1. Vaidya, T., Zhang, Y., Sherr, M., Shields, C.: Cocaine noodles: exploiting the gap between human and machine speech recognition. In: 9th {USENIX} Workshop on Offensive Technologies ({WOOT} 2015) (2015)
2. Carlini, N., et al.: Hidden voice commands. In: 25th {USENIX} Security Symposium ({USENIX} Security 2016), pp. 513–530 (2016)
3. Hu, S., Shang, X., Qin, Z., Li, M., Wang, Q., Wang, C.: Adversarial examples for automatic speech recognition: attacks and countermeasures. IEEE Commun. Mag. 57(10), 120–126 (2019)
4. Audhkhasi, K., Ramabhadran, B., Saon, G., Picheny, M., Nahamoo, D.: Direct acoustics-to-word models for English conversational speech recognition, arXiv preprint arXiv:1703.07754 (2017)
5. Xiong, W., Wu, L., Alleva, F., Droppo, J., Huang, X., Stolcke, A.: The Microsoft 2017 conversational speech recognition system. In: 2018 IEEE International Conference on Acoustics, Speech and Signal Processing (ICASSP), pp. 5934–5938. IEEE (2018)
6. Povey, D., et al.: The kaldispeech recognition toolkit. In: IEEE 2011 Workshop on Automatic Speech Recognition and Understanding, no. CONF. IEEE Signal Processing Society (2011)
7. Kaldi. https://github.com/kaldi-asr/kaldi
8. Schönherr, L., Kohls, K., Zeiler, S., Holz, T., Kolossa, D.: Adversarial attacks against automatic speech recognition systems via psychoacoustic hiding, arXiv preprint arXiv:1808.05665 (2018)
9. Hannun, A., et al.: Deep speech: scaling up end-to-end speech recognition, arXiv preprint arXiv:1412.5567 (2014)
10. DeepSpeech. https://github.com/mozilla/DeepSpeech
11. Du, T., Ji, S., Li, J., Gu, Q., Wang, T., Beyah, R.: Sirenattack: generating adversarial audio for end-to-end acoustic systems, arXiv preprint arXiv:1901.07846 (2019)
12. Graves, A., Fernández, S., Gomez, F., Schmidhuber, J.: Connectionist temporal classification: labelling unsegmented sequence data with recurrent neural networks. In: Proceedings of the 23rd International Conference on Machine Learning, pp. 369–376 (2006)
13. Szegedy, C., et al.: Intriguing properties of neural networks, arXiv preprint arXiv:1312.6199 (2013)
14. Papernot, N., McDaniel, P., Goodfellow, I., Jha, S., Celik, Z.B., Swami, A.: Practical black-box attacks against machine learning. In: Proceedings of the 2017 ACM on Asia Conference on Computer and Communications Security, pp. 506–519 (2017)

15. Moosavi-Dezfooli, S.M., Fawzi, A., Fawzi, O., Frossard, P.: Universal adversarial perturbations. In: Proceedings of the IEEE Conference on Computer Vision and Pattern Recognition, pp. 1765–1773 (2017)
16. Su, J., Vargas, D.V., Sakurai, K.: One pixel attack for fooling deep neural networks. IEEE Trans. Evol. Comput. **23**(5), 828–841 (2019)
17. Dong, Y., et al.: Efficient decision-based black-box adversarial attacks on face recognition. In: Proceedings of the IEEE Conference on Computer Vision and Pattern Recognition, pp. 7714–7722 (2019)
18. Mozilla common voice (2017). https://voice.mozilla.org/en
19. Warden, P.: Speech commands: a public dataset for single-word speech recognition, vol. 1 (2017). Dataset. http://download.tensorflow.org/data/speech_commands_v0.01.tar.gz
20. Panayotov, V., Chen, G., Povey, D., Khudanpur, S.: Librispeech: an ASR corpus based on public domain audio books. In: 2015 IEEE International Conference on Acoustics, Speech and Signal Processing (ICASSP), pp. 5206–5210. IEEE (2015)
21. Busso, C., et al.: Iemocap: interactive emotional dyadic motion capture database. Lang. Resour. Eval. **42**(4), 335 (2008)
22. Zhang, G., Yan, C., Ji, X., Zhang, T., Zhang, T., Xu, W.: Dolphinattack: inaudible voice commands. In: Proceedings of the 2017 ACM SIGSAC Conference on Computer and Communications Security, pp. 103–117 (2017)
23. Yuan, X., et al.: Commandersong: a systematic approach for practical adversarial voice recognition. In: 27th {USENIX} Security Symposium ({USENIX} Security 2018), pp. 49–64 (2018)
24. Cisse, M., Adi, Y., Neverova, N., Keshet, J.: Houdini: fooling deep structured prediction models, arXiv preprint arXiv:1707.05373 (2017)
25. Amodei, D., et al.: Deep speech 2: end-to-end speech recognition in English and mandarin. In: International Conference on Machine Learning, pp. 173–182 (2016)
26. Iter, D., Huang, J., Jermann, M.: Generating adversarial examples for speech recognition. Stanford Technical Report (2017)
27. Abdullah, H., Garcia, W., Peeters, C., Traynor, P., Butler, K.R., Wilson, J.: Practical hidden voice attacks against speech and speaker recognition systems, arXiv preprint arXiv:1904.05734 (2019)
28. Carlini, N., Wagner, D.: Audio adversarial examples: targeted attacks on speech-to-text. In: 2018 IEEE Security and Privacy Workshops (SPW), pp. 1–7. IEEE (2018)
29. Yakura, H., Sakuma, J.: Robust audio adversarial example for a physical attack, arXiv preprint arXiv:1810.11793 (2018)
30. Qin, Y., Carlini, N., Cottrell, G., Goodfellow, I., Raffel, C.: Imperceptible, robust, and targeted adversarial examples for automatic speech recognition, arXiv preprint arXiv:1903.10346 (2019)
31. Shen, J., et al.: Lingvo: a modular and scalable framework for sequence-to-sequence modeling, arXiv preprint arXiv:1902.08295 (2019)
32. Schönherr, L., Zeiler, S., Holz, T., Kolossa, D.: Robust over-the-air adversarial examples against automatic speech recognition systems, arXiv preprint arXiv:1908.01551 (2019)
33. Szurley, J., Kolter, J.Z.: Perceptual based adversarial audio attacks, arXiv preprint arXiv:1906.06355 (2019)
34. Liu, X., Zhang, X., Wan, K., Zhu, Q., Ding, Y.: Towards weighted-sampling audio adversarial example attack. arXiv, Audio and Speech Processing (2019)

35. Kwon, H.W., Kwon, H., Yoon, H., Choi, D.: Selective audio adversarial example in evasion attack on speech recognition system. IEEE Trans. Inf. Forensics Secur. **15**, 526–538 (2020)
36. Abdoli, S., Hafemann, L.G., Rony, J., Ayed, I.B., Cardinal, P., Koerich, A.L.: Universal adversarial audio perturbations, arXiv, vol. abs/1908.03173 (2019)
37. Vadillo, J., Santana, R.: Universal adversarial examples in speech command classification, arXiv, vol. abs/1911.10182 (2019)
38. Moosavi-Dezfooli, S.M., Fawzi, A., Frossard, P.: Deepfool: a simple and accurate method to fool deep neural networks. In: 2016 IEEE Conference on Computer Vision and Pattern Recognition (CVPR), pp. 2574–2582 (2015)
39. Neekhara, P., Hussain, S., Pandey, P., Dubnov, S., McAuley, J., Koushanfar, F.: Universal adversarial perturbations for speech recognition systems, arXiv, vol. abs/1905.03828 (2019)
40. Gong, Y., Poellabauer, C.: Crafting adversarial examples for speech paralinguistics applications, arXiv, vol. abs/1711.03280 (2017)
41. Kreuk, F., Adi, Y., Cissé, M., Keshet, J.: Fooling end-to-end speaker verification with adversarial examples. In: 2018 IEEE International Conference on Acoustics, Speech and Signal Processing (ICASSP), pp. 1962–1966 (2018)
42. Alzantot, M., Balaji, B., Srivastava, M.: Did you hear that? Adversarial examples against automatic speech recognition, arXiv, vol. abs/1801.00554 (2018)
43. Taori, R., Kamsetty, A., Chu, B., Vemuri, N.: Targeted adversarial examples for black box audio systems. In: 2019 IEEE Security and Privacy Workshops (SPW), pp. 15–20 (2018)
44. Khare, S., Aralikatte, R., Mani, S.: Adversarial black-box attacks on automatic speech recognition systems using multi-objective evolutionary optimization, arXiv preprint arXiv:1811.01312 (2018)
45. Zagoruyko, S., Komodakis, N.: Wide residual networks, arXiv preprint arXiv:1605.07146 (2016)
46. Sun, S., Yeh, C.-F., Ostendorf, M., Hwang, M.-Y., Xie, L.: Training augmentation with adversarial examples for robust speech recognition, arXiv preprint arXiv:1806.02782 (2018)
47. Zeng, Q., et al.: A multiversion programming inspired approach to detecting audio adversarial examples. In: 2019 49th Annual IEEE/IFIP International Conference on Dependable Systems and Networks (DSN), pp. 39–51. IEEE (2019)
48. Latif, S., Rana, R., Qadir, J.: Adversarial machine learning and speech emotion recognition: utilizing generative adversarial networks for robustness, arXiv preprint arXiv:1811.11402 (2018)
49. Rajaratnam, K., Shah, K., Kalita, J.: Isolated and ensemble audio preprocessing methods for detecting adversarial examples against automatic speech recognition, arXiv preprint arXiv:1809.04397 (2018)
50. Rajaratnam, K., Kalita, J.: Noise flooding for detecting audio adversarial examples against automatic speech recognition. In: 2018 IEEE International Symposium on Signal Processing and Information Technology (ISSPIT), pp. 197–201. IEEE (2018)
51. Samizade, S., Tan, Z.-H., Shen, C., Guan, X.: Adversarial example detection by classification for deep speech recognition, arXiv preprint arXiv:1910.10013 (2019)
52. Yang, Z., Li, B., Chen, P.-Y., Song, D.: Characterizing audio adversarial examples using temporal dependency, arXiv preprint arXiv:1809.10875 (2018)
53. Kwon, H., Yoon, H., Park, K.-W.: Poster: detecting audio adversarial example through audio modification. In: Proceedings of the 2019 ACM SIGSAC Conference on Computer and Communications Security, pp. 2521–2523 (2019)

54. Ma, P., Petridis, S., Pantic, M.: Detecting adversarial attacks on audio-visual speech recognition, arXiv preprint arXiv:1912.08639 (2019)
55. Esmaeilpour, M., Cardinal, P., Koerich, A.L.: A robust approach for securing audio classification against adversarial attacks. IEEE Trans. Inf. Forensics Secur. **15**, 2147–2159 (2019)
56. Goodfellow, I., et al.: Generative adversarial nets. In: Advances in Neural Information Processing Systems, pp. 2672–2680 (2014)
57. Roy, N., Hassanieh, H., Roy Choudhury, R.: Backdoor: making microphones hear inaudible sounds. In: Proceedings of the 15th Annual International Conference on Mobile Systems, Applications, and Services, pp. 2–14 (2017)
58. Tamura, K., Omagari, A., Hashida, S.: Novel defense method against audio adversarial example for speech-to-text transcription neural networks. In: 2019 IEEE 11th International Workshop on Computational Intelligence and Applications (IWCIA), pp. 115–120. IEEE (2019)
59. Yang, C.-H., Qi, J., Chen, P.-Y., Ma, X., Lee, C.-H.: Characterizing speech adversarial examples using self-attention u-net enhancement, arXiv preprint arXiv:2003.13917 (2020)

Enhancing Adversarial Examples with Flip-Invariance and Brightness-Invariance

Wanping Liu$^{(\boxtimes)}$ and Zhaoping Li

College of Computer Science and Engineering, Chongqing University of Technology,
Chongqing 400054, China
wpliu@cqut.edu.cn

Abstract. Despite of achieving remarkable success in computer vision tasks, convolutional neural networks still face the threat of adversarial examples, crafted by adding small human-invisible perturbations on clean inputs. Usually, most of existing black-box adversarial attacks show extremely low transferability while encountering powerful defense models. In this paper, based on the observed invariant property of convolutional neural networks (i.e., the models could maintain accuracy to transformed images), we propose two new methods to improve the transferability which are called as the flip-invariant attack method (FIM) and the brightness-invariant attack method (BIM), respectively. Both the novel approaches derive multiple different logit outputs by inputting the transformed copies of the original image into the white-box model. Simultaneously, the ensemble of these outputs is attacked to avoid overfitting the white-box model and generating more transferable adversarial examples. Moreover, the newly-proposed FIM and BIM methods can be naturally combined with other gradient-based methods. Extensive experiments on the ImageNet dataset prove that our methods achieve higher attack success rate and higher transferability than previous gradient-based attack methods.

Keywords: Adversarial attacks · Transferability · Convolutional neural networks · Adversarial examples · Cybersecurity

1 Introduction

In recent years, convolutional neural networks are extremely vulnerable to adversarial examples [1], although they have achieved great success in computer vision tasks, including image recognition [2–4], object detection [5,6] and semantic segmentation [7]. Adversarial examples are very beneficial to evaluate the robustness of alternative models [8] and strengthen the vulnerabilities of existing algorithms [9]. Besides, adversarial examples have the property of transferability [1,10,11]. That is, adversarial examples generated for one model may

Supported by the Science and Technology Research Program of Chongqing Municipal Education Commission (Grant no. KJQN201901101), and the National Natural Science Foundation of China (Grant no. 61603065).

be effective for another model, making black box attacks possible in practical applications and posing serious security problems [12,13]. Thus, how to generate adversarial examples with high transferability has attracted much attention in the research.

Several methods for crafting adversarial examples have been proposed recently, such as the fast gradient symbol method [9], the basic iterative method [14] and the C&W method [15]. Although the above methods can achieve a high success rate for a white-box attack (which can fully access the target model), the lack of transferability in a black box environment (which cannot access the target model) poses only a limited threat. For the transferability, there existed various attempts, such as attacking an ensemble of multiple varied models [10], momentum boosting [16], diverse input [17], and translation invariance [18]. These methods have some effects, however, they still need to be improved, especially for defense models, such as adversarial training and input transformation.

In this work, the generation of transferable adversarial examples is considered as an optimization process to improve the generalization ability. We newly propose the brightness-invariant attack method and the flip-invariant attack method, both of which can improve the transferability of adversarial examples. Our work can be divided into the following three parts:

1) We find that deep learning models have flip invariance and brightness invariance, and thus we propose an invariance-based model augmentation method. This approach improves the transferability of the adversarial examples by simultaneously optimizing the adversarial perturbance on multiple copies of the input image.
2) We have conducted extensive experiments on the ImageNet dataset [19], including models that are normally trained and have defenses. The results indicate that our proposed method can effectively improve the attack success rate.
3) We find that combining the flip invariant attack method and the brightness invariant attack method with existing gradient-based attack methods (such as attacking an ensemble of multiple alternative models [10], momentum boosting [16], diverse input [17], and translation invariance [18]) can hugely improve the attack success rate and the latest transferability benchmark.

2   Related Work

2.1   Generating Adversarial Examples

Szegedy et al. [1] firstly found adversarial examples with a box-constrained LBFGS method and indicated the fragility of CNN. Due to the expensive calculations, the fast gradient sign method that can craft adversarial examples faster by performing a step along the gradient direction was proposed by Goodfellow et al. [9]. Kurakin et al. [14] extended this method to an iterative version. An iterative algorithm that was based on momentum was proposed by Dong et al. [16] to improve the transferability of adversarial examples. Attacking a group of networks at the same time can also improve the transferability [10].

2.2 Defending Adversarial Examples

A large number of defense methods to resist adversarial examples have been proposed.

Adversarial Training. One of the most popular methods is the adversarial training [9]. This method augments training data by adding adversarial examples during the training process. Tramer et al. [20] pointed out the vulnerability of this method and proposed ensemble adversarial training, which uses disturbances passed from other models to increase training data so as to further improve the robustness of the network.

Input Transformation. In addition, Guo et al. [21] found that a series of image transformations are used to eliminate adversarial interference while retaining the information of the image. Xie et al. [22] applied the random transformation to reduce adversarial affects. Liu et al. [23] attempted to correct the adversarial examples, thus proposed a framework based on JPEG compression without affecting the accuracy of the original data. Liao et al. [24] proposed an advanced notation guided noise reducer to filter adversarial examples. Jia et al. [25] defended against adversarial examples with an end-to-end image compression model. Cohen et al. [26] used random smoothing to get a classifier with proven adversarial robustness.

3 Methodology

3.1 Gradient-Based Methods

Consider a clean image x with ground truth label y_{true} and the model f to be attacked, and let $J(x, y_{true})$ be the loss function. Our goal is to find an adversarial example that can mislead the model into misclassification (e.g. $f(x_{adv}) \neq y_{true}$), while still remaining in the ϵ-ball centered at x (e.g., $\|x_{adv} - x\|_\infty \leq \epsilon$).

Fast Gradient Sign Method (FGSM) [9]. FGSM craft adversarial example for one step along the gradient direction by the amount of ϵ:

$$x_{adv} = x + \epsilon \cdot \text{sign}\left(\nabla_x J\left(x, y_{true}\right)\right). \tag{1}$$

Projected Gradient Descent (PGD) [27]. PGD perturbs clean image x for T steps with small step size. When adversarial example goes beyond the ϵ-ball, PGD projects it back into the ϵ-ball of x after each step:

$$x_{adv}^{t+1} = \prod_\epsilon \left(x_{adv}^t + \alpha \cdot \text{sign}\left(\nabla_x J\left(f\left(x_{adv}^t\right), y_{true}\right)\right)\right), \tag{2}$$

where $\prod_\epsilon()$ is the projection operation, and the step size is set as $\alpha = \epsilon/T$.

Momentum Iterative Boosting Method (MIM) [16]. MIM incorporates a momentum term into the gradient to boost the transferability:

$$x_{adv}^{t+1} = \prod_{\epsilon} \left(x_{adv}^t + \alpha \cdot \text{sign}\left(g^{t+1}\right) \right),$$

$$g^{t+1} = \mu \cdot g^t + \frac{\nabla_x J\left(f\left(x_{adv}^t\right), y_{true}\right)}{\left\| \nabla_x J\left(f\left(x_{ddv}^t\right), y_{true}\right) \right\|_1},$$

(3)

where g^t indicates the gradient at the t-th step, $\alpha = \epsilon/T$ is the step size for a total of T steps, μ is a decay factor, and $\|.\|_1$ is the L_1 norm.

Diverse Input Method (DIM) [17]. DIM proposes to craft adversarial exampels using gradient with respect to the randomly-transformed input example:

$$x_{adv}^{t+1} = \prod_{\epsilon} \left(x_{adv}^t + \alpha \cdot \text{sign}\left(\nabla_x J\left(f\left(H\left(x_{adv}^t; p\right)\right), y_{true}\right)\right) \right), \quad (4)$$

where $H\left(x_{adv}^t; p\right)$ is a stochastic transformation function on x_{adv}^t for a given probability p.

Translation Invariant Method (TIM) [18]. TIM attempts to avoid robustly trained DNNs by producing less reactive adversarial examples for the surrogate model's discriminative regions. In particular, TIM calculates the gradients for a number of translated versions of the original input:

$$x_{adv}^{t+1} = \prod_{\epsilon} \left(x_{adv}^t + \alpha \cdot \text{sign}\left(W * \nabla_x J\left(f\left(x_{adv}^t\right), y_{true}\right)\right) \right), \quad (5)$$

where W is a predefined kernel (e.g., Gaussian) matrix. This kernel convolution is equivalent to the weighted sum of gradients over $(2k+1)^2$ number of shifted input examples.

MIM, DIM, and TIM can not only improve the transferability of adversarial examples, but also have their own advantages. Specifically, MIM can speed up the search of adversarial examples, DIM can prevent input transformation defense, and TIM can limit the perturbance to low-frequency space and invalidate the defense model. However, when encountering stronger defense models, these methods usually need to be combined with ensemble-based attack methods(attacking a group of different models at the same time), but the training of different models consumes a lot of resources.

3.2   Motivation

The process of generating adversarial examples is similar to the process of training neural networks. We can consider improving the transferability of adversarial examples as improving neural networks' generalization ability. In the optimization stage, the white-box model we attacked to craft adversarial examples could be regarded as training data in the training procedure, thus the adversarial examples could be regarded as the model's training parameters. During the testing stage, the black-box model that is used to evaluate the adversarial examples could be considered as test data for the model.

In general, ensemble-based attack methods [10] have better performance than non-ensemble attack methods. The top teams in the competition have basically adopted ensemble-based method, so they have received more attention. We call this method as model augmentation. However, for better accuracy and diverse models, people usually need to train them independently from scratch, which will consume a lot of time and resources. How to implement model augmentation at a lower cost to generate adversarial examples with high transferability is the focus of our attention.

3.3 Flip-Invariant and Brightness-Invariant Attack Method

The formal definition of model augmentation and accuracy-maintained transformations is first introduced, as follows:

Definition 1. *Accuracy-maintained transformation.* *Given an input image x and a classifier $f(x) : x \in \mathcal{X} \rightarrow y \in \mathcal{Y}$, if there is always $argmax(f(x)) \approx argmax(f(\mathcal{T}(x)))$ for any $x \in \mathcal{X}$, then we say that $\mathcal{T}(.)$ is accuracy-maintained transformation.*

Definition 2. *Model augmentation.* *Given a model $f(x) : x \in \mathcal{X} \rightarrow y \in \mathcal{Y}$, an input image x and an accuracy-maintained transformation $\mathcal{T}$, if we can derive a new model from the original model by $f'(x) = f(\mathcal{T}(x))$, we define such a model derivation as a model augmentation.*

Attacking more models simultaneously to improve the transferability of adversarial examples is analogous to improving the generalization ability of the model through data augmentation.

In our work, we do not need to train a set of different models from scratch to attack, but derive more models from the raw model through model augmentation. This is an efficient method to obtain multiple model copies by accuracy-maintained transformation, saving a lot of computing costs. At the same time, we observe that the image will be affected by light and direction during the shooting process, so we guess that the deep neural network may have flip invariance and brightness invariance. Specifically, the original image on the one model has the same prediction as the image after flip and brightness adjust, which is verified in Sect. 4.2.

Therefore, the flip transformation and the brightness transformation can be used as accuracy-maintained transformations, thereby achieving model augmentation. Based on the above analysis, we propose the flip-invariant attack method and the brightness-invariant attack method, which optimize the adversarial perturbation on the input images' copies generated by flip-transformation and brightness-transformation:

$$\arg\max \frac{1}{n} \sum_{k=0}^{n} J\left(\mathcal{T}_k\left(x_{adv}\right), y_{true}\right), \text{s.t.} \|x_{adv} - x\|_\infty \leq \epsilon, \tag{6}$$

where $\mathcal{T}_k$ represents the flip transformation and brightness transformation, and n represents the number of image copies.

Using flip-invariance attack and brightness-invariance attack, it is unnecessary to train a new set of models from scratch. We can effectively attack varied models through model augmentation. Furthermore, it prevents overfitting on the white-box model, thereby achieving the purpose of improving the transferability of the adversarial examples.

3.4 Attack Algorithm

For the ensemble-based attack method, FIM and BIM can import model augmentation function to craft adversarial examples through flip transformation and brightness transformation, respectively. Multiple models can be derived from only a single model for attack. FIM and BIM can be naturally combined to a stronger attack method, which is called as FI-BIM (Flip and Brightness Invariant Attack Method). Algorithm 1 summarizes the algorithm of FI-BIM attack.

Algorithm 1. FI-BIM

Input: A classifier f with loss function J; a clean example x with label y_{true};
Input: Perturbation size ϵ; iterations T; decay factor μ and number of copies n.
Output: An adversarial example x_{adv}

1: $\alpha = \epsilon/T$
2: $g_0 = 0; x_{adv}^0 = x$
3: **for** $t = 0$ to $T - 1$ **do**
4:    **for** $k = 0$ to $n - 1$ **do**
5:       Get the gradients as $g_k = \nabla_x J\left(\mathcal{T}_k\left(x_{adv}^t\right), y_{true}\right)$
6:    **end for**
7:    Get average gradients as $g = \frac{1}{n} \cdot \sum_{k=0}^{n} g_k$
8:    Update g_{t+1} by $g_{t+1} = \mu \cdot g_t + \frac{g}{\|g\|_1}$
9:    Update x_{adv}^{t+1} by $x_{adv}^{t+1} = \text{Clip}_x^\epsilon \left\{x_{adv}^t + \alpha \cdot \text{sign}\left(g_{t+1}\right)\right\}$
10: **end for**

In addition, to greatly improve the transferability, DIM (Diversified Input), TIM (Translate Invariant) and TI-DIM (Translate Invariant Diversified Input Method) can also be integrated with FI-BIM as FI-BI-DIM, FI-BI-TIM and FI-BI-TI-DIM, respectively. The detailed algorithms for these attack methods are provided in Appendix A.

4 Experiments

In this section, experimental results are presented to demonstrate the proposed method's effectiveness. The experimental settings are first specified in Sect. 4.1. The flip-invariance and brightness-invariance of convolutional neural networks are then validated in Sect. 4.2. We then compare the results of baseline methods with our method in Sect. 4.3 and 4.4 on both normally trained models and adversarial trained models. In addition to the defense models based on adversarial training, the effectiveness of our proposed methods is also quantified on more advanced defense in Sect. 4.5.

4.1 Experiment Setup

Data. It is less meaningful to attack wrongly classified examples. Therefore, we randomly build our test dataset that contains 1000 images from the ImageNet validation dataset [19], which are almost aright classified by all the networks we applied. In advance, those images are all resized to $299 \times 299 \times 3$.

Networks. We have considered seven common networks that are available to the public, InceptionV3 (IncV3) [28], InceptionV4 (IncV4) [29], ResnetV2 (ResV2) [3] and InceptionResnetV2 (IncResV2) [29] are all normally trained networks, Ens4-Adv-Inception-V3 (IncV3ens4) and Ens-Adv-InceptionResNet-V2 (IncResV2ens) [20] are all adversarial trained networks.

We also consider other defense models: resizing and padding (R&P) [22], high-level guided denoiser (HGD) [24], image compression model purification (Comdefend) [25], feature distillation (FD) [23] and randomized smoothing (RS) [26].

Baselines. We integrate DIM, TIM, and TI-DIM with our methods, to prove the FI-BIM performance boost over these baselines. We denote our FI-BIM integrated with other method as FI-BI-TIM, FI-BI-DIM and FI-BI-TI-DIM, respectively.

Hyper-Parameters. We follow the settings for the hyper-parameters in MIM with the iteration number $T = 16$, maximum disturbance as $\epsilon = 16$, and step size $\alpha = 1.6$. We adopted the MIM's decay factor $\mu = 1.0$. For DIM, we set the default ratio of transformation is 0.5. We adopt the Gaussian kernel for TIM with the kernel size is 7×7. The number of invariant copies of our FI-BIM is set to $m = 10$.

4.2 Flip-Invariance and Brightness-Invariance of CNNs

We randomly select 1,000 raw images from the ImageNet validation dataset to validate the flip-invariance and brightness-invariance of deep neural networks. Specifically, we keep the pixel size of the brightness adjustment within the range of $[-150, 150]$ with a step size 30 and flip the images horizontally and vertically.

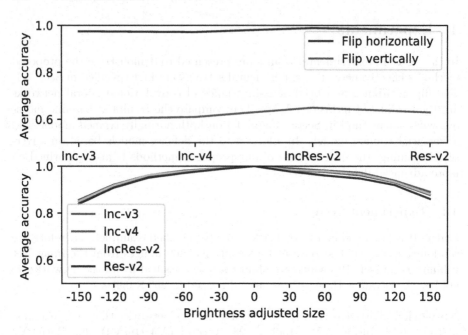

Fig. 1. The average accuracy for Inc-v3, Inc-v4, IncRes-v2 and Res-101 when images be flipped and brightness adjusted.

We then input the transformed images to the test networks, including IncV4, IncV3, IncResV2, and ResV2, to get an average accuracy of all 1,000 images.

As shown in Fig. 1, when the pixel size of the brightness adjustment is within the range $[-100, 100]$, we could easily observe that the accuracy curves are stable and smooth. That is, the accuracy for both the raw and the transformed images are very similar. We can also observe that the accuracy after flipping horizontally is almost the same as the raw. Thus, we assume that the brightness-invariance of deep learning models is held within $[-100, 100]$, and we optimize adversarial perturbations over the transformed copies of input images rely on the brightness-invariance and flip-invariance.

4.3 Attacking a Single Network

In this section, we compare flip-brightness-invariant based black-box attack success rates with baseline attacks. We first apply DIM, TIM and TI-DIM to execute adversarial attacks for IncV3, IncV4, IncResV2, and ResV2, respectively, through integrating them with our method as FI-BI-DIM, FI-BI-TIM, and FI-BI-TI-DIM. Black-box attack success rates are reported in Table 1(a) for DIM and FI-BI-DIM, Table 1(b) for TIM and FI-BI-TIM, and Table 1(c) for TI-DIM and FI-BI-TI-DIM, respectively.

Table 1. Attack success rates (%) of adversarial attacks against six models under single model setting. The adversarial examples are crafted on IncV3, IncV4, IncResV2 and ResV2, respectively. * indicates the white-box attacks.

(a) Comparison of DIM and FI-BI-DIM

Model	Attack	IncV3	IncV4	IncResV2	ResV2	IncV3$_{ens4}$	IncResV2$_{ens}$
IncV3	DIM	99.5*	59.1	54.9	51.7	38.7	27.6
	FI-BI-DIM	**99.8***	**81.2**	**79.2**	**73.8**	**63.9**	**49.1**
IncV4	DIM	64.2	97.2*	59.4	52.8	38.4	32.6
	FI-BI-DIM	**83.5**	**98.6***	**76.5**	**70.8**	**59.2**	**51.9**
IncResV2	DIM	63.2	58.8	91.0*	56.9	42.6	43.9
	FI-BI-DIM	**80.1**	**76.6**	**94.7***	**73.6**	**61.2**	**63.8**
ResV2	DIM	70.8	63.7	64.1	99.4*	50.3	43.1
	FI-BI-DIM	**89.1**	**84.2**	**84.7**	99.3*	**75.2**	**66.9**

(b) Comparison of TIM and FI-BI-TIM

Model	Attack	IncV3	IncV4	IncResV2	ResV2	IncV3$_{ens4}$	IncResV2$_{ens}$
IncV3	TIM	99.9*	44.4	39.4	39.0	32.2	21.6
	FI-BI-TIM	99.9*	**69.4**	**66.4**	**61.7**	**54.0**	**41.4**
IncV4	TIM	52.5	98.9*	44.5	41.9	34.0	28.2
	FI-BI-TIM	**75.7**	**99.3***	**69.5**	**60.3**	**52.6**	**45.9**
IncResV2	TIM	58.7	51.3	96.0*	49.7	36.9	40.0
	FI-BI-TIM	**79.9**	**74.0**	**97.0***	**68.8**	**61.2**	**65.6**
ResV2	TIM	58.2	52.3	50.6	99.3*	44.0	37.3
	FI-BI-TIM	**80.6**	**75.1**	**76.7**	**99.4***	**69.5**	**61.9**

(c) Comparison of TI-DIM and FI-BI-TI-DIM

Model	Attack	IncV3	IncV4	IncResV2	ResV2	IncV3$_{ens4}$	IncResV2$_{ens}$
IncV3	TI-DIM	99.0*	61.4	58.5	54.6	45.4	35.6
	FI-BI-TI-DIM	**99.6***	**83.0**	**81.5**	**75.9**	**69.9**	**58.1**
IncV4	TI-DIM	67.3	97.4*	61.5	54.0	45.6	40.6
	FI-BI-TI-DIM	**83.5**	**98.2***	**80.4**	**72.5**	**66.8**	**60.7**
IncResV2	TI-DIM	70.6	65.1	92.7*	61.1	51.8	54.3
	FI-BI-TI-DIM	**82.9**	**79.4**	**94.7***	**75.5**	**70.3**	**73.2**
ResV2	TI-DIM	75.4	68.0	70.2	99.2*	62.1	56.2
	FI-BI-TI-DIM	**88.7**	**85.4**	**86.3**	**99.4***	**81.6**	**76.5**

It can be observed from the table that no matter which attack algorithm or white box model is used, the success rate of the black box model is greatly improved by using the proposed method. The FI-BIM method generally outperforms baseline attacks consistently by 10% to 30%. In particular, the resulting adversarial examples have about 83.7% success rates against the black box models when using FI-BI-TI-DIM, the combination of FI-BIM and TI-DIM, to attack the IncResV2 model (as shown in Table 1(c)). It reveals current models' vulnerability to black-box attacks. The efficiency of the proposed method is also validated by the results.

Table 2. Attack success rates (%) of adversarial attacks against six models under multimodel setting. ∗ indicates the white-box models being attacked.

Attack	IncV3*	IncV4*	IncResV2*	ResV2*	IncV3$_{ens4}$	IncResV2$_{ens}$
DIM	99.8	99.2	98.7	98.7	60.1	42.1
FI-BI-DIM	**100.0**	**99.9**	**99.8**	**99.7**	**84.8**	**70.3**
TIM	99.5	99.1	98.8	99.6	65.1	52.1
FI-BI-TIM	**99.6**	**99.7**	**99.5**	**100.0**	**88.1**	**81.2**
TI-DIM	99.6	99.1	98.9	99.0	79.8	72.1
FI-BI-TI-DIM	**100.0**	**100.0**	**99.8**	**99.9**	**91.4**	**87.5**

Table 3. Attack success rates (%) of adversarial attacks against the advanced defense models.

Attack	HGD	R&P	FD	ComDefend	RD	**Average**
MIM	35.8	28.4	50.1	46.2	25.6	37.2
TI-DIM	83.5	74.6	82.9	79.4	50.3	74.1
FI-BI-TI-DIM	**92.4**	**89.6**	**92.5**	**92.1**	**68.9**	**87.1**

4.4 Attacking an Ensemble of Networks

In this section, we further present the results for an ensemble of models when adversarial examples are generated. Liu et al. [10] showed that attacking multiple models simultaneously could improve the transferability of the generated adversarial example. This is because that if an example is still against various models, it is more probable to move to other black box models. The ensemble method proposed in [10] is used to integrate logit activations of various models. We use DIM, FI-BI-DIM, TIM, FI-BI-TIM and TI-DIM and FI-BI-TI-DIM to attack the ensemble of IncV3, IncV4, IncResV2 and ResV2 with same ensemble weight.

The results of black-box attacks against the three adversarial trained models are shown in Table 2. The success rates are also improved by the proposed method over all baseline attacks across all experiments. It should be noticed that the adversarial examples crafted by FI-BI-TI-DIM could deceive the adversarial trained models at an average success rate of 89.5%. This shows that when using FI-BI-TI-DIM as a black-box attack, these adversarial trained models provide little robustness guarantee.

4.5 Attacking Advanced Defensive Models

In addition to above models that are normally trained and adversarially trained, we consider to test the effectiveness of our methods on other advanced defense models, such as high-level guided denoiser (HGD), resizing and padding (R&P), feature distillation (FD) purifying perturbations via image compression (Comdefend) and randomized smoothing (RS).

We compare our FI-BI-TI-DIM with the state-of-the-art attack method TI-DIM [18]. First, we use MIM, TI-DIM and FI-BI-TI-DIM to respectively craft adversarial examples on the ensemble of IncV4, IncV3, IncResV2 and ResV2. Second, we test the adversarial examples by attacking those defensive models.

As indicated in Table 3, our FI-BI-TI-DIM reaches an mean attack success rate of 87.1%, which exceeds the state-of-the-art method by a large 13.0% margin. FI-BI-TI-DIM could deceive the adversarial trained models and other advanced defensive models by attacking the normally trained models and only relying on adversarial examples' transferability, raising a new security problem for more robust development of deep learning models.

5   Conclusion

In this work, we proposed two novel attack methods to improve the transferability of adversarial examples, namely flip-invariant attacks and brightness-invariant attacks. The flip-invariant attack and brightness-invariant attack are designed to enhance the model by using the model's flip invariance and brightness invariance to avoid the generated adversarial examples from overfitting the current white box replacement model. Extensive experiments on ImageNet dataset show that our method greatly improves the transferability of adversarial examples. In addition, the combination with existing methods can achieve higher attack success rates on adversarial training models and also penetrate other powerful defense models. Our work poses new challenges to the security of deep neural networks.

Appendix A: Details of the Algorithms

The algorithm of FI-BI-TI-DIM attack is summarized in Algorithm 2.

Algorithm 2. FI-BI-TI-DIM

Input: A classifier f with loss function J; a clean example x with label y_{true};
Input: Perturbation size ϵ; iterations T; decay factor μ and number of copies n.
Output: An adversarial example x_{adv}

1: $\alpha = \epsilon/T$
2: $g_0 = 0; x_{adv}^0 = x$
3: **for** $t = 0$ to $T - 1$ **do**
4:    **for** $k = 0$ to $n - 1$ **do**
5:       Get the gradients as $g_k = \nabla_x J\left(H\left(\mathcal{T}_k\left(x_{adv}^t\right);p\right),y_{true}\right)$
6:    **end for**
7:    Get average gradients as $g = \dfrac{1}{n} \cdot \sum_{k=0}^n g_k$
8:    Convolve the gradient by $g = \boldsymbol{W} * g$
9:    Update g_{t+1} by $g_{t+1} = \mu \cdot g_t + \dfrac{g}{\|g\|_1}$
10:   Update x_{adv}^{t+1} by $x_{adv}^{t+1} = \text{Clip}_x^\epsilon \left\{x_{adv}^t + \alpha \cdot \text{sign}\left(g_{t+1}\right)\right\}$
11: **end for**

References

1. Szegedy, C., et al.: Intriguing properties of neural networks. In: Proceedings of 2nd International Conference on Learning Representations (ICLR 2014) (2014)
2. Girshick, R.: Fast R-CNN. In: Proceedings of 2015 IEEE International Conference on Computer Vision (ICCV), pp. 1440–1448 (2015)
3. He, K., Zhang, X., Ren, S., Sun, J.: Identity mappings in deep residual networks. In: Leibe, B., Matas, J., Sebe, N., Welling, M. (eds.) ECCV 2016. LNCS, vol. 9908, pp. 630–645. Springer, Cham (2016). https://doi.org/10.1007/978-3-319-46493-0_38
4. Krizhevsky, A., Sutskever, I., Hinton, G.E.: ImageNet classification with deep convolutional neural networks. Commun. ACM **60**(6), 84–90 (2017)
5. Long, J., Shelhamer, E., Darrell, T.: Fully convolutional networks for semantic segmentation. In: Proceedings of the IEEE Conference on Computer Vision and Pattern Recognition, pp. 3431–3440 (2015)
6. Ren, S., He, K., Girshick, R., Sun, J.: Faster R-CNN: towards real-time object detection with region proposal networks. IEEE Trans. Pattern Anal. Mach. Intell. **39**(6), 1137–1149 (2017)
7. Simonyan, K., Zisserman, A.: Very deep convolutional networks for large-scale image recognition. In: Proceedings of 3rd International Conference on Learning Representations (ICLR 2015) (2015)
8. Arnab, A., Miksik, O., Torr, P.H.: On the robustness of semantic segmentation models to adversarial attacks. In: Proceedings of the IEEE Conference on Computer Vision and Pattern Recognition, pp. 888–897 (2018)
9. Goodfellow, I.J., Shlens, J., Szegedy, C.: Explaining and harnessing adversarial examples. In: Proceedings of 3rd International Conference on Learning Representations (ICLR 2015) (2015)
10. Liu, Y., Chen, X., Liu, C., Song, D.: Delving into transferable adversarial examples and black-box attacks. In: Proceedings of 5th International Conference on Learning Representations (ICLR 2017) (2017)
11. Moosavi-Dezfooli, S.M., Fawzi, A., Fawzi, O., Frossard, P.: Universal adversarial perturbations. In: Proceedings of the IEEE Conference on Computer Vision and Pattern Recognition, pp. 1765–1773 (2017)
12. Liu, W., Zhong, S.: Web malware spread modelling and optimal control strategies. Sci. Rep. **7**, (2017) Article no. 42308
13. Liu, W., Zhong, S.: Modeling and analyzing the dynamic spreading of epidemic malware by a network eigenvalue method. Appl. Math. Model. **63**, 491–507 (2018)
14. Kurakin, A., Goodfellow, I., Bengio, S.: Adversarial examples in the physical world. In: Proceedings of 5th International Conference on Learning Representations (ICLR 2017) (2017)
15. Carlini, N., Wagner, D.: Towards evaluating the robustness of neural networks. In: Proceedings of the IEEE Symposium on Security and Privacy, pp. 39–57 (2017)
16. Dong, Y., et al.: Boosting adversarial attacks with momentum. In: Proceedings of the IEEE Conference on Computer Vision and Pattern Recognition, pp. 9185–9193 (2018)
17. Xie, C., et al.: Improving transferability of adversarial examples with input diversity. In: Proceedings of the IEEE Conference on Computer Vision and Pattern Recognition, pp. 2730–2739 (2019)
18. Dong, Y., Pang, T., Su, H., Zhu, J.: Evading defenses to transferable adversarial examples by translation-invariant attacks. In: Proceedings of the IEEE Conference on Computer Vision and Pattern Recognition, pp. 4312–4321 (2019)

19. Russakovsky, O., et al.: Imagenet large scale visual recognition challenge. Int. J. Comput. Vision **115**(3), 211–252 (2015)
20. Tramer, F., Kurakin, A., Papernot, N., Goodfellow, I., Boneh, D., McDaniel, P.: Ensemble adversarial training: attacks and defenses. In: Proceedings of 6th International Conference on Learning Representations (ICLR 2018) (2018)
21. Guo, C., Rana, M., Cisse, M., Van Der Maaten, L.: Countering adversarial images using input transformations. In: Proceedings of 6th International Conference on Learning Representations (ICLR 2018) (2018)
22. Xie, C., Wang, J., Zhang, Z., Ren, Z., Yuille, A.: Mitigating adversarial effects through randomization. In: Proceedings of 6th International Conference on Learning Representations (ICLR 2018) (2018)
23. Liu, Z., et al.: Feature distillation: DNN-oriented jpeg compression against adversarial examples. In: Proceedings of the IEEE Conference on Computer Vision and Pattern Recognition, pp. 860–868 (2019)
24. Liao, F., Liang, M., Dong, Y., Pang, T., Hu, X., Zhu, J.: Defense against adversarial attacks using high-level representation guided denoiser. In: Proceedings of the IEEE Conference on Computer Vision and Pattern Recognition, pp. 1778–1787 (2018)
25. Jia, X., Wei, X., Cao, X., Foroosh, H.: Comdefend: an efficient image compression model to defend adversarial examples. In: Proceedings of the IEEE Conference on Computer Vision and Pattern Recognition, pp. 6084–6092 (2019)
26. Cohen, J.M., Rosenfeld, E., Kolter, J.Z.: Certified adversarial robustness via randomized smoothing. In: Proceedings of 7th International Conference on Learning Representations (ICLR 2019) (2019)
27. Madry, A., Makelov, A., Schmidt, L., Tsipras, D., Vladu, A.: Towards deep learning models resistant to adversarial attacks. In: Proceedings of 6th International Conference on Learning Representations (ICLR 2018) (2018)
28. Szegedy, C., Vanhoucke, V., Ioffe, S., Shlens, J., Wojna, Z.: Rethinking the inception architecture for computer vision. In: Proceedings of the IEEE Conference on Computer Vision and Pattern Recognition, pp. 2818–2826 (2016)
29. Szegedy, C., Ioffe, S., Vanhoucke, V., Alemi, A.: Inception-v4, inception-ResNet and the impact of residual connections on learning. In: Proceedings of the Thirty-first AAAI Conference on Artificial Intelligence, pp. 4278–4284 (2017)

MLAB-BiLSTM: Online Web Attack Detection Via Attention-Based Deep Neural Networks

Jun Yang[1], Mengyu Zhou[1(✉)], and Baojiang Cui[2]

[1] School of Computer Science, Beijing University of Posts and Telecommunications, Beijing, China
{junyang,manassehzhou}@bupt.edu.cn
[2] School of Cyberspace Security, Beijing University of Posts and Telecommunications, Beijing, China
cuibj@bupt.edu.cn

Abstract. With the continuous development of Web threats such as SQL injection and Cross-Site Scripting, Numerous web applications have been plagued by various forms of security threats and cyber attacks. And web attack detection has always been the focus of web security. Because the attacking payloads are often multiple small segments hidden in the long original request traffics, traditional machine learning based methods may have difficulties in learning useful patterns from the original request. In this study, we proposed an MLAB-BiLSTM method that can precisely detect Web attacks in real time by using multi-layer attention based bidirectional LSTM deep neural network. Firstly, due to the malicious payloads contains similar keywords, we used a keyword enhanced embedding method to transfer the original request to feature vectors. Then the features are divided into different segments. The words in the segments are firstly inputted into the bidirectional LSTM model with an attention mechanism to generate a encoded representation of different segments. Then the segments of the requests are input into another BiLSTM model with an attention mechanism to generate the encoded representation of the original request. Finally, the generated features are input into the Convolutional Neural Network to find out which kind of attack payload it is. The MLAB-BiLSTM model was tested on CSIC dataset and CTF competition traffic, the experiment results show that the accuracy of the model is above 99.81%, the recall of 99.56%, the precision of 99.60%, and the F1 Score is 0.9961, which outperformed both traditional rule-based methods like Libinjection or deep learning based methods like OwlEye.

Keywords: Network security · Malicious request detect · Long-short term memory · Attention

1 Introduction

With the rapid expansion of the Internet, more and more devices are connected to the Internet. In recent years, the majority of enterprises chose to save their data

© Springer Nature Singapore Pte Ltd. 2020
S. Yu et al. (Eds.): SPDE 2020, CCIS 1268, pp. 482–492, 2020.
https://doi.org/10.1007/978-981-15-9129-7_33

or provide service through web applications. Due to the flexibility of Web applications, there are many known or unknown ways to attack it, leading to leakage of user sensitive data. Symantec Internet Security Report [11] reveals that more than 1.3 million unique web attacks were blocked on endpoint machines every day in 2018. While analyzing all the URLs, 1 in 10 URLs analyzed was identified as being malicious. All these facts show that web security deserves to be taken seriously.

Given the severity to protect web attacks, there are many methods to detect web attack through malicious URLs proposed by scholars from all over the world. In summary, these methods can be divided into three categories, which are traditional rule based methods, machine learning based, and deep learning based. In rule based methods, such as ModSecurity [6], the web application firewall (WAF) usually used regular expression to match the requests, and the advantage of rule based detection is the low false alarm rate and the speed. However, this method is highly based on the experiences of the creator of the rule database, resulting in the weakness in detecting novel attack payloads. The machine learning based methods are based on the features extracted with artificial experiences and statistical models, giving them the ability to detect new types of intrusion as deviations from normal behavior [1]. But due to the selection of large amount of artificial features needed to be extracted and the performance of different detection methods, it's hard to use such methods in real life detection tasks. Lately, deep learning methods have achieved promising performance in malicious URLs classification tasks [14]. By learning and extracting features from the original web requests, it is significantly more efficient and more flexible to adapt to more complex attack behaviors due to the absence of the most time-consuming feature engineering phase. But during extracting, it usually treats all words with same weight, but in the real world, the researchers can classify the request with only few keywords in the URL.

In this paper, we proposed MLAB-BiLSTM model that can detect web attacks with both attention from word level and segment level. In our approach, we firstly used the word level attention to focus on which of the words are important in different segments of the web requests. Then the segment level attention focus on where the attacking payload may exist. The extracted features are fed into a CNN based classification network to decide which kind of attack this request belongs to.

To evaluate the model, we chose web requests both from CSIC dataset and CTF competition web traffic as training set. These requests including web attack methods such as XSS, SQLi. We compared proposed model with other web attack detect methods. The experimental results show that compared to other models the detection model we proposed is very effective and can obtain 99.7% accuracy.

The remaining parts of this article are organized as follows. In Sect. 2 we firstly summarized the related works. Section 3 considers the architecture of the proposed MLAB-BiLSTM neural network. In Sect. 4, we used both data from CSIC dataset and real-world traffic captured during CTF competitions. Finally, we draw our conclusion and discussions in Sect. 5.

2   Related Works

In this section, we analyzed different kinds of methods to detect web attacks. We divided these methods into three categories and discusses the advantage and disadvantages of these methods.

2.1   Rule Based Methods

Traditional rule based methods including blacklisting and heuristic approaches. Blacklisting means generating their rules by collecting a large amount of web traffics that contains malicious traffic. When a new visit was made, it tries to look up the database to find whether the request is in the database or not. Blacklist based rules need to keep obtaining different web attack traffic in real life, and with the growth of the malicious traffic database, the performance becomes worth. Future more, it is easy for attackers to find different payloads with same function to bypass the detection of the WAF [12], which is critical for protecting sensitive user data in big companies. Despite the weakage in generalization, nowadays there are still a large number of WAFs that use these approaches thanks to their simplicity and efficiency. To improve the ability of generalization, run-time application self-protection (RASP) approaches are proposed [4]. Instead of collecting the malicious traffic, extract the function call signature among those traffics with artificial experience and check if the traffic match any malicious signature, then raise an alarm to indicate the request is malignant. While the types of attacks and the flexibility of the web applications, it's pretty easy for attackers to find different ways to bypass the detection. As well as there is many kind of languages to develop a web application, so it's hard to develop a RASP firewall for each language.

2.2   Machine Learning Based Methods

Various machine learning methods have been used to detect malicious web attacks over the years. These approaches try to extract feature representations of web requests and training a prediction model on training data of both malicious and benign URLs. Some researchers have used statistical methods to locate key elements of malicious requests, extracted features for machine learning models [13]. Chandrasekhar et al. suggested a technique that combines Support Vector Machine classifier, K-means along with fuzzy neural network [2]. Chen et al. [3] proposed hybrid flexible neural-tree-based IDS with the help of flexible neural tree, evolutionary algorithm, and particle swarm optimization. Test results proved that their method is high-efficiency. With the help of machine learning methods, the models can detect new kinds of attacks with only the request traffic. But the requirement of expert experience and the difference between the systems make it hard for today's real world.

2.3   Deep Learning Based Methods

Nowadays deep learning [9] models have achieved great success in data-driven learning. Compared with knowledge-driven methods, data-driven approaches usually have a better generalization ability in detecting unseen attacks. Compared to machine learning methods, they don't need artificial feature extraction. Besides, they are more friendly in quick deployment and capable of rapid updating. Anomaly detection methods such as the HMM-Web [5] have shown their ability to capture unseen web attacks. And with the improvements of feature extraction such as convolutional gated-recurrent-unit [15], the speed of deep learning methods is improving.

2.4   Related Work: Summary

After a review of available technologies, we found out most deep learning based methods treat the word in the web requests with same weight. But in real world web attack traffic, there will only 5%–20% of the web requests contains the payloads used to attack the website which result in the speed was compromised in real world usage. We proposed an MLAB-BiLSTM method, it firstly generates a encoded representation of the original request to rule out the noise in the request and focusing on the more suspicious part that contains attacking payloads. Then the Text-CNN classify which kind of attack this attacking payload is. After experimental verification, the proposed method performs well in speed and accuracy of detecting both known and unknown web attacks.

3   Method

In this section, we described our proposed MLAB-BiLSTM model for detecting web attacks. The model contains two parts, firstly, the MLAB-BiLSTM generate a encoded representation contains the suspicious web attack from web request traffic, then a Text Convolution Neural Network is used to judge whether the requests contain valid attacking payload or not, and classify it to different types. In Fig. 1 is the brief structure of proposed MLAB-BiLSTM network.

To generate a encoded representation from the original web request, which is like the idea of document summarizing in neural language process works. It can find the key element from the document, which in our case is the malicious payload. Supposing we denote the original web request as R, and we can divide the original web traffic into several segments (S_i) by URL delimiter, \n for headers and delimiter for post data. The MLAB-BiLSTM is used to firstly choose suspicious parts from each segment S_i, then select the most suspicious segments from the request R. It firstly processes the document with a keyword enhanced traffic embedding module, then uses generated result as input of a multi-layer neural network, then it outputs the encoded representation containing suspicious attacking payload of the original request. Finally, the generated structure is feed into a Text-CNN model to evaluate which category of attack type this request may belong to.

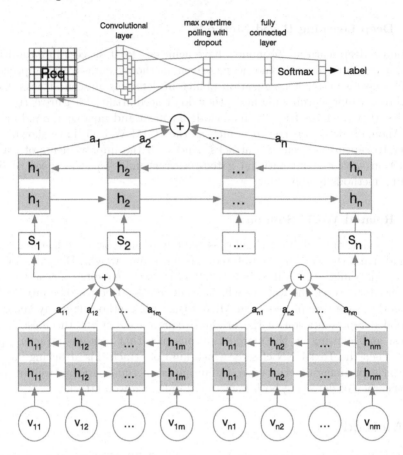

Fig. 1. MLAB-BiLSTM: the first layer is a word-level encoder for every segment in the original request, followed by a segment-level encoder. There is an attention layer after each encoder. Finally, the generated encoded representation will be fed into a Text-CNN network to output the original request into different attack types.

3.1 Keyword Enhanced Traffic Embedding

In most cases, the web requests contain such as URL addresses, methods, header, post data and etc., and most of the detect methods the web request are embedded in character level or 1-gram format. Using the letters of printable English characters, the original request is mapped to its corresponding vector representation, which is then embedded into the multidimensional feature space. It treats characters independently, but in web attack payloads the words are not completely independent, such as "script" for XSS payloads, "union", "select" for SQLi payloads. To keep more key information as possible, in our implementation, we firstly collected a keyword list with artificial experience as briefly shown in Table 1, and then used it for request embedding.

Table 1. Web request keywords list

Type	List
SQLi	and, or, union, select, substr, xp_, hex, ascii, concat, order, exec, benchmark, sleep, information_schema
XSS	script, iframe, eval, alert, onerror, onclick, cookie, document, href, src
Normal	GET, POST, GET, OPTIONS, HTTP/1.1, HTTP/2

3.2 Word Feature and Attention

Suppose we have a request (R) with n segments, let $R = (s_1, s_2, \cdots, s_n)$. Each segment contains m words. After word embedding, the segment was transformed into a vector of $d * m$ dimension, let denote $S = (w1, w2, \cdots, w_m)$. The w_i is a d dimensional word embedding for the ith word. In this paper, we use a bidirectional LSTM is used to encode the words in the segments with the focus on information from both forward and backward direction. So the hidden state h_t that contains the general information of the whole segment including both the forward and the backward part.

$$h_t = [\overrightarrow{LSTM}(w_t, \overrightarrow{h_{t-1}}), \overleftarrow{LSTM}(w_t, \overleftarrow{h_{t-1}})]$$

Supposing each unidirectional LSTM contains u hidden units, $H_s \in \mathbb{R}^{m \times 2u}$ can denote the whole LSTM hidden states.

$$H_s = (h_1, h_2, \cdots, h_m)$$

What we want is to extract the suspicious payload sequence from the original segment. Instead of treating all the words with same weight, an attention mechanism is introduced, paying more or less attention to words that affect the function of the segment. To achieve this goal, we used the hidden states as input, and output the weight of each word.

$$a_s = softmax(w_{s_2} tanh(w_{s_1} H_s^T))$$

Where $w_{s_2} \in \mathbb{R}^{k \times 2u}$ and $w_{s_1} \in \mathbb{R}^k$ is learned from the data; k is a manually set hyperparameter. Finally we uses softmax to normalize the attention weights.

Then we can obtain a weighted representation of original segment s_i which is the weighted sum of the attention vector a_s and LSTM hidden states H_s (Fig. 2).

$$s_i = a_s H_s$$

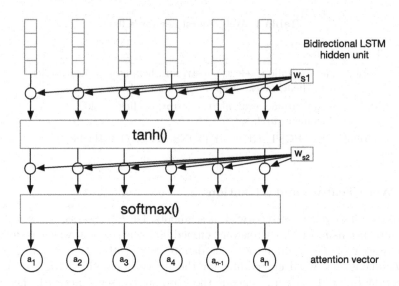

Fig. 2. The attention units take bidirectional LSTM hidden state as input, and output the attention vector a_s. The circles in the graph represent for unit in MLP layer. w_{s1} is a $k \times 2u$ dimensional matrix, and w_{s2} is a k dimensional vector. k is a manually set hyperparameter.

3.3 Segment Feature and Attention

To prevent hackers from hiding the payloads separately in two segments of the web request, we also focus on the relationship between the segments in the requests. Now we have the segment vector s_i, similarly, we can get the request LSTM hidden state representing as h_{st}.

$$h_{st} = [\overrightarrow{LSTM}(s_i, \overrightarrow{h_{t-1}}), \overleftarrow{LSTM}(s_i, \overleftarrow{h_{t-1}})]$$

With the forward and backward hidden states, it has the ability to focus on the adjacent segment information around i^{th} segment. Supposing each unidirectional LSTM contains u hidden units, the overall hidden state for the request can be represented as following.

$$H_r = (h_{s1}, h_{s2}, \cdots, h_{sn})$$

To extract important segment from the request, we also use an attention mechanism to take H_r as input to generate an output of attention vector representing the importance of the segments.

$$a_r = softmax(w_{s2} tanh(w_{s1} H_r^T))$$

Finally, we can obtain a encoded representation of the original request r which is the weighted sum of the attention vector a_r and the LSTM hidden states.

$$r = a_r H_r$$

3.4 Classification Network

After the multiple attention based bidirectional LSTM, the suspicious web request will be presented in a encoded representation. Then a convolutional neural network is applied to analyze the request is malicious or not. It performs a text classification task with input of the extracted request feature vector, and output the attack type of the given web requests.

The model architecture of the is similar to the Text-CNN proposed by Kim [8]. A 5-layer convolutional neural network with different filters and a max-pooling layer with dropouts. The different filters give CNN the ability to identify payloads accurately with multiple features. These features are reshaped and passed into three fully connected layers with Rectified Linear Unit. The output is probabilities of different attack types after being processed by a softmax layer. The loss function is composed of a multi-class cross entropy loss and a L_2 regular term.

$$L = -\frac{1}{N}\sum_i^N \sum_j^K y_{ij} log(p_{ij}) + \lambda \|W\|$$

4 Implementation and Experiments

To evaluate our proposed model, we used CSCI dataset and web traffic collected from CTF competitions. We prepared our proposed model with traditional rule base methods such as Libinjection, and HMM based methods like OwlEye [10].

4.1 Implementation Details

The train of MLAB-BiLSTM is optimized with Adam optimizer. The learning rate and weight decay was set to 1e−6 and 0.99. For the input of the neural network, the word embedding layer has a dimension of 8, and the hidden state of the LSTM is set to 100. So the segment encoder and request encoder in our model will output a 400 dimension combination from both forward and backward LSTM. The word and sentence attention context vector also have a dimension of 400. We split the segments firstly by the '\n' in the requests, and split the URL with '&' symbol. During training, the batch size was set to 64. The requests we selected has a maximum segment count of 150, and each segment contains no more than 200 words.

4.2 Performance on CSCI Dataset

The CSCI database is a publicly available labeled dataset contains web traffic to an e-Commerce Web Application contains 36,000 normal requests and more than 25,000 anomalous requests [7]. After reviewing the dynamic attacks among the anomalous traffic, we found there are 2000 SQLi and 1500 XSS samples.

As our model only detects SQLi and XSS attacks, other attacks are classified as benign traffics.

The results in Table 2 shows that our proposed model performs better than OwlEye and better recall rate than Libinjection. In terms of the F1-Score, our proposed model performs better than the other two methods.

Table 2. Test result on CSCI dataset

Method	Accuracy	Precision	Recall	F1-score
Libinjection	95.84%	99.81%	55.59%	0.7060
OwlEye	99.30%	96.21%	95.91%	0.9606
Proposed method	99.69%	98.23%	98.34%	0.9828

4.3 Performance on CTF Competition Traffic

To evaluate the MLAB-BiLSTM model, we also captured web traffic during different CTF competitions. In the dataset we collect 1 million web traffic logs with 245,000 attack samples collected from XSS and SQLi problems. The attack samples are labeled as SQLi or XSS by artificial experience.

Results. The performance of the selected methods are listed in Table 3. Our method obtains the second highest precision. OwlEye obtains the highest recall, slightly better than LTD, while it suffers from high False Positive Rate (FPR), while high FPR in production environment can interfere with normal user operation, so it is usually required to be less than 0.01%. For cyber attack detection tasks, there is a balance between FPR and recall, but low FPR is an important prerequisite in a production environment. Therefore it is unacceptable considering a system with high FPR may block normal user requests. In this experiment, OwlEye's FPR was considerably higher than our proposed approach. This is because, as an anomaly-based approach, OwlEye will classify anything not previously seen as malicious. In addition, if the web application is updated, OwlEye must be retrained with a new sample to conform to the new user behavior patterns, or the FPR will increase significantly. For these reasons, the OwlEye method is not suitable for real-time detection but is a good choice for offline analysis.

Rule based method Libinjection is widely used by many Internet corporations, such as Google. It is being known as first successful WAF. In our experiment, it achieves 100% precision (almost zero FPR), which is slightly better than our proposed method. However, due to the incomplete rule set, it has a recall rate of just over 85%, while our proposed method can detect over 99% of the attacks. So the over all accuracy of our method is much higher than Libinjection. In Table 4, we list some key element from misclassified samples by

Table 3. Test result on CTF competition dataset

Method	Accuracy	Precision	Recall	F1-score
Libinjection	96.37%	100%	85.20%	0.9201
OwlEye	99.65%	98.89%	99.69%	0.9929
Proposed method	99.81%	99.60%	99.56%	0.9961

Libinjection, the first two samples contain obvious SQLi features but the Libinjection missed. And the fourth and the fifth sample contains SQLi keywords such as "GRANT" and "Union", which appears in a lot of rules in the database lead to the misclassification of these examples. The last example was a normal session in PHP language, while Libinjection classified it as an XSS attack vector. As we can see from the above examples, even though the Libinjection method analyzed the lexical and syntax content of the request, it still cannot avoid certain misclassifications. Compared to Libinjection, our method based on deep learning methods exhibit better flexibility, better generalization and higher adaptability to avoid these misclassifications. Finally, in term of the F1-score, the LTD method outperforms all other three methods.

Table 4. Misclassified examples by Libinjection

Payload	Libinjection	MLAB-BiLSTM
1337) INTO OUTFILE 'xxx'–	N	Y
or 1<@. union select 1,version()#	N	Y
2104 GRANT AVE #A	Y	N
Manufacturing Workers' Union (MMWS)	Y	N
ONLINETOOLS_PHPSESSID = 3	Y	N

5   Conclusion

In this paper, we proposed an MLAB-BiLSTM method that can precisely detect Web attacks in realtime by using multi-layer attention based bidirectional LSTM deep neural network. Due to the malicious payloads contains similar keywords, we used a keyword enhanced embedding method to transfer the original request to feature vectors. Then we used a bidirectional LSTM model with attention to generate the encoded representation of the segments in the original request. Then uses the similar method to generate a encoded representation of the original requests. Then the structures are input into the CNN network to output the category of the attack. Moreover, the experimental results show that the MLAB-BiLSTM model can achieve better results on web attack detection than traditional methods. Later on, we would modify the model to add more malicious classes, adjust parameters, and minimize the use of parameters between networks to achieve better performance.

References

1. Chandola, V., Banerjee, A., Kumar, V.: Anomaly detection: a survey. ACM Comput. Surv. (CSUR) **41**(3), 1–58 (2009)
2. Chandrasekhar, A., Raghuveer, K.: Intrusion detection technique by using k-means, fuzzy neural network and SVM classifiers. In: 2013 International Conference on Computer Communication and Informatics, pp. 1–7. IEEE (2013)
3. Chen, Y., Abraham, A., Yang, B.: Hybrid flexible neural-tree-based intrusion detection systems. Int. J. Intell. Syst. **22**(4), 337–352 (2007)
4. Čisar, P., Čisar, S.M.: The framework of runtime application self-protection technology. In: 2016 IEEE 17th International Symposium on Computational Intelligence and Informatics (CINTI), pp. 000081–000086. IEEE (2016)
5. Corona, I., Ariu, D., Giacinto, G.: HMM-web: a framework for the detection of attacks against web applications. In: 2009 IEEE International Conference on Communications, pp. 1–6. IEEE (2009)
6. Firewall, A.: Modsecurity (2009)
7. Giménez, C.T., Villegas, A.P., Marañón, G.Á.: HTTP data set CSIC 2010. Information Security Institute of CSIC (Spanish Research National Council) (2010)
8. Kim, Y.: Convolutional neural networks for sentence classification. arXiv preprint arXiv:1408.5882 (2014)
9. LeCun, Y., Bengio, Y., Hinton, G.: Deep learning. Nature **521**(7553), 436–444 (2015)
10. Liu, X., Yu, Q., Zhou, X., Zhou, Q.: OwlEye: an advanced detection system of web attacks based on HMM. In: 2018 IEEE 16th International Conference on Dependable, Autonomic and Secure Computing, 16th International Conference on Pervasive Intelligence and Computing, 4th International Conference on Big Data Intelligence and Computing and Cyber Science and Technology Congress (DASC/PiCom/DataCom/CyberSciTech), pp. 200–207. IEEE (2018)
11. O'Gorman, B., et al.: Internet security threat report. Technical report. Symantec Corporation (2019)
12. Sheng, S., Wardman, B., Warner, G., Cranor, L., Hong, J., Zhang, C.: An empirical analysis of phishing blacklists (2009)
13. Torrano-Gimenez, C., Nguyen, H.T., Alvarez, G., Franke, K.: Combining expert knowledge with automatic feature extraction for reliable web attack detection. Secur. Commun. Netw. **8**(16), 2750–2767 (2015)
14. Vinayakumar, R., Soman, K., Poornachandran, P.: Evaluating deep learning approaches to characterize and classify malicious URL's. J. Intell. Fuzzy Syst. **34**(3), 1333–1343 (2018)
15. Yang, W., Zuo, W., Cui, B.: Detecting malicious URLs via a keyword-based convolutional gated-recurrent-unit neural network. IEEE Access **7**, 29891–29900 (2019)

A Moving Target Tracking Algorithm Based on Motion State Estimation and Convolutional Neural Network

Yongmei Zhang[1], Jianzhe Ma[2(✉)], Qian Guo[1], and Weifeng Lv[1]

[1] School of Information Science and Technology, North China University of Technology,
Beijing 100144, China
zhangym@ncut.edu.cn, gqhannah@163.com, 774381239@qq.com
[2] Department of Electronic and Information Engineering, The Hong Kong Polytechnic
University, Hong Kong 00852, China
421955907@qq.comx

Abstract. Moving target tracking is widely used in different fields. In practical applications, it faces the complex situations such as mutual occlusions among targets and rapid movement of targets, and needs to solve the problems of tracking accuracy and real time for the algorithms. To address the problems, the paper takes the moving targets of ships, yachts, and aircraft carriers at sea as the research objects, studies the maritime moving target tracking models under big data and small sample data environments, presents a tracking algorithm combining motion state estimation and convolutional neural network (CNN). Integrating Edge Boxes with CNN to realize multi-target detection at sea, the recall rate and accuracy of target detection are improved under the condition of higher detection efficiency. The target recommendation areas are generated based on the motion state estimation, and continuous information between video frames is used to improve estimation accuracy and effectively deal with occlusions among targets through efficient prediction of target states. The training model is utilized to detect and track the targets in the recommended areas. Compared with the tracking method of Fast R-CNN, as well as the tracking method based on histogram of oriented gradient (HOG) and support vector machine (SVM), the experiment results show the proposed algorithm has higher tracking accuracy and better real time even in the scenes of mutual occlusions among targets and rapid movement of targets.

Keywords: CNN · Motion state estimation · Big data · Small sample · Target tracking

1 Introduction

Video target tracking is a key technology of image understanding and an important research topic of computer vision. It has been widely used in intelligent traffic, military, automatic driving, video surveillance, and other fields. The basic task of target tracking is to estimate the task trajectory of the target image sequences in the following consecutive frames under the given initial state of the target [1].

© Springer Nature Singapore Pte Ltd. 2020
S. Yu et al. (Eds.): SPDE 2020, CCIS 1268, pp. 493–517, 2020.
https://doi.org/10.1007/978-981-15-9129-7_35

The tracked targets are usually multi-target in a complex scene with one or more interference factors such as occlusion, background clutter, rapid movement, illumination change, rotation, scale change, motion blur, etc. Therefore, how to accurately and efficiently track the targets remains an urgent problem to be solved.

Since the 21st century, mankind has entered a period of large-scale exploitation and utilization of the sea. The role of the sea in the pattern of national economic development and opening to the outside world is more important, and it is more prominent in safeguarding national sovereignty, security and development interests. China is a long coastline country with 18,400 km of continental coastline and more than 300 coastal ports.

Ships, speedboats, and aircraft carriers are the only transport carriers and the main military combat equipment on the sea. Automatic detection and tracking are of great significance and have broad application prospects in both civil and military fields. In the civil field, it can be used for the intelligent monitoring of maritime traffic in various ports and sea areas within the jurisdiction, to track maritime moving targets such as ships, speedboats, and aircraft carriers for auxiliary salvage, to facilitate the positioning of maritime moving targets and the early warning of dangerous situations, and to cooperate with the maritime police and customs in monitoring and combating various maritime violations and regulations. In military application, it can monitor the deployment and dynamics of ships, speedboats and aircraft carriers in key ports and sea areas of the enemy, analyze the hostile maritime combat strength, evaluate the wartime maritime hitting effect, and form operational information at sea [2].

The core idea of traditional target tracking methods is to extract simple and effective visual features such as color, texture and so on by artificial design features, and realize tracking algorithms through combining the features with feature matching or classification model. Due to the inability to extract high-level semantic information and the need for strong prior information, it is often highly adaptable to specific scenes. However, in the process of tracking in complex environments, the factors such as occlusion, fast motion, deformation of the target will cause these traditional artificial features to change too violently, leading to tracking failure.

In 2006, Hinton proposed the concept of deep learning [3]. Its powerful learning ability and excellent feature expression ability show great potential in the field of computer vision such as image classification and target detection. Since 2013, deep learning has been used for target tracking.

Convolutional neural network (CNN) simulates the learning process of human brain and constructs a multi-layer neural network. As the number of layers increases, the acquired features become more and more abstract. CNN has been used for tracking usually in two strategies, one is to use it as a feature extractor incorporating with a good classifier and the other is to use a unified deep structure for object tracking.

Dong etc. presented an approach to detect and track UAVs from a single camera mounted on a different UAV [4]. Initially, estimate background motions via a perspective transformation model and then identify moving object candidates in the background subtracted image through deep learning classifier trained on manually labeled datasets. For each moving object candidates, find spatio-temporal traits through optical flow matching and then prune them based on their motion patterns compared with the background.

Kalman filter is applied on pruned moving objects to improve temporal consistency among the candidate detections. The algorithm can effectively detect and track small UAVs with limited computing resources. Unfortunately, when there are occlusions in the video, the algorithm cannot detect and track the targets, the algorithm is slower.

Söderlund etc. proposed a real-time solution for detection and tracking of moving objects which adopted deep learning-based 3D object detection [5]. Utilize the predictability of Kalman Filters to infer object properties and semantics to the object detection algorithm, present a 3D object detection network YOLO++ on point clouds only, propose a Multi-threaded Object Tracking (MTKF) solution for multiple object tracking. Each unique observation is associated to a thread with a novel concurrent data association process. Each of the threads contains an Extended Kalman Filter that is used for predicting and estimating an associated object's state over time. Furthermore, a LiDAR odometry algorithm was used to obtain absolute information about the movement of objects. However, the method is based only on LiDAR data, fails to track the rapid moving objects on the ground, and more testing has to be done in order to argue whether the proposed method of inferring semantic information is feasible or not.

In [6], Wang and Ying firstly proposed deep learning tracker (DLT) to offline learn genetic features from auxiliary natural images. Although the work performed well, when significant temporal changes of a moving object occur the approach fails to effectively learn these changes. In [7], Wang et al. improved CNN architecture to learn hierarchical features for model-free object tracking which can handle temporal variations and do efficiently online tracking. Next, Wang et al. [8] took advantage of CNN features extracted from different layers and used a selection method by adding two pre-defined convolutional layers to filter out noisy, irrelevant or redundant features. Zhai et al. [9] used a Bayesian classifier as a loss layer in CNN tracker and updated the network parameters in online tracker. By doing this, appearance variations of a moving object over time were taken into account.

More recently, an exhaustive comparison of tracking methods based on deep learning has been done in [10]. In general, the CNN for tracking is trained in a simple an effective way which provides good features for object tracking. However, training of a robust CNN requires a considerable large number of annotated samplers and learning process is very time consuming.

In general, object tracking methods based on deep learning cannot provide accurate information on the silhouette of tracked moving object in the sequence. Meanwhile, multiple object tracking is also a challenging problem. The introduction of deep learning significantly improves the accuracy of target tracking, but once the target detection fails, the targets will be lost, resulting in tracking failure. In addition, speed is an important index to evaluate the target tracking algorithms. Due to the high computational complexity of deep learning algorithms, most of target tracking algorithms based on deep learning are very slow.

How to improve the real-time performance of the algorithms under the premise of ensuring the accuracy is a major challenge [11, 12]. Aiming at poorer accuracy of the traditional target tracking algorithms and slower speed of the existing deep learning tracking algorithms, the paper takes the moving targets of ships, yachts, and aircraft carriers at sea as the research objects, studies the maritime moving target tracking models under big data and small sample data environments, presents a tracking algorithm combining motion state estimation and CNN.

The algorithm effectively utilizes continuous information between video frames to obtain the potential target regions by analyzing the motion states of the target, improves the search efficiency, reduces the occurrence of target loss, and ensures the stability of tracking. Because deep learning models cannot converge under the condition of small sample, the fine-tuning method of transfer learning is adopted to train the model, and good convergence effects are achieved. Experiments show the tracking algorithm in this paper has good accuracy and running speed.

The rest of this paper is organized as follows. In Sect. 2, the proposed tracking algorithm combining motion state estimation and CNN is discussed in detail. The experiment results and analysis on real data are given in Sect. 3. Finally, some conclusions are drawn in Sect. 4.

2 A Tracking Algorithm for Maritime Moving Targets in Multiple Data Environments

According to the different numbers of target tracking, target tracking can be divided into single-target and multi-target tracking. This paper mainly studies the multi-target tracking algorithm. Maritime targets chiefly include ships, speedboats, and aircraft carriers, which vary greatly in shape and size. The paper studies the tracking algorithm of moving objects at sea under big data and small sample data environments, presents a tracking algorithm combining motion state estimation and CNN.

2.1 A Maritime Target Detection Method Based on Edge Boxes and CNN

For multi-target tracking methods on the basis of detection, the accuracy of detection algorithm plays an important role in tracking effects. Traditional object detection methods can only detect single target, while multi-target detection methods need longer offline time to learn templates or features, and most algorithms cannot balance efficiency while ensuring accuracy.

Zitnick et al. proposed an Edge Box method [13] in 2014 that can quickly and accurately locate target candidate regions. This method can improve the efficiency of existing target detection and determine the region position with high precision. It is an important algorithm in the field of candidate region detection. It has strong robustness to image illumination change and local contrast difference, and also has good detection effects in the case of larger color difference within the candidate regions. However, the method has lower recall rate and accuracy.

With the continuous development of deep learning, CNN has been widely used in the fields of target recognition and target tracking. However, the traditional deep convolution neural network models can only judge the target category with the highest score in a single image, ignoring the target category with less than the highest score. And it cannot obtain the determined position of multiple targets in the image.

To solve the above problems, this paper proposes a maritime multi-target detection method combining Edge Boxes with CNN. The Edge Box method is used to roughly locate the multi-target candidate regions, and the candidate regions are finely screened by CNN to improve the detection performance of marine multi-target candidate regions.

2.1.1 A Rough Location Method of Candidate Areas Based on Edge Boxes

Edge Box method uses the edge information of the image and the sliding window method to generate candidate objects, determines the number of contour in the frame body and the number of contour overlapped with the boundary of the frame body. Then it scores the bounding box according to the number of complete contour in each frame body. To a large extent, it gives the possibility that the box contains a target and obtains target information based on the size of the resulting score [14, 15]. Compared with the traditional multi-scale sliding window scanning detection methods, Edge Boxes can remove redundant windows and get high-quality and less candidate areas. Therefore, the outstanding advantage of this method is the detection speed is very fast.

The specific steps of Edge Boxes method include edge detection of input images, calculating the size and direction of edges to obtain sparse edge images, constructing edge sets and calculating the similarity of each edge, enumerating and calculating candidate region scores, setting thresholds to remove candidate regions with lower scores, and output candidate target regions.

Edge Boxes utilizes the structure edge detection method in [16] to calculate the edge response of each pixel in the images. This edge detection method can effectively detect the target boundary, and its computing efficiency is very high. After obtaining the edge response, adopt non-maximum suppression method on the edge response to find the boundary peaks, then get a relatively sparse edge image. Each pixel p has an edge size m_p and a direction θ_p, and the edge is defined as $m_p > 0.1$. A contour is defined as a related boundary, curve, or line formed by a group of edges.

The goal of Edge Boxes is to identify contours that overlap with the boundary of the bounding box, so it is unlikely to contain objects belonging to the bounding boxes. Given a box b, identify these edges by calculating the maximum similarity between each $p \in b$ for $m_p > 0.1$ and the edges on the box boundary.

Edge Boxes believed that the direct connection through the edge contour should have high similarity, where those that are not connected or through contour connections with high curvature should have low similarity. The specific way to calculate the edge set is to use a simple greedy method to keep looking for eight connected edge points to form the edge set S, until the sum of their directional differences exceeds the threshold (namely $\pi/2$). Given a set of edge groups $s_i \in S$, calculate an affinity between each pair of adjacent groups. For a pair of edge groups s_i and s_j, the affinity is computed according to their mean positions x_i and x_j, as well as mean orientations θ_i and θ_j. Intuitively, edge groups have high affinity if the angle between the groups means in similar to the orientations of the groups. Specifically, adopt Eq. (1) to calculate the affinity $a(s_i, s_j)$.

$$a(s_i, s_j) = |\cos(\theta_i - \theta_{ij})\cos(\theta_j - \theta_{ij})|^\gamma \tag{1}$$

Where θ_{ij} is the angle between x_i and x_j. The value of γ can be used to adjust the sensitivity of affinity to orientation change. The larger the γ value is, the more sensitive it is to the orientation change of the edge group. In the Edge Box method, the value of γ is 2. If two edge groups are separated by more than 2 pixels, the affinity is set to be zero. To improve computational efficiency, only the affinities above the small threshold (namely 0.05) are stored, and the rest are assumed to be zero.

Given the set S of edge groups and their similarity, the object proposal score for any candidate bounding box b can be calculated. Edge Boxes calculates a continuous value $w_b(s_i) \in [0, 1]$ for each edge group s_i, which indicates whether s_i is wholly contained in b when $w_b(s_i) = 1$, or not when $w_b(s_i) = 0$.

Let S_b be the set of edge groups that overlap the boundary of box b, and $\bar{x}_i$ is an arbitrary pixel position in edge group s_i. Then for all $s_i \in S_b$, $w_b(s_i)$ is set to be 0. Similarly, $w_b(s_i) = 0$ for all s_i when $\bar{x}_i \notin b$. For the remaining edge groups for $\bar{x}_i \in b$ and $s_i \notin S_b$, $w_b(s_i)$ is calculated using the Eq. (2).

$$w_b(s_i) = 1 - \max_T \prod_j^{|T|-1} a(t_j, t_{j+1}) \tag{2}$$

Where T is an ordered path of edge groups with a length of $|T|$ that begins with some $t_1 \in S_b$ and ends at $t_{|T|} = s_i$. If no such path exists, define $w_b(s_i) = 1$. Thus, find the path with the highest affinity between the edge group s_i and edge group that overlaps the boundaries of boxes by Eq. (2). Since most pairwise affinities are zero, the calculation efficiency of this process is very high.

Using the value of $w_b(s_i)$, the score of the box body is calculated by the Eq. (3) and Eq. (4).

$$h_b = \frac{\sum_i w_b(s_i) m_i}{2(b_w + b_h)^k} \tag{3}$$

$$m_i = \sum_{p \in s_i} m_p \tag{4}$$

Where b_w and b_h are the width and height of box b_k, k is the parameter used to counteract the larger window deviation that usually contains more edges. Experiment results show the effect is best when $k = 1.5$. The edge strength m_i of the edge group is obtained by summation of the edge size for each pixel in the ith edge group s_i surrounded by the box b_k.

Considering that the contribution of the edge group closer to the bounding box boundary is greater, Eq. (5) is used to subtract the edge value of the central box b_b^{in} from the box b_k to speed up the calculation.

$$h_b^{in} = h_b - \frac{\sum_{p \in b^{in}} m_p}{2(b_w + b_h)^k} \tag{5}$$

Where b_b^{in} is a box centered in box b_k, and its width and height are $b_w/2$ and $b_h/2$ respectively, m_p indicates the edge size of each pixel.

To locate the candidate areas in the image, the paper adopts the smoothing window search strategy to traverse the candidate bounding boxes in different positions, scales and aspect ratios of pixels, and calculates the voting scores. Sort by voting scores, and store the position of the bounding box with the maximum voting scores more than 0.5 and the corresponding scores. After the non-maximum suppression of the sorted bounding boxes, the remaining positions of the bounding boxes are candidates for coarse location.

2.1.2 A Fine Screening Method for Multi-object Candidate Areas Based on CNN

In the field of computer vision, deep convolutional network has been widely used and achieved good results. Krizhevsky etc. [17] performed image classification by training deep CNN and efficient Graphics Processing Unit (GPU) through large-scale datasets, which significantly improved classification performance. CNN has achieved great success in target detection and recognition, and more and more researchers begin to apply the convolution feature to target tracking [18, 19]. Convolutional network features have the advantages of simple extraction, rich features, and strong generalization ability. But there are also obvious deficiencies, such as high feature dimension, a lot of redundancy between features, and low signal-to-noise ratio.

Although CNN has achieved great success, the performance of the tracking algorithms has not been greatly improved due to lack of large-scale training data. Early CNN-based tracking algorithms could only handle predefined target object classes, such as humans. Since CNN can offline train and then predict, many algorithms have emerged. For example, the authors proposed a learning method based on the pool of CNN in [20]. But this method lacks the deep network of training data, and its accuracy is not particularly better compared with the methods based on manual extraction features. Some of the methods proposed in recent years [21] have transferred the pre-trained CNN to the large data sets constructed for image classification, but the basic difference between classification and tracking may not be obvious. Different from the existing methods, this paper adopts large-scale data to pre-train CNN and obtains effective detection results.

The detection efficiency of the candidate region coarse location method based on Edge Boxes is very high, but it has the problems of lower recall rate and accuracy. Aiming at the problems, this paper adopts two-level detection, takes the candidate regions detected based on the Edge Boxes as coarse location regions to obtain several maritime moving target candidate regions. Then for these regions, CNN are used for further fine screening.

Each candidate region is extracted features and classified by using the trained CNN model, and the candidate regions classified as moving targets at sea are marked, the overlapped rectangular boxes are screened through non-maximum suppression method, and the best detection boxes are retained to achieve the fine screening of candidate areas. In this way, the recall rate and accuracy of the target detection in the candidate region are improved while the high detection efficiency of the candidate region coarse location method based on Edge Boxes is guaranteed.

With the rapid development of high-performance computing devices, more and more deep neural network architectures have emerged, such as AlexNet, ResNet, and VGG-Net. These deep architecture models can realize end-to-end feature extraction and detection, and the performance is much better than that of traditional target detection methods.

VGG-Net is a deep convolutional neural network developed by the computer vision group at Oxford University and researchers from Google DeepMind. VGG-Net constructed 16–19 layer deep neural network by repeatedly stacking the small convolution kernel of 3 * 3 and the maximum pooling layer of 2 * 2 [22], which has strong detection capability. While the error rate is greatly reduced, it has strong scalability, good generalization ability to migrate to other image data, and simple structure. In order to pre-train deep CNN, the paper adopts the model structure of the VGG-Net-16 CNN to construct the target detection network, VGG-Net-16 network structure is shown in Fig. 1.

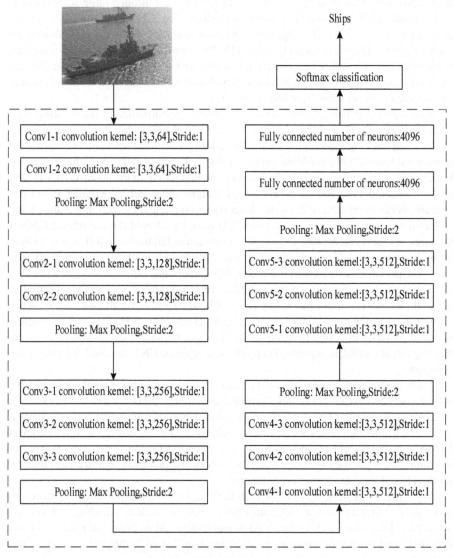

Fig. 1. VGG-Net-16 network structure

As can be seen from Fig. 1, the VGG-Net-16 network structure consists of 5 convolutional layers and 3 fully connected layers. The Softmax layer of the original VGG-Net-16 network was designed for 1000 target categories, with a total of 1000 neurons. In this paper, the targets at sea are taken as the detection objects. Therefore, the number of neurons at the Softmax layer is set according to the category of the ships.

2.2 A Regional Recommendation Method Based on Motion State Estimation

When the targets are partially occluded, the effective target features are reduced during the detection process, which easily leads to tracking failure. When the targets are seriously occluded or even completely occluded, the effective target features are few, and most algorithms cannot track the targets efficiently. Many excellent target tracking algorithms have good detection effects for complete targets. Once the occlusion is encountered, the tracking performance of these algorithms will be greatly reduced. Therefore, solving occlusion is the key to improve the performance of tracking algorithms. The key to solve partial occlusion is how to correctly calculate the target position through the parts without occlusion, and the key to solve the serious and utter occlusion is how to estimate the target position according to the target motion trajectory and state before the occlusion.

This paper proposes a regional recommendation method based on motion state estimation according to the characteristics of target tracking to better predict the moving state of the targets and deal with the occlusion between the targets. In the analysis of a large number of target video frames, it is found that the targets of a video frame do not need to be searched globally in the image, and the target movement is a dynamic state prediction problem [23]. The effective prediction of the target state can greatly reduce the search ranges of the targets, decrease the computation, improve real time of the tracking algorithms, and facilitate the rapid extraction of high-quality target recommendation areas.

Establish the state equations of the tracking targets in target tracking systems. Assuming they are Eq. (6) and Eq. (7).

$$X(t+1) = A(t)X(t) + T(t)W(t) \tag{6}$$

$$Z(t) = H(t)X(t) + V(t) \tag{7}$$

Where $X(t+1)$ and $X(t)$ are the target state vectors at time $t+1$ and time t respectively, $A(t)$ is a state transition matrix, representing the target mode motion from previous moment to the current moment, $T(t)$ is an interference matrix, the statistical characteristics of the noises $W(t)$ in the moving systems are consistent with the normal distribution, $Z(t)$ represents the observation state of the system at time t, observation matrix $H(t)$ represents the corresponding relationship between the internal states of the system and the observed values, $V(t)$ is the measurement noise in the process of observation motion, and it conforms to the normal distribution.

When the targets are seriously or even completely occluded, the appearance information is seriously missing. Adopting the appearance information methods cannot achieve tracking, at the moment, the effective information is the historical tracks of the targets. The video target tracking is a process of sequential processing of multiple image sequences, the time interval between adjacent video frames is extremely short, and the instantaneous motion velocity changes little. Therefore, it is assumed that the target motion form between adjacent video frames is uniform linear motion when estimating the motion states of the tracking targets.

A state vector x of each frame contains information such as target position, motion velocity, scale size, which is expressed as $x = \begin{bmatrix} l_x, l_y, s, r, v_x, v_y, v_s \end{bmatrix}^T$. Where l_x and l_y are the coordinate of the upper left of the target, v_x and v_y are the horizontal and vertical decomposition of the target motion speed, r is the aspect ratio of the target, s represents the area, v_s is the rate of area change. Considering multiple continuous video frames, the relationship between the elements of the target motion can be denoted as Eq. (8).

$$\begin{cases} L(t) = L(t-1) + \Delta t v(t-1) \\ S(t) = S(t-1) + \Delta t v_S(t-1) \\ v(t) = v(t-1) \\ v_S(t) = v_S(t-1) \end{cases} \tag{8}$$

Where L is the position of the tracking target, v is the moving speed of the target, S is the size of the object tracking box body, v_s is the area change rate of the tracking box, Δt is a time interval.

According to the information in the existing moving target state vectors, each target state in the future frame can be predicted in the video tracking. The way of target prediction and update can be obtained by solving the state equation in Eq. (6) and Eq. (7).

$$x^-_{t|t-1} = A_{t|t-1} x^u_{t-1} \tag{9}$$

$$P^-_{t|t-1} = A_{t|t-1} P_{t-1} A^T_{t|t-1} + Q_{t-1} \tag{10}$$

$$K_t = P^-_{t|t-1} H^T (H P^-_{t|t-1} H^T + R_t)^{-1} \tag{11}$$

$$x^u_t = x^-_{t|t-1} + K_t(z_t - H x^-_{t|t-1}) \tag{12}$$

$$P_t = P^-_{t|t-1} - K_t H P^-_{t|t-1} \tag{13}$$

In Eq. (9), x^u_{t-1} is the optimal estimation state of the target at time $t-1$, $x^-_{t|t-1}$ is the prediction state of the optimal estimation, and this equation is utilized to predict state. Equation (10) is to predict the covariance of the error. P_{t-1} is the updated error covariance matrix at time $t-1$, and $P^-_{t|t-1}$ is the predicted value of the error covariance. In Eq. (11), K_t is the filtering gain matrix, which is used to predict the target state value of Eq. (9) and the value of the error covariance of Eq. (10), and to optimize the gain of the two values. In Eq. (12), x^u_t is the optimal predicted value at time t. Equation (13) is represented as the optimization mode of error covariance, and P_t is the optimal estimation value at time t.

Obtain the potential target regions and realize the prediction of the target position in the light of the predicted state vectors. According to the area and aspect ratio, the predicted state vectors can get the size of the predicted box body. The size and the predicted upper left corner coordinates are combined into the initial quaternion. Based on this quad amplification, the potential areas are extracted. The Edge Box method is used to sample the potential regions, and 0.8 times the target size of the previous frame is used as the threshold to screen the recommended regions, generating the recommended regions for CNN detection. Furthermore, when multiple targets exist in the video, the paper separately establishes a state estimate for each target, generates target recommendation areas, and improves the estimation accuracy. Whether the objects in the video are occluded or not, the complete trajectories of the video targets can be better obtained, it is beneficial to enhance the accuracy of the video target tracking.

2.3 A Maritime Moving Target Tracking Algorithm

Aiming at poorer accuracy of traditional target tracking algorithms and slower speed of existing tracking methods based on deep learning, this paper proposes a tracking algorithm combining motion state estimation and CNN. The specific steps of the algorithm list as follows.

(1)   Offline training. Train the ship target detection network VGG-Net-16-based architecture to obtain the representation ability of common features. This paper separately trains the detection network for big data and small sample data environments.
(2)   Target detection. Load the video, and input the first frame image of the video. The Edge Box method is used to coarsely locate the multi-objective candidate regions of the whole frame image. The rough positioning regions are input into the CNN ship detection network to improve CNN detection speed. The targets in the first frame image are detected, and the target motion state estimation model is initialized by the detection results.
(3)   Target tracking. After the targets are detected, a new frame of video image is read. Adopt the regional recommendation method based on motion state estimation to predict the target state by Eq. (9), and obtain the potential regions of the targets. Then use the Edge Box method for sampling of the potential areas, and generate recommended areas. Input the recommended regions into the CNN detection network to detect the target location, and output the tracking results of the current frame. If the video is not finished, turn (3), otherwise, the algorithm is over.

3   Experiment Results and Analysis

3.1   Experiment Environment Configuration and Data Characteristic Analysis

In this paper, the experiment results and analysis of maritime moving target tracking under big data and small sample data environments are given. The experiment is configured as Intel Xeon 3.00 GHz, NVIDIA Tesla K40c GPU, 64G memory, Windows10 operating system, MATLAB 2016a experiment platform, and Matconvnet deep learning framework is adopted to realize the tracking algorithms.

(1) Big data training sets

This paper adopts Imagenet2012 data set, one of the most famous data sets in the field of image processing, as well as the self-built training sets to train the big data model. Imagenet2012 dataset includes 140 GB of image samples with a total of 1000 categories. The self-built training sets are established for maritime target tracking, including ships, speedboats, aircraft carriers, and other maritime targets, with a total of 1 GB of training samples. Some self-built training samples are shown in Fig. 2.

Fig. 2. Some self-built training samples

The traditional training images only include the whole targets. For example, there is a ship in one image. After analyzing a lot of ship target images, it is found that the ship targets are of larger shapes, and there are many separate areas, such as sharp bows, the ship fences, and ship roofs. In view of these characteristics of ship targets, this paper adds local images of ship hulls in the training sets. Some local graphs of ship hulls are shown in Fig. 3. Considering most of the whole ship targets appear in the field of vision, such labeled samples in the self-built ship training sets just account for the proportion of 5% to avoid the influence of the local testing on the overall detection.

(2) Small sample training set

In contrast to the concept of big data, the small sample problem is common in the application of machine learning algorithms. However, in many scenarios, it is difficult to collect sufficient data to train the model. Small sample learning provides a solution to this problem. The literal meaning of "small" in small sample learning is that the total

Fig. 3. Some local graphs of ship hulls

number of samples used for model training is small, but the essential meaning is that the existing training samples are not enough to make the model characterize the feature space well. This paper assumes that the carrier targets are small sample targets and establishes a training set containing 200 carrier samples.

3.2   Model Training and Detection Results in Multi-data Environment

The size of training data in deep learning has a great influence on the training accuracy of the model. This paper studies the training of big data model, the amount of data is sufficient to make the model converge. For the self-built training set data, the weight attenuation is set to be 0.0005, and the batch size is set to be 32. The results of 300 iterations of big data model training are shown in Fig. 4 objective represents the model loss function value for each iteration of the model, and top1err is the error rate of model classification after each epoch. It can be seen that the loss value and error rate of the model in the training process are generally decreasing.

The advantages of deep learning depend on big data. Driven by big data, machines can effectively learn. However, insufficient amount of data may lead to the problems such as over-fitting of models. Although simple data augmentation and regularization can alleviate the problem, the problem has not been completely solved [24]. Small sample learning for small data sets becomes the key technology to solve such problems.

Under the condition of small sample data, the deep learning model training will be unable to converge due to the small number of training samples. As shown in (a) of Fig. 5, when the model is randomly initialized with a value conforming to the gaussian distribution and trained, the loss value declines with the training of the model. But the error rate of the model always fluctuates greatly, and it is impossible to train effectively.

Using transfer learning can reduce the cost of model training while achieving the purpose of adapting CNN to small sample data [25]. Because transfer learning utilizes existing knowledge to learn new knowledge, and the core is to find the relationship between existing knowledge and new knowledge for modeling. According to the existing studies, transfer learning is beneficial to the rapid convergence of model parameters, and it can improve the generalization ability of the model. This paper adopts a fine tune method of transfer learning for model training with small samples, and obtains good convergence effects. The specific steps are as follows.

(1) Select a big data model similar to the small sample problem to be studied.
(2) Initialize the small sample model with selected parameters of the big data model.
(3) Set learning rate to be 0.0001, weight attenuation to be 0.0005 for training, batch size to be 4.

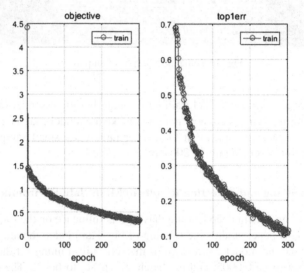

Fig. 4. Training convergence results under big data conditions

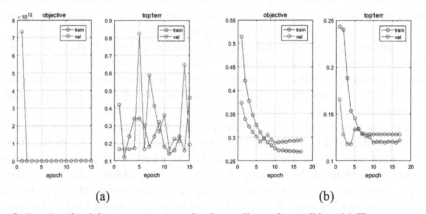

(a)   (b)

Fig. 5. Results of training convergence under the small sample condition. (**a**) The convergence results of non-transfer learning training. (**b**) The convergent results of transfer learning training in this paper.

The convergence of the small sample training is shown in (b) of Fig. 5. It can be seen that the model loss converges, and the loss value and error rate of the model both reach a stable state after 11 iterations.

The training of deep learning model is the process of solving the model by gradient descent algorithm. In the environment of small sample data, applying a randomly initialized model for training will cause the gradient calculated by the model to be corrected in the direction of the batch gradient each time, so the gradient does not converge. When the model is initialized by the parameters with certain classification ability, the gradient direction suitable for this class will be calculated in each iteration of the model, so that the model can reach the convergence state.

Figure 6 shows the detection results of various target scenarios by the marine target detection method combined Edge Boxes and CNN in this paper, (a) and (b) are the detection results of the big data model, (c) and (d) are the detection results of the small sample model. It can be seen that the detection effect of this method is better. However, in the scenario (a), too small targets cannot be detected, because the detection algorithm in this paper suppressed too small detection boxes. In the small-sample model test of (d), the ship is detected as the aircraft carrier, resulting in false detection. This is due to the training method of similar sample migration in the training process of small samples. Ship and carrier targets are similar samples, so there is some error detection for ship targets.

In order to comprehensively evaluate detection methods, this paper sets 2000 test samples under the condition of big data, and 200 test samples under the condition of small sample. All test samples are marked with accurate target position, mainly adopt the accuracy and recall rate to evaluate the detection method. The calculation method is shown in Eq. (14) and Eq. (15).

$$Acc = \frac{1}{n} \sum_{i=1}^{n} \frac{TT_i}{TT_i + TF_i} \tag{14}$$

$$Rec = \frac{1}{n} \sum_{i=1}^{n} \frac{TT_i}{TT_i + FT_i} \tag{15}$$

Where TT is the number of boxes correctly detected for the targets, TF is the number of the correct category boxes that are misdetected as the boxes in other categories, FT is the number of other category boxes that are misdetected as the boxes in correct category. The detection results under various data environments are shown in Table 1. It demonstrates that the detection method in this paper can accurately and in real time detect the targets at sea. For the small sample model, the detection accuracy of this method is lower, but the recall rate for the determinate target detection is higher.

3.3 Experiment Results and Analysis of Tracking Method Comparison

In order to verify the effectiveness of the proposed algorithm, the paper designs comparison experiments of the regional recommendation methods and tracking algorithms. The maritime moving target tracking scenes mainly include fast motion, occlusion, background clutter, giant waves of single target and multi-target.

(a) Speedboat target scene   (b) Ship target scene

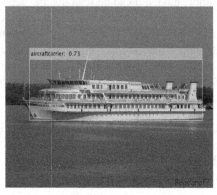

(c) Carrier target scene   (d) Ship target scene

Fig. 6. Results of maritime target detection combined with Edge Boxes and CNN

Table 1. Detection results under various data environments

Data environments	Average accuracy	Average recall rate	Average running time (seconds)
Big data	85.3%	76.4%	1.26
Small sample	72.2%	86.4%	1.26

The regional recommendation comparison experiments are based on motion state estimation and selective search region recommendation. In the tracking performance comparison experiment, Method$_b$ represents a method combining the region recommendation method based on motion state estimation in this paper with the Fast R-CNN detection model. Fast R-CNN utilizes multi-task loss function to train deep CNN network, Softmax classifiers and bounding box regressors together. In addition to the extraction of candidate areas, Fast R-CNN realizes end-to-end training and detection [26].

Therefore, the training speed, detection speed and average detection accuracy of Fast R-CNN have been significantly improved.

Method$_c$ represents a method combining the proposed regional recommendation method based on motion state estimation and the HOG-SVM detection model. HOG-SVM detection model extracts Histogram of Oriented Gradient (HOG) feature widely used in object detection, HOG feature is robust to translation, rotation, and illumination changes. Detect targets using HOG features in combination with a linear SVM classifier.

(1) Comparative experiments of regional recommendation methods

Due to the limited space, two sets of experiment results in the case of single target and multiple target are presented in this paper, which are based on motion state estimation and selective search recommendation methods, as shown in Fig. 7 and Fig. 8. It can be seen that the proposed region recommendation method based on motion state estimation makes full use of motion information between video frames and effectively reduces the search range of targets during tracking.

(a)   (b)

Fig. 7. Comparison of results of the single-target region recommendation methods. (a) Results of the regional recommendation method in this paper. (b) Results of selective search region recommendation method

The two groups of experiments are region recommendation under the condition of single-target and multiple-targets respectively. It can be seen that the region recommendation method based on motion state estimation in this paper makes full use of the motion information between video frames and effectively reduces the search range of the target in the tracking process. The selective search recommendation method is on the basis of the target position hierarchy and feature diversity in the image, multiple merging strategies are used to merge and cluster the pixel blocks obtained by image segmentation [27], thus obtaining candidate regions that may contain the targets, so the selective search recommendation method will produce a large number of overlapping redundant candidate regions. A lot of candidate regions increase the computation.

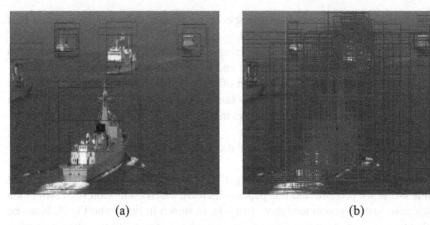

(a)   (b)

Fig. 8. Comparison results of the multiple-target region recommendation methods. (**a**) Results of the regional recommendation method in this paper. (**b**) Results of selective search region recommendation method

(2) Comparison experiment of big data training model

The parameters of the detection model used in the experiment are obtained by big data training, shown in Figs. 10 and 11. The scenes of Fig. 9 show the rapid movement of the speedboat target. It can be seen that the proposed tracking algorithm can track the target stably. When the detection model fails to detect the target at 99th frame, the model uses the predicted position as the tracking target position to update, making the tracking process more stable. In Method$_b$, the detection effect of the target is poor. It cannot detect the target from 99th frame, and the tracking target is lost. In Method$_c$, there is a false check in the tracking process, resulting in tracking target number 2. The presented algorithm combines target detection with motion state estimation to ensure the stability of the tracking process.

Figure 10 shows the ship moving in the scene of giant waves. It can be seen that the proposed tracking algorithm can track the target stably. At 12th frame, only part of the hull is covered by waves. The algorithm can effectively detect and track the hull. At 156th frame, the hull disappears with only the mast of the ship, and the model uses the predicted position as the tracking target position to update, which makes the tracking process more stable. Method$_b$ has poor detection effects on the targets. In the spray scene on 12th frame, the target cannot be detected and the target position is predicted. In the tracking process of Method$_c$, the single target is detected as 2 targets, resulting in false detection. However, the tracking process for the two targets is stable. Training and tracking experiment of small sample model. The presented algorithm combines target detection with motion state estimation to ensure the accuracy and stability of the tracking process.

Figure 11 are multi-target tracking scenes, including 4 ship targets. It can be seen that the proposed algorithm has good detection and tracking effects on all 4 targets. In the tracking results of Method$_b$ and Method$_c$, there are cases of missing and false detection. Especially there are overlaps in the Method$_c$ detection results. This is because the two boxes of the same target are divided into different categories, which cannot be eliminated, leading to false detection results.

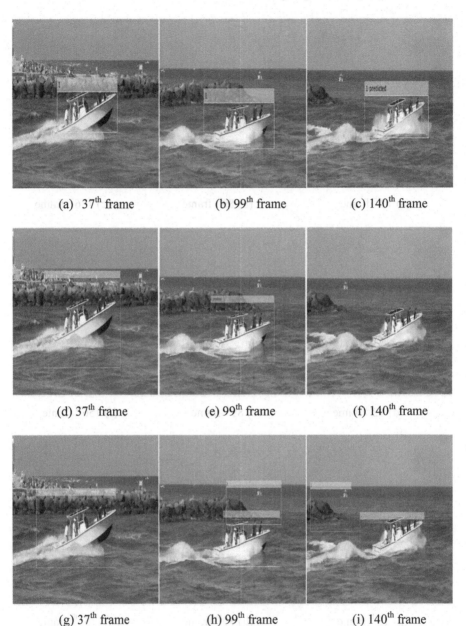

(a) 37th frame   (b) 99th frame   (c) 140th frame

(d) 37th frame   (e) 99th frame   (f) 140th frame

(g) 37th frame   (h) 99th frame   (i) 140th frame

Fig. 9. Comparison results of the fast-moving scene tracking. **(a)-(c)** Results of the proposed algorithm. **(d)–(f)** Results of Method$_b$. **(g)–(i)** Results of Method$_c$.

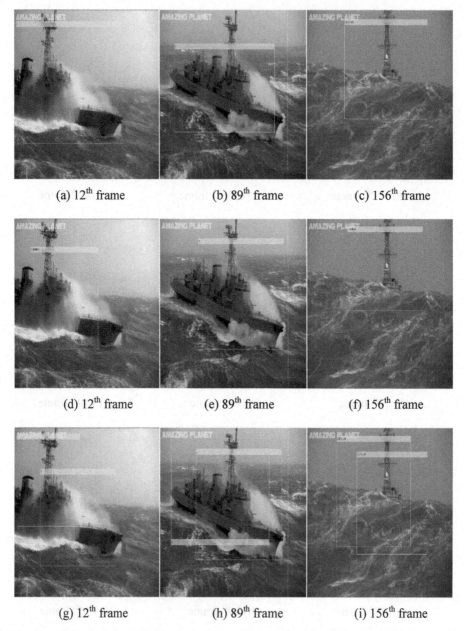

(a) 12th frame   (b) 89th frame   (c) 156th frame

(d) 12th frame   (e) 89th frame   (f) 156th frame

(g) 12th frame   (h) 89th frame   (i) 156th frame

Fig. 10. Comparison results of the giant wave scene tracking. (**a**)–(**c**) Results of the presented algorithm. (**d**)–(**f**) Results of Method$_b$. (**g**)–(**i**) Results of Method$_c$.

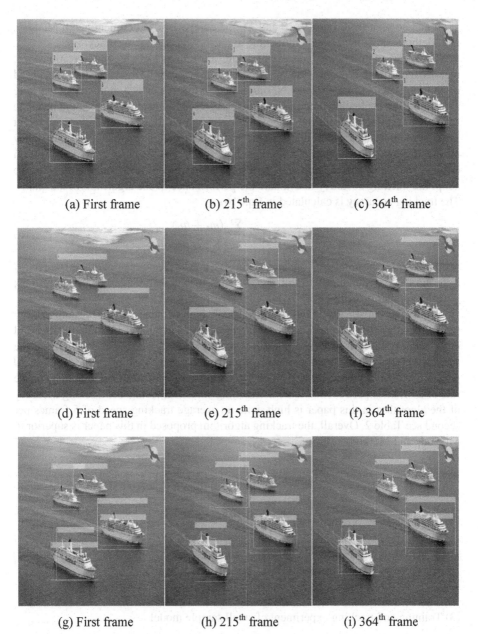

(a) First frame   (b) 215th frame   (c) 364th frame

(d) First frame   (e) 215th frame   (f) 364th frame

(g) First frame   (h) 215th frame   (i) 364th frame

Fig. 11. Comparison results of the multi-target scene tracking. (**a**)–(**c**) Results of the presented algorithm. (**d**)–(**f**) Results of Method$_b$. (**g**)–(**i**) Results of Method$_c$

It can be seen from Figs. 9, 10 and 11, the comparison experiments with Method$_b$ and Method$_c$ show the presented tracking algorithm has higher accuracy.

The common evaluation indexes of tracking algorithms include center position error, region overlap degree, and tracking accuracy. The moving target tracking algorithm based on motion state estimation and CNN proposed in this paper is a multi-target tracking algorithm. The evaluation index of a multi-objective tracking algorithm should meet the following requirements: all the emerging targets can be found in time; find the target location as consistent as possible with the real target location; maintain the consistency of tracking and avoid the jump of tracking targets [28, 29]. Because the center position error and region overlap degree cannot meet the above requirements at the same time, we adopt the tracking accuracy to evaluate the performance of the algorithm in this paper. The tracking accuracy is calculated in Eq. (16).

$$Acc = 1 - \frac{\sum_t (m_t + fp_t)}{\sum_t g_t} \tag{16}$$

Where m_t is the number of undetected targets, that is, the number of missed targets; p_t is the number of redundant detected targets, that is, the number of missed false detections; g_t is the number of real targets.

This paper statistically analyzes 20 groups of video sequences in the big data training model including local target occlusion, target rapid movement, background clutter and other scenes. Table 2 gives the statistical results of tracking. In order to ensure the accuracy of the statistical comparison, we marked the exact position of the target of 20 groups of video sequences, all of which had the resolution of 1280 * 720 and the frame rate of 29 frames per second. Table 2. Tracking statistical results the tracking accuracy of the algorithm in this paper is high, with an average tracking speed of 5 frames per second see Table 2. Overall, the tracking algorithm proposed in this paper is superior to Method$_b$ and Method$_c$.

Table 2. Tracking statistical results

Tracking methods	Tracking accuracy	Average tracking speed (frame/s)
Method$_b$	81.4%	3
Method$_c$	70.5%	28
The proposed algorithm	92.5%	5

(3) Training and tracking experiment of small sample model

In this paper, the small-sample model is only for the carrier-class target experiment. Due to the particularity of the small samples, only give the experimental results of the proposed tracking algorithm. The detection and tracking model obtained by the transfer learning method in this paper can effectively detect and track the aircraft carrier target (see Fig. 12). In (c), when the aircraft carrier target moves to the edge of the video, the lower-left aircraft carrier target has only part of the hull and loses the lower-left aircraft carrier target.

(a) First frame result   (b) 123th frame result   (c) 180th frame result

Fig. 12. The experiment results of small sample tracking adopting the presented algorithm.

The experiment results show that the CNN model can be effectively trained in the big data environment, and the model needs to be trained in the small samples environment in combination with transfer learning. In this paper, we combine two environmental training models of big data and small samples with the Edge Boxes and the regional recommendation method based on motion state estimation to realize the detection and tracking of moving targets at sea. Compared with Fast R-CNN and SVM detection and tracking algorithms, the experiment shows that the presented tracking algorithm has higher accuracy.

4   Conclusion

In view of the slower speed of target tracking in existing deep learning algorithms and the problems of missing targets during tracking and tracking failure, this paper studies two models of big data and small sample environments, and proposes a maritime moving target tracking algorithm based on motion state estimation and CNN. Detect the potential tracking target of the first frame of the video by combining the Edge Boxes with the multi-classification network based on the VGG-Net-16 structure. In order to better predict the motion state of the target and deal with the occlusion between the targets, recommend regions based on motion state estimation, track the targets combining the motion information and CNN. The experiment results show that the proposed algorithm has good tracking accuracy and real-time performance for both single target and multiple targets under the conditions of mutual occlusion and rapid movement of targets.

Acknowledgement. This paper was supported by National Natural Science Fund of China (Grant No. 61371143).

References

1. Hassabis, D., Kumaran, D., Summerfield, C., et al.: Neuroscience-inspired artificial intelligence. Neuron **95**(2), 245–258 (2017)
2. Zhang, P.H., Zhen, D., Jang, C., et al.: Fast fourier transform networks for object tracking based on correlation filter. Inst. Electr. Electron. Eng. Access **34**(4), 2169–2171 (2017)
3. Hinton, G.E., Salakhutdinov, R.R.: Reducing the dimensionality of data with neural networks. Science **313**(5786), 504–507 (2006)
4. Ye, D.H., Li, J., et al.: Deep learning for moving object detection and tracking from a single camera in unmanned aerial vehicles (UAVs). Electron. Imaging, **2018**(10), 466-1-466-6 (2018)
5. Söderlund, H.: Real-time Detection and Tracking of Moving Objects Using Deep Learning and Multi-threaded Kalman Filtering. Umeå University (2019)
6. Wang, N., Yeung, D.Y.: Learning a deep compact image representation for visual tracking. In: Advances in Neural Information Processing Systems, pp. 809–817 (2013)
7. Wang, L., Liu, T., Wang, G., Chan, K.L., Yang, Q.: Video tracking using learned hierarchical features. IEEE Trans. Image Process. **24**(4), 1424–1435 (2015)
8. Wang, L., Ouyang, W., Wang, X., Lu, H.: Visual tracking with fully convolutional networks. In: Proceedings of the IEEE International Conference on Computer Vision, pp. 3119–3127 (2015)
9. Zhai, M., Roshtkhari, M.J., Mori, G.: Deep learning of appearance models for online object tracking, arXiv preprint arXiv:1607.02568 (2016)
10. Li, P., Wang, D., Wang, L., Lu, H.: Deep visual tracking: review and experimental comparison. Pattern Recogn. **76**, 323–338 (2018)
11. Haitao, W., Rongyao, W., Wenhao, W.: A survey on recent advance and trends in object tracking. Comput. Measur. Control **28**(4), 1–7 (2020)
12. Yazdi, M., Bouwmans, T.: New trends on moving object detection in video images captured by a moving camera: a survey. Comput. Sci. Rev. **28**, 157–177 (2018)
13. Zitnick, C.Lawrence, Dollár, P.: Edge boxes: locating object proposals from edges. In: Fleet, D., Pajdla, T., Schiele, B., Tuytelaars, T. (eds.) ECCV 2014. LNCS, vol. 8693, pp. 391–405. Springer, Cham (2014). https://doi.org/10.1007/978-3-319-10602-1_26
14. Liu, J., Ren, T., Bei, J.: Elastic edge boxes for object proposal on RGB-D images. In: Tian, Q., Sebe, N., Qi, G.-J., Huet, B., Hong, R., Liu, X. (eds.) MMM 2016. LNCS, vol. 9516, pp. 199–211. Springer, Cham (2016). https://doi.org/10.1007/978-3-319-27671-7_17
15. Diao, W., Dou, F., Fu, K., et al.: Aircraft detection in sar images using saliency based location regression network. In: IEEE International Geoscience and Remote Sensing Symposium. IEEE (2018)
16. Dollar, P., Zitnick, C.L.: Structured forests for fast edge detection. In: Proceedings of the IEEE International Conference on Computer Vision (2013)
17. Krizhevsky, A., Sutskever, L., Hinton, G.E.: Imagenet classification with deep convolutional neural networks. In: Conference and Workshop on Neural Information Processing Systems (2012)
18. Licheng, J., Shuyuan, Y., Fang, L., et al.: Seventy years beyond neural networks: retrospect and prospect. Chin. J. Comput. **39**(8), 1697–1716 (2016)
19. Feiyan, Z., Linpeng, J., Jun, D.: Review of convolutional neural network. Chin. J. Comput. **40**(6), 1229–1251 (2017)
20. Li, H., Li, Y., Porikli, F.: DeepTrack: learning discriminative feature representations by convolutional neural networks for visual tracking. In: British Machine Vision Conference, Nottingham (2014)

21. Kristan, M., et al.: The visual object tracking VOT2016 challenge results. In: Hua, G., Jégou, H. (eds.) ECCV 2016. LNCS, vol. 9914, pp. 777–823. Springer, Cham (2016). https://doi. org/10.1007/978-3-319-48881-3_54

22. Li, L., Zhao, L., Chengyu, G., et al.: Texture classification: state-of-the-art methods and prospects. Acta Automatica Sinica **44**(4), 10–33 (2018)

23. Witrisal, K.: Belief propagation based joint probabilistic data association for multipath-assisted indoor navigation and tracking. In: International Conference on Localization & GNSS. IEEE (2016)

24. Vinyals, O., Blundell, C., Lillicrap, T., Koray, K.: Matching networks for one shot learning. In: Proceedings of the 30th International Conference on Neural Information Processing Systems, Barcelona, Spain, pp. 3630–3638. MIT Press (2016)

25. Aytar, Y., Zisserman, A.: Tabula rasa: model transfer for object category detection. In: 2011 International Conference on Computer Vision, Barcelona, Spain, pp. 2252–2259. IEEE (2011)

26. Girshick, R.: Fast R-CNN. Comput. Sci. (2015)

27. Uijlings, J.R.R., Sande, K.E.A.V.D., Gevers, T., et al.: Selective search for object recognition. Int. J. Comput. Vis. **104**(2), 154–171 (2013)

28. Doellinger, J., Prabhakaran, V.S., Fu, L., et al.: Environment-aware multi-target-tracking of pedestrians. IEEE Robot. Autom. Lett. **5**(2), 56–67 (2019)

29. Yu, S., Liu, M., Dou, W., et al.: Networking for big data: a survey. IEEE Commun. Surv. Tutor. **197**(1), 531–549 (2017)

Detecting Advanced Persistent Threat in Edge Computing via Federated Learning

Zitong Li, Jiale Chen, Jiale Zhang, Xiang Cheng, and Bing Chen[(✉)]

College of Computer Science and Technology,
Nanjing University of Aeronautics and Astronautics, Nanjing 211106, China
{lizitong,chenjl,jlzhang,xcheng_1988,cb_china}@nuaa.edu.cn

Abstract. Advanced Persistent Threat (APT) is one of the most men-
acing and stealthy multiple-steps attacks in the context of information
systems and IoT-related applications. Recently, with increasing losses to
organizations caused by APT, its detection has attracted more attention
in both academia and industry. However, conventional attack detection
methods cannot be used to defense APT ideally for the following reasons: 1) *misuse-based* mechanisms require too much expert knowledge of
APT attacks; 2) *anomaly-based* strategies lead to many false positives;
3) *machine learning-based* solutions lack training dataset that describes
APT patterns. Thus, we propose a novel detection system in edge computing systems based on federated learning, named FLAPT, to detect
APT attacks. The federated model can learn various APT attack patterns by maintaining a global model across multiple clients. The experimental results demonstrate that our proposed system can detect various
attacks including real-life APT campaigns with high detection accuracy
and low false alarm rate.

Keywords: APT · Federated learning · Alert correlation · Edge
computing

1 Introduction

Nowadays, with the continual escalation of attacks conducted by sophisticated
adversaries, the situation of information systems becomes far more dangerous. In
particular, Advanced Persistent Threats (APTs) have raised increasing attention
as the most serious attack type [1]. Driven by the vigorous development of IoT [2],
plenty of low-security devices are connected to the Internet which provides more
entry points for attackers [3]. Against increasingly disguised and complicated
APT attacks, technologies such as intrusion detection and prevention systems,
firewalls, etc. [4]. have been incapable of preventing sophisticated attackers [5].

Supported in part by the National Key R&D Program of China, under Grant
2019YFB2102000, in part by the National Natural Science Foundation of China, under
Grant 61672283, and in part by the Postgraduate Research & Practice Innovation
Program of Jiangsu Province under Grant KYCX18_0308.

© Springer Nature Singapore Pte Ltd. 2020
S. Yu et al. (Eds.): SPDE 2020, CCIS 1268, pp. 518–532, 2020.
https://doi.org/10.1007/978-981-15-9129-7_36

For that reason, more effective methods are desired to detect and defense against APT attacks.

APT refers to a long-lasting, targeted cyber intrusion process and is performed in several phases. Many approaches in APT detection are misuse-based, yet such methods require a lot of expert knowledge [6]. Besides, anomaly-based detection will generate many false positives [7]. With the emergence of machine learning as a novel and practical method in the area of APT detection [8], the bottleneck lies in the lack of sufficient datasets describing multiple APT patterns to train a powerful detection model [9]. As a result, APT defense work is only carried out within the organization which makes the machine learning-based method inefficient.

As different organizations suffered from different APT attacks and it is difficult for a single organization to obtain sufficient and diverse attack data, hence the cooperation between organizations on data is a promising way to defense against APT [10]. However, organizations are reluctant to disclose their data considering the data privacy [11,12]. Federated learning [13] is a distributed deep learning solution that trains a model across multiple decentralized edge servers and ensures data confidentiality [14–16]. Therefore, models can be trained without exchanging their data samples between organizations and multiple APT attack patterns can be learned through federated learning.

In this paper, we propose FLAPT, an attack detection system based on federated learning to defense against APT in the edge computing environment. The FLAPT performs in three phases: 1) **Model Training via Federated Learning**, in which the edge servers in organizations play the role of participants in federated learning. Each edge server uses its traffic datasets and shared algorithms to train the local model and continuously interacts with the cloud server for iterative learning. After the training phase, the cloud server will distribute a model to all edge servers for detecting attacks. 2) **Attack Detection**, in which the detection model obtained through federated learning has learned comprehensive APT attack patterns and can be used for attack detection within the organization. The output of this phase is a set of alerts, which represents the detailed information of the detected attacks. 3) **APT Scenario Reconstruction**, in which the generated alert set is correlated to generate an APT scenario describing the causality between APT stages. The main contributions of this paper are as follows:

- We propose an APT detection method based on federated learning, which can effectively learn various APT attack patterns from different organizations by training a global model across multiple participants. The solution also can effectively solve the problem of imbalance and confidentiality of APT data.
- To reduce the overheads of computation and communication, we integrate the detection system into the edge computing which the edge server can share the load with the cloud server and provide computing capabilities.
- We also present an APT scenario reconstruction algorithm to match the detection method and an APT attack scenario will be presented to provide global comprehension and guide the defense against APTs.

The rest of this paper is organized as follows: In Sect. 2, we introduce the related works about APT detection and federated learning. In Sect. 3, we present the system model of our APT detection method. The proposed FLAPT system is described in Sect. 4. Extensive experimental evaluations are conducted in Sect. 5. Finally, Sect. 6 summarizes the whole paper.

2 Related Work

2.1 APT Detection

The traditional APT detection approach is to detect malicious behaviors by defining a set of rules [17]. In recent years, since machine learning has made remarkable achievements in many fields, it is natural to apply it to detect malicious behaviors [18].

Traditional Detection Methods. *Misuse-based* detection method [1,3], which defines a set of rules that indicate attack behaviors. The organization is considered to be under attack once the behavior that matches the rule is detected. However, this type of method requires too much expert knowledge and only works well for known attacks. Because of the high-class and disguise APT techniques, the predefined rules are easily bypassed by the sophisticated attackers. In addition, the rule base will be tremendous and complex if the defender wants to detect a variety of different attacks comprehensively. *Anomaly-based* detection method refers to modeling benign behavior and treating all outliers that deviate from benign behavior as malicious [7,17]. But the disadvantage of this method is that the false positives rate is too high.

ML-Based Detection Methods. In order to address the challenges in traditional detection methods, intelligence-driven detection methods relying on machine learning have become the mainstream research direction for APT detection. This method requires little expert knowledge as a result of few artificially defined rules are needed. It has the capability to learn multiple and changeable APT behavior patterns relying on the powerful learning ability of machine learning. An intrusion detection system based on CNN and LSTM was proposed in [6] which can classify the traffic to identify malicious behavior. But for APT attacks, it is necessary to further correlate the attack behaviors to form a complete attack scenario. MLAPT [8] put forward a complete APT detection, correlation, and prediction framework, which is of great significance to our research.

However, one of the biggest obstacles in machine learning methods is the lack of public datasets. And organizations may be reluctant to share their datasets due to data privacy, which greatly hinders the use of machine learning methods for APT detection. As a consequence, our method adopts the federated learning architecture to aggregate detection models.

2.2 Federated Learning

When it comes to how to enable massive data and APT detection nodes to be linked under the premise of meeting data privacy, security, and regulatory requirements, we adopt federated learning. Zhao et al. [19] proposed a method to improve the training effect by sharing a small subset of data globally, which offers a scheme for the case of non-IID data in federated learning. A distinctive feature of federated learning is that it can protect the privacy of data. But this does not mean that the federated learning is completely safe [20], even parameters can be analyzed to obtain a lot of confidential information. In strengthening privacy protection, Bhowmick et al. [21] introduced a relaxed version of local privacy by restricting the power of potential opponents. It provides a stronger privacy guarantee than global privacy and has better model performance than strict local privacy.

3   System Model

3.1   Design Rationale

The main purpose of our approach is to build an APT attack detection model through federated learning so that it can classify incoming traffic as attack types, such as *Shellcode, Command-and-Control (C&C), Backdoor*, etc. The reason why we adopt federated learning can be summarized as follows. Firstly, it is difficult for a single node to obtain sufficient and diverse attack data since many attacks are characterized by stages, resulting in unbalanced data distribution during a wide time period. Secondly, it is probable that all the detection nodes are not affiliated with the same institution, hence, different institutions may reluctant to share their monitoring data but willing to train shared parameters jointly. At last, the aggregation mechanism benefiting from federated learning has higher security than distributed machine learning. Multi-nodes collect data and train collaboratively, then share a common model. The model composes of various APT behavior patterns and can be used to detect APT attacks and generate alerts.

It is worth noting that APT is a multi-step and slow attack, thus an effective detection model should be used in all stages of the APT life cycle to detect the most commonly used techniques. But it needs to be distinguished that the detection of a single stage of APT does not mean the detection of APT attacks. Even if the alert of a single attack indicates that there is a technique used in an APT attack, the technique can be used for other types of attacks, and may not even be an attack. For example, *domain flux, port scanning*, and *C&C communication* used in APT attacks can also be used for botnet attacks. In addition, when data leakage in an APT attack will suddenly increase the amount of data transmission, it may also be caused by changes of enterprise normal business. Therefore, the information of all single-step attacks detected should be correlated to construct complete information about APT attacks.

3.2   Overview of FLAPT Architecture

Based on the design rationale, the architecture of FLAPT is shown in Fig. 1. The proposed system runs through three main phases:

Model Training via Federated Learning. Initially, a model for detecting various attack techniques used in APT will be trained. The edge servers of each organization act as participants for federated learning defense against APT attacks in the edge computing environment. Each edge server safely uses its own dataset and shares the same learning algorithm to train the detection model through federated learning. There is no need to consider the confidentiality of the datasets that trained locally. In the wake of cloud server aggregation and iterative training, a global model that aggregates comprehensive APT attack data from multiple institutions is obtained and the problem of data privacy is resolved. Each participant eventually synchronizes the identical global detection model which capable of detecting attacks in a complex network environment.

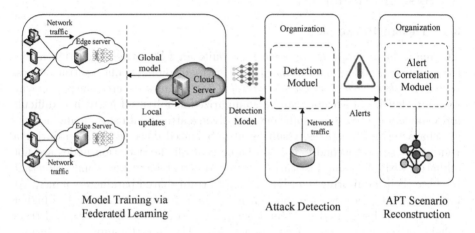

Fig. 1. System architecture of FLAPT

Attack Detection. After that, each organization deploys a detection model, and the detection nodes scan and process network traffic continuously to detect specific techniques used in one of the attack steps of APT. The output of this stage is various types of alerts, also known as malicious events, which contain detailed information describing specific attacks.

APT Scenario Reconstruction. At last, the alerts from the detection module are fed to the correlation module which associates the alerts that may be relevant and belong to an APT attack campaign. The process of this stage is divided into three main steps: 1) **Alert Mapping.** Alerts indicating attacks are mapped to the APT attack stages according to the adversarial tactics of each stage and the techniques of each attack event. 2) **Alert Correlation.** Associate alerts that are most likely to belong to the same APT attack campaign. Several correlation functions are defined to measure the correlation between the alerts by analyzing the various features of alerts. The output of this step is a set of clusters that indicating APT full-campaign or sub-campaign. 3) **Attack scenario Presentation.** All alert clusters are correlated to generate a complete APT scenario, which indicates the probability of an attack transferring to another attack. With the assistance of the APT attack scenario, security analysts can aware security situation roundly and predict the following behaviors of APT attackers accurately.

4 Proposed FLAPT Method

4.1 Model Training via Federated Learning and Attack Detection

As shown in Fig. 2, suppose that there are N participants in a federated learning system, and each participant P is ready to join in the synchronously updated federated training. In the selection phase of the federated learning, the cloud server selects participants randomly and partly to engage in the current round of training. Each selected participant P downloads the same parameters θ_d to train its own model. After the local training, the cloud server waits for each participant to return the trained gradient parameters θ_u in the subsequent reporting phase. Once receiving parameters, the cloud server uses a specific algorithm to aggregate them and notifies participants of the next request time. Iterating until the model converges, the cloud server distributes the global model to all participants for storage.

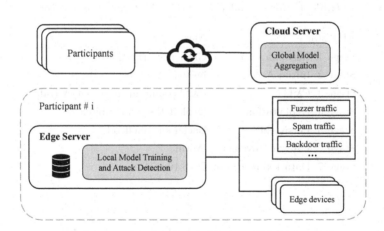

Fig. 2. Model training via federated learning

There is a pace control module in the entire process, called *Pace Steering*, which can manage the connection of all the participants. When there are enough participants returning gradients before the timeout, this round of training is successful, otherwise, it fails. If the number of participants N is large, *Pace*

Steering will randomize the request time of the participants to avoid a large number of simultaneous requests which may cause exceptions. Additionally, the models trained by each participant do not interfere with each other during the training process.

After the model training via federated learning, the detection model is deployed in the organizations for APT attack detection. The APT detection model takes network traffic as input and output a set of alerts for suspicious behaviors. The alert generated in this phase is expressed in the form of tuples with seven attributes, i.e., *alert_type*, *timestamp*, *src_ip*, *src_port*, *dest_ip*, *dest_port*, and *infected_host*.

4.2 APT Scenario Reconstruction

Map Alert to Kill-Chain. The alerts generated during the attack detection phase are mapped to the APT attack stages in order to additionally understand the attack process and effectively associate alerts. The mapping process from alerts to APT stages is based on MITRE's ATT&CK framework, which is an integration of tactics and techniques formed by summarizing real-world attacks. ATT&CK lists the techniques that may be used for specific tactical purposes in the form of a matrix and the APT attack stage can be summarized from these tactics. The APT stage can be determined for each alert through the mapping. As shown in Table 1, we define 7 APT attack stages and map each type of alert to the corresponding stage.

Table 1. Correspondence between APT stages and alerts

APT stage	Alert type
Stage 1: Reconnaissance	Gather information
Stage 2: Initial Access	Fuzzer, Analysis
Stage 3: C&C	C&C communication, DGA traffic
Stage 4: Exploitation	Exploit the vulnerability
Stage 5: Persistent	Backdoor, Shellcode
Stage 6: Lateral Movement	Worm
Stage 7: Data Exfiltration	DNS tunnel

Alert Correlation. After the alert set is obtained and the APT stage to which each alert belongs is determined, alerts with causality will be associated and form an alert cluster. The final output of this step is a number of attack clusters. Alert correlation is based on the similarity score which is used to measure the causality between two alarms. The similarity score is calculated in the following equation:

$$Sim(a_i, a_j) = (\sum_{k=1}^{m} W_k \cdot F_k(a_i, a_j))/m, \tag{1}$$

where m represents the number of features used to associate alerts, F_k indicates the correlation function of the alerts a_i and a_j about the k-th feature, and W_k is the weight of the corresponding feature. In order to improve the effect of alert correlation, we follow the information gain method, described in [22], to select features. Therefore, alert features *alert_type*, *ip_address*, *timestamp*, *port_number* are selected for alert correlation.

Alert a_i is processed by four correlation functions $F(a_i, a_j)$ where a_j is the last alert in each alert cluster in chronological order. The calculation of $F_{alert\_type}(a_i, a_j)$ is based on the difference of two APT stages that a_i and a_j belong to. There is a strong correlation between two alerts if a_i and a_j belong to the same APT stage, or the APT stage of a_i is the next of a_j. $F_{ip}(a_i, a_j)$ and $F_{port}(a_i, a_j)$ represent the similarity of IP address and port number respectively. For instance, if the source IP of a_i and a_j are quite similar, these two alerts are more likely triggered by the same attacker's APT process. $F_{timestamp}(a_i, a_j)$ is negatively related to the difference of timestamp between a_i and a_j. The shorter the time difference between two alerts, the higher the probability that two attacks belong to the same APT stage.

In the wake of the similarity score $Sim(a_i, a_j)$ is calculated through the four correlation functions described above, a_i is added to the alert cluster to which a_j belongs when $Sim(a_i, a_j)$ exceeds the threshold δ. After processing all the alerts, a collection of alert clusters AC is obtained which expressed in Eq. 2. Alerts in each alert cluster are sorted in temporal order, and each cluster is represented by an attack sequence graph as shown in Fig. 3.

$$AC_i = \{a_1, a_2, \cdots, a_n\}. \tag{2}$$

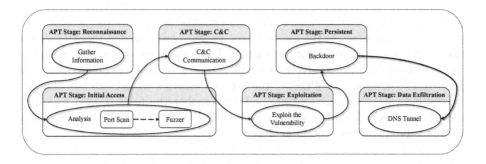

Fig. 3. Attack sequence graph

Attack Scenario Presentation. In the end, we create a probability transition matrix that the row and column indexes are the detected attack events. Traversing each attack sequence graph, the corresponding position in the matrix increases by 1 if there is a directed edge from the attack i to j. The non-zero elements in the matrix are converted to the proportion of its value in the corresponding row after the traversal is completed. Based on the probability transition matrix, an APT attack scenario is presented in the form of a weighted directed graph. As shown in Fig. 4, the weight of each directed edge in the graph is the transition probability of the attack state. Security analysts dynamically maintain the attack scenario which provides guidance for detecting and defending APT attacks.

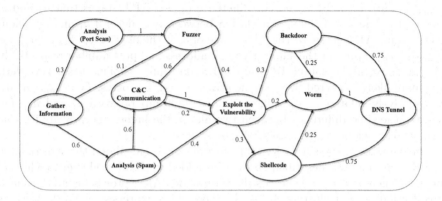

Fig. 4. APT attack scenario

5 Experimental Evaluation

In this section, the efficacy of FLAPT is explored from multiple perspectives, including the accuracy of the federated model, the correctness of the APT detection, and the comparison between the FLAPT system and other machine learning models. To comprehensively illustrate our method, we set the following two goals of experiments: 1) Whether the attack detection model can be enhanced by the federated learning scheme; and 2) Whether the fully trained federated model can precisely detect various steps of the APT attack and pave the way for the subsequent correlation analysis.

5.1 Experimental Setup

We implemented the federated learning by using the PyTorch 1.2.0 and Python 3.6. All experiments are carried out in the Ubuntu 16.04 LTS with NVIDIA Quadro P4000 GPU and 32 GB RAM. We set up five participants and they all subordinate to the same central server. In each round of the federated training, participants' local models are trained separately, then they upload their updates into a new global model synchronously.

Since there are scarce public datasets that record complete APT processes or exactly suitable for APT detection, we are dedicated to building simulation datasets in addition to utilizing the latest UNSW-NB15 datasets. Table 2 shows the UNSW-NB15 and synthetic datasets, in which the synthetic data uses *flight-sim* to simulate *DNS tunnel, C&C communication,* and *DGA traffic.* Moreover, 10 full APT attacks spanning seven stages are simulated in a virtual environment and the network traffic during the attacks is collected in order to evaluate the performance of our method. We use 80% of data in Table 2 for training in federated learning and the rest of the data in Table 2 for testing the detection accuracy of the federated model. Additionally, 10 APT full campaign datasets to evaluate the FLAPT performance both in attack classification and scenario reconstruction.

Table 2. Attack data records distribution from UNSW-NB15 and flightsim

Attack type	Description	Amount
Gather information	Gather information of target organization	13987
Fuzzer analysis	Vulnerabilities mining Port scan, Spam and HTML files penetrations	24246 2677
C&C communication	Communicate with C&C server	15627
DGA traffic	Bypass the detection of the domain blacklist	5215
Exploit the vulnerability	Exploit the security holes of the operating system	44525
Backdoor Shellcode	Bypass stealthily to access a computer	2329 1511
Worm	Replicate itself to spread	174
DNS tunnel	Covert channel for remote control and file transfer	5007

5.2 Model and Training Configurations

According to the previous introduction, a deep learning model referred to as Fed-CNN-LSTM is designed to construct the APT detection classifier. The preprocessed data in matrix form is first passed to the CNN network, which captures multiscale features of network traffic. The convolution kernels of the CNN are designed as 1×1, 2×2, and 3×3, and adopted 2×2 max-pooling. Several convolution and pooling layers learn the spatial features of the data by same padding, and subsequently, the spatial features are passed to the LSTM network to capture the temporal patterns. LSTM inputs data through the "cell" structure which uses three "gates" to achieve information selection, i.e., input gate, forget gate, and output gate. Each gate completes the tasks through a neural layer containing the *sigmoid* function and *Hadamard product* operation. For each participant, the training configurations are epoch $E = 500$ with the initial learning rate $\eta = 0.1$. Besides, we run the experiment for 400 communication rounds of federated learning.

5.3   Experimental Metrics

The experiment is evaluated in terms of model training Accuracy (ACC), the True Positive Rate (TPR), and the False Positive Rate (FPR). The parameters involved in the evaluations are $\{TP, FP, TN, FN\}$, which present the quantity of true-positive, false-positive, true-negative, and false-negative of APT alerts, respectively. Consequently, the APT detection effect measurement indicators can be formalized as follows:

$$\begin{cases} Accuracy\ (ACC) = \frac{TP+TN}{TP+FP+FN+TN} \\[2mm] True\ Positive\ Rate\ (TPR) = \frac{TP}{TP+FN} \\[2mm] False\ Positive\ Rate\ (FPR) = \frac{FP}{FP+TN} \end{cases} \tag{3}$$

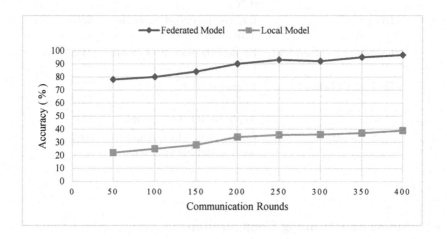

Fig. 5. Model accuracy comparison

5.4   Performance Evaluation of FLAPT

Figure 5 shows the variation curve of model classification accuracy as the number of iterations (communication rounds) increases. We compare the results of the federated model with the average accuracy of 5 participants' local models that training without communication. It is obvious that the training effect of the federated learning is better than the models trained in isolation. In the end, the accuracy of the federated learning model reaches 96.7%, while the average accuracy of 5 local models is only 38.9%. This proves the reinforcement scheme based on federated learning not only solves the inherent problem that the confidentiality and unbalanced distribution of APT data, but also enhances the classification precision of models of all participants significantly.

To dive into the effectiveness of our approach, we compare Fed-CNN-LSTM with three deep learning based baselines. The sets of comparative experiments are composed of three neural networks, i.e., Lenet-5 [23], MSCNN, and HAST network proposed by Wang et al. [24]. The Lenet-5 network is a classic CNN architecture and the MSCNN uses various convolutional kernels so as to aggregate multi-scale local features. The HAST network deployed in an intrusion detection system which in the light of hierarchical spatial-temporal features to conduct anomaly detection. The comparative experiment results are shown in Fig. 6, and the test data is taken 20% from Table 2. We can draw a conclusion that the model of our scheme has higher accuracy and lower false-positive rate than other models, which benefits from the combination of CNN and LSTM algorithms.

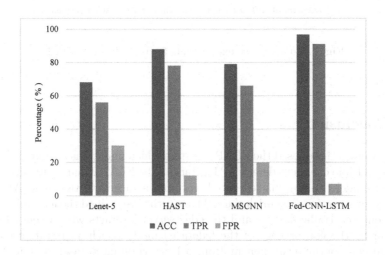

Fig. 6. Comparative experiments for test dataset

When facing a real-life APT attack, whether the model can correctly identify the entire APT attack chain is the most critical indicator to measure the detection model. Consequently, we use the 10 simulated APT attacks dataset to evaluate the FLAPT method. The experimental results are shown in Fig. 7. Obviously, our Fed-CNN-LSTM based APT detection model is superior to other models in terms of all indicators. This indicates the integrated detection model is more suitable for intrusion detection systems and has a great generalization ability of rare attacks. In future work, we will continue to study how to design a more powerful and generalized model. Another crucial issue is the communication of federated learning could leak some sensitive information on the traffic that was used to build the model. Hence, the model security and data privacy mechanisms should be further considered to defend attacks.

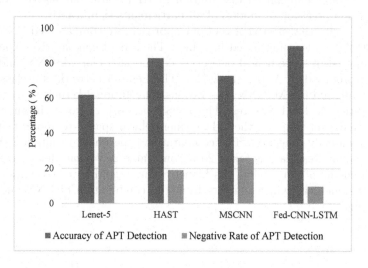

Fig. 7. Comparative experiments for real-life APT attacks

6   Conclusion

In this work, we proposed the FLAPT system which maintains a federated model across multiple clients to detect APT attacks. The FLAPT mainly involved three phases: model training via federated learning, attack detection, and APT scenario reconstruction. To enrich the APT patterns, we trained the federated model on a collected traffic dataset and the edge server interacts with a central server to improve the convergence of the federated model. Such an iterative training method can continuously benefit from a large training dataset contributed by massive participants. Moreover, we also presented a corresponding APT attack detection and scenario reconstruction method, where the formal one can generate alert set from the learning results, and the latter one is used to correlate multiple APT stages by analyzing the detailed information of the detected attacks. The extensive experimental results demonstrated that our proposed FLAPT system can achieve high detection accuracy with low false alarm rates.

Acknowledgment. This work was supported in part by the National Key Research and Development Program of China under Grant 2017YFB0802303, in part by the

National Natural Science Foundation of China under Grant 61672283 and Grant 61602238, in part by the Natural Science Foundation of Jiangsu Province under Grant BK20160805, and in part by the Postgraduate Research & Practice Innovation Program of Jiangsu Province under Grant KYCX18_0308.

References

1. Milajerdi, S.M., Gjomemo, R., Eshete, B., et al.: Holmes: real-time apt detection through correlation of suspicious information flows. In: Proceedings of 2019 IEEE Symposium on Security and Privacy (SP), pp. 1137–1152 (2018)
2. Qu, Y., Yu, S., Peng, S., Wang, G., Xiao, K.: Privacy of things: emerging challenges and opportunities in wireless Internet of Things. IEEE Wireless Commun. **25**(6), 91–97 (2018)
3. Milajerdi, S.M., Eshete, B., Gjomemo, R., et al.: Poirot: aligning attack behavior with kernel audit records for cyber threat hunting. In Proceedings of 2019 ACM SIGSAC Conference on Computer and Communications Security (CCS 2019), pp. 1795–1812 (2019)
4. Xiao, L., Xu, D., Xie, C., Mandayam, N.B., Vincent, P.H.: Cloud storage defense against advanced persistent threats: a prospect theoretic study. IEEE J. Sel. Areas Commun. **18**(1), 99–109 (2017)
5. Cheng, X., Zhang, J., Chen, B.: Cyber situation comprehension for IoT systems based on apt alerts and logs correlation. Sensors **19**(18), 4045–4064 (2019)
6. Zhang, J., Ling, Y., Fu, X., et al.: Model of the intrusion detection system based on the integration of spatial-temporal features. Comput. Secur. **89**(2), 1–9 (2020)
7. Manzoor, E., Milajerdi, S., Akoglu, L.: Fast memory-efficient anomaly detection in streaming heterogeneous graphs. In: Proceedings of 22nd ACM SIGKDD International Conference on Knowledge Discovery and Data Mining (KDD), pp. 1035–1044 (2016)
8. Ghafir, I., Hammoudeh, M., Prenosil, V., et al.: Detection of advanced persistent threat using machine-learning correlation analysis. Future Gener. Comput. Syst. **89**(12), 349–359 (2018)
9. Roschke, S., Cheng, F., Meinel, C.: A new alert correlation algorithm based on attack graph. CISIS **6694**(11), 58–67 (2017)
10. Mach, P., Becvar, Z.: Mobile edge computing: a survey on architecture and computation offloading. IEEE Commun. Surv. Tutor. **19**(3), 1628–1656 (2017)
11. Yu, S.: Big privacy: challenges and opportunities of privacy study in the age of big data. IEEE Access **4**, 2751–2763 (2016)
12. Zhang, J., Zhao, Y., Wang, J., Chen, B.: FedMEC: improving efficiency of differentially private federated learning via mobile edge computing. Mob. Netw. Appl. 1–13 (2020). https://doi.org/10.1007/s11036-020-01586-4
13. Smith, V., Chiang, C.-K., Sanjabi, M., Talwalkar, A.S.: Federated multi-task learning. In: Proceedings of 32nd Annual Conference on Neural Information Processing Systems (NIPS), pp. 4427–4437 (2017)
14. Zhang, J., Zhao, Y., Wu, J., Chen, B.: LPDA-EC: a lightweight privacy-preserving data aggregation scheme for edge computing. In: Proceedings of 15th International Conference on Mobile Ad Hoc and Sensor Systems, pp. 98–106 (2018)
15. Yang, Q., Liu, Y., Chen, T., Tong, Y.: Federated machine learning: concept and applications. ACM Trans. Intell. Syst. Technol. **10**(2), 1–19 (2019)

16. Zhang, J., Chen, B., Yu, S., Deng, H.: PEFL: a privacy-enhanced federated learning scheme for big data analytics. In: Proceedings of 2019 IEEE Global Communications Conference (GLOBECOM), pp. 1–6 (2019)
17. Berlin, K., Slater, D., Saxe, J.: Malicious behavior detection using windows audit logs. In: Proceedings of 8th ACM Workshop on Artificial Intelligence and Security, pp. 35–44 (2015)
18. Alshamrani, A., Myneni, S., Chowdhary, A., Huang, D.: A survey on advanced persistent threats: techniques, solutions, challenges, and research opportunities. IEEE Communi. Surv. Tutor. 21(2), 1851–1877 (2019)
19. Zhao, Y., Li, M., Lai, L., Suda, N., Civin, D., Chandra, V.: Federated learning with non-IID data. https://arxiv.org/abs/1806.00582 (2018)
20. Zhang, J., Zhao, Y., Wu, J., Chen, B.: LVPDA: a lightweight and verifiable privacy-preserving data aggregation scheme for edge-enabled IoT. IEEE Internet of Things J. 7(5), 4016–4027 (2020)
21. Bhowmick, A., Duchi, J., Freudiger, J., Kapoor, G., Rogers, R.: Protection against reconstruction and its applications in private federated learning. https://arxiv.org/abs/1812.00984v1 (2018)
22. Ahmed, A,T., Md, S.M., Anazida, Z., et al.: Feature selection using information gain for improved structural-based alert correlation. PLoS ONE. 11(12), e0166017 (2016)
23. Lecun, Y., Bottou, L.: Gradient-based learning applied to document recognition. Proc. IEEE 86(11), 2278–2324 (1998)
24. Wang, W., Sheng, Y., Wang, J., Zeng, X., Huang, Y., Zhu, M.: HAST-IDS: learning hierarchical spatial-temporal features using deep neural networks to improve intrusion detection. IEEE Access 6, 1792–1806 (2017)

Covert Communication

Data Computing in Covert Domain

Zhenxing Qian[1]([⊠]) [iD], Zichi Wang[2] [iD], and Xinpeng Zhang[2] [iD]

[1] Shanghai Institute of Intelligent Electronics and Systems, School of Computer Science, Fudan University, Shanghai 201203, People's Republic of China
zxqian@fudan.edu.cn
[2] Shanghai Institute for Advanced Communication and Data Science, Key Laboratory of Specialty Fiber Optics and Optical Access Networks, Joint International Research Laboratory of Specialty Fiber Optics and Advanced Communication, Shanghai University, Shanghai 200444, People's Republic of China
{wangzichi,xzhang}@shu.edu.cn

Abstract. This paper proposes an idea of data computing in the covert domain (DCCD). We show that with information hiding some data computing tasks can be executed beneath the covers like images, audios, random data, etc. In the proposed framework, a sender hides his source data into two covers and uploads them onto a server. The server executes computation within the stego and returns the covert computing result to a receiver. With the covert result, the receiver can extract the computing result of the source data. During the process, it is imperceptible for the server and the adversaries to obtain the source data as they are hidden in the cover. The transmission can be done over public channels. Meanwhile, since the computation is realized in the covert domain, the cloud cannot obtain the knowledge of the computing result. Therefore, the proposed idea is useful for secure computing.

Keywords: Information hiding · Covert computation

1 Introduction

With the development of big data and cloud computing, many security problems appear, e.g., privacy disclosure [1], data abuse [2], malicious attacks [3]. Therefore, many data protection algorithms have been proposed for data storage and computing. One important task of protection is to conceal the content of sensitive data. For example, during cloud computing the users always hope that the cloud can process the committed data without knowing its content [4]. Data encryption is one of the most effective and popular means of privacy protection [5]. However, protection by encryption would inevitably impact the utility of cloud computing.

As present, the most popular approaches to achieve secure computation for cloud is signal processing in encrypted domain [6–9]. As shown in Fig. 1, a sender encrypts his source data (the sensitive information that cannot be exposed to the others) and uploads the encrypted versions to the cloud sever. The server executes computing within the encrypted data without knowing the content of source data and returns the computing

S. Yu et al. (Eds.): SPDE 2020, CCIS 1268, pp. 535–545, 2020.
https://doi.org/10.1007/978-981-15-9129-7_37

results to a receiver. Finally, the receiver decrypts the returned results to obtain the computation results of source data. Homomorphic encryption algorithms were proposed to achieve these goals. After encrypting the data into a ciphertext with tremendous bits, additive or multiplicative operations can be done in encrypted domain. As the computation complexity [10–12] is very large, homomorphic encryption is not convenient for common users or mobile devices.

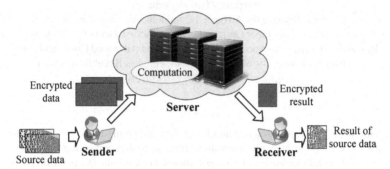

Fig. 1. Computation in encrypted domain using encryption.

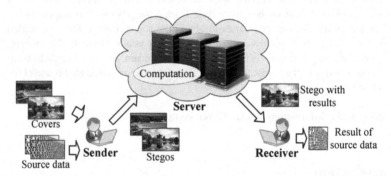

Fig. 2. Computation in covert domain using information hiding.

In this paper, we propose a novel idea of secure computation, i.e., data computing in the covert domain (DCCD). Different from the encrypted domain, the covert domain is a space generated by information hiding that can accommodate data inside a cover. The covers can be images, videos, audios, noise, or even random data, etc. Traditionally, information hiding is also called steganography, which is used to transmit secret message covertly over public channels. Many works have been done on steganography, e.g., LSB, JSteg, ZZW, STC, etc. We find that information hiding can also be used for cloud computing. On the one hand, data privacy can be protected since the data are embedded inside the covers. On the other hand, both the additive and multiplicative operations can be realized in the covert data. As shown in Fig. 2, a sender embeds his source data into covers, and then uploads the obtained stegos to a server. For the ease of illustration, we use images as covers for example.

The server executes computing within the covers and returns the stego with computing result to the receiver. The receiver extracts the computation result of the source data. In this framework, no information of the original data can be obtained by the server. Meanwhile, the computation complexity is much smaller than the homomorphic encryption. Besides, the source data are secure to be transmitted over public channels since the data are hidden inside the covers.

2 Proposed Method

The proposed framework of DCCD is shown in Fig. 3. We use digital images as covers to show the process of DCCD. A sender hopes to calculate $\varphi(\mathbf{m}_1, \mathbf{m}_2)$ in the server, and keep $\mathbf{m}_1$ and $\mathbf{m}_2$ secret to the server, where $\mathbf{m}_1$ and $\mathbf{m}_2$ are the source data, and $\varphi(\cdot)$ is a calculation operator.

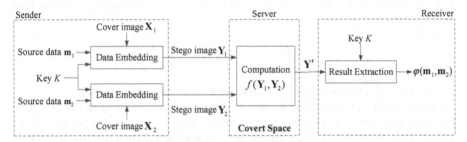

Fig. 3. Framework of the proposed method.

To achieve this goal, the sender embeds $\mathbf{m}_1$ and $\mathbf{m}_2$ into the cover images $\mathbf{X}_1$ and $\mathbf{X}_2$ with data hiding key K, respectively. The stego images $\mathbf{Y}_1$ and $\mathbf{Y}_2$ are then uploaded onto the server. The server executes the computation $f(\mathbf{Y}_1, \mathbf{Y}_2)$ using $\mathbf{Y}_1$ and $\mathbf{Y}_2$ without any knowledge of $\mathbf{m}_1$ and $\mathbf{m}_2$. After that, the stego $\mathbf{Y}'$ containing computation result is obtained. With $\mathbf{Y}'$ the receiver is able to extract the computation result $\varphi(\mathbf{m}_1, \mathbf{m}_2)$.

The computation is done in the covert domain generated by data hiding. Many algorithms can be used to realize the proposed DCCD. For the ease of explanation, we use the matrix embedding in LSB (Least Significant Bitplane) as examples to illustrate the proposed idea, since LSB is one of the most representative approachs of data hiding.

2.1 Source Data Embedding

Let the source data be binary sequences, i.e., $\mathbf{m}_1 = [m_1(1), m_1(2), ..., m_1(k)]^{\mathrm{T}} \in \{0, 1\}^{k \times 1}$, $\mathbf{m}_2 = [m_2(1), m_2(2), ..., m_2(k)]^{\mathrm{T}} \in \{0,1\}^{k \times 1}$. To conceal $\mathbf{m}_1$ and $\mathbf{m}_2$, two cover images $\mathbf{X}_1 = [x_1(i, j)]^{w \times r}$ and $\mathbf{X}_2 = [x_2(i, j)]^{w \times r}$ is used, where $i \in \{1, 2, ..., w\}, j \in \{1, 2, ..., r\}$. The LSB $\mathbf{c}_1 = [c_1(i, j)] \in \{0,1\}^{w \times r}$ and $\mathbf{c}_2 = [c_2(i, j)] \in \{0,1\}^{w \times r}$ of $\mathbf{X}_1$ and $\mathbf{X}_2$ are used for embedding, as shown in (1) and (2).

$$c_1(i, j) = \mod(x_1(i, j), 2) \tag{1}$$

$$c_2(i, j) = \mod(x_2(i, j), 2) \tag{2}$$

Next, we use matrix embedding method [13] to embed $\mathbf{m}_1$ into $\mathbf{c}_1$. With a data hiding key K, we generate a binary matrix $\mathbf{H} = [h(u, v)] \in \{0, 1\}^{k \times wr}$, where $u \in \{1, 2, ..., k\}$, $v \in \{1, 2, ..., wr\}$. The data hiding key is shared by the sender and the receiver. The process of data embedding is to make (3) true by modifying the elements in $\mathbf{c}_1$ to generate $\hat{\mathbf{c}}_1$.

$$\mathbf{m}_1 = \mathbf{H}\hat{\mathbf{c}}_1 \tag{3}$$

During the embedding, $\hat{\mathbf{c}}_1 = [\hat{c}_1(1), \hat{c}_1(2), ..., \hat{c}_1(wr)]^{\mathrm{T}} \in \{0,1\}^{wr \times 1}$ is obtained by cascading the rows in $\mathbf{c}_1$, as shown in (4), $t \in \{1, 2, ..., wr\}$ and "$\lfloor \cdot \rfloor$" is the floor rounding operator.

$$\hat{c}_1(t) = c_1\left(\left\lfloor \frac{t-1}{w} \right\rfloor + 1,\ t - \left\lfloor \frac{t-1}{w} \right\rfloor w\right) \tag{4}$$

Subsequently, we substitute the LSB $\mathbf{c}_1$ in $\mathbf{X}_1$ to achieve the stego $\mathbf{Y}_1$.

The procedure of embedding $\mathbf{m}_2$ into $\mathbf{c}_2$ is the same as embedding $\mathbf{m}_1$ into $\mathbf{c}_1$. After cascading the rows in $\mathbf{c}_2$ to obtain $\hat{\mathbf{c}}_2 = [\hat{c}_2(1), \hat{c}_2(2), ..., \hat{c}_2(wr)]^{\mathrm{T}} \in \{0, 1\}^{wr \times 1}$, we make (5) true by modifying the elements in $\mathbf{c}_2$ to achieve $\hat{\mathbf{c}}_2$. Therefore, the stego $\mathbf{Y}_2$ is obtained.

$$\mathbf{m}_2 = \mathbf{H}\hat{\mathbf{c}}_2 \tag{5}$$

After the data embedding, we upload the stego images $\mathbf{Y}_1$ and $\mathbf{Y}_2$ to the server. Without the data hiding key, the content of $\mathbf{m}_1$ and $\mathbf{m}_2$ cannot be revealed. This security performance will be demonstrated in Subsect. 3.3.

2.2 Computation in Covert Domain

With the stego images $\mathbf{Y}_1$ and $\mathbf{Y}_2$, the server can execute the computation task $f(\mathbf{Y}_1, \mathbf{Y}_2)$, which is equivalent to $\varphi(\mathbf{m}_1, \mathbf{m}_2)$ in the plaintext domain. Next, we discuss three cases of binary calculations $\varphi(\cdot)$ in the covert domain, i.e.,

$$\varphi_1(\mathbf{m}_1, \mathbf{m}_2) = \mathbf{m}_1 + \mathbf{m}_2,$$

$$\varphi_2(\mathbf{m}_1, \mathbf{m}_2) = \mathbf{m}_1 \mathbf{m}_2^{\mathrm{T}},$$

$$\varphi_3(\mathbf{m}_1, \mathbf{m}_2) = \mathbf{m}_1^{\mathrm{T}} \mathbf{m}_2.$$

These operations are widely used in outsourcing computation [14, 15], image retrieval [16, 17], privacy protection [18, 19], etc.

i) *Case One*

For the case of $\varphi_1(\mathbf{m}_1, \mathbf{m}_2)$, we use

$$f(\mathbf{Y}_1, \mathbf{Y}_2) = \hat{\mathbf{c}}_1 + \hat{\mathbf{c}}_2 \tag{6}$$

In this way, the LSB $\mathbf{c}' = [c'(i,j)] \in \{0,1\}^{w \times r}$ of $\mathbf{Y}'$ is

$$c'(i,j) = y_1(i,j) + y_2(i,j) \tag{7}$$

After cascading, the obtained binary sequence $\hat{\mathbf{c}}' = [\hat{c}'(1), \hat{c}'(2), \ldots, \hat{c}'(wr)]^{\mathrm{T}} \in \{0, 1\}^{wr \times 1}$ is

$$\hat{c}'(t) = c'\left(\left\lfloor \frac{t-1}{w} \right\rfloor + 1, \ t - \left\lfloor \frac{t-1}{w} \right\rfloor w\right) \tag{8}$$

which satisfies

$$\hat{\mathbf{c}}' = \hat{\mathbf{c}}_1 + \hat{\mathbf{c}}_2 \tag{9}$$

After that, the server replaces the LSB of $\mathbf{Y}_1$ by $\hat{\mathbf{c}}'$ to generate the final $\mathbf{Y}'$, which is sent to the receiver.

According to (3) and (5), the receiver can obtain

$$\mathbf{H}\hat{\mathbf{c}}' = \mathbf{H}\hat{\mathbf{c}}_1 + \mathbf{H}\hat{\mathbf{c}}_2 = \mathbf{m}_1 + \mathbf{m}_2 \tag{10}$$

Therefore, the result extracted from $\mathbf{Y}'$ is $\varphi_1(\mathbf{m}_1, \mathbf{m}_2) = \mathbf{m}_1 + \mathbf{m}_2$.

ii) *Case Two*

For the case of $\varphi_2(\mathbf{m}_1, \mathbf{m}_2)$, we calculate

$$f(\mathbf{Y}_1, \mathbf{Y}_2) = \hat{\mathbf{c}}' = \hat{\mathbf{c}}_1 \hat{\mathbf{c}}_2^{\mathrm{T}},$$

and put back the results into the LSB of $\mathbf{Y}_1$ to generate $\mathbf{Y}'$.

The receiver can obtain the result of $\mathbf{m}_1 \mathbf{m}_2^{\mathrm{T}}$ by $\mathbf{H}\hat{\mathbf{c}}' \mathbf{H}^{\mathrm{T}}$ because of

$$\mathbf{m}_1 \mathbf{m}_2^{\mathrm{T}} = \mathbf{H}\hat{\mathbf{c}}_1 (\mathbf{H}\hat{\mathbf{c}}_2)^{\mathrm{T}} = \mathbf{H}\hat{\mathbf{c}}_1 \hat{\mathbf{c}}_2^{\mathrm{T}} \mathbf{H}^{\mathrm{T}} = \mathbf{H}\hat{\mathbf{c}}' \mathbf{H}^{\mathrm{T}} \tag{11}$$

iii) *Case Three*

For the case of $\varphi_3(\mathbf{m}_1, \mathbf{m}_2) = \mathbf{m}_1^{\mathrm{T}} \mathbf{m}_2$, we use

$$f(\mathbf{Y}_1, \mathbf{Y}_2) = \hat{\mathbf{c}}' = \hat{\mathbf{c}}_1^{\mathrm{T}} \hat{\mathbf{c}}_2.$$

The server calculates

$$\mathbf{m}_1^{\mathrm{T}} \mathbf{m}_2 = (\mathbf{H}\hat{\mathbf{c}}_1)^{\mathrm{T}} \mathbf{H}\hat{\mathbf{c}}_2 = \hat{\mathbf{c}}_1^{\mathrm{T}} \mathbf{H}^{\mathrm{T}} \mathbf{H}\hat{\mathbf{c}}_2 \tag{12}$$

Once the embedding matrix $\mathbf{H}$ is an orthogonal matrix, i.e.,

$$\mathbf{H}^{\mathrm{T}} \cdot \mathbf{H} = \mathbf{I}$$

The result of (12) is equal to

$$\mathbf{m}_1^T \mathbf{m}_2 = \hat{\mathbf{c}}' = \hat{\mathbf{c}}_1^T \hat{\mathbf{c}}_2$$

After that, the server replaces LSB of $\mathbf{Y}_1$ by $\hat{\mathbf{c}}'$ to generate the final $\mathbf{Y}'$. As $\hat{\mathbf{c}}'$ is equal to $\mathbf{m}_1^T \mathbf{m}_2$, the server can obtain the calculation result. In order to protect the result, the sender can multiply the source data $\mathbf{m}_1$ and $\mathbf{m}_2$ with two factors, respectively. On the other side, the receiver can remove these factors to obtain the real result. Therefore, the security of data computation can be guaranteed. In addition, binary operations among more than two source sequences can be achieved using DCCD two by two.

3 Experimental Results

We have conducted many experiments to verify the DCCD idea. In this section, we show the feasibility, imperceptibility, security performance, and computational complexity of the proposed paradigm.

3.1 Feasibility

We use two random binary sequences with 1000 bits as $\mathbf{m}_1$ and $\mathbf{m}_2$. As shown in Fig. 4, the test images Lena and Baboon sized 512×512 are used as the cover $\mathbf{X}_1$ and $\mathbf{X}_2$. After data embedding, $\mathbf{m}_1$ and $\mathbf{m}_2$ are embedded into $\mathbf{X}_1$ and $\mathbf{X}_2$ to generate the stego images $\mathbf{Y}_1$ and $\mathbf{Y}_2$, as shown in Fig. 5. The stego images are indistinguishable from cover images. Therefore, the imperceptibility of the source data can be realized. More analysis about the imperceptibility of $\mathbf{m}_1$ and $\mathbf{m}_2$ are shown in Fig. 6.

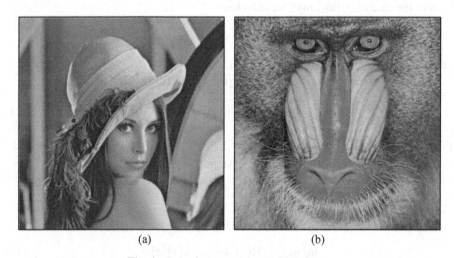

(a)   (b)

Fig. 4. Cover images (a) Lena; (b) Baboon.

Fig. 5. Stego images (a) Lena containing m_1; (b) Baboon containing m_2.

Next, we process DCCD with $\mathbf{Y}_1$ and $\mathbf{Y}_2$ using the algorithms described in subsection II.B. The result extract form the covert domain are then compared with $\varphi(\mathbf{m}_1, \mathbf{m}_2)$. The difference ratio between $\varphi(\mathbf{m}_1, \mathbf{m}_2)$ and the extracted result are shown in Table 1. For all cases, the difference ratio is zero. It means the receiver can obtain $\varphi(\mathbf{m}_1, \mathbf{m}_2)$ after data extraction. Hence, the proposed method is feasible.

Table 1. Difference ratio between $\varphi(m_1, m_2)$ and the extracted result.

$\varphi(\mathbf{m}_1, \mathbf{m}_2)$	$\mathbf{m}_1 + \mathbf{m}_2$	$\mathbf{m}_1 \mathbf{m}_2^{\mathrm{T}}$	$\mathbf{m}_1^{\mathrm{T}} \mathbf{m}_2$
Difference ratio	0	0	0

3.2 Imperceptibility

To verify the imperceptibility of the source data statistically, we use all 1338 images sized 512×384 in UCID [20] as cover images. Each image is embedded with capacity 1000, 2000, 3000, 4000, and 5000 bits respectively using the proposed method. The imperceptibility of the source data can be checked by modern steganalytic methods which are based on the supervised machine learning [21]. Specifically, we employ the popular steganalytic feature extraction methods SPAM [22], SRMQ1 [23], SRM [23], and PSRM [24] with an ensemble classifier [25]. One half of the cover and stego feature sets are used for training, while the remaining sets are used for testing. The criterion of evaluating the performance of feature sets is the minimal total error P_E with identical priors achieved on the testing sets [25].

$$P_E = \min_{P_{FA}} \left(\frac{P_{FA} + P_{MD}}{2} \right) \tag{13}$$

where P_{FA} is the false alarm rate and P_{MD} the missed detection rate. The performance is evaluated using the average of P_E over ten random tests. A higher P_E value stands for a better imperceptibility.

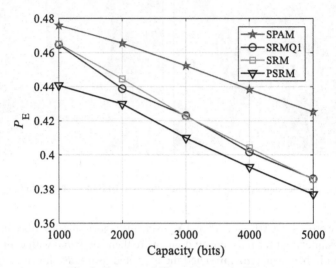

Fig. 6. Imperceptibility of data embedding.

The imperceptibility of data embedding is shown in Fig. 6. The values of P_E keep a high level for all cases. It is difficult to discover the embedded source data from the stego images. Thus, the imperceptibility can be guaranteed. In addition, the values of P_E are close to 0.5 (the bound of P_E) for small capacity (such than 1000 bits). The result indicates that the existence of source data is completely undetectable using the modern steganalysis tools when capacity is less than 1000 bits. Therefore, the specific attention and unwanted attack existing in encrypted domain can be avoided in the covert domain.

3.3 Security Performance

In the proposed framework of DCCD, the content of source data should not be leaked to the server. In other words, the content of $\mathbf{m}_1$ and $\mathbf{m}_2$ cannot be obtained without data hiding key. To verify the security of source data, we also use the images in UCID as covers. Each image is embedded with capacity 1000, 2000, 3000, 4000, and 5000 bits, respectively. Next, a binary matrix with random bits (without data hiding key) is generated for each stego image to extract source data. Meanwhile, a binary matrix generated using data hiding key is used for data extraction. The average ratio of data extraction error is shown in Table 2.

The result shows that the data extraction error is around 50% (the bound of extraction error) for all cases. It means the content of source data would not be leaked without the data hiding key. On the other hand, the source data can be extracted correctly (data extraction error is 0%) when data hiding key is known. Therefore, the security of the proposed method can be guaranteed.

Table 2. Data extraction error with/without data hiding key.

Capacity (bits)	1000	2000	3000	4000	5000
Error with data hiding key (%)	0	0	0	0	0
Error without data hiding key (%)	50.02	49.96	49.97	49.96	49.95

3.4 Computational Complexity

While the complexity of computation in the encrypted domain is huge, the complexity of computing in the covert domain is smaller. To verify the efficiency of the proposed DCCD scheme, source data with 1000, 2000, 3000, 4000, and 5000 bits are embedded into image Lena, respectively. Meanwhile, the same source data is encrypted using RSA with the key sized 256 bits. The complexity comparison between the proposed DCCD and the RSA is shown in Fig. 7. These results are generated on a serve with 1.8 GHz CPU, 8 GB memory and windows 10. The type of system is 64 bits and the version of MATLAB is R2017b.

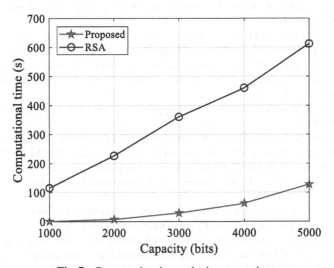

Fig. 7. Computational complexity comparison.

The result shows that the computational complexity of DCCD is much smaller than that of RSA for all cases. In addition, the computational complexity of RSA increases when a longer key is used. Thus, the proposed DCCD idea performs more potential convenience for cloud computing.

4   Conclusions

We propose a new idea of achieving secure computation in the covert domain using data hiding. A practical method is designed to implement the binary additive and multiplication calculations. As the source data are hidden in the covers, it is imperceptible for the cloud and the adversaries to obtain the data. Meanwhile, as the computation is realized in the covert domain, the cloud cannot obtain the computation data and the result. On the recipient side, the computation result can be obtained after data extraction. Experimental results show the effectiveness of the proposed DCCD idea. The proposed paradigm can also be extended to the covert domain generated by JSteg, F5, etc. To the best of our knowledge, it is the first work on computing in covert domain. More works on this topic can be done in the future.

Acknowledgement. This work was supported by the Natural Science Foundation of China (Grant U1736213, 62002214).

References

1. Chen, J., Ping, J., Xu, Y., Tan, B.: Information privacy concern about peer disclosure in online social networks. IEEE Trans. Eng. Manage. **62**(3), 311–324 (2015)
2. Liu, G., Wang, C., Peng, K., Huang, H., Li, Y., Cheng, W.: SocInf: membership inference attacks on social media health data with machine learning. IEEE Trans. Comput. Soc. Syst. **6**(5), 907–921 (2019)
3. Mustafa, A., Khan, S., Hayat, M., Shen, J., Shao, L.: Image super-resolution as a defense against adversarial attacks. IEEE Trans. Image Processing **29**, 1711–1724 (2020)
4. Puteaux, P., Puech, W.: An efficient MSB prediction-based method for high-capacity reversible data hiding in encrypted images. IEEE Trans. Inf. Forensics Secur. **13**(7), 1670–1681 (2018)
5. Zhang, X.: Reversible data hiding in encrypted image. IEEE Signal Process. Lett. **18**(4), 255–258 (2011)
6. Qian, Z., Xu, H., Luo, X., Zhang, X.: New framework of reversible data hiding in encrypted JPEG bitstreams. IEEE Trans. Circ. Syst. Video Technol. **29**(2), 351–362 (2019)
7. Ren, Y., Zhang, X., Feng, G., Qian, Z., Li, F.: How to extract image features based on co-occurrence matrix securely and efficiently in cloud computing. IEEE Trans. Cloud Comput. **8**(1), 207–219 (2020)
8. Zhang, Q., Yang, L., Chen, Z.: Privacy preserving deep computation model on cloud for big data feature learning. IEEE Trans. Comput. **65**(5), 1351–1362 (2016)
9. Zhang, X., Wang, Z., Yu, J., Qian, Z.: Reversible visible watermark embedded in encrypted domain. In: 2015 IEEE China Summit and International Conference on Signal and Information Processing (ChinaSIP2015), Chengdu, China, pp. 826–830, July 2015
10. Li, M., Li, Y.: Histogram shifting in encrypted images with public key cryptosystem for reversible data hiding. Signal Process. **130**(9), 190–196 (2017)
11. Zhang, X., Long, J., Wang, Z., Cheng, H.: Lossless and reversible data hiding in encrypted images with public key cryptography. IEEE Trans. Circ. Syst. Video Technol. **26**(9), 1622–1631 (2016)
12. Chen, Y., Shiu, C., Horng, G.: Encrypted signal-based reversible data hiding with public key cryptosystem. J. Vis. Commun. Image Represent. **25**(5), 1164–1170 (2014)
13. Fridrich, J., Soukal, D.: Matrix embedding for large payloads. IEEE Trans. Inf. Forensics Secur. **1**(3), 390–395 (2006)
14. Ren, Y., Dong, M., Qian, Z., Zhang, X., Feng, G.: Efficient algorithm for secure outsourcing of modular exponentiation with single server. IEEE Trans. Cloud Comput. (2018). https://doi.org/10.1109/TCC.2018.2851245

15. Dong, M., Ren, Y., Zhang, X.: Fully verifiable algorithm for secure outsourcing of bilinear pairing in cloud computing. KSII Trans. Internet Inf. Syst. **11**(7), 3648–3663 (2017)
16. Liang, H., Zhang, X., Cheng, H.: Huffman-code based retrieval for encrypted JPEG images. J. Vis. Commun. Image Represent. **61**, 149–156 (2019)
17. Cheng, H., Zhang, X., Yu, J.: AC-coefficient histogram- based retrieval for encrypted JPEG images. Multimed. Tools Appl. **75**(21), 13791–13803 (2016)
18. Peng, T., Liu, Q., Wang, G.: Enhanced location privacy preserving scheme in location-based services. IEEE Syst. J. **11**(1), 219–230 (2017)
19. Li, S., Chen, X., Wang, Z., Qian, Z., Zhang, X.: Data hiding in iris image for privacy protection. IETE Tech. Rev. **35**(S1), 34–41 (2018)
20. Schaefer, G., Stich, M.: UCID - an uncompressed colour image database. In: Proceedings of Conference on Storage and Retrieval Methods and Applications for Multimedia, San Jose, CA, USA, pp. 472–480, January 2004
21. Wang, Z., Qian, Z., Zhang, X., Yang, M., Ye, D.: On improving distortion functions for JPEG steganography. IEEE Access **6**, 74917–74930 (2018)
22. Pevny, T., Bas, P., Fridrich, J.: Steganalysis by subtractive pixel adjacency matrix. IEEE Trans. Inf. Forensics Secur. **5**(2), 215–224 (2010)
23. Fridrich, J., Kodovsky, J.: Rich models for steganalysis of digital images. IEEE Trans. Inf. Forensics Secur. **7**(3), 868–882 (2012)
24. Holub, V., Fridrich, J.: Random projections of residuals for digital image steganalysis. IEEE Trans. Inf. Forensics Secur.ty **8**(12), 1996–2006 (2013)
25. Kodovsky, J., Fridrich, J., Holub, V.: Ensemble classifiers for steganalysis of digital media. IEEE Trans. Inf. Forensics Secur. **7**(2), 432–444 (2012)

Post-processing for Enhancing Audio Steganographic Undetectability

Xueyuan Zhang, Rangding Wang$^{(\boxtimes)}$, Li Dong, and Diqun Yan

College of Information Science and Engineering of Ningbo University, Ningbo, China
1098262448@qq.com
{wangrangding,dongli,yandiqun}@nbu.edu.cn

Abstract. Currently, the conventional steganography method often only perform data embedding, without additional post-processing to enhance undetectability. In this work, we propose a new audio post-processing steganography model, which further hiding the traces to a certain extent. Specifically, we design the Signal-to-Noise Ratio (SNR) threshold to determine whether the current stego is suitable for adding disturbance or not, and use JS divergence to decide whether the added disturbance is kept or not, respectively. The designed two measures will process the traces frame-by-frame by adding appropriate disturbances on needed sampling points of the stego audio. Experimental results illustrate that, with the proposed post-processing, the undetectability can be successfully improved without affecting the message extraction.

Keywords: Steganographic traces · Post-processing · JS divergence.

1 Introduction

Digital steganography aims at embedding the secret message into the cover (e.g., audio, image, video, etc.) while attaining the undetectability of the embedded message. In the past decade, for the mainstream steganography schemes, one long-standing crucial problem is how to minimize the distortion during embedding. Designing a distortion cost function to minimize the embedded distortion became the most popular solution, since Filler *et al.* [3] proposed the seminal Syndrome-Trellis Codes (STCs) framework, in 2011.

Inspired by Filler's work, in the field of image steganography, there were many excellent algorithms under this STC framework, e.g., HUGO [13], WOW[5], UNI-WARD [6], HILL [7], and MiDOP [15], to name a few. Those methods sequentially embedded message into low-cost regions of the image and update the cost to minimize it dynamically. In the field of audio steganography, there also were some representative works developed audio steganography schemes under a similar framework. Luo *et al.* [10] used the residual of the signal before and after Advanced Audio Coding compression to calculate the possible distortion. Gong *et al.* [4] used the short-term stability of pitch delay and the statistical distribution of adjacent subframe to design a distortion function for the

© Springer Nature Singapore Pte Ltd. 2020
S. Yu et al. (Eds.): SPDE 2020, CCIS 1268, pp. 546–559, 2020.
https://doi.org/10.1007/978-981-15-9129-7_38

Adaptive Multi-Rate (AMR) speech stream. Yi *et al.* [17] considered integrating the psychoacoustic model of intra-frame with frame-level perceptual distortion of inter-frame as a distortion function. Chen *et al.* [2] proposed a rule named "large-amplitude-first," which would assign low modification distortion to large amplitude audio samples. All the above methods involved the cover selection, which evaluates the possible distortion cost of each pixel or sampling point, and designing a distortion cost function. By adaptively selecting suitable areas for embedding, all methods are able to find the most reasonable embedding strategy with minimal total distortion.

Currently, however, the conventional steganography model steganography methods only perform data embedding, without further post-processing to enhance undetectability (as shown in the first row of Fig. 1). Current researches tend to reduce the distortion during the embedding, to improve the performance of the steganography. It is rare to find research on stego processing (or steganographic trace hiding) after embedding. In 2019, Chen *et al.* proposed a primary method for stego post-processing on image steganography [1]. The basic idea is as follows. Computing the two residual differences of the original cover, stego with the post-stego, respectively (here the residual is the absolute difference between the original signal and filtered signal). Then, by modifying every pixel of the stego image, it can reduce the residual difference under some criterion, and enhance steganography security. However, this method is not suitable for audio, and the evaluation criterion is based on residuals only. Namely, the criterion used incite is not precise enough, which requires a more secure and audio-suitable post-processing method.

In this paper, we propose a new audio post-processing steganography model, which hides the steganographic traces after message embedding, by adding proper disturbances. As seen in Fig. 1, the steganographic trace hiding includes three main parts: 1) hide the steganographic traces, 2) guarantee secret message extraction, 3) enhance the undetectability of the message. Specifically, we use the SNR (Signal-to-Noise Ratio) threshold and JS divergence in our method. The former one will determine whether the current stego is suitable for adding disturbance or not. The latter one will decide whether the added disturbance is kept or not. Our method will complete the optimization of steganographic traces frame-by-frame by adding appropriate disturbances on needed sampling points. Extensive experimental results illustrate that, after post-processing, the undetectability can be successfully improved to a certain extent without affecting the message extraction. The method proposed in this paper focuses on optimizing the steganographic traces of stegos, instead of distortion cost function design. Unlike the existing steganography methods, adding simple post-processing will improve the undetectability of post-stego. The main contributions of this work can be summarized as follows.

- We propose the audio post-processing steganography model, which can effectively select the size and position of the disturbance.
- The proposed method uses JS divergence as a criterion, which is suitable for audio cases to determine the rationality of the disturbance.

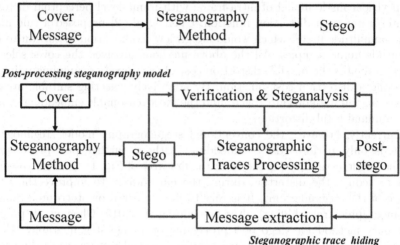

Fig. 1. Conventional steganography model VS Post-processing steganography model. The red-line part is the framework of the steganographic trace hiding method. (Color figure online)

- We evaluate the performances, limitations, and potential improvements for the current post-processing model.

The rest of this paper is organized as follows. Section 2 briefly describes two parameters of the proposed method. Section 3 presents our method and its algorithm in detail. Section 4 gives the experimental results and its analysis. Finally, Sect. 5 gives the conclusion and future works.

2 Preliminary

2.1 Location of Post-processing

In [1], when Syndrome-Trellis Codes (STCs) was used as a practical coding method, Chen *et al.* observed that if the parity-check matrix was fixed, the message extraction entirely relied on the Least Significant Bit (LSB) of the stego. It means that the location of post-processing can not be the LSB of the stego. Otherwise, the extraction of the secret message will be disturbed. In binary cases, the location should be (or higher) the 3rd LSB, meaning the value of the post-processing must be an integer multiple of 4.

In this paper, we use audio cover as a steganographic cover. Without changing the message extraction, the location of post-processing will also be adjusted according to the Signal-to-Noise Ratio (SNR). Specifically, we design an adaptive SNR threshold T to measure whether the SNR of the disturbance and stego is appropriate or not. The value of SNR can be calculated using the current disturbance and stego. The formula is as follows.

$$\text{Snr}(y_i, \Delta_i) = 20 \cdot log_{10} \left| \frac{y_i}{\Delta_i} \right| \tag{1}$$

where, y_i denotes the current stego value, Δ_i denotes the current disturbance suitable for y_i, $\text{Snr}(\cdot)$ denotes the standard SNR calculation formula.

If the calculated SNR is lower than T, no disturbance will be added or vice versa. We believe that the current stego position is not suitable for adding disturbance because it will make the perceived audio quality of the post-processing stego decrease. The SNR threshold T can be determined according to experimental results. In the following experiments for evaluating the performance of the post-processing model, we will discuses the post-processing effects under different thresholds.

2.2 JS Divergence

Jensen-Shannondivergence (JS divergence [11]) is a method of measuring the similarity between twoprobability distributions. It is based on theKullback-Leibler divergence (KL divergence), with some notable and useful differences, including that it is symmetric, and it is always a finite value. The JS divergence is a symmetrized and smoothed version of theKL divergence. It is defined by

$$\text{JS}(P||Q) = \frac{1}{2} \left(\text{KL} \left(P|| \frac{P+Q}{2} \right) + \text{KL} \left(Q|| \frac{P+Q}{2} \right) \right) \tag{2}$$

where, the KLD can be computed as

$$\text{KL}(P||Q) = \sum_{\text{all } i} P_i \cdot log \frac{P_i}{Q_i} \tag{3}$$

where, P and Q are two different data distributions. Compared with the KL divergence, the JS divergence has triangular symmetry, which means the JS divergence can be used to compare the distance (similarity) among three different data distributions. In the proposed post-processing model, we can simply send two different audio clips directly into (3) to calculate the similarity between the two audio clips. The lower the calculated value, the closer the distance between the two distributions, that is, the higher the similarity.

2.3 Stego Post-processing of Chen's

At the IH & MMSec conference in 2019, Chen *et al.* proposed a post-processing scheme for image steganography [1]. The basic idea is: by comparing the two residuals difference (as (5) of the original cover x and the stego y, post-stego z (the residual can be calculated through the filter, as (4). Then, feedback to the post-stego and make certain modifications (as (6)) on its non-cryptographic embedding bits (ij-th pixel). Finally, by traversing all pixels, the post-processing will be completed.

$$R_x = x \otimes f, \ R_y = y \otimes f, \ R_z = z \otimes f \tag{4}$$

$$D_{xy} = |R_x - R_y|, \ D_{xz} = |R_x - R_z| \tag{5}$$

$$z_{k+1} = \begin{cases} z'_k, & D_{xz'_k} < D_{xz} \\ z_k & D_{xz'_k} > D_{xz} \end{cases} \tag{6}$$

where, $R_{(.)}$ represents a filtered residual of a signal, and f represents the filter for image, which can be customized in size and parameters. $D_{(.)}$ denotes the difference between two signals. z'_k denotes the k-th updated post-stego, if $D_{xz'_k}$ is smaller than D_{xz}, it means that the post-processing makes post-stego's performance improved. Thus, the latest post-stego z'_k will be reserved, otherwise, z_k will be reserved.

For the audio case, however, the sampling value of audio has a larger value range than images', and it is a one-dimensional signal. The processing for such post-stego is different from the image. In the following experiments, we will use this method for comparative experiments. To adapt for audio, we change its filter to a one-dimensional filter.

3   Proposed Method

We propose to incorporate the SNR threshold T and JS divergence (JSD) into our audio steganographic traces processing model (the JSD-Based Trace Optimization Model). The former one is to determine whether the current stego is suitable for adding disturbance or not. The latter one is to determine whether the added disturbance is kept or not. In this section, we first give the overall framework of the proposed method, and then gradually illustrate the algorithm of our proposed post-processing model.

3.1   Overall Framework

We will determine the SNR threshold T, which can help us to select the locations of the added disturbance, and prevents added disturbance from becoming a new steganography risk. A large number of experiments [2,4,6,7,10,15,17] have proved that when the disturbance (or the noise) is added into the low-complexity areas, it might be detected more easily. On the other hand, we will compare two JS divergences of the stego and the post-stego with the original cover, respectively, to ensure that the resultant post-stego is closer to the original cover.

First, we will describe how to use the proposed method to perform post-processing optimization on audio stego. As illustrated in Fig. 2, x denotes the original cover, y denotes the stego (after message embedding), z denotes the

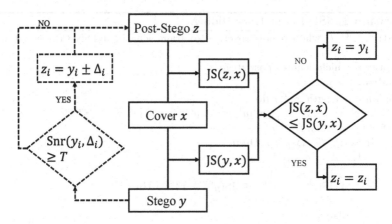

Fig. 2. The proposed framework of optimizing stego elements. The post-stego will be obtained by the stego with disturbances. The SNR threshold T will control the size and location of the disturbance. JS divergence will measure the justifiability of the disturbance.

post-stego, i denotes the subscript. The dotted-line part indicates the part that using the SNR threshold to determine what disturbance is available. The solid-line part indicates the part that using JS divergence to determine whether the added disturbance Δ_i remains or not. When the SNR of the stego and disturbance $\mathrm{Snr}(y_i, \Delta_i)$ is lower than the SNR threshold T, the target i-th value of the post-stego z_i will be updated by adding Δ_i to y_i. Otherwise, the z_i will equal to y_i. Next, the justifiability of the added disturbance will be tested by comparing two JS divergences of the stego and the post-stego with the original cover, respectively. If the updated post-stego one is lower, the added disturbance remains or vice versa. It traverses all the sample values of the audio one by one. In order to run this post-processing framework, we design the following implementation algorithm.

3.2 The Algorithm

Algorithm 1 summarizes the pseudo-code of our proposed method. Notably, in practical applications, when using the JS divergence to evaluate the justifiability of the disturbance, we will segment the audio into several frames. Because the difference between JS divergences of two long audio clips is too small to be captured, especially there is only one sample value changed. In the algorithm, $length(\cdot)$ denotes the function for computing the length of the subject, num denotes the number of frames, a denotes the value of the disturbance.

As one can see in Algorithm 1, the inputs include the cover, the stego, the frame length, and the SNR threshold. The stego will be initialized as post-stego at the beginning. There are three iterations in the proposed algorithm, i.e., lines 1–15, lines 3–14, lines 5–12, respectively.

Algorithm 1. JSD-Based Trace Hiding.

Input: x, y, fl, T, where denote cover, stego, frame length, and SNR threshold, respectively.

Output: z, which denotes post-stego.

Initialize: $z = y$.

1: **for** $num = \text{length}(x)/fl$ **do**
2: $\quad x = [x^1, x^2, ..., x^{num}]; y = [y^1, y^2, ..., y^{num}]; z = [z^1, z^2, ..., z^{num}]$
3: $\quad$ **for** $i = [1, 2, ..., fl]$ **do**
4: $\quad\quad$ **if** $\text{Snr}(y_i^{num}, \Delta_i) \geq T$ **then**
5: $\quad\quad\quad$ **for** $\Delta_i = a \times [-1, 1]$ **do**
6: $\quad\quad\quad\quad z_i^{num} = y_i^{num} + \Delta_i$
7: $\quad\quad\quad\quad$ **if** $\text{JS}(z^{num}, x^{num}) \leq \text{JS}(y^{num}, x^{num})$ **then**
8: $\quad\quad\quad\quad\quad z_i^{num} = z_i^{num}$
9: $\quad\quad\quad\quad$ **else**
10: $\quad\quad\quad\quad\quad z_i^{num} = y_i^{num}$
11: $\quad\quad\quad\quad$ **end if**
12: $\quad\quad\quad$ **end for**
13: $\quad\quad$ **end if**
14: $\quad$ **end for**
15: **end for**
16: **return** z.

- In the first loop, the three audio clips (x, y, z) are divided into several frames. The length of each frame is fl (num denotes the number of frames). The algorithm runs frame-by-frame.
- In the second loop, the SNR threshold T determines whether the size and location of the disturbance are suitable or not. The algorithm runs point by point, in each frame.
- In the last loop, disturbance times two wights (i.e., $-1, 1$), so that two types of post-stegos will be produced. By comparing $JS(z_1^{num}, x)$, $JS(z_{-1}^{num}, x)$, $JS(y^{num}, x)$, final disturbance will be determined.

Finally, after these three loops, the algorithm has dealt with all sampling points in the stego to optimize the steganographic traces and returns a post-stego, which has a higher similarity with the original cover. The complexity of this algorithm consists of three parts, where, the complexity of JS divergence is $(O)(log(fl))$, and the complexity of the remaining two loops are $(O)(fl)$ and $(O)(num)$, respectively. Therefore, the complete complexity $(O)(fl \cdot num \cdot log(fl))$ can be obtained.

It should be noted that there are two critical parameters in this proposed method, the frame length for zooming JS divergence and the SNR threshold for selecting the disturbance. These two parameters will be analyzed and determined through experiments to prove the reasonability of them. In the next section, we will provide some experimental results for further illustrating the method performance. Meanwhile, we will also provide the results of optimizing steganographic traces on audio stego and the perceived quality of the post-stego. Some limitations of the existing post-processing steganography model will be briefly discussed as well.

4 Experiments, Results and Analysis

4.1 Setup

We design the following three comparative experiments to evaluate the usability of the proposed post-processing steganography model:

1. Under different parameters (i.e. fl, T), respectively, compare the effects of the proposed steganographic trace optimization model.
2. Use our method to optimize the traces of different stegos. Compare the undetectability with another post-processing method [1] via steganalysis methods.
3. Use different methods to process stegos, and then compare the perceived audio quality of the resultant post-stegos.

In our experiments, we use two types of audio as steganographic cover. First is music cover (MUSIC), we manually crawl $5,000$ audio clips from publicly available websites, where each clip is of 1 s at 44.1KHz in WAV format. Second is speech cover, we use the TIMIT database, which is wildly used in the field of audio steganography. We manually cut $5,000$ clips, where each clip is of 1 s at 16KHz in WAV format.

Two representative steganographic schemes are used in this work for testing, i.e., LSB matching (LSBm) steganography[12] and STC-based steganography (i.e., optimal simulator [3]). To evaluate the undetectability of the resultant stegos (performing the audio steganalysis), two modern state-of-the-art audio steganalysis methods are employed, i.e., the feature-based steganalysis [9] and the CNN-based steganalysis [8]. For the LSB matching, the payload of embedded data is set in between the interval $[0.6, 1.0]$bps. For the STC-based method, the payload is set in between the interval $[0.1, 0.5]$bps. The data will be embedded in the Least Significant Bit (LSB).

In this work, to evaluate the subjective perceived audio quality, we employ the PEAQ (Perceptual Evaluation of Audio Quality) evaluation system [14,16]. In this system, each audio clip receives an ODG score to represent its human-audible quality, whose dynamic range is $[-4.5, 0.5]$. It is worth pointing out that with the ODG score increases, the perceived quality of the tested audio is better.

Please note that the original Chen's method was designed for image [1]. To adapt to the audio cover and stego, we simply modify this post-processing method. Compared with the original code, we only change the matrix filter to a one-dimensional vector filter, $f = [-1, 4, -6, 4, -1]$, to make it suitable for audio and retain its integrity as much as possible.

4.2 Results and Analysis

Parameters Selection

Under different frame lengths fl and different SNR thresholds T, the effects of the JS divergence steganography optimization model will be different. Taking the TIMIT database as an example, the message payload of stego is 1.0bps. Under different $T = [10, 20, 30, 40, 50, 60]$(dB) and fixed $fl = 20$(bit),

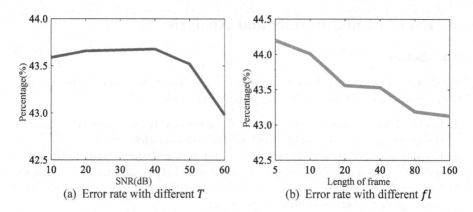

(a) Error rate with different T (b) Error rate with different fl

Fig. 3. Influence of the proposed method with two different parameters. Subgraph-(a) and -(b) denote the error rates under different SNR thresholds and different frame lengths, respectively. The undetectability increases w.r.t. error rate grows.

we use proposed method to generate post-stegos and give the steganalysis results (error rate, %) of them. Then, under fixed $T = 30(dB)$ and different $fl = [5, 10, 20, 40, 80, 160](bit)$, we use proposed method to generate post-stegos and give the steganalysis results.

The results are illustrated in Fig. 3. It shows the error rate of the post-stego against the MFCCF-based steganalysis. As one can see in Fig. 3(a), the undetectability of our proposed method decreases, when T is lower than 30dB or higher than 40dB. This is because when T is too high (i.e. larger than 40dB), the number of added disturbances will decrease, causing few steganographic traces of the stego can not be optimized effectively. On the other hand, if T becomes lower than 30dB, stego will be added too many disturbances, which part of them becomes new traces for steganalysis. In Fig. 3(b), as the frame length decreases, the undetectability increases dramatically. This means that as the JS divergence measurement range decreases, the difference between frames is amplified more obviously. This helps to zoom the differences between different frames, and makes selecting suitable disturbances more easily. However, notably, if the fl is too low (i.e. lower than 1ms, for TIMIT, it is 16 bits), the running time will increase.

In general, we believe that when T is between 25 and 45 dB, our proposed method has a better optimization performance. As well as fl is the integer divisor of the cover sampling rate.

Undetectability Performance

After embedding data into MUSIC and TIMIT audio cover, we use the proposed method (where, $fl_{timit} = 30, fl_{music} = 63, T = 30$) to process the steganographic traces of the stego. To test the undetectability of the post-stego, we used two steganalysis methods to run the experiment. However, the CNN-based steganalysis method cannot detect effectively. The detection accuracy rates for stego and post-stego are all 49.12% (on TIMIT) or 50.25% (on MUSIC), without any fluctuations. One possible reason is that the message is embedded in the high-value areas. Due to the large amplitude, the cover-to-message ratio becomes extremely low. This makes the steganographic traces very imperceptible and invalidates the CNN-based steganalysis.

For the feature-based (i.e. MFCCF) steganalysis, despite the detection capability is normal, one can easily see the trend of change, which proves the effectiveness of the proposed method. The result can be seen in Table 1, where presents the error rates of the steganalysis. It can be seen that in most cases, the proposed method has better performance. The optimization ability can reach up to twice of Chen's maximum.

Table 1. Experimental results of the proposed model on two audio databases. The upper half of the table uses the simulator to embed, and the lower half uses LSBm. We compare the undetectability of the stego and two post-stegos (Chen's method and our JSD model). Bold text indicates the best performance.

Payload (bps)	MUSIC			TIMIT		
	Simulator	Chen's	JSD model	Simulator	Chen's	JSD model
0.1	49.90	49.93	**50.01**	46.39	46.61	**46.77**
0.2	49.33	**49.67**	49.63	46.44	46.78	**46.81**
0.3	48.80	49.53	**49.55**	46.57	46.77	**46.91**
0.4	48.40	49.24	**49.55**	46.33	46.69	**46.88**
0.5	48.00	48.97	**49.42**	46.25	**46.67**	46.55
Payload	LSBm	Chen's	JSD model	LSBm	Chen's	JSD model
0.6	53.06	52.87	**53.12**	47.13	47.24	**47.53**
0.7	52.42	52.51	**52.76**	46.18	46.51	**46.68**
0.8	51.35	51.67	**51.97**	45.48	45.49	**45.74**
0.9	51.09	51.10	**51.31**	44.14	44.25	**44.56**
1.0	50.49	50.54	**50.76**	43.09	43.36	**43.56**

We believe the reason is that our method is better at measuring the location and the effect of the disturbance. As a followed example (one TIMIT audio clip, under 1.0bps) illustrates, in Fig. 4, the added disturbances are in the complex areas (Fig. 4(b)). Due to the SNR threshold T, our model selects a more suitable location and size of the disturbance. Meanwhile, the proposed method ensures that the JS divergence of the post-stego and cover is closer, after adding the disturbance. For residual signal performance (compare Fig. 4(d) and Fig. 4(e)), the residuals of our post-stego and the original cover are smoother.

Quality of Post-processed Audio Stegos
We compared the perceived audio quality of all post-stegos generated in the last experiment. The result can be seen in Table 2, the ODG scores of the proposed method are more substantial than Chen's. However, there is a unique phenomenon. After simulator embedding and post-processing, no matter what

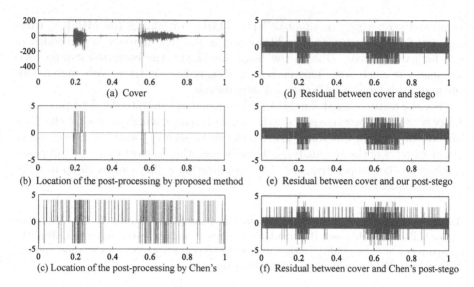

Fig. 4. Comparison of the details of the two methods. (a) is the original cover. (b) is our location of the added disturbance. (c) is Chen's location of the added disturbance. (d) is the residual of stego and cover. (e) is the residual of cover and our post-stego. (f) is the residual of cover and Chen's post-stego. For all subgraphs, the horizontal coordinate is time, and the vertical coordinate is the magnitude of the sampling value.

kind of post-processing, the ODG scores of post-stego are displayed the same on each payload. We believe that this is due to the simulator, the number of changed elements is limited, and those elements mainly concentrate on complex areas of the audio. Therefore, after steganographic traces optimization, the differences of all post-stegos and covers tend to be consistent, under each payload, in both Chen's and our evaluation systems.

4.3   Limitation and Cost

In [1], Chen *et al.*. used image as steganographic cover, and modified some specific values of the stego to enhance the undetectability of the message in image cover. According to the experimental results, we can find that under $0.5-0.1$bpp payloads, the undetectability (error rate) has increased from 40.19%, 31.71%, 25.75%, 20.72%, 16.94% to 40.39%, 32.00%, 26.41%, 21.73%, 17.88%, respectively. (with SRM and maxSRMd2 features, ensemble classifier.) One can see that the undetectability has only increased by about $0.2 - 0.8\%$. In the field of the audio, as shown in Table 1, we are facing the same problem. Through analysis, we believe that a possible limitation is: the post-processing can not change the **sensitive areas** where the message is embedded, which determines the upper limit of the optimization capability. Since these "real traces" (i.e. costs after embedding) have not been completely eliminated, the undetectability is inevitably improved slightly.

Table 2. The perceived audio quality of all post-stegos. The upper half of the table uses the simulator to embed, and the lower half uses LSBm. Bold text indicates the best performance.

Payload (bps)	Simulator			
	MUSIC		TIMIT	
	Chen's	JSD model	Chen's	JSD model
0.1	0.1470	**0.1478**	0.1570	**0.1588**
0.2	0.1470	**0.1478**	0.1571	**0.1587**
0.3	0.1469	**0.1478**	0.1571	**0.1588**
0.4	0.1470	**0.1478**	0.1571	**0.1587**
0.5	0.1470	**0.1478**	0.1571	**0.1587**
Payload	LSBm			
	Chen's	JSD model	Chen's	JSD model
0.6	0.1500	**0.1514**	0.1608	**0.1614**
0.7	0.1476	**0.1490**	0.1571	**0.1583**
0.8	0.1454	**0.1467**	0.1547	**0.1554**
0.9	0.1431	**0.1445**	0.1512	**0.1521**
1.0	0.1411	**0.1424**	0.1476	**0.1485**

The steganography post-processing proposed in this paper requires some time costs from steganographers (the time complexity of the algorithm has been discussed in Subsect. 3.2, which is acceptable). There is no additional cost for the message extractor because this method will not change the area of embedding-used cover. The threshold T guarantees that the modified sampling points in the proposed post-processing method will not interfere with the transmission and extraction of embedded messages.

5 Conclusion

In this paper, we propose an audio steganography post-processing method to optimize the steganographic traces by enhancing JS divergence between cover and stego. In three experiments, we test our proposed method with several different SNR thresholds and frame lengths to illustrate the impacts of these parameters on the performance of our method. We also evaluate it on music and speech, respectively, with two widely-used steganography methods. Experimental results prove that the proposed method is very promising to improve the undetectability and reduce steganographic traces. However, meanwhile, we analyze the limitation of the existing post-processing methods. For future works, several essential issues in post-processing are worthing further researching, such as reducing the steganographic traces in sensitive areas and combining with Generative Adversarial Network (or Adversarial Samples) for learning the location and strategy of the disturbance addition. Furthermore, it is expected that the proposed method can be extended to compressed audio steganography.

Acknowledgments. This work was supported by the National Natural Science Foundation of China (Grant No. U1736215, 61672302, 61901237), Zhejiang Natural Science Foundation (Grant No. LY20F020010, LY17F020010), Ningbo Natural Science Foundation (Grant No. 2019A610103) and K.C. Wong Magna Fund in Ningbo University.

References

1. Chen, B., Luo, W., Zheng, P.: Enhancing steganography via stego post-processing by reducing image residual difference. In: Proceedings of the ACM Workshop on Information Hiding and Multimedia Security, pp. 63–68 (2019)
2. Chen, K., Zhou, H., Li, W., Yang, K., Zhang, W., Yu, N.: Derivative-based steganographic distortion and its non-additive extensions for audio. IEEE Trans. Circuits Syst. Video Technol. **30**, 2027–2032 (2019)
3. Filler, T., Judas, J., Fridrich, J.: Minimizing additive distortion in steganography using syndrome-trellis codes. IEEE Trans. Inf. Forensics Secur. **6**(3), 920–935 (2011)
4. Gong, C., Yi, X., Zhao, X.: Pitch delay based adaptive steganography for AMR speech stream. In: Yoo, C.D., Shi, Y.-Q., Kim, H.J., Piva, A., Kim, G. (eds.) IWDW 2018. LNCS, vol. 11378, pp. 275–289. Springer, Cham (2019). https://doi.org/10.1007/978-3-030-11389-6_21
5. Holub, V., Fridrich, J.: Designing steganographic distortion using directional filters. In: 2012 IEEE International Workshop on Information Forensics and Security (WIFS), pp. 234–239. IEEE (2012)
6. Holub, V., Fridrich, J.: Digital image steganography using universal distortion. In: Proceedings of the first ACM workshop on Information Hiding and Multimedia Security, pp. 59–68. ACM (2013)
7. Li, B., Tan, S., Wang, M., Huang, J.: Investigation on cost assignment in spatial image steganography. IEEE Trans. Inf. Forensics Secur. **9**(8), 1264–1277 (2014)
8. Lin, Y., Wang, R., Yan, D., Dong, L., Zhang, X.: Audio steganalysis with improved convolutional neural network. In: Proceedings of the ACM Workshop on Information Hiding and Multimedia Security, pp. 210–215. ACM (2019)
9. Luo, W., Li, H., Yan, Q., Yang, R., Huang, J.: Improved audio steganalytic feature and its applications in audio forensics. ACM Trans. Multimedia Comput. Commun. Appl. (TOMM) **14**(2), 43 (2018)
10. Luo, W., Zhang, Y., Li, H.: Adaptive audio steganography based on advanced audio coding and syndrome-trellis coding. In: Kraetzer, C., Shi, Y.-Q., Dittmann, J., Kim, H.J. (eds.) IWDW 2017. LNCS, vol. 10431, pp. 177–186. Springer, Cham (2017). https://doi.org/10.1007/978-3-319-64185-0_14
11. Menéndez, M., Pardo, J., Pardo, L., Pardo, M.: The jensen-shannon divergence. J. Franklin Inst. **334**(2), 307–318 (1997)
12. Mielikainen, J.: LSB matching revisited. IEEE Signal Process. Lett. **13**(5), 285–287 (2006)
13. Pevný, T., Filler, T., Bas, P.: Using high-dimensional image models to perform highly undetectable steganography. In: Böhme, R., Fong, P.W.L., Safavi-Naini, R. (eds.) IH 2010. LNCS, vol. 6387, pp. 161–177. Springer, Heidelberg (2010). https://doi.org/10.1007/978-3-642-16435-4_13

14. Recommendation, ITUR: Methods for objective measurements of perceived audio quality. ITU-R BS, vol. 13871 (2001)
15. Sedighi, V., Cogranne, R., Fridrich, J.: Content-adaptive steganography by minimizing statistical detectability. IEEE Trans. Inf. Forensics Secur. $11(2)$, 221–234 (2015)
16. Thiede, T., et al.: PEAQ-the ITU standard for objective measurement of perceived audio quality. J. Audio Eng. Soc. $48(1/2)$, 3–29 (2000)
17. Yi, X., Yang, K., Zhao, X., Wang, Y., Yu, H.: Ahcm: Adaptive huffman codemapping for audio steganography based on psychoacoustic model. IEEE Trans. Inf. Forensics Secur. 14, 2217–2231 (2019)

Steganalysis of Adaptive Steganography Under the Known Cover Image

Jialin Li, Xiangyang Luo$^{(\boxtimes)}$, Yi Zhang, Pei Zhang, Chunfang Yang, and Fenlin Liu

State Key Laboratory of Mathematical Engineering and Advanced Computing,
Zhengzhou, China
jlli233@163.com, {luoxy_ieu,tzyy4001}@sina.com, 991378175@qq.com,
chunfangyang@126.com, liufenlin@vip.sina.com

Abstract. Digital image steganography is one of the important ways to achieve covert communication to protect users' data privacy. Steganalysis technology is the key technology to check the security of steganography, and the extraction of embedded messages is an important challenge for image steganalysis technology. Existing methods are for plain text embedding or only for certain special scenarios, they are not applicable to the extraction under the known cover image. To this end, this paper proposes a method of extracting embedded messages under the condition of the known cover images. First, the STCs encoding process is analyzed using the syndrome trellis. Second, a path in the syndrome trellis can be obtained by using the stego sequence and a certain parity-check matrix. Meanwhile, the embedding process can also be partially simulated using the cover sequence and the parity-check matrix. By comparing whether the paths are consistent, the coding parameters can be quickly filtered to find the correct submatrices and extract the correct embedded messages. This algorithm avoids the second embedding of all possible secret messages, which significantly improves the efficiency of coding parameter recognition. The experimental results show that the proposed method can identify STCs parameters of stego images using HUGO steganography in a short time, so as to realize the extraction of embedded messages.

Keywords: Information security · Image steganography · STC coding · Parameter recognition

1 Introduction

In the Internet era, the development of information technology and the advancement of digital multimedia have made the interaction on the network increasingly frequent and convenient, and also brought many challenges to information security and privacy protection. As one of the important means to protect information security, information hiding techniques [1] have received more and more attention. The digital steganography technology [2] is to embed secret data into the redundant signal of the public digital multimedia file, and transmit it through the public channel, so as not to be discovered by third parties. With the rapid development of social media, people are increasingly keen to

© Springer Nature Singapore Pte Ltd. 2020
S. Yu et al. (Eds.): SPDE 2020, CCIS 1268, pp. 560–574, 2020.
https://doi.org/10.1007/978-981-15-9129-7_39

share texts, pictures, videos on social platforms. Compared to the traditional encryption of text, which is easy to detect and the operation of video encryption is complex, hiding the secret messages in the picture is a better choice. Sometimes, in order to facilitate operation and not to cause suspicion, users would choose the pictures already on the Internet as a carrier, embed secret messages in it and transfer them on the network, so as to realize secret communication.

Image steganography technology includes spatial domain steganography algorithm and frequency domain steganography algorithm. The spatial steganography algorithm implements message embedding by changing the pixel value of the image, while the frequency domain steganography algorithm embeds secret messages in the transform domain (such as DCT and DWT domain). In traditional steganography algorithms, the change caused by the modification of different elements of the carrier is regarded as the same. With the development of image steganography, people gradually realize that the influence caused by changing the carrier image elements in different positions is different. It is more difficult to find the hidden information in the region with complex texture. The image adaptive steganography algorithm came into being. It uses the distortion function combined with steganography coding mode to realize the embedding and extraction of secret information, and the detection resistance has been improved. The fast and universal syndrome-trellis codes (STCs) proposed by Filler et al. [3] is a coding method that can find an embedded path theoretically close to the optimal boundary, and is widely used in adaptive steganography algorithms. Representative spatial adaptive steganography algorithms include HUGO [4], WOW [5], S-UNIWARD [6], HILL [7], MiPOD [8] etc., whose distortion functions are defined based on pixels. Frequency domain adaptive steganography algorithms include MOD [9], UED [10], UERD [11], J-UNIWARD [6], etc., whose distortion is usually defined on the DCT coefficients.

The adaptive steganography algorithm defines different distortion values for different carrier elements according to the characteristics of the image. STCs provides a method to find the best stego sequence when the distortion is minimum. STCs weakens the relationship between secret messages and stego images, while achieving minimum global distortion, high efficiency and good results. The parameters of STCs are very important. The recipient can easily extract the secret information using the encoding parameters, which also means that once the attacker gets the encoding parameters, the secret information will be exposed. Due to the change of the embedding method, most of the extraction methods for traditional image steganography algorithms are no longer applicable to stego images with adaptive image steganography. At present, there are few publicly published methods for extracting embedded information for adaptive image steganography. A theoretical method of STCs encoding key recovery in two special scenarios is proposed [12]. One is when there are a large number of stego images with the same size and the same embedded key, and their corresponding message sequences. The other is when there are stego images with the same size, the same embedded messages and the same embedded key. Ref. [13] proposes a method for parameter identification of STCs when the embedded information is plain text. This method is based on the non-randomness of plain text messages. By exhausting the submatrix, the correctness of the coding parameters is judged according to the randomness of possible secret obtained by different submatrices. Therefore, when the embedded message is encrypted, the randomness of the ciphertext and the randomness of the error messages cannot be distinguished, making this extraction method ineffective. Ref. [14] proposed a method of information extraction under the condition that some information is known. The structural characteristics of the parity-check matrix in STCs are analyzed, and the same deformation of the matrix operation is used to simplify the decoding equation. The unknown and relatively complex matrix is transformed into a column vector that is easy to solve. Combined with a good code judgment standard, the impossible submatrix is eliminated to avoid exhaustive traversal of the submatrix, which improves the efficiency of identifying STCs parameters.

Since the methods in the existing literature are for plain text embedding or only for certain special scenarios, they are not applicable to the extraction under the known cover image. Nowadays, the emergence of image search engines makes "searching for pictures" become a reality. We can find other pictures similar to it by searching for a picture. Considering that two communicating parties will use public images on the Internet as cover images, it is possible for an attacker to obtain the cover images. Moreover, if the attacker intercepts the image library of the communicator and obtains the carrier image, the secret communication will no longer be secure. Figure 1 shows the communication process. Therefore, in order to achieve better and safer secret communication, it is necessary to study the extraction of secret information when the cover image is known. Under the condition that the cover image is known, we take HUGO as an example to study the secret information extraction of the adaptive steganography algorithm embedded in plaintext and ciphertext. Since the adaptive steganography algorithm reduces the relevance of secret messages and some elements in the stego sequence, the embedded messages are related to each stego elements. Therefore, despite that the cover image is known, we know the fact that the two parties communicate secretly, it is still very difficult to extract the embedded messages in the stego image. In such a scenario, through the research on the distortion function and the STC encoding process, we realize the fast and effective encoding parameter identification of the dense image, then extract the embedded secret information.

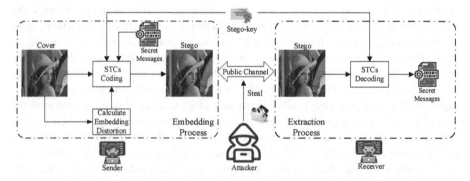

Fig. 1. Schematic diagram of stealth communication with adaptive steganography.

The rest of this paper is organized as follows. In Sect. 2, the basic principles and encoding process of STCs are introduced. Section 3 elaborates on the algorithm of STCs parameter identification and the main steps under the known conditions of the carrier image. Section 4 gives the experimental results and analysis of STCs parameter identification are presented. Finally, the paper is concluded in Sect. 5.

2 STCs Method

2.1 Basic Principles of STCs

Classic spatial image steganography algorithm realizes the embedding of secret messages by modifying the pixel value of the cover image, while adaptive steganography is to adaptively select an appropriate position according to the content of the cover image and embed it in combination with coding. When the original cover image is known, for the traditional steganography algorithm, a partial secret message can be determined by comparing pixel values. When the keyspace is given, the steganographic key can be uniquely determined as long as there are enough pixels modified. For the adaptive steganography algorithm, instead of simply matching and replacing pixel values, it is implemented using STCs, so that the embedded messages are related to all stego images pixels. Therefore, when extracting a message, we need to find the relationship among the original cover image, the stego image, and the embedded messages.

In recent years, due to the high efficiency and good performance of STCs, spatial adaptive steganography algorithms such as HUGO, WOW, S-UNIWARD, HILL, and JPEG domain adaptive steganography algorithms such as MOD, UED, UERD, J-UNIWARD, etc. use different distortion functions combined with STCs [3] to achieve the embedding and extraction of secret messages. The cover sequence is defined as $x = (x_1, x_2, \cdots, x_n) \in \{0, 1\}^n$, the secret sequence $y = (y_1, y_2, \cdots, y_n) \in \{0, 1\}^n$, and $\mathbf{m}$ are the secret messages to be embedded. The process of STCs encoding and decoding is shown in formulas (1) and (2):

$$Emb(\mathbf{x}, \mathbf{m}) = \arg \min_{\mathbf{y} \in C(\mathbf{m})} D(\mathbf{x}, \mathbf{y}) \tag{1}$$

$$\mathbf{m} = Ext(\mathbf{y}) = \mathbf{Hy} \tag{2}$$

where $D(\mathbf{x}, \mathbf{y})$ is the embedding distortion function. $C(\mathbf{m}) = \{\mathbf{z} \in \{0, 1\}^n | \mathbf{Hz} = \mathbf{m}\}$ is the coset of the embedded messages, and $\mathbf{H} \in \{0, 1\}^{m \times n}$ is the parity-check matrix. It can be seen that the process of STCs is to find a satisfying vector $\mathbf{Hy} = \mathbf{m}$ and minimize the embedding distortion $D(\mathbf{x}, \mathbf{y})$. The parity-check matrix $\mathbf{H}$ is formed by the sub-parity check matrix $\hat{\mathbf{H}}$ in row h and column w in order of main diagonal. The height and width of the submatrix are the size parameters of the code, and the values of the elements in the submatrix are the content parameters of the code. The secret sequence can be obtained by the Viterbi algorithm [3].

According to the principle of STC encoding, we can explain the encoding process shown in Fig. 2 as follows. First, the initial state is 00. Because of $\mathbf{Hy} = \mathbf{m}$, each row in the matrix H is respectively related to the embedded messages m = (m_1, m_2, m_3, m_4),

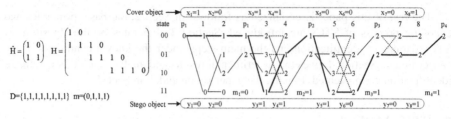

Fig. 2. STC coding process.

and every embedded message is related to each value of the stego sequence y. In this example, the solution process can be understood as follows:

If $y_1 = 0$, the equivalent is that 0 is respectively multiplied by the first column (11) of the submatrix to get the result (00). So the result (00) XOR with the initial state to get the corresponding temporary results of m_1 and m_2, that is, the state $m_2m_1 = 00$. If $y_1 = 1$, the equivalent is that 1 is respectively multiplied by the first column (11) of the submatrix to get the result (11). Similarly, the result (11) XOR with the initial state to get the corresponding temporary results of m_1 and m_2, that is, the state $m_2m_1 = 11$.

Then, under the condition of $y_1 = 0$, the current state is $m_2m_1 = 00$. If $y_2 = 0$, the equivalent is that 0 is respectively multiplied by the second column (01) of the submatrix to obtain the result (00) which XOR with the current state to get the new state $m_2m_1 = 00$. If $y_2 = 1$, 1 would be respectively multiplied by the second column (01) of the submatrix to obtain the result (01) which XOR with the current state to get the new state $m_2m_1 = 10$. Similarly, if $y_1 = 1$, the state $m_2m_1 = 11$ can be obtained when $y_2 = 0$ and the state $m_2m_1 = 01$ can be obtained when $y_2 = 1$.

Because y_1 and y_2 determine m_1 and $m_1 = 0$, we need to choose the corresponding state, so $m_2m_1 = 00$ and $m_2m_1 = 10$ are retained. The latter process is similar. Through this process, many paths and their corresponding distortions can be obtained. Finally, the state with the least distortion is selected for backtracking, and an optimal path with the smallest global distortion can be obtained.

It can be seen that if the stego sequence is known, a certain check matrix can be combined to obtain a path in the fence diagram. When this path happens to correspond to the path with the least distortion, the check matrix is the correct matrix corresponding to the original cover image. In other words, each cover sequence and the determined parity-check matrix will determine the only optimal route. This route corresponds to the stego image, and the route with the least distortion is the stego sequence y. From this we can determine whether a matrix is correct by judging whether a path is the best path.

2.2 STC Coding Parameter Identification

In the case of the known cover image, a conventional solution (Scheme 1) can naturally be thought of, as shown in Fig. 3. First of all, the submatrix is exhausted, and the matrix combined by the submatrix is multiplied by the stego sequence to obtain possible secret messages. Then, the possible secret messages are re-embedded into the original cover sequence to obtain a possible stego sequence. It is judged whether the submatrix is correct by comparing the possible stego sequence with the original stego sequence.

Through experiments, we found that this method takes more time. Because to obtain a possible secret sequence, it is equivalent to embedding the secret information every time.

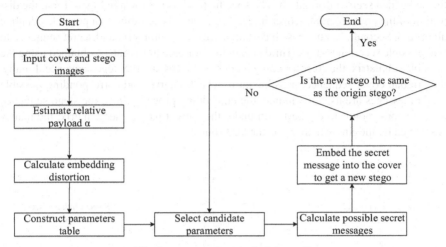

Fig. 3. A general method (Scheme 1).

Since the stego sequence can be obtained by the Viterbi algorithm, we consider the relationship between the original sequence and the stego sequence. The stego sequence corresponds to an optimal route in the fence diagram of the Viterbi algorithm, and the correct parity-check matrix can be identified by judging whether the sequence is the optimal route. So we considered the relationship between the original cover sequence and the stego sequence and found a faster method described in the next section. Therefore, it is possible to judge whether the submatrix is correct or not without obtaining all possible stego sequences by secondary embedding.

3 Proposed Method

Common adaptive steganography algorithms usually use the "distortion function + STCs" mode for embedding and extracting secret information. Different adaptive steganography algorithms have different methods of measuring the distortion function. In the communication process, both parties need to share two important parameters, STCs coding submatrix and the length of the embedded messages, to ensure that the receiver can correctly obtain the embedded secret messages. Since the height h and width w of the main parameters of the submatrix are limited, it is possible to construct a coding parameter table. By traversing the size parameters, and combining the stego sequence, we can obtain possible secret information.

In actual communication, the communicator may use some pictures published on the network to hide information, and the attacker may steal the communicator's image database to obtain the cover image. Therefore, we study the extraction of secret information under the condition that the cover image is known.

3.1 Method Principle and Main Steps

This method is based on the situation that the original cover image is known, by identifying the STC encoding parameters, recovering the encoding parameters and extracting the embedded secret information. The specific process is shown in Fig. 4. First, the distortion of the corresponding cover image is calculated according to a possible adaptive algorithm. Second, exhaust possible submatrices. Use submatrix and secret sequence to find possible secret messages. Third, a path in syndrome trellis can be obtained using the possible submatrix, the corresponding hidden messages and the stego sequence. Finally, the original cover sequence, possible parity-check matrix, and corresponding possible secret messages are used to emulate the embedding process. Since the stego sequence actually corresponds to the best path under the correct parity-check matrix, the matrix is selected by judging whether it is the best route.

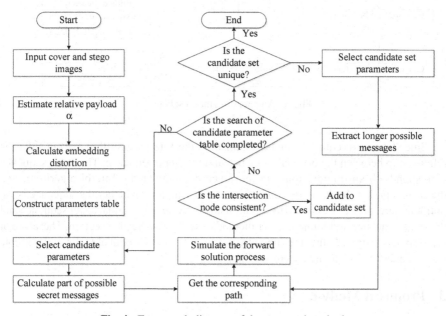

Fig. 4. Framework diagram of the proposed method.

The main steps of the algorithm are as follows:

Step 1: Read cover sequence and stego sequence. Read the cover image and the stego image, obtain the LSB of each pixel, and obtain the cover and the stego sequence.

Step 2: Estimate the length of embedded messages. The existing embedding estimation method in Ref. [15] is used to estimate the embedding rate of the image to be extracted, and then the length of the embedding information is calculated.

Step 3: Calculate image embedding distortion. Calculate the distortion corresponding to each pixel using the original cover image.

Step 4: Construct the coding parameter table. The value range of the code size parameter is determined according to the length of the embedded information, and the code size parameter table is constructed.

Step 5: Calculate some possible secret messages. Exhaustive submatrix, using submatrix and stego sequence to calculate some possible secret messages, such as 500bit.

Step 6: Get the corresponding path. Use the stego sequence and the submatrix to get a corresponding path.

Step 7: Simulate the forward solution process. Using the submatrix, part of the possible secret information, and the stego sequence, then paths for solving the stego sequence are obtained.

Step 8: Determine whether the submatrix is correct. At the intersection node, determine whether the corresponding path in step 6 is consistent with the path in step 7; if so, save the submatrix into set A, and if not, return to step 5.

Step 9: Exhausts the candidate set. Enumerate the matrix in A, extract longer possible embedded messages, and repeat steps 6 and 7.

3.2 Solving the Submatrix

STCs is used to solve the stego sequence which is implemented by the Viterbi algorithm. The following will show the feasibility of the proposed method through the analysis of this algorithm process.

The syndrome trellis in the above Fig. 5 shows the path of the correct stego sequence obtained under the correct parity-check matrix. Assume the cover sequence $x = \{1, 0, 1, 1, 0, 0, 0, 1\}$, the distortion $D = \{2, 1, 2, 1, 2, 1, 2, 1\}$ of each pixel, the secret information $m = \{0, 1, 1, 1\}$, and the parity-check matrix H as shown above. The secret sequence $y = \{0, 0, 1, 1, 1, 0, 0, 1\}$ can be obtained. And the thick black line in the syndrome trellis shows the best path corresponding to the stego sequence.

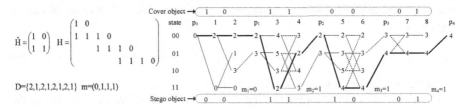

Fig. 5. Corresponding route when the check matrix is correct.

In Fig. 6, we assume another different submatrix H'. Using the submatrix H' and the secret sequence y, we can find the corresponding message m'. Combining the carrier image can simulate the embedding process. The distortion in the process is shown in Fig. 6 above. At the same time, using the submatrix H' and the stego sequence y can find a corresponding path in the syndrome trellis, which is indicated by the bold red line in the diagram. We can see that at the cross node at the red circle, the corresponding distortion on the bold black line should be 2. It shows that this path is not the best path corresponding to the parity-check matrix. Through such situation analysis, we find that only the correct parity-check matrix corresponds to the path and the path obtained by the correct solution matches.

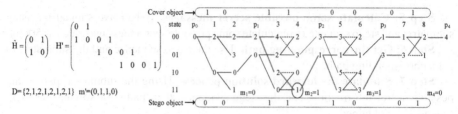

$$\hat{H} = \begin{pmatrix} 0 & 1 \\ 1 & 0 \end{pmatrix} \quad H' = \begin{pmatrix} 0 & 1 & & \\ 1 & 0 & 0 & 1 \\ & 1 & 0 & 0 & 1 \\ & & 1 & 0 & 0 & 1 \end{pmatrix}$$

D={2,1,2,1,2,1,2,1}   m'=(0,1,1,0)

Fig. 6. Corresponding route when the check matrix is wrong.

Therefore, we can use the cover sequence, a certain parity-check matrix and its corresponding partial possible secret information to simulate the embedding process, and then use the stego sequence and the same parity-check matrix to obtain a corresponding route in the syndrome trellis. At the intersection node, the correctness of the parity-check matrix is determined by judging whether the distortion of the state when embedded here is consistent with the distortion on the corresponding path.

3.3 Algorithm Complexity Analysis

This section will analyze the performance of this algorithm. When identifying STCs parameters, it is necessary to construct a coding parameter table according to the situation. For an estimated value of a certain embedding ratio, the search range of the sub-check matrix parameters is composed of all possible submatrices, including submatrices of various heights and widths. For a sub-check matrix with a height of h and a width of w, all possible value spaces $N = 2^{h*w}$. According to the experimental results in Ref. [3], a good sub-check matrix should satisfy that both the first row and the last row are 1 and any two columns are different. Therefore, the search range N can be expressed as:

$$N = 2^{(h-2)\cdot w} - 2^{h-2} \cdot (C_w^2 + C_w^3 + \cdots + C_w^w) \tag{3}$$

In the case of the known cover image, the time complexity of scheme 1 in the second section mainly lies in the complete solution process of STCs. We use a to denote the length of all secret messages, a' to denote the length of partial secret messages used in this article, b to represent the width of the submatrix, and c to represent the height of the submatrix. We can conclude that the time complexity of scheme 1 is $O(a \times b \times 2^c)$, and the time complexity of the method proposed in this paper is $O(a' \times b \times 2^c)$. We can see from the later experimental results that a' is much smaller than a, so the efficiency of the method in this paper has been improved.

4   Experimental Results and Analysis

In this chapter, the classic HUGO steganography is used to extract the secret messages. In order to verify the effectiveness of the algorithm, the following experiments are carried out. The experimental platform is window 7, Intel i7 processor, using C language programming, and the compiling platform is VS2015.

4.1 Generate Stego Image

In order to verify the feasibility of the extraction algorithm under the known cover image proposed in the article, the cover images in this experiment is from BossBase1.01 image library, and the ciphertext is chapters in "War and Peace" encrypted by the RC4 algorithm. When HUGO steganography is performed, it is assumed that the cover sequence is obtained from the cover image by sequentially obtaining the lowest bit of the pixel according to the line scanning method. The size of the cover and the stego image is 512 × 512, and the embedding rate of the stego image is $\alpha = 0.5$, that is, the number of embedded messages is 131072. The submatrix $\hat{H} = [109, 71]$ used is shown in Fig. 7 whose height $h = 7$ and width $w = 2$. After the secret messages are embedded in the cover image shown in Fig. 8 (a), the stego image shown in Fig. 8 (c) is obtained.

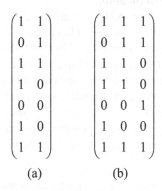

$$
\begin{pmatrix} 1 & 1 \\ 0 & 1 \\ 1 & 1 \\ 1 & 0 \\ 0 & 0 \\ 1 & 0 \\ 1 & 1 \end{pmatrix}
\qquad
\begin{pmatrix} 1 & 1 & 1 \\ 0 & 1 & 1 \\ 1 & 1 & 0 \\ 1 & 1 & 0 \\ 0 & 0 & 1 \\ 1 & 0 & 0 \\ 1 & 1 & 1 \end{pmatrix}
$$

(a)   (b)

Fig. 7. Submatrix used in the experiment.

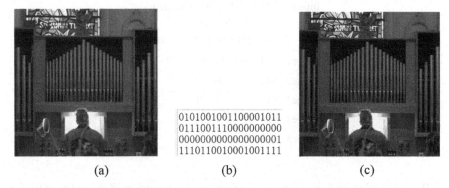

(a)   (b)   (c)

Fig. 8. Cover image, secret messages, stego image.

4.2 STC Encoding Parameter Identification and Message Extraction

When the cover image is known, the STCs parameter identification is based on the relationship between the cover image and the stego image. The correct coding parameter is identified according to the difference in the route in the syndrome trellis. When search-ing for STCs parameters, the range of the embedding ratio must be estimated first, and then the submatrix search begins. The following describes the process of STC encoding parameter identification and the extraction process and feasibility of embedded secret information. According to the recognition step in Sect. 3.1, first, read in the image to be detected and the length of its embedded information. Second, according to the estimated length of the embedded messages, a code size parameter table is constructed. Then, the submatrix is exhausted, and some possible embedded messages are calculated. Use the possible embedded messages and stego sequence to get the path in the syndrome trellis. Then, part of the possible embedded messages is used to simulate the embedding cover sequence. Finally, judge the correctness of the submatrix at the intersection node.

STC Coding Parameter Identification.
When the cover image is known, STCs parameters can be identified by the method in this paper. When the length of the possible embedded messages extracted is short, sometimes multiple possible submatrices are identified, but there must be a correct sub-check matrix. At this time, we can add multiple possible submatrices to the candidate set, and continue to extract longer messages for the submatrix in the candidate set. The length of the extracted partial secret information is different, and the number of identified submatrices is different. We randomly selected 5 pictures in the BossBase1.01 image library, for testing. For a single image, the number of possible submatrix parameters that can be identified by different lengths is shown in Table 1 below, and Fig. 9 is drawn.

Table 1. The number of submatrices identified for the secret information of different lengths in a single image.

Image	The length of the extracted possible messages					
	100	200	300	400	500	600
image1	284	76	14	5	2	1
image2	342	65	30	7	2	1
image3	117	3	1	1	1	1
image4	184	25	1	1	1	1
image5	113	12	4	1	1	1

We can see that for a single image, the number of submatrices identified by extracting embedded messages of different lengths is different. When the length of the extracted embedded messages is 400, the range of the sub-check matrix has been greatly reduced. When the length of the extracted embedded messages is 600, a unique sub-check matrix can be identified. Based on the above foundation, we randomly select 3000 pictures in the BossBase1.01 image library. When the lengths of the extracted possible embedded messages are 500, 600, 700, 800, 900, and 1000, respectively, the number of images that the identified sub-check matrix is not unique is as follows (Table 2).

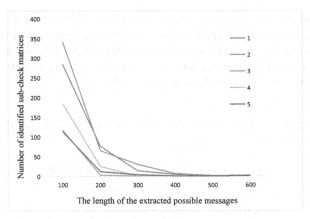

Fig. 9. The number of submatrices identified for the secret information of different lengths in a single image.

Table 2. Number of images with unique identification parameters when extracting secret information of different lengths.

Payload (bpp)	The length of the extracted possible messages					
	500	600	700	800	900	1000
0.50	209	53	10	0	0	0

According to the experimental results, we can find that after the exhaustive sub-check matrix obtains possible embedded messages, most pictures (93%) can use the first 500 bits of possible messages to uniquely determine the sub-check matrix. The range is greatly reduced. If the first 800 bit possible messages are used, all the pictures can uniquely determine the sub-check matrix. By analyzing the situation where the identified parameters are not unique, we find that the identified parameters are unique only when there is a pixel with less distortion after the changed pixel. Considering the actual situation, this situation certainly exists. The distortion distribution of each pixel is fluctuating, so the method in this paper is feasible in reality. In the general scheme 1 shown in Fig. 3, all 131072 bit possible messages need to be embedded in the cover image for comparison. By contrast, the efficiency of the proposed algorithm is greatly improved. At the same time, the method in this paper is also applicable to encrypted information, because it has nothing to do with message encryption or not.

STC Coding Parameter Recognition Efficiency
When the cover image is known, the submatrix needs to be searched for STCs parameter identification, which is very time-consuming. The proposed method in this paper avoids re-embedding all possible embedded messages obtained after exhausting the sub-check matrix into the cover image to judge whether the sub-check matrix is correct. Using part of the possible embedded messages can greatly reduce the range of the candidate

matrix, and the efficiency is greatly improved. The reason is that the method proposed in this paper can use one percent of all possible embedded messages to identify STCs parameters, avoiding the calculation of re-embedding all possible messages. When the proposed method in this paper uses 800-bit possible messages for identification, the time comparison between the two methods is shown in Table 3.

Table 3. Average time required to extract all possible messages and identify STC encoding parameters (unit: seconds).

Payload (bpp)	Scheme1	Proposed method
0.35	944973.78	72528.90
0.40	944973.94	72529.70
0.45	944974.56	72529.06
0.50	10.78	2.87

Compare the embedded messages extraction method proposed in this paper and the methods of Ref. [12–14] in 3 cases (Plaintext embedded, ciphertext embedded with partially known information, ciphertext with the known cover image). The extraction performance is compared and shown in Table 4. Among them, $\sqrt{}$ means that the extraction method has this ability, while $\times$ means that the extraction method does not have this ability. The comparison results show that only the proposed method can realize the extraction of plaintext and ciphertext of adaptive steganography under the condition that the cover image is known.

Table 4. Applicability of different extraction algorithms.

	Plaintext embedded	Ciphertext embedded	
		Partially known plaintext	The cover image is known
Method in [12]	$\times$	$\times$	$\times$
Method in [13]	$\sqrt{}$	$\times$	$\times$
Method in [14]	$\sqrt{}$	$\sqrt{}$	$\times$
Proposed method	$\sqrt{}$	$\times$	$\sqrt{}$

5 Conclusion

For the scene where the cover image is known, this paper proposes an adaptive steganography information extraction algorithm, based on the characteristics of the STC encoding process and the relationship between the cover and stego image. The correct parity-check matrix and stego sequence correspond to the best path in the syndrome trellis. The possible embedded messages are obtained through the exhaustive sub-check matrix, corresponding to a path in the syndrome trellis. Then embed part of the possible embedded messages into the cover sequence, and judge the correctness of the sub-check matrix at the cross node. It avoids the low efficiency caused by the second embedding of all possible embedded messages, so that the coding parameters can be quickly and effectively identified, and then the embedded messages can be extracted. However, when the embedding ratio is low, the time consumption caused by the exhaustive matrix is still very large. How to further compress the solution space of the sub-check matrix according to the characteristics of the encoding to better improve the efficiency is our future research direction.

Acknowledgement. This work was supported by the National Natural Science Foundation of China (No. U1804263, 61772549).

References

1. Wayner, P.: Disappearing Cryptography: Information Hiding: Steganography and Watermarking. Morgan Kaufmann, Burlington (2009)
2. Cheddad, A., Condell, J., Curran, K., et al.: Digital image steganography: survey and analysis of current methods. Sig. Process. **90**(3), 727–752 (2010)
3. Filler, T, Judas, J, Fridrich, J.: Minimizing embedding impact in steganography using trelliscoded quantization. In: Proceedings of SPIE, Media Forensics and Security II[C], SPIE 7541, pp. 0501–0514 (2010)
4. Pevný, T., Filler, T., Bas, P.: Using high-dimensional image models to perform highly undetectable steganography. In: Böhme, R., Fong, P.W.L., Safavi-Naini, R. (eds.) IH 2010. LNCS, vol. 6387, pp. 161–177. Springer, Heidelberg (2010). https://doi.org/10.1007/978-3-642-16435-4_13
5. Holub, V., Fridrich, J.: Designing steganographic distortion using directional filters. In: Proceedings of the 4th IEEE International Workshop on Information Forensics and Security, pp. 234–239 (2012)
6. Holub, V., Fridrich, J.: Digital image steganography using universal distortion. In: Proceedings of the 1st ACM Information Hiding and Multimedia Security Workshop, pp. 59–68 (2013)
7. Li, B., Wang, M., Huang, J., et al.: A new cost functions for spatial image steganography. In: Proceeding of 21st IEEE International Conference on Image Processing, pp. 4206–4210 (2014)
8. Sedighi, V., Cogranne, R., Fridrich, J.: Content-adaptive steganography by minimizing statistical detectability. IEEE Trans. Inf. Forensics Secur. **11**(2), 221–234 (2016)
9. Filler, T., Fridrich, J.: Design of adaptive steganographic schemes for digital images. In: Proceedings of SPIE, Electronic Imaging, Media Watermarking, Security, and Forensics XIII, SPIE 7880, pp. 0F01–0F14 (2011)
10. Guo, L., Ni, J., Shi, Y.Q.: An efficient JPEG steganographic scheme using uniform embedding. In: Proceedings of the 4th IEEE International Workshop on Information Forensics and Security, pp. 169–174 (2012)
11. Guo, L., Ni, J., Su, W., et al.: Using statistical image model for jpeg steganography: uniform embedding revisited. IEEE Trans. Inf. Forensics Secur. **10**(12), 2669–2680 (2015)
12. Liu, W., Liu, G., Dai, Y.: On recovery of the stego-key in syndrome-trellis codes. Innov. Comput. Inf. Control Express Lett. **8**(10), 2901–2906 (2014)

13. Luo, X., Song, X., Li, X., et al.: Steganalysis of HUGO steganography based on parameter recognition of syndrome-trellis-codes. Multimedia Tools Appl. **75**(21), 13557–13583 (2016)
14. Gan, J., Liu, J., Luo, X., et al.: Reliable steganalysis of HUGO steganography based on partially known plaintext. Multimedia Tools Appl. **8**, 1–21 (2017)
15. Kodovský, J., Fridrich, J.: Quantitative steganalysis using rich models. In: Proceedings of SPIE, Electronic Imaging, Media Watermarking, Security and Forensic XV, SPIE 8665, pp. 86650O (2013)

Security Protocol

Improving Communication Efficiency for Encrypted Distributed Training

Minglu Zhang[1,2], Qixian Zhou[1], Shaopeng Liang[1], and Haomiao Yang[1,2(✉)]

[1] School of Computer Science, University of Electronic Science and Technology of China,
Chengdu 611731, China
haomyang@uestc.edu.cn
[2] State Key Laboratory of Cryptology, P.O. Box 5159, Beijing 100878, China

Abstract. Secure Multi-Party Computation (SMPC) is usually treated as a special encryption way. Unlike most encryption methods using a private or public key to encrypt data, it splits a value into different shares, and each share works like a private key. Only get all these shares, we can get the original data correctly. In this paper, we utilize SMPC to protect the privacy of gradient updates in distributed learning, where each client computes an update and shares their updates by encrypting them so that no information about the clients' data can be leaked through the whole computing process. However, encryption brings a sharp increase in communication cost. To improve the training efficiency, we apply gradient sparsification to compress the gradient by sending only the important gradients. In order to improve the accuracy and efficiency of the model, we also make some improvements to the original sparsification algorithm. Extensive experiments show that the amount of data that needs to be transferred is reduced while the model still achieves 99.6% accuracy on the MNIST dataset.

Keywords: Distributed training · Secure Multi-Party Computation · Gradient compression

1 Introduction

Distributed training enables larger datasets and more complex models [1] which allows multiple participants to train a model, each with its local dataset. Each participant trains a local model on each round and sends the updates to the server to construct the global model. However, recent evidence reveals that private information can be leaked by the process of transferring updates. Notable examples include collecting periodic updates and use Data Representatives (DR) and Generative Adversarial Network (GAN) to recover the original data [1] and inferring unintended feature from a malicious participant [2]. While training a model through different participants, there is inevitable exist malicious attackers, to protect the privacy of each participant, preventive action must be done in advance. Since some prior work has been done to protect the privacy in machine learning [3–7] using Secure Multi-Party Computation, but we notice that the communication cost can be high, since after encryption, larger amounts of data need to be transferred.

© Springer Nature Singapore Pte Ltd. 2020
S. Yu et al. (Eds.): SPDE 2020, CCIS 1268, pp. 577–590, 2020.
https://doi.org/10.1007/978-981-15-9129-7_40

For simplicity, we consider synchronized algorithms for encrypted distributed training where a typical round consists of the following steps:

1. A subset of the participants is selected, and each participant downloads the global model from the server.
2. Each participant locally computes the gradient updates based on its dataset.
3. The encrypted gradient updates are computed and sent from the participants to the server
4. The server aggregates the encrypted updates and applies the updates to the global model using stochastic gradient descent (SGD).

A bottleneck of the whole training process is internet connection speeds, and that extends the communication time. We especially notice that the uplink speed is much slower than the download speed. For example, the fixed broadband of the global [8] was 74.4Mbps download vs. 40.0Mbps upload, while China Telecom's average broadband speed was 79.4Mbps download vs. 30.5Mbps upload (speedtest.net, 2020). Besides, prior work [9] has been done to reduce the bandwidth necessary to download the current model.

In this paper, we focus on improving upload communication efficiency with encrypted data. Gradient Sparsification reduces the upload communication cost by compressing the gradients, as shown in Fig. 1. In this case, we only select a small percentage of the gradients for uploading. Besides, our experiment proves that Gradient Sparsification also plays a great role in protecting the data privacy, since less information can be leaked during the training process. But compressing the upload gradients reduces the performance of the model, so in our model we have added three methods to improve the performance and efficiency. Besides, we also evaluate and analyze the impact on the performance and efficiency of different methods.

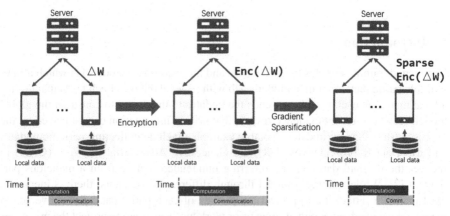

Fig. 1. Gradient Sparsification reduces the communication cost and finally improve the training efficiency.

2 Related Work

Many studies have been done to improve the communication efficiency. To reduce the upload bandwidth demand, the most common method is to compress the gradient before sending it to the server. In this paper, we summarize three methods of gradient compression.

Low Rank. The basic idea for gradient compression using low rank is to enforce every update of the local model $M \in \mathbb{R}^{n \times m}$ and express M as the product of the two matrices: $M = PQ^\top$, where $P \in \mathbb{R}^{n \times r}$ and $Q \in \mathbb{R}^{m \times r}$. In subsequent computation, Q is initialized from an i.i.d. standard normal distribution [10]. Through this method, we only need to send P and Q instead of M and can get a similar result while saving n/r in communication since Q can be compressed in the form of a random seed [11].

Probabilistic Quantization. Instead of splitting the update into two matrices, there is another method for gradient compression. Jakub et al. [11] introduced an algorithm of quantizing each update scalar to one bit. One can also generalize the update to more than 1 bit. Alistarh et al. [12] proposed QSGD which has lower bandwidth requirements and it is highly competitive with the full-precision variant.

Gradient Sparsification. Another method of compressing the updates is gradient sparsification. Jakub et al. [11] send the random mask and the values of the non-zero entries of the update gradients to reduce the data to be transferred. Lin et al. [13] proposed an algorithm named Deep Gradient Compression (DGC) which allows only sending the important gradients (sparse update) to reduce the communication cost. DGC can achieve the same accuracy as the original model with a high compression ratio using momentum correction and local gradient clipping.

Besides, we consider using distributed learning with synchronized gradient updates, since it reduces the computation time by separating the large dataset into many small subsets to different participants. During the training process, each participant downloads the current model and trains the updates based on the local dataset, then sends the encrypted update to the server for aggregation.

3 Problem Statement

In this section, we give the problem statement, including models and design goals.

3.1 System Model and Threat Model

Assume in the distributed training setting, there are N participants and an adversary server to collaboratively train a model, and one of the participants is the target for the adversary. The participants' main goal is to train a local update and sends it to the server in every iteration. And the server's main goal is to collect the updates from every participant and aggregates them for updating the current model. In this setting, we assume the server is semi-honest. The server updates the global model honestly but still wants to speculate on the dataset information of the target participant. There also exist some participants who are not the target. In this case, we have summarized the two major problems that need to be solved.

- The dataset information of all participants, including the gradient update in every iteration, must not be leaked without permission.
- Since the encrypting process increases the communication cost, corresponding solutions must be proposed to solve the problem.

3.2 Design Goals

The overarching goal is to do the distributed training efficiently while keeping the privacy of the participants. In this case, the following design goals need to be achieved.

- Accuracy. The final model should have high accuracy on the test dataset.
- Security. The security of the participants needs to be guaranteed. Since the malicious server can analyze the relevant privacy information through the gradient uploaded by the participants, the gradient of all participants needs to be effectively protected.
- Efficiency. The total training time and communication cost need to be limited.

4 Proposed Scheme

This section demonstrates the overview of our model and the privacy protecting scheme using Secure Multi-Party Computation (SMPC). To improve the performance, we also introduce a few methods and there will be a detailed explanation in the corresponding section.

4.1 Architecture Overview

Figure 2 briefly illustrates our architecture of gradient sparsification for protected updates. For the scenarios we propose, assume there are N participants in the distributed training scenarios, each of them owns a local private dataset. The participants are selected to jointly train a global model. To protect the privacy of the update gradients, we add a Secure Multi-Party Computation (SMPC) model to this architecture. Before sending the protected gradients, gradient sparsification is implemented for reducing the communication bandwidth demand by sending only the important gradients.

A detailed process of our gradient sparsification for privacy protected updates on a specific participant is shown in Algorithm 1. It calculates the local update G^k, then selects the location of the upload gradient according to the gradient ratio to be uploaded, and uploads the update after using SMPC model for privacy protection.

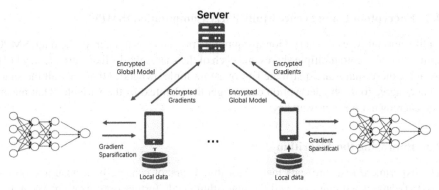

Fig. 2. The architecture of gradient sparsification for privacy protected updates

---

Algorithm 1 Gradient Sparsification for privacy protected updates on participant k

---

Input. Local dataset X
Input. The selected subset of the participants S
Input. The number of the participants in S is N
Input. Batch size b for each node
Input. Initial global parameters w_0

1.   initialize G^k
2.   **for** t = 0,1, ... T **do**
3.   **for** i = 1, ..., b **do**
4.   Sample data x from X
5. $G_t^k \leftarrow \frac{1}{Nb} \boxed{} f(x; w_t)$
6.   **end for**
7.   Select threshold: threshold $\leftarrow$ s% of $|G_t^k|$
8.   Mask $\leftarrow |G_t^k| >$ threshold
9. $G_t^k \leftarrow G_t^k \odot$ Mask
10.   Secure Multi-Party Computation: $\widetilde{G_t^k} \leftarrow Encryption(G_t^k)$
11. $G_t \leftarrow \sum_{k=1}^{N} Decryption(\widetilde{G_t^k})$
12. $w_{t+1} \leftarrow SGD(w_t, G_t)$

Let one iteration of the local updates be $G_t^1, G_t^2, ..., G_t^N$. We use synchronized SGD for the updates, and to aggregate all the local updates we do the following steps:

$$G_t = \frac{1}{N} \sum_{k \in S} G_t^k \tag{1}$$

$$w_{t+1} = w_t + \eta_t G_t \tag{2}$$

The learning rate η_t is chosen by the server. In our experiment we choose $\eta_t = 0.01$.

4.2 Encryption Using Secure Multi-Party Computation (SMPC)

Unlike normal types of encryption using public/private keys to encrypt the data, SMPC splits a variable into multiple shares and each of the shares works like a private key [14]. Besides, these shares are distributed amongst multiple owners so that only all the share owners agree to do the decryption can we get the plaintext of the variable. That means that each owner has a private key.

4.3 Improving the Algorithm

The experiment result reveals that Algorithm 1 cannot achieve high accuracy on the MNIST dataset without care and the algorithm needs further optimization. We notice that there are a few steps we can do to reduce the negative impact of compression on accuracy.

Momentum SGD. Momentum SGD is usually modified by vanilla SGD. Unlike the traditional SGD, the momentum SGD method can accelerate the convergence and reduce the shock during the convergence process.

The following steps show implementing momentum SGD on the distributed training scenario [15].

$$G_t = mG_{t-1} + \sum_{k \in S} G_t^k \tag{3}$$

$$w_{t+1} = w_t - \eta G_t \tag{4}$$

where m is the momentum parameter and we set $m = 0.9$. S is the subset of the participants participant in the training process.

To apply momentum SGD to gradient sparse scenes, a few changes need to be done.

$$G_t = mG_{t-1} + \sum_{k \in S} sparse(G_t^k) \tag{5}$$

$$w_{t+1} = w_t - \eta G_t \tag{6}$$

where $sparse()$ function is shown in Algorithm 1.

Learning Rate Decay. If the learning rate is large in the early stage of the algorithm optimization, the model is easy to approach the local or global optimal solution. However, there will be large fluctuation in the later stage, and even the value of the loss function will hover around the minimum value. The fluctuations are very large and it is always difficult to achieve the optimal. Therefore, the concept of learning rate decay is introduced. At the early stage of model training, a larger learning rate will be used for model optimization. As the number of iterations increases, the learning rate will gradually decrease, ensuring the model does not have too much fluctuation and it is closer to the optimal solution.

Warm-up Training. In our early experiments, we found that the final accuracy was unsatisfactory. After the analysis, we conclude that in the early stage of training, the gradients are more aggressive and diverse, and doing the gradient sparsification at that time greatly affects the subsequent training. It prolongs the training period, therefore extending the total training time. This violates our original goal. We introduce warm-up training [16], and find it is helpful to overcome this problem. More proportional gradients are transmitted during the warm-up training period, and in the later stage of the training process, we upload fewer gradients to achieve gradient sparseness. But this strategy brings another problem—the participant's local data can be more vulnerable in the early stage of the training process. Our SMPC strategy solves this problem and protect the privacy.

5 Security Analysis

Distributed training is not always safe. Since it is impossible to ensure that all parties involved in the training are honest, the original distributed training has the risk of privacy leakage. SMPC solves this problem by increasing the difficulty of obtaining plaintext information. It needs all the share owners agree to do the decryption.

Besides, prior works [18] have proved that gradient compression can well protect the private information of the participants. In our system, the participants only send a small subset of the gradient, and it becomes more difficult for the malicious attacker to infer the private information from the gradient after sparseness, and this conclusion has also been proved in our experiments. Only in this way can the participants be active to participate in the training.

6 Experiments

6.1 Default Setting

We evaluate our system on the MNIST dataset. It has handwritten digits formatted as 28×28 images and composed of 60,000 training examples and 10,000 test examples. The default experimental setting is described in the table. All experiments were performed on a computer equipped with a 2.70 GHz CPU i7-7500U, 24 GB RAM. Training our model for one epoch only takes about one minute on average and does not needs a GPU to accelerate the training process. Besides, we use PyTorch [17] and PySyft [3] as our computing framework.

Multi-layer perceptron (MLP) is used in our experiment, it is a neural network architecture which is popular in doing image classification works. We provide a detailed example of our MLP architecture in Fig. 3, where ReLU means rectifier function (Table 1).

6.2 Results and Analysis

6.2.1 Accuracy

The Effect of Momentum SGD. We first evaluate the effect of momentum SGD with different learning rates and different gradient sparsity. The result (Fig. 4) shows that when the gradient sparsity is 99.9% (only 0.1% is non-zero), the model can achieve

```
nn.Sequential {
    [ input → (1) → ... → (5) → output ]
    (1): nn.Reshape(784)
    (2):nn.Linear(784 → 500)
    (3):nn.ReLU
    (4):nn.Linear(500 → 10)
    (5):nn.LogSoftMax
}
```

Fig. 3. The architecture of MLP

Table 1. Default experimental setting

Dataset	MNIST
Architecture	MLP
Momentum	0.9
Learning rate	10^{-2}
LR decay	/10 from epoch 5 to 40
LR warm-up	Before sixth epoch
Epochs	40

higher accuracy using momentum SGD (blue). But the momentum SGD can also cause the drop of accuracy with the increase of the epoch when the learning rate is 0.01 and the gradient sparsity is 99%.

The Effect of Learning Rate Decay. We also evaluate the effect of learning rate decay using different learning rates when the gradient sparsity is 99.9%. Figure 5 reveals that the learning rate decay can solve the problem of overfitting well. In the early stage of training, the accuracy increases rapidly in every model, and the models without learning rate decay can even reach higher accuracy. But in the subsequent training process, we find that the learning rate decay helps the model maintain accuracy at a high level.

The Effect of Warm-Up. Warm-up is also pretty important for improving the performance after our analysis. We choose to update all the gradients in the early 5 epochs (called warm-up period), besides, we also prohibit the use of learning rate decay during that period. Figure 6 compares the effect of warm-up on different gradient sparsity on the MNIST dataset. The learning rate in this experiment is set to 0.001. The result shows that warm-up can help the model achieve higher accuracy with less epoch. Besides, without warm-up, the accuracy rate may fluctuate greatly.

We also test the accuracy of MLP on MNIST using different gradient sparsity. Given the gradient sparsity of 99.95%, 99.9% and 99%, Fig. 7 shows the variation curve of the training set accuracy under different learning rates (0.001 vs. 0.01). Table 2 shows the detailed accuracy. During our experiments, we noticed that the momentum SGD, warm-up, and learning rate decay can help improve the performance of our system in different

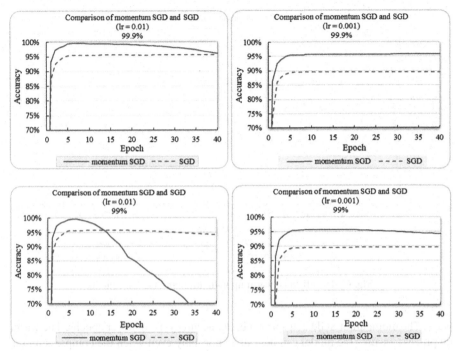

Fig. 4. Comparison of momentum SGD and SGD with different learning rate and gradient sparsity

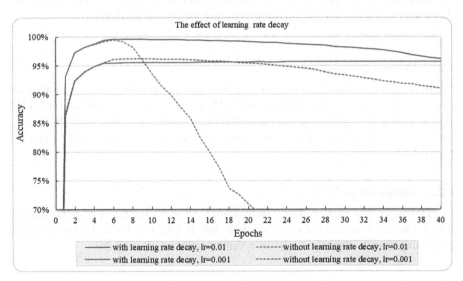

Fig. 5. The effect of learning rate decay (gradient sparsity = 99.9%)

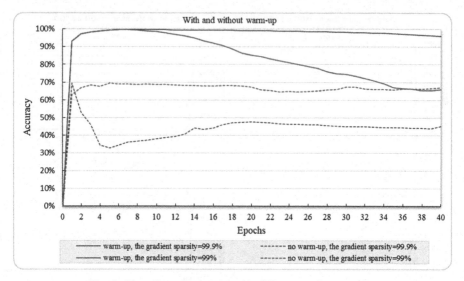

Fig. 6. The effect of warm-up with different gradient sparsity

ways. The momentum SGD helps us get better accuracy using fewer epochs. The warm-up process ensures the model can be trained normally even when the compression rate is high. And the learning rate decay can reduce the negative effects of overfitting. These three methods let the gradient sparsification algorithm be possible to be added in the distributed training of SMPC, therefore reducing the communication cost.

6.2.2 Communication Cost

We theoretically evaluated the impact of different gradient sparsity on the communication cost (see Fig. 8). It is worth noting that some additional information needs to be uploaded, such as a mask matrix representing the zeroed elements during compression. We believe this mask matrix can be replaced by a random seed, so its communication impact is negligible.

6.2.3 Computation Time

In addition, we also measured the computation time of our system (Table 3). Although it has a higher computation time, we think this is tolerable for using the increased computing time in exchange for lower communication cost.

6.2.4 Security

In addition to reducing the communication cost, we also made relevant experiments on the protection of the original data information using gradient compression. Our experiment uses the iDLG method [19] to perform gradient privacy analysis on the MNIST and CIFAR100 datasets. As shown in Fig. 9, after fixing a single picture and increasing

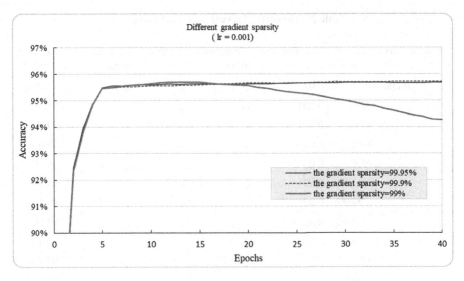

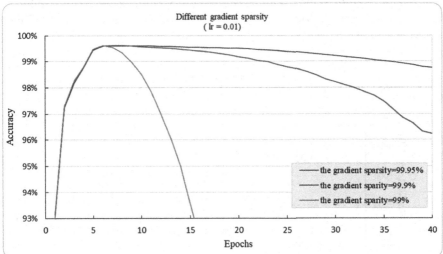

Fig. 7. Comparison at different gradient sparsity

the gradient compression ratio (gradient upload ratio from 100% to 10%), the final effect of restoring the image becomes worse as the gradient compression ratio increases.

In these experiments, we detected an obvious problem in our system, that is, compared with the model without gradient compression, although our model can also achieve similar accuracy during the training process, after several epochs, it is easier to encounter the phenomenon of overfitting. We analyze that this is due to the negative effects of momentum SGD and the reduction of the gradient updates.

Table 2. The detailed accuracy in the training set

Gradient sparsity	Learning rate	Momentum SGD	Warm-up	Learning rate decay	Accuracy
0% (no compression)	0.01	√	√	√	99.99%
99%	0.001	√	√	√	95.7%
99%	0.001	–	√	√	89.7%
99%	0.01	√	√	√	99.6%
99%	0.01	–	√	√	95.7%
99.9%	0.001	√	√	√	95.7%
99.9%	0.001	–	√	√	89.5%
99.9%	0.01	√	√	√	99.6%
99.9%	0.01	√	–	√	69.4%
99%	0.01	√	–	√	69.4%
99.9%	0.01	√	√	–	99.6%
99.9%	0.001	√	√	–	96.2%

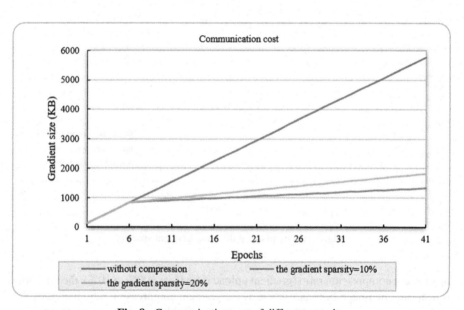

Fig. 8. Communication cost of different sparsity

Table 3. Comparison of computation time

	Computation time for one epoch (seconds)
With compression	63.53
Without compression	25.85

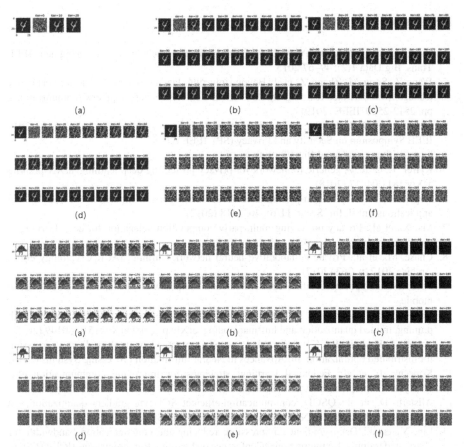

Fig. 9. As the compression rate increases, it becomes more difficult for an attacker to guess the original data from the limited gradient information both on MNIST and CIFAR100 dataset

7 Conclusion

In this paper, we have made corresponding solutions to the increase in communication costs caused by SMPC encryption. The core idea of our solution is selecting only a small percentage of gradients for uploading to achieve the goal of reducing communication bandwidth requirements. But we also notice that the original algorithm will bring a serious negative impact on the performance of the model. To improve the performance and efficiency, we add three methods to the original model, that are, momentum SGD, the learning rate decay and warm-up. Experiments show that these three methods are very helpful for improving the performance of our model. After choosing a suitable learning rate, our model can achieve similar accuracy as the uncompressed gradient model, and the computation time for one epoch is only 37.7 s longer than the uncompressed one on average, which is caused by the extra calculation cost.

References

1. Xing, E.P., et al.: Petuum: a new platform for distributed machine learning on big data. IEEE Trans. Big Data 1(2), 49–67 2015
2. Wang, Z., Song, M., Zhang, Z., et al.: Beyond inferring class representatives: user-level privacy leakage from federated learning. In: 2019-IEEE Conference on Computer Communications, pp. 2512-2520. IEEE (2019)
3. Melis, L., et al.: Exploiting unintended feature leakage in collaborative learning. In: 2019 IEEE Symposium on Security and Privacy (SP). IEEE (2019)
4. https://github.com/OpenMined/PySyft
5. Ryffel, T., et al.: A generic framework for privacy preserving deep learning. arXiv preprint arXiv:1811.04017 (2018)
6. Bogdanov, D., et al.: High-performance secure multi-party computation for data mining applications. Int. J. Inf. Secur. 11(6), 403–418 (2012)
7. Ma, X., et al.: Privacy preserving multi-party computation delegation for deep learning in cloud computing. Inf. Sci. 459, 103–116 (2018)
8. Chase, M., et al.: Private collaborative neural network learning. IACR Cryptology ePrint Archive 2017, p. 762 (2017)
9. Speedtest.net: Speedtest market report, March 2020. https://www.speedtest.net/global-index#mobile
10. Han, S., Mao, H., Dally, W.J.: Deep compression: Compressing deep neural networks with pruning, trained quantization and huffman coding. arXiv preprint arXiv:1510.00149 (2015)
11. Vogels, T., Karimireddy, S.P., Jaggi, M.: PowerSGD: practical low-rank gradient compression for distributed optimization. In: Advances in Neural Information Processing Systems (2019)
12. Konečný, J., et al.: Federated learning: strategies for improving communication efficiency. arXiv preprint arXiv:1610.05492 (2016)
13. Alistarh, D., et al.: QSGD: communication-efficient SGD via gradient quantization and encoding. In: Advances in Neural Information Processing Systems (2017)
14. Lin, Y., et al.: Deep gradient compression: reducing the communication bandwidth for distributed training. In: International Conference on Learning Representations (ICLR) (2018)
15. Ryffel, T., et al.: A generic framework for privacy preserving deep learning. arXiv preprint arXiv:1811.04017 (2018)
16. Qian, Ning: On the momentum term in gradient descent learning algorithms. Neural Netw. 12(1), 145–151 (1999)
17. Goyal, P., et al.: Accurate, large minibatch sgd: Training imagenet in 1 hour. arXiv preprint arXiv:1706.02677 (2017)
18. https://github.com/torch/nn
19. Shokri, R., Shmatikov, V.: Privacy-preserving deep learning. In: Proceedings of the 22nd ACM SIGSAC Conference on Computer and Communications Security (2015)
20. Zhao, B., Mopuri, K.R., Bilen, H.: iDLG: improved deep leakage from gradients. arXiv preprint arXiv:2001.02610 (2020)

A PoL Protocol for Spatiotemporal Blockchain

Yiwenjin Fu⬤, Huahui Chen⁽✉⁾, Jiangbo Qian⬤, and Yihong Dong

Ningbo University, Ningbo 315211, China
chenhuahui@nbu.edu.cn

Abstract. Spatiotemporal data is the foundation of technologies such as the supply chain industry and autonomous driving. Recent years, the processing of spatiotemporal data has become a hot issue. The current processing method of spatiotemporal data is mainly a single point of centralized storage, which brings certain problems such as data islands. The blockchain is a peer-to-peer distributed ledger, which can ensure that the data is decentralized and not tampered. Using blockchain to process spatiotemporal data can solve important problems in the field of spatiotemporal data processing. A very important part of this process is that the proof-of-location (*PoL*) is created by consensus. This paper proposes a blockchain protocol for spatiotemporal data. The protocol includes the creation of *PoL*, consensus and block sequencing. We propose a *PoL* generation algorithm to generate *PoL* and create transactions. Further, a consensus algorithm for *PoL* is proposed to verify *PoL* and transaction and create blocks. We used a parallel DAG architecture to generate the topology of the blockchain for storing blocks. Finally, we conducted a threatening analysis of the proposed protocol. We simulated a supply chain case to evaluate the throughput, scalability, and fault tolerance of the protocol.

Keywords: Spatiotemporal data · Blockchain · Parallel DAG · Proximity test

1 Introduction

Spatiotemporal data is a kind of data with two-dimensional properties of time and space. Spatiotemporal data mainly represents the amount of geographic information that changes with time. The most typical spatiotemporal data is logistics data, which is denoted as latitude and longitude data that changes with time. Spatiotemporal data is the foundation of the supply chain industry. Recent years, the supply chain industry developed rapidly, and its dependence on spatiotemporal data has greatly increased. The supply chain industry includes spatiotemporal data from the original state of the product or service to the end customer. These spatiotemporal data are often of a continuous property [1]. In the whole supply chain industry, the entities include manufacturers, sellers, warehouses, transportation companies, distribution centers and retailers etc.

The important information about the supply chain often includes the source of the transported object, the transshipment location and a reasonable transportation route [2]. Based on this information, the end customer can trace the source of the transportation object obtained, the logistics companies can track the logistics process, select the most

S. Yu et al. (Eds.): SPDE 2020, CCIS 1268, pp. 591–605, 2020.
https://doi.org/10.1007/978-981-15-9129-7_41

costly and reasonable transportation route, and the regulatory body can track the legality and authenticity of the transportation object based on these data etc. [3] Fig. 1 shows the basic architecture of a supply chain.

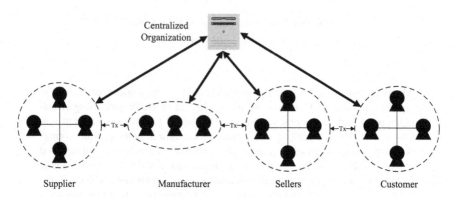

Fig. 1. Basic architecture of supply chain

At present, the existing storage methods of spatiotemporal data are mainly single-point centralized storage [4]. Large companies store their spatiotemporal data in their own servers. The biggest problem caused by this storage method is the problem of information islands [5, 6]. Recent years, there have been a lot of missing key spatiotemporal data in the cases of toxic milk powder, drain oil, counterfeit and shoddy commodities, which has brought difficulties for the regulatory authorities to obtain evidence later.

Blockchain is proposed by Satoshi Nakamoto in 2008 as the basic technology of Bitcoin. In the blockchain, the block header of each block has a hash value. At the same time, each block has a hash pointer, and through this hash pointer, each block links its previous blocks, thereby forming a blockchain [7]. The block is the most basic structural unit of the blockchain, which includes the block header and the block body. The storage method is through the Merkle tree [8]. By encrypting each transaction and storing it on the Merkle tree, the block ensures that the global data needs to be modified when the data is modified and written [9]. This ensures the security of the data and its non-tampering.

The problems caused by the single-point centralized storage of spatiotemporal data have already emerged. The emergence of blockchain and its own characteristics plays an important role in solving these problems. The blockchain itself has the characteristics of information transparency and is difficult to tamper with [10]. Combining blockchain with spatiotemporal data will effectively meet the needs and pain points of spatiotemporal data processing.

Traditional blockchain architecture cannot support the processing of the spatiotemporal data. One of the most important problem is that the spatiotemporal data needs the proof-of-location (*PoL*) to ensure the data security and integrity. So, it is important to propose a protocol with *PoL* for the blockchain. Now we present the content of our work:

- We proposed an algorithm for blockchain nodes to generate *PoL*. The algorithm first selects miner nodes through the *PoS* consensus algorithm, and then the miner nodes generate *PoL* and write transactions to create blocks, then send blocks to the blockchain nodes for consensus.
- We proposed a *PoL* consensus algorithm between the blockchain nodes on the generated transactions and send blocks to the blockchain topology for ordering.
- We proposed a parallel DAG architecture based on the *blockDAG* and using the staining algorithm to sort the order of blocks.
- We made a threat analysis of the proposed protocol and analyzed the reliability of the protocol by defining the opponent model and the corresponding defense mechanism.
- We simulated a supply chain model using the proposed spatiotemporal blockchain protocol and evaluated the security and processing performance of the proposed protocol in the presence of malicious actors.

The structure of this article is as follows:

Section 1 is an introduction. The introduction introduces the research background of the subject studied in this article. Section 2 provides a detailed review of domestic and foreign research content on issues. In Sect. 3 we formalize the problem. In Sect. 4, we propose a location proof generation algorithm for generating location proofs and creating blocks. In Sect. 5, we propose a consensus algorithm for proof of location, which is used for consensus verification of the generated blocks. In Sect. 6, we propose a parallel DAG architecture model based on the third generation blockchain architecture and propose a sorting algorithm for the ranking of blocks on the blockchain topology. In Sect. 7, we conducted a threat analysis of the proposed protocol. In Sect. 8, we simulated a supply chain case to evaluate the performance of the proposed protocol in terms of throughput, scalability, and fault tolerance. In Sect. 9, we summarize the work and look forward to the future work.

2   Related Works

Blockchain technology was proposed by Satoshi Nakamoto in 2008 [11]. As the basic architecture of Bitcoin, it is essentially an encrypted distributed account book. In the traditional blockchain, the heavy node has a copy of the full transaction information, while the light node only saves the block header data of the Bitcoin network. When writing, modifying, or deleting content, nodes will vote according to the consensus mechanism to ensure data security and tamper resistance. The traditional blockchain architecture mainly includes two generations of blockchain. The main representative of the blockchain 1.0 architecture is Bitcoin, which uses the UTXO account model [12]. The main representative of the blockchain 2.0 system architecture is Ethereum adopting the Account model [13]. The two traditional blockchain architectures have certain disadvantages in terms of processing efficiency and support for spatiotemporal data, which will be elaborated later. *blockDAG* architecture the blockchain was proposed by the Hebrew University of Jerusalem, Israel in 2018, and it is regarded as the blockchain 3.0 architecture [14].

There are some studies currently optimizing these issues. Carl R. Worley, Anthony Skjellum, et al. proposed using sidechain techniques to improve the efficiency of the blockchain to support spatiotemporal data [15]. The main idea is to store data on different blockchains, store time data and spatial data on two chains, and improve transaction efficiency through parallel voting of the two chains. Jiaping Wang and Hao Wang proposed a block expansion architecture, which aims to achieve block expansion through a forwarding queue [16]. Shin Morishima, Hiroki Matasutani et al. proposed that after the spatiotemporal data is stored in a side chain structure [17]. Qingling Zhao, Zonghua Gu, et al. proposed a blockchain architecture based on SegWit technology to achieve block expansion through forwarding queues to better improve the spatiotemporal data processing capability of the blockchain [18]. Sven Helmer, Matteo Roggia et al. proposed an Ethernity DB architecture for the slow query of spatiotemporal blockchain, adding an analytical layer to the data layer and consensus layer of the blockchain [19]. Most of these tasks are optimized based on the traditional blockchain architecture, while the traditional blockchain architecture determines its limited support for spatiotemporal data. FOAM2 and XYO3, provide reliable spatiotemporal information based on Ethereum smart contracts [20, 21]. The main idea of the FOAM protocol is to create a spatial index with encrypted spatial coordinates by assigning unforgeable indexes to each object. In contrast, XYO Network assumes of a shared network, where each participant plays a clear role and gets the motivation to forward, collect or store location data [22].

3   Problem Formulation

Proof of location (PoL) is a verifiable digital certificate that is used to prove that an object σ exists at the time t with $(\emptyset, \lambda)$ as the latitude and longitude at the location of l, and is signed by an authoritative miner ω.

Definition 1 (Integrity). The integrity of proof of location (*PoL*) refers to having a proof object σ provided by an authoritative miner ω at time t whose location is the location l with $(\emptyset, \lambda)$ as latitude and longitude.

Definition 2 (Stability). The stability of proof of location (*PoL*) means that when the actual location of a proved object σ at time t is not the location l with $(\emptyset, \lambda)$ as the latitude and longitude, it cannot obtain the location proof.

Definition 3 (Non-Temper Proof). The proof of location (*PoL*) cannot be tampered with, which means that when tampering with the proof of location occurs, all nodes in the network can discover and prevent this behavior in time.

Definition 4 (Non-Transferable). The non-transferability of proof of location (*PoL*) means that the proof of location created by a miner node ω_i for the proved object σ_j is invalid for other proven objects.

Definition 5 (Security). The security of Proof of Location (*PoL*) refers to that *PoL* is safe when it proves that it has integrity, stability, non-temper proof and non-transferable (Table 1).

Table 1. Important notations

Notation	Meaning
G	Transaction set
$P = [\gamma_1 \dots \gamma_n]$	Blockchain peer set
$S = [\sigma_1 \dots \sigma_k]$	Being proved object
$W = [\omega_1 \dots \omega_m]$	Alternative miners set
Z	Proposal set
f	*PoL* generation rate
τ	Transaction
l	Announced location
(φ, λ)	(latitude, longitude)
t	Timestamp
δ	Network delay
Δ	Network imprecision
θ	Proximity threshold
k_s, k_p	Cryptographic Keypair

4 PoL Generation

In this chapter we will introduce the process of the miner node generating *PoL*. The specific steps are as follows. When the proven object wants to obtain the *PoL*, it sends a proximity test request to the "alternative miner", and after obtaining the list of the "alternative miner" nodes, it waits for the results of the *PoS* consensus of Generate miner nodes. After that, the node that created the *PoL* (i.e., the miner node) generates the proof of location of the being proved object according to the *PoL* generation algorithm and broadcasts it to the full blockchain node network for consensus verification.

We use the *DPOS* consensus algorithm to verify and vote on the validity of the *PoL* proof of location, write the proof of location into the transaction after the voting procedure is completed, and then create a block. The whole process is completed by the being proved object and its multiple nodes within the distance threshold. The purpose of adopting the *DPOS* consensus algorithm is to ensure the "long-term purity" principle of the blockchain network, thereby ensuring the security of the network. This chapter will focus on the generation of *PoL*, and the next chapter will introduce the verification and consensus algorithm of *PoL* in detail. Figure 2 shows the generation of *PoL*.

PoL needs to obtain a certain fault tolerance in a distributed environment, which will be completed through the interaction of multiple untrusted or semi-trusted parties. In a blockchain system, miners are responsible for generating transactions and creating blocks and recording transaction times. Consider that in a supply chain system, there are both dynamic and static entities. Dynamic entities include the goods being transported which is the being proved objects, etc. Static entities include manufacturers, customers

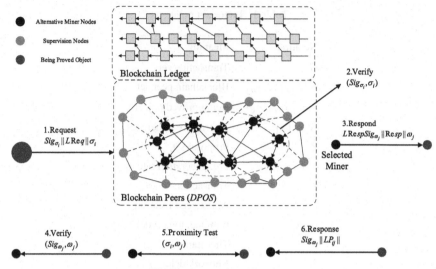

Fig. 2. Generation of the *PoL*

with fixed locations, etc. We consider arranging miner nodes at specific spatial locations (φ_i, λ_i) These miner nodes may be the fixed manufacturers, fixed customers, transfer centers, etc. Algorithm 1 is used to generate *PoL* from the being proved objects requesting *PoL* to confirm their current *pos*itions. Consider deploying a pair of key pairs on the being proved object, and when it joins the network in the current period, its public key is broadcasted to all blockchain nodes and is used as the blockchain address. The blockchain node uses the public key to identify the certified and verified objects.

Algorithm 1. *PoL* Generation
1   **function** SENDPROPOSAL $(\sigma_i; \tau; \theta)$
2    $Z \leftarrow \emptyset$
3   **for all** $[\sigma_1 \dots \sigma_k] \in S$ **do**
4       $LReq\|\|\sigma_i\|\|sig_{\sigma_i}\{LReq\}$
5   **function** PROCESSPROPOSAL $(\sigma_i, \tau, \theta, f)$
6   **for all** $[\omega_1 \dots \omega_m] \in W$ **do**
7   PROXIMITYCHECK $(\sigma_i, [\omega_1 \dots \omega_j])$
8   if $dist_{harv} \leq \theta \wedge sig_{\sigma_i}$ **do**
9   SEND $LRespsig_W\|\|Resp\|\|W$ to σ_i
10   **if** $sig_{\omega_j} \wedge f_{\omega_j} > [f_{\omega_1} \dots f_{\omega_{j-1}}]$ **do**
11   PROXIMITYCHECK (σ_i, ω_j)
12   if $dist_{harv} \leq \theta \wedge sig_{\sigma_i} \wedge sig_{\omega_j}$ **do**
13   SEND $sig_{\omega_j}\|\|LP_{ij}\|\|$ to σ_i
14   **end**
15   **return** LP_{ij}

For the being proved object σ_i, define the following request function $PoLR(\sigma_i)$ as:

$$PoLR(\sigma_i) = LReq||\sigma_i||sig_{\sigma_i}\{LReq\} \tag{1}$$

The object σ_i selects the miner node to send the request $LReq||\sigma_i||sig_{\sigma_i}\{LReq\}$ (line 4). $LReq$ is used to initialize the proximity test and declare its location (φ, λ) at time t. The signatures sig_{σ_i} and σ_i are used to verify the request. The format of $PoLR(\sigma_i)$ can be expressed as:

$$Req_{i \rightarrow j} : \left\{ \begin{array}{c} sig_{\sigma_i} \\ \langle \varphi_{\sigma_i}, \lambda_{\sigma_i} \rangle \\ t \end{array} \right\} \tag{2}$$

Normally, the miner node and the being proved object perform a fast information exchange, in which the miner node sends some generated secrets and waits for a response from the prover with the same secret. Every message is signed to prevent being attacked. The miner node processes the PoL request (line 5-line 11) by verifying the encrypted addresses corresponding to the signature sig_{σ_i}, spatial location (φ, λ), time stamp t and σ_i.

The format of the PoL response can be expressed as:

$$Res_{j \rightarrow i} : \left\{ \begin{array}{c} Req_{i \rightarrow j} \\ sig_{\omega_j} \\ \langle \varphi_{\omega_j}, \lambda_{\omega_j} \rangle \\ t \end{array} \right\} \tag{3}$$

After the series of tests above, the miner node ω_j confirms the actual spatial location and time data declared by the being proved object σ_i, and sends the lp_{ij} to the proven object σ_i (line 12). lp_{ij} includes the spatial *position* declared by the being proved object σ_i, the location of the miner node ω_j, and the current timestamp t_{ω_j}. Finally, the being proved object signs the received location proof lp_{ij} and sends it to other network nodes in the blockchain network. The network nodes share the PoL and run the PoL consensus algorithm to verify it and execute the vote procedure to create a block and send it to the blockchain ledger.

For the proximity test, the calculation between spatial data can use the Haversine formula [23]. The Haversine formula is used to solve the distance $dist_{harv}$ between two coordinates. The formula for calculating the distance between two coordinates is given following, where $r_e = 6371$ km is the radius of the earth:

$$dist_{harv} = 2r_e \arcsin\left(\min\left[1, \sqrt{sin^2\left(\frac{\varphi_2 - \varphi_1}{2}\right) + cos\varphi_i cos\varphi_2 sin^2\left(\frac{\lambda_2 - \lambda_1}{2}\right)} \right] \right) \tag{4}$$

Define $LReq$ as the proximity test function:

$$LReq = \theta - dist_{harv} \tag{5}$$

The being proved object checks the distance to some of the alternative miners' nodes pre-defined nearby. When $dist_{harv} \leq \theta$ is satisfied, select the "alternative miners" node $\omega = \{\omega_1 \ldots \omega_j\}$ and send a request. The alternative miner node selects the miner node according to the DPOS consensus algorithm to generate the PoL and write it into the transaction information to create a block. Figure 3 shows Prover σ_i chooses "Alternative Miner".

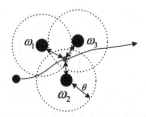

Fig. 3. Prover σ_i chooses "Alternative Miner"

For the verification of the spatial position (φ, λ), the miner node requires the proved object to meet the proximity test. For the verification of time t, the miner node verifies the timestamp of the being proved object, and its verification function is defined as follows:

$$t_{now} - \delta \leq t \leq t_{now} + \delta + \Delta \tag{6}$$

Where δ is the minimum network delay, Δ is the error value, and t_{now} is the clock time of the local miner node. That is, the timestamp t must be within the range before the miner node can provide proof of location. After the verification is completed, the miner node ω_j replies to the being proved object with a response message *Resp*, and the encrypted address and signature of ω_j are also packaged into *Resp* and used to confirm identity verification to generate the *PoL*.

5   PoL Consensus Mechanism

Section 4 has introduced the process of generating *PoL* for a being proved object by defining miner nodes, and proposed Algorithm 1. After generating the *PoL*, the miner nodes write the *PoL* into a transaction, and then creates a new block. In this chapter, we will propose an algorithm for the verification and consensus of blockchain nodes on the *PoL* to ensure the reliability of the generated *PoL*.

The traditional blockchain architecture uses *PoW* and *PoS* algorithms as the consensus mechanism to generate blocks and record transaction content. With *PoW*, nodes compete for the right to create a block by calculating a complexity problem, and the nodes that obtain the right to create block can obtain certain rewards, such as the electronic cryptocurrency Bitcoin and Ether.

The selected miners perform *PoL* generation and complete block creation. The blockchain nodes considers *DPOS* to achieve consensus. *DPOS* is a blockchain consensus algorithm which means delegated proof of stake. It is like the board system of a company, that is, the miner nodes are like the directors of a company, while other nodes vote to select these miner nodes. If the selected miner node fails to generate a *PoL* or fails to create a block, or the generated *PoL* and the created block are not discarded through system consensus, the node will lose the right to be a miner. Figure 4 shows the flow of the *PoL* consensus algorithm. When at least 51% of the nodes confirm the validity of the *PoL*, the *PoL* is written into the transaction. The miner records himself to provide the number of proofs of location serves as the basis for consensus.

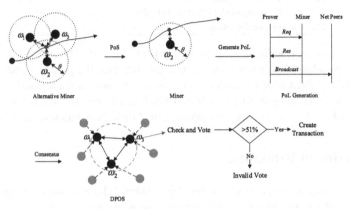

Fig. 4. *PoL* consensus algorithm flow

As shown in Fig. 4, the being proved object first selects a group of "alternative miners". The distance between these "alternative miners" and the being proved object is less than the preset maximum verification radius θ. For these "alternative miners", we consider using the *PoS* consensus algorithm to select the miners in the "alternative miners", which determined the number of miners who create blocks by judging the number of *PoL* created by each "alternative miner" before. As showed in Fig. 4, suppose that when the proved object σ_i requests to obtain a *PoL* at the red dot *position*, there are $[\omega_1, \omega_2, \omega_3]$ three "alternative miner" nodes. Their distance to σ_i is less than θ. Assuming that among the three nodes, in a certain period of time T, ω_2 has generated the most *PoL*, after the *PoS* consensus, ω_2 becomes a miner node and executes algorithm 4.1 to generate *PoL* and broadcast it to the blockchain network. The network of the blockchain nodes checks the signature validity and timestamp of the generated *PoL* and vote via *DPOS* consensus. Algorithm 2 represents the consensus algorithm for *PoL*.

Algorithm 2. *PoL* Consensus
1   **function** PROCESSVOTE $(\omega_0 \dots \omega_k)$
2   Vote (h_k, sig_{ω_j}) received from ω_j
3   **if** $\omega_j \in W \wedge sig_{\omega_j}$ **then**
4   votes $[h_k]$ = votes $[h_k] \cup \omega_k$
5   **if** $|h_k| > k/2$ **then**
6   Send block
7   **function** PROCESSBLOCK $(G; W)$
8   **if** BLOCKVALIDATION $(G; \omega_k)$ **then**
9   *NewState* = APPLY (State (ω_k), G)
10   **return** *NewState*
11   *NewState*←SYNCHRONISE (P)
12   **return** *NewState*

Algorithm 2 represents the consensus algorithm for *PoL*. The process of the entire location proof algorithm is as follows: The nodes received the proposal and started the vote procedure. Each node checks the signature, time stamp in the transaction information, and makes a corresponding vote (line 1-line10), The *PoL* forms a brand-new block (line 7–10). Finally, store the received block in the blockchain database (line 11-line 12).

6   Experiment Evaluation

Consider evaluating the proposed protocol in a supply chain scenario. A supply chain is a system of people, activities, information, and resources that involves transferring products or services from suppliers to customers. Generally, a supply chain can be represented as a transition sequence from producer to consumer with multiple intermediate points. Figure 5 shows a schematic diagram of a supply chain. It represents the process of transporting commodities from producers to consumers (consumers are not the same as end users in the actual supply chain here). Miner node $\omega = \{\omega_1 \dots \omega_9\}$ exists in different pre-arranged spatial locations. Proof of location. Its entire *pos*ition proves that it is generated, used and confirmed in the supply chain as follows:

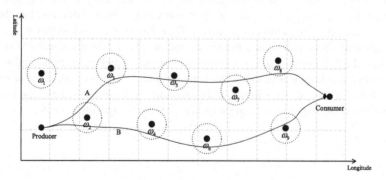

Fig. 5. Example of a supply chain

First, the manufacturer and the consumer reach a smart contract through an initial exchange of information, that is, the commodity P is delivered to the consumer through a transportation method. When the consumer receives the product at the location (φ_i, λ_i) at t_1 and the verification is completed, the manufacturer immediately receives the payment from the consumer. After the definition of the smart contract is completed, the commodity P begins to be transported. In the transportation process, there may be multiple transportation routes such as route A and route B. The transportation costs involved in different routes are not the same. With the transportation of commodities, the miner node performs proximity testing on the proof object close to its maximum verification radius θ and reports on the blockchain node during this process. After that, the *PoL* is sent to the nodes of the blockchain, and each node performs consensus verification on it, and writes the result into the basic data storage of the blockchain. Finally, when the product P reaches the consumer's location (φ_i, λ_i), the consumer ends the transaction and provides proof of time and *pos*ition, and receives the product P at the *pos*ition (φ_i, λ_i) at time t_2 and sends it to the producer pay for transportation and goods.

The experiment uses a PDAG network topology based on a *blockDAG* infrastructure and runs on a cluster of 24 nodes. The environment of each node is Intel Core Duo i5-7500 3.40 GHz CPU, 4 GM RAM, 500G hard disk, running Ubuntu 16.04 64, and interconnected by 1 GB switch. The experiment used the spatial and temporal data set in the Montreal region provided by the Canadian logistics company BiXi Open Platform.

The experiment will evaluate the following performance to measure the PSTB protocol. (1) Transaction generation throughput: the number of transactions generated per second, that is, the number of transactions generated by the miner node per unit time including the *PoL*; (2) Transaction confirmation throughput: the number of transactions that can complete the confirmation per second. (3) Scalability: the impact of new nodes joining the blockchain node network on transaction generation and confirmation throughput; (4) Fault tolerance: changes in transaction generation and confirmation throughput when some nodes fail.

We divided 24 nodes into 8 "alternative miner" nodes and 12 companion nodes to implement *DPOS* consensus. 8 "alternative miners" nodes have all been defined with the initial spatial data.

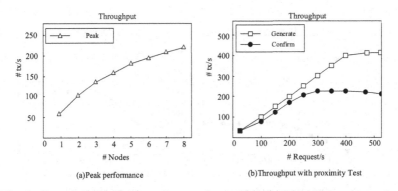

(a)Peak performance   (b)Throughput with proximity Test

Fig. 6. Throughput performance of transaction generation with multiple miner nodes

We considered the generation of transactions where there are multiple miner nodes $[\omega_0 \ldots \omega_7]$. We first tested the scalability, from a single node to the full node for the throughput of transaction generation. Figure 6(a) shows the peak transaction generation for different numbers of nodes.

As shown in Fig. 6(b), as the number of nodes increases, the throughput of transaction generation does not increase linearly. This is because as the number of nodes increases, both *PoS* consensus and proximity testing cause a certain delay, thus affecting transaction generation throughput. Unlike the traditional blockchain system architecture, we use a parallel mining mechanism to improve the overall throughput of the protocol.

We also evaluated the impact of proximity testing and miner consensus selection on transaction generation. We selected 8 "alternative miners" nodes for evaluation. For the case of no proximity test and miner consensus selection, we first send the transaction request equally and randomly to each node to create a transaction, and then we record the throughput of the generated transaction. Then we require miners to perform proximity testing on the request and use it for miner selection according to the PoS consensus mechanism. Figure 6(b) shows the comparison of these two situations.

As shown in Fig. 6(b), for 8 candidate miner nodes $[\omega_0 \ldots \omega_7]$, firstly use Formula 5 and Formula 6 to conduct proximity test to select the miner nodes needed to process the transaction. When the number of transaction requests per second is less (less than 100), the proximity test has less effect on transaction generation. As the number of requests increases, the miner selection delay caused by proximity testing causes a decrease in the throughput of transaction generation per second. When the number of requests generated by the transaction sent per second is close to 300, the throughput of transaction generation It will hardly grow anymore, that is, the throughput reaches its peak.

After a transaction containing content such as proof of location is generated, the miner node packages the transaction and writes it to the block for broadcasting. Other miner nodes receive and vote, and the voting is conducted using the *DPOS* consensus algorithm. Blocks that have received more than 51% of the votes are sent to the blockchain network. We separately tested the transaction confirmation throughput of block consensus using *PoW* consensus algorithm and *PoS* consensus algorithm to measure the impact of consensus algorithm on transaction confirmation throughput. Figure 7 shows the transaction confirmation throughput changes as the number of requests increases.

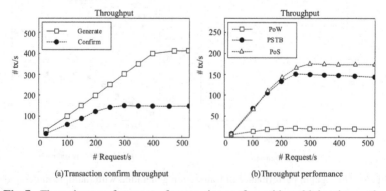

(a) Transaction confirm throughput   (b) Throughput performance

Fig. 7. Throughput performance of transaction confirm with multiple miner nodes

As shown in Fig. 7(a), when there are 8 "alternative miners" nodes, as the number of transaction requests increases, when the number of requests is small, the throughput of transaction confirmation increases with the number of requests. Then with the further growth of transaction requests, when the number of transaction requests reaches a certain threshold, the processing of transaction requests by the node network reaches the upper limit. We set the rate of block creation to create one block per second and count all confirmed transactions in the block. Regardless of the network transmission and delay, when there are 8 miner nodes, a maximum of approximately 157 transaction confirmations can be completed per second. In actual applications, due to the network transmission delay, the actual number of transactions that can be confirmed per second will be less than this value.

As shown in Fig. 7(b), we use the traditional blockchain consensus algorithm as a comparison to test the impact of the consensus algorithm on the transaction confirmation throughput. Among them, the *PoW* algorithm is Bitcoin's consensus algorithm, and the *PoS* algorithm is Ethereum's consensus algorithm. For the *PoS* algorithm, we also designated 8 miner nodes as voting nodes. Unlike our protocol, the *PoS* algorithm's consideration of voting weight is determined by the number of transactions created by the miner node. In our protocol, the companion node is responsible for supervising the voting node, and the voting weight of the voting node is the same.

In addition, we also tested the scalability and fault tolerance of the protocol. We tested the transaction confirmation throughput under different numbers of nodes to measure the impact of the addition of new nodes on the protocol.

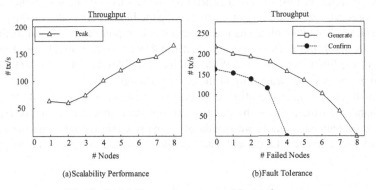

Fig. 8. Scalability performance and fault tolerance

As shown in Fig. 8(a), we tested the throughput of transaction confirmation with different numbers of nodes. When there is only a single miner node, the transaction is confirmed after it is created. With the addition of nodes, transaction requests are processed and confirmed by different miners simultaneously. However, due to the delay caused by proximity testing and consensus, the transaction confirmation throughput at the beginning has decreased. Later, with the addition of more nodes, the throughput of transaction confirmation gradually increased, and until the 8 miner nodes simultaneously processed transaction requests, the throughput of the blockchain node network for transaction confirmation reached its peak.

We also tested the fault tolerance of the protocol. We consider that when 8 miner nodes are running normally, a node is suddenly disconnected to measure the impact of the protocol's throughput. We make requests to the blockchain node network at a rate of 250 transaction requests per second. After a period, disconnect several of the nodes to test the fault tolerance of the system protocol. Figure 8(b) shows the impact of node failure on protocol throughput.

As shown in Fig. 8(b), we tested the impact of disconnecting miner nodes on the throughput of the node network. When the network of running blockchain nodes is disconnected, due to the protocol, multiple miners are used to mine in parallel. The throughput of transaction confirmations gradually declined. As for the throughput of transaction confirmation, it has been defined in the *DPOS* consensus algorithm that more than 51% of nodes must pass to create blocks. Therefore, when the number of failed nodes reaches more than 4, the confirmation of the transaction cannot continue.

7 Conclusion

This paper proposes a reliable spatiotemporal blockchain protocol to solve the problem of proof of location faced by the blockchain when processing spatiotemporal data. We have designed a *PoL* algorithm for blockchain nodes to generate proofs of position. This algorithm first selects miner nodes through the *PoS* consensus algorithm, and then the miner nodes generate position proofs and write transactions to create blocks, and then send the blocks to the blockchain node network for consensus sorting.

Further, after the position proof generation and block creation, this chapter proposes a *PoL* consensus algorithm for consensus among the blockchain nodes on the generated block and sends it to the blockchain account book for topology update and sorting. This consensus algorithm is used to ensure that reliable transaction blocks are sent to the ledger of the blockchain, and the PDAG architecture based on the *blockDAG* staining algorithm ensures high scalability of the blockchain topology.

In addition, we made a validity threat analysis of the proposed protocol and analyzed the reliability of the protocol by defining the opponent model and the corresponding defense mechanism. Finally, we simulated a supply chain model using the proposed protocol, and evaluated the throughput, scalability, and fault tolerance of the proposed protocol.

References

1. Yuan, Y., Wang, F.-Y.: Blockchain: the state of the art and future trends. Acta Autom. Sinica **42**(4), 481–494 (2016)
2. Weili, C., Zibin, Z.: Blockchain data analysis: a review of status, trends and challenges. J. Comput. Res. Dev. **55**(9), 1853–1870 (2018)
3. Zhang, L., Liu, B., Zhang, R., Jiang, B., Liu, Y.: Overview of blockchain technology. Comput. Eng. **45**(5), 1–12 (2019)
4. Tsai, W.T., Yu, L., Wang, R., Liu, N., Deng, E.Y.: Blockchain application development techniques. J. Softw. **28**(6), 1474–1487 (2017). (in Chinese)
5. Abe, R., Nakamura, K., Teramoto, K., Takahashi, M.: Attack incentive and security of exchanging tokens on proof-of-work blockchain. In: AINTEC 2018, pp. 32–37 (2018)

6. Fernández-Caramés, T.M., Fraga-Lamas, P.: A review on the use of blockchain for the internet of things. IEEE Access **6**, 32979–33001 (2018)
7. Atzei, N., Bartoletti, M., Lande, S., Zunino, R.: A formal model of bitcoin transactions. Financ. Cryptogr. 541–560 (2018)
8. Carminati, B.: Merkle trees. Encycl. Database Syst. 1714–1715 (2009)
9. Helo, P., Hao, Y.: Blockchains in operations and supply chains: a model and reference implementation. Comput. Ind. Eng. **136**, 242–251 (2019)
10. Jayaraman, R., Saleh, K., King, N.: Improving opportunities in healthcare supply chain processes via the internet of things and blockchain technology. IJHISI **14**(2), 49–65 (2019)
11. Nakamoto, S.: Bitcoin: a peer-to-peer electronic cash system (2009)
12. Delgado-Segura, S., Pérez-Solà, C., Navarro-Arribas, G., Herrera-Joancomartí, J.: analysis of the bitcoin UTXO set. IACR Cryptology ePrint Archive 2017: 1095 (2017)
13. Buterin, V.: Ethereum and the decentralized future. Future Thinkers Podcast. 21 April 2015. Accessed 13 May 2016
14. Lewenberg, Y., Sompolinsky, Y., Zohar, A.: Inclusive block chain protocols. In: Böhme, R., Okamoto, T. (eds.) FC 2015. LNCS, vol. 8975, pp. 528–547. Springer, Heidelberg (2015). https://doi.org/10.1007/978-3-662-47854-7_33
15. Worley, C.R., Skjellum, A.: Blockchain tradeoffs and challenges for current and emerging applications: generalization, fragmentation, sidechains, and scalability. iThings/GreenCom/CPSCom/SmartData, pp. 1582–1587 (2018)
16. Wang, J., Wang, H.: Monoxide: scale out blockchains with asynchronous consensus zones. In: NSDI 2019, pp. 95–112 (2019)
17. Morishima, S., Matsutani, H.: Accelerating blockchain search of full nodes using GPUs. In: PDP 2018, pp. 244–248 (2018)
18. Zhao, Q., Zonghua, G., Yao, M., Zeng, H.: HLC-PCP: A resource synchronization protocol for certifiable mixed criticality scheduling. J. Syst. Archit. – Embedd. Syst. Design **66–67**, 84–99 (2019)
19. Helmer, S., Roggia, M., El Ioini, N., Pahl, C.: EthernityDB - integrating database functionality into a blockchain. In: ADBIS (Short Papers and Workshops), pp. 37–44 (2018)
20. Muzammal, M.: Renovating blockchain with distributed databases: an open source system. Futur. Gener. Comput. Syst. **90**, 105–117 (2019)
21. Pham, A., Huguenin, K., Bilogrevic, I., Dacosta, I., Hubaux, J.P.: SecureRun: cheat-proof and private summaries for location-based activities. IEEE Trans. Mob. Comput. **15**(8), 2109–2123 (2016)
22. Wan, J., Zou, C., Ullah, S., Lai, C., Zhou, M., Wang, X.: Cloud-enabled wireless body area networks for pervasive healthcare. IEEE Netw. **27**(5), 57–61 (2013). pp. 292–293 (2018)
23. Alkan, H., Celebi, H.: The implementation of positioning system with trilateration of haversine distance. In: PIMRC, pp. 1–6 (2019)

Deep Learning-Based Reverse Method
of Binary Protocol

Chenglong Yang[1,2], Cai Fu[1,2], Yekui Qian[3(✉)], Yao Hong[1,2], Guanyun Feng[1,2],
and Lansheng Han[1,2]

[1] School of Cyber Science and Engineering,
Huazhong University of Science and Technology, Wuhan 430074, China
stand_fucai@126.com
[2] Hubei Engineering Research Center on Big Data Security, Wuhan 430074, China
[3] Department of Command and Control,
Air Defence Forces Academy of PLA, Zhengzhou 450052, China
qyk1129@hotmail.com

Abstract. With the growth of network equipment, the security of network access environment becomes particularly important. Many network security technologies, such as vulnerability mining, fuzzy testing and intrusion detection, have attracted more and more attention. However, the effectiveness of these security technologies will be greatly reduced in the face of unknown protocols. By automatically extracting the format information of unknown protocols through the protocol reverse technology, the processing capability of the above security technologies in the face of unknown protocols can be enhanced. In this paper, by analyzing the changing characteristics of protocol fields, a field sequence coding method is proposed, which is suitable for reflecting the field sequence characteristics of different protocols and can improve the generalization ability of the model. Using the above field sequence coding method, a field classification model for unknown protocols is implemented based on the LSTM-FCN network, which is widely used in time series classification tasks. Finally, a binary protocol reverse method based on deep learning is proposed. The method is based on the field classification model and realizes the division and type identification of unknown protocol fields according to the classification results. In the experiment, the field classification model has high accuracy and recall in different protocols, which shows that the model has the ability to identify the field type according to the changing characteristics of the field. The proposed protocol reverse method also accurately and quickly identifies the field and its type, proving the reverse ability of the method to unknown binary protocols.

Keywords: Binary protocol reverse · Protocol field classification · Deep learning

1 Introduction

Network protocols are the basic guarantee for communication in the network. Many common security technologies, such as intrusion detection, vulnerability

© Springer Nature Singapore Pte Ltd. 2020
S. Yu et al. (Eds.): SPDE 2020, CCIS 1268, pp. 606–624, 2020.
https://doi.org/10.1007/978-981-15-9129-7_42

mining and fuzzy testing, usually require a certain understanding of protocol technology standards [1–3]. When faced with unknown protocols, their accuracy and efficiency will be seriously affected. The protocol reverse technology can extract the format fields of the protocol by analyzing the message sequence, instruction execution and system state in the actual communication process without the protocol standard document [4]. The most primitive of the protocol reverse techniques is the manual protocol reverse. However, the manual protocol reverse is very time-consuming and energy-consuming, and its accuracy depends almost entirely on the professionalism of the reverse personnel. In addition, the network protocol is not static and is always improved, so the manual reverse method is costly. Therefore, the highly efficient and automated protocol reverse method has high research significance and broad application prospects, and is the research direction of many scholars [5, 6].

In addition to traditional manual analysis methods, protocol reverse techniques can be roughly divided into two categories: message sequence analysis and binary instruction execution analysis [7]. The message sequence analysis technology takes the protocol session data stream obtained by Wireshark, Tcpdump and other sniffing tools as the analysis object. The most commonly used algorithms are multi-sequence alignment algorithms and sequence clustering algorithms. The core of these algorithms is the comparison of sequence similarity [8]. The comparison of sequence clustering algorithms is mainly based on keywords, editing distance and probability model [9]. However, the common problem of these algorithms is that they can not give an accurate similarity evaluation criterion, and clustering algorithms usually needs high-dimensional clustering calculation, which will bring great difficulty in calculation. The instruction execution analysis technique takes the terminal program that parses or constructs the message as the analysis object. It monitors the instruction sequence and propagation process of protocol data parsing by means of dynamic stain tracking [10]. But this technology needs to obtain the terminal program of protocol parsing, which is usually difficult.

Both kinds of protocol reverse analysis techniques have made much progress and have their own advantages and limitations. In terms of processing objects, the message sequence is easier to obtain than the terminal program of protocol parsing. In terms of analysis depth, the message sequence analysis technology analyzes the characteristics and changing rules of field values, so it is difficult to realize the semantic analysis of message fields, while the instruction sequence analysis technology can realize the recognition of field semantics and hierarchical relationship [11]. In terms of analysis speed, the speed of message sequence analysis is much faster than that of instruction execution sequence analysis.

In this paper, we pay more attention to the universality and speed of the protocol reverse, so we choose the message sequence analysis technology and realize the binary protocol reverse method based on deep learning. Firstly, by analyzing the changing characteristics of protocol fields, a field sequence coding method is proposed, which is suitable for reflecting the field sequence characteristics of different protocols and can improve the generalization ability of the model. Second, using the above field sequence coding method, and based on the LSTM-FCN network which is widely used in time series classification tasks, a field classification model for unknown protocols is implemented. Finally, the field classification results and the field partition algorithm are used to complete the division and type identification of unknown protocol fields, and the reverse of binary protocol is realized.

Our contributions can be summarized as follows:

- We propose a reverse method of binary protocol based on deep learning. Compared with the statistical and rule-based algorithms such as clustering and multi-sequence alignment in the traditional protocol reverse method, deep learning can extract higher-dimensional features of data, so better results can be achieved. Moreover, through the pre-training of the deep learning model, the prediction speed of the model will be fast.
- Our method is based on the dynamic characteristics of fields, and we propose a field sequence coding method according to the changing characteristics of fields. The traditional sequence clustering algorithms do not consider the dynamic characteristics of protocol packets in time series. In comparison, our scheme can obtain more information in theory.
- Our method is for binary protocols. The traditional protocol reverse methods based on message sequence analysis depend on the similarity comparison between sequences, and usually fail to get good analysis results on pure binary protocols. The reverse object of our solution is binary protocols.

The rest of this paper is organized as follows. We introduce the preliminaries of our work in Sect. 2, describe the field classification model in Sect. 3, expound the binary protocol reverse method in Sect. 4, present experimental results in Sect. 5 and conclude our work in Sect. 6.

2   Preliminaries

Convolution Neural Network (CNN) is a kind of neural network designed to deal with grid structure data. It is widely used in image processing, speech analysis and other fields [12,13]. However, CNN has encountered challenges in the task of image semantic segmentation. In order to solve the task of semantic segmentation, the concept of Full Convolution Network (FCN) is proposed in paper [14]. FCN is the first end-to-end network for semantic segmentation which is realized by pixel-level prediction. Unlike classical CNN, FCN allows inputs of different sizes. In the last layer of FCN, the transposed convolution layer is used to up-sample the feature map to restore the original input size and retain the information of the spatial position. Therefore, FCN can generate a prediction for each pixel and finally perform pixel-by-pixel classification.

Long Short-Term Memory (LSTM) is a classical model for time series tasks [15], which is widely used in natural language processing, machine translation, timing prediction and other fields [16,17]. In recent years, FCN-based deep learning models have also begun to be applied to the tasks of time series classification and prediction [18, 19]. Karim F [20] proposes a new end-to-end time series classification network model: LSTM-FCN. The model uses a combination of FCN and LSTM network, and has the advantages of high time efficiency and no need for additional feature extraction. Also, in multiple tests of time series classification, the model shows better accuracy than other classification methods. The network structure of LSTM-FCN is shown in Fig. 1. LSTM-FCN uses a Full Convolution Network composed of multiple convolution layers to extract sequence features, and uses the global pooling layer to reduce parameters, which speeds up the training. A small LSTM network is used to enhance the Full Convolution Network. Finally, the output results of the two parts are concatenated and input to Softmax for classification. The detailed description and use of the model is in Sect. 3.3.

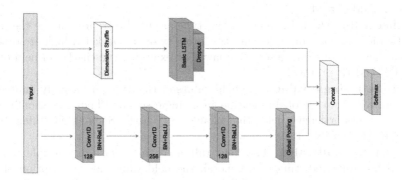

Fig. 1. Network structure of LSTM-FCN

3   Field Classification Model

3.1   Field Type Selection

The ultimate purpose of field classification is to identify the fields of unknown protocols, and do not need to focus on the specific meaning of field values. Therefore, when selecting the field type, we only need to pay attention to the changing law of the field sequence. The field types should not be too fine, which will lead to the difference between different types being too small, thus making the subsequent training more difficult. The field types should also not be too rare, which will lack the practicality and may affect the generalization ability of the training model. Therefore, it is necessary to ensure that the selected field types are common, have differentiation, and can be classified more accurately.

After statistics and analysis of the field types in the common network protocols, the following field types are selected.

1. **Incremental sequence.** The field values of this type generally change in an incremental manner, and the subsequent values always increase or remain the same, and may also be a loop similar to the TCP serial number. This field type usually appears in the serial number and index, such as the seq and ack fields of the TCP protocol, and the id field of the IP protocol.
2. **Identifier.** Fields of this type are usually used as identifiers for a single session. Theoretically, the field values are the same in a single session and different in different sessions, which can be used to distinguish between multiple parallel sessions. For example, the port field of the TCP protocol and the address field of the IP protocol.
3. **Fixed value.** The field values of this type are fixed throughout the protocol. Therefore, the field of this type can be used as a unique flag of the protocol, such as the version field of the IPv4 protocol, which is fixed to 4, or an aligned zero-padded field.
4. **Checksum.** The field values of this type are used to represent the checksum of a piece of data and to ensure the integrity of the packet, which are random and have no obvious descriptive law. For example, the checksum field of the TCP and IP protocols.
5. **Discrete single value.** The field values of this type are usually limited, so there will be a lot of duplication in a single session. They are usually used as flag bits or length fields that change very little. Such as TCP flag: SYN, ACK, RST, FIN, etc.
6. **Discrete multivalue.** The field values of this type are multiple discrete and less repeated values. In general, the field values are description of certain attributes, such as specific parameters and the length of message. For example, the length fields of the TCP protocol and the IP protocol.

To simplify the presentation of the experimental results, the following conventions are made: D for discrete single value type, M for discrete multivalue type, S for incremental sequence type, C for checksum type, ID for identifier type, and F for fixed value type.

3.2   Field Sequence Coding Method

Message Preprocessing. Wireshark is used to obtain network communication messages. But the protocol messages intercepted by this software are generally mixed with various protocols, such as TCP, UDP, ICMP, etc. So the following processing is required to make the messages useful. *(1) Protocol classification extraction.* The messages are processed according to different protocols. The unnecessary protocols are deleted, and the required protocols are stored according to the protocol. After this step, the original protocol messages are processed into network message groups divided by protocol types. *(2) Session grouping.* Session-based protocols usually consist of one or more sessions per protocol interaction. Session grouping can make the changing mode of messages in the session clearer. The specific method is to divide the messages by parsing the identification fields of protocols, such as the port field of the TCP protocol and the ip address field of the IP protocol. For the obtained messages of a single session, the identities are added according to the sending and receiving. *(3) Data deletion of underlying protocol stack.* Protocols usually do not work alone because network communication requires multiple protocols to work together. Therefore, for the captured messages, it is necessary to delete the unrelated underlying encapsulations and protocol headers according to their protocol stacks.

Protocol Field Sequence Combination. Each protocol consists of multiple fields and each field has a separate definition and range of values. So the message byte stream can be divided into multiple sets of fields through the field boundary.

As shown in Fig. 2, in an $N \times M$ protocol session, each message contains M fields and the session contains N protocol messages. Each time the same fields in M fields are extracted to form a field sequence of length N, which is a final field sequence sample. An $N \times M$ protocol session can extract M sequences of length N.

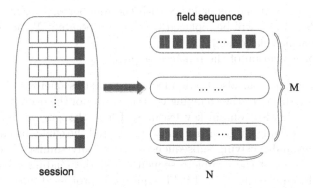

Fig. 2. Protocol field sequence combination process

After the protocols are divided according to the sessions, the messages in each session are further divided according to the field types. The same fields of messages in a single session are combined into a field sequence. Taking TCP protocol as an example, all source ports in a single TCP session are combined into a field sequence, and fields such as destination ports and serial numbers are also combined into field sequences separately. The final protocol field sequences are the key features of the field classification model.

Sequence Coding. A sequence of the same fields in a single session is a data form similar to a time series. A single field sequence is a numerical sequence arranged according to the transmission time, which is a change in a field over a certain period of time.

The proposed classification model will eventually be used to identify the field types of different protocols. Different protocols mean that the values of the fields may be completely different, so the field types can only be determined by the changing mode of the field values. For example, an incremental sequence number field whose incremental starting value affects the size of all subsequent values. But this field should be classified under the same class regardless of the starting value. Also, the TCP port number field and the IP address field have completely different values: the former has only 2 bytes, while the latter uses 4 bytes. But in the classification task, the two will be considered the same type.

In order to eliminate the interference of field values on the classification model, it is necessary to design a method to encode the original field sequences. By numbering the field values according to the size relationship in the sequence, the interference of the field values can be removed while the key features will be retained. Given field sequence $S = s_1, s_2, s_3, \cdots, s_m$, the specific field sequence coding method is as follows:

1. Statistics of all different value sets V in sequence S.
2. Arranging V in numerical ascending order and numbering it incrementally from 1 to N.
3. Replacing the original sequence S with the number of V. For example, if a value in S is V_x, it will be replaced by its corresponding N_x according to the transformation relationship.
4. Linear normalization of the replaced sequence.

A field sequence can also be divided into two subsequences of sending and receiving. In addition to the changing characteristics of the overall sequence, the subsequences will also contain key features of field changes in some cases. The length of the receiving subsequence may be zero, and the changing characteristics of the sending and receiving subsequences are usually similar. Therefore, only the characteristics of the complete sequence and the sending subsequence are considered. Finally, each original field sequence is processed into two sequences after coding: the overall sequence T and the sending sequence T_s. In order to keep the length fixed, the sequence T_s is filled or cropped to a fixed length.

3.3 Classification Model Network Structure

The coded field sequences are very similar to the traditional time series in data form, and they are all real value series arranged according to the time relationship. Therefore, the LSTM-FCN network, which has been proved to be excellent in processing time series, can be used to construct the field sequence classification model. As mentioned in Sect. 3.2.3, each field sequence is processed into two sequences of different lengths: the overall sequence T and the sending sequence T_s. The classification model needs to extract the features of the two sequences at the same time, so two LSTM-FCN networks are used to process the overall sequence and the sending sequence side by side. Finally, the outputs of the two LSTM-FCN networks are concatenated and input to the Softmax layer for multi-classification. The overall network structure of the classification model is shown in Fig. 3.

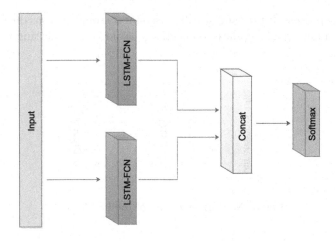

Fig. 3. Overall network structure of the classification model

LSTM-FCN network can be divided into two parts: FCN and LSTM. The network structure of the FCN part is shown in Fig. 4. When processing sequence data, FCN is usually used to extract the features of original sequences. The basic convolution block of FCN is composed of convolution layer, batch standardization layer and activation layer. Convolution operation consists of three one-dimensional convolutions with size 8, 5, 3 and step size 1. After the last convolution block, the global pooling layer is used to reduce the number of parameters and speed up training.

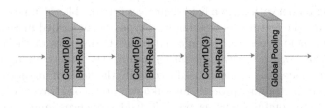

Fig. 4. Network structure of the FCN part

The network structure of the LSTM part is shown in Fig. 5, including the Dimension shuffle layer, the LSTM layer and the Dropout layer. Unlike the structure of traditional LSTM, a dimension shuffle operation is first performed on the input sequence of LSTM in LSTM-FCN. In fact, the dimension shuffle operation is to transform the input series with dimension $N \times 1$ into the form of $1 \times N$, the central idea of which is to transform a time series into a single time step of a multivariable time series. This is one of the key reasons for the high performance of LSTM-FCN. In practical applications, the Dropout layer is usually added after the LSTM layer, which is a regularization method used in the training process. It probabilistically disconnects some neurons during forward propagation and weight update to effectively avoid the over-fitting problem.

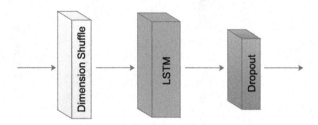

Fig. 5. Network structure of the LSTM part

4   Binary Protocol Reverse Method

4.1   Method Overview

The binary protocol reverse method uses the field classification model given in Sect. 3 to learn the features of the existing field types. After the training, the model is used to classify the unknown field sequences. Then the optimal classification is selected from the classification results of all the field sequences, and finally the field division of the protocol is given.

As shown in Fig. 6, the binary protocol reverse method consists of three core parts: *(1) Field classification model training.* The purpose of training the field classification model with known field sequences is to enable the final classification model to learn the features of existing field types (as described in Sect. 3). Thus, the unknown field types can be inferred from the features of the known field types. *(2) Unknown protocol field classification.* After the training of the field classification model, the model is used to classify the fields of unknown protocols. Different from the training process, for unknown protocols, traversing all possible continuous byte combinations as possible field sequences, and then using the classification model to classify all sequences and record the classification results. *(3) Field division.* After obtaining the classification results of all combinations, the field division algorithm is used to obtain the optimal classification method, and the protocol field division manner is calculated according to the optimal classification.

The complete scheme of the field classification model has been described in detail in Sect. 3. The unknown protocol field classification and field division are detailed below.

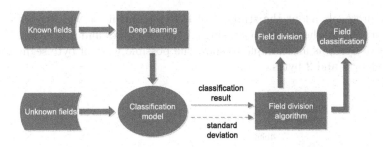

Fig. 6. Overview of binary protocol reverse method

4.2   Unknown Protocol Field Classification

Message Interception. Data interception is the first step, and the quality of the obtained data will affect the accuracy of all subsequent steps. There are three issues to be focused on when obtaining raw data: *(1) Protocol session partition.* Unlike the collection of network messages used as training data, unknown protocols do not have explicit document information, so the session identifiers cannot be obtained and the data cleaning and classification cannot be performed after all data has been collected. Therefore, when collecting test data, it is necessary to distinguish between sessions in order to avoid multiple sessions in parallel. *(2) Integrity of protocol session.* The integrity of the field sequences is very important. The more complete a sequence is, the more field changing characteristics (that is, type features) will be contained, which is helpful to the accuracy of field classification. *(3) Diversity of session state.* The message state change in a single session is a subset of the whole protocol state change. Therefore, in order to obtain a complete protocol state changing relationship, it is necessary to obtain as many protocol sessions in different states as possible.

Message Preprocessing. The preprocessing removes the data of the unrelated underlying protocol stacks. Each message is processed into a byte sequence of a certain length, and each byte sequence only contains the target protocol message.

Byte Segmentation. After preprocessing, the unknown protocol messages have been converted to byte sequences. Then, the byte sequences need to be segmented to form the field sequences.

In order to find out the most likely segmentation of the real protocol fields from all possible segments, it is necessary to imitate the commonly used protocol field segmentation method as much as possible. Most of the commonly used binary protocols adopt the strategy of byte alignment, so we choose four byte segmentation methods: half byte, single byte, two bytes and four bytes. Figure 7 takes two bytes as an example to show the possible ways of byte segmentation: 4 bits, 1 byte and 2 bytes.

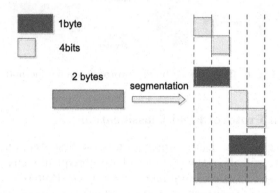

Fig. 7. An example of byte segmentation

After segmenting the unknown protocol byte sequences, the same segmented "field" can be sequenced in units of sessions. Finally, the field sequences are transformed into vectors to be input to the classification model, and the field classification results are recorded.

4.3   Field Division

The field division algorithm is used to compare the classification results of all the segmented field sequences (obtained by Sect. 4.2.3). The results which best conform to the known field types are selected to form the final protocol field division. In theory, the same field sequences in a protocol will show the same sequence characteristics in different sessions. In the actual classification, it will be shown that the classification results of most or even all the samples will belong to the same class. For two different byte segmentation methods, the more centralized the distribution of type prediction results is, the more likely that the samples are the real field sequences. Standard deviation is a measure of the degree of data discreteness. The more centralized the data is, the greater the standard deviation is. Taking the standard deviation as the scoring function, the final field division algorithm is shown as Algorithm 1.

Algorithm 1. The field division algorithm

Input: Initial byte segmentation method set F(each element in F is a class that contains four attributes: start, length, type, score).

Output: Field division result R.

1: Sort elements in F by the attribute "score" from large to small;

2: $R \leftarrow \{\}$;

3: **while** F is not null **do**

4:     Select the first element f in set F,

5:     Add f to the set R,

6:     Remove f and the elements which partially coincide with f from F;

7: **end while**

8: Sort elements in R by the attribute "start" from small to large.

The core idea of the algorithm is to select the best byte segmentation method from the byte segmentation method set F each time, and then remove the segmentation methods which partially coincide with the current best segmentation method from the set. Repeating this process until the set F is empty. All the selected byte segmentation methods make up the final field division result R. Each byte segmentation method is represented by a class which records specific information about a byte segmentation method, including starting byte, length, field type and score (based on standard deviation).

5   Experiments

5.1   Experiment Setup

Our experiments are conducted on a server with 16 GB memory, 2.80 GHz CPU, and NVIDIA GeForce GTX 1050. The method is implemented using Keras with TensorFlow as the backend.

Data Sets. Protocol reverse technology is usually used to analyze the format, state machine and other information of an unknown protocol. In order to test the accuracy and effectiveness of the protocol reverse method, the most appropriate way is to use unknown protocols for reverse analysis. However, it is difficult to obtain unknown protocols, and it is also difficult to give accurate criteria to evaluate the experimental results. Therefore, known protocols are usually selected for test in experiments.

Two common binary type protocols, IPv4 and TCP, are selected in the experiment. Training sets and test sets use different types of protocols. It is guaranteed that the protocol used to test is unknown to the whole protocol reverse method to simulate the reverse process of the real unknown protocols.

Performance Metrics. For classification problems, there may be three different classification results for each sample to be classified: TP (True Positive) refers to the correctly classified samples, that is, the predicted type is the same as the true type of a sample. FP (False Positive) means that a sample whose real type is A is not classified as A. FN (False Negative) means that a sample whose real type is not A is incorrectly classified as A. The following performance metrics which are commonly used in classification tasks are used in the experiment. *(1) Precision* $P = \frac{TP}{TP+FP}$. Precision describes the ratio at which a certain type of samples are correctly predicted. *(2) Recall* $R = \frac{TP}{TP+FN}$. Recall describes the ratio of correct samples in all samples that are predicted to be a certain type. *(3) F1-Score* $F_1 = 2 \cdot \frac{precision \cdot recall}{precision+recall}$. F1-Score is the harmonic average of Precision and Recall, which is a comprehensive measure of a classification model. *(4) Micro-F1 and Macro-F1.* The total F1-Score of the multi-classification model can be divided into two types according to the different calculation methods: Micro-F1 calculates the total accuracy and total recall of all categories, and then calculates the overall F1-Score. Macro-F1 calculates the separate F1-Score value for each category, and then takes the average F1-Score for all categories.

5.2   Field Classification Result

For the field classification model, the TCP protocol field data is used as the training set and validation set, and the IP protocol field data is used as the test set. The length of the field sequence is 256. The results on the validation set are shown in Table 1, and the results on the test set are shown in Table 2.

Table 1. Field classification results of TCP protocol

Validation set	TCP		
Performance metrics	Precision	Recall	F1-score
Discrete multivalue	0.94	0.99	0.96
Incremental sequence	0.98	0.98	0.98
Checksum	0.98	0.93	0.95
Identifier	1.00	1.00	1.00
Fixed value	1.00	1.00	1.00
Discrete single value	0.93	0.99	0.96
Micro-F1	0.98		
Macro-F1	0.97		

Table 2. Field classification results of IP protocol

Test set	IP		
Performance metrics	Precision	Recall	F1-score
Discrete multivalue	0.95	0.90	0.93
Incremental sequence	0.95	0.79	0.86
Checksum	0.80	0.84	0.82
Identifier	0.89	0.80	0.84
Fixed value	1.00	1.00	1.00
Discrete single value	0.85	0.95	0.90
Micro-F1	0.89		
Macro-F1	0.89		

On the validation set, which uses the same TCP protocol as the training set, the Precision and Recall of all field types are more than 90%, even 100% on the types of fixed value and identifier, and the F1-Score is greater than 0.95. This shows that the model has excellent performance in identifying the protocol field types of the training set.

On the test set which uses the IP protocol field data, the Precision of each field type is more than 80%, the Recall is higher than 79%, and the F1-Score is greater than 0.82. Compared with the validation results of TCP protocol, the Precision and Recall of IP protocol data are reduced to a certain extent. However, they are acceptable considering that the test data comes from the real network environment and do not participate in training.

The comparison of F1-Score between the validation set and the test set is shown in Fig. 8. Generally speaking, the field classification model performs better on the training set which uses the TCP protocol, but it also performs well on the IP protocol.

5.3   Protocol Reverse Result

Firstly, training the field classification model by using the initial learning rate of 1e-3 and Adam optimizer. In order to prevent the classification model from over-fitting on a single protocol, the intermediate model of each epoch is retained and the best model is selected through testing. When dividing unknown protocol fields, each protocol uses a variety of byte segmentation methods to obtain a large number of field sequences for classification. Finally, the fields are divided according to the classification results of all sequences and the field division algorithm in Sect. 4.3. Two typical binary format protocols, IPv4 protocol and TCP protocol, are used in the experiment, and all the test data comes from the real network environment.

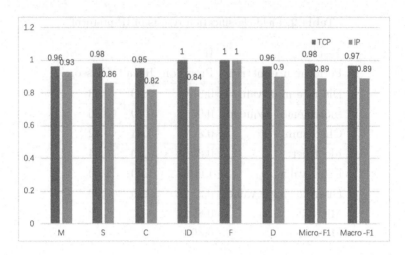

Fig. 8. The comparison of F1-Score

TCP Protocol. In order to compare with the real results, the actual field information of the TCP protocol header is shown in Table 3. The reverse result of the TCP protocol is shown in Table 4.

Table 3. Actual field information of TCP protocol

Bits	0–3	4–7	8–11	12–15	16–19	20–23	24–27	28–31
Type	Source port				Destination port			
	SEQ							
	ACK							
	Length	Reserve	6-bit flag		Window			
	Checksum				Emergency pointer			

There are some differences between the experimental results and the actual results, but most of the differences are understandable and acceptable. For the source port and destination port fields of the TCP protocol, each field consists of one 2-byte identifier type in the actual results, but in the experiment, it is divided into two 1-byte identifier type fields. Considering the characteristics of the identifier type: it is immutable in a one-way packet for a single session, so it is reasonable to divide it arbitrarily. For the window fields of the TCP protocol, the law of their actual values is not particularly obvious, so they are divided into two fields in the experiment.

IP Protocol. In order to simulate the unknown protocol, the IP protocol data which does not interfere with the training data of the model is selected to replace the "unknown protocol". The most representative two groups of reverse results

Table 4. Reverse result of TCP protocol

Bits	0–3	4–7	8–11	12–15	16–19	20–23	24–27	28–31
Type	ID		ID		ID		ID	
	S							
	S							
	D	F	D		D		ID	
	C				F		F	

are chosen and analyzed from several groups of tests, which are shown in Table 5 and Table 6. The real field division and field types of the IPv4 protocol are shown in Table 7.

Table 5. Reverse result 1 of IP protocol

Bits	0–3	4–7	8–11	12–15	16–19	20–23	24–27	28–31
Type	F		F		F	M		
	S				D	F	F	
	ID		D		C			
	ID		ID		ID			
	ID							

Table 6. Reverse result 2 of IP protocol

Bits	0–3	4–7	8–11	12–15	16–19	20–23	24–27	28–31
Type	F		F		ID		M	
	S				D	F	F	
	ID		D		C			
	ID		ID		ID		ID	
	ID				ID			

Comparing the real results of IPv4 protocol (Table 7) with the experimental results of Table 5 and Table 6, we can see that the field classification results are basically the same as the real field classification of IPv4 protocol. Some fields of the same type will be divided into multiple segments because of the algorithm, such as the source and destination address fields. They are divided into multiple identifier types (represented by ID) since this type itself is divisible, so getting different ways of dividing according to the data is in line with the actual results.

Table 7. Actual field information of IP protocol

Bits	0–3	4–7	8–11	12–15	16–19	20–23	24–27	28–31
Type	Version	Length	TOS		Total length			
	Identification				3-bit flag	13-bit offset		
	TTL		Protocol number		Checksum			
	Source IP							
	Destination IP							

From the experimental results, it is found that there are two ways to divide the total length field of IPv4, but neither of them is completely the same as the real division. After the analysis of the actual data, the reason is that the actual maximum length of the IPv4 packet is only 1500, and the hexadecimal form is 0x05dc. The four bits of its highest bit are always zero, so it is divided into a fixed value (F). When the message length is generally short, the value of the field is between 0x00ff and 0x01ff, so the previous byte will be divided into the identifier (ID), which is also in line with the objective law of the data.

In the experimental results, the 3-bit flag and 13-bit offset fields are not consistent with the real field. This is because the algorithm does not consider the unusual byte segmentation method of 3+13 and the value of the 13-bit offset field is always zero and remains the same in the test data. So these two fields are eventually divided into 4-bit discrete single value field (D), 4-bit fixed value field (F), and 8-bit fixed value field (F).

From the above experimental results, it can be seen that the field divisions of TCP protocol and IP protocol are basically consistent with the actual results. Therefore, the proposed binary protocol reverse method has generally achieved the expected goal in the actual situation.

6   Conclusion

In this paper, a reverse method of binary protocol based on deep learning is implemented. Based on the knowledge of the types of known protocol fields, it uses neural networks to learn the characteristics of known fields to implement the field classification model. Then, the possible byte segmentation of the unknown protocol is carried out, and the result of field division is given by looking for the optimal byte segmentation method. Finally, the reverse result of the protocol is given according to the results of field classification and field division. The core part is using the method of deep learning to realize the field classification model, which is based on LSTM-FCN network. This avoids the manual feature extraction of the original sequences and realizes the automatic protocol reverse.

References

1. Yusheng, W., Kefeng, F., Yingxu, L.: Intrusion detection of industrial control system based on modbus TCP protocol. In: Proceedings of the 13th IEEE International Symposium on Autonomous Decentralized System, Bangkok, Thailand, 22–24 March 2017 (2017)
2. Zhang, S., Zhang, L.: Vulnerability mining for network protocols based on fuzzing. In: Proceedings of the 2nd International Conference on Systems and Informatics, Shanghai, China, 15–17 November 2014 (2014)
3. Zhao, J., Su, Z., Ma, J., Cui, B.: Fuzzing test method based on constraint-conditions priority for LTE-EPC protocol. In: Barolli, L., Javaid, N., Ikeda, M., Takizawa, M. (eds.) CISIS 2018. AISC, vol. 772, pp. 465–475. Springer, Cham (2019). https://doi.org/10.1007/978-3-319-93659-8_41
4. Narayan, J., Shukla, K., Clancy, T.: A survey of automatic protocol reverse engineering tools. CSUR 48, 40:1–40:26 (2016)
5. Xiao, M., Luo, Y.: Automatic protocol reverse engineering using grammatical inference. J. Intell. Fuzzy Syst. 32, 3585–3594 (2017)
6. Ji, R., Wang, J., Tang, C.: Automatic reverse engineering of private flight control protocols of UAVs. Secur. Commun. Netw. 2017, 1308045:1–1308045:9 (2017)
7. Sija, B.D., Goo, Y.H., Shim, K.S.: A survey of automatic protocol reverse engineering approaches, methods, and tools on the inputs and outputs view. Secur. Commun. Netw. 2018, 8370341:1–8370341:17 (2018)
8. Xing, S., Wang, B., Zhou, C., Zhang, Q.: RNA sequences similarities analysis by inner products. In: Bikakis, A., Zheng, X. (eds.) MIWAI 2015. LNCS (LNAI), vol. 9426, pp. 329–339. Springer, Cham (2015). https://doi.org/10.1007/978-3-319-26181-2_31
9. Hu, Y.-J.: Instruction sequences clustering and analysis of network protocol's dormant behaviors. 3PGCIC 2016. LNDECT, vol. 1, pp. 639–649. Springer, Cham (2017). https://doi.org/10.1007/978-3-319-49109-7_61
10. Liu, M., Jia, C., Liu, L. Extracting sent message formats from executables using backward slicing. In: Proceedings of the 4th International Conference on Emerging Intelligent Data and Web Technologies, Shaanxi, China, 9–11 September 2013 (2013)
11. Caballero, J., Song, D.: Automatic protocol reverse-engineering: message format extraction and field semantics inference. Comput. Netw. 57, 451–474 (2013)
12. Krizhevsky, A., Sutskever, I., Hinton, G.E.: ImageNet classification with deep convolutional neural networks. Commun. ACM 60, 84–90 (2017)
13. Zhang, X., Sun, H., Wang, S., Xu, J.: Speech signal classification based on convolutional neural networks. In: Sun, F., Liu, H., Hu, D. (eds.) ICCSIP 2018. CCIS, vol. 1006, pp. 281–287. Springer, Singapore (2019). https://doi.org/10.1007/978-981-13-7986-4_25
14. Long, J., Shelhamer, E., Darrell, T.: Fully convolutional networks for semantic segmentation. IEEE Trans. Pattern Anal. Mach. Intell. 39, 640–651 (2017)
15. Hochreiter, S., Schmidhuber, J.: Long short-term memory. Neural Comput. 9, 1735–1780 (1997)
16. Jia, Y., Feng, Y., Luo, B., Ye, Y., Liu, T., Zhao, D.: Transition-based discourse parsing with multilayer stack long short term memory. In: Lin, C.-Y., Xue, N., Zhao, D., Huang, X., Feng, Y. (eds.) ICCPOL/NLPCC -2016. LNCS (LNAI), vol. 10102, pp. 360–373. Springer, Cham (2016). https://doi.org/10.1007/978-3-319-50496-4_30

17. Anava, O., Hazan, E., Mannor, S.: Online learning for time series prediction. In: Proceedings of the 26th Annual Conference on Learning Theory, NJ, USA, 12–14 June 2013 (2013)
18. Han, Y., Zhang, S., Geng, Z.: Multi-frequency decomposition with fully convolutional neural network for time series classification. In: Proceedings of the 24th International Conference on Pattern Recognition, Beijing, China, 20–24 August 2018 (2018)
19. Wang, Z., Yan, W., Oates, T.: Time series classification from scratch with deep neural networks: a strong baseline. In: Proceedings of the 2017 International Joint Conference on Neural Networks, Anchorage, AK, USA, 14–19 May 2017 (2017)
20. Karim, F., Majumdar, S., Darabi, H.: LSTM fully convolutional networks for time series classification. IEEE Access **6**, 1662–1669 (2018)

Analysis Toward RLWE-Based Key Exchange Protocol Based on Automatic Learning Structure

Shuaishuai Zhu[1]([✉]) and Yiliang Han[1,2]

[1] College of Cryptography Engineering,
Engineering University of People's Armed Police, Xi'an 710086, China
zhu_sama@126.com
[2] Key Laboratory of Network and Information Security under the People's Armed
Police, Xi'an 710086, China

Abstract. We analyzed one of the NIST post-quantum cryptography candidates: NewHope-Key-Exchange, the post-quantum key exchange protocol, using an automatic analysis strategy to attack the security properties of the scheme. Our analysis approach mainly concentrates on the Number Theory Transform (NTT) as well as the RLWE assumption applied in NewHope. The influences of security and efficiency toward NewHope are analyzed based on specially designed attack models applying an automatic analysis oracle. Under the assumption of full security indistinguishability model and partial leakage security indistinguishability model, we configure the key exchange protocol respectively, and evaluate different security strength and efficiency in different scenarios to validate the influences of NTT structure. The quantitative results show that the NTT process performs an signaficent role in the key exchange protocol.

Keywords: Post-quantum cryptography · Key exchange protocol · Indistinguishability model · Security model

1 Introduction

1.1 Background

NewHope [1–4] is one of the most promising post-quantum candidates in the final contest round that covers public key encryption (PKE), key encapsulation mechanisms (KEM) [1,2] and key exchange protocols (KEP). In the official documentation, the passively CPA security level of PKE, NewHope-CPA-PKE is the

Supported by the National Natural Science Foundation of China (No. 61572521,U1636114), National Key Project of Research and Development Plan (2017YFB0802000), Innovative Research Team Project of Engineering University of APF (KYTD201805),Fundamental Research Project of Engineering University of APF (WJY201910).

S. Yu et al. (Eds.): SPDE 2020, CCIS 1268, pp. 625–639, 2020.
https://doi.org/10.1007/978-981-15-9129-7_43

essential conponent of NewHope in the continual practical primitives that the subscribors claim semantically security. The NewHope-CPA-KEM is designed by calling the PKE key generation, encryption and decryption algorithms. By applying FujisakiCOkamoto transform, the adaptively secure NewHope-CCA-KEM can be constructed with PKE algorithms. Also, the NewHope key exchange scheme is constructed by basic PKE algorithms, including the NewHope with reconciliation [4] and NewHope without reconciliation [3]. The former one is a complex two-pass key exchange protocol with key encapsulation direct relying on RLWE hardness. The later one is a much simple key exchange with the reuse of NewHope-CPA-PKE. Both of them are theoretically proved semantically secure under quantum oracle model. More specifically, the NewHope key exchange protocol is claimed to be semantically secure under CCA model, and now applied in online key negotiation [18] of Google Chrome browser. As in a key exchange protocol, a major security concern is the identity extraction from all the participators, which is specially considered in adaptively selective identity model that much more weaker than selective ciphertext model in indistinguishability attack. As the NewHope without reconciliation is a CPA-KEM wrap, we only consider the security of the former key exchange protocol under adaptively secure model. The interactions of the two-pass messages is compact and quite effective, but it covers the phases of public seed sampling, an uniform Number Theoretic Transform (NTT), and a negotiation round of reconciliation vectors which generated from the same noise distribution.

In this paper, three contributions are made surrounding the analysis of a post-quantum key exchange protocol candidate in the second round of NIST submissions. Firstly, compared with traditional theoretical provable analysis, we firstly explore the automatic analysis approach in the evaluation of security models, which will benefit the development of quantitative analysis of cryptographic protocols. Secondly, applying the automatic learning approach, we quantitatively analyzed the influences of NTT component toward security levels and system efficiency under different attack configuration. Thirdly, a standard methodology of cryptographic protocol is developed with practical steps to handle in real instantiations. By generalizing these steps, any theoretically secure primitives can be detected and evaluated in case of potential weak points. The rest of the paper is organized in five sections. In Sect. 2 and Sect. 3, we give some necessary preliminaries and related works. The attack structure and simulation oracle are explained in details in Sect. 4. Some results of the quantitative tests are demonstrated Sect. 5. The paper concludes in the final section.

2   Preliminaries

2.1   Notations

All our working space is in the polynomial ring noted as $R_q = \mathbb{Z}_q[x]/x^n + 1$, s.t. $n \in \mathbb{Z}$ and $q \equiv 1 \mod 2n$. G is an intelligent learning system, namely, a guess system to yield a result given enough samples of specified set. One of the most important benchmarks of G is accuracy of its results, noted as $\text{Acc}(G)$. All bold variables are vectors or matrices or a serial of coordinates.

2.2   Number Theoretic Transform(NTT)

For any $m \in \mathbb{Z}^+$, let $n = 2^m$, $q = 1 \bmod 2n$, and R_q be the polynomial ring. The NTT result of polynomial $p = \sum_{i=0}^{n-1} x^i$, $p \in R_q$ is defined as,

$$\text{NTT}(p) = \sum_{i=0}^{n-1} \hat{p}_i x^i,$$

in which $\hat{p}_i = \sum_{i=0}^{n-1} p^j w^{j(2i+1)}$ and w satisfies $w^{2n} = 1 \bmod 2n$.
    Similarly, the inverse result NTT^{-1} is defined as,

$$p = \text{NTT}^{-1}(\hat{p}) = \sum_{i=0}^{n-1} p_i x^i = \sum_{i=0}^{n-1} (n^{-1} \sum_{j=0}^{n-1} \hat{p}_j w^{i(2j+1)}) x^i$$

NTT transform is sort of similar to the discrete Fourier transform to simplify and speed up polynomial multiplication over finite fields.

2.3   Ring-LWE Based Security Models

Definition 1 (R-LWE). A $(R_q, n, \mathbb{D})$–LWE problem defined on a R_q : $\mathbb{Z}_q[x]/(x_n + 1)$ is the access to a challenge oracle $\mathcal{O}$ which is either a pseudorandom oracle $\mathcal{O}_p$ or a truly random oracle $\mathcal{O}_t$. $\mathcal{O}_p$ and $\mathcal{O}_t$ are defined as follows:
    $\mathcal{O}_p$ generates a value $(u_i, v_i) = (u_i, u_i^T s + e_i) \in R_q \times R_q$, where s is a uniformly random vector in $\mathbb{R}_q$, u_i are randomly picked vectors in $\mathcal{D}_{\mathcal{L},s}$, and $e_i \in \mathbb{Z}_q$ are fresh noise samples in $\Psi_{q,n}$.
    $\mathcal{O}_p$ generates a truly uniform random sample from $R_q \times R_q$.
    Then the decisional R-LWE problem is to distinguish source oracle of the outputs, and the computational R-LWE problem is to recover s from (u_i, v_i).

Definition 2 (Search problem on Ring-LWE with partial key leakage, R-SLWE). R-SLWE is defined on the parameter tuple (n, n', S, χ) in which $n' \in \{1, 2, 4, \cdots, n\}$, $S \subseteq \mathbb{Z}_{2n'}^+$ shows the set of index of possible leakage. $s \leftarrow \chi$ is a randomly sampled secret key, and let $\hat{s} = \text{NTT}(s)$. Given the partial leakage $(\hat{a}, \hat{u} = \hat{a} \cdot \hat{s} + \hat{e}, [\hat{s}_i]_{i \equiv \alpha \bmod 2n', \alpha \in S})$ in which a is a public matrix chosen from χ, and e is the noise vector sampled from χ, the R-SLWE problem is to recover s.

Definition 3 (Decisional problem on Ring-LWE with partial key leakage, R-DLWE). R-DLWE is defined on the parameter tuple (n, n', S, χ) in which $n' \in \{1, 2, 4, \cdots, n\}$, $S \subseteq \mathbb{Z}_{2n'}^+$ shows the set of index of possible leakage. $s \leftarrow \chi$ is a randomly sampled secret key, and let $\hat{s} = \text{NTT}(s)$. Given the partial leakage $(\hat{a}, \hat{u} = \hat{a} \cdot \hat{s} + \hat{e}, [\hat{s}_i]_{i \equiv \alpha \bmod 2n', \alpha \in S})$ in which a is a public matrix sampled from χ, and e is the noise vector sampled from χ, the R-DLWE problem is to distinguish $(\hat{a}, \hat{u} = \hat{a} \cdot \hat{s} + \hat{e}, [\hat{s}_i]_{i \equiv \alpha \bmod 2n', \alpha \in S})$ from $(\hat{a}, \hat{u} \leftarrow \mathbb{Z}_q, [\hat{s}_i]_{i \equiv \alpha \bmod 2n', \alpha \in S})$.

We note INS_{real} and INS_{presdu} as the real samples and the samples constructed in primitives respectively. For all the R-LWE based secure instances, the following theorem holds. **Theorem 1.** [12] If a cryptographic primitive is polynomial time secure, then for an instance I,

(1) $P\{I \in INS_{real}^{R-LWE}\}$-$P\{I \in INS_{presdu}^{R-LWE}\} = \epsilon_1$;

(2) $P\{I \in INS_{real}^{R-SLWE}\}$-$P\{I \in INS_{presdu}^{R-SLWE}\} = \epsilon_2$;

(3) $P\{I \in INS_{real}^{R-DLWE}\}$-$P\{I \in INS_{presdu}^{R-DLWE}\} = \epsilon_3$,

in which ϵ_1, ϵ_2 and ϵ_3 are negligible.

A key encapsulation mechanism consists three algorithms: $(pk, sk) \leftarrow KeyGen(1^k)$,$(v, c) \leftarrow Encap(pk)$, and $v \leftarrow Decap(sk, c)$, in which k is the security parameter. An IND-CCA secure KEM is defined by the following game between a challenger C and an adversary A.

Definition 4 (In Sect. 2 of [22]). (IND-CCA secure KEM) C establishes (pk, sk) by running $KeyGen(1^k)$, then uniformly samples a bit $m \in 0, 1$, and generates (v_m^*, c^*) by $Encap(pk)$. C sends (v_m^*, c^*, pk) as a challenge message. For any $c_i \neq c^*$, A adaptively choose to query the coordinate v_i. Finally, A makes a guess m' on m. If $m' = m$, A wins the IND-CCA game. The advantage of A is defined as,

$$Adv_{A,KEM}^{IND-CCA}(k) = |P[m' = m] - 1/2|$$

The KEM is IND-CCA secure if the advantage is bounded by $n(k)$, which is a negligible polynomial of k.

2.4   Attack on Indistinguishability of Output

To avoid identity forge and message re-sending, indistinguishability is a basic property of the output of key exchange protocols. In this subsection, we define the indistinguishability security model of NewHope acending the security model defined in Definition 4 and [3,4]. Then the indistinguishability security characters are fully evaluated by instances of the model. We assume the two-pass key exchange protocol as a black box which is given a pair of identities, such as the tuple $\{id_a, id_b\}$, and yields two messages $(\hat{a}, \hat{b})$, $(\hat{u}, \hat{r})$. Then in the adversary's view on communication channels, he gets an instance of NewHope protocol as follows,

$$\{(\hat{a}, \hat{b}), (\hat{u}, \hat{r})\} \leftarrow INS(id_a, id_b)$$

Basic Attack. For $id^* = (id_0, id_1)_i \in \{(id_a, id_b), (id_c, id_d)\}$, in which $i \in \{0, 1\}$, the basic attack is a multiple rounds of interactions between a challenger and an adversary with the following steps.

Step 1. The challenger initiates two instances of key exchange protocol in which one is a real protocol $INS_{real}(\cdot)$ and the other one is an ideal random generator $INS_{sim}(\cdot)$.

Step 2. The adversary launches queries with $id = (id_0, id_1) \in S_{id}$, and the challenger takes id as an input of $\text{INS}_{real}(\cdot)$ and sands the outputs back to the adversary.

Step 3. The adversary randomly selects $\{(id_a, id_b), (id_c, id_d)\} \in S_{id}$ and sends it to the challenger. The challenger flips a coin to get a random bit $i \in \{0, 1\}$, and then he takes $id^* = (id_0, id_1)_i \in \{(id_a, id_b)_0, (id_c, id_d)_1\}$ as the challenged identities. Finally, the challenger sends the output $\{(\hat{a}^*, \hat{b}^*), (\hat{u}^*, \hat{r}^*)\}$ back to the adversary.

Step 4. The adversary makes more additional queries with $id = (id_0, id_1) \in S_{id}$. If $id = id^*$, the challenger returns

$$\{(\hat{a}, \hat{b}), (\hat{u}, \hat{r})\} \leftarrow \text{INS}_{sim}(id_a, id_b),$$

else it returns

$$\{(\hat{a}, \hat{b}), (\hat{u}, \hat{r})\} \leftarrow \text{INS}_{real}(id_a, id_b)$$

Step 5. Finally, the adversary outputs a guess $b \in \{0, 1\}$. If $b = i$, the adversary wins in the attack.

Definition 5 (Indistinguishability security on selective identities of NewHope key exchange). For two group of randomly selected users $\{(id_a, id_b), (id_c, id_d)\} \in S_{id}$, two instances are generated as follows,

$$\{(\hat{a}, \hat{b}), (\hat{u}, \hat{r})\} \leftarrow \text{INS}(id_a, id_b),$$

$$\{(\hat{a}', \hat{b}'), (\hat{u}', \hat{r}')\} \leftarrow \text{INS}(id_c, id_d)$$

Given the outputs, the probability that the adversary can win in the Basic Attack with the above two instances is a negligible variable $\epsilon(k)$, in which k is the security parameter.

3   Related Works

Post-quantum Key Exchange Mechanisms. We assume that key exchange mechanism is a special instantiation for key encapsulation mechanisms (KEM). The post-quantum KEM usually includes the authenticated protocols like [15, 23], in which signatures or additional verifying structures are applied, and the direct KEM which is much brief and efficient, such as Ding [13], Peikert [20], and Alkim's NewHope [2,4] that built on Ring-LWE assumption. Also, there are KEM based on standard LWE assumption, which makes the scheme more brief, such as Frodo protocol [7] and Kyber protocol [8]. Schemes in the first categray can easily satisfy strong security like IND-CCA and IND-CCA2 in quantum security model, despite there complex steps and heavy bandwidth costs. KEMs in the second and the third categray may only achieve passively secure, unless safe hash functions or FO transformation [14] are applied, such as Alkim's NewHope.

Attack on the Lattice Problem. Theoretically, security guarantees of lattice based cryptographic primitives including NewHope are the hardness of SVP,

CVP and their variants. For efficiency reason, LWE and Ring-LWE problems are intriguing the attention of both designers and analyzers. Many works have been down in designing attack and analysis models against LWE problem and primitives based on it [5,10,19,21]. A basic approach is to focus on attacking the SVP structure by basis enumeration or sieve under classic or quantum reduction, such as LLL [19] and BKZ [21] types of attacks. In basis reduction attacks, the purpose is to design an realizable and efficient SVP oracle by implementing a classic or a quantum algorithms. Then the oracle is applied in acquiring a ideal basis to fulfill the SVP problem in LWE instances.

BKZ and BKZ2.0 [10] in classic settings run in the exponential time complex of $2^{\mathcal{O}(n \log n)}$ with approximate factor complex of $O((6k^2)^{n/k})$. To the state-of-the-art, for $k-$demension lattice, the best approximate factor is reduced on the level of $((1+\epsilon)\gamma_k)^{(n-k)/(k-1)}$, and is still accelerating. But according to the proof of Chen [10], the complex of enumerations and their variants is lower-bounded by blocksizes (or demension size $k \geq 250$).

Recent quantum sieve algorithms based on Locality Sensitive Hashing has reduced the complexity of reduction to $2^{0.292n}$ [6,16], which brings a further advance scope in basis reduction. But the work in [17] shows that the best performance of quantum SVP algorithm may still have time complexity worse that $2^{0.2075n}$.

Semantic Security. Semantic security analysis initiated by Cramer [11] is now a standard way of proving and evaluating the security strength of cryptographic primitives and protocols. The security strength or the costs of attacks are normally reduced to the costs of solving an open hard problems by mathematically implementing an attack between a challenger $\mathcal{C}$ and an adversary $\mathcal{A}$. NewHope PKE scheme is semantically proved CPA secure under decisional Ring-LWE hard problem assumption in [9] with the following advantage for the adversary.

$$Adv_{NewHope-PKE}^{IND-CPA}(\mathcal{A}) \leq Adv_{n,q,\chi}^{dRLWE}(\mathcal{B}_1) + Adv_{n,q,\chi}^{dRLWE}(\mathcal{B}_2)$$

in which $\mathcal{B}_1$ and $\mathcal{B}_2$ are quantum algorithms of solving decisional RLWE problems.

According to the work in [1,2], the KEM schemes based on NewHope CPA PKE can be reduced to IND-CCA secure level both under classic random oracle model and quantum random oracle model. Then the key exchange protocol constructed both from NewHope SIMPLE [3] (based on NewHope CPA KEM) and NewHope USEIX [4] (based on NewHope CPA PKE) are at least CCA secure.

Leaky RLWE Assumptions. As partial key leaky attack is an important attack in security resilient evaluation, [12] introduced the computational and decisional assumptions of leaky RLWE assumptions, focusing on the NTT and NTT^{-1} coefficients leakage during key exchange process. The partial key leakage attack indicates that under certain combinations of coefficient exposure, the secret keys can be recovered with noneligible probability, applying the techniques of constructing local CVP solvers and partial linear equation system of partial coefficients of secret keys or noise vectors.

4   Construction of Automatic Guess Oracle

4.1   An Automatic Analysis Framework

In this section, our main analysis framework to implementing the indistinguishability in details is introduced. The framework is constructed by a guess oracle including two alternative subroutines to adjust different attack models configured below. Each subroutine is a learning system controlled by instance configuration as well as time and memory boundaries to preprocess the query results. Subroutine 1 is partial leakage attack to boost the attack speed on NTT coefficients. Subroutine 2 is designed for the original key exchange protocol with noise decoder to enhance the significance of features in each queries. We will discuss the design of the two components in the next section. It takes queries under attack models as input, and outputs the guess result, see Fig. 1.

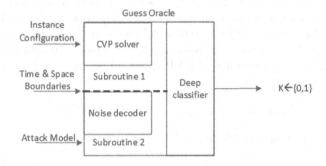

Fig. 1. Automatic analysis framework

As in our attack framework, we mainly focus on the features exposed by NTT, NTT^{-1} and the two-pass messages, we have the following three heuristics to support the availability of the above framework.

Heuristic 1. In NTT, the co-efficients can be transformed into small CVP problems.

According to Lemma C.1 [3] and the construction of linear system of coefficients in Sect. 3 in [12], the secret vector can be detected with significant probability with speicially chosed leakage points.

Heuristic 2 (Advantage over enumeration and guess). A solution to a linear system is learnable with accurate confidence of ϵ.

The method of solving the linear system in partial leakage attack is vector searching, such as the instances in Sect. 3 of [12]. But the success rate is quite low with approximate 0.57% in one fourth leakage instances under a confidence of 98%. A learning system solves linear equations by constructing coefficient candidate from input samples of local CVP instances. So a solver based on learning system performs as good as searching secret keys in the worst cases.

For a linear system that can be solved with an noneligible probability ϵ, there exists a learning system that can solve the linear system efficiently with success rate of at least ϵ.

Heuristic 3 (Existence of automatic analysis oracle to the linear system). A guess oracle based on learning system exists for identity distinguishability attacks in NewHope key exchange protocols.

By applying automatic learning approach to realize the heuristics, the attack framework acts like a detecting needle in revealing the weak points during the indistinguishability attack. Then following the framework, the details of each subroutine will be designed in the next section.

4.2   Subroutine 1: Neural Network Based $\text{CVP}_{D_n'}$ Solver

For the key leakage attack, a basic way to recover all the secret key s is by constructing linear systems from $u = a \cdot s + e$ as mentioned in Sect. 2. In this section, we construct a full connection neural network as the $\text{CVP}_{D_n'}$ solver to improve the probability in searching solutions to the linear equations. The solver is basically a dynamic denoising model, by which n' coordinates of e^j are generated under the constrains of CVP on D_n'. The model is expressed by the following processing method,

$$S_{\text{CVP}}(u_i, a, [e_i]_{i \equiv \alpha \bmod 2n'}, , v_i \in D_{n'}) = \text{NN}(W, F(\cdot))$$

in which the loss function $F(\cdot)$ is,

$$F([e_i]_{i \equiv \alpha \bmod 2n'}) = \arg_w c_0(\min||e_i^j - y_i||^2) + c_1(\min||e_i^j - \omega||^2), j \in \{1, \cdots, n'\}$$

In the linear system L_i, the output e_i^* of $S_{\text{CVP}}(\cdot)$ that supervised by the leakage e_i satisfies L_i, meanwhile, we gain $P\{e_i^*$ is a correct guess$\}$ is significantly higher than the direct enumeration in Sect. 3.1 and 3.2 of [12] according to Heuristic 3.

Then we can construct the guess oracle using the $\text{CVP}_{D_{n'}}$ solver with the following three phases.

Initial Phase: For a RLWE instance $(a, u = a \cdot s + e)$ and leakage $[s]_{i \equiv \alpha \bmod 2n'}$, $S_{\text{CVP}}(u_i, a, [e_i]_{i \equiv \alpha \bmod 2n'}, v_i \in D_{n'})$ instances are created based on a full connection neural network to hold the latent parameters in expressing the solution to L_i. We have n/n' solver instances in parallel.

Training Phase: Given a RLWE instance set S, for e_i^j of the linear equation L_i of the j-th RLWE instance, the solver S_{CVP}^i takes a random noise vector $v \in \Psi$ to optimize the latent connection in the neural network until the output of the solver satisfies L_i with the required confidence ϵ. For a chosen $\alpha \in 1, 2, \cdots, 2n'$, such as $\alpha = 1$, all the linear equation solver output the correct solution with the confidence of ϵ.

Generating Phase: Let $V = \{v_1, \cdots, v_{n/n'}\}$ be randomly generated noise vectors. The parallel solvers take V as input, and take $[u, e]_{i \equiv \alpha \bmod 2n'}$ as the optimizing constrains of $F(\cdot)$. Finally, the solvers output all the e_i for the RLWE secret key. The final state of all solvers is capsulated as a guess oracle for the RLWE noise vector e.

As the input of the solver is random noise, it can applied as a CVP searcher for "the confident solutions" for each linear system. Loss function $F(\cdot)$ may be turbulent during training phase because of dispersion of target noise vectors. To partially avoid the turbulence, the training phase can be divided into two steps. In the first step, let $c_0 = 1$ and $c_1 = 0$. Then in the second step, candidates of solutions are fed back to input end to train the solver again, while let $c_0 = 0$ and $c_1 = 1$.

A adversary can launch a partial key leakage attack by applying the above guess oracle, and generate a more likely secret key compared with the random generated keys as the preprocessed results to win the indistinguishability attack. We will initiate the attack in Sect. 4.5.

4.3   Subroutine 2: A Wide Noise Decoder

Another category of attack configuration is the direct attack interaction without any knowledge of the secret key or the noise vectors. We use an automatic noise decoder to partially expose the coordinate information of secret key. A wide noise decoder is a deep structured classifier, such as learning network, which is designed for automatic guess on all the coordinates of secret key from attack queries both in scenarios with NTT and without NTT process. But it's also applicable for the original scheme of NewHope, in which the adversary takes the output of CVP solver as the input of the decoder.

The noise decoder is expressed by the following processing method,

$$S_{BD}(u, r, a, b) = NN(W, F(\cdot))$$

in which the loss function $F(\cdot)$ is,

$$F(INS(\cdot)) = \arg_w c_0(\min||b - a \cdot s||^2) + c_1(\min||u - a \cdot s'||^2) + c_2[\min(Rec(b \cdot s', r) - Rec(a \cdot s \cdot s', r))]$$

If the input of the noise decoder is from instances without NTT, then $c_2 = 0$, and the decoder is a pure boundary linear decoder for $s \leftarrow (a, b)$ and $s' \leftarrow a, u$, which is NP-hard to get correct solution, but is helpful to identify boundaries in distinguishing potentially correct secret from those selected from random instances. If the input is from instances with NTT, then $c_2 \neq 0$, and the potential s and s' are decoded by $Rec(\cdot)$ which is defined in [3]. The accuracy of the noise decoder can be allocated by a parameter γ defined as $\gamma = c_0 + c_1 + c_2$. We will discuss the value of γ in the implementations of different attacks.

Then we construct the noise decoder of guess oracle with an self-decoding network shaped learning system to capture the noise pattern by the following three phases.

Initial Phase: For a RLWE instance, let (a, b, u, r) and two selected identities $\{id_a, id_b\}$ as the input of the noise decoder based on two symmetric full connection neural networks to hold the latent parameters in expressing noise pattern of e and e'. We can process (a, b) and (u, r) in parallel simultaneously or independently, and the learning results may slightly different.

Training Phase: Taking a set $S = \{(\text{INS}_i, s, s'\}$ of query results as input, the noise decoder extracts features of noise sampling from the two-pass message under the supervision of the loss function $F(\text{INS}(\cdot))$ until the query limitation reached or the required confidence of decoding ϵ' is achieved.

Decoding Phase: Let $\text{INS}^* = \{(a^*, b^*, u^*, r^*)\}$ be challenged instance. The trained decoder takes INS^* as input, and outputs an expected $a^* \cdot s^*$ and $a^* \cdot s'^*$.

As NTT transform is applied in the original NewHope key exchange protocol, the above construction of the noise decoder can be easily changed to comply with NTT variables by switching (a, b, u, r) to $(\hat{a}, \hat{b}, \hat{u}, \hat{r})$ in the initial phase and offering $S = \{(\text{INS}_i, \hat{s}, \hat{s}'\}$ in training phase. Finally, the noise decoder yields the expected $\hat{a}^* \cdot \hat{s}^*$ and $\hat{a}^* \cdot \hat{s}'^*$ with a confidence ϵ'.

4.4 Deep Classifier

As the preprocess components of guess oracle, the CVP solver and the noise decoder offer an preliminary guess of s and s'. In the query phase of the basic attack, the adversary constructs a simulation of challenge phase which is also a realization of basic attack taking the out layer attack result as its challenge message $\text{INS}(s^*, s'^*)$ to train an applicably expressive structure in the guess oracle. Then it means that the adversary chooses a proper subroutine to train a guess oracle that can express the basic features of current system parameters. The deep classifier in the backend of the guess oracle takes the role as the above simulator accepting preprocessed candidates of s and s'. In the query phrase of basic attack, the simulator takes the following steps to get a guess.

Step 1. For a set of query results $\{\text{INS}_i^{id^*}\}$ of selected id^*, the simulator pick a subroutine to preprocess $\{\text{INS}_i^{id^*}\}$ with a batch size of $|\{\text{INS}_i^{id^*}\}|$. Then a $\text{INS}(s^*, s'^*)$ is generated at the end of handling the batch of queries.

Step 2. The simulator requests more batches of query results $\{\text{INS}_i^{id^*}\}$ of reselected id^*, in which i is bounded by time or memory limitations.

Step 3. The simulator learns on the set $\{\text{INS}(s^*, s'^*)_j\}$, in which j is the number of batches and is bounded by time or memory limitations.

Step 4. The simulator initiates j simulating instances of id^{**}, $\text{INS}(id^*)$, and generates s^{**}, s'^{**}. If the the guess results are significant on distinguishing secret keys of id^* and id^{**}, the simulator terminates the query phase, or else goto Step 1.

In fact, the above steps describe a guess simulation for the instance randomly picked by the adversary. If the simulation returns a satisfactory results, the query phase ends. Note that $id^* = \{id_a^*, id_b^*\}$ is independently selected in each query batch, the outputs of preprocess components are independently generated secret key candidates $\{s^*, s'^*\}$.

5 Evaluation

5.1 Configuration

To fully evaluate the effectiveness and system costs, we designed a instantiation platform of our attack model. The platform contains a challenger terminal and a computationally powerful adversary backend. The challenger terminal accepts queries and generates the coordinate responses according to the four different attack instances in Sect. 4.5. The adversary's backend collects all the responses for each key exchange process, and builds the guess oracles for four attack instances respectively.

For objectiveness in each attack instance, we assume the adversary not only make queries from the challenger, but also can naturally acquire the passed messages on public channels to enhance the knowledge of the adversary. During the constructing of guess oracle, the adversary can arbitrarily make transformation on collected samples. One of the most simple transformations is global shifting or shrinking on features of samples. In each instance, we maintain a shrink rate to point the proportion of transformation. Obviously, these messages cannot change the alter the procedures of the original indistinguishability game defined in Sect. 2.

5.2 Results

Significance. From the results in Table 1, it's obvious that NTT component has an important influence in both partial leakage instances (attack i and ii) and tactic instances (attack iii and iv). Without NTT and partial leakage, the significance of guess oracle is so negligible (attack iv) that we have to increase the optimal shrink rate to quantitatively evaluate it. We can safely draw the conclusion that the NTT component can increase the advantage of adversary, especially in PKE based KEM instances. In Rec. based KEM, NTT shows a weaker influence toward the advantage in the attack. Naturally, for the comparison of instances with and without partial leakage (attack ii and iv), the adversary gains overwhelming advantage in the former attacks, which complies with the theoretical results. But the influence of NTT, NTT^{-1} and partial key leakage does not seem to accumulate the advantage for the guess oracle to compute advantage from the results of attack i,ii and iii.

Cost of Adversary. Table 2 shows the overall costs of adversary in constructing guess oracle, including space and time costs. Each sample in query phase consists of at least four major feature points which are encapsulations of polynomial coefficients. Restricted by computing power, the adversary is only allowed to make less than 10000 queries in each attack instance to avoid system crash. Compared with attack ii and iv, attack i and iii only cost about 1/3 time in period T1 (querying and training), which shows NTT and NTT^{-1} play important role in enhancing system efficiency. In period T2 (challenge and guess), although the performance varies for different attack instance, time cost of all instances is less

Table 1. The overall significance of the guess oracle

Attack models	Schemes	Optimal shrink rate	Significance
Attack (i)	PKE based KEM	0.19997	0.23333
Attack (ii)	PKE based KEM	0.19997	0.23416
Attack (iii)	PKE based KEM	0.24997	0.20667
Attack (iv)	PKE based KEM	0.54997	0.01258
Attack (i)	Rec. based KEM	0.19997	0.02416
Attack (ii)	Rec. based KEM	0.19997	0.21750
Attack (iii)	Rec. based KEM	0.24997	0.01500
Attack (iv)	Rec. based KEM	0.19997	0.00416

then 0.01 ms, which is undoubtedly acceptable. Instances based on reconciliation cost an average of extra 20% time more than the PKE based KEM.

So far as we know, there no similar quantitative measurement mechanism for us to make a full comparison, such that we only demonstrated an average computing resource costs in our attack instances in Table 3. The peak memory is the maximum available ram space on the rim of system crash, and it shows that attack iv (original scheme without NTT) gains the most significant memory cost, while instances with partial leakage reaches the least memory cost (attack ii). The storage in Table 3 is volume of samples after they are pre-processed to fit coordinate learning models. As we only realized a prototype of our guess oracle on a platform with limited computing resources, the peak memory and storage costs are both in controllable levels.

Table 2. The overall cost of adversary

Attack models	Schemes	Query	T1 (seconds)	T2 (seconds)
Attack (i)	PKE based KEM	10000	1317	0.00100
Attack (ii)	PKE based KEM	10000	4213	0.00083
Attack (iii)	PKE based KEM	10000	1615	0.00902
Attack (iv)	PKE based KEM	10000	4509	0.00041
Attack (i)	Rec. based KEM	10000	1401	0.00002
Attack (ii)	Rec. based KEM	10000	3889	0.00021
Attack (iii)	Rec. based KEM	10000	1570	0.00285
Attack (iv)	Rec. based KEM	10000	3716	0.00033

Table 3. The maximum computing power cost of adversary

Attack models	Schemes	Peak memory (Gb)	Storage (Gb)
Attack (i)	PKE based KEM	5.56022	0.27459
Attack (ii)	PKE based KEM	4.95308	0.27493
Attack (iii)	PKE based KEM	5.59003	0.28948
Attack (iv)	PKE based KEM	5.95913	0.28998
Attack (i)	Rec. based KEM	5.57011	0.27446
Attack (ii)	Rec. based KEM	5.65902	0.27470
Attack (iii)	Rec. based KEM	5.20087	0.28820
Attack (iv)	Rec. based KEM	5.89022	0.29001

6   Conclusions and Future Works

Quantized security analysis is an important aspect of cryptographic primitives. Post-quantum cryptographic designs of PKE, KEM and KTM schemes are usually only proved semantically secure under the assumptions of post-quantum hard problems. But it's hard to fully evaluate the influence of certain components in a complex cryptographic scheme because of the constrains of mathematical reduction in the semantic proof. So the construction of quantized security analysis system is quite necessary. In this paper, we explored the availability of quantized security analysis toward a post-quantum key exchange protocol (NewHope key exchange protocol with reconciliation) by applying an automatic learning methodology. Based on the routine of the challenge games in semantic proof, we carefully designed a serial of attack models, in which the adversary is granted the power of using a guess oracle to distinguish each instances based on automatic and statistical learning.

The evaluation results showed that different security strength under different circumstances (NTT & NTT^{-1}, partial key leakage, sampling methods) as we had expected. We can safely draw the conclusion that the NewHope key exchange protocol probabilistically do not satisfy selective identity CCA security in each circumstances. The application of NTT

There are still many unsolved problems in quantized security analysis, especially in cryptographic protocols, such as secure KEM and secure multi-party computing. These protocols are hard to compactly and universally describe in analysis systems. Artificial Intelligence is a powerful infrastructure in analysis systems, but how to mathematically design a rigid theory to achieve the optimal learning result in revealing the security level is also the leverage part in the exploration.

References

1. Alkim, E., et al.: Newhope-algorithm specifications and supporting documentation. First Round NIST PQC Project Submission Document (2017)
2. Alkim, E., et al.: Newhope-algorithm specifications and supporting documentation. Second Round NIST PQC Project Submission Document (2019)
3. Alkim, E., Ducas, L., Pöppelmann, T., Schwabe, P.: Newhope without reconciliation. IACR Cryptology ePrint Archive 2016:1157 (2016)
4. Alkim, E., Ducas, L., Pöppelmann, T., Schwabe, P.: Post-quantum key exchange'a new hope. In: 25th {USENIX} Security Symposium ({USENIX} Security 16), pp. 327–343 (2016)
5. Aono, Y., Wang, Y., Hayashi, T., Takagi, T.: Improved progressive BKZ algorithms and their precise cost estimation by sharp simulator. In: Fischlin, M., Coron, J.-S. (eds.) EUROCRYPT 2016. LNCS, vol. 9665, pp. 789–819. Springer, Heidelberg (2016). https://doi.org/10.1007/978-3-662-49890-3_30
6. Becker, A., Ducas, L., Gama, N., Laarhoven, T.: New directions in nearest neighbor searching with applications to lattice sieving. In: Proceedings of the Twenty-Seventh Annual ACM-SIAM Symposium on Discrete Algorithms, pp. 10–24. Society for Industrial and Applied Mathematics (2016)
7. Bos, J., Costello, C., Ducas, L., et al.: Frodo: take off the ring! Practical, quantum-secure key exchange from LWE. In: Proceedings of the 2016 ACM SIGSAC Conference on Computer and Communications Security, pp. 1006–1018 (2016)
8. Bos, J., et al.: CRYSTALS-kyber: a CCA-secure module-lattice-based KEM. In: 2018 IEEE European Symposium on Security and Privacy (EuroS&P), pp. 353–367. IEEE (2018)
9. Bos, J.W., Costello, C., Naehrig, M., Stebila, D.: Post-quantum key exchange for the TLS protocol from the ring learning with errors problem. In: 2015 IEEE Symposium on Security and Privacy, pp. 553–570. IEEE (2015)
10. Chen, Y., Nguyen, P.Q.: BKZ 2.0: better lattice security estimates. In: Lee, D.H., Wang, X. (eds.) ASIACRYPT 2011. LNCS, vol. 7073, pp. 1–20. Springer, Heidelberg (2011). https://doi.org/10.1007/978-3-642-25385-0_1
11. Cramer, R., Shoup, V.: Design and analysis of practical public-key encryption schemes secure against adaptive chosen ciphertext attack. SIAM J. Comput. 33(1), 167–226 (2003)
12. Dachman-Soled, D., Gong, H., Kulkarni, M., Shahverdi, A.: Partial key exposure in ring-lwe-based cryptosystems: Attacks and resilience. IACR Cryptology ePrint Archive 2018:1068 (2018)
13. Ding, J.: New cryptographic constructions using generalized learning with errors problem. IACR Cryptology ePrint Archive 2012:387 (2012)
14. Fujisaki, E., Okamoto, T.: Secure integration of asymmetric and symmetric encryption schemes. In: Wiener, M. (ed.) CRYPTO 1999. LNCS, vol. 1666, pp. 537–554. Springer, Heidelberg (1999). https://doi.org/10.1007/3-540-48405-1_34
15. Jiang, H., Zhang, Z., Chen, L., Wang, H., Ma, Z.: IND-CCA-secure key encapsulation mechanism in the quantum random oracle model, revisited. In: Shacham, H., Boldyreva, A. (eds.) CRYPTO 2018. LNCS, vol. 10993, pp. 96–125. Springer, Cham (2018). https://doi.org/10.1007/978-3-319-96878-0_4
16. Laarhoven, T.: Sieving for shortest vectors in lattices using angular locality-sensitive hashing. In: Gennaro, R., Robshaw, M. (eds.) CRYPTO 2015. LNCS, vol. 9215, pp. 3–22. Springer, Heidelberg (2015). https://doi.org/10.1007/978-3-662-47989-6_1

17. Laarhoven, T., Mosca, M., Van De Pol, J.: Finding shortest lattice vectors faster using quantum search. Designs, Codes Cryptogr. **77**(2–3), 375–400 (2015)
18. Langley, A.: Cecpq1 results. Imperial Violet (2016)
19. Lenstra, A.K., Lenstra, H.W., Lovász, L.: Factoring polynomials with rational coefficients. Math. Ann. **261**(4), 515–534 (1982)
20. Peikert, C.: Lattice cryptography for the internet. In: Mosca, M. (ed.) PQCrypto 2014. LNCS, vol. 8772, pp. 197–219. Springer, Cham (2014). https://doi.org/10.1007/978-3-319-11659-4_12
21. Schnorr, C.-P., Euchner, M.: Lattice basis reduction: improved practical algorithms and solving subset sum problems. Math. Program. **66**(1–3), 181–199 (1994)
22. Boyen, X., Li, Q.: Direct CCA-secure KEM and deterministic PKE from plain LWE. In: Ding, J., Steinwandt, R. (eds.) PQCrypto 2019. LNCS, vol. 11505, pp. 116–130. Springer, Cham (2019). https://doi.org/10.1007/978-3-030-25510-7_7
23. Zhang, J., Zhang, Z., Ding, J., et al.: Authenticated key exchange from ideal lattices. In: Annual International Conference on the Theory and Applications of Cryptographic Techniques, pp. 719–751 (2015)

Anonymous Communication

AnonyTrust: An Anonymous Trust Authentication System for Pervasive Social Networking

Pu Wang[1], Limei He[1], Zheng Yan[1,2(✉)], and Wei Feng[1]

[1] Xidian University, Xi'an 710071, Shaanxi, China
wangpu03@gmail.com, zyan@xidian.edu.cn
[2] Aalto University, 02150 Espoo, Finland
zheng.yan@aalto.fi

Abstract. Pervasive social networking (PSN) is facilitating and enriching people's life at any time and in any place. One of the most important issues in PSN is its security and privacy, since users hope their privacy not to be disclosed in social activities. Trust relationship plays a crucial role in the PSN system, and can be utilized to support trustworthy PSN system with anonymous authentication. Thus, this paper proposes an anonymous trust authentication (AnonyTrust) scheme that can simultaneously authenticate identities and trust levels of users with privacy preservation. It also can achieve conditional traceability with a trusted server (TS), and can switch online and offline states with multiple authorized access points (APs). The security analysis and performance evaluation show the scheme is secure and efficient regarding security, anonymity, computational complexity, and communication cost. To verify the feasibility of the proposed scheme, a lightweight secret chat application called AnonyChat is developed in practice. The results show AnonyChat performs well and efficiently in Android devices.

Keywords: Anonymous authentication · Trust management · Pervasive social networking

1 Introduction

With the advent of the Internet era, pervasive social networking (PSN) supports instant social activities anywhere and anytime in an intelligent and context-aware manner. With PSN, not only people socially connected, but also strangers physically in proximity can form a social group to perform various social activities [1–3]. One of the most important issues in PSN is its trust, security and privacy [4–6]. For example, users want to perform identity authentication to ensure their personal and property security. Meanwhile, users also hope their privacy, such as identity information and geographical location, not to be disclosed. From sociological definition, trust can help people overcome perceptions of uncertainty and risk by evaluating the trust relationship with communication parties. Thus, the integration of anonymous authentication and social trust

© Springer Nature Singapore Pte Ltd. 2020
S. Yu et al. (Eds.): SPDE 2020, CCIS 1268, pp. 643–660, 2020.
https://doi.org/10.1007/978-981-15-9129-7_44

relationship is an attractive technique to ensure the security and privacy of PSN systems. However, anonymous authentication brings risks to the network, that is, malicious users may abuse anonymity to do illegal activities. The existence of malicious users and unknown social trust relationships make it hard to verify the trust of users and their messages in PSN. Therefore, how to authenticate the identity and trust of users while keeping anonymity to preserve privacy becomes an important issue in PSN systems.

However, few existing works studied this issue in the literature [7,8]. Traditional anonymous authentication schemes mainly focus on protecting identities of users, such as pseudonyms-based [9], group signature [10,11] and blind signature [12]. For example, pseudonyms are applied in social networking to hide real identities and avoid privacy tracking [9]. The frequently changed pseudonyms will negatively influence the efficiency of authentication and pseudonyms management. Shao et al. [13] proposed a group signature protocol that realizes a threshold authentication for privacy preservation, but brings a group revocation problem. Nevertheless, most of the existing schemes only realize the anonymous authentication, yet not considering to build the trust relationship among PSN users. Thus, they are unable to completely satisfy the security and performance requirements of PSN due to its specific features, such as heterogeneous and mobility. Besides, natural trust relationships among PSN users are not utilized to enhance the security and reliability of PSN.

To address the above issue, Yan and Feng et al. [14] firstly proposed an anonymous authentication scheme based on the trust value issued by a centralized TS with a trust evaluation system. Users can authenticate each other about both identity and trust without disclosing any private information. But the centralized structure cannot adapt to the heterogeneous and complex PSN topology so that it cannot support the scalability and flexibility. Yan and Wang et al. [15] proposed a distributed scheme that alleviates the dependence of the trusted TS, but the computational and communication overhead still needs further improvement. Notably, it is necessary to verify the feasibility and efficiency of such anonymous trust authentication scheme in practical systems, especially for devices with limited resources, such as computation, storage and network.

In this paper, we propose a semi-distributed anonymous trust authentication system (AnonyTrust) to secure PSN and assist user social decisions. In such a system, TS and/or APs evaluate the trust value of each user, and issue up-to-date trust lists for anonymously identity and trust authentication. The proposed scheme can flexibly support the online state with TS and the offline state with APs for users, which is appropriate to PSN features. With trust value monitored by TS, APs and even some PSN users, the malicious users can be rapidly detected and their message will be rejected. Besides, the complexity and consumption are reduced to satisfy PSN requirements. Specifically, the contributions of this paper can be summarized as below:

- We propose an anonymous trust authentication scheme in PSN systems that can realize authentication and privacy preservation. It also adopts a semi-distributed architecture to support users with online and offline states.

- We confirm the security of the proposed scheme by extensive analysis and security proof, and validate the advantages through the simulation-based evaluation and comparison.
- A lightweight secret chat application called AnonyChat is developed in Android devices to show the feasibility and performance, such as message delay, CPU utilization, memory usage and communication cost.

The remainder of the paper is organized as follows. A summarization of related work is given in Sect. 2. Section 3 overviews the system model of AnonyTrust and details of the anonymous trust authentication scheme. Section 4 gives the security analysis and performance evaluation. A secret chat APP based on AnonyTrust is presented in Sect. 5. Section 6 concludes the paper.

2   Related Work

Lindell [16] formally defined the anonymous authentication, which has been widely studied in Vehicular Ad Hoc Networks (VANETs) and Wireless Body Area Networks (WBANs) to preserve privacy without exposing real identities. But most anonymous authentication schemes mainly focused on security requirements and performance promotion. Pseudonym-based authentication, as one of the methods, has widely been applied in mobile networks to protect privacy while communicating without real identities [17,18]. Emura et al. [18] proposed a secure and anonymous communication protocol with pseudonym for user authentication based on identity-based encryption solutions. Lin and Li [19] proposed a cooperative message authentication scheme for VANETs. Vehicles can verify an evidence token from a Trusted Authority (TA) and check whether other vehicles truly verify the message their claimed with pseudonyms.

On the other hand, group signature and blind signature are other common techniques of anonymous authentication [8,20,21]. Shao et al. [13] presented an authentication protocol for VANETs with the group signature to achieve a threshold authentication. Besides, an anonymous authentication scheme was proposed based on the group signature for authenticating trust levels rather than identities to avoid privacy leakage in PSN [22]. These schemes can well resist selective plaintext attacks, but the revocation of group members is still a difficult problem. With the integration of blind signature and hash chain, Ren and Lou [12] designed an anonymity scheme with privacy preservation in pervasive computing environments. Users get blind signature certificates from service providers to prove their legitimacy without providing the real identity. Based on the blind signature, Huszti [23] proposed a multi-supplier that provides anonymity for the customers. In such a micro-payment system, customers can be authenticated anonymously by multiple vendors. However, these solutions mainly depend on a central server, which distributes and manages the key pairs and certificates. They cannot support decentralized authentication when the server is offline, as well as the scalability and flexibility.

Trust relationship among users can be applied to support anonymous authentication in PSN, such as the distributed reputation system [24], securing communication [25], and cloud access control [26,27]. Zhao et al. [28] proposed a

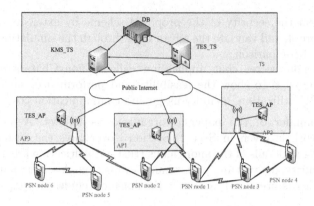

Fig. 1. System model of AnonyTrust.

trust model of VANET to theorize the trust relationship in the dynamic traffic environment. In such a system, vehicles can perform verification through a trust chain with the evaluated trustworthiness. However, this scheme only focuses on the design of the trust evaluation model to provide trust verification. Yan et al. [14] proposed an anonymous authentication scheme based on the evaluated trust which is issued by a centralized TA. But it cannot support a distributed PSN topology where APs can play a role like TS to issue the trust value. Besides, an anonymous trust authentication scheme [15] can alleviate the dependence of the server, but the computational and communication overhead still needs further improvement. Furthermore, all solutions above only analyzed the performance with simulation, without implementing in a real system, especially for mobile devices with limited resources, such as computation, storage and network.

3   Anonymous Trust Authentication Scheme

3.1   Overview of AnonyTrust

As shown in Fig. 1, all entities in the model are divided into TS (Trusted Server), AP (Authorized Party) and PSN nodes (or users). This paper assumes that TS is trustworthy and will not reveal user privacy due to business motivation. Its functions are mainly divided into three parts: KMS_TS (Key Management Server of TS), TES_TS (Trust Evaluation Server of TS) and DB (DataBase).

KMS_TS handles registration requests from APs and PSN users and manages their identities and the corresponding long-term keys. For nodes whose trust value does not satisfy the condition, KMS_TS will not grant them access permission. TES_TS is responsible for collecting feedback from all users in the network, and evaluating and updating their trust. According to evaluation results, TES_TS publishes $token_{TS}$ and $list_{TS}$ related to trust values to all trusted users. DB is responsible for storing the identity information, key information and user feedback of APs and PSN nodes.

AP is semi-trusted, a stable and reliable service device. Its main function is to evaluate and update the trust value of PSN nodes within its coverage. Similarly, it will issue $token_{AP}$ and trust value related $list_{AP}$. The purpose of this design is to enable users to authenticate each other when TS is not available, to achieve a semi-distributed manner. On the other hand, the introduction of AP can support users to authenticate offline, thus reducing the dependence of TS. Although AP is responsible for the trust evaluation of PSN nodes, it does not know the real identity of users, but only the temporary identity.

PSN nodes will authenticate each other regarding the identity and trust value with $list_{TS}$ or $list_{AP}$ issued from TS or AP, correspondingly. Notably, nodes can switch between off-line only with APs and on-line state with both TS and APs according to their communication needs. To better understand the online and offline states of PSN nodes, we named and labeled PSN nodes in Fig. 1 where PSN node 1 connects AP1 and AP2 simultaneously. When it is online, it can anonymously authenticate with all online PSN nodes through TS. When it is offline, it can only anonymously authenticate with local user PSN node 2 through AP1, as well as PSN nodes 3 and 4 through AP2. It should be noted that in rare cases, PSN node 1 hopes to anonymously authenticate with PSN nodes 5 and 6, at which time it must adopt an online state with the assistance of TS. Thus, the offline state can only support anonymous authentication between users within the coverage of the same APs. On the one hand, it enhances the stability of the system and prevents users from being unable to authenticate each other, when they cannot connect to the TS. On the other hand, it can reduce the communication and computing overhead between users and the TS, when users only communicate with each other within the coverage of the same APs.

Besides, the behavior of PSN nodes is uncertain, and there may be malicious behavior, such as eavesdropping other people's private information. PSN nodes hope that their identity will not be disclosed in the communication, meanwhile authenticating the trust and identity of others. Thus, TS is responsible for trust evaluation and distribution, which can be utilized for authentication at PSN nodes. In some scenarios, PSN nodes can only obtain incomplete trust information from multiple APs without TS. On the other hand, the PSN nodes can evaluate the trust value of other nodes according to the anonymous messages and their behavior, which is finally uploaded to TES_AP or TES_TS as feedback for trust evaluation. Therefore, the trust value of PSN nodes can be periodically updated with all new feedback.

This paper only focuses on the secure and reliable anonymous authentication and communication between PSN nodes with the assistance of TS and APs. The communication between TS and PSN nodes, AP and PSN nodes, and between AP and TS is assumed to be based on secure channels, such as Diffie-Hellman protocol.

Table 1. Notations

Notation	Description
sk_{TS}, pk_{TS}	Secrete and public key of TS
ID_i, ID_{ap}	Identity of user i and ap
sk_{ap}, pk_{ap}	Private and public key of ap
$cert_{ap}$	Public key certificate of ap
$tempID_i$	Temp identity of i
$info_i$	Personal information of i
sk_i, pk_i	Long-term private and public key of i
$cert_i$	Long-term public key certificate of i
s_i	Secret between i and TS
Q_i	Multi-scalar multiplication of s_i and P
tv_i_TS, tv_i_ap	Trust value of i from TS and ap
$token_i$	Token of i's trust value
$secre\_token_i$	Token of $token_i$
$list$	Trust related list
$\boldsymbol{P}_i$	Short-term public key vector of i
$\boldsymbol{temp\_sk}_i$	Short-term private key vector of i

3.2 Preliminaries

Bilinear pair is a powerful tool for constructing digital signatures. Assume q is a large prime number related to a given security constant k, G is a cyclic additive group with the generation element P, GT is a cyclic multiplicative group, $|G| = |GT| = q$. Bilinear map $e : G \times G \to GT$ satisfies the following properties:

- **Bilinear:** For $\forall P, Q \in G$, $a, b \in Z_q^*$, $e(aP, bQ) = e(P, Q)^{ab}$.
- **Non-degenerate:** There exist $P, Q \in G$ that $e(P, Q) \neq 1_{GT}$.
- **Computable:** For $\forall P, Q \in G$, $e(P, Q)$ can be computed by polynomial-time algorithm.

The following cryptographic problems ensure that bilinear pairings can be used to construct digital signatures safely:

- **Discrete Logarithm Problem (DLP):** Given $P, Q \in G$, compute $a \in Z_q^*$ that $Q = aP$.
- **Computational Diffie-Hellman Problem (CDH Problem):** Given P, $aP, bP \in G$, in which $a, b \in Z_q^*$, compute $abP \in G$.

The notations that are usually used in this paper are summarized in Table 1.

3.3   The Proposed Scheme

Each step of the anonymous trust authentication scheme is described in detail below. Assuming that the sender i requires anonymous communication, and its corresponding authorized access point is ap (i may connect with multiple AP but with the same operation), the receiver j will verify i's trust level and authenticate the message.

System Setup: Give security parameter k and generate q, G, GT, Z_q^*, P, and e. TS chooses master private key $sk_{TS} \in Z_q^*$ and computes the corresponding public key $pk_{TS} = sk_{TS} \cdot P$. Besides, it also chooses $H_1 : \{0,1\}^* \rightarrow \{0,1\}^n$, $H_2 : G \rightarrow \{0,1\}^n$, $H_3 : \{0,1\}^n \rightarrow G, H_4 : \{0,1\}^* \rightarrow G$. The system parameters contains $\{q, G, GT, e, P, pk_{TS}, H_1, H_2, H_3, H_4\}$.

AP Registration: ap registers at TS with its own ID_{ap}. TS generates private key $sk_{ap} \in Z_q^*$, public key $pk_{ap} = sk_{ap} \cdot P$ and the certificate $cert_{ap} = pk_{ap} \cdot sk_{TS}$ for ap.

User Registration

- User i registers at TS with his real ID (such as phone number or mailbox) and sends his necessary information $info_i$ required by TS.
- TES_TS uses $info_i$ and previous information to generate the trust value tv_i_TS for user i. If tv_i_TS reaches the desired threshold, TS generates the unique temporary identification $tempID_i$. Then it chooses private key $sk_i \in Z_q^*$, public key $pk_i = sk_i \cdot P$ and public key certificate $cert_i = pk_i \cdot sk_{TS}$ for user i.
- TS sends $\{tempID_i, sk_i, pk_i, cert_i\}$ to user i through a secure channel.

Trust Evaluation: When the user swicthes to the offline state, only APs connected by the user work. If the user selects online, TS and all APs connected by the user will conduct trust evaluation with its $tempID_i$.

- TS chooses s_i as the secret of user i, and calculates $Q_i = s_i \cdot P$.
- TS/ap periodically updates tv_i, and generates $token_i = H_1(tv_i \| tempID_i)$. Users will provide the Q_i to ap for trust evaluation services.
- TS/ap first calculates $secret\_token_i = H_1(Q_i \| H_1(token_i))$ and puts it into the $list = \{secret\_token_i, ..., secret\_token_j\}$. Secret tokens are arranged in ascending order of the corresponding trust values.
- TS sends $\{token_i\_TS, s_i, Q_i\}$ to i, and publishes $list_{TS}$ to all users of the network; ap sends $token_i\_ap$ to i and publishes $list_{ap}$ to local users.

Short-Term Key Pair Generation: Users will generate its short-term public and private keys based on $token_i$ and $token_i\_ap$. Table 2 shows the short-term key pair generation algorithm with $token_i$ from TS (if with AP, replacing with $token_i\_ap$ in algorithm). It should be noticed that user i will choose either online or offline mode. It will receive multiple tokens from TS and/or APs to generate multiple short-term public keys. Accordingly, i's public key is a vector $\boldsymbol{P_i}$ with

Table 2. Short-term key generation

Input: $token_i$, s_i, Q_i

Output: $temp\_pk_i$, $temp\_sk_i$

a) compute $temp\_pk_i$

$temp\_pk_i\_1 = H_1(a \oplus H_2(Q_i))$

$temp\_pk_i\_2 = temp\_pk_i\_1 \oplus H_1(token_i)$

b) compute $temp\_sk_i$

$temp\_sk_i = s_i \cdot H_3(|P_i\_1|) + s_i \cdot H_3(|P_i\_2|)$

---

several elements $temp\_pk_i$, composed of $temp\_pk_i\_1$ and $temp\_pk_i\_2$. User i's secret key is $temp\_sk_i$. $|P_i\_k|$ is the XOR result of all $temp\_pk_i\_k(k = 1, 2)$.

Signature Generation: User i uses $temp\_sk_i$ to generate the signature of message m, $sig(m) = temp\_sk_i + H_4(m) \cdot s_i$. User i sends $\{m, sig, P_i, Q_i\}$.

Signature Verification: The whole process of message verification is shown in Table 3.

Table 3. Signature verification

Input: P_i, Q_i, m, sig

Output: true, false

1) if (at least one $secret\_token$ was found) goto 2);

else return false;

2) if $(e(sig, P) = e(H_3(|P_i\_1|) + H_3(|P_i\_2|) + H_4(m), Q_i))$ goto 3);

else return false;

3) if $(tv_i > threshold)$ return true;

else return false;

- a) Verify the identity legitimacy of message signers. First calculate $H_1(token) = temp\_pk_i\_2 \oplus temp\_pk_i\_1$, and calculate $secret\_token = H_1(Q_i||H_1(token))$. Then check if there is any $secret\_token$ can be found in $list$. If no $secret\_token$ is found in $list$, the verification will be terminated.
- b) Determine whether the equation $e(sig, P) = e(H_3(|P_i\_1|) + H_3(|P_i\_2|) + H_4(m), Q_i)$ is satisfied. If the validation result is correct, the message is complete; otherwise, the message may be tampered.
- c) Obtain signer's global trust level TV_i as $tv_i = \sum_{x=1}^{k}(rank(x) \cdot 0.5 + 0.5)/k$.
- d) Check if the global trust level is satisfying, users can judge if the message sender is trustworthy based on the trust threshold.

The whole procedure of the anonymous trust authentication scheme is summarized in Fig. 2.

4   Security Analysis and Performance Evaluation

In this section, the security of the proposed scheme is proved theoretically and analyzed to show the correctness, anonymity, unforgeability, traceability and nonrepudiation. Then, we analyze and evaluate its performance about computation and communication cost.

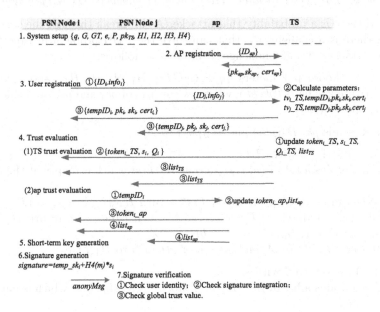

Fig. 2. The procedure of anonymous trust authentication.

4.1   Security Analysis

1) Correctness: the correctness of the signature verification can be proved as follows:

$$
\begin{aligned}
e(sig, P) &= e(temp\_sk_i + H_4(m) \cdot s_i, P) \qquad (1) \\
&= e(s_i \cdot H_3(|\boldsymbol{P}_i\_1|) + s_i \cdot H_3(|\boldsymbol{P}_i\_2|) + H_4(m) \cdot s_i, P) \\
&= e(H_3(|\boldsymbol{P}_i\_1|) + H_3(|\boldsymbol{P}_i\_2|) + H_4(m), P \cdot s_i) \\
&= e(H_3(|\boldsymbol{P}_i\_1|) + H_3(|\boldsymbol{P}_i\_2|) + H_4(m), Q_i)
\end{aligned}
$$

2) Anonymity: The receiver can get are Q_i, $temp\_pk_i\_1$, $temp\_pk_i\_2$, $list_{ap}$, $list_{TS}$, m, sig, and compute $H1(token_i)$ and $secret\_token_i$. Q_i is an element on G and has nothing to do with real identity because of DLP problem. $temp\_pk_i\_1$ and $temp\_pk_i\_2$ generated by $token_i$, random number a and Q_i, are hash value that seems to be a random value for receiver. Besides, $H_1(token_i)$, $secret\_token_i$, $list_{ap}$ and $list_{TS}$ are only related to the hash value of $token_i$, so the receiver can not determine the identity of the sender.

3) Unforgeability: the commonly used definition of digital signature security is Existence Unforgebility under Adaptive Selective Message Attacks (EUF-CMA) [29]. EUF-CMA of AnonyTrust can be proved under the random oracle model. The proof is as follows,

Theorem 1. *For a given security parameter k, the anonymous trust authentication scheme (TAS) is secure under a random oracle model if the CDH problem holds.*

Proof. If there is a probability that attacker A can break through the scheme in time t, there is a challenger $\mathcal{C}$ that can solve the CDH problem in time t'. We assume Attacker $\mathcal{A}$ and Challenger $\mathcal{C}$ interact as follows:

Step 1: $\mathcal{C}$ choose parameters $\{q, P, G, GT, e, H_1, H_2, H_3, H_4\}$ and calculates public-private key pairs (pk, sk), where pk consists of pk_1 and pk_2, and calculates $H_3(pk_1)$ and $H_3(pk_2)$.

Step 2: $\mathcal{C}$ sends pk, $H_3(pk_1)$ and $H_3(pk_2)$ to $\mathcal{A}$;

Step 3: $\mathcal{A}$ queries $\mathcal{C}$ with $H_4(x)$.

a) $\mathcal{C}$ maintains a list of $(n, x, H_4(x))$ as H_4_List which is empty at the beginning.

b) When input x^* appears in H_4_List, return $H_4(x^*)$. If not, $rand^* \in 0, 1$ is randomly generated, where $Pr[rand^* = 1] = \delta$. If $rand^* = 0$, return $H_4(x^*) = nP$; else, $rand^* = 1$, $H_4(x^*) = nP + bP$, $n \in Z_q^*$.

c) Return $H_4(x^*)$ to $\mathcal{A}$, and add $(n, x^*, H_4(x^*)$ to H_4_List.

Step 4: $\mathcal{A}$ queries to $\mathcal{C}$ with $sig(m)$

a) $\mathcal{C}$ maintains a list of $(m^*, H_4(m^*), sig(m^*))$ as $signList$ which is empty at the beginning.

b) $\mathcal{A}$ should ask for $H_4(m^*)$ before inquiring for $sig(m^*)$ from $\mathcal{C}$. If $H_4(m^*)$ is not inquired before, the $\mathcal{C}$ will answer generate $(m^*, H_4(m^*))$.

c) When the input m^* appears in the list $signList$, it returns $sig(m^*)$; when the input m^* is not in the list, if $rand^* = 0$, it calculates $\sigma = a \cdot H_3(pk_1) + a \cdot H_3(pk_2) + a \cdot H_4(m^*)$; else, terminates the response.

d) Returns $sig(m^*)$ to $\mathcal{A}$ and adds $(m^*, H_4(m^*), sig(m^*))$ to the list.

Step 5: if $\mathcal{A}$ forges $sig(m')$, then $rand^* = 1$, the following equation holds: $\sigma' = a \cdot H_3(pk\_1) + a \cdot H_3(pk\_2) + abp + anp$.

Thus, $abp = \sigma' - a \cdot H_3(pk\_1) - a \cdot H_3(pk\_2) - anp$. So $\mathcal{C}$ can obtain abp as a solution of CDH problems. If $\mathcal{A}$ breaks the scheme with a non-negligible probability ϵ in time t, then $\mathcal{C}$ can solve the probability of CDH with probability $\epsilon' >= \delta(1-\delta)^{q_S}\epsilon >= \epsilon/(q_S\rho)$, rho is a natural number. Then, $\epsilon <= q_S \cdot rho \cdot \epsilon'$.

4) Conditional Traceability: TS can determine the signer of a message through the corresponding relationship between temporary ID and user's real ID. Thus, the scheme achieves conditional traceability, which is one of the acceptable and desired properties in PSN. But if TS is not involved in the PSN, such a dispute cannot be solved. Thus, we suggest that for crucial PSN communications, TS should be involved in order to guarantee system safety and preserve node privacy at the same time.

4.2 Performance Analysis

1) Computation Cost

We mainly focus on the computation cost of key algorithms, such as short-term key generation, signature generation and signature verification. By comparing our scheme with [7] and [30], the analysis results are summarized as shown in Table 4. We define cost of pairing as C_e, as well C_G, C_{GZ}, C_{GT} is the cost of add and multiplication operation of G and multiplication operation of GT, respectively. $\oplus$, $|\cdot|$ and other operations are not considered here because they are simple operation in groups compared operations above. According to implementation in next subsection, we obtain that the C_{GZ} and C_e are most time-consuming operations. The compared result will be given with the evaluation results.

Table 4. Analysis and comparison of computation cost

Scheme	Short-term key	Signature	Verification
AnonyTrust	$2C_{GZ} + C_G$	$C_{GZ} + C_G$	$2C_G + 2C_e$
[7]	$2C_{GZ}$	$C_{GZ} + C_G$	$C_{GT} + 3C_e$
[30]		$3C_{GZ}$	$2C_{GZ} + C_G + C_e$

2) Communication Cost

The data frequently transmitted in this scheme are *token*, *list* and *anonymsg*. With n users and k APs, we can obtain the communication cost as Table 5. Only data length of *list* is linear with the number user, but it is distributed by TS while registering and only updated when needing. Besides, the number of APs is not large. Thus, communication cost in the proposed scheme is acceptable.

Table 5. Communication data length

Data type	Content	Data length
token	MD5	16
list	$\{secret\_token_1, ...,\}$	$16n$
anonymsg	P_i, Q_i, sig, m	$16 + 16k + 64 + m + 64$

Table 6. Operation time comparison (ms))

Scheme	Short-term key	Signature	Verification
1 token	14.724	3.268	46.402
5 token	16.981	3.275	47.453
[7]	14.127	3.142	65.051
[30]	8.045	9.076	27.029

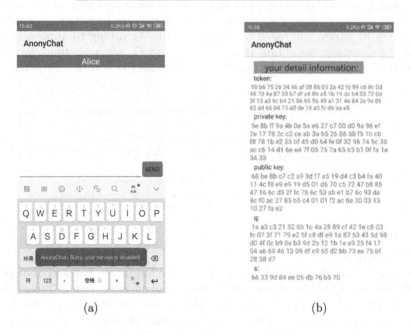

(a)   (b)

Fig. 3. Access control based on user trust

4.3   Performance Evaluation

We implemented the proposed scheme in Java language using the JPBC library on a desktop (running 64-bit Windows OS, equipped with Intel Core i5-3230M @2.60 GHz). We mainly focus on the computational performance of short-term key generation, signature generation and signature verification.

We assume that users use $num = 1$ (only TS) or $num = 5$ tokens (for TS and 4 APs) to authenticate anonymously, and then test their performance compared with [7] and [30]. The average computational time for each stage is shown in Table 6. The time of short-term key generation of 5 tokens is a little longer than that in 1 token, but the computing time of other stages is very close. Thus, multiple tokens do not affect the computing performance of the scheme.

Besides, compared with [7] and [30], the short-term key generation time of our scheme is the longest. This is because the public key is generated in two parts to realize anonymity, message verification and trust value authentication. The signature generation is the same as [7], but more efficient than [30] because of less C_{GZ} operations. For signature verification, our scheme is faster than [7], but longer than [30]. That is because our scheme realizes both authenticating the identity based on the trust level and integrity of the message at the same time. As can be seen from the above analysis and evaluation results, our scheme can achieve trust authentication at a low computational cost.

5 Implementation and Experimental Results

This section implements a secret chat APP: AnonyChat on Android devices and then gives the experimental results, such as running efficiency, message delay, CPU occupancy, memory occupancy and communication overhead.

5.1 Function Design

1) Access Control Based on User Trust
As shown in Fig. (3a), when a user sends a login request, the server will verify his/her trust value. If the user's trust value is lower than the threshold (set to 0.56), a pop-up window will prompt the user that he/she has been denied. As shown in Fig. (3b), a user can check his/her detailed information like the token, short-term key.

2) Anonymous Chat
Figure (4b) and Fig. (4b) shows the chat interface. After receiving a message, a user first verifies the identity of the sender by checking whether its *secret_token* is in the trust-related list. If it does not exist, the message bubble is red and "an illegal message" is displayed. Then the correctness of the signature is verified. If it fails, the bubbles are shown in red and "a fake message" is displayed. Finally, the trust value of the sender is computed. If lower than the threshold (0.6), the bubble of the message is yellow, and the normal content of the message is displayed. Otherwise, the bubble of the message is green.

3) Rating Feedback
As shown in Fig. (4c), when a user clicks on a certain message, AnonyChat will pop up a scoring dialog box for users to score the corresponding message. The score results will be sent as feedback to TS or APs for updating the trust value list.

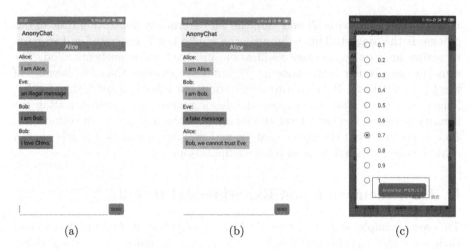

(a)   (b)   (c)

Fig. 4. (a)(b) Anonymous chat interface, (c) Trust rating feedback interface

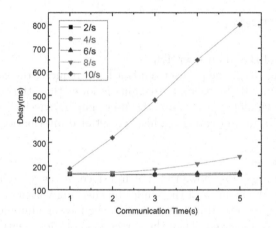

Fig. 5. Performance evaluation on message delay

5.2   Experimental Results

1) Message Delay
In this paper, AnonyChat is tested on the Android device (Xiaomi 6, 6G RAM,
835 @2.45 GHz CPU). When the density of messages is 2/s– 10/s, the average
delay of messages changes with time as shown in Fig. 5. When the message
density is less than 8/s, the delay keeps stable as 150 ms. When reaching 8/s,
the message delay will increase slightly, but the delay lasting for 5 s is only 240
ms. When reaching 10/s, the message delay can rise to 800 ms in 5 s, which
is unfriendly for users. Thus, 10/s can be viewed as the limit of AnonyChat's
message density. This is because the time interval between messages transmission
is less than the time needed for encryption and decryption, so there is a blockage

of message processing in the client. In practice, sending and receiving messages at a density of 8/s can already meet the actual needs of users for most of the time, but it is necessary to improve it in the future.

2) CPU Usage, Memory Usage and Communication Consumption

CPU usage, memory usage and communication consumption are three commonly used performance indicators for mobile applications. This paper will assume an extreme situation is the density of messages is 10/s to test performance. From Fig. 6, AnonyChat occupies lower than 4% of the CPU even in extreme cases, so it does not consume too much system resources of Android devices. As shown in Fig. 7, AnonyChat generally occupies about 4M–5M of memory even in extreme cases, so it is very lightweight. For communication cost, the traffic consumption of AnonyChat is less than 5 KB/s, very little traffic even in extreme cases, as shown in Fig. 8. Therefore, the resource usage of AnonyChat can be accepted for present smartphones.

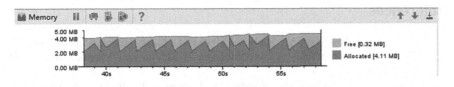

Fig. 6. Performance evaluation on CPU usage

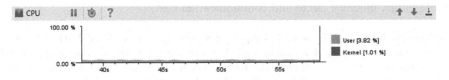

Fig. 7. Performance evaluation on memory

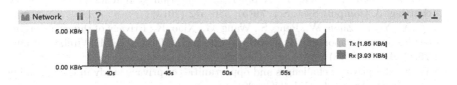

Fig. 8. Performance evaluation on communication

6   Conclusion

This paper proposed an anonymous trust authentication scheme, which can ensure the security of user messages and the anonymity of identity by verifying the trust level of anonymous users. In the proposed scheme, TS is responsible for the management of all PSN entities, evaluates and issues the trust value of PSN users along with APs. Based on the token of trust value, cryptographic algorithms and the authentication protocol were constructed to realize anonymous trust authentication for PSN users. This scheme adapted a semi-distributed architecture and introduced authorized APs to overcomes the problem of over-reliance on central TS. Thus, PSN users can switch online and offline states to authenticate with each other. Through security analysis and performance evaluation, the scheme realized secure and trusted anonymous authentication among users with high computational efficiency. Last, AnonyChat was developed to verify the feasibility and performance in Android devices. The results demonstrated that the application is very lightweight and performs well about message delay, CPU usage, memory usage and communication cost.

Acknowledgment. The work is supported in part by the National Natural Science Foundation of China under Grants 61672410 and 61802293, the Academy of Finland under Grants 308087 and 314203, the Key Lab of Information Network Security, Ministry of Public Security under grant No. C18614, the open grant of the Tactical Data Link Lab of the 20th Research Institute of China Electronics Technology Group Corporation, P.R. China under grant CLDL-20182119, the Shaanxi Innovation Team project under grant 2018TD-007, and the 111 project under grant B16037.

References

1. Yan, Z., Zeng, K., Xiao, Y., Samarati, P., et al.: Guest editorial special issue on trust, security, and privacy in crowdsourcing. IEEE Internet Things J. **5**(4), 2880–2883 (2018)
2. Ahtiainen, A., Kalliojarvi, K., Kasslin, M., Leppanen, K., Richter, A., Ruuska, P., Wijting, C.: Awareness networking in wireless environments. IEEE Veh. Technol. Mag. **4**(3), 48–54 (2009)
3. Shen, X., Yu, H., Buford, J., Akon, M. (eds.): Handbook of Peer-to-Peer Networking, vol. 34. Springer, Boston (2010). https://doi.org/10.1007/978-0-387-09751-0
4. Yan, Z., Chen, Y., Shen, Y.: A practical reputation system for pervasive social chatting. J. Comput. Syst. Sci. **79**(5), 556–572 (2013)
5. Qu, Y., Yu, S., Zhou, W., Peng, S., Wang, G., Xiao, K.: Privacy of things: emerging challenges and opportunities in wireless Internet of Things. IEEE Wirel. Commun. **25**(6), 91–97 (2018)
6. Yu, S.: Big privacy: challenges and opportunities of privacy study in the age of big data. IEEE Access **4**, 2751–2763 (2016)
7. Zhang, C., Lu, R., Lin, X., Ho, P., Shen, X: An efficient identity-based batch verification scheme for vehicular sensor networks. In: IEEE INFOCOM 2008-The 27th Conference on Computer Communications, pp. 246–250. IEEE (2008)

8. Wasef, A., Shen, X.: Efficient group signature scheme supporting batch verification for securing vehicular networks. In: 2010 IEEE International Conference on Communications, pp. 1–5. IEEE (2010)

9. Liu, J., Zhang, Z., Chen, X., Kwak, K.: Certificateless remote anonymous authentication schemes for wirelessbody area networks. IEEE Trans. Parallel Distrib. Syst. **25**(2), 332–342 (2013)

10. Boneh, D., Boyen, X., Shacham, H.: Short group signatures. In: Franklin, M. (ed.) CRYPTO 2004. LNCS, vol. 3152, pp. 41–55. Springer, Heidelberg (2004). https://doi.org/10.1007/978-3-540-28628-8_3

11. Lee, Y., Han, S., Lee, S., Chung, B., Lee, D.: Anonymous authentication system using group signature. In: 2009 International Conference on Complex, Intelligent and Software Intensive Systems, pp. 1235–1239. IEEE (2009)

12. Ren, K., Lou, W., Kim, K., Deng, R.: A novel privacy preserving authentication and access control scheme for pervasive computing environments. IEEE Trans. Veh. Technol. **55**(4), 1373–1384 (2006)

13. Shao, J., Lin, X., Lu, R., Zuo, C.: A threshold anonymous authentication protocol for VANETs. IEEE Trans. Veh. Technol. **65**(3), 1711–1720 (2015)

14. Yan, Z., Feng, W., Wang, P.: Anonymous authentication for trustworthy pervasive social networking. IEEE Trans. Comput. Soc. Syst. **2**(3), 88–98 (2015)

15. Yan, Z., Wang, P., Feng, W.: A novel scheme of anonymous authentication on trust in pervasive social networking. Inf. Sci. **445**, 79–96 (2018)

16. Lindell, Y.: Anonymous authentication. J. Priv. Confidentiality **2**(2) (2011). https://doi.org/10.29012/jpc.v2i2.590

17. Lin, X., Sun, X., Wang, X., Zhang, C., Ho, P., Shen, X.: TSVC: timed efficient and secure vehicular communications with privacy preserving. IEEE Trans. Wireless Commun. **7**(12), 4987–4998 (2008)

18. Sato, F., Takahira, H., Mizuno, T.: Message authentication scheme for mobile ad hoc networks. In: 11th International Conference on Parallel and Distributed Systems (ICPADS 2005), vol. 1, pp. 50–56 (2005)

19. Lin, X., Li, X.: Achieving efficient cooperative message authentication in vehicular ad hoc networks. IEEE Trans. Veh. Technol. **62**(7), 3339–3348 (2013)

20. Zhang, L., Wu, Q., Solanas, A., Domingo-Ferrer, J.: A scalable robust authentication protocol for secure vehicular communications. IEEE Trans. Veh. Technol. **59**(4), 1606–1617 (2009)

21. Hao, Y., Cheng, Y., Zhou, C., Song, W.: A distributed key management framework with cooperative message authentication in VANETs. IEEE J. Sel. Areas Commun. **29**(3), 616–629 (2011)

22. Feng, W., Yan, Z., Xie, H.: Anonymous authentication on trust in pervasive social networking based on group signature. IEEE Access **5**, 6236–6246 (2017)

23. Huszti, A.: Anonymous multi-vendor micropayment scheme based on bilinear maps. In: International Conference on Information Society (i-Society 2014), pp. 25–30. IEEE (2014)

24. Yan, Z., Zhang, P., Vasilakos, A.: A survey on trust management for Internet of Things. J. Netw. Comput. Appl. **42**, 120–134 (2014)

25. Li, N., Yan, Z., Wang, M., Yang, L.: Securing communication data in pervasive social networking based on trust with KP-ABE. ACM Trans. Cyber Phys. Syst. **3**(1), 1–23 (2018)

26. Yan, Z., Shi, W.: Cloudfile: a cloud data access control system based on mobile social trust. J. Netw. Comput. Appl. **86**, 46–58 (2017)

27. Yan, Z., Wang, M.: Protect pervasive social networking based on two-dimensional trust levels. IEEE Syst. J. **11**(1), 207–218 (2014)

28. Zhao, H., Sun, D., Yue, H., Zhao, M., Cheng, S.: Dynamic trust model for vehicular cyber-physical systems. IJ Netw. Secur. **20**(1), 157–167 (2018)
29. Goldwasser, S., Micali, S., Rivest, R.: A digital signature scheme secure against adaptive chosen-message attacks. SIAM J. Comput. **17**(2), 281–308 (1988)
30. Cao, X., Zeng, X., Kou, W., Hu, L.: Identity-based anonymous remote authentication for value-added services in mobile networks. IEEE Trans. Veh. Technol. **58**(7), 3508–3517 (2009)

Transaction Deanonymization in Large-Scale Bitcoin Systems via Propagation Pattern Analysis

Meng Shen[1,2(✉)], Junxian Duan[1], Ning Shang[1], and Liehuang Zhu[1]

[1] School of Computer Science, Beijing Institute of Technology, Beijing 100081, China
{shenmeng,duanjx,liehuangz}@bit.edu.cn, shangning128@163.com
[2] Cyberspace Security Research Center, Peng Cheng Laboratory,
Shenzhen 518000, China

Abstract. Bitcoin is a digital currency payment system, which bases on the property of decentralization and anonymization of Blockchain. Researches on transaction deanonymization for the Bitcoin system may not associate anonymous transactions with the IP addresses (physical identity) of the originator accurately and may consume network resources excessively. In this paper, we propose an approach to obtain the originating transactions through analyzing the propagation information. We calculate a pattern matching score by combining the propagation pattern extraction and the node weight assignment. Through carrying out the experiments in the real Bitcoin system, we effectively match the originating transactions with the target node, which reaches a precision of 81.3% and is 30% higher than the state-of-the-art method.

Keywords: Bitcoin transactions · Deanonymization · Data analytics · Propagation path · Empirical probability distribution

1 Introduction

Bitcoin system has been recently emerging as a world-wide decentralized anonymous digital currency system [1]. It works without a centralized administrator, where all transactions are verified by nodes in a peer-to-peer (P2P) Bitcoin network and recorded in public distributed ledger (i.e., Blockchain) [7,15–17]. The total number of nodes (a.k.a., peers) in the Bitcoin P2P network is estimated to exceed 10,300. At the same time, the system generates a block every ten minutes and 2,000 transactions per block on average. In the complex system, assuming to track who issued a specific transaction, we need to match the transactions with the nodes [19,23]. However, matching large-scale transactions with their

This work is partially supported by Key-Area Research and Development Program of Guangdong Province (No. 2019B010137003), Zhejiang Lab Open Fund with No. 2020AA3AB04, National Natural Science Foundation of China under Grants 61972039 and 61872041, and Beijing Natural Science Foundation under Grant 4192050.

© Springer Nature Singapore Pte Ltd. 2020
S. Yu et al. (Eds.): SPDE 2020, CCIS 1268, pp. 661–675, 2020.
https://doi.org/10.1007/978-981-15-9129-7_45

originating nodes needs a massive information collection and extraction, which may lead to prohibitively expensive computational and storage costs [20–22].

We aim to design an effective and efficient method to identify the Bitcoin transaction of originators (i.e., peers who generate transactions) with its IP addresses. Existing studies on Bitcoin transaction deanonymization can be roughly classified into two categories. The *first* category mainly focuses on discovering the relationship among Bitcoin anonymous peers from publicly available transactions, e.g., extracting user relationships through transaction graph analysis [5,11,18], or clustering transaction addresses belonging to the same user [6,24]. This category only analyzes the transaction characteristics of anonymous peers. The *second* category aims at linking transactions to its real-world originating IP address by analyzing transaction propagation data [2,3]. However, existing methods often require always requesting transaction information for massive calculations, which may cause severe disruption to the Bitcoin network.

To address the problem of existing studies, there still exist two main challenges: 1) *Effectiveness*: the transaction prorogation information in Bitcoin network vary significantly due to network dynamics (e.g., network topology and transmission delay), making the originated and forwarded transactions less distinguishable. Thus, it is non-trivial to identify originated transactions in such an error-prone scenario accurately. 2) *Efficiency*: transaction deanonymization requires the frequent collection of Bitcoin network information, such as the network topology and transaction prorogation paths, which may introduce an interference with the network functionalities and cause high communication overhead. Therefore, it remains a challenging task to conduct the information collection process more efficient.

To tackle these challenges, we choose probability analytics to match the originating transactions with the IP address of Bitcoin nodes. Since the nodes are using the forwarding dynamics in the underlying network, a regular pattern of forwarding paths still exists. To handle the effect of the dynamics of network and forwarding, we calculate the square error as the loss function and obtain a suspected probability distribution of the originating transactions. In addition, we also propose a node weight model to improve the matching precision and output the originating transactions without knowledge of specific neighbor nodes.

Our main contributions can be briefly summarized as follows.

- We propose a propagation pattern extraction model to identify suspicious transactions that are probably to be originated from the target node with lower interference to the network.
- We improve the precision of matching the target node IP address with its anonymous Bitcoin transactions by assigning nodes weight, which does not rely on the specific neighbor nodes of the target.
- We verify the effectiveness of the proposed method in the real-world Bitcoin system. The results show that it achieves 81.3% precision on average, which is 30% higher in comparison with the state-of-the-art method.

To the best of our knowledge, this is the first attempt to combine the propagation pattern of transactions and nodes weight assignment for Bitcoin deanonymization. The rest of this paper is organized as follows. Section 2 introduces the relevant background and summarizes the previous works. The system architecture of our method is presented in Sect. 3, which is followed by the design details of the matching score calculation via propagation pattern speculation in Sect. 4. After evaluating the performance of our method in Sect. 5, the conclusion of this study is presented in Sect. 6.

2 Background and Related Work

In this section, we provide a brief introduction of the Bitcoin system with a particular focus on the transaction forwarding mechanism. Then, we present an overview of existing deanonymization methods.

2.1 Transaction Propagation in Bitcoin System

A transaction in the Bitcoin system consists of one or more input addresses and one or more output addresses. These addresses are known as pseudonyms of Bitcoin users for authenticating transactions [12].

When a transaction is generated by an originator, it will be broadcasted to all the other nodes in the Bitcoin network. To forward transactions, each node connects to a limited number of nodes, which are referred to as neighbors [3]. The originator first sends the transaction to its neighbors (i.e., 1st-neighbor nodes), who, in turn, forwards the transaction to their neighbors (i.e., 2nd-neighbor nodes). The forwarding process continues until the transaction reaches every node in the network.

Based on the characteristics of the Bitcoin system, a transaction needs to be forwarded by other nodes from the originator, and the transaction is broadcasted in the whole network. Actually, the forwarding of a transaction does not happen immediately when a peer receives the transaction. Every 100 milliseconds, one neighbor node is randomly selected from the list of all peers' neighbors, and the queue for outgoing forwarding messages is flushed for this node [3]. In the meanwhile, the mechanism may prevent the other neighbor nodes from receiving the forwarded transaction.

2.2 Summary of Existing Studies

We briefly summarize the existing studies on Bitcoin deanonymization, which can be classified into two categories. The first category attempts to discover the relationship among users from publicly available transaction information. The second category aims to analyze the transaction propagation information in the underlying network.

Correlation Analysis of Transaction-Layer Information. Reid et al. [13] and Liao [10] speculated the source Bitcoin address and the funds' flow of transaction from public transaction address. DuPont [5] determined the frequent period of the transaction according to the consumption habits of the public. Zhao [24] proposed a clustering process for Bitcoin transaction data through analyzing 35,587,286 addresses in the global Bitcoin account. Dmitry Ermilov [6] proposed two heuristics to cluster the address associated. Cazabet [14] used complex network analysis and community detection to match multiple addresses with its Bitcoin users. Moreover, the precision of these approaches will be significantly affected when users adopt a one-off address strategy or transaction obfuscation.

Linkability Analysis of Network-Layer Propagation Information. Koshy et al. [9] classified distinct transaction relay patterns and designed heuristics to hypothesize transaction ownership. Dan Kaminsky et al. [2] proposed the Sybil attack to assume that the first forwarding node IP address of a new transaction is owned by the original sender. Biryukov et al. [3] put forward a transaction traceability mechanism based on neighbor nodes and developed a TOR middleman attack and "Address cookies" to identify specific clients [4]. Ethan used a set of IP address controlled to form an unsolicited incoming connection with the victim and sent false network information continuously to obtain the transaction address [8]. In the above discussion, the solution might cause serious interference to the underlying network, even requiring more computing resources.

3   System Overview

Based on the existing researches, we have optimized the traceability scheme via the propagation pattern analysis. In this section, we propose an innovative deanonymization architecture and introduce the workflow of each step in it.

3.1   System Architecture

Due to the characteristics of the anonymity and dynamics of nodes in the Bitcoin system, we have designed a traceability scheme based on the network topology to track the originating transactions based on the node's IP address. We are trying to reduce the interference to the network, which focuses on a specific target node with a known IP address in advance. To select its originating transactions from all available transactions in the Bitcoin network, we obtain the characteristics of the transaction retransmission mode. Then, based on the problem that neighbor nodes are uncontrollable, a weight calculation method is adopted to improve the accuracy of tracing effectively. An overview of the system architecture is shown in Fig. 1, which consists of three main components.

The first component collects forwarding information of all transactions in the Bitcoin network, and then feeds this information to the rest two components for further analysis. The second component, referred to as the propagation pattern extraction model fits a probability distribution that provides the probability of occurrence of different peers on each position in the transaction forwarding path of the target node. The probability distribution can be used to identify suspicious transactions that are probably to be originated from the target node. The

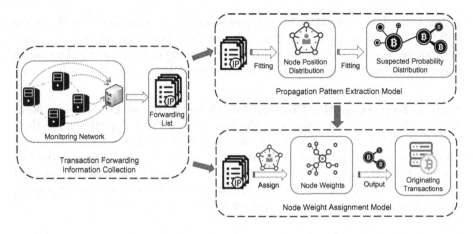

Fig. 1. An overview of system architecture.

third component, which is referred to as the node weight assignment model, assigns a node weight for each forwarding node according to originating transactions. Through calculating the matching score for all captured transactions, the transaction that has score above the threshold is identified to the suspected originating transaction.

We develop the probe program based on the Bitcoin open source code to monitor the target node and obtain the forwarding information for each transaction. The Bitcoin node realizes the connection with the target node or other nodes by saving the IP address, the port of neighbor nodes, the forwarding transaction information, and the block information. The probe is a Bitcoin Network Crawler, which dose not modify the existed network connection, including neighbor nodes of all nodes. A probe node which can receive transaction information rather than generating transaction to collect the propagation path passively. The probe will not cause interference to the network.

3.2   Description of Workflow

This section describes the details involved in the architecture in Sect. 3.1, including the process from acquiring transactions in the network to finding the originating transactions, which can reduce errors caused by propagation delays and applies to uncontrollable nodes.

Suppose it is required to match an uncontrollable target node with its originating transactions. After establishing the monitoring network to collect transaction information, we use propagation pattern extraction and node weight assignment to output the suspected originating transactions through a threshold.

Step 1. Collecting the Individual Transaction by Probe. To extract the underlying propagation pattern mainly relies on the forwarding path characteristics. We use a probe to record the transactions associated with the target node. The information of each forwarded transaction arrives at the probe will be recorded, including the hash value of the transaction, the forward node IP address, and the arrival time. Then, we sort the different forwarding nodes according to the time when the forwarded transaction reaches the probe.

Step 2. Extracting the Propagation Pattern in the Underlying Network. The transaction created by the target node will be firstly sent to their neighbors. When we know about the neighbor nodes' information of the target node, we can count the probability that the neighbor node appears in the forwarding path of one originating transaction. The parameter to fit is illustrated in Sect. 4. Then, we extract the pattern that the transaction is an originating transaction when a certain node appears in a particular position.

Step 3. Outputting the Suspected Originating Transactions. As the dynamic of neighbor nodes that are not easily to be continuously connected, we assign the node weight depending on the probability where the node appears in the originating transaction forwarding path. Then, we calculate the matching score for each collected transaction with the pattern extracted. When the score of a transaction is higher than the threshold, it is regarded as a suspected originating transaction and output it.

4   Matching Score Calculation via Propagation Pattern Speculation

Since the nodes are using the step-by-step forwarding mechanism in the underlying network, a regular pattern of forwarding paths still exists. To handle the effect of the dynamics of network, we calculate the square error as the loss function to speculate the propagation pattern of the originating transactions. In addition, we also propose a node weight model to improve the matching precision for the suspected originating transactions without knowledge of specific nodes.

4.1   Propagation Pattern Extraction Using Forwarding Path

We assume that an originating transaction had a similar propagation pattern when it forwarded in the underlying network, and it will inevitably be forwarded by important nodes (such as neighbor nodes). We deploy probes and sort the collected forwarding information in order of time arrival to obtain a forwarding path list for a transaction.

By analyzing the forwarding path of each transaction through the forwarding information in the underlying network, we find that several nodes which forward information advanced are important nodes in most cases. We can empirically judge the probabilities $\hat{b}_p$ of the position in which these important nodes appear in the forwarding path of the originating transaction $\mathbb{T}^{(o)}$. That is, each position in the forwarding path list has a $\hat{b}_p$ corresponding to the important node. Similar to the propagation pattern in the originating transactions, we can assume that the non-originating transaction $\mathbb{T}^{(n)}$ also has a specific propagation pattern. In the collected forwarding path list of non-original transactions, we can find out that the position of important nodes is generally more backward. Consequently, we define the $\hat{a}_p$ is the probability of a position that corresponds to the important node in the forwarding path list of the non-originating transactions.

We extract the propagation pattern by analyzing the forwarding path list. We calculate the probability of the transaction being originated when a position corresponds to an important node, through the $\hat{b}_p$ and $\hat{a}_p$ of two forwarding path lists from different transactions. In the following, we call this probability $d_{iscount}$. With that in mind, if the forwarding path list of a transaction is similar to the propagation pattern we extract, then the transaction is more likely to be the originating transaction we are looking for. Based on the above idea, we focus on how to extract the propagation pattern by calculating the $d_{iscount}$. We define the process of calculation, as shown in Algorithm 1.

Algorithm 1. Propagation pattern speculation through $d_{iscount}$

Require:
transactions M, controllable node A, probe k
Ensure:
suspected probability $d_{iscount}$
  1: Deploy the probe k and obtain forwarding path list.
  2: Use a controllable node A as the target node to originate total of M transactions;
  3: Capture originating transactions $\mathbb{T}^{(o)}$ and non-originating transactions $\mathbb{T}^{(n)}$;
  4: **for each** $T_i \in \mathbb{T}^{(o)}$ **do**
  5:    Calculate $\hat{b}_p$ by Eq. (1);
  6: **end for**
  7: **for each** $T_i \in \mathbb{T}^{(n)}$ **do**
  8:    Calculate $\hat{a}_p$ by Eq. (2);
  9: **end for**
10: Use Eq. (3) to speculate the $d_{iscount}$;
11: Through Eq. (4), the loss functions by the square error are selected to fit r_p.

We conduct an analysis of $d_{iscount}$ according to the forwarding path information of the known originating transactions collected by the probe. First of all, we use Eq. (1) to calculate the probability of the position p corresponding to the neighbor node in the originating transaction, where the $L_{\mathbb{T}^{(o)},p}$ represents the node IP address on position p in the forwarding path of transaction $\mathbb{T}^{(o)}$.

$$\hat{b}_p = \frac{1}{|\mathbb{T}^{(o)}|} \sum_{i=1}^{|\mathbb{T}^{(o)}|} \sigma_{\mathbb{D}^{(n)}}(L_{\mathbb{T}^{(o)},p}) \tag{1}$$

In addition, the $\sigma_{\mathbb{D}^{(n)}}$ is the characteristic function represents the node $L_{\mathbb{T}^{(o)},p}$ whether is a neighbor node. As the same, we define the function $\hat{a}_p$ for non-original transactions as shown in Eq. (2), where the $L_{\mathbb{T}^{(n)},p}$ represents the node

IP address on position p in the forwarding path of transaction $\mathbb{T}^{(n)}$.

$$\hat{a}_p = \frac{1}{|\mathbb{T}^{(n)}|} \sum_{i=1}^{|\mathbb{T}^{(n)}|} \sigma_{\mathbb{D}^{(n)}} \left(L_{\mathbb{T}^{(n)}, p} \right) \tag{2}$$

Then, we combine the $\hat{b}_p$ and $\hat{a}_p$ to speculate the propagation pattern as the discrete empirical probabilities function $\hat{r}_p$. When the neighbor nodes from $\mathbb{T}^{(o)}$ appear in position p of forwarding path list, the function is expressed in Eq. (3).

$$\hat{r}_p = \frac{\hat{b}_p}{\hat{b}_p + \hat{a}_p} \tag{3}$$

Next, we need to fit appropriate r_p represents the $d_{iscount}$ according to the distribution of empirical probability $\hat{r}_p$. We calculate the square error as the loss function, which is shown in Eq. (5).

$$r_p = f_r(p, \alpha) \tag{4}$$

$$min \sum_{i=1}^{p_{max}} (r_p - \hat{r}_p)^2 \tag{5}$$

The Levenberg-Marquardt method is employed to fit the parameter vectors α. The p_{max} represents the max length of the forwarding path list, where equals 100 in our experiment. Subsequently, we can obtain r_p by real-word Bitcoin network.

4.2   Weight Assignment for Forwarding Nodes

We assume that transactions forwarded by important nodes (neighbor nodes) can be presumed to be originating transactions, while transactions forwarded by more important nodes are more like originating transactions. After knowing the $d_{iscount}$ for each position p, if the node at this position is not a neighbor node, we assign the weight w_{d_i} for every node d_i to confirm the degree of importance in the forwarding path list. We propose a method to assign nodes weight, which is described in Algorithm 2.

Through analyzing the forwarding path of the transactions sent by the controllable node B, we can fit the probability function b_p of the neighbor nodes appearing in different positions p as shown in Eq. (6).

$$b_p = f_b(p, \beta) \tag{6}$$

The Levenberg-Marquardt method is employed to fit the parameter vectors β. The loss function by calculating the square error is shown in Eq. (7).

$$min \sum_{i=1}^{p_{max}} (b_p - \hat{b}_p)^2 \tag{7}$$

Algorithm 2. Nodes weight assignment

Require:
Transactions M, controllable node B, probe k
Ensure:
w_{d_i}
1: Deploy the probe k, use another controllable node B to connect the target node
   with a single point and originate total of M transactions;
2: Capture originating transaction set $\mathbb{T}^{(o)}$;
3: Take Eqs. (6) and (7) to fit the probability function b_p of the neighbor nodes
   appearing in different position p;
4: **for each** $T_j \in \mathbb{T}^{(o)}$ **do**
5: $\quad \mathcal{L} \leftarrow \mathcal{L} \cup \left\{ L_{\mathbb{T}_j^{(o)},p} \right\}$;
6: **end for**
7: Calculate the node weight w_{d_i} according to Eq. (8);
8: Get the node weight set $\mathcal{W}$ of captured nodes by probe k.

After fitting the parameter vector β of b_p, we can define the weight assignment
for node d_i as shown in Eq. (8).

$$w_{d_i} = \sum_{j=1}^{|\mathbb{T}^{(o)}|} \sum_{p=1}^{p_{max}} \sigma_{d_i}(L_{\mathbb{T}_j^{(o)},p}) \cdot b_p \qquad (8)$$

Obviously, the w_{d_i} depends on the $d_{iscount}$ that the node appears in the originating transactions and the frequency of occurrence. And the $d_{iscount}$ needs to be universally applicable to all forwarding transactions. The node appears in more forwarding paths; the cumulative weight is greater.

4.3 Matching Score Calculation

In order to accurately evaluate whether a transaction is an originating transaction, we use the $d_{iscount}$ and the weight w_{d_i} of the node corresponding to a certain position p to calculate the matching score. When the matching score of a transaction is high, the transaction is closer to the propagation pattern we extracted, and it is more likely to be the originating transaction.

$$S_{T_i} = \sum_{p=1}^{p_{max}} r_p w_{L_{T_i,p}} \qquad (9)$$

The threshold is used to determine the suspected transaction originated from the target node. When the matching score of a transaction exceeds the threshold, the transaction is considered to belong to the target node. Choosing the optimal solution of the threshold is very important for improving the precision of traceability. In order to choose the appropriate threshold, we use the receiver-side operating characteristic (ROC) curve to select the threshold. The specific process of threshold selection will be introduced in Sect. 5.3.

5 Performance Evaluation

In this section, we evaluate the performance of the proposed method. In order to present a comprehensive understanding of the contribution of our approach, we will employ the method proposed by Biryukov et al. [3] for comparison, which is referred to as **Neigh** hereafter. The method we proposed is referred to as **Prow** hereafter.

5.1 Experimental Settings

In our experiments, we use two controllable nodes to verify the effectiveness of the method. The controllable node A is used as the target node under the real network environment. Another controllable node B is used to single-point connect with the controllable node A and originate transactions to calculate the probability distribution of neighboring nodes. A probe node is adopted in the experiment to monitor the Bitcoin network. Among them, the probe node can effectively collect the transaction information forwarded in the underlying network. The controllable nodes can independently create the transaction and check the information of the neighboring nodes.

To avoid interference with the Bitcoin system, we only conduct experiments on one target node. To ensure data authenticity and universality, the partial transactions are originated during the dispersed time period of one day, and different neighbors are selected between different sessions.

5.2 Evaluation of Propagation Pattern Effectiveness

In our preliminary considerations, in order to accurately identify whether a transaction is originated by the target, we need to verify whether the r_p is universal in the Bitcoin network. We first use controllable node A to originate 100 transactions as different groups in different time periods intermittently. And we know the neighbor nodes of the controllable nodes in these groups of transactions. When the probe monitors the network, we have received more than 120,000 transactions forwarded by all nodes. Based on the position of known neighbors in the forwarding list, we calculate the probability b_p and a_p of neighbors appearing in each location, as shown in Fig. 2.

The (a) shows the probability b_p of neighbors appearing in each position in the list. According to the probability of b_p, we find the higher the position, the more probably it is the neighbor node. Therefore, we assume the inverse function $\hat{p}_N(k, c)$ in the Eq. (10). We can obtain the $c_1 = 0.3963$, $c_2 = -0.3601$, $c_3 = -0.0005$.

$$\hat{p}_N(k, c) = \frac{c_1}{k - c_2} - c_3 \qquad (10)$$

In the view of the feasibility of the neighbor probability in forwarding lists, we select 3,000 non-originating transactions. The (b) shows the probability a_p of neighbors appearing in each position in the list. Similarly, we describe the probability of neighbors appearing in each position in non-originating transaction as

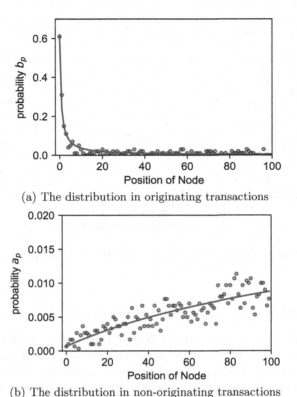

(a) The distribution in originating transactions

(b) The distribution in non-originating transactions

Fig. 2. The distribution of known neighbors appearing in each location of the forwarding list in originating transactions and non-originating transactions.

$\hat{p}_N(k, d)$. We assume the exponential function to fit the parameter d as presented in Eq. (11). We obtain the $d_1 = 0.0081$, $d_2 = 56.5202$, $d_3 = -0.0321$.

$$\hat{p}_N(k, d) = d_1 \times ln(k + d_2) + d_3 \tag{11}$$

Under the Eq. (10) and Eq. (11), we can calculate the probability whether the transaction is originated when neighbor nodes appear in a certain position. Then, we describe the function $p_N(k, b)$ as shown in Eq. (12), where the $p_N(k, b)$ equals to the r_p.

$$p_N(k, b) = \frac{\hat{p}_N(k, c)}{\hat{p}_N(k, c) + \hat{p}_N(k, d)} \tag{12}$$

According to the transaction collection and probability analytics in the real Bitcoin network, the probability distribution of the originating and non-originating transactions is matched with the propagation pattern extracted in Sect. 4.

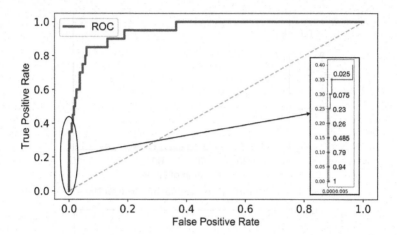

Fig. 3. The receiver-side operating characteristic (ROC) curve and its partial enlargement.

5.3   Evaluation of Threshold and Precision

This experiment aims to compare the **Neigh** method with our **Prow** method in terms of precision and recall rate by outputting the originating transactions. We assume that the two methods have the same transaction propagation paths. In order to implement the previous method, we mark the six neighbors of the target node. If the top ten of the forwarding list has three neighbors, we output the suspected originating transactions. Additionally, we obtain the matching score of each transaction through our method. Besides, we output the originating transactions over the threshold.

We use the receiver-side operating characteristic (ROC) curve to select the threshold. By traversing the threshold, the true positive rate and the false positive rate at different thresholds are obtained, and the ROC curve is drawn as shown in Fig. 3.

To efficiently realize the deanonymization, we intend to reach higher precision while requiring a general recall rate, which requires a threshold corresponding to a higher TPR and a lower FPR. Through observing the partial enlargement of the ROC curve in Fig. 3, there is a part of the TPR that almost grows vertically (c.f., TPR from 0.25 to 0.30). We choose the point with obvious inflection and get the value of 0.075 as the threshold, which is also employed in the later experiments. In addition, we use the area under the ROC curves (AUC) for model evaluation. The calculated AUC is 0.95, indicating that we have a probability of 95% to make the score of the originating transaction larger than the non-originating transaction in our model.

In order to clearly compare the two methods, we select six rounds of experimental transaction data for conducting comprehensive analytics. The number of transactions in per round is recorded. On average, the probe received 5,925

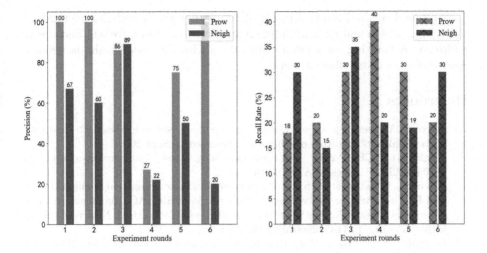

Fig. 4. Comparison of our method and existing studies.

transactions on each round of experiments. We estimate the precision and recall rate of two methods on average of six rounds.

As shown in Fig. 4, the average precision reached up to 81.3%, and the recall rate was 26.3%. In the case of the same network environment and experimental settings, the precision was 51.3%, and the recall rate was 24.8% through the application of the previous method. Although rarely correct transactions are found in the previous method, it represents that the strategy can ignore most abnormal transactions. Comparing the precision and the recall rate of the previous method, we can find that our method has higher precision.

Our method has the advantage that we do not depend on the network environment and known neighbors. It is difficult to guarantee continuous connection to the whole network, and there are some non-originating transactions and some uncontrollable forwarded transactions in the real environment. Therefore, we may get an inaccurate forwarding list when the neighbor node forwards with random delay. Especially, we calculate the whole forwarding node rather than the neighbors who may not be connected. Besides, the recall rate was not higher than the previous method. For different requirements, we can select different thresholds referring to the ROC curve.

6   Conclusion

In this paper, we proposed an effective method to realize the deanonymization of large-scale Bitcoin transactions based on propagation pattern analysis in the underlying network. By extracting the transaction propagation pattern and assigning the forwarding nodes weight, we could output the originating Bitcoin transactions from large-scale captured transactions. In addition, we reduced the deviation caused by forwarding delay. The experimental results showed that the proposed method is more practical compare with the existing methods in terms of precision and network interference. In future work, we will find the IP addresses by tracking the related transactions with the node weight assignment model or other more efficient methods.

References

1. Bitcoin: A peer-to-peer electronic cash system—satoshi nakamoto institute. https://nakamotoinstitute.org/bitcoin/. Accessed 15 Sept 2019
2. Black ops of TCP/IP 2011—dan kaminsky's blog. https://dankaminsky.com/2011/08/05/bo2k11/. Accessed 8 Oct 2019
3. Biryukov, A., Khovratovich, D., Pustogarov, I.: Deanonymisation of clients in bitcoin P2P network. In: Proceedings of the 2014 ACM SIGSAC Conference on Computer and Communications Security, CCS 2014, pp. 15–29. ACM, New York (2014). https://doi.org/10.1145/2660267.2660379
4. Biryukov, A., Pustogarov, I.: Bitcoin over tor isn't a good idea. In: 2015 IEEE Symposium on Security and Privacy, pp. 122–134, May 2015. https://doi.org/10.1109/SP.2015.15
5. DuPont, J., Squicciarini, A.C.: Toward de-anonymizing bitcoin by mapping users location. In: Proceedings of the 5th ACM Conference on Data and Application Security and Privacy, CODASPY 2015, pp. 139–141. ACM, New York (2015). https://doi.org/10.1145/2699026.2699128
6. Ermilov, D., Panov, M., Yanovich, Y.: Automatic bitcoin address clustering. In: 2017 16th IEEE International Conference on Machine Learning and Applications (ICMLA), pp. 461–466, December 2017. https://doi.org/10.1109/ICMLA.2017.0-118
7. Gao, F., Zhu, L., Shen, M., Sharif, K., Wan, Z., Ren, K.: A blockchain-based privacy-preserving payment mechanism for vehicle-to-grid networks. IEEE Netw. 32(6), 184–192 (2018)
8. Heilman, E., Kendler, A., Zohar, A., Goldberg, S.: Eclipse attacks on bitcoin's peer-to-peer network. In: 24th USENIX Security Symposium (USENIX Security 15), pp. 129–144. USENIX Association, Washington, D.C. (2015)
9. Koshy, P., Koshy, D., McDaniel, P.: An analysis of anonymity in bitcoin using P2P network traffic. In: Christin, N., Safavi-Naini, R. (eds.) FC 2014. LNCS, vol. 8437, pp. 469–485. Springer, Heidelberg (2014). https://doi.org/10.1007/978-3-662-45472-5_30
10. Liao, K., Zhao, Z., Doupe, A., Ahn, G.J.: Behind closed doors: measurement and analysis of cryptolocker ransoms in bitcoin. In: 2016 APWG Symposium on Electronic Crime Research (eCrime), pp. 1–13, June 2016. https://doi.org/10.1109/ECRIME.2016.7487938
11. Narayanan, A., Shmatikov, V.: Robust de-anonymization of large sparse datasets. In: 2008 IEEE Symposium on Security and Privacy (SP 2008), pp. 111–125, May 2008. https://doi.org/10.1109/SP.2008.33
12. Ober, M., Katzenbeisser, S., Hamacher, K.: Structure and anonymity of the bitcoin transaction graph. Future Internet 5(2), 237–250 (2013). https://doi.org/10.3390/fi5020237
13. Reid, F., Harrigan, M.: An analysis of anonymity in the bitcoin system. In: 2011 IEEE Third International Conference on Privacy, Security, Risk and Trust and 2011 IEEE Third International Conference on Social Computing, pp. 1318–1326, October 2011. https://doi.org/10.1109/PASSAT/SocialCom.2011.79

14. Remy, C., Rym, B., Matthieu, L.: Tracking bitcoin users activity using community detection on a network of weak signals. In: Cherifi, C., Cherifi, H., Karsai, M., Musolesi, M. (eds.) COMPLEX NETWORKS 2017 2017. SCI, vol. 689, pp. 166–177. Springer, Cham (2018). https://doi.org/10.1007/978-3-319-72150-7_14

15. Shen, M., Deng, Y., Zhu, L., Du, X., Guizani, N.: Privacy-preserving image retrieval for medical iot systems: a blockchain-based approach. IEEE Netw. **33**(5), 27–33 (2019)

16. Shen, M., Duan, J., Zhu, L., Zhang, J., Du, X., Guizani, M.: Blockchain-based incentives for secure and collaborative data sharing in multiple clouds. IEEE J. Sel. Areas Commun. **38**(6), 1229–1241 (2020)

17. Shen, M., et al.: Blockchain-assisted secure device authentication for cross-domain industrial IoT. IEEE J. Sel. Areas Commun. **38**(5), 942–954 (2020)

18. Shen, M., Ma, B., Zhu, L., Mijumbi, R., Du, X., Hu, J.: Cloud-based approximate constrained shortest distance queries over encrypted graphs with privacy protection. IEEE Trans. Inf. Forensics Secur. **13**(4), 940–953 (2017)

19. Shen, M., Zhang, J., Zhu, L., Xu, K., Tang, X.: Secure svm training over vertically-partitioned datasets using consortium blockchain for vehicular social networks. IEEE Trans. Veh. Technol. (2019)

20. Yu, S.: Big privacy: challenges and opportunities of privacy study in the age of big data. IEEE Access **4**, 2751–2763 (2016)

21. Yu, S., Gu, G., Barnawi, A., Guo, S., Stojmenovic, I.: Malware propagation in large-scale networks. IEEE Trans. Knowl. Data Eng. **27**(1), 170–179 (2014)

22. Yu, S., Zhao, G., Dou, W., James, S.: Predicted packet padding for anonymous web browsing against traffic analysis attacks. IEEE Trans. Inf. Forensics Secur. **7**(4), 1381–1393 (2012)

23. Zhang, C., Zhu, L., Xu, C., Liu, X., Sharif, K.: Reliable and privacy-preserving truth discovery for mobile crowdsensing systems. IEEE Trans. Dependable Secure Comput. (2019). https://doi.org/10.1109/TDSC.2019.2919517

24. Zhao, C., Guan, Y.: A graph-based investigation of bitcoin transactions. In: Peterson, G., Shenoi, S. (eds.) DigitalForensics 2015. IAICT, vol. 462, pp. 79–95. Springer, Cham (2015). https://doi.org/10.1007/978-3-319-24123-4_5

User Privacy-Preserving Scheme Based on Anonymous Authentication in Smart Grid

Qichao Lai[1,2], Li Xu[1,2(✉)], Manli Yuan[1,2], Feng Wang[1,2], and He Fang[3]

[1] College of Mathematics and Informatics, Fujian Normal University, Fuzhou, China
xuli@fjnu.edu.cn
[2] Fujian Provincial Key Laboratory of Network Security and Cryptology,
Fujian Normal University, Fuzhou, China
[3] Department of Electrical and Computer Engineering,
The University of Western Ontario, London, Canada

Abstract. One of the main functions of smart meter is to assist utility companies charge from users intelligently. To save computation and communication resources, while protecting the privacy of users, many data aggregation schemes for privacy protection have been proposed. However, the real-time power consumption data collected by utility companies may be insufficiently fine-grained (individual user electricity consumption data at time slot t, usually, t is 15 min) in these schemes, resulting in low data availability. For example, the collected data cannot be used for anomaly detection. To overcome this difficulty, we propose a new anonymous authentication scheme using Boneh-Schacham group signature which supports fine-grained data collection. Through this scheme, even though the gateway receives user's electricity consumption information, it can protect the privacy of the user. Moreover, dynamic price, lower secret key management difficulty and track of the faulty smart meters can also be realized in our scheme.

Keywords: Smart grid · Anonymous authentication · Privacy preservation · Fine-grained · Signature

1 Introduction

Smart grid refers to development of the traditional electrical grid, which is consisted of traditional grid, modern communication technology, sensor technology, and control technology and so on [1]. It helps the utility companies to flexibly regulate the operation of the whole electrical grid and to charge from users remotely. In smart grid, the smart meter is an important component, which is a two-way communication device and deployed at user's home [2]. As many non-intrusive load monitoring techniques [3,4] have been proposed, which are applied to smart

This work is supported by the National Natural Science Foundation of China (Grant No. U1905211, NO. 61771140).

S. Yu et al. (Eds.): SPDE 2020, CCIS 1268, pp. 676–691, 2020.
https://doi.org/10.1007/978-981-15-9129-7_46

meters to measure the amount of electricity used by a single appliance at specific time slot t (e.g., 2019. 03. 28, 09: 00–09: 15). The utility companies can use these data to calculate electricity bill of users, as well as future complex data analysis, like anomaly detection [5,6], which aims to help electricity consumers to identify unusual behaviors, e.g., forgetting to turn off the lights after leaving; and help utility companies detect abnormal events, e.g., electricity stealing and leakage. It should be emphasized that anomaly detection requires the data receiver to collect fined-grained data. Furthermore, the pressure of power transmission increased with users demand for electricity, however, the dynamic price strategy is an effective way to warn users to save electricity and balance power transmission. Meanwhile, the smart grid can increase the transparency of users' electricity consumption, that is, users can view their dynamic electricity consumption. Beneficially, users can adjust the habit of using electricity to reduce daily power consumption. Therefore, collecting users' fine-grained data to formulate dynamic electricity pricing strategies is of great significance to utility companies.

Although the smart grid can bring many benefits, the privacy leakage is a main concern from the users perspective [7–9]. This is because the malicious third party may obtain their private information from the electricity data submitted. For example, a malicious adversary can find out when users leave home and when they are at home by analyzing customer electricity data. Further, the adversary can know from the lighting electricity data when the user gets up and when to sleep. He can also know when the user starts cooking from the electricity data of the rice cooker. So it is very important to preserve users' privacy.

1.1 Related Work

In recent years, relevant scholars have made some achievements in the protection of user privacy in smart grid. The scenarios of privacy protection mainly include traditional user power consumption [10–18,20] and Vehicle-to-Grid [21,22]. In order to protect users' privacy, The most straightforward way to hide communication content and protect the privacy of the user is that users encrypt the electricity data and transmit it to utility companies, but this will eventually bring huge computational cost to utility companies during the decryption process. Data aggregation schemes [10–12] and anonymous authentication [13,16,19] can solve the problem that the message receiver needs enormous computation cost. Apart from the utility companies should ensure the availability of data, i.e., ensure that the data is complete during the communication process.

In 2017, Ni *et al.* [11] proposed a differentially private data aggregation scheme with fault tolerance and range-based filtering in smart grid. Utility companies can get that the user's measurements within an acceptable range without knowing the exact readings. But this protocol does not have the function of dynamic pricing charging. Gope and Sikdar [18] introduced an efficient data aggregation scheme (EDAS), which support dynamic pricing-based billing. In order to reduce the computation load of utility companies in existing aggregation schemes, Xue *et al.* [12] outsourced the time-sensitive computation in real-time pricing demand response (e.g., dynamic prices predictions) to a third-party service provider to improve the effectiveness of demand response program and reduce the computation complexity on the utility companies. Gope and Sikdar [20] designed a lightweight data aggregation scheme by using one way Hash functions and XOR operations. However, the more remarkable problem characteristics in those data aggregation schemes are that the data collected by utility companies is not fine enough to make anomaly detection, dynamic price and so on.

Compared with collecting aggregated data, electricity consumption data collected by utility companies for individual users is more practical. In 2015, Diao et al. [13] established privacy-preserving smart metering scheme in which users upload real-time electricity consumption data anonymously. gateway can not know its corresponding user identity even if it gets all users' electricity consumption information. At the same time, the protocol can verify the data and track the faulty smart meters. Due to network fault, or smart meter aging during it long-term use, etc., the user may fail to upload the power data. Tracking these users identities becomes a necessity. Unfortunately, Qu et al. [14] pointed out this protocol can not resist forgery attack and malicious attacker could inject false data into smart grid. In 2016, a privacy-preserving scheme for data collection based pseudonym was proposed by Tang et al. [15]. In 2017, Kishimoto et al. [16] adopted group signature as a tool, and presented an anonymous authentication protocol scheme, but they did not analyze the performance of the scheme in detail. Gope and Sikdar [17] considered a lightweight and privacy-preserving data aggregation scheme (LPDA) which based on single-pass authenticated encryption implementing lightweight data aggregation for dynamic pricing billing. However, this scheme suffers from the difficulties in management due to the large number of user key certificates.

1.2   Contribution

In this paper, under the scenario of traditional electricity consumption, we utilize Boneh-Schacham (BS) group signature technology to propose a Privacy-Preserving Scheme based on Anonymous Authentication (PPS2A). The theoretical and simulation results of PPS2A scheme show that our scheme is more efficient in computation overhead at utility companies. Specifically, our contributions can be summarized as follows:

1. To preserve the users privacy in smart grid, we explore the BS group signature for anonymous authentication, the proposed PPS2A scheme prevents the gateway from knowing user's identity during the authentication process. Besides, gateway can also verify the integrity of the collected data.
2. The proposed PPS2A scheme supports utility companies collect fine-grained data. In order to improve the practicality of the data, in our scheme, the utility companies finally collects the real-time electricity consumption data of a single user.
3. The proposed PPS2A scheme supports real-time electricity pricing, which can level off peak period of electricity consumption and balance grid power transmission. Moreover, in our scheme, we can effectively track the faulty smart meters.

The rest of this paper is organized as follows. In Sect. 2, we present the technologies relating to our scheme. In Sect. 3, we describe the system model and the security requirements. In Sect. 4, we propose the PPS2A scheme. In Sect. 5, we give the security analysis. In Sect. 6, we provide the performance analysis. In Sect. 7, we conclude our work.

2   Preliminaries

In this section, we briefly review the necessary complexity assumptions and the BS group signatures [23], and both of them will serve as the basis of the proposed scheme.

2.1   Complexity Assumption

In this subsection, we recall the following two complexity assumptions, which related to the security of our scheme.

Definition 1. q-Strong Diffie-Hellman (q-SDH) assumption. Let g_1, g_2 be a generator of $\mathbb{G}_1$ and $\mathbb{G}_2$, respectively. Input a $(q + 2)$-tuple $(g_1, g_2, g_2^{\gamma}, g_2^{(\gamma^2)}, ..., g_2^{(\gamma^q)})$, output a pair $(g_1^{\frac{1}{\gamma+x}}, x)$, where γ, $x \in \mathbb{Z}_q^*$. Any probabilistic polynomial time algorithm $\mathscr{A}$ has advantage ϵ in solving the q-SDH assumption in $(\mathbb{G}_1, \mathbb{G}_2)$ is defined as

$$\Pr[\mathscr{A}(g_1, g_2, g_2^{\gamma}, g_2^{(\gamma^2)}, ..., g_2^{(\gamma^q)}) = (g_1^{\frac{1}{\gamma+x}}, x)] = \epsilon \tag{1}$$

The q-SDH assumption is that, for any probabilistic polynomial time algorithm $\mathscr{A}$, the ϵ is negligibly small.

2.2   BS Group Signature

The BS group signature can achieve anonymity of identity. Concretely, the BS signature is comprised of three algorithms: key generation, signature, verification.

1) *Key Generation*: Given the security parameter κ, the parameter generation algorithm $\mathcal{G}en(\kappa)$ outputs a tuple $(q, \mathbb{G}_1, \mathbb{G}_2, \mathbb{G}_T, e)$. It proceeds as follows: Selecting generator g_1, g_2 in $\mathbb{G}_1$ and $\mathbb{G}_2$, respectively. Randomly choosing $\eta \in \mathbb{Z}_q$ and computes $\omega = g_2^{\eta}$. then, selecting $x_i \in \mathbb{Z}_q$ such that $x_i + \eta \neq 0$, and computing $A_i = g_1^{1/(\eta+x_i)}$. After that, the group public key is $gpk = (g_1, g_2, \omega)$. Each user's private key is tuple $gsk_i = (A_i, x_i)$.
2) *Signature*: Given a message m, user picks a random number $r \in \mathbb{Z}_q$, and computes generators $(\hat{u}, \hat{v})$ in $\mathbb{G}_2$ from $H_0 : \{0, 1\}^* \rightarrow \mathbb{G}_2^2$ as

$$(\hat{u}, \hat{v}) = H_0(gpk \,||\, m \,||\, r) \in \mathbb{G}_2^2. \tag{2}$$

The user also computes $u = \varphi(\hat{u})$, $v = \varphi(\hat{v})$, where, φ is an efficiently computable isomorphism from $\mathbb{G}_2$ to $\mathbb{G}_1$. After that, user selects $\alpha \in \mathbb{Z}_q$ and computes $T_3 = u^\alpha$, $T_4 = A_i v^\alpha$. Then, he/she sets $\delta = x_i\alpha \in \mathbb{Z}_q$, and randomly picks r_0, r_1, $r_2 \in \mathbb{Z}_q$ and computes

$$R_1 = u^{r_0}, \qquad\qquad R_3 = T_3^{r_1} \cdot u^{-r_2},$$
$$R_2 = e(T_4,\ g_2)^{r_1} \cdot e(v,\ w)^{-r_0} \cdot e(v,\ g_2)^{-r_2}. \tag{3}$$

Finally, chooses a hash function $H : \{0,\ 1\}^* \to \mathbb{Z}_q$ and computes

$$c = H(gpk \,\|\, m_i \,\|\, r \,\|\, T_3 \,\|\, T_4 \,\|\, R_1 \,\|\, R_2 \,\|\, R_3), \tag{4}$$

$s_0 = r_0 + c\alpha$, $s_1 = r_1 + cx_i$ and $s_2 = r_2 + c\delta$. The signature on message m_i is $\sigma_i = (r,\ T_3,\ T_4,\ c,\ s_0,\ s_1,\ s_2)$.

3) *Verification*: Firstly, verifier computes $\hat{u}$ and $\hat{v}$ according Eq. (1) and $u = \varphi(\hat{u})$, $v = \varphi(\hat{v})$. Then, in term of σ rederives R_1, R_2, R_3 as

$$\hat{R}_1 = u^{s_0}/T_3^c, \qquad\qquad \hat{R}_3 = T_3^{s_1} u^{-s_2},$$
$$\hat{R}_2 = e(T_4,\ g_2)^{s_1} e(v,\ w)^{-s_0} e(v,\ g_2)^{-s_2}\Big(\frac{e(T_4,\omega)}{e(g_1,g_2)}\Big)^c, \tag{5}$$

and checks

$$c \stackrel{?}{=} H(gpk \,\|\, m_i \,\|\, r \,\|\, T_3 \,\|\, T_4 \,\|\, \hat{R}_1 \,\|\, \hat{R}_2 \,\|\, \hat{R}_3). \tag{6}$$

If this equation holds, verifier accepts the signature. Otherwise, verifier rejects the signature.

Correctness of signatures:

$$\hat{R}_1 = u^{s_0}/T_3^c = u^{r_0+c_1\alpha}/(u^\alpha)^{c_1} = u^{r_0} = R_1; \tag{7}$$

$$\hat{R}_3 = T_3^{s_1}u^{-s_2} = (u^\alpha)^{s_1} \cdot u^{-r_2-c_1x_i\alpha} = (u^\alpha)^{r_1+c_1x_i} \cdot u^{-r_2-c_1x_i\alpha}$$
$$= (u^\alpha)^{r_1} \cdot u^{-r_2} = (T_3)^{r_1} \cdot u^{-r_2} = R_3; \tag{8}$$

$$\hat{R}_2 = e(T_4,g_2)^{s_1} e(v,w)^{-s_0} e(v,g_2)^{-s_2}\Big(\frac{e(T_4,\omega)}{e(g_1,g_2)}\Big)^c$$
$$= (e(T_4,\ g_2)^{r_1} e(v,\ w)^{-r_0} e(v,\ g_2)^{-r_2}) \cdot (e(T_4,g_2)^{x_i} e(v,\ w)^{-\alpha}$$
$$e(v,\ g_2)^{-x_i\alpha}\big(\frac{e(T_4,\ \omega)}{e(g_1,\ g_2)}\big))^c \tag{9}$$
$$= R_2 \cdot \Big(\frac{e(T_4v^{-\alpha},\ wg_2^{x_i})}{e(g_1,\ g_2)}\Big)^c = R_2 \cdot \Big(\frac{e(A_i,\ wg_2^{x_i})}{e(g_1,\ g_2)}\Big)^c$$
$$= R_2 \cdot \Big(\frac{e(g_1^{\frac{1}{\eta+x_i}},\ g_2^\eta \cdot g_2^{x_i})}{e(g_1,\ g_2)}\Big)^c = R_2.$$

If the above Eq. (8), (9), and (10) hold, then, equation (7) holds, and the signatures is valid. Otherwise, the signatures is invalid.

3 System Model, Security Requirements and Design Goals

In this section, we first describe the system model for our proposed PPS2A scheme. Then we explicate the security requirement. Finally, the design goals of our scheme are presented.

3.1 System Model

When users broadcast real-time electricity data, they always care about privacy. In this work, the protection of user privacy is also our research focus. Specifically, according to [10], a smart grid system model including smart meter (also mentioned as user, SM/U), gateway (GW), control center (CC), as shown in Fig. 1.

Smart Meter/User (SM/U). Each user is equipped with a smart meter, which is used to measure the user's electricity consumption data. The smart meter also broadcasts signed data to GW periodically. In our scheme, we suppose there are n users (i.e., $U = \{U_1, U_2, ..., U_n\}$) in a residential area.

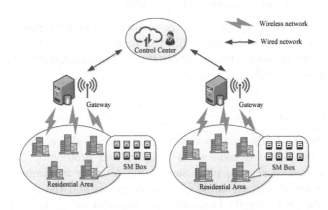

Fig. 1. System model.

Gateway (GW). GW is an entity close to the user, which has powerful computational capacity. It connects user and CC into a network. The main responsibilities of GW are to verify the validity of messages from users and assist in forwarding the communication between user and CC.

Control Center (CC). The CC is also the utility companies which we mentioned earlier. It is a trusted entity, whose duties are stated as follows: Firstly, it takes the responsibility for users registration and system initialization. Secondly, it collects the users' electricity consumption data. Thirdly, it calculates the electricity price of the next period of time slot t for users, and then, announces it to them. Besides, CC charges from each user after a billing period.

3.2   Security Requirements

We intend to design a fine-grained data collection scheme that can guarantee users' privacy preserving when users are anonymous broadcast electricity consumption data. Therefore, the security requirements should be satisfied as the following three aspects:

Identity Anonymity. In order to protect individual residential users' privacy from $\mathcal{A}$ eavesdropping in which all the identities of users should be hidden from GW during the SM broadcasts electricity consumption data, that is, even if the $\mathcal{A}$ and GW get the information, they can not know anything about the user identity. In other words, except CC, no other entity can match the user's identity and the corresponding electricity consumption data. Therefore, user privacy is guaranteed. In addition, the user's private key only be used by himself, and can not lent to others without CC's permission.

Sender Authentication and Data Integrity. Authenticating a signed message is sent indeed by a legitimate user and has not been altered or even replaced during the transmission. In other words, if an adversary $\mathcal{A}$ attempts to modify a message, the malicious behavior can be detected, which means that only the correct broadcasts can be accepted by the GW.

Identity Extracting. Once CC receives users' electricity consumption data from GW, it extracts the identity of SM to match with the corresponding electricity consumption data. Then it can obtain the fine-grained data and effectively find out the broken SM.

3.3   Design Goals

In addition to the basic security requirements stated above, we are committed to achieving the following goals when designing our protocol.

1) The proposed scheme must satisfy the security requirements described above. If the users' privacy could be compromised, and the real-time electricity data could be replaced. Then, the development of smart grid will not go far. Therefore, the proposed scheme must achieve identity anonymity, sender authentication and data integrity. Besides, only the CC can extract the identity for users.

2) The proposed scheme should provide fine-grained data collection and dynamic electricity pricing strategy. Nowadays, the increase in demand for electricity has led to the sharp decrease of resource, at the same time, to balance and stabilize the power transmission of the grid, and improve the practicality of the data. In our work, we must have the function of fine-grained data collection and dynamic electricity price charging.

3) The proposed scheme should track the fault SMs. Due to SMs may be damaged and malfunction after them work for a long time, they will fail to broadcasts electricity consumption data. When this happens, the CC in the proposed scheme must have the ability of finding out the user's identity.

4 Our PPS2A Scheme for Privacy Preservation

In this section, our proposed PPS2A scheme mainly consists of the following five stages: system initialization, smart meter setup, user report generation, verification, and data processing.

4.1 System Initialization

This step is operated by CC. Because CC is the only fully trusted entity in a smart grid system, it is reasonable that regard it as the beginning of the bootstrap program. Specifically, in the system initialization phase, given the security parameters κ, CC running $\mathcal{Gen}(\kappa)$ out put $\{\mathbb{G}_1,\ \mathbb{G}_2,\ \mathbb{G}_T,\ q,\ g,\ g_1,\ g_2,\ e\}$, where q is a large prime. $\mathbb{G}_1,\ \mathbb{G}_2,\ \mathbb{G}_T$ are multiplicative cyclic groups of order q. g, g_1, g_2 are generator of $\mathbb{G}_T,\ \mathbb{G}_1$ and $\mathbb{G}_2$, respectively. After that, CC randomly selects $\lambda,\ \eta \in \mathbb{Z}_q$, and sets $\lambda,\ \eta$ as its private key, and computes $\mu = g^\lambda$, $\omega = g_2^\eta$ as its public key. CC also chooses $E_\pi(\cdot)/D_\pi(\cdot)$ and two Hash functions H, H_0, where $E_\pi(\cdot)/D_\pi(\cdot)$ is the symmetric encryption algorithm (e.g., AES), π is the symmetric key, and $H : \{0, 1\}^* \rightarrow \mathbb{Z}_q, H_0 : \{0,1\}^* \rightarrow \mathbb{G}_2^2$. Finally, the system parameters are $Pars = \{\mathbb{G}_1,\ \mathbb{G}_2,\ \mathbb{G}_T,\ q,\ g,\ g_1,\ g_2,\ e,\ \mu,\ \omega,\ E_\pi(\cdot)/D_\pi(\cdot),\ H,\ H_0\}$.

4.2 Smart Meter Setup

At this stage, a user obtains a private key pair of signature from CC after it provides ID to CC. Firstly, CC chooses $x_i \in \mathbb{Z}_q(i = 1,\ 2,\ ...,\ n)$ as the private key for every SM $_i$, where x_i satisfy $x_i + \eta \neq 0(i = 1,\ 2,\ ...,\ n)$ and every SM$_i$'s other. Then, CC computes $A_i = g_1^{1/(\eta+x_i)}$, $D_i = g^{x_i}$ and sets user's registration log $Reg(ID_i) = D_i$, and each user's private key is the tuple $sk_i = (A_i,\ x_i)$. After that, CC assigns sk_i and $Reg(ID_i)$ to U$_i$ through a secure channel, and it adds all of users' $Reg(ID_i)$ and the correspond of ID$_i$ to registration log list ($Regl$).

4.3 User Report Sign Message

Suppose one user's electricity usage data are $m_{i,t}$ at time slot t. SM$_i$ generates a signature for the message $m_{i,t}$ as follows:

1) SM$_i$ random chooses $r, \gamma \in \mathbb{Z}_q$, computes $t_0 = H(T_s)$, where T_s is the current timestamp, $T_{i,1} = D_i g^{\gamma t_0}$, $T_{i,2} = \mu^\gamma$, $H_0(gpk\,||\,m_{i,t}\,||\,r) = (\hat{u},\ \hat{v}) \in \mathbb{G}_2^2$, $u = \varphi(\hat{u})$, $v = \varphi(\hat{v})$.

2) SM$_i$ random selects $\alpha \in \mathbb{Z}_q$ and computes $T_3 = u^\alpha$, $T_4 = A_i v^\alpha$.

3) SM$_i$ random picks $r_0,\ r_1,\ r_2 \in \mathbb{Z}_q$, and computes

$$R_1 = u^{r_0}, \qquad\qquad R_3 = T_3^{r_1} \cdot u^{-r_2},$$
$$R_2 = e(T_4, g_2)^{r_1} \cdot e(v, \omega)^{-r_0} \cdot e(v, g_2)^{-r_2}. \tag{10}$$

4) SM$_i$ computes

$$c_1 = H(gpk||m_{i,t}||r||T_{i,1}||T_{i,2}||T_3||T_4||R_1||R_2||R_3), \tag{11}$$

$s_0 = r_0 + c_1\alpha, s_1 = r_1 + c_1 x_i, s_2 = r_2 + c_1\delta \in \mathbb{Z}_q$, where $\delta = x_i\alpha$.

5) Finally, SM_i outputs the signature of $m_{i,t}$ i.e., $\sigma_{i,t} = (r,\ T_{i,1},\ T_{i,2},\ T_3,\ T_4,\ c_1,\ s_0,\ s_1,\ s_2,\ T_s)$, then broadcasts $(m_{i,t},\ \sigma_{i,t})$ to GW.

4.4 Verifications

After GW receives user's $(m_{i,t},\ \sigma_{i,t})$ for $i = 1,\ 2,\ ...,\ n$, the GW firstly checks the timestamp T_s. If it does hold, then, GW performs the following steps to check the validity of signatures.

1) GW computes $H_0(gpk\,\|\,m_{i,t}\,\|\,r) = (\hat{u},\ \hat{v}) \in \mathbb{G}_2^2$, $u = \varphi(\hat{u})$, $v = \varphi(\hat{v})$.
2) According to the U_i provides σ_i, GW rederives $R_1,\ R_2,\ R_3$, i.e.,

$$\hat{R}_1 = u^{s_0}/T_3^{c_1}, \qquad \hat{R}_3 = T_3^{s_1} u^{-s_2},$$
$$\hat{R}_2 = e(T_4, g_2)^{s_1} e(v,\omega)^{-s_0} e(v, g_2)^{-s_2}\left(\frac{e(T_4,\omega)}{e(g_1,g_2)}\right)^c, \tag{12}$$

and checks

$$c_1 \overset{?}{=} H(gpk\,\|\,m_{i,t}\,\|\,r\,\|\,T_{i,1}\,\|\,T_{i,2}\,\|\,T_3\,\|\,T_4\,\|\,\hat{R}_1\,\|\,\hat{R}_2\,\|\,\hat{R}_3). \tag{13}$$

If equation holds, accept, otherwise, reject.

If all of the signatures are validity. Then, GW random selects two secret number $\theta,\ \tau \in \mathbb{Z}_q^*$, computes $\pi = \omega^\theta$, $h = g_2^\theta$, $\Delta = E_\pi(\tau)$ and $c_2 = H(m_{1,t}\,\|\,m_{2,t}\,\|\,...\,\|m_{n,t}\,\|\,\tau\,\|\,T_s)$. Finally, it sends $\{(m_{1,t}, T_{11}, T_{12}), (m_{2,t}, T_{21}, T_{22}), ..., (m_{n,t}, T_{n1}, T_{n2}),\ h,\ \Delta,\ c_2\}$ to CC.

If some of the signatures are invalidity or some users due to the malfunctioning smart meters can not broadcasts electricity consumption data normally, and we denote those users as $\bar{U} \subset U$. Then GW sends all of the U_i's data $\{(m_{1,t}, T_{11}, T_{12}), (m_{2,t}, T_{21}, T_{22}), ..., (m_{\bar{n},t}, T_{\bar{n}1}, T_{\bar{n}2}),\ h,\ \Delta,\ c_2\}$ to CC, where $U_i \in U/\bar{U}(i = 1,\ 2,\ ...,\ \bar{n})$.

4.5 Data Processing

When CC receives $\{(m_{1,t}, T_{11}, T_{12}), (m_{2,t}, T_{21}, T_{22}), ..., (m_{n,t}, T_{n1}, T_{n2}),\ h,\ \Delta,\ c_2\}$ from GW. It first computes $\pi = h^\eta$, $D_\pi(\Delta)$ to get τ and checks $c_2 \overset{?}{=} H(m_{1,t}\,\|\,m_{2,t}\,\|\,...\|m_{n,t}\,\|\,\tau\,\|\,T_s)$, if the equation holds, accept, otherwise, requests GW to send message again. After that, CC processing U_i's message during the specific time period as following stages.

ID Extract. For every U_i's $(m_{i,t},\ T_{i1},\ T_{i2})$, CC extracts T_{i1} and T_{i2}, then, uses private key λ and $t_0 = H(T_s)$ to compute $T_{i,1}/T_{i,2}^{t_0/\lambda} = g^{x_i}$, and searches $Regl$ for i with $D_i = g^{x_i}$. After that, CC constructs a list of user's ID and the corresponding of electricity usage, denoted by $(ID_i,\ t,\ m_{i,t})$.

When the number of messages received is less than n, which means that at time slot t have users don't broadcast electricity consumption data normally. CC will extract the identity list of those users according to the $Regl$ and $\bar{U} \subset U$.

Then, CC finds out the faulty meter and requests them to resend the electricity consumption information.

Price Forecasting. After recovers user's Identity, CC sums all of the $m_{i,t}$ ($i = 1, 2, ..., n$), denoted by $M_t = \sum_{i=1}^{n} m_{i,t}$. CC utilizes its adopted algorithm, such as the algorithm in [13], denoted as $p_{t+1} = \mathcal{F}(parameters)$, where $\mathcal{F}$ is the function of generate price. CC generates the electricity price of the next period of time slot t as follows:

$$p_{t+1} = \mathcal{F}(M_t, other\ parameters). \tag{14}$$

Then, CC broadcasts p_{t+1} to users through GW. After receiving the electricity price, user can artificially or automatically adjust its electricity consumption behavior.

Charging process. For charging every U_i, the CC performs Eq. (16) to compute electricity bill at time slot t.

$$b_{i,t} = m_{i,t} \cdot p_t. \tag{15}$$

After that, CC adds $b_{i,t}$ to U_i's account, i.e., $Acc_{U_i} : \{(ID_i,\ t,\ m_{i,t},\ p_t,\ b_{i,t}),...\}$, then, it storages Acc_{U_i} to cloud server that user can inquire their own real-time electricity usage and bills on line.

5 Security Analysis

In this section, we show that the proposed PPS2A scheme meets all the security requirements defined in Sect. 3.2.

The proposed protocol achieves identity anonymity. SM broadcasts electricity data anonymously, and the adversary $\mathcal{A}$ cannot match the user's identity with their messages. As described in our security requirement, an adversary $\mathcal{A}$ may reside in the residential area to eavesdrop the communication between the users and GW. Suppose $\mathcal{A}$ has eavesdropped a U_i's messages ($m_{i,t}$, $\sigma_{i,t}$), cause of the user is anonymity broadcasts electricity consumption data, $\mathcal{A}$ has no idea who broadcasts the messages. Besides, GW reports to the users the price forecast, which does not contain any information of users, so it does not reveal users' privacy. Therefore, our scheme successfully preserves the user privacy.

Table 1. Function comparison between our scheme and the existing schemes.

	Privacy preserving	Data Integrity	Sender Authentication	Dynamic Price	Fine-grained data collection	sk Management Difficulty
DiPrism [11]	Yes	Yes	No	No	No	Easy
LPDA [17]	Yes	Yes	Yes	Yes	No	Hard
UDP [25]	Yes	No	No	Yes	No	Hard
PPS2A	Yes	Yes	Yes	Yes	Yes	Easy

Table 2. Comparison of computation complexity[a,b].

	DiPrism [11]	PPS2A
User	$6C_{e1} + 2C_e + C_{m1} + C_m$	$5(C_{e1} + C_e) + 2(C_{m1} + C_m) + 3C_p$
GW	$(n+4)C_p + (2n+2)C_{e1} + (4n-5)C_{m1}$ $+(2n-2)C_m$	$4nC_p + 4n(C_{e1}+C_m) + 2nC_{m1} +$ $(n+1)C_{e2} + (3n+1)C_e$
CC	$2C_{e1} + 4C_e + 2C_{m1} + 4C_m + D_e{}^{a,b}$	$(n+1)C_e + nC_m$

a Since the structure of our scheme is different from LPDA scheme, we have not compare our scheme with LPDA scheme in computation complexity.

b D_e represent the time for executing decryption in reference [11].

The proposed protocol achieves sender authentication and data integrity. GW can ensure that the received actually from legitimate users. In our proposed PPS2A scheme, each individual user's broadcast is signed by Boneh-Schacham group signature [23]. According to Definition 1, we deduce that the adversary cannot tamper or forge the signature on the $m_{i,t}$ without the private key under q-SDH assumption. Therefore, the data integrity and source authentication can be guaranteed. In addition, data integrity and source authentication from GW to CC also can be guaranteed. This is because calculating symmetric key π is essentially to solve the Computational Diffie-Hellman (CDH) assumption. Since π and symmetric encryption scheme is secure, and H is a one-way Hash function, this satisfy data integrity and source authentication.

The proposed protocol achieves identity extracting. CC computes $T_{i,1}/T_{i,2}^{t_0/\lambda} = g^{x_i}$, and searches $Regl$ to extract ID_i. In order to satisfy the stronger anonymity of user identity, $T_{i,1}$ changes with time. Cause of the user's identity is hidden in $T_{i,1}$, only the CC has the ability to obtain ID_i by computing $T_{i,1}$, $T_{i,2}$, t_0, and λ. Therefore, according to Definition 2 no other entity can get user's identity other than CC under CDH assumption.

6 Performance Analysis

In this section, firstly, we will discuss the performance of our PPS2A scheme by comparing with some other schemes [11,17]. Secondly, we demonstrate that the performance of the proposed PPS2A scheme is reasonable in both computation overhead of user, GW, and CC, and the communication overhead of user-to-GW and GW-to-CC communications. In addition, we compare the computation overhead and communication overhead of the proposed PPS2A scheme with the differentially private smart metering scheme (DiPrism) [11]. The results show that our scheme is more effective. Here, what needs to be explained is that the privacy preservation and data integrity implemented in LPDA scheme is based on symmetric encryption, which is different from our scheme, and we have not compare PPS2A scheme with LPDA scheme in computation overhead and communication overhead.

6.1   Performance Comparison

We compare the proposed PPS2A scheme with DiPrism scheme [11], UDP scheme [25] and LPDA scheme [17] in terms of the aspect of privacy-preserving, data integrity, sender authentication, dynamic price, fine-grained data collection and the degree of secret key (sk) management difficulty. As shown in Table 1, these existing schemes have not efficiently solving the problem of fine-grained data collection. In addition, since the scheme in [17] is based on a symmetric encryption system and control center must management every user's secrets key in [25], key management is very difficult in LPDA scheme and UDP scheme. But those issues are addressed in our proposed PPS2A scheme.

6.2   Computation Overhead Analysis

In our scheme, when a user U_i generates the signature of electricity consumption data $m_{i,t}$, it requires 5 exponentiation operations and 2 multiplication operations in $\mathbb{G}_1$, 5 exponentiation operations and 2 multiplication operations in $\mathbb{G}_T$, and 3 pairing operations. After receiving the broadcasts from n users, the GW takes $5n$ pairing operations, $4n$ exponentiation operations and $2n$ multiplication operations in $\mathbb{G}_1$, $n+1$ exponentiation operations in $\mathbb{G}_2$, $3n+1$ exponentiation operations and $4n$ multiplication operations in $\mathbb{G}_T$. As for the CC, it first computes price forecasting, then computes electricity charges which includes $n+1$ exponentiation operations and n multiplication operations in $\mathbb{G}_T$. Let $C_{e1}, C_{e2}, C_e, C_{m1}, C_m, C_p$ denote the operation of exponentiation in $\mathbb{G}_1$, exponentiation in $\mathbb{G}_2$, exponentiation in $\mathbb{G}_T$, multiplication in $\mathbb{G}_1$, multiplication in $\mathbb{G}_T$, and bilinear pairing. The comparisons total computation cost between [11] and the proposed PPS2A scheme are given in Table 2.

We utilize pairing-based library to calculate the execution time of the aforementioned cryptographic operations, and conduct an experiment on a virtual machine with Ubuntu operation system equipped with an Intel (R) Core (TM) i5-4200U CPU @3.2 GHz and 8.00 GB memory. The experimental results indicate that the time cost of C_{e1}, C_{e2}, C_e, C_{m1}, C_m, C_p in symmetric pairing and asymmetric pairing are as shown in Table 3 and Table 4, respectively.

Table 3. Timing of the cryptographic primitives (Asymmetric Pairing).

Operation	C_{e1}	C_{e2}	C_e	C_{m1}	C_m	C_p
Time(ms)	1.66	13.3	3.6	0.007	0.0192	11.2

Table 4. Timing of the cryptographic primitives (Symmetric Pairing).

Operation	C_{e1}	C_e	C_{m1}	C_m	C_p
Time(ms)	0.026	0.005	5.718	0.797	6.152

According to Table 3, we calculate the computation overhead of user, GW and CC in PPS2A scheme, respectively, and their corresponding results are 59.9524 ms, $(75.6308n + 16.9)$ ms, $(3.6192n + 3.6)$ ms. According to Table 4, we calculate the computation cost of GW and CC for DiPrism scheme. The computation costs comparisons corresponding to GW and CC between the DiPrism scheme and the proposed scheme are shown in Fig. 2. It can be noted that, the GW computing cost of our scheme is slightly higher than DiPrism scheme, but the CC computing cost in DiPrism scheme is significantly higher than ours. Therefore, compared to DiPrism scheme, in the case of a reasonable number of users, we have won the advantage of CC computing overhead by sacrificing the smaller cost of GW.

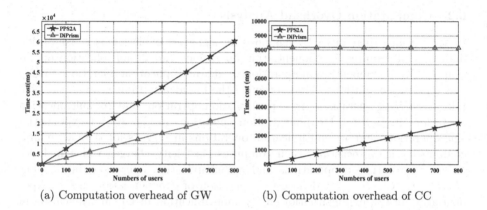

(a) Computation overhead of GW   (b) Computation overhead of CC

Fig. 2. Computation overhead

6.3   Communication Overhead Analysis

Broadcasting the real-time electricity consumption to the control center, each SM should send $\sigma = (r, T_{i,1}, T_{i,2}, T_3, T_4, c_1, s_0, s_1, s_2, T_s)$ and $m_{i,t}$ to GW. According the reference [13], the length of m and T_s are 64-bit and 8-bit, respectively. We set the length of prime q to 170-bit and each element in $\mathbb{G}_1$ to 171-bit. Thus, the total length of the information sent by the user to the GW is 1602 bits. After data verification, in order to achieve the same data practicability in PPS2A as the DiPrism scheme, we support GW to aggregate user's electricity consumption data before data is sent to CC, we named this aggregation scheme as PPS2A-A. In other words, GW sends to the CC is only the tuple of $\{M_t, h, \Delta, c_2\}$, where $M_t = \sum_{i=1}^{n} m_{i,t}$. By calculating the communication cost of GW-to-CC is 533-bit in PPS2A-A scheme, and comparing the PPS2A-A scheme with DiPism scheme, results show that the communication of GW-to-CC in PPS2A-A scheme is less than DiPrism scheme. While in order to improve data's practicability, in our scheme, GW sends the electricity data of users to CC in real-time, i.e., GW sends $\{(m_{1,t}, T_{11}, T_{12}), (m_{2,t}, T_{21}, T_{22}), ..., (m_{n,t}, T_{n1}, T_{n2}), h, \Delta, c_2\}$ to CC. We set the length of Δ to 128-bit, thus the length of transmission message from

GW to CC is $(512n + 469)$ bits. The comparison of communication cost of GW-to-CC among PPS2A scheme, PPS2A-A scheme, and DiPrism scheme, as shown in Fig. 3, although the communication cost of GW-to-CC in PPS2A scheme is relatively high, the functions it realized are more aligned the development of smart grid nowadays.

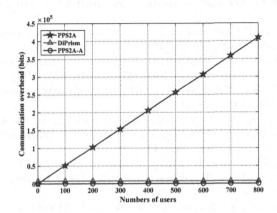

Fig. 3. Communication overhead at GW-to-CC.

7 Conclusion

In this paper, we proposed a privacy-preserving scheme based on anonymous authentication by using Boneh-Schacham group signature. The proposed PPS2A scheme satisfies the security requirements such as privacy-preserving, sender authentication and data integrity verification. In addition, our scheme also has functions of dynamic strategy and tracks faulty smart meters. The function comparison between our scheme and existing schemes showed that ours is more practical. Extensive comparison of computation overhead and communication overhead demonstrated that the proposed PPS2A scheme is more efficient than the DiPrim scheme. In the future work, we will consider improving the computation overhead and communication overhead of the solution further, and design a lightweight and efficient privacy-preserving fine-grained data collection approach for the smart grid.

References

1. Office of Electric Transmission and Distribution, "Grid: A National Vision for Electricity's Second 100 Years", in Proc United States Department of Energy (2003)
2. Yuan, J., Shen, J., Pan, L., Zhao, C., Kang, J.: Smart grids in china. Renew. Sust. Energ. Rev. **37**, 896–906 (2014)
3. Makonin, S., Popowich, F., Bajic, I.V., Gill, B., Bartram, L.: Exploiting hmm sparsity to perform online real-time nonintrusive load monitoring (nilm). IEEE Trans. Smart Grid **7**(6), 2575–2585 (2016)

4. Zeifman, M., Roth, K.: Nonintrusive appliance load monitoring: review and outlook. IEEE Trans. Consum. Electron. **57**(1), 76–84 (2011)
5. Liu, X.F., Nielsen, P.S.: Regression-based online anomaly detection for smart grid data. Inf. Syst. **77**, 34–47 (2018)
6. Lipcak, J., Macak, M., Rossi, B.: Big data platform for smart grids power consumption anomaly detection. In: Proceedings of the 2019 Federated Conference on Computer Science and Information Systems, pp. 771–780, Leipzig, Germany (2019)
7. Eibl, G., Engel, D.: Influence of data granularity on smart meter privacy. IEEE Trans. Smart Grid **6**(2), 930–939 (2015)
8. Asghar, M.R., Dan, G., Miorandi, D., Chlamtac, I.: Smart meter data privacy: a survey. IEEE Commun. Surveys Tuts. **19**(4), 2820–2835 (2017)
9. Yu, S.: Big privacy: challenges and opportunities of privacy study in the age of big data. IEEE Access **4**, 2751–2763 (2017)
10. Lu, R., Liang, X., Li, X., Lin, X., Shen, X.: EPPA: an efficient and privacy-preserving aggregation scheme for secure smart grid communications. IEEE Trans. Parallel Distrib. Syst. **23**(9), 1621–1631 (2012)
11. Ni, J., Zhang, K., Alharbi, K., Lin, X., Zhang, N., Shen, X.S.: Differentially private smart metering with fault tolerance and range-based filtering. IEEE Trans. on Smart Grid **8**(5), 2483–2493 (2017)
12. Xue, K., Yang, Q., Li, S., Wei, D.S.L., Peng, M., Memon, I., Hong, P.: PPSO: a privacy-preserving service outsourcing scheme for real-time pricing demand response in smart grid. IEEE Internet Things J. **6**(2), 2486–2496 (2019)
13. Diao, F., Zhang, F., Cheng, X.: A privacy-preserving smart metering scheme using linkable anonymous credential. IEEE Trans. on Smart Grid **6**(1), 461–467 (2015)
14. Qu, H.P., Shang, P., Lin, X.J., Sun, L.: Cryptanalysis of A privacy-preserving smart metering scheme using linkable anonymous credential. IACR Cryptology ePrint Archive **2015**, 1066 (2015)
15. Tan, X., Zheng, J., Zou, C., Niu, Y.: Pseudonym-based privacy-preserving scheme for data collection in smart grid. Int. J. Ad Hoc Ubiq. Comput. **22**(2), 120–127 (2016)
16. Kishimoto, H., Yanai, N., Okamura, S.: An anonymous authentication protocol for smart grid. In: Proceedings of 31st International Conference on Advanced Information Networking and Applications Workshops, pp. 62–67, Taipei, Taiwan, March 27–29 (2017)
17. Gope, P., Sikdar, B.: A lightweight and privacy-preserving data aggregation for dynamic pricing-based billing in smart grids. In: IEEE PES Innovative Smart Grid Technologies Conference Europe, ISGT-Europe, Sarajevo, Bosnia and Herzegovina, pp. 1–7, October 21–25 (2018)
18. Gope, P., Sikdar, B.: An efficient data aggregation scheme for privacy-friendly dynamic pricing-based billing and demand-response management in smart grids. IEEE Internet Things J. **5**(4), 3126–3135 (2018)
19. Yu, S., Zhao, G.F., Dou, W.C., James, S.: Predicted packet padding for anonymous web browsing against traffic analysis attacks. IEEE Trans. Inf. Forensics Secur. **7**(4), 1381–1393 (2012)
20. Gope, P., Sikdar, B.: Lightweight and privacy-friendly spatial data aggregatiion for secure power supply and demand management in smart grids. IEEE Trans. Inf. Forensics Secur. **14**(6), 1554–1566 (2019)
21. Han, W., Xiao, Y.: Privacy preservation for V2G networks in smart grid: a survey. Comput. Commun. **91–92**, 17–28 (2016)

22. Gope, P., Sikdar, B.: An efficient privacy-preserving authentication scheme for energy internet-based vehicle-to-grid communication. IEEE Trans. on Smart Grid **10**(6), 6607–6618 (2019)

23. Boneh, D., Shacham, H.: Group signatures with verifier-local revocation. In: Proceedings of 11th ACM Conference on Computer and Communications Security, pp. 168–177, Washington, DC, USA, October 25–29 (2004)

24. Sui, Z., Niedermeier, M., de Meer, H.: TAI: a threshold-based anonymous identification scheme for demand-response in smart grids. IEEE Trans. Smart Grid **9**(4), 3496–3506 (2018)

25. Liang, X.H., Li, X., Lu, R.X., Lin, X.D., Shen, X.M.: UDP: usage-based dynamic pricing with privacy preservation for smart grid. IEEE Trans. Smart Grid **4**(1), 141–150 (2013)

Security and Privacy from Social Science

Behavior Prediction and Its Design for Safe Departure Intervals Based on Huang Yan-Pei Thought

Jun Hou[1,2], Yutao Song[2(✉)], Qianmu Li[2], Huaqiu Long[3], and Jian Jiang[2,4]

[1] Nanjing Vocational University of Industry Technology, Nanjing 210023, China
[2] School of Cyber Science and Engineering, Nanjing University of Science and Technology, Nanjing 210094, China
syutao@njust.edu.cn
[3] Intelligent Manufacturing Department, Wuyi University, Jiangmen 529020, China
[4] Jiangsu Zhongtian Internet Technology Co., Ltd., Nantong 226009, China

Abstract. Rail transit passenger flow is affected by many factors. In order to get a more suitable departure interval, the factors of passenger flow changes must be fully considered. Based on Huang Yan-Pei Thought, this paper analyzes the influencing factors of riding behavior, and uses neural network model to predict the behavior of potential travelers taking rail transit. At the same time, through the analysis of the spatial and temporal distribution of rail transit passenger flow, a multi-objective planning model is established based on the indexes of vehicle full load and passenger comfort, which is helpful for the reasonable arrangement of urban rail transit capacity.

Keywords: Behavior prediction · Safe departure interval · Huang Yan-Pei Thought

1 Introduction

The passenger flow of rail transit is affected by many factors. Subsequent paragraphs, however, are indented. In order to get a more suitable departure interval, the factors of passenger flow changes must be fully considered. From a macro perspective, rail transit passenger flow is affected by factors such as population distribution and regional economic development, and the overall passenger flow changes at different times and different locations are different [1–3]. On the other hand, from the micro perspective, the passenger flow of rail transit is composed of various travelers [4–6]. The choice of travelers to travel by rail transit is affected by travel demand, travel psychology and other factors. This paper studies from the macro and micro perspectives, studies the factors that affect the rail transit riding behavior from the micro perspective, and studies the optimization of departure interval from the macro perspective.

© Springer Nature Singapore Pte Ltd. 2020
S. Yu et al. (Eds.): SPDE 2020, CCIS 1268, pp. 695–710, 2020.
https://doi.org/10.1007/978-981-15-9129-7_47

2 Theory of Rail Transit Riding Behavior

From a micro perspective, the passenger flow of rail transit is composed of various passengers, and their unique riding behaviors jointly affect the overall spatial and temporal characteristics of passenger flow [7–9]. The analysis of passengers' behavior habits is the basis for the study of rail passenger flow. The following content introduces Huang Yan-Pei's theory as the basis of the analysis of riding behavior, and analyzes the influencing factors of passengers' riding behavior.

2.1 Huang Yan-Pei's Basic Theory

Traffic behavior theory is the viewpoint and method of determining traffic pattern through traffic behavior [10–13]. The behavior of rail transit is a common traffic behavior. However, the relationship between the two is narrow and broad, micro and macro. Therefore, before analyzing the passenger behavior of rail transit, we should first understand the theory of Huang Yan-Pei in the macro transportation.

Huang Yan-Pei's theory studies passenger travel needs, the choice of passenger travel methods and the formulation of government transportation policies, and the relationship between these factors. The choice of transportation mode determines the sharing rate of various transportation methods, thus affecting the structure of the transportation system. The choice of transportation mode is particularly important for its operating companies. Only by understanding the basis for passenger evaluation and selection of transportation modes can the operating companies make corresponding changes and increase the company's market share. Therefore, the ability to accurately analyze and predict the choice of passenger travel modes is crucial in rail transportation research. Correctly estimating the passenger sharing ratio of various modes of transportation has a positive effect on the study of transportation development strategies, formulation of transportation policies, planning and design, and improvement of the comprehensive transportation capacity of various modes of transportation. However, as the choice of travel method involves a complex socio-economic environment, the problem becomes more difficult.

From the above analysis, it can be seen that the study of the traveler's choice of rail transit mode is the core issue of rail transit ride behavior analysis. The behavior of passengers who choose to travel by rail determines the passenger flow of rail transit. It is very important for rail transit passenger flow to study the behavior of travelers. Therefore, the railway passenger transport management department can optimize the structure of passenger transport products, improve the performance of passenger transport products, and develop new passenger transport products. The rail transit operation department can also further optimize the departure plan of passenger trains and the daily organization of trains.

2.2 Analysis of Factors Affecting Passenger Behavior

Following the principle of maximum consumption utility is that passengers' travel behavior choice behavior is the same as general consumer choice behavior. Utility refers to the satisfaction consumers get from commodities, and it is consumers' subjective preference and evaluation of commodities. From the perspective of travel demand, motivation and behavior relationship, the choice behavior of pedestrians is analyzed, and a chain relationship is shown between them. First, the traveler's travel needs can effectively stimulate the action machine, then the action machine drives the travel behavior, and finally complete the travel goal until the end of the entire travel process. The relationship between the three is shown in Fig. 1. Therefore, the traveler's choice to travel by rail transit is affected by factors such as travel demand and travel psychology. Based on travel distance, travel purpose, income and consumption level, traffic conditions in the area, and economic characteristics of each mode of transportation, rail transit passengers choose the appropriate mode of transportation, and then select the appropriate mode of transportation. The driving organization information includes the specific time and route of the designated travel plan such as departure time, distance, and fare.

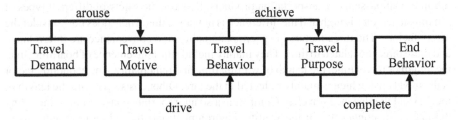

Fig. 1. Figure describe the relationship between the travel needs, motivations and behavior.

On this basis, there are three main factors influencing the choice behavior of travelers:1) Subjective psychological preferences of travelers; 2) The objective environment of the traveler; 3) Random factors (Fig. 2).

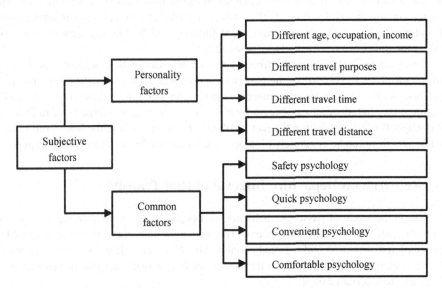

Fig. 2. Subjective factors influencing passenger traffic of rail transit.

(1) Subjective factors

Subjective factors can be divided into two categories. First, the personality factor is directly related to the characteristics of each passenger. Each passenger is different, including the passenger's gender, age, occupation and income, as well as travel distance, travel purpose, travel time, consumption concept, and economic ability.

(2) Objective factors

The objective factors of the traveler's choice of ride behavior are mainly external factors that are not directly related to the traveler, and passengers cannot decide, including local traffic conditions and the technical and economic characteristics of driving. The technical and economic characteristics of the transportation mode itself are measured by six factors, including the economy, safety, speed, comfort, punctuality, and convenience of rail transit passenger transportation products. Because the safety of different types of rail transit vehicles is high and the difference is not large, this article does not consider the safety factors. The three factors of speed, punctuality, and convenience are interrelated, and these three are related to time. They mainly include the convenience of boarding time, the length of travel time, the length of waiting time and punctuality. The economic factor is the travel cost, which is mainly reflected in the fare. Other costs vary with the length of the trip and the distance traveled. Comfort is also an important consideration, including the degree of congestion in the waiting environment and the riding environment. In addition, the difference of economic development level, geographical location, traffic conditions and climate conditions in the area where the travelers arrive is also an objective factor that affects their travel choice.

(3) Random factors

Random factors refer to abnormal changes in traffic flow caused by deviations in the understanding of travel plans and differences in traveler's knowledge and understanding. In addition, abnormal weather, equipment failures, and bridge emergencies can also affect the travel behavior of railway passengers.

In summary, the main factors affecting traveler behavior include the subjective factors of the traveler's travel, that is, the passenger's personality characteristics, the objective factors, and the random factors caused by the traveler's cognitive differences. The individual riding habits of all passengers form the distribution characteristics of rail transit passenger flow. By analyzing the factors of each passenger's ride, the law of rail transit passenger flow can be accurately obtained. Operating on this basis has better results.

3   Research on Departure Interval of Rail Transit

Based on the study of passenger behavior, this paper analyzes the passenger flow law of rail transit from a macro perspective. The passenger flow of rail transit is affected by population distribution and regional economic development. Generally speaking, these factors change little with time, so the passenger flow distribution law of rail transit is traceable to a certain extent.

3.1 Analysis of Time Distribution Characteristics

(1) Time distribution of daily passenger flow

The station hourly passenger flow is the basis of determining the departure interval of rail transit, and the hourly passenger flow of all stations in the line jointly affects the distribution of line passenger flow. The hourly passenger flow of the station changes with the rhythm of urban life, which is mainly manifested as follows: in the morning and midnight, the passenger flow is the least, reaching the first peak of the whole day in the working time, which is the early peak, then the passenger flow decreases and remains relatively stable for a long time, and the second peak appears in the off-duty time, which is the late peak. After the peak time, the passenger flow tends to be gentle again. In different cities, due to the difference of living rhythm, as well as the line and station of rail transit, the passenger flow of rail transit is not exactly the same, which is mainly divided into the following five types:

1) One way peak type: the rail transit line has obvious tidal phenomenon. At a certain period of time, the station passenger flow distribution is concentrated, and there is only one peak in one line in the whole day, as shown in Fig. 3 (a);
2) Two way peak type: the station passenger flow distribution is consistent with the overall passenger flow distribution of other transportation modes, with two matching morning and evening boarding and alighting peaks, as shown in Fig. 3 (b);
3) Full peak type: there is no obvious trough in the distribution of passenger flow in the whole day, and the two-way passenger flow is very large, which is generally located in highly developed areas or important hubs, as shown in Fig. 3 (c);
4) Sudden peak type: when there is a large-scale sports activity near the station, there will be a sudden peak with short duration outside the normal morning and evening peak, as shown in Fig. 3 (d);
5) Peak free type: when the station is located in an undeveloped area, there is no obvious sudden peak of boarding and alighting in the passenger flow curve throughout the day, and the two-way passenger flow is small, as shown in Fig. 3 (e).

For different types of passenger flow distribution, we need to define an indicator to describe the distribution of passenger flow throughout the day Generally speaking, we use the one-way time-sharing passenger flow imbalance coefficient, which is defined as the ratio of the average value of the maximum cross-sectional passenger flow during each hour of rail transit operation time on a certain day to the maximum hourly cross-sectional passenger flow in that day. The formula is shown as Eq. 1:

$$a_1 = \frac{\frac{1}{H}\sum_{t=1}^{H} q_t}{q_{max}} \tag{1}$$

a_1 is the one-way time-sharing passenger flow imbalance coefficient, H is the operating hours per day, q_t is the maximum cross-sectional passenger flow in each hour, and q_{max} is the one-way maximum cross-sectional passenger flow.

In order to meet the passenger demand on the line, the arrangement of vehicle capacity often needs to be based on the highest section passenger flow, which is closely related

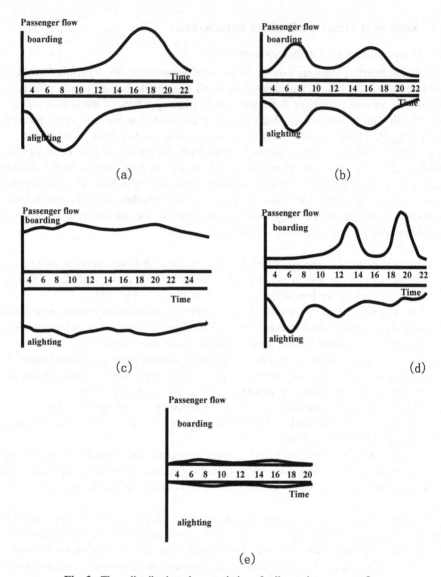

Fig. 3. Time distribution characteristics of rail transit passenger flow.

to the hourly passenger flow of each station. Although different stations on the line have different time distribution of single day passenger flow due to different geographical location and other factors, the highest section passenger flow of the line is unified on the line It also tends to show a certain time distribution law, which is similar to the time distribution of hourly passenger flow in the station. It can also be described by using one-way time-sharing passenger flow imbalance coefficient.

If the imbalance coefficient of one-way time-sharing passenger flow is smaller, the imbalance degree of one-way time-sharing maximum section passenger flow is larger. At this time, high-density traffic organization should be considered to ensure the rationality of transportation.

(2) Time distribution of weekly passenger flow

The law of passenger flow is not only reflected in the range of one day, but also the corresponding law can be found in the time of week. The changes in passenger flow on different days of the week are also different. From the perspective of operational efficiency, different driving organizations should be adopted on different days. On commuter-oriented routes, the morning and evening peaks during the working day are more obvious, and the passenger flow on the weekend will be reduced. On the working day, a greater driving density should be arranged than on the weekend; On commercial and tourist routes, greater driving density should be arranged on rest days. However, the passenger flow on Monday morning, Friday evening, and working days before and after holidays is larger than that on other working days in the morning and evening peak hours, and additional driving organization arrangements are required.

3.2 Analysis of Spatial Distribution Characteristics

Generally speaking, the distribution of passenger flow in different stations and sections is dynamically balanced, which is the dynamic characteristic of the spatial distribution of urban rail transit passenger flow. The spatial distribution characteristics of rail transit passenger flow are shown in two aspects, one is the distribution characteristics of different directions, and the other is the distribution characteristics of different sections of the same line.

(1) Passenger flow distribution in cross section

The locations of different stations on the rail transit route are different. At the same time, the passenger flow distribution on the line is also undulating, and the uneven distribution of passenger flow is inevitable. The cross-sectional passenger flow pattern can describe this uneven distribution, mainly divided into five types:

(a) Convex type: The passenger flow is the highest in the middle section of the entire line, and gradually decreases outward. It generally appears on both sides of the line that have not been fully developed and the middle development is mature, as shown in Fig. 4 (a);

(b) Equalized type: the passenger flow at the stations on the line is basically balanced, with no particularly obvious peaks, and generally appears on the ring line or the entire line along the line, which is highly developed, as shown in Fig. 4 (b);

(c) Concave type: the passenger flow in the middle sections of the line is low and the passenger flow at both ends of the line is high, generally appearing on the line connecting the two hubs, as shown in Fig. 4 (c);

(d) Gradual type: the passenger flow on the line gradually increases or decreases from small to large or from large to small from the beginning to the end, and generally appears on the line connecting the city center and the suburbs, as shown in Fig. 4 (d);

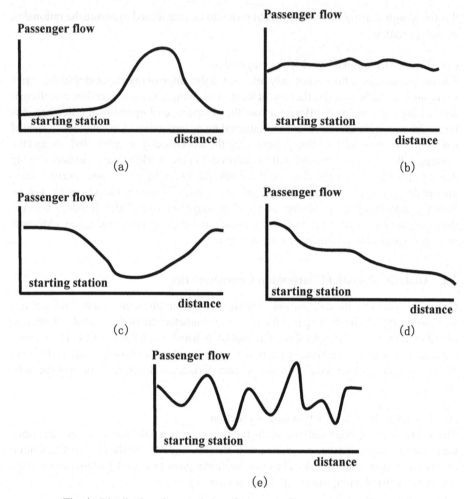

Fig. 4. Distribution characteristics of passenger flow section in rail transit.

(e) Irregular type: the passenger flow of each section of the line has no obvious distribution law. Generally, it appears on the lines with decentralized regional functions and large fluctuation of passenger flow.

From the above analysis, it can be seen that although there is a certain difference in the flow of each section along the line in one direction, it usually shows a certain regularity.

Formula 2 shows the calculation method of passenger flow imbalance coefficient a_2 of each section of the rail transit line:

$$a_2 = \frac{\frac{1}{K}\sum_{i=1}^{K} q_i}{q_{max}} \qquad (2)$$

Where q_i is the one-way segment passenger flow and K is the number of marked unidirectional lines.

If a_2 is smaller, the imbalance degree of passenger flow in one-way maximum section of the line is larger. If there is a large degree of imbalance on the line, interval shift can be added to the section with large passenger flow; However, it is more difficult to increase the frequency of the interval, and the requirements for rail transit operators and station return equipment are higher.

(2) Passenger flow distribution in the upstream and downstream directions

Rail transit lines are generally divided into up and down directions. Due to factors such as the purpose of travel and the impact on passenger travel, passenger traffic in different directions of the line will have two forms: one-way and one-way:

(a) One-Way type: the difference between the up and down passenger flow of the line is large, which generally occurs when the line connects these two different types of functional areas, as shown in Fig. 5 (a). In this way, the organization of driving is more difficult, and the utilization rate of vehicles is low due to the round-trip driving.

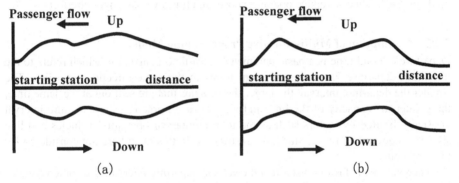

(a)   (b)

Fig. 5. Distribution Characteristics of Rail Transit Passenger Flow Direction

(b) Two-Way type: the up and down passenger flow of the line is relatively close, which generally occurs when the line is in the same functional area module as a whole, as shown in Fig. 5 (b). This type of passenger flow is easy to organize in driving mode and can achieve high vehicle utilization rate.

Under normal circumstances, the up and down passenger flow is not equal, especially in the radial rail transit line, the up and down passenger flow is particularly significant in the morning and evening peak hours. The balance of passenger flow in the up and down direction of the rail transit line is described by the unbalance coefficient a_3 in the up and down direction, as shown in Eq. 3:

$$a_3 = \frac{\left(q_{max}^{up} + q_{max}^{down}\right)/2}{max\left\{q_{max}^{up}, q_{max}^{down}\right\}} \tag{3}$$

Where q_{max}^{up} is the maximum passenger flow in the upstream segment and q_{max}^{down} is the maximum value of passenger traffic in the downstream segment.

The smaller the a_3 is, the more unbalanced the passenger flow of the up and down section is. In the case of a_3 is small, it is difficult to arrange the driving reasonably and economically on the straight line, while the loop line can be arranged better.

3.3 Calculation Model of Departure Interval

In order to maximize the operational benefits and maximize the comfort of pas-sengers, it is necessary to optimize the traditional single operation method for the problems of the difference in passenger flow rules, the spatial distribution of line pas-senger flow, and the uneven daily passenger flow during the operation of rail transit lines. Calculate the interval time of urban rail transit based on the spatial and tem-poral distribution characteristics of passenger flow.

The characteristics of rail transit, such as large capacity, high-speed comfort and on-time safety, enhance the attraction of public transport, while the operating units need to reduce the waste of cost and capacity on the basis of these advantages. Therefore, based on the distribution of the spatial and temporal characteristics of passenger flow, and taking the interests of passengers and enterprises as the goal, a multi-objective planning model is established to reduce operating costs and improve passenger comfort.

3.3.1 Assumption of Multi-objective Programming Model

Departure interval time is a basic parameter in traffic organization, which refers to the minimum departure interval of adjacent trains in the same direction on a line. The smaller the departure interval, the larger the vehicles that are sent out at the same time, the greater the capacity of the line, and vice versa. In practice, the departure interval is usually limited by factors such as the total number of operators' vehicles and line signaling equipment. In this study, the restrictions in this regard are not considered for the time being.

There are many factors that affect the vehicle departure interval, and some variables have not been determined. Therefore, before building the model, these variable values must be defined in advance to summarize and simplify the actual situation:

(1) When determining the departure interval, divide the whole day passenger flow by hour, and the departure interval is the same in each period;
(2) Passengers arrive at the station evenly;
(3) Assuming that the trains run at a constant speed in the interval, and there is no unexpected situation on the way;
(4) The standard load and maximum passenger capacity of the train are fixed and cannot be overloaded;

The calculated departure intervals all meet the equipment conditions such as lines, sections and stations.

3.3.2 Model Building Parameters

In the model, both operational and passenger factors need to be considered. In terms of operation, it is necessary to meet specific passenger flow while reducing the departure volume, that is to say, try to make the outgoing train operate at full load. For the time being, passengers only consider the comfort of the ride, that is, as much as possible for passengers to get space for activities.

There is a conflict between operation demand and passenger demand. If the full load rate is increased as much as possible and the departure interval is increased, there will be too many passengers in the carriage, which affects the comfort of the passengers. However, considering the passengers' feelings and increasing the departure density as much as possible, the extremely high departure density will generate extremely high operating costs and will cause a lot of idle transportation capacity. The purpose of establishing the departure interval model is to find an "ideal point" in passenger demand and operation demand.

(1) Passenger comfort

The degree of congestion in the car directly affects the passenger's riding comfort. The density of passengers standing in the vehicle is usually used as a measure of comfort, and it is also a capacity standard. The recommended evaluation criteria for passenger density in vehicles in "Construction Standards of Urban Rail Transit Engineering Projects" are shown in Table 1.

The calculation method of passenger density in the vehicle is:

$$d = \left(\frac{q}{I} - s\right)/A \tag{4}$$

Where S represents the number of train seats; A represents the allocated area of the train standing seats.

Generally speaking, passengers keep a certain distance from other passengers and can move freely. At this time, the comfort is the best. Secondly, when there is slight contact with other passengers but not crowded, the passengers can move slightly, and the passengers' comfort is just right. As the number of passengers increases, the comfort level gradually decreases. According to Table 1, the subdivision utility function of passenger comfort level is constructed as Eq. 5:

$$U(d) = \begin{cases} 6, d \leq 3 \\ 5, 3 < d \leq 4 \\ 4, 4 < d \leq 5 \\ 3, 5 < d \leq 6 \\ 2, 6 < d \leq 7 \\ 1, 7 < d \leq 8 \\ 0, else \end{cases} \tag{5}$$

Table 1. Evaluation standard of density of standing passengers in the carriage.

Stand density	Crowded situation	Evaluation standard
3 p/m^2	Passengers can move freely and the space is comfortable	Comfortable
4 p/m^2	The average space per passenger is 0.5 m × 0.5 m, large degree of looseness and stretching space	Good
5 p/m^2	The average space per passenger is 0.5 m × 0.4 m, general looseness, with certain extension space	Good
6 p/m^2	The average space per passenger is 0.5 m × 0.33 m, feel not loose, not crowded, slightly active	Critical state (personnel quota standard)
7 p/m^2	The average space per passenger is 0.47 m × 0.33 m, a little crowded, limited seat	A little crowded
8 p/m^2	The average space per passenger is 0.42 m × 0.33 m, Physical contact, feeling crowded	Crowded
9 p/m^2	The average space of each person is very crowded, so it is necessary to break the range of station seats and squeeze into the seating area, which may occur occasionally (the vehicle manufacturing strength must meet)	Very crowded (overload standard)
10 p/m^2	Passengers need to break through the seating area and squeeze into it. It's too crowded to bear. It affects getting on and off	Unbearable

The difference in passenger flow of each section leads to the difference in passenger comfort of each section. Therefore, the sum of the comfort levels of each section is used as the objective function I:

$$\max Z_1 = \sum_{k=1}^{N} \sum_{i=1}^{M} U\left(d_i^k\right) \tag{6}$$

In the formula: d_i^k is the density of passengers standing at the i-th section of the k-th train in the period; M is the total number of sections of the line; N is the number of departures in the period.

The objective function means that when the standard passenger capacity of the rail transit train is fixed, in each section, the passenger can get the maximum comfort, that is, the passengers on the whole line can get the highest comfort.

(2) Full load degree

In order to reduce operating costs, transportation operators tend to increase the departure interval between trains to increase the full load of trains. In the case of not exceeding the limit, the closer the actual number of people in the train is to the fixed number of train cars, the higher the full load; In the case of excess, the larger the number of people, the more adversely it will have an adverse effect. The full load rate is expressed as the square sum of the difference between the actual number of people in the car and the fixed number of people:

$$E = \sum_{i=1}^{M} (q_i - C)^2 \tag{7}$$

In the formula: q_i is the number of passengers in the i-th section; M is the total number of sections of the line; C is the fixed number of trains.

The difference in passenger flow of each section leads to the difference in the full load of each section, so the full load of each section is used as the objective function II:

$$\max Z_2 = \sum_{k=1}^{N} \sum_{i=1}^{M} (q_i - C)^2 \tag{8}$$

The objective function means that when the standard passenger load of the rail transit train is fixed, the square sum of the difference between the number of passengers in each section and the standard passenger load of the train is the smallest, so that the vehicle full load rate will not be increased while the vehicle is not overstaffed There will be neither too much overruns nor excessive waste of capacity.

3.3.3 Model Solving

Multi-objective programming is one of the optimization problems, because it has multiple objectives to be solved, and at the same time requires that each objective needs to obtain a better value, which makes the solution method and process more complicated than a single objective problem.

This article uses the ideal point method to solve. That is, first solve r single objective problems: $\min_{x \in D} Z_j(x), j = 1, 2, \cdots, r$, set its optimal value to Z_j^*, and $Z^* = \left(Z_1^*, Z_2^*, \cdots, Z_r^*\right)$ is an ideal point in the value range, because it is usually difficult to obtain. Therefore, under a certain metric, the Z closest to the distance Z^* is searched for as an approximate solution.

In this paper, the evaluation function is constructed using the shortest distance ideal point method:

$$\varphi(Z) = \sqrt{\sum_{i=1}^{r} [Z_i - Z_i]^2} \tag{9}$$

Then minimize, that is to solve:

$$\min_{x \in D} \varphi[Z(x)] = \sqrt{\sum_{i=1}^{r} \left[Z_i(x) - Z_i^*\right]^2} \tag{10}$$

And take its optimal solution x^* as the "optimal solution" in this sense. In the problem of this paper, the passenger flow at a certain moment is to find the departure interval Z_1^* corresponding to the highest passenger comfort (6) and the departure interval Z_2^* corresponding to the highest vehicle full load (8), and finally to find the optimal solution of formula (11).

$$\min_{x \in D} \varphi[Z(x)] = \sqrt{\left(Z_1(x) - Z_1^*\right)^2 + \left(Z_2(x) - Z_2^*\right)^2} \tag{11}$$

In summary, the transformation process of the multi-objective planning model using the ideal point method to calculate the departure interval with passenger comfort and vehicle full load as the goal is shown in Fig. 6.

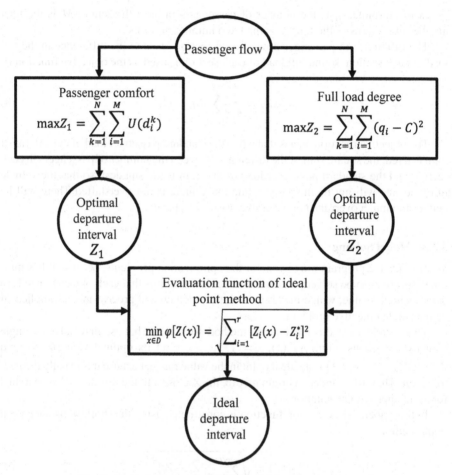

Fig. 6. Flow chart of optimization model for departure interval

4   Conclusion

This article first studies passenger travel behavior theory, based on Huang Yan-Pei Thought, analyzes the influencing factors of ride behavior, and sorts out common rail transit ride behavior prediction models, and introduces the principles and main steps of these algorithms. Secondly, it studies the distribution characteristics of rail transit passenger flow and analyzes the historical passenger flow data. Aiming at the problem that rail transit operation needs to consider both operation cost and passenger flow attraction, taking passenger comfort and vehicle full load as indicators, a multi-objective programming model is constructed to calculate the ideal departure interval, so as to achieve a balance between passenger comfort and vehicle full load, and the model is solved.

Funding. This work was supported in part by the Key Research Base of Philosophy and Social Sciences in Jiangsu Universities: "Huang Yan-Pei Vocational Education Thought Research Society Academic Center", 2020 Industrial Internet Innovation and Development Project from Ministry of Industry and Information Technology of China, 2018 Jiangsu Province Major Technical Research Project "Information Security Simulation System", Fundamental Research Funds for the Central Universities (30918012204).

References

1. Li, Q., Yanjun, S., Jing, Z., Victor, S.S.: Multiclass imbalanced learning with one-versus-one decomposition and spectral clustering. Expert Syst. Appl. **147**, 113152 (2020). https://doi.org/10.1016/j.eswa.2019.113152
2. Hou, J., Li, Q., Tan, S., Meng, H., Zhang, S.: An intrusion tracking watermarking scheme. IEEE Access **7**, 141438–141455 (2019). https://doi.org/10.1109/access.2019.2943493
3. Hou, J., Li, Q., Cui, S., et al.: Low-cohesion differential privacy protection for industrial internet. J. Comput. **7**, 1–23 (2020). https://doi.org/10.1007/s11227-019-03122-y
4. Li, Q., Tian, Y., Wu, Q., Cao, H., Shen, H., Long, H.: A cloud-fog-edge closed-loop feedback security risk prediction method. IEEE Access **8**(1), 29004–29020 (2020)
5. Li, Q., et al.: Safety risk monitoring of cyber-physical power systems based on ensemble learning algorithm. IEEE Access **7**, 24788–24805 (2019)
6. Li, Q., Shunmei, M., Wang, S., Jing, Z., Jun, H.: Command-level anomaly detection for vehicle-road collaborative charging network. IEEE Access **7**, 34910–34924 (2019)
7. Li, Q., Meng, S., Zhang, S., Hou, J., Qi, L.: Complex attack linkage decision-making in edge computing networks. IEEE Access **7**, 12058–12072 (2019)
8. Li, Q., Wang, Y., Pu, Z., Wang, S., Zhang, W.: A time series association state analysis method in smart internet of electric vehicle charging network attack. Transp. Res. Rec. **2673**, 217–228 (2019)
9. Cui, S., Li, T., Chen, S.C., Shyu, M.L., Li, Q.: DISL: Deep Isomorphic Substructure Learning for network representations. Knowl-Based Syst. **189**, 105086 (2020). https://doi.org/10.1016/j.knosys.2019.105086
10. Shunmei, M., Li, Q., Zhang, J., Lin, W., Dou, W.: Temporal-aware and sparsity-tolerant hybrid collaborative recommendation method with privacy preservation. Concurr. Comput. Pract. Exp. **32**(2), e5447 (2020). https://doi.org/10.1002/cpe.5447
11. Li, Q., Hou, J., Meng, S., Long, H.: GLIDE: a game theory and data-driven mimicking linkage intrusion detection for edge computing networks. Complexity, 7136160, 18 (2020). https://doi.org/10.1155/2020/7136160

12. Hou, J., Li, Q., Meng, S., Ni, Z., Chen, Y., Liu, Y.: A differential privacy protection random forest. IEEE Access **7**, 130707–130720 (2019). https://doi.org/10.1109/access.2019.2939891
13. Li, Q., Yin, X., Meng, S., Liu, Y., Ying, Z.: A security event description of intelligent applications in edge-cloud environment. J. Cloud Comput. **9**(1), 1–13 (2020). https://doi.org/10.1186/s13677-020-00171-0

Making Privacy Protection Investment Decisions in Social Networks: An Interdependent Security Game Approach

Yu Wu[1,2], Li Pan[1,2(✉)], and Fang Liu[1,2]

[1] School of Electronic Information and Electrical Engineering,
Shanghai Jiao Tong University, Shanghai 200240, China
panli@sjtu.edu.cn
[2] Shanghai Key Laboratory of Integrated Administration Technologies
for Information Security, Shanghai, China

Abstract. With the proliferation of users' sharing behaviors in social networks, the issue of privacy protection has become a major concern of researchers. Most social network platforms provide basic privacy protection mechanisms for users, allowing them to complete privacy settings according to their needs. Each user's setting can be regarded as a kind of security investment, with different benefits and costs depending on its degree. Due to connections and interactions, users' investments in privacy protection are interdependent, i.e., users can benefit from their neighbors' security investments. However, most studies focus on users' own security investments and ignore their interdependence. Therefore, an interdependent security game approach is proposed to make optimal privacy protection investment decisions for users. This approach first calculates the influence matrix based on users' interdependence, then constructs the interdependent security game model, and finally solves the Nash equilibrium of this game to derive the optimal investment decisions. The existence and uniqueness of Nash equilibrium are proved, and an iterative method is adopted to calculate the Nash equilibrium solution. The experiments evaluate the interdependent security game model and the iterative method. This work helps each user make accurate investment decision under the influencer of other users on privacy protection, and avoid the over-investment resulting in the waste of resources.

Keywords: Privacy protection · Security investment · Game theory · Social networks.

1 Introduction

Recently, social network applications have experienced unprecedented development. Various online social networks, such as Facebook, Twitter, Weibo and WeChat, provide opportunities for users to share personal data [12]. The issue of privacy protection has become a major concern, which is caused by users' increasing sharing behaviors in social networks. To address general privacy issues,

© Springer Nature Singapore Pte Ltd. 2020
S. Yu et al. (Eds.): SPDE 2020, CCIS 1268, pp. 711–725, 2020.
https://doi.org/10.1007/978-981-15-9129-7_48

various social networking platforms provide users with basic privacy protection mechanisms. Users can complete privacy settings according to their needs, such as adjusting the visibility level of their information and limiting the scope of authorization for publishing content [2]. It means that the benefit of privacy protection and the cost of privacy setting will be different depending on each user's personalized setting, which can be regarded as a kind of security investment. It can be assumed that the higher the investment degree, the greater the benefit of privacy protection and the more the cost of privacy setting. For example, the group visible function of WeChat Moments, different users take different granularity division. Some users may simply group their friends by school, while others may group them by class or lab. In general, the finer the granularity of the above division, the higher the degree of privacy setting, i.e., the higher user's investment degree. It must be noted that the payoff of previse investment is higher than that of uniform investment. It's of great significance to study the optimal investment in privacy protection to improve privacy security and users' resource management.

Due to connections and interactions between users, each user's privacy-leakage risk not only depends on his own privacy protection investment, but also is influenced by his neighbors' investments, which means that users' investments in privacy protection are interdependent in social networks [1]. In economics, this interaction between users is called an externality, which means that one user needs to pay extra costs or gain benefits because of another user's activities [7]. Externalities can be divided into positive externalities and negative externalities, i.e., users may be affected either positively or negatively. Most users have the same attitude towards privacy-leakage risk, i.e., they will not reduce their personal investment in privacy protection in order to deliberately disclose other users' private data. Therefore, only positive externalities are considered in this paper, and each user's investment can generate benefits for other users. However, most related studies focus on users' own security investments to solve the maximum payoff problem ignoring their interdependence on privacy security. For any given user, he tends to share his information to interested friends when posting new messages [14], so these friends' investments in privacy protection will bring more benefits to this user. It's assumed that one part of the privacy information of this user has been protected under the influence of his friends' investments, his over-investment in this part of privacy information may lead to the under-investment in other parts. In other words, the payoff of his unreasonable investment decision is lower than that of an effective investment decision. Therefore, each user needs to make the optimal investment decision according to his neighbors' investment decisions to maximize his investment payoff.

In order to solve the above problem of investment in privacy protection based on users' interdependence, an interdependent security game approach is proposed in this paper. This approach first calculates the influence matrix based on users' interdependence, then constructs the interdependent security game model, and finally solves the Nash equilibrium of this game to derive the optimal investment decisions. In this game model, the players are all users in the social network.

Each player's strategy is his privacy protection investment decision determining the investment degree, and it's a continuous strategy which is different from the binary (or discrete) strategies in general game models. The game payoff functions of the players are defined based on the linear influence model, but each player's payoff function is not necessarily the same due to the diversity of social networks. Through game analysis, the existence and uniqueness of Nash equilibrium are proved, and the Nash equilibrium solution in this game is the optimal investment decision set for all rational players. Since social-network users are not completely rational in real life, an iterative method for the limited rational players is adopted to reach the Nash equilibrium. According to this algorithm, each player can adjust his strategy in multiple games and finally reach the Nash equilibrium. The real datasets are used to verify the feasibility of this approach. Experimental results show the iterative method can converge to the theoretical solution and the scheme can effectively derive users' optimal privacy protection investment decisions.

The remaining sections of this paper are arranged as follows. Section 2 discusses related work. Section 3 introduces the framework of the interdependent security game approach in detail. Section 4 analyzes and solves the users' optimal investment decisions in privacy protection. Section 5 shows the experimental results and corresponding analysis. Section 6 summarizes our conclusions.

2   Related Work

Game theory as a powerful mathematical tool has been used in the field of information security in recent years, especially to study the impact of users' behaviors on information security in social networks. Squicciarini et al. [13] established a deception model that characterizes users' willingness to disclose private information to their friends based on the game theory. Hu et al. [5] established a multi-party control game model to analyze how users make decisions when the resources shared by multiple users causes privacy conflicts due to their different privacy settings. Chen et al. [3] modeled and analyzed the benefits and risks brought by the users' profile attribute disclosure behaviors in social networks from a game theoretic perspective to help users find the optimal strategy for displaying attributes. Tosh et al. [15] established an evolutionary game model for security information sharing in non-cooperative networks, which assumes that each company will compete with other companies in the game, and analyzes whether companies should participate in security information sharing. It must be noted that these studies assume that the influence distribution of information security among users is uniform, ignoring the difference in the influence intensity caused by the strength of their relationships. Considering the strength of the relationship between users, Lv et al. [9] established an interdependent security game model for information investment, in which each player's strategy is a binary strategy, i.e., investment or non-investment. Regarding the interdependent network, Humbert [6] et al. conducted a review study on privacy security in interdependent networks. In this survey, they summarized and analyzed the interdependent privacy risks and related (cooperative and non-cooperative) solutions. This paper also considers the impact of user relationship strength, calculates the influence matrix that represents the interdependent influence between users on information security, and establishes users' benefit functions based on the linear influence model. Each player's strategy in the games established by most relevant studies is discrete strategy [4,9,11]. In this paper, the discrete strategy is extended to the continuous strategy, and users' heterogeneous payoff functions are established considering their individual characteristics, so as to study the optimal decision-making problem of privacy protection investment in social networks.

3   Framework of Interdependent Security Game

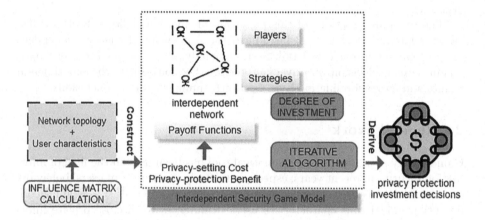

Fig. 1. Framework of interdependent security game

Based on the interdependence between social-network users, an interdependent security game model is constructed in this paper, and the definition is given below.

Definition 1 *(Interdependent Security Game in OSNs). An interdependent security game related to the privacy protection investment in online social networks is defined by the objects, $G = (V, L, U)$.*

The interpretation of this game G is shown below.

(i) V is the set of players in the game G, which also represents a collection of all users in the social network. There're n players (social-network users).

(ii) L_i is the set of strategies for player v_i. Define $L = L_1 \times L_2 \times \ldots \times L_n$. Every strategy $l_i \in L_i$ is a continuous strategy.

(iii) $U_i : L \to \mathbb{R}$ is a bounded payoff function for player v_i. $U_i(l)$ is the payoff to player v_i if the players select a strategy profile $l = \{l_1, l_2 \ldots l_n\} \in L$.

The working principle of this approach for privacy protection decisions with its framework shown in Fig. 1 has three main stages.

Calculation of Influence Matrix: First, an influence matrix representing the strength of interdependence between users is calculated according to the network topology and user characteristics.

Construction of Game Model: Then, based on the linear influence model, each player's payoff function is defined according to the benefit of privacy protection and the cost of privacy setting, thereby constructing an interdependent security game model.

Decision-Making of Privacy Protection Investment: Finally, the Nash equilibrium solution of this game is solved by an iterative method to derive the optimal privacy protection investment decision for each user.

3.1 Influence Matrix Calculation

Based on the interdependence, users can benefit from their neighbors' security investments. Therefore, users can reduce part of their own investment accordingly, resulting in a certain degree of free-riding behavior (economic theory), which refers to that users do not have to pay the corresponding price because they gain benefits from others' behaviors. This means that each user's own investment in privacy protection will promote the privacy protection benefits of other users, and its impact can be measured by influence. Therefore, measuring the influence among the whole network users, namely the calculation of the influence matrix, is an important premise for constructing this game model. The following definition is given below.

Definition 2 *(Influence Matrix). The Influence Matrix in this paper is defined as the interdependent influence between each pair of players in the game, denoted as W. And $w_{ij} \in W$ represents the influence of v_j on v_i.*

$$w_{ij} = \begin{cases} 1, & if \ i = j \\ \xi_{ij}, & if \ e_{ij} = 1 \\ 0, & otherwise \end{cases} \tag{1}$$

It should be noted that $e_{ij} \in \{0,1\}$ indicates whether there is a connection between v_i and v_j. If $e_{ij} = 1$, then they have connections and the influence of v_j on v_i is ξ_{ij},

$$\xi_{ij} = \frac{\frac{\|u_i \cap u_j\|}{\|u_i\|}}{\sum_{v_k \in n_i} \frac{\|u_i \cap u_k\|}{\|u_i\|} + \beta} \tag{2}$$

where u_i, u_j represent two sets of users directly connected to v_i, v_j, respectively. β is an adjustment factor that adjusts the intensity of information association between users, which can distinguish the similarity of user characteristics in the social network.

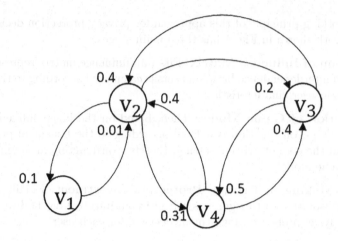

Fig. 2. An example of influence network

According to Eq. 2, the strength of influence among users is related to the proportion of two users' common friends to the total number of their friends. The more common friends there are, the stronger the strength of influence will be. Figure 2 is a sample network, which contains four users. The value on the line refers to the influence of the origin user on the target user, and the corresponding influence matrix is shown in Eq. 3.

$$W = \begin{bmatrix} 1 & 0.1 & 0 & 0 \\ 0.01 & 1 & 0.4 & 0.4 \\ 0 & 0.2 & 1 & 0.4 \\ 0 & 0.31 & 0.5 & 1 \end{bmatrix} \tag{3}$$

3.2   Interdependent Security Game Formulation

The interdependent security game model for privacy protection investment is actually a n-person weighted game model. For users who are not directly connected, their privacy protection investments have no influence with each other, and the payoffs to the users who are directly connected depend on the influence strength of them.

It is assumed that this game is a complete information game in which all players know the influence matrix and make rational decisions. When considering privacy protection investment, each user does not discuss with each other but makes decisions according to the knower information. Although the players do not necessarily determine their game strategies at the same time, but each does not know the other's strategy, so this game is a non-sequential game. In this game, each player gives his own privacy protection investment decision according to all players' payoff functions which depend on the above calculated influence matrix. It should be noted that the Nash equilibrium solution in this game is the optimal investment decision set for all rational players. The basic elements of the game $G = (V, L, U)$ are described in detail as follows.

The set of players $V = \{v_i | i \in [1, n]\}$ consists of all the users in the social network. For each player v_i, he uses a continuous strategy $l_i \in L_i$ in the game, which represents the degree of his investment in privacy protection. In order to facilitate the calculation of payoff functions, the vector $\mathbf{l} = [l_1, l_2, \ldots, l_n]$ is used to represent the corresponding strategy profile, which is the privacy protection investment strategy of all players. The payoff to v_i can be obtained as $U_i(\mathbf{l})$,

$$U_i(\mathbf{l}) = B_i\left(\left(W\mathbf{l}^T\right)_i\right) - c_i l_i$$
$$(W\mathbf{l})_i = \sum_{j \in [1,n]} e_{ij} \cdot l_j \qquad (4)$$

where $\left(W\mathbf{l}^T\right)_i$ represents the total interdependent investment of v_i in privacy protection, $B_i(\cdot)$ is a mapping function from security investments to privacy protection benefit, and $c_i > 0$ is the privacy setting cost.

Considering the diversity of social networks, the benefit function $B_i(\cdot)$ and cost c_i of each player v_i are not necessarily the same. It should be noted that $B_i(\cdot)$ satisfies the following properties.

(i) $B_i(\cdot)$ is continuous.
(ii) $B_i(\cdot)$ is monotonically increasing convex function.
(iii) $B_i(0) = 0$.
(iv) $B_i'(0) > c_i$.
(v) $\lim_{l \to \infty} B'_i(l) < c_i$.

These properties are in line with actual application scenarios. The higher investment degree, the greater the benefit, but the benefit is limited. Among them, Property(iv) refers to that the setting cost should not be too large so that users do not adopt any investment decision, and Property(v) guarantees that each user's optimal investment degree is limited.

4   Privacy Protection Investment Decisions in Interdependent Security Game

In this section, we first prove the existence and uniqueness of Nash equilibrium, and discuss that the Nash equilibrium solution in this game is the optimal investment decision set for all rational players. Finally, an iterative method for the limited rational players is adopted to reach the Nash equilibrium. According to this algorithm, each player can adjust his strategy in multiple games and finally reach the Nash equilibrium.

4.1 Existence of Nash Equilibrium

The Nash equilibrium refers to that no player has an inventive to deviate from his chosen strategy after considering the opponents' choices, i.e., the current strategies of the players attain their optimal payoffs in this game. Thus, the Nash equilibrium solution in this game is the optimal investment decision set for all rational players, which is also called the best response of every player. The optimal investment decision l_i^* of player v_i is shown below.

$$U_i\left(l_i^*, \mathbf{1}_{-i}^*\right) \geq U_i\left(l_i, \mathbf{1}_{-i}^*\right), \forall i \in N, l_i \in [0, +\infty) \tag{5}$$

where $\mathbf{1}_{-i}^*$, is the optimal investment strategy vector $\mathbf{1}^*$ of the players except v_i.

Therefore, we can obtain the optimal investment strategy vector $\mathbf{1}^* = [l_1^*, l_2^*, \ldots, l_n^*]$ for all players by solving the Eq. 6,

$$l_i^* = \arg\max_{l_i \geq 0} U_i\left(l_i, \mathbf{1}_{-i}^*\right), \forall i \in N \tag{6}$$

Let b_i be the investment decision of v_i under the condition of $B_i'(\cdot) = c_i$, i.e., it's the extreme value point. The following equation can be obtained by Eq. (6) and properties of $B_i(\cdot)$.

$$\begin{cases} \left(W\mathbf{1}^T\right)_i = b_i, & if \; l_i > 0 \\ \left(W\mathbf{1}^T\right)_i > b_i, & if \; l_i = 0 \end{cases} \tag{7}$$

In other words, the feasible solutions of Eq. 7 can be the candidates of the optimal investment strategy vector $\mathbf{1}^*$, i.e., the Nash equilibrium. Then looking back at Eq. 1, we can obtain

$$\sum_{k \neq i} w_{ik} < 1 = w_{ii} \tag{8}$$

From Eq. 8, we can know that the influence matrix W is a strictly diagonally dominant matrix. Thus the matrix W is a non singular matrix, i.e., $|W| \neq 0$. It means that there is a unique solution to Eq. 7 whose coefficient matrix is W. Therefore, the game model has the unique Nash equilibrium solution. The existence and uniqueness of Nash equilibrium solution of the game model are proved, thus the optimal investment strategy vector $\mathbf{1}^*$ (decisions for all players) can be obtained.

More importantly, the influence matrix represents the degree of interdependence of each player's investment in the social network, and the diagonal elements represent the influence of the user's investment on himself. Although each player can benefit from other players' security investments, these benefits from other players should be less than the benefit from his own investment in privacy protection. Therefore, the strictly diagonally dominant matrix W corresponds to the actual scenario.

4.2   Privacy Protection Investment Decisions with Nash Equilibrium

Cournot oligopoly game [10] is a classic example of Nash equilibrium applied in economics. This section will calculate the Nash equilibrium solution of this game model based on the calculation method in Cournot oligopoly game, i.e., the users' optimal investment decisions. The derivative of payoff function of each player can be obtained:

$$\frac{\partial U_i(\mathbf{l})}{\partial l_i} = B_i' \left((W\mathbf{1}^T)_i \right) - c_i \tag{9}$$

Since the Nash equilibrium exists and is unique, let $\frac{\partial U_i(\mathbf{l})}{\partial l_i} = 0$ get the following equation.

$$W\mathbf{1}^T = (B_i)^{-1}(c) \tag{10}$$

From Eq. 10, it can be deduced that each player's response function is shown in Eq. 11.

$$(\mathbf{l}^*)^T = (B_i)^{-1}(c) - (W - I)\mathbf{1}^T \tag{11}$$

The completely rational players can directly calculate their optimal investment decisions based on the global information. However, social-network users are not completely rational in real life, and each user may not know the response function of other users, so it is impossible to directly calculate the optimal investment decisions. In fact, the game between the players can be regarded as a repeated game where each player can know other players' investment decisions and his own payoff at the end of each subgame. Thus, all players can learn from the results of subgames and continuously adjust their strategies until they reach the optimal investment decisions, i.e., the Nash equilibrium. Therefore, an iterative method for the limited rational players is proposed, as shown in Algorithm 1.

Algorithm 1. Iteration Method for Solving Nash Equilibrium

Input: initial strategy vector $\mathbf{l}(0)$.
Output: optimal strategy vector $\mathbf{l}^*$.
1: **for** $t = 1$ to T **do**
2:     **for** $v_i \in V$ **do**
3:         $l_i(t) = R_i(\mathbf{l}_{-i}(t-1));$ // $R_i(\mathbf{l}_{-i})$ is the response function of player i
4:     **end for**
5:     **if** $\mathbf{l}(t) == \mathbf{l}(t-1)$ **then**
6:         break;
7:     **end if**
8:     t=t+1;
9: **end for**
10: **return** $\mathbf{l}^* = \mathbf{l}(t)$.

According to Eq. 11, the following equation can be obtained:

$$\mathbf{l}^T(t) = (B_i')^{-1}(c) - (W - I)\mathbf{l}^T(t-1) \tag{12}$$

In fact, the matrix $(W - I)$ is an iterative matrix, and since the spectral radius of the matrix is not greater than any norm, thus we can get

$$\rho \le \|W - I\|_\infty = \max_{1 \le i \le N} \sum_j (W - I)_{ij} = \max_{1 \le i \le N} \sum_{k \ne i} w_{ik} < 1 \qquad (13)$$

Since the spectral radius of the iterative matrix is less than 1, this iterative method converges.

5   Experiment and Analysis

5.1   Experimental Settings

In order to verify the feasibility of this interdependent security game approach, four datasets are used in our experiments, including two artificial datasets and two real network datasets [8]. In the experiments, the influence matrix is calculated based on the given network structures and user characteristics, and then the optimal investment decision for each user is calculated based on the iterative method. At the same time, the theoretical results are compared with the results of the iterative method. The machine parameters used in the experiments are: Intel Xeon e5-1620 3.5 GHz processor, 16.0 GB memory, 64-bit Windows 10 operating system.

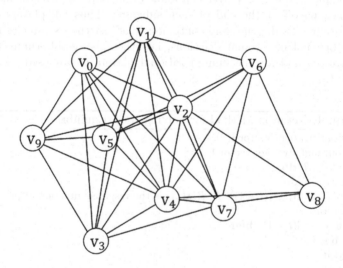

Fig. 3. The network of Synthetic dataset

The artificial datasets include the regular structure dataset and the non-regular structure dataset. And the network of the non-regular structure (Synthetic) dataset is shown in Fig. 3. The information for all datasets is shown in Table 1.

Table 1. The information for all datasets

Dataset	Nodes	Edges
Synthetic dataset	10	35
Regular-graph	4039	80780
Ego-Facebook	4039	88234
Wiki-vote	7115	103689

In order to verify the effectiveness of the iterative method, the MAE (Mean Absolute Error) is used to measure the Error between the iterative results and the theoretical results. The calculation method is shown in Eq. 14.

$$MAE = \frac{1}{N} \sum_{i=1}^{N} |theoretical_i - nash_i| \qquad (14)$$

where $theretical_i$ represents the theoretical optimal investment decision of v_i, and $nash_i$ represents the investment decision of v_i calculated by iteration method.

5.2 Analysis of Experimental Results

In an environment where the users are not completely rational, they adjust their strategies until they reach the optimal investment decisions, according to their payoff functions. Assume that the payoff function of users is shown in the following equation.

$$U_i(1) = 2\ln\left(\left(W1^T\right)_i + 1\right) - l_i, i = 1, \ldots, N \qquad (15)$$

According to Eq. 15, the benefit is $2\ln\left(\left(W1^T\right)_i + 1\right)$ and the cost is $c_i = 1$, satisfying all the properties of the benefit function $B_i(\cdot)$.

Table 2. Simulation results of synthetic dataset

User	Theoretical result	Iteration result
0	0.542843743	0.542843738
1	0.53649912	0.536499115
2	0.53322072	0.533220715
3	0.542843743	0.542843738
4	0.53322072	0.533220715
5	0.546763822	0.546763818
6	0.563291583	0.563291589
7	0.552576632	0.552576628
8	0.59081694	0.590816945
9	0.550640018	0.550640013

Table 2 shows the simulation results of the Synthetic dataset with $\beta = 1$, including the comparison of the iteration results and the theoretical results. This dataset is extracted from the subgraph data of the real dataset, and the connection relationship between users is shown in Fig. 3. It can be seen that the connection between users is nearly a complete graph, i.e., each user is a friend of other users, indicating that this group has a close internal connection with a high degree of information correlation and strong interdependent influence. The optimal investment results show that in a closely connected group, users can get the best results with a small investment if all users adopt privacy settings. According to Eq. 14, the dataset satisfies $MAE = 4.82125 \times 10^{-9}$, so the error is very small.

Table 3. MAE of three datasets

Dataset	MAE
Regular-graph	5.06292×10^{-9}
Ego-Facebook	1.69624×10^{-7}
Wiki-vote	2.80736×10^{-9}

Table 3 shows the MAE of the other three datasets with $\beta = 1$, and their errors are also small, indicating that under the condition of $\beta = 1$, all users keep adjusting their strategies according to the results of subgames, and the optimal investment strategies can be finally reached.

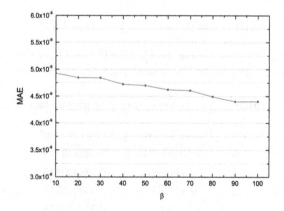

Fig. 4. MAE of Ego-Facebook dataset

Taking Ego-Facebook as an example, Fig. 4 shows the trend of MAE decreasing with the increase of β. First of all, it can be seen from the figure that β does not affect the convergence of the iterative method to the theoretical result, indicating that the social network platform environment does not affect the applicability of our approach. Whether it is the social platform with a large impact or other social platform with a small impact, users will eventually adjust their strategies to the optimal investment decisions after several subgames, which verifies the correctness of the iterative method. The increase of β means that the interaction between users will be less intense, and the fewer friends that can influence users' investments, the faster the users can reach their optimal strategies. Therefore, under the same number of iterations, the bigger β is, the smaller MAE is.

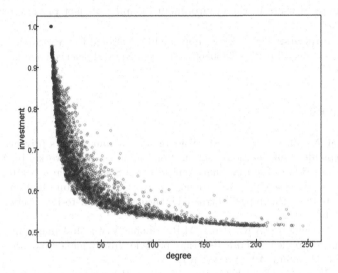

Fig. 5. Optimal investment decisions in Ego-Facebook dataset with $\beta = 10$

Figure 5 shows the distribution of Ego-Facebook dataset's optimal investment decisions and the number of friends with $\beta = 10$. The horizontal coordinate is the number of friends (degree), where the translucent blue circle represents the users. The same number of friends will overlap with the same number of invested users, so the darker the color is, the more users there are. As can be seen from the figure, the investment has a downward trend with the increase of friends, i.e., when all users in the social network adopt the privacy settings, users with a higher degree need less investment. However, when the number of friends exceeds 50, the curve becomes flat, indicating that even if users can get benefits from the investment of friends, the privacy settings of friends cannot fully protect their own privacy information, and users still need to take privacy protection investments. The above experimental results are consistent with the actual situation.

6 Conclusion

Based on the interdependence between social-network users, the influence matrix is calculated in this paper, and then an interdependent security game is constructed to derive users' optima investment decisions in privacy protection. We prove the existence and uniqueness of the Nash equilibrium of this game model, and derives the theoretical solution. An iterative method is given to show how limited rational users can invest to achieve Nash equilibrium in social networks. Experimental results show that the iterative method can effectively converge to the theoretical solution, proving the effectiveness of our approach. In the future, the research will study the optimal investment decisions under the limited resources of users in the environment of multi-project privacy protection.

Acknowledgments. This work is supproted by National Key Research and Development Plan in China (2018YFC0830500), National Natural Science Foundation of China (U1636105).

References

1. Alsarkal, Y., Zhang, N., Xu, H.: Your privacy is your friend's privacy: Examining interdependent information disclosure on online social networks. In: Proceedings of the 51st Hawaii International Conference on System Sciences (2018)
2. Arnaboldi, V., La Gala, M., Passarella, A., Conti, M.: Information diffusion in distributed osn: the impact of trusted relationships. Peer-to-Peer Netw. Appl. **9**(6), 1195–1208 (2016)
3. Chen, J., Kiremire, A.R., Brust, M.R., Phoha, V.V.: Modeling online social network users' profile attribute disclosure behavior from a game theoretic perspective. Comput. Commun. **49**, 18–32 (2014)
4. Du, J., Jiang, C., Chen, K.C., Ren, Y., Poor, H.V.: Community-structured evolutionary game for privacy protection in social networks. IEEE Trans. Inf. Forensics Secur. **13**(3), 574–589 (2017)
5. Hu, H., Ahn, G.J., Zhao, Z., Yang, D.: Game theoretic analysis of multiparty access control in online social networks. In: Proceedings of the 19th ACM Symposium on Access Control Models and Technologies. pp. 93–102 (2014)
6. Humbert, M., Trubert, B., Huguenin, K.: A survey on interdependent privacy. ACM Comput. Surveys (CSUR) **52**(6), 1–40 (2019)
7. Laszka, A., Felegyhazi, M., Buttyan, L.: A survey of interdependent information security games. ACM Comput. Surveys (CSUR) **47**(2), 1–38 (2014)
8. Leskovec, J., Krevl, A.: Snap datasets: Stanford large network dataset collection (2014)
9. Lv, J., Qiu, W., Wang, Y.: An analysis of games of information security investment based on interdependent security. Chinese J. Manage. Sci. **14**(3), 7–12 (2006)
10. Maskin, E., Tirole, J.: A theory of dynamic oligopoly, iii: Cournot competition. Eur. Econ. Rev. **31**(4), 947–968 (1987)
11. Panaousis, E., Fielder, A., Malacaria, P., Hankin, C., Smeraldi, F.: Cybersecurity games and investments: a decision support approach. In: Poovendran, R., Saad, W. (eds.) GameSec 2014. LNCS, vol. 8840, pp. 266–286. Springer, Cham (2014). https://doi.org/10.1007/978-3-319-12601-2_15

12. Rathore, S., Sharma, P.K., Loia, V., Jeong, Y.S., Park, J.H.: Social network security: Issues, challenges, threats, and solutions. Inf. Sci. **421**, 43–69 (2017)
13. Squicciarini, A.C., Griffin, C.: An informed model of personal information release in social networking sites. In: 2012 International Conference on Privacy, Security, Risk and Trust and 2012 International Conference on Social Computing. pp. 636–645. IEEE (2012)
14. Sun, J., Tang, J.: Models and algorithms for social influence analysis. In: Proceedings of the Sixth ACM International Conference on Web Search and Data Mining. pp. 775–776 (2013)
15. Tosh, D., Sengupta, S., Kamhoua, C., Kwiat, K., Martin, A.: An evolutionary game-theoretic framework for cyber-threat information sharing. In: 2015 IEEE International Conference on Communications (ICC). pp. 7341–7346. IEEE (2015)

De-anonymizing Social Networks with Edge-Neighborhood Graph Attacks

Hongyan Zhang[1,2,3], Li Xu[1,2(✉)], Limei Lin[1,2], and Xiaoding Wang[1,2]

[1] Fujian Provincial Key Laboratory of Network Security and Cryptology,
Fujian Normal University, Fujian, China
xuli@fjnu.edu.cn
[2] School of Mathematics and Informatics, Fujian Normal University, Fujian, China
[3] Concord University College Fujian Normal University, Fujian, China

Abstract. Social networks have a great influence in business, for which the data of social networks are usually released for research purpose. Since the published data might contain sensitive information of users, the identities of which are removed for anonymity before release. However, adversaries could still utilize some background knowledge to re-identify users. In this paper, we propose a novel attack model named edge-neighborhood graph attack (ENGA) against anonymized social networks, in which adversaries are assumed to have background knowledge about targets and their two-hop neighbors represented by 1-neighborhood graph and 1*-neighborhood graphs respectively. Based on such model, a de-anonymous approach is proposed to re-identify users in anonymous social networks. Theoretical analysis indicate that ENGA has a higher de-anomymization rate. And experiments conducted on synthetic data sets and real data sets illustrate the effectiveness of ENGA.

Keywords: Social networks · Edge-Neighborhood Graph (ENG) · Re-identify · Graph matching.

1 Introduction

With the development of communication technologies, i.e., Twitter, Facebook, WeChat etc., social networks have become an indispensable part of people's lives. Every day, a great amount of data generated by social networks can be released for various purpose, including targeted advertising, academic research and public competition [5,6,14]. Because social network data might contain significantly sensitive and private information of users, e.g. identity, income, phone number, etc., data should be "processed" before release for privacy protection.

Studies on social networks are usually graph based, where nodes represent the users of social networks and edges represent the relationships between them. Although many privacy protection strategies have been proposed, they

This work is supported by the National Natural Science Foundation of China (Grant No. 61771140, No. U1405255, No. U1905211, No. 61702100, No. 171061).

© Springer Nature Singapore Pte Ltd. 2020
S. Yu et al. (Eds.): SPDE 2020, CCIS 1268, pp. 726–737, 2020.
https://doi.org/10.1007/978-981-15-9129-7_49

are designed against certain attacks. A naïve anonymization for social networks is to remove the users' idetntities, however it can hardly resist the node re-identification, where adversaries have some knowledge about the targets. Liu et al. [10] propose a vertex degree attack with node degrees known by adversaries. Zhou et al. [19] propose a neighborhood attack, in which adversaries have some knowledge about victims and their neighbors which is presented by 1−neighorhood graph (NG). Ying et al. [16] propose an attack based on edge probability and vertices similarity. Narayanam et al. [12] propose an attack which combines multiples graphs, in which adversaries have an auxiliary graph whose members overlap with anonymous networks, such that adversaries can re-identify the victim through the auxiliary graph in anonymous networks. Sharad et al. [15] propose an machine learning based automated approach to re-identify the nodes, which matches pairs of nodes in disparate anonymized subgraphs. Liu et al. [11] propose a weighted 1*-neighborhood attack, which assume the adversary has knowledge not only the victim's 1-neighborhood graph but the neighbors' degrees as well. Qian et al. [13] propose a knowledge graph based attack, where the adversary possesses some prior knowledge about a certain node and the knowledge graph is used to construct a posterior attack graph to re-identify the node. Chiasserini et al. [3] present a de-anonymization algorithm that exploits an initial set of users as seeds, employing the bootstrap percolation theory and a novel graph slicing technique. To prevent the re-identification attacks, the work in [10] proposed the k-anonymity model, where each node should be indistinguishable with at least $k − 1$ other nodes in terms of attribute and structural information. This model prevents the adversary from re-identifying any node in published networks with a probability higher than $1/k$.To defend these attacks, many approaches [1,4,7,8,10,17–20] have been put forward. *Therefore, under the protection of these anonymous schemes, the effect of using existing attack models to de-anonyize users is greatly reduced.*

Different from previous works, we propose a novel Edge-Neighborhood Graph Attack (ENGA) against anonymous social network. In social networks, an important person always have some important neighbors. Although node itself has no directly influence on the whole network, the influence is constructed by local networks around this node [2], thus, we focus on structure attacks. If the adversary not only has the background knowledge about the victim's NG but one of his 1-hop neighbor's NG as well, then a k-degree or k-neighbor anonymous social graph still suffers from edge-neighborhood graph attacks. On this model, we propose a seed graph matching based de-anonymous approach. First, choose candidate set in which the node pairs are similar to victims, it can reduce search scope of target victims. Meanwhile, we use graph matching algorithm to de-anomymize users, members in candidate set can be regarded as matching seeds, it can reduce the time cost.

The contributions of this paper are summarized below.

- We propose a novel edge-neighborhood graph attack to re-identify the users in anonymous social networks, it can capture more graph topological information, and more efficient than other attacks.

...

- On this attack model, we propose a seed based de-anonymization approach to show how to de-anonymize the anonymous social networks. The time costs of de-anonymizing social networks can be reduced by starting graph matching with pairs of matched seeds of the two graphs instead of randomly selecting nodes.
- The theoretical analysis show that our attack model is more efficient than degree attack, 1-neighoborhood and 1*-graph attack, and we give experiment on synthetic data sets and real data sets to show our attack model is more powerful.

2   Preliminaries and Modeling

In this paper, a social network is modeled as an undirected graph $G =< V, E >$, where V is the a set of nods, E is a set of edges. The nodes represent the individuals in the social networks, while the edges represent the relationships such as friendship, partnership between these individuals. The cardinalities of V and E are denoted by $|V|$ and $|E|$ respectively. We assume that $|V| = n$, $|E| = m$. Figure 1 is a well-known and much-used Zachary karate club network. Each node represents a member of the club, and each edge denotes relationship between two members. Here is the naïvely anonymized social network, the node identities are replaced by a random numbers.

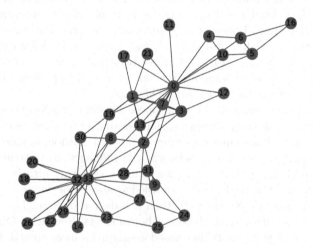

Fig. 1. Karate club graph

2.1   Attack Model

The adversary has certain background knowledge about the victims, i.e., 1-Neighborhood Graph and 1*-Neighborhood Graph. The corresponding definitions are given as follows.

Definition1 (1-Neighborhood Graph). $G(v) = < V(v), E(v) >$, where $V(G(v))$ is the set of neighbors of v and $V(G(v)) = \{u|(u,v) \in E\} \cup v$, $E(G(v))$ is the set of edges between the nodes in $V(G(v))$, and $E(v) = \{(u,v)|u,v \in V(v) \wedge (u,v) \in E\}$.

Definition2 (1*-Neighborhood Graph). $G^*(v) = < G(v), D(v)) >$, $G(v)$ is the 1-Neighborhood Graph of v. $D(v) = \{d_1, d_2 \cdots d_m\}$, d_i is the degree of v_i, $D(v)$ is the degree sequence of nodes in $G(v)$. In Fig. 1, if an adversary knows the degree of node 0, the only 16 degree node, he can re-identify node 0, therefore the anonymous social network can not resist degree attack. Figure 2a, Fig. 2b shows the NG of node 1 and 24. Because of the uniqueness of background knowledge, it can resist degree attack but can not resist the NG attack. Due to the small world phenomenon of social networks, the diameters of social networks are small, it is difficult to collect information of d-hop neighbors, when d is large. However, the adversary may collect information about the neighbors of two users, who are also neighbors. The adversary can utilize this information to form a edge-neighborhood graph attack (ENGA), then, de-anonymize an anonymous social network with this attack.

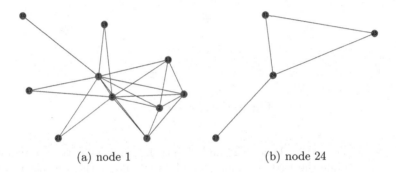

(a) node 1   (b) node 24

Fig. 2. NG of 1, 24

3 Edge-Neighborhood Graph Attack and De-anonymization

In this section, we present the edge-neighborhood graph attack model and a de-anonymizing scheme based on the ENGA.

3.1 Edge-Neighborhood Graph Attack

We give the definition of edge-neighborhood graph attack first and then Fig. 3 is utilized as example to show how an adversary conduct ENGA.

Definition3 (Edge-Neighborhood Graph (ENG)). The edge-neighborhood graph of node u is denoted by $G(u,v) = < G(u), G(v) >$, $(u,v) \in E$, where $G(u)$, $G(v)$ is the 1*-Neighborhood Graph of u and v.

Definition4 (Edge-Neighborhood Graph Attack (ENGA)). In an anonymous graph $\widetilde{G}$, the adversary utilize ENG in the original graph to re-identify users.

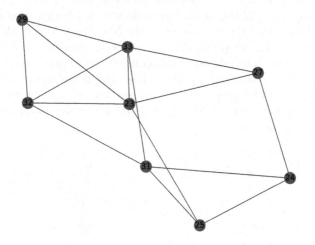

Fig. 3. ENG between 23, 24

For example, in Fig. 1, node 24 and 25 has the same NGs, thus, it can resist NG attack. While the ENG of node 23 and 24 is unique, the adversary can re-identity the 23 and 24 by ENG attack, Fig. 3 shows the ENG between node 23 and 24.

3.2   De-anonymization on Anonymous Social Networks

In the de-anonymizing step, the adversary tries to map the target users in the original graph G to nodes in anonymous graph $\widetilde{G}$. We propose a three step processing scheme. The adversary first find a candidate set in which the node pairs are similar to victims according to node similarity. The node pairs in the set are regarded as seeds in the graph matching step, this can reduce time complexity without having to match nodes in the whole graph $\widetilde{G}$. Next, from the candidate set S, for each member in S, construct its ENG, compute node similarities with victim pair's ENG in original graph to construct the weighted bipartite graph. At last, we perform maximum graph matching algorithm to obtain the optimal matching M, its the result we looking for.

Before presenting the de-anonymizing algorithm, we first define the node similarity to measure node structure similarity.

Node Similarity. For a given graph $G = <V, E>$, each node $u \in G$, we consider the following metrics: local clustering coefficient, in-degree distribution, out-degree distribution.

Local Clustering Coefficient: $C_u = \alpha(u)/\beta(u)$, where $\alpha(u)$ is the numbers of triangles, $\beta(u)$ is the numbers of triples in $G(u)$.

In-degree Distribution: $ID_w = |E_w^+|_{w \in V(G(u))}$, where E_w^+ is the set of edges which are between node w and the nodes inside $G(u)$. The maximum in-degree in $V(G(u))$ is denoted as $Max_{IDD}(u)$. Then, the in-degree distribution can be defined as $IDD(u) = \{ID_w\}/Max_{IDD}(u)|w \in V(G(u))\}$.

Out-degree Distribution: $OD_w = |E_w^-|_{w \in V(G(u))}|$, where E_w^- is the set of edges which are between node w and the nodes outside $G(u)$. The maximum out-degree in $V(G(u))$ is denoted as $Max_{ODD}(u)$. Then the out-degree distribution of node u is $ODD(u) = \{OD_w/Max_{ODD}(u)|u \in V(G(u))\}$.

We regard local clustering coefficient, in-degree distribution, out-degree distribution of node u as a measurement vector $T(u) = <C_u, IDD(u), ODD(u)>$. Note that we compute the Euclid distance between nodes u and v denoted as $Dist(u, v)$.

$$Dist(u, v) = \sqrt{(C_u - C_v)^2 + (IDD(u) - IDD(v))^2 + (ODD(u) - Odd(v))^2} \tag{1}$$

According to node distance, we provide the definition of node similarity.

Definition5 (Node similarity). For a given threshold δ, two nodes u and u' are node similar if the distance between them is less than a given threshold $Dist(u, u') < \delta$. Node similarity can be defined as

$$Sim(u, u') = 1 - Dist(u, u') \tag{2}$$

Seeded Graph Matching. The adversary knows the ENG $G(u, v)$ of node u and v, which are two endpoints on one edge (u, v). The goal of de-anonymization is to find a bijection function π between $G(u, v)$ and $\widetilde{G}(u', v'), \pi : V(G(u, v)) \rightarrow V(\widetilde{G}(u', v'))$, such that the nodes in $G(u, v)$ can map to the nodes in $\widetilde{G}(u', v')$. To address this problem, we construct a weighted bipartite graph $G_B = <V_1, V_2, E>$, where $V_1 = V(G(u, v))$, $V_2 = V(\widetilde{G}(u', v'))$. Therefore, the de-anonymization is transformed to find a bipartite graph matching in G_B.

The first step is to select an appropriate node set $S = \{(u', v')|(u', v') \in E(\widetilde{G})\}$ from anonymous graph $\widetilde{G}$, S is composed of node pairs u' and v', which are similar to target node pair u and v in the original graph G. Algorithm 1 shows the process of how to determine the candidate set S. Sort the nodes in $\widetilde{G}$ with descending order of degrees. According to the node degrees in original graph and the anonymous graph, give appropriate thresholds $k1$, $k2$, if the degree pair

(u', v') satisfy the given thresholds, then, compute the distance $dist(u, u')$ and $Dist(v, v')$, if they satisfy the threshold $\delta 1$, $\delta 1$, add them to the candidate set S. The process continues until all vertices in the graph are computed.

Algorithm 1. Candidate Set Construction

Input: $G(u, v)$, $\widetilde{G}$, $k1$, $k2$, $\delta 1$, $\delta 2$
Output: candidate set S

1: compute clustering coefficient, in-degree distribution, Out-degree distribution of node u and v in $G(u, v)$
2: set $S = \phi$
3: sort the nodes with descending order of degrees in $\widetilde{G}$, save as $D = d_{v_1}, d_{v_2}, \cdots d_{v_n}$
4: **for** $u' \in D$ **do**
5:     **if** $|d(u') - d(u)| < k1$ and $|d(v') - d(v)| < k2$ **then**
6:         compute $T(u')$ and $T(v')$
7:         **if** $Dist(u, u') < \delta 1$ and $Dist(u, u') < \delta 2$ **then**
8:             $S = S \cup \{u', v'\}$
9: **return** S

The second step is to construct top-K weighted bipartite graphs for node u, v and each node pair in candidate set S, where $G_B = < V_1, V_2, E, W >$, V_1 is consist of the nodes in $G(u, v)$, V_2 is consist of the nodes in $G(u', v')$, (u', v') is the member of candidate S, E is the edge set and W is the weight set of edges in G_B. Then we compute the measurement vectors of all the nodes in G_B. For each node u in V_1, compute the similarity $Sim(u, u')$s with all the nodes in V_2, then link u to the top-K similarity nodes in V_2, considering these similarities as the weight of these edges. The process repeat until all the nodes in V_1 have edges with nodes in V_2. Algorithm 2 shows the process of the top-K weighted bipartite graph construction.

Algorithm 2. Top-K Weighted Bipartite Graph Construction

Input: $G(u, v)$, $\widetilde{G}(u', v')$
Output: G_B

1: set $V_1 = V(G(u, v))$, $V_2 = V(\widetilde{G}(u', v'))$
2: **for** $u_i \in V_1$ **do**
3:     **for** $u_j' \in V_2$ **do**
4:         compute $w_{ij} = Sim_{ij} = 1 - dist(u_i, u_j')$
5:         select the top-K similar nodes in V_2 denoted as SN_i
6:         link node (u_i with u_j') in SN_i with weight w_{ij}
7: **return** G_B

The last step is to find the maximal bipartite graph matching in G_B as shown in algorithm 3. For each node pair in candidate S, we construct a bipartite graph, then, utilize Kuhn-Munkres algorithm to obtain the optimal matching and matching cost. Thus, the graph corresponding to the minimum matching cost is the result we're looking for.

Algorithm 3. Optimal Graph Matching

Input: G_B
Output: the optimal Matching M in G_B
1: set $Cost = \phi$ and $M = \phi$
2: using algorithm 1 to find candidate S
3: **for** e **do**ach pair of nodes $s_i = (u^{'}, v^{'}) \in S$
4:    construct bipartite graph G_B^i
5:    using Kuhn-Munkres algorithm to compute the matching cost $Cost_i$ and to find maximum graph matching M_i
6:    add $Cost_i$ and M_i into $Cost$ and M, respectively
7: find the minimum value in $Cost$
8: find the corresponding matching in M
9: **return** M

---

4   Performance Analysis

In this section, we analysis the performance of our ENG attack and compare it with the degree, NG and $1^{*}-$NG attacks.

4.1   Theoretical Analysis

Theorem 1. *Edge-neighborhood graph attack (ENGA) has higher deanomymization rate than degree, $1-$neighborhood and $1*-$neighborhood attacks.*

Proof 1. *The adversary want to re-identify the target node u and v, it means that the adversary have knowledge about ENG. ENG contains node degree and NG even $1^{*}-$NG of u and v, therefore, ENG attack include degree, NG and $1^{*}-$NG attacks. That is to say, the ENG attack is more powerful than degree, NG and $1^{*}-$neighborhood graph attack.*

5   Validation Experiment

We conducted experiments to evaluate the performance of our proposed attack model on synthetic and real data sets. Experiments are conducted on a local machine, running the Microsoft Windows 10 ultimate operating system. The programs are implemented Python.

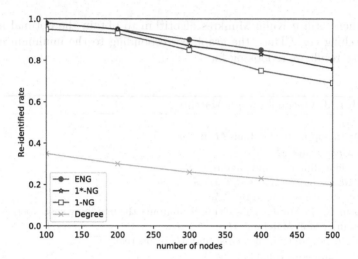

Fig. 4. Re-identification on anonymized networks

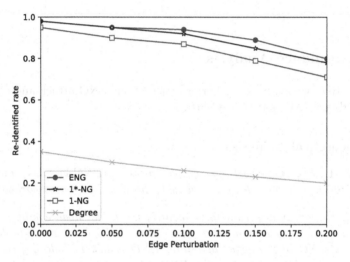

Fig. 5. Edge perturbed anonymization

We use Stanford Snap Platform [9] to generate synthetic data sets. In this model, nodes' degree distribution follows power-law distribution. In our experiment, the synthetic social network contains $100 - 500$ nodes, the average node degree is 10, anonymized with 10% edges perturbed. We compare our attack model with degree, NG and $1^* - NG$ attack models, consider the re-identification rate of nodes as the metric. The rate of re-identification is defined as $r = \|V^r\|/\|V\|$, where $\|V^r\|$, $\|V\|$ are the number of re-identified nodes and the whole nodes, respectively. From Fig. 4, we can see that as the number of

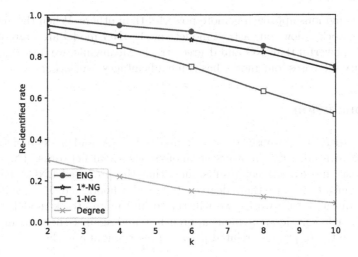

Fig. 6. k-degree anonymization

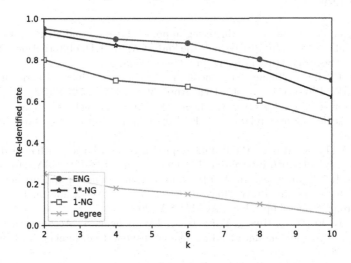

Fig. 7. k-neighborhood graph anonymization

nodes in networks increases, the re-identification rate decreases, however our model is more powerful than other three attack models.

We evaluate our attack model on Jazz musician social network, comparing with three attack models with different anonymous methods, edge perturbed, k-degree, k-NG anonymity. Figure 5, Fig. 6, Fig. 7 show the efficiency of these four attack models under three anonymous methods, respectively. The figures show that from degree anonymous approach to NG anonymous approach, the anonymity increases, no matter which attack model of the four models, the re-identification rates reduce. However, We can see, no matter in which picture, our de-anonymous approach is more powerful than others. When the anonymity of the network is low, our attack model and 1*−NG model are quite effective, but more powerful than NG and degree attack. Meanwhile, we investigate when anonymity increases, our model has some advantages over others.

6 Conclusion

In this paper, we propose an attack model ENGA and a de-anonymization approach to re-identify the users on anonymous social networks. The theoretical analysis and experiment results show that the proposed ENGA has higher de-anomymization rate than degree, 1−neighborhood and 1*−neighborhood attacks. In our future works, we will try to find more attack models and propose more efficient de-anonymous approaches, and against these de-anonymous attacks, we try to propose related privacy preserving approaches.

References

1. Campan, A., Truta, T.: A clustering approach for data and structural anonymity in social networks. In: Proceedings the 2nd ACM SIGKDD International Workshop Privacy Security Trust in KDD, pp. 33–54 (2008)
2. Chen, D., Lü, L., Shang, M., Cheng, Y.: Identifying influential nodes in complex networks. Physica A Statist. Mech. Appl. **39**(4), 1777–1787 (2012)
3. Chiasserini, C.F., Garetto, M., Leonardi, E.: Social network de-anonymization under scale-free user relations. IEEE/ACM Trans. Networking **24**(6), 3756–3769 (2016)
4. Day, W., Li, N., Min, L.: Publishing graph degree distribution with node differential privacy. In: the 2016 International Conference, pp. 123–138. USA (2016)
5. Gross, R., Acquisti, A., Iii, H.J.H.: Information revelation and privacy in online social networks. In: Proceedings of the 2005 ACM Workshop on Privacy in the Electronic Society, pp. 71–80. ACM, USA (2005)
6. Jung, T., Li., X.Y., Huang, W.C., Qian, J.W., Cheng, S.: Accounttrade: accountable protocols for big data trading against dishonest consumers. In: IEEE INFOCOM (2017)
7. Kiabod, M., Dehkordi, M.N., Barekatain, B.: Tsram: a time-saving k-degree anonymization method in social network. Expert Syst. Appl. **125**, 378–396 (2019)
8. Langari, R.K., Sardar, S., Mousavi, S.A., Radfar, R.: Combined fuzzy clustering and fifireflfly algorithm for privacy preserving in social networks. Expert Syst. Appl. **141**, 1–15 (2020)
9. Leskovec, J.: Stanford large network dataset collection. http://snap.stanford.edu/data/
10. Liu, K., Terzi, E.: Towards identity anonymization on graphs. In: Proceedings ACM SIGMOD International Conference Management Data, pp. 93–106 (2008)
11. Liu, Q., Wang, G., Li, F., Yang, S., Wu, J.: Preserving privacy with probabilistic indistinguishability in weighted social networks. IEEE Trans. Parallel Distrib. Syst. **28**(5), 1417–1429 (2017)
12. Narayanan, A., Shmatikov, V.: De-anonymizing social networks. In: Proceedings of the 30th IEEE Symposium on Security and Privacy, pp. 173–187 (2009)

13. Qian, J., Li, X., Zhang, C., Chen, L., Jung, T., Han, J.: Social network de-anonymization and privact inference with knowledge graph model. IEEE Trans. Dependable Secure Comput. **99**, 1–14 (2017)
14. Shah, C., Capra, R., Hansen, P.: Collaborative information seeking: guest editors' introduction. IEEE Trans. Comput. **47**(3), 22–25 (2014)
15. Sharad, K., Danezis, G.: An automated social graph de-anonymization technique. Computer Science, pp. 47–58 (2014)
16. Ying, X., Wu, X.: Randomizing social networks: a spectrum preserving approach. In: In Proceedings of the 2008 SIAM International Conference on Data Mining, no. 12, pp. 739-750. SIAM (2008)
17. Yuan, M., Chen, L., Yu, P.S., Yu, T.: Protecting sensitive lables in social network data anonymization. IEEE Trans. Knowl. Data Eng. **25**(3), 633–647 (2013)
18. Zheng, X., Luo, G., Cai, Z.: A fair mechanism for private data publication in online social networks. IEEE Transactions on Network Science and Engineering, pp. 1–11 (2018)
19. Zhou, B., Pei, J.: Privacy preservation in social networks against neighborhood attacks. In: ICDE, pp. 506–515. IEEE, USA (2008)
20. Zou, L., Chen, L., Ozsu, M.: K-automorphism: A general framework for privacy preserving network publication. In: Proceedings of the VLDB Endowment, vol. 2, pp. 946–957 (2009)

User Grouping Privacy-Preserving Strategy Based on Edge Computing for Mobile Crowdsensing

Peng Yang[1,2,3,4]($\boxtimes$) (iD), Yan Zhang[1], Qiming Wu[2,3,4] (iD), Dapeng Wu[2,3,4] (iD), and Zhidu Li[2,3,4] (iD)

[1] Chongqing Academy of Information and Communications Technology, Chongqing 401336, China
yangpeng@caict.ac.cn
[2] School of Communication and Information Engineering, Chongqing University of Posts and Telecommunications, Chongqing 400065, China
[3] Key Laboratory of Optical Communication and Network in Chongqing, Chongqing 400065, China
[4] Key Laboratory of Ubiquitous Sensing and Networking in Chongqing, Chongqing 400065, China

Abstract. At present, the data information is uploaded to the platform by a large number of users in mobile crowdsensing, which can be processed in the sensing platform. As a result, the sensing platform not only a target for attackers, but also greatly increases time delay and high bandwidth costs. To solve this problem, a user clustering privacy-preserving scheme based on edge servers (UPPE) is proposed. Firstly, the task requester sends the tasks to the platform, publishes the task after sensing the platform's scalar task attributes, and the sensing user uploads the user task request to the edge server. Then, the edge server utilizes the clustering method to hide the information related users, taking the edge server as a clustering to sign the users and upload it to the platform. Finally, the platform randomly matches the users and selects the user set in the clustering. The edge server notifies the user to upload the sensing data after signature verification. The simulation results show that the proposed mechanism verifies the user availability to upload data and protect the identity of user.

Keywords: Mobile crowdsensing · Privacy-preserving · User grouping · Edge computing.

1 Introduction

Due to the rapid development of sensing, computing and communication technologies, many mobile devices embedded various sensors are used by more and

This work was supported by the National Key Research and Development Project of China under Grant 2018YFB2100200.

more people. Mobile crowdsensing can use millions of mobile devices to sense, collect and analyze data while no need to deploy thousands of static sensing equipment [1]. Crowdsensing has been widely applied in healthcare [2], traffic monitoring [3], smart city [4] and environmental monitoring [5]. The typical crowdsensing application service implementation is based on the centralized cloud, the user task matching process is executed by the platform, which is located on the remote cloud server, the user must upload their task quotation and sensing data to the cloud to complete task allocation process. This not only generates long communication delays, but also comes with many privacy issues [6]. Therefore, the problems of high latency and high risk in traditional crowdsensing based on centralized cloud servers make it particularly important to change the existing crowdsensing system architecture.

Some researchers have combined edge computing models to study privacy protection in crowdsensing. In Ref. [7,8] uses an anonymous method to prevent sensing data from being associated with its provider, thereby protecting the privacy of users when participating in tasks. In Ref. [9,10] uses cryptographic methods to encrypt the sensing data The solution can provide higher privacy protection performance. Considering the characteristics of user-generated content and the heterogeneity of resources, Yang et al. [11] designed a smart edge computing framework based on cloud-user-edge collaboration, which protects the user's sensitive data and can reduce network traffic. Zhou et al. [12] proposed an crowdsensing task allocation framework suitable for edge computing scenarios, where the edge server optimizes the task allocation strategy based on the user's real-time information. The emergence of edge computing paradigm makes it possible to solve the time delay of transmitting large amounts of complex data and solve the problem of privacy protection. The basic idea of edge computing is to calculate the uplink data on the uplink network on behalf of the data source, and to calculate the downlink data on behalf of the cloud server [13,14].

In this paper, we propose the UPPE introduces edge computing architecture into the crowdsensing system, the edge server is used to cluster and group the users, and the identity of the group management is used to sign and verify the selected user set. The sensing platform will group the matching users and select the user set to realize the identity information protection of the sensing users and complete the task allocation process.

2   System Model

A typical mobile crowdsensing mainly includes three entities: sensing platform, task requester and sensing user. As shown in Fig. 1, this paper introduces an edge layer between the sensing platform as a cloud layer and a user layer composed of users. The specific operation of the system is as follows: the sensing platform sorts out the task request of the task requester, sends it to the edge server, and the edge server broadcasts it to the user layer. For the perceptive user participating in the task, the user generates the corresponding user task attribute according to the task attribute and uploads it to the edge server. Since each attribute has a certain weight influence on the sensing task, with the cooperation of the edge server, the attributes of the participating users are used as input, and the clustering method of the Gaussian mixture model is used to cluster into clusters, and the users are grouped within the cluster. After the edge server signs the users in the group as the group management identity, it uploads it to the sensing platform according to group. The sensing platform randomly calculates the group matching users and selects the user set optimally, and sends the results to the edge server. As a group management, the edge server can verify the identity of participating users and notify them to upload sensing data.

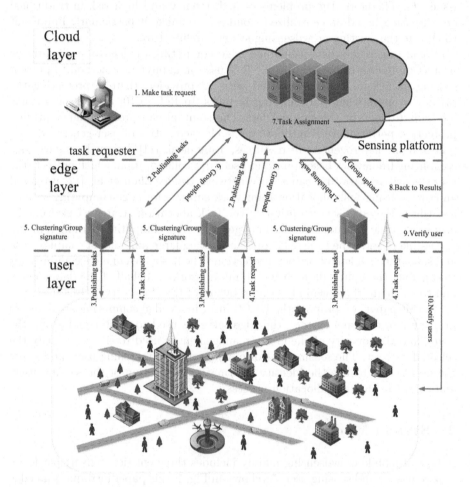

Fig. 1. Group intelligence sensing system model under the edge.

3 Group Signature Algorithm Based on User Grouping

3.1 User Grouping Based on Clustering

In crowdsensing system, the attribute values of users present a Gaussian distribution, so we propose a method based on multi-dimensional feature clustering. The edge server can use Gaussian mixture model to cluster users into groups. Users are clustered according to the attributes of users, so that users are divided into different categories, and users in the same category have a higher similarity. According to the multi-dimensional attributes of users, a multivariate Gaussian distribution is formed by:

$$N\left(x\,\Big|\,\mu, \sum\right) = \frac{1}{(2\pi)^{\frac{n}{2}}|\sum|^{\frac{1}{2}}} e^{-\frac{1}{2}(x-\mu)^{\mathrm{T}}\sum^{-1}(x-\mu)} \tag{1}$$

where μ is a n-dimensional mean vector, $\sum$ is a $n \times n$ covariance matrix, and $|\sum|$ is a determinant of $\sum$.

The Gaussian mixture model is a linear combination of several Gaussian distributions. Assuming that there existing K Gaussian distributions, these K Gaussian distributions are mixed into a Gaussian mixture model with a certain probability, there are:

$$p(x) = \sum_{k=1}^{K} p(k)\, p(x\,|k) = \sum_{k=1}^{K} \pi_k N\left(x\,\Big|\,\mu_k, \sum_k\right) \tag{2}$$

where μ_k denotes the average value of the sample data of the k th category, $\sum_k$ denotes covariance of the sample data of k th category, π_k denotes mixing coefficient, $0 \le \pi_k \le 1$ and $\sum_{k=1}^{K} \pi_k = 1$.

When clustering, only the observation data X is actually known, and there is no result label, so one is usually randomly selected as a hidden variable Z. In order to make the hidden variable as the final result, the EM algorithm is used to estimate the hidden variable, so that the Gaussian mixture model can fit the probability density of the original data as perfectly as possible. The EM algorithm is divided into step E and step M. Step E is to calculate the probability of data points generated by each Gaussian according to the current parameters. A hidden variable is defined as $z = (z_1, z_2, z_3, ..., z_k)$, in which only one z_k is 1 and the rest elements are 0, namely:

$$z_k = \begin{cases} 1, the\ data\ come\ from\ kth\ model \\ 0, the data does not come from the kth model \end{cases} \tag{3}$$

We define π_k as the priori probability of selecting k th sub-model, namely $\pi_k = p(z_k = 1)$, corresponding $N(x\,|\mu_k, \sum_k) = p(x\,|z_k = 1)$. In addition, each x_n corresponds to a hidden variable z_{nk}. Based on Bayesian theory, x_n belongs to the posterior probability of k th sub-model, defined as $\gamma(z_{nk})$:

$$\gamma(z_{nk}) = p(z_{nk} = 1 \,|x_n) = \frac{\pi_k N(x_n \,|\mu_k, \Sigma_k)}{\sum\limits_{j=1}^{K} \pi_j N\left(x_n \,\Big|\mu_j, \Sigma_j\right)} \tag{4}$$

Step M is the probability estimated by step E to improve the mean, variance, and weight of each distribution, namely, μ_k, Σ_k, and π_k are solved respectively. The improvement method is to find the maximum likelihood, and fix the likelihood function obtained by step E. The log-likelihood function is obtained by taking the logarithm of Eq. (2), and then the derivatives of μ_k and Σ_k are obtained, and finally μ_k^{new} and Σ_k^{new} are obtained:

$$\mu_k^{new} = \frac{\sum\limits_{n=1}^{N} \gamma(z_{nk}) x_n}{\sum\limits_{n=1}^{N} \gamma(z_{nk})} \tag{5}$$

$$\Sigma_k^{new} = \frac{\sum\limits_{n=1}^{N} \gamma(z_{nk})(x_n - \mu_k^{new})(x_n - \mu_k^{new})^T}{\sum\limits_{n=1}^{N} \gamma(z_{nk})} \tag{6}$$

For the mixing coefficient π_k, due to the restriction condition $\sum\limits_{k=1}^{K} \pi_k = 1$, the Lagrange multiplier method is used to transform into an unconstrained optimization problem, and finally π_k^{new} is obtained, namely:

$$\pi_k^{new} = \frac{\sum\limits_{n=1}^{N} \gamma(z_{nk})}{N} \tag{7}$$

Finally, step E and step M are repeated until the convergence. For a small positive number ε, the iteration condition is as follows:

$$\left\| \left[N\left(x \,\Big|\mu_k, \sum_k\right) \right]^{i+1} - \left[N\left(x \,\Big|\mu_k, \sum_k\right) \right]^{i} \right\| < \varepsilon \tag{8}$$

After clustering in the edge server, the number of users included in the cluster may be different. In order to make users in the group within the same number and protect user privacy by user grouping, assuming that each user that has been clustered will be grouped into h groups, can be denoted as $G_1^k, G_2^k, G_3^k, \ldots G_h^k$, the number of clusters is j, which is denoted $C_1, C_2, C_3, \ldots, C_j$. The number of user groups is divided according to the weighting for all clusters, then the number of groups of the n th cluster N_n^G can be obtained:

$$N_n^G = h \frac{C_n}{\sum\limits_{n=1}^{j} C_n} \tag{9}$$

In order to allow the sensing platform to choose fairly within the group, the users in each cluster are classified according to the corresponding group number N_n^G, and the user grouping is defined as follows:

$$f^k = \min \max_{n=1}^{h} |G_n^k|, s.t. |G_n^i| \max_{u_i \in G_n^k} \Upsilon(u_i) \tag{10}$$

where $\Upsilon(u_i)$ refers to the number of each group. Since clustering has divided all users who want to participate in the task into categories, f^k is to minimize the size of the largest group, and the constraint is that the number of users in each group must be greater than or equal to the maximum number of any users in the group. All users in the cluster are sorted into list L, assuming that $h = 1$. Creating the first group with user $\Upsilon(u_1)$ in list and deleting it from L. Traversing all the users in the cluster in turn, the group number G_h^k of these members are set to h, and $h = h + 1$, and then traversing all the clusters to get all user groups.

3.2 Secure Matching Based on Group Signature

As shown in Fig. 2, the user privacy protection scheme based on group signature can be described as: in the initialization phase of the system, the public/private key pair generated by the edge server broadcasts the group public key to the users in each group, and users sign their identity information, then feed it back to the edge server, and finally edge server uploads it to the sensing platform. After the sensing platform verifies the signature, it will perform task matching for the users in each group and return the selection result to the edge server. The edge server can track the true signature of users as an administrator and determine whether it is a legitimate user, and finally users selected by the platform to participate in the task are notified, thus the task assignment process is completed. The specific steps can be described as:

System initialization: The edge server randomly selects five big prime numbers p_1, p_2, p_3, p_4, p_5, which satisfies $p_1 = 2p_3p_4 + 1$ and $p_2 = 2p_3p_5 + 1$. Multiplicative group Z^* is generated by calculating $n = p_1p_2$. Selecting random integers $e, g \in Z^*$, the order is f. The edge server generates private key $sk_G \in Z^*$ and public key $pk_G = g^\sigma \bmod n$, and public parameters $(n, e, g, f, ID_G, h(\cdot))$, ID_G is the edge server ID $h(\cdot)$ is the hash function.

User coefficient generation: If the user wants to participate in the task, selecting random number $s \in Z^*$ to generate identity $ID_{u_i} = g^s \bmod n$. Then selecting random number $\delta \in Z^*$ and calculating $r = g^\delta \bmod n$, $t = \delta + r\sigma \cdot h(ID_{u_i}) \bmod f$, $v = ID_G r(pk_G)^{rh(ID_{u_i})} ID_{u_i}$, and (r, t, v) is set as group membership certificate.

Group signature generation: After the edge server groups the users, for the user request task message m, two random numbers $q_1, q_2 \in Z^*$ are selected. Calculating $r_1 = q_2^e g^{q_1} \bmod n$, $r_2 = h(r_1, m)$, $r_3 = q_1 + (t + \sigma)r_2 \bmod f$, $r_4 = q_2 w^{r_2} \bmod n$ and finally group signature can be denoted as (r_1, r_2, r_3, r_4).

744   P. Yang et al.

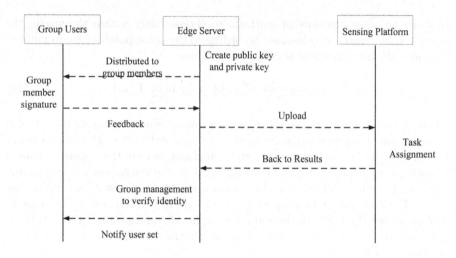

Fig. 2. Group signature process.

Signature Verification: When the sensing platform receives the group signature (r_1, r_2, r_3, r_4), calculating $r_1' = ID_G{}^{r_2} g^{r_3} r_4{}^e \bmod n$ and $r_2' = h(r_1', m)$, and verifying whether $r_2 = r_2'$ is valid. If true, it means that the group signature is a valid group signature.

User Selection: After grouping the users after clustering, they still have similar attributes. A user is randomly selected to perform the task matching calculation with the task of the sensing platform. The calculated user is marked as $flag = 1$, which refers to that the matching calculation has been completed. Then the next user is selected randomly, and then determine whether $flag$ is equal to 1. If $flag = 1$, then re-select a new user until the selected users $flag$ is equal to 1, thus the selection of users within the group is completed. The sensing platform selects the appropriate sensing users by ranking the matching degree of the users in the group.

Verify User identity: By calculating $\eta = r_2 \bmod n$ and $\gamma = ID_G{}^{r_2} g^{r_3} \bmod n$, the edge server verifies the group membership certificate (r, t, v), ID_{u_i} and group signature (r_1, r_2, r_3, r_4), and verifies $ID_{u_i} = \left(g^{r_3}\left(\gamma g^{ID_G}\right) - 1\right)^\eta v^{-e} \bmod n$, if true, the user is the real signer, and notifies the user to participant in the task and uploads the sensing data.

3.3 Security Analysis

Anonymity: The user combines the public-private keys published by the edge server and his own private key to generate the user identity ID_{u_i}, and then uploads the request message to the sensing platform after grouping. The platform can use the group public key to verify the message, but any verifier cannot determine which member of the group the sender is.

Untraceability: Given a group signature (r_1, r_2, r_3, r_4), for any user u_i in the group and its corresponding qualification certificate $(r_{u_i}, t_{u_i}, v_{u_i})$, user identity ID_{u_i} and group identity ID_G. By calculating $g^{t_{u_i}} = r_{u_i}(pk_G)^{r_{u_i}h(ID_{u_i})}$, $v_{u_i}{}^e = (ID_G g^{t_{u_i}} ID_{u_i}) - 1 \bmod n$, and $v_{u_i} = ID_G r_{u_i}(pk_G)^{r_{u_i}h(ID_{u_i})} ID_{u_i} \bmod n = ID_G g^{t_{u_i}} ID_{u_i} \bmod n$, the following equation can be obtained:

$$
\begin{aligned}
&(g^{r_3}(\gamma g^{r_2 t_{u_i}}) - 1)^\eta v_{u_i}{}^{-e} \bmod n \\
&= g^{r_3 \eta}(ID_G{}^{r_2 \eta} g^{r_3 \eta} g^{r_2 \eta t_{u_i}}) - 1 v_{u_i}{}^{-e} \bmod n \\
&= ID_G g^{t_{u_i}} ID_{u_i}(ID_G g^{t_{u_i}}) - 1 \bmod n \\
&= ID_{u_i}
\end{aligned}
\tag{11}
$$

there are $ID_{u_i} = (g^{r_3}(\gamma g^{r_2 t_{u_i}}) - 1)^\eta v_{u_i}{}^{-e} \bmod n$ for any user u_i. In this way, even if the attacker obtains relevant information, he cannot confirm the member of the signature.

Non-repudiation: Users who participate in group signatures cannot deny their signed messages. As a group management, the edge server can prove the user authenticity through $ID_{u_i} = (g^{r_3}(\gamma g^{r_2 t_{u_i}}) - 1)^\eta v_{u_i}{}^{-e} \bmod n$ for any user u_i, so user cannot deny the process of participating in the group signature and cannot deny the signed message.

4   Simulation

In this paper, we use the Python simulation environment to verify the performance of the proposed UPPE. The main performance indicators include the running time and data accuracy of the number of users under different iterative conditions during the clustering, as well as the communication success rate under different similarities for the users after the selection is successful, the message exposure rate and the network of different malicious users Load rate. Among them, the communication success rate refers to the ratio of the perceived user who is finally selected by applying to the perception platform for the perception task, the message exposure rate refers to the amount of perception data submitted by the perception user to the perception platform and the total amount of data perceived, and the network load rate indicates incomplete The ratio of the number of perceived users of the task to the number of perceived users who completed the task. The simulation data set we used is derived from the real data set collected in the GeoLife project [15]. The data points in this data set are collected by GPS recorders with different collection frequencies, and contain a total of 18670 GPS track records and 24.87 million data from 182 users. point. The data is recorded from April 2007 to August 2012, which is a typical spatio-temporal data set. Under the same conditions, the algorithm in this paper is compared with CS-DMP in Ref. [16] and LoPub in Ref. [17].

Figure 3 and Fig. 4 reflects the influence of the positive number ε of iteration conditions on the clustering running time and data accuracy in different number of users. Reflects the influence of the positive number of iteration conditions on the clustering running time and data accuracy in different number of users. It can be found from Fig. 3 that as the number of users increases, the running time increases. This is because the training data needs to be processed for a larger number, and as the positive number decreases, the EM algorithm. The number of iterations increases, resulting in an increase in runtime. It can be found from Fig. 4 that when the positive number $\varepsilon = 0.1$, $\varepsilon = 0.01$ and $\varepsilon = 0.001$ of the iteration condition, the data accuracy increases with the increase of the users number, and when $\varepsilon = 0.0001$, after the peak value is reached, the data accuracy decreases as the amount of users increases, the reason is that the smaller the positive number of the iteration condition is, the more clusters that need to be classified by the user are increased, resulting in a decrease in data accuracy.

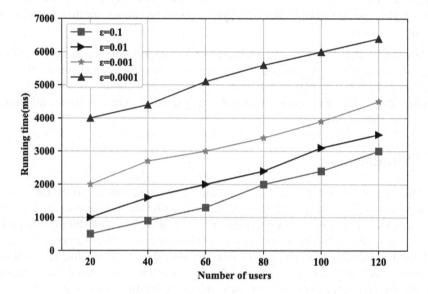

Fig. 3. Running time under different iteration conditions.

Figure 5 shows how the similarity of different users changes the communication success rate when using the three schemes. The user similarity indicates the similarity of the user's action trajectory and interests in daily life. The higher the similarity, the more similar the attributes among users. It can be seen from the figure that the CS-DMP and LoPub mechanisms increase and decrease in communication success rate as the user similarity increases. This is because the CS-DMP and LoPub mechanisms do not consider the similarity between users. As a result, with the increase of user similarity, UPPE's communication success rate shows an upward trend. This is because UPPE uses an edge server to first calculate the similarity of users participating in the task. With the cooperation of the edge server, not only the communication delay is reduced, but also the communication quality is improved.

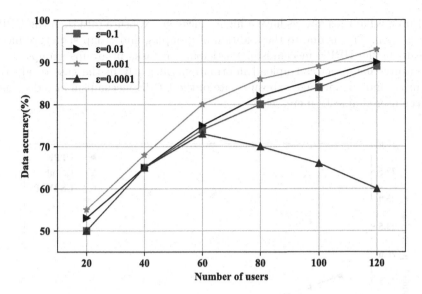

Fig. 4. Data accuracy under different iteration conditions.

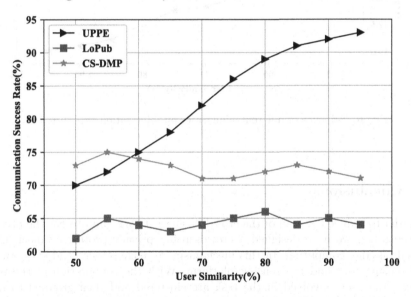

Fig. 5. The influence of different similarity degree on communication success rate.

Figure 6 shows the changes in message exposure rates of different user similarities when using the three schemes. The higher the similarity between users, the more obvious the edge server is in clustering and clustering, and the more stable the communication topology when the platform selects users. It can be seen from the figure that with the increase of user similarity, the CS-DMP and

LoPub mechanisms always have a higher message exposure rate than the UPPE mechanism. This is due to the addition of grouping and group signature mechanisms in the UPPE mechanism. Participate in tasks in groups/groups, so as to ensure that users can upload information efficiently in the case of identity security, and the message exposure rate of the UPPE mechanism also decreases as the user similarity increases.

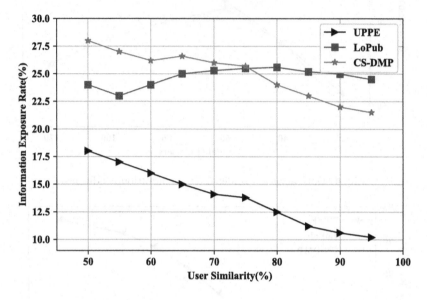

Fig. 6. Influence of different similarities on information exposure rate.

5   Conclusions

In order to reduce the load of the crowdsensing network and protect the privacy of the users, we have designed a crowdsensing privacy protection mechanism based on edge computing. In this mechanism, an edge server is added between the sensing user and the sensing platform. With the cooperation of the edge server, the users involved in the task are clustered and then grouped to hide the user information. In addition, the edge server can not only use the group signature to the users in the group as the group management, but also verify the final selected user set. Through experimental verification, the user's identity information protection is realized, and the user's task allocation process is completed efficiently.

References

1. Yang, D., et al.: Incentive mechanisms for crowdsensing: crowdsourcing with smartphones. IEEE/ACM Trans. Networking **24**(3), 1732–1744 (2015)
2. Hicks, J., et al.: AndWellness: an open mobile system for activity and experience sampling. Wireless Health **2010**, 34–43 (2010)
3. Ni, J., et al.: Security, privacy, and fairness in fog-based vehicular crowdsensing. IEEE Commun. Mag. **55**(6), 146–152 (2017)
4. Zhao, Y., et al.: Greendrive: a smartphone-based intelligent speed adaptation system with real-time traffic signal prediction. In: 2017 ACM/IEEE 8th International Conference on Cyber-Physical Systems (ICCPS). IEEE (2017)
5. Mun, M., et al.: PEIR, the personal environmental impact report, as a platform for participatory sensing systems research. In: Proceedings of the 7th International Conference on Mobile Systems, Applications, and Services, pp. 55–68 (2009)
6. Marjanovic, M., Aleksandar, A., Zarko, I.P.: Edge computing architecture for mobile crowdsensing. IEEE Access **6**, 10662–10674 (2018)
7. Li, Y., et al.: Privacy-preserving location proof for securing large-scale database-driven cognitive radio networks. IEEE Internet Things J. **3**(4), 563–571 (2015)
8. Wang, X.O., et al.: Enabling reputation and trust in privacy-preserving mobile sensing. IEEE Trans. Mobile Comput. **13**(12), 2777–2790 (2013)
9. Fan, J., Li, Q., Cao, G.: Privacy-aware and trustworthy data aggregation in mobile sensing. In: 2015 IEEE Conference on Communications and Network Security (CNS), pp. 31–39. IEEE (2015)
10. Zhang, Y., Chen, Q., Zhong, S.: Efficient and privacy-preserving min and k th min computations in mobile sensing systems. IEEE Trans. Dependable Secure Comput. **14**(1), 9–21 (2015)
11. Li, Q., Cao, G., La Porta, T.F.: Efficient and privacy-aware data aggregation in mobile sensing. IEEE Trans. Dependable Secure Comput. **11**(2), 115–129 (2013)
12. Yang, B., Dapeng, W., Wang, R.: CUE: an intelligent edge computing framework. IEEE Network **33**(3), 18–25 (2019)
13. Shi, W., et al.: Edge computing: vision and challenges. IEEE Internet Things J. **3**(5), 637–646 (2016)
14. Li, T., et al.: Participant grouping for privacy preservation in mobile crowdsensing over hierarchical edge clouds. In: 2018 IEEE 37th International Performance Computing and Communications Conference (IPCCC). IEEE (2018)
15. Zheng, Yu., Xie, X., Ma, W.-Y.: GeoLife: a collaborative social networking service among user, location and trajectory. IEEE Data Eng. Bull. **33**(2), 32–39 (2010)
16. Song, Z., Li, Z., Chen, X.: Local differential privacy preserving mechanism for multi-attribute data in mobile crowdsensing with edge computing. In: 2019 IEEE International Conference on Smart Internet of Things (SmartIoT). IEEE (2019)
17. Ren, X., et al.: LoPub: high-dimensional crowdsourced data publication with local differential privacy. IEEE Trans. Inf. Forensics Secur. **13**(9), 2151–2166 (2018)

Author Index

Printed in the United States
By Bookmasters